TWEAKING THE NOSE
OF THE RUSSIANS:

FIFTY YEARS OF
AMERICAN-ROMANIAN RELATIONS,
1940-1990

by

Joseph F. Harrington
and
Bruce J. Courtney

EAST EUROPEAN MONOGRAPHS, BOULDER
DISTRIBUTED BY COLUMBIA UNIVERSITY PRESS, NEW YORK

1991

EAST EUROPEAN MONOGRAPHS, NO. CCXCVI

CONTENTS

FOREWORD

A word about the book's organization. Following a brief sketch of Romanian-Allied relations from 1940-1947, this book examines post World War II American-Romanian relations within the following context. Whenever documentation is available, the American side considers first, the larger perspective of East-West trade, which at the outset focused on restricting commerce through export controls; second, American's national security policy, which normally addressed the issue of Soviet-American relations; third, America's policy toward Eastern Europe, which at times differed from its approach toward the Soviet Union; and fourth, specific relations with Romania, first as a satellite and later as a nation, somewhat independent of Moscow. Romania's relations with America are considered within the framework of Bucharest-Moscow relations and Romania's internal developments which affect her foreign policy toward Washington.

A note of thanks to many people. After five years of archival research, the authors are most grateful to the staffs at the National Archives in Washington, D.C. and in Suitland, Maryland, for helping us find Department of State Legation Files and Joint Chiefs of Staff papers. Special thanks are due a number of people without whose help we would have wasted considerable time and energy. Thank you Irwin Mueller at the Harry S. Truman Library; James Leyerzapf at the Dwight D. Eisenhower Library; Will Johnson at the John F. Kennedy Library; Bonnie Baldwin and Scott Parnham at the Nixon Presidential Materials Project; William Stewart at the Gerald R. Ford Library; and, Martin Elzy at the Jimmy Carter Library. We are also grateful to the staffs at the Framingham State College Library and to those at the government depositories at Lamont Library, Harvard University, and at Stonehill College, Easton, Massachusetts. A special thanks to Paul Hudon for his editorial suggestions and for typing the footnotes and bibliography, and to Ted Karns for his help in indexing.

Among those we interviewed, no one was more helpful than Corneliu Bogdan, the Romanian Ambassador to the United States from 1967 to 1976, and most recently the Deputy Foreign Minister of the National Salvation Front government in Romania. We were terribly saddened by his sudden death on January 1, 1990. He was a loyal Romanian, fine scholar and a wonderful gentleman. Further, the title of this book stems from a comment he made to us on April 11, 1987. He suggested that one of the reasons Nixon decided to visit Romania in 1969 was to "tweak the nose of the Russians." We also thank Ambassadors William Crawford, Harry Barnes and O. Rudolph Aggrey for their insights and comments.

Finally, we thank those we love, who kindly let us ignore some of our duties so we could live in archives, sit at microfilm readers and type on word processors. Special thanks to Brenda, Christopher and Megan Harrington, Bruce, Mary, Brian, Karen and Scott Courtney, and Jodi Rafus.

CHAPTER I

BACKGROUND: WAR AND PEACE

Romania Between Berlin and Moscow, 1939-1941

With the advantage of hindsight, the German-Soviet Pact of August 23, 1939, designed the ultimate fate of Romania as a Soviet satellite. By the August agreement, the Germans gave the Soviets a free hand in Romania. Ribbentrop recalled his confidential conversations with Molotov during the negotiations of the Non-Aggression Pact. The Fuhrer had instructed him to declare Germany's "complete political disinterest" in the area of Bessarabia and in Southeastern Europe. Ribbentrop did insist that Germany maintain an economic interest in the area, but both sides clearly understood that Romania was in the Soviet sphere of influence as was Western Poland in Germany's sphere.[1]

Hitler's rapid invasion of France, and Italy's belated declaration of war against Paris, prompted the Soviets to seize their promised lands in Romania. On June 26, 1940, the Soviets demanded the return of Bessarabia and the cession of Northern Bukovina from Bucharest. With encouragement from Germany to cooperate, the government of King Carol acquiesced on June 28. Four days later, Soviet troops marched into Bessarabia and settled on the river Pruth.[2]

In September, King Carol fled Romania. His son, Michael, assumed the throne and Marshal Antonescu formed a new cabinet. Within a month, German forces arrived in Romania, ostensibly to train Romanian soldiers and to protect Romania's oil wells against British designs. The German interest in these wells had been secured by the German-

Romanian treaty of March 23, 1939, which created a mixed Romano-German Company to prospect for petroleum and carry out a program of extraction and manufacture.[3]

On November 23, 1940, Romania joined the Rome-Berlin-Tokyo alliance. As Germany's ally, Bucharest accepted Hitler's *volte face*, and too attacked the Soviet Union in June, 1941. At the outset of the campaign, Romania wanted primarily to regain Bessarabia and Northern Bukovina, recently seized by Moscow. This accomplished, and with encouragement from Berlin, General Antonescu moved his Romanian troops across the Dneister River onto Soviet territory. While this produced some concern among moderate Romanians, most of the people supported Antonescu's move. Furthermore, Germany's control over Bucharest was "too strong to permit Antonescu to halt his armies even had he wished to do so."[4] The Romanian army would occupy Soviet territory until the Spring of 1944.

Moscow's Territorial Goals in Romania

Meanwhile, the European war quickly became part of a global conflict. Japan's attack on Pearl Harbor, and Hitler's war declaration against the United States on December 11, 1941, enormously enlarged the battle zone. However, these developments did not prevent Stalin from making his new allies aware of his precise territorial intentions toward Romania. Within a week of Germany's declaration of war against America, Stalin met with the British Foreign Minister, Sir Anthony Eden. The Soviet leader demanded British recognition of the Soviet frontiers as they existed on June 21, 1941, prior to the German invasion. This meant that Bessarabia and northern Bukovina belonged to the Soviets. In addition, Stalin wanted to establish Soviet airbases in Romania. In return, he would permit Britain to have bases in France, Belgium, the Netherlands, Norway or Denmark.[5]

When informed, Churchill rejected the proposal pointing out that territorial demands were in direct contradiction to the Atlantic Charter, a document which the Soviet Union had just subscribed to on September 24.[6] Britain would make no such agreement "secret or public, direct or implied, without prior agreement with the United States." Eden left Moscow on December 28 promising Stalin he would discuss the territorial demands with the United States and the British Dominions. As Averell Harriman later noted, "the Soviet territorial demands, in short, had not been rejected, only deferred."[7]

Since the Soviets had never recognized the cessation of Bessarabia to Romania, Stalin continued to demand its return. Correctly sensing that the British were not as wedded to the literal interpretation of the Atlantic Charter as were the Americans, Molotov renewed Moscow's claims on Bessarabia and Northern Bukovina in his May, 1942, meeting with Eden. Molotov suggested that the two countries sign a secret agreement guaranteeing the Soviet Union her Romanian claims. Eden refused. America would not support any wartime territorial changes.[8]

From Stalingrad to Tehran

The Soviet victory at Stalingrad forced Roosevelt and Churchill to take Stalin's claims for Romanian territory more seriously. Soviet troops would soon move into Eastern Europe. As a result, when Eden came to Washington in March, 1943, he noted that the President was more open than ever before to negotiating territorial settlements with the Soviets. Both men agreed that Stalin "would want, and should get, boundary concessions" from Romania.[9]

The Soviet victory at Stalingrad and the subsequent German loses to Red Army troops also impressed Mihai Antonescu, the Romanian Vice-Premier and Foreign Minister.[10] Romania was aware that the West, especially the United States, viewed Bucharest's involvement in the war as accidental. Roosevelt had certainly indicated this in January of 1942. He told Cordell Hull that rather than respond to the declarations of war made by Hungary, Romania, Bulgaria and Siam against the United States with a similar declaration, he should send a letter to the House Committee on Foreign Affairs and the Senate Committee on Foreign Relations to inform them of the declarations. Roosevelt hoped that no additional action either by Congress or the Executive Office would be necessary. Roosevelt maintained this position until June, 1942, when he finally agreed to declare war against the belligerents.[11] The Romanians hoped to capitalize on this attitude and began to send out peace feelers in mid-1943 to Britain and America. Bucharest hoped that the West would protect Romania against Soviet efforts to seize Bessarabia and Northern Bukovina.

However, Bucharest failed to see that the war had made Washington, London and Moscow into temporary bedfellows. Consequently, Romania's surrender proposals would ultimately require three power approval. The Allies had first addressed the issue of an enemy surrender at Casablanca. At this January, 1943 meeting, Roosevelt and Churchill decided on unconditional surrender as the sole basis for negotiating with an enemy state. Eight months later, at the Foreign Ministers Conference in October, Molotov accepted the Casablanca decision.[12] The Allies further agreed that any and all negotiations concerning the surrender of an enemy nation would be conducted jointly.[13]

One month later, in November, 1943, the Allies made a decision at Teheran that would place Romania's future firmly in the hands of Moscow. Although Roosevelt did not want to make any post-war political or territorial decisions during the war, military decisions which he accepted frequently carried considerable political-territorial significance. From November 27 to December 2, Roosevelt, Churchill and Stalin met to consider military strategies to end the war. Stalin persuaded Roosevelt that American forces in Italy should move north and west and prepare to invade southern France simultaneously with the Anglo-American invasion of Normandy. Roosevelt and Churchill's consent meant that the Soviet army alone would liberate the Balkans.[14]

Surrender Terms: Western and Soviet Views

Meanwhile, the Romanians continued to send peace feelers to British and American legations in neutral countries, while the Soviets began informal talks with representatives of the Antonescu regime. The Soviets knew of Romania's talks with the Western Allies and were determined to prevent Romania from making a separate peace with them, which would have "jeopardized its scheme to use Antonescu's surrender as justification for setting up a government of occupation of its own making and choice."[15]

In Washington, the State Department's Working Security Committee began studying Romanian surrender terms in January and February of 1944. They were approved by the Joint Chiefs of Staff and forwarded to the American representatives on the European Advisory Commission in London. These terms called for the "incorporation of Northern Bukovina and Bessarabia within the Soviet Union," and an adjustment of the Hungarian-Romanian frontier in Tranyslvania along ethnic lines. Further, if the Romanian people agreed to resist the Germans, and established a democratic government friendly toward the United Nations, "military occupation. . . would not be necessary." Romania would pay reparations in kind and emerge from the war as an independent state, with its economy and foreign commerce open to all nations.[16]

Of the many Romanian peace overtures, none was as celebrated as that of the former Premier, Prince Barbu Stirbei. With the consent of Bucharest, he visited Cairo on March 17, 1944, and met with British and American representatives.[17] However, his attempt at secret diplomacy with the West never materialized. The press announced his arrival in Cairo which forced the Anglo-American representatives to report the talks to their Soviet counterpart. The Western representatives told Stirbei that an armistice would include Romania's collaboration in the war against Germany, and freedom for Allied prisoners. Stirbei also met with the Soviet representative who indicated that an armistice would include Romania's cessation of Bessarabia and Northern Bukovina to Moscow along with reparation payments. Stirbei rejected the terms and left Cairo.[18]

If nothing else, the Cairo talks revealed differences between the Western allies and the Soviets concerning the future of Romania.[19] According to John Campbell, who worked on the American armistice terms, the State Department's draft armistice terms were "more or less discarded, because it didn't fit the kinds of drafts the Russians were producing."[20] In fact, the Soviet armistice terms were "in some respects, terms of peace." They dealt with territorial changes and reparations. Consequently, they were not easily reconcilable with the American principle of leaving such matters to a post-war conference.[21]

During the remainder of March, 1944, representatives of the Big Three allied powers worked on Romanian armistice terms. The American and Soviet delegations came to loggerheads over the issue of territory. The Americans saw territorial settlements and reparations as the province of a peace settlement, rather than terms for an armistice. The Soviets wanted Bessarabia and Northern Bukovina for themselves, and the restoration of most, if not all, of Transylvania to Romania. In addition, they wanted specific reparations.

Although the State Department balked, they would ultimately accept the Soviet terms. The Joint Chiefs of Staff simply wanted Romania out of the war, and were not concerned with the political and territorial particulars of the arrangement.[22] In addition, the Soviets played upon the fact that Romania had invaded their territory, and waged war for three years. As Campbell explained, "it was very difficult, from a political and moral view, for us to say to the Russians: 'You can't ask these Romanians not to pay for the fact that they were invading the Soviet Union and were allies of Hitler.' We found ourselves not in a position to take a very strong line."[23] As a result, the only concession the Soviets gave to the Americans was to include the phrase "subject to confirmation at the peace settlement" following the armistice provision on the Romanian-Hungarian border. This saved face for the Western allies, but "actually it didn't change the *de facto* situation."[24]

The armistice terms were essentially Soviet peace terms. The British and American delegations accepted the Soviet proposals on April 8, 1944. They departed from "unconditional surrender" by providing for a status tantamount to cobelligerency if Romania actively fought the Germans. Romania was encouraged to fight Hungary with a view to restoring all, or, the major part, of Transylvania to Romania. In turn, Romania recognized Soviet acquisition of Bessarabia and Northern Bukovina.[25]

Meanwhile on April 1, Soviet troops moved onto Romanian soil near Iasi. On the following day, Molotov publicly announced that the Soviets had no intention of annexing Romanian territory or of "changing the existing social order in Romania." Translated, this meant that Bessarabia and Northern Bukovina were parts of the Soviet Union, and that the Pruth River was the Romanian-Soviet border.[26]

Churchill was not pleased. Efforts to convince the Romanians to accept an armistice had failed. Neither Marshal Antonescu nor Iuliu Maniu, the leader of one of the "tolerated opposition" parties, the National Peasants, were willing to make the moves necessary to bring Romania into the war against the Axis powers.[27] Churchill feared that unless something were done, the Soviets would seize all of the Balkans. Aware that Roosevelt did not want to discuss post-war issues until hostilities ceased, Churchill decided to negotiate bilaterally with Stalin to curb Soviet control of the Balkans. Eden broached the question of delimiting post-war zones in the Balkans to Soviet Ambassador Gusev on May 5, 1944.[28] The Foreign Minister suggested that the Soviets should take the lead in Romanian affairs while Britain would take the lead in Greek affairs. On May 18, the Soviets accepted Eden's proposal for delimiting zones, but insisted that the United States had to agree to the arrangement. Stalin did not trust his Western Allies, and since he was not yet in control of the Balkans, he did not want to forfeit future control on the basis of an Allied "misunderstanding."

Churchill notified Roosevelt on May 31 of his talks with Stalin and urged the President to "give this proposal your blessing." The zones were logical for in the light of the existing military situation, "Romania falls within the sphere of the Russian armies and Greece within the Allied command under General Wilson in the Mediterranean." Churchill also noted that this arrangement only applied "to war conditions" and did not affect postwar settlements.[29]

The American Secretary of State, Cordell Hull, learned of these talks through the British Ambassador to the United States, Lord Halifax. Hull was furious and adamantly opposed the suggestion. Roosevelt listened to Hull and notified Churchill on June 10 that his State Department would not approve the plan since it would most likely lead to spheres of influence. The President suggested that some consultative machinery be made to avoid the development of spheres of influence.[30] Churchill responded. The events in the Balkans were moving too quickly to permit consultative committee deliberations.

> It seems to me, considering the Russians are about to invade Romania in great force and are going to help Romania recapture part of Transylvania from Hungary. . . it would be a good thing to follow the same leadership considering that neither you nor we have any troops there at all and that they will probably do what they like anyhow.

Since the Soviets were "doing all the work in the area," Churchill requested that Roosevelt accept this delimiting arrangement for a trial period of three months," after which it must be reviewed by the three powers."[31]

Churchill's appeal succeeded. Unbeknownst to Hull, the President agreed to the three months trial on June 12. In fact, the Secretary of State did not know about Roosevelt's decision until June 30, which proved to be an example of Roosevelt's impromptu approach to foreign policy.[32] On July 1, Soviet Ambassador Gromyko sent an aide-memoire to Hull to confirm America's agreement to the Anglo-Soviet proposal. On July 15, Hull reaffirmed America's commitment, but noted that it was only given in consideration of the present war strategy. The consent should not be viewed as precedent setting and it "would be unfortunate if any temporary arrangement should be so conceived as to appear to be a departure from the principle adopted by the three governments at the Moscow Conference definitely rejecting the spheres-of-influence idea."[33]

A Romanian Coup

Meanwhile, armistice talks had continued at Cairo between Iuliu Maniu and representatives of the Big Three.[34] At the same time in Stockholm, secret talks were underway between the Soviets and Antonescu. However, neither set of talks came to fruition. Maniu thought he was in a stronger position to bargain than he was, while Antonescu ultimately feared the Soviets too much to cooperate. With both sets of talks collapsed,[35] the Soviets launched a major offensive into Romania on August 20. The attack came as a surprise to both the Germans and the Romanians. The Red army quickly overran the fortifications along the Dniester River, seized Iasi on the 22nd, and two days later secured most of Bessarabia. By August 23, the Soviets surrounded fifteen German divisions.[36]

King Michael met with Maniu and Constantine "Dinu" Bratianu, leader of the National Liberals, the other "tolerated opposition" party, on August 21. They quickly prepared their finals plans for the overthrow of Marshal Antonescu. On August 23, the King summoned Antonescu to Casa Noua, a villa on the grounds of the Royal Palace in Bucharest. Antonescu did not know what to expect. Michael arrested the Marshal and within a few hours formed a government of "national union" headed by General Constantine Sanatescu, the Marshal of the Palace and intimate of the King.[37] Later that evening, Michael broadcast the new government change over the radio. Further, he declared an end to hostilities, and announced that he was willing to accept an armistice offered by the Big Three.[38]

The Allies and the Armistice Terms

The Allies were surprised at the speed of the coup. On August 24, Clark Kerr, British Ambassador to the Soviet Union, notified Moscow that Britain and the United States would like to participate in drafting the armistice terms.[39] Churchill was primarily concerned with the lack of specificity in the armistice terms drafted the previous April. Nothing was stipulated about Allied control in Romania following the armistice, and the Prime Minister wanted to make sure that Britain maintained some leverage in Romania and influence in the Balkans. Kerr demanded Allied representation in the control of Romania. Averell Harriman, the American Ambassador agreed, but the United States was less demanding than Britain. Once again, the predominant influence of the Joint Chiefs of Staff overshadowed State Department proposals. The Joint Chiefs wanted Romania out of the war.

On August 25, Romania declared war on Germany, and the British notified the Soviets that two points needed special clarification in the armistice. The armistice had to provide for both an Allied Control Commission with British and American representation as well as the precise amount of reparations that Moscow intended to demand. Since this would take some negotiating, Molotov suggested giving Romania a preliminary armistice based on the terms rejected the previous April. On August 27 King Michael accepted the terms which ended Soviet-Romanian hostilities, but which did not end the Soviet military advance against the German army in Romania. On September 1, the Soviets entered Bucharest. On the next day, they continued their advance South toward the Bulgarian border.

Meanwhile, Molotov, Kerr and Harriman negotiated the final armistice terms. The Anglo-American representatives accepted Molotov's demand for $300 million in reparations. Churchill considered the demand very reasonable. Hull, in contrast, opposed any reparation stipulation in an armistice, preferring to leave such matters for the peace treaty. Nonetheless, he accepted the Soviet proposal noting that it was not precedent setting.[40] As for the Control Commission, the Soviets were reluctant to share power with the Western powers in Romania. Molotov found a solution. "The Control Commission in Romania would operate in the same way as the Control Commission in Italy."

Molotov knew that Britain and America had guaranteed Western control over Italy by limiting Soviet participation in the Allied Control Commission. Molotov decided to make Romania Moscow's Italy. His proposals insured Soviet domination of the Allied Control Commission and its subcommittees. London and Washington had awarded Moscow a political representative in Italy, independent of the Commission. Molotov offered Britain and America the same representation.[41] Confronted with the same terms they had given Moscow in Italy, the Western powers accepted the Soviet armistice proposal.

The Armistice

On September 12, Romania signed the Allied armistice terms. The 20 articles and annexes provided for Romania's: withdrawal from the war against the United Nations; entrance into the war against Germany and Hungary; cessation of Bessarabia and Northern Bukovina to the Soviet Union; repatriation of prisoners of war; release of all persons held in confinement on account of their activities or sympathies in favor of the United Nations; surrender of all war material of Germany and her satellites including military vessels and Romania's merchant fleet; payment of $300 million in reparations in kind over six years; restoration to the Soviet Union of all materials taken while the Romanian army occupied Soviet lands; agreement that all forms of communication would be subject to Allied (Soviet) High Command; restoration of all legal rights and interests of the United Nations and their nationals as they existed before the war, including the return of their property in good order; assistance in the arrest and trial of war criminals; dissolution of all Fascist organizations; and, restoration of Romanian civil control to most areas for the purpose of implementing instructions from the Allied (Soviet) High Command. Further, subject to confirmation at a peace conference, the terms annulled the Vienna Decree which returned Transylvania to Romania.[42]

One of the most significant parts of the Armistice was Article 18. It established the Allied Control Commission which would regulate and control the execution of the Armistice terms under the direction and orders of the Allied (Soviet) High Command until the conclusion of the peace. Article 18 proved to be the key to Soviet control of Romania. Washington naively understood the phrase "Allied (Soviet) High Command" to mean that the "military command there just happens to be a Soviet general. . . It doesn't mean that they do everything without regard to the wishes of the other two members of the Control Commission, the British and American generals."[43] However, Molotov knew exactly what the phrase would mean in light of the Soviet military presence in Romania. The Soviet representative alone would have the authority to issue orders to the Romanian government; the Soviet representatives of the Commission would exercise executive power; and, the Anglo-American representatives would be as inconsequential in the decision making process as the Soviet representatives were on the Italian Allied Control Commission.[44]

No sooner had Romania accepted the armistice than Harriman and Churchill began to have second thoughts. The American representative cabled Hull that he feared that the armistice terms would enable the Soviets to dominate Romania.[45] Churchill had a greater fear. The continued drive of the Soviet-Romanian armies toward Yugoslavia, Bulgaria and Hungary could give Moscow total control of the Balkans, including Greece.[46] The Prime Minister wanted at all costs to prevent the fall of Greece and was quite willing to bargain away Romania, in order to establish an Anglo-Soviet balance in Southeastern Europe. On October 9, Eden and Churchill flew to Moscow and quickly met with Stalin. The Prime Minister immediately got to the point. He wanted spheres of influence in the Balkans with the Soviets having a 90%

predominance in Romania, 50% in Hungary and Yugoslavia, and 75% in Bulgaria, while Britain had 90% in Greece, 50% in Hungary and Yugoslavia, and 25% in Bulgaria. After writing these percentages on a half sheet of paper, he pushed it across the table to Stalin. The Premier "took his blue pencil and made a large tick upon it, and passed it back to us. It was all settled in no more time than it takes to set down."[47] Churchill was aware that this arrangement could appear callous, and two days later he notified Stalin that the percentages "could not be the basis of any public document, certainly not at the present time."[48] When Roosevelt learned of the arrangement, he notified Churchill that whatever had been done could only be viewed as preliminary, pending another Big Three conference.[49]

The Communists and the New Romanian Government

Meanwhile in Bucharest, the "national union" government struggled to survive against external pressures from the Allies as well as from internal dissension. The conservative government of General Sanatescu included a large number of army officers in important ministries, along with Maniu and Bratianu, leaders of the former "tolerated opposition," and Lucretiu Patrascanu from the Communist party.[50]

Communism had never had a strong tradition in Romania. It had first appeared there at the end of the nineteenth century in the person of Mikhail Katz, a Jewish emigre from Russia. Later known as Constantine Dobrogeanu-Gherea, he became the party theoretician, but without a large following. The internationalism of Soviet Marxism lacked appeal to the nationalistic Romanians who feared Russia. According to J. F. Brown, "it was doubtful whether the Romanian Communist party ever had more than 1,000 members."[51] However, the Soviet victory at Stalingrad and Moscow's subsequent Western offensive produced a power struggle among party members. On the one hand, there were those Romanian Communists who had spent much of the war in the Soviet Union. Foremost among them were Ana Pauker, Vasile Luca and Emil Bodnaras. Pauker, the daughter of a Moldavian Rabbi, arrived in Moscow as part of a prisoner exchange with Bucharest in 1940. Luca was a Transylvanian who served as a Major in the Soviet Army, and Bodnaras was a Ukrainian-Romanian deserter. In a strongly nationalistic society, none of these "Moscow" Communists were viewed as truly ethnic Romanians.

On the other hand, there was the Romanian faction of the Romanian Communist party led by Gheorghe Gheorghiu-Dej. He was imprisoned in the 1930s for his involvement in a railroad workers union. He spent sufficient time in a prison in Transylvania to add the prison town's name, Dej, to his own surname.[52] Other members of this so-called "native" Communist group were Lucretiu Patrascanu, Gheorghe Apostol, Chivu Stoica, Nicolae Ceausescu and Miron Constantinescu, all of whom spent most of the war in jail in Romania. Although both groups of Communist supported Soviet policies, the Kremlin preferred dealing with the "Moscow" group.[53] Consequently, Gheorghiu-Dej and his "native" party followers accepted the role assigned them, carried out Soviet orders, but never surrendered their nationalistic beliefs that the Romanian Communist Party ought to be an independent Communist party.[54]

Having only one portfolio in the new government, the Communists decided to move to increase their party strength. In October, the Communists allied with a leftist farmers party called the Plowmen's Front, splinter elements of the Social Democrats, various labor unions, several social welfare organizations such as the Patriotic Defense, and "front" organizations such as the Union of Patriots to form the National Democratic Front, or FND.[55] Of these allies, the Plowmen's Front would play the largest role principally because of its founder and leader Petru Groza. He was a wealthy landowner and industrialist, who held a cabinet post in the 1920s and who founded the Plowmen's Front in 1933.[56] Neither the National Peasant Party nor the National Liberal Party joined the FND.

On November 5, the first cabinet of General Sanatescu collapsed due to protests from the Soviet Control Commissioner General Vinogradov, on alleged non-fulfillment of the armistice terms. Sanatescu formed a new government which included four representatives from each of the National Liberal and National Peasant parties, three representatives from the Socialists, and one Communist. This cabinet passed several significant measures, such as arresting former Iron Guardists and repealing all anti-Jewish legislation.[57] Nonetheless, the FND bitterly attacked the Minister of the Interior, Nicolae Penescu, a member of the National Peasant Party. They attacked the conservative Penescu, accusing him of protecting Fascists. The government collapsed.[58] General Radescu replaced Sanatescu as Premier, and assumed the Minister of

Interior post. The Communists had secured their first government victory.

The Washington Response

Meanwhile in Washington, the State Department was trying to develop a new policy toward Eastern Europe in light of the successful Soviet offensive in the Balkans. In November, 1944, a State Department report concluded that the Soviets would assume a dominant position in the Balkans similar to the United States position in the Americas. The Soviets needed to strengthen their military security to insure access to the Black Sea.[59] In its analysis of Soviet foreign policy, the Department believed that the Soviets wanted economic and political cooperation with all states on the basis of sovereign equality and independence, and non-interference in the internal affairs of other states.[60] In projecting the future of each Balkan state, the Department believed that if Romania felt secure with her neighbors, "a democratic regime, which would possess the elements of stability, resting on the peasantry, might be developed."[61] In a subsequent study, on November 28, the State Department anticipated that the Soviet Union might try to construct a *cordon sanitaire* in the Balkans, so that no country or group of countries could threaten Russia in the future. However, the report noted, that designs for Balkan unions have been "as common as olives at a Greek table," but due to mutual animosities among the states, no union had yet evolved.[62]

On November 8, Secretary of State Edward Stettinius sent his department a memo for their consideration outlining six goals he thought American foreign policy should pursue. The United States should work to ensure self-determination of peoples, equality of opportunity in commerce, unrestricted access to all forms of media and public information vehicles, freedom for American philanthropic and educational organizations to carry on their work on the basis of most-favored-nation treatment,[63] protection of American citizens and property, and that all territorial settlements be left until the end of the war.[64] Two months later, in anticipation of the Yalta Conference, the State Department adopted five of Stettinius's recommendations.[65] The last was dropped so that Roosevelt, if needed, could offer Stalin territorial concessions to entice him into the war against Japan.

By January, 1945, the State Department had prepared a report on Romania in preparation for the forthcoming Big Three meeting. America's goal was to establish an independent Romania, which offered equal economic opportunities for all states.[66] Washington accepted Moscow's leading role during the Armistice period, because the Soviets had a "more direct interest in Romania" than did the other Allied powers.

However, in the execution of the Armistice, the United States did not intend to surrender its responsibilities. The principal American representative on the Allied Control Commission, Brigadier General Schuyler, had the right to be informed of the policy directives issued in the name of the Commission before they were communicated to the Romanian government.[67] However, this was not always done. John Campbell noted that people in the State Department and the Pentagon "were being bombarded" by cables saying "What kind of an Allied Control Commission is this? We don't have any say about anything. The Russians are running the whole show."[68] The Department was especially concerned by the January, 1945, Soviet decision to deport "racial" Germans from Romania for labor service in the USSR. The Commission had issued orders to this effect, when, in fact, the United States had no knowledge of the decision.[69]

In addition to Schuyler's reports, the State Department also received complaints from Burton Y. Berry, the American political representative in Romania who worked independently of the Commission. Berry was especially upset at the Soviet decision to remove petroleum refinery equipment from the American owned Romano-Americana oil company. As a result, the State Department urged the President to get assurances that the Soviets would consult with the Anglo-American representatives on the Control Commission on all decisions, especially those including reparations and boundaries.[70]

Roosevelt had the opportunity to deal directly with the Soviets at Yalta, in February, 1945. However, he chose not to raise the Romanian issue. Instead, the Yalta talks focused on the United Nations, postwar Germany, Soviet participation in the war against Japan, and the boundaries and government of Poland. Much of the attention focused on the Polish questions, because their resolution would indicate the extent of Soviet control in Eastern Europe.

With this in mind, the State Department drafted a "Declaration on Liberated Europe" for the approval of the Big Three. The Declaration called for the three powers to work jointly to help the liberated peoples

to "create democratic institutions of their own choice," by forming interim "governmental authorities broadly representative of all democratic
elements in the population and pledged to the earliest possible establishment through free elections of governments responsive to the will of
the people." If problems arose, the Declaration provided that "when in
the opinion of the three governments, conditions. . . make such actions
necessary, they will immediately consult together on the measures necessary to discharge the joint responsibilities set forth in this declaration."[71]

In the initial draft, the Department had recommended that the Big
Three establish a European High Commission to enforce the Declaration's provisions. However, the President rejected the idea because he
did not want another commission.[72] Without an enforcement apparatus,
Stalin, Churchill and Roosevelt quickly approved the Department's proposal with little modification. The Big Three agreed that this declaration reaffirmed their commitment to the Atlantic Charter and their
determination to build a world of peace, security and freedom.[73] State
Department officials were excited. The Declaration appeared to provide
a vehicle to recoup some of the losses of the Armistice agreement.[74]

The Radescu Government

Meanwhile in Bucharest, the Communists worked to overthrow the
Radescu government. The war had left Romania without institutions
and with socio-economic-political chaos. In fact, government control
scarcely extended beyond Wallachia and Southern Transylvania. The
Soviets maintained order in Bessarabia, later renamed the Moldavian
SSR, and in Northern Transylvania, where Bucharest officials were unable to prevent Romanians from avenging four years of persecution
under Hungarian occupation.[75]

In January, 1945, Ana Pauker and Gheorghiu-Dej went to Moscow.
The Kremlin encouraged them to be more aggressive. Radescu's government was ripe for overthrow. The conservative parties viewed him as
too liberal, while the leftists groups saw him as too conservative. Upon
their return, the Communist party called for a new government and
hinted that were the FND in power, Romania might regain Northern
Transylvania.[76] The Communists continued to harass Radescu. He
eventually ignored the fact that he was a "nonpolitical appointee," and
assumed leadership of those forces which opposed the left. On February
20, National Peasants and Communists waged a bloody battle at the

Malaxa Metullurgical Works in Bucharest. On the following day, both the British and American representatives on the Control Commission protested to General Vinogradov about the threatening situation. However, the British action was more for form than substance. Their Moscow "percentage" agreement the previous October undermined the strength of their protest. Vinogradov blamed the Fascist Radescu government for all of Romania's problems.[77]

The final crisis occurred on February 24. The Communist-led FND sponsored a major demonstration in Bucharest. Shots killed several demonstrators. That evening Radescu attacked Pauker and Luca over the radio. He denounced them as "horrible hyenas" and as "foreigners without God or country," clearly referring to their Jewish and Hungarian origins. The FND called Radescu a murderer,[78] and at ten o'clock that evening, General Vinogradov, the Soviet head of the Allied Control Commission, took Radescu to task.[79]

On the same day, Harriman told the Soviet government that the United States wanted order restored in Romania, or else there should be consultations among the Big Three.[80] On February 27, Molotov gave his answer. His deputy, Andrei Vyshinski, went to Bucharest and saw the King. With his customary "quick, abrupt gestures and rapid speech,"[81] he told Michael that Radescu had to be replaced by a new government "truly representative of the democratic forces of the country."[82] Vyshinsky returned the following day, and in a celebrated meeting with the King gave Michael 2 hours and 5 minutes to announce to the public Radescu's replacement. The King tried to have Prince Stirbei form a government, but the Communists refused to join. Vyshinsky quickly sent word that Petru Groza was the Soviet choice.[83] Michael procrastinated until March 1, when under strong Soviet pressure, he conceded and asked Groza to form a new government.[84] The crisis had forced the King to consider abdication, but he decided to remain "to see what he could do for his people."[85] On March 2, Soviet tanks drove down the streets of Bucharest.[86] On March 6, the Groza government officially took office. There were no loyal members of the National Peasant party or the National Liberals in the Cabinet.

However, not all the members were Communists. The Cabinet also included George Tatarescu, a former premier and leader of a dissident Liberal group. However, his past involvement with anti-Semitic movements and his pro-German position during the war, so compromised him that he would be a docile instrument of the left. There were other dissident Liberals and Peasant party members, but there were none that would oppose Communist leadership. One striking feature of the new Cabinet was that all of the members were ethnically Romanian. Stephen Fischer-Galati believes that this was due to Moscow's accepting the advice of the "moderates" in the Romanian Communist Party, who "urged the pursuit of policies of 'persuasion' of Romanians by Romanians with a view to gaining the support of the masses for 'progressive reforms'."[87] Three days later, on March 9, the Soviets approved the reannexation of Northern Transylvania to Romania; Romania received her reward for accepting the Groza regime.

Western Reaction to the Groza Regime

Neither Churchill nor Roosevelt liked these developments, nor did the American Minister, Burton Berry, who cabled Washington that the Groza regime did not represent the Romanian people. If the Yalta Declaration of Liberated Europe meant anything, there should be consultation among the Big Three to alter the Romanian situation.[88] Berry was frustrated. He had chased Vyshinsky all over Bucharest, trying to get him to talk about the Yalta Declaration, but without success. He was genuinely ready to resign. In fact, the inability of the United States to affect any change in Romania had reached the point that Berry and two other young Foreign Service officers on his staff, Roy Melbourne and Charles Hulick seriously contemplated resigning *en masse*.[89]

Part of their frustration came from a lack of direction from Washington. Neither Roosevelt nor Churchill wanted to save Romania and lose Poland.[90] On March 8, Churchill wrote the President. He recognized Soviet control of Romania and admitted that Britain had been hampered in its protests because at Moscow, Eden and he had surrendered Romania to save Greece. Now, "we have on our hands the much more important issue of Poland, and I do not therefore want to do anything as regard [to] Romania which might prejudice our prospects of reaching a Polish settlement." Churchill was willing to support Roosevelt in a message to Stalin urging him not to "immediately" purge all political opposition in Romania.[91]

Three days later Roosevelt replied. He agreed with the Prime Minister. Romania was not a good place for a test case. Poland was more important.[92] However, Roosevelt did decide to have Harriman talk with the Soviets about the need for a Big Three meeting to ensure that the Yalta Declaration was implemented in Romania.[93] Harriman understood that Romania was of secondary importance.[94] On March 16, Harriman talked to the Soviets. He urged them to call a meeting of the Big Three to discuss the present political situation in Romania and her future form of government. Both of these issues were outside the province of the Allied Control Commission, and therefore were appropriate for a Big Three meeting. The Soviets refused, and since implementation of the Yalta Declaration required consultation by all three powers, the Western Allies had no recourse available to affect change.[95] Instead, the Americans decided to show their displeasure with the Groza regime by having as limited contact with it as possible.[96] The Soviet decision not to live by the Yalta Declaration became the first major source of dissension between the Soviet Union and her Western allies. Ironically, Romania had proved to be the first major problem the Soviets had with their German "ally" in 1940.

Moscow and Romania's Oil

One reason that the United States was so upset about not having a voice in Romania was economics. Implementation of the reparation provisions in the Armistice gave the Soviets a dominant position in the Romanian economy, and enabled her to secure control over the oil industry, an area that had been largely developed by American and British petroleum companies. Since the turn of the century American oil companies had invested in Romania. Principal among them was Romano-Americana owned by the Standard Oil Company of New Jersey. America had used her influence over the years to insure that the Romanian oil industry remained available to American development. In the 1920s, when Romania intended to pass a law designed to reduce foreign control over her oil industry, the State Department threatened diplomatic action forcing Bucharest to reconsider.[97] In February, 1926, America signed a trade agreement granting Romania most-favored-nation trade status, and thereafter American-Romanian economic relations improved. By the outbreak of the war, America controlled 13.8% of Romania's oil production.[98] This ended abruptly during the war when Germany seized control of Romania's oil industry. Consequently, when the Soviets moved into Romania in the Summer of 1944, they viewed oil and all oil-related equipment, including pipes and refineries, as German owned war booty, and later as in kind reparation payments.[99]

Moscow viewed Eastern Europe as a warehouse from which they

could rebuild the devastated Soviet economy. The German invasion had destroyed the farmland of the Ukraine and the coal fields in the Don Basin. Over 30,000 industrial plants were destroyed along with over 40,000 miles of railroad track. Iron production stood at 65% of the pre-war level.[100] Reparations was a rapid means to reconstruct and rein-dustrialize the Soviet Union, and to provide her economic security. Romanian oil and industry was one part of that reparations program. To guarantee continued economic relations with Romania, the Soviets signed an Armistice Agreement and Reparations Convention with Bucharest on January 16, 1945, reserving 40% of the oil output for themselves during each of the next six years. Subsequently, the Soviets built a pipe line from Ploesti directly to Odessa using, in the process, material from a former German pipe line which had run between Ploesti and Giurgiu on the Danube.[101]

Washington and London protested Moscow's seizure of the oil equipment. They maintained that the equipment belonged to British and American oil companies and had been illegally taken by the Ger-mans. The Soviets ignored these complaints until the January treaty with Bucharest, when they agreed that they would not remove any more oil equipment from Western firms, even though they contended that such material was legal war booty.[102] In early March the United States again protested that the Soviets were unwilling to let American oil busi-nessmen enter Romania.[103] However, the protests were not followed up because both Roosevelt and the State Department were focused on the Polish problem.[104]

On April 12, 1945, Franklin Delano Roosevelt suffered a massive brain hemorrhage and died. The new President, Harry S. Truman, was inexperienced in foreign affairs and received numerous briefings. On May 2, he met with General Schuyler, the American representative on the Allied Control Commission in Bucharest. Truman was furious at the way the Americans were treated. His initial reaction was to remove all United States representatives from Romania. However, Joseph Grew, the Acting Secretary of State, counseled against it, noting that by doing so America would surrender what little influence she still had.[105] Rec-ognizing that the new President appeared willing to pursue a more ag-gressive Romanian policy, Schuyler made four recommendations to Truman. He should seek first, to create a truly tripartite Allied Control Commission, with equal representation by each of the three members; second, to broaden the Groza government to include proportional representation of all political parties; third, to resume commercial relations between Romania and the other Allied nations, especially Britain and America; and fourth, to have the Commission institute economic reforms to restore stability to Romania.[106]

On May 8, Victory in Europe day, Romania and the Soviet Union signed an economic accord providing for the development of mixed Soviet-Romanian companies, or Sovroms. Following Bucharest's ratification, the agreement took effect on July 17, the opening day of the Potsdam Conference. There were numerous Sovroms including Sovromtransport, and Sovrombanc. However, the one Sovrom that particularly interested the Western Allies was Sovrompetrol, which legally cemented Soviet control of the Romanian oil industry.

Sovrompetrol was responsible for the exploration, refining, and marketing of all oil and oil products.[107] The Soviet contribution to the joint company consisted, to a large degree, simply of shares of oil companies seized as reparations by Moscow, despite the protests of former owners.[108] The Romanian contribution consisted of the shares and assets of the two largest Romanian oil companies, at least 50% of all crude oil royalties paid to Romania, and Sovrompetrol's inclusion under the Petroleum Law of 1942. This meant that Bucharest recognized Sovrompetrol as a company indigenous to Romania and as such entitled to all discriminatory privileges exercised by Romanian owned companies, including preference to purchase oil exploration rights. The 1942 Petroleum Law reserved for Sovrompetrol one-fourth of all new oil lands and granted it a variety of tax and credit privileges.[109]

Sovrompetrol also included considerable equipment taken from American oil companies. By March, 1945, the Romano-Americana oil company complained that the Soviets had taken nearly seven thousand tons of equipment, or 65% of their total equipment stock. In May, the Soviets seized additional stock. The State Department objected, but the Soviets reassured Washington that they were only taking equipment which was considered excess, or had been brought into Romania by Germany during the Nazi occupation. The Soviets said that all equipment seized bore German markings, had not been paid for by Romano-Americana, and had been destined for the Baku oilfields. Hence, all material came under Article 7 of the Armistice as "war trophies." The State Department notified the Soviets that should the equipment not be returned, American owned oil companies would be compensated by either Romania through reparations, or by the Soviet Union by direct payment.[110]

Potsdam and Romania

Meanwhile, in an effort to further solidify Soviet control over Romania, Stalin urged his allies to join him in reestablishing diplomatic relations with Romania, as well as with Bulgaria and Finland.[111] This May 27th offer stirred considerable discussion in Washington. Six days later Truman agreed to resume diplomatic relations with Finland because she had not been at war with the United States, and had adopted democratic principles and procedures. However, the latter was not true in Romania or Bulgaria. Truman reminded Stalin that in March, the United States had suggested tripartite consultation to resolve some of the political problems in Romania, but the Soviets had refused to implement the Yalta Declaration. Consequently, the United States would not resume diplomatic relations with Bucharest.[112] While Stalin repeated his request on June 9, neither Truman nor Churchill budged. Rather, the President suggested that the entire issue be discussed at their forthcoming meeting in Potsdam.[113]

By early July, the positions of the three Allied powers had become hardened toward Romania. Soviet interests in descending order were: to see that Romania paid its debts and made restitution for damage caused to the Soviet Union during the war; to obtain all possible economic benefits from Romania; to insulate Romania from Western capitalist penetration; and, to maintain and perpetuate a regime friendly to Moscow.

London had been reluctant to protest Soviet actions in Romania primarily because she had accepted Soviet primacy in Romania. Nevertheless, Britain wanted to prevent Soviet domination of Eastern Europe, and to limit the spread of Communism. In addition, Britain had special economic interests. While her prewar trade with Romania had been small, her financial investments, especially in oil, were large. Britain hoped to resume her financial relations with Romania and as Europe's major industrial power, London wanted to expand her export trade to Bucharest.

The United States interests in Romania were even less defined than those of Britain. Washington wanted Romania to be politically independent with a government of the people's choice. Economically, America had little at stake in Romania save some oil investments. However, America wanted an "open-door" policy everywhere in order to take advantage of her economic power. Finally, America was in a better position to complain about Soviet policies than Britain, because London could be criticized about her Greek interests, a risk not shared by the United States.[114]

Notwithstanding these differences, the United States prepared for the upcoming meeting at Potsdam. There were several areas of special concern. First was Allied recognition of the governments of Romania, Bulgaria and Hungary. There appeared to be three courses of action possible: first, to accept Stalin's proposal for immediate recognition; second, to support a British proposal for the immediate conclusion of peace treaties with the present governments, which would implicitly grant them recognition; and, third, to insist on the reorganization of the present government through free general elections as a condition to establishing diplomatic relations and later peace.

The State Department immediately dismissed the first option. As for the second, Washington did not share London's view that a peace treaty would end Soviet domination. More importantly, a peace treaty would legitimatize the present governments. Consequently, the State Department recommended the third option which would be consistent with the Atlantic Charter and the Yalta Declaration on Liberated Europe. There would be no recognition until there was tripartite consultation to insure free and democratic elections.[115]

The second area of concern involved economics. The American representatives in Bucharest wanted the Allies to establish a total dollar value of Romania's obligations to Moscow as required under Article 10 of the Armistice. This article required Romania to underwrite the costs of all Soviet troops on Romanian soil. During the first ten months of the Armistice, Romania had already paid approximately 800 billion lei. The German defeat, ironically, increased Romania's obligation. The Soviets interpreted Article 10 to mean that Bucharest had to pay the expenses of the Red Army as it marched home through Romania. As a result, the Bucharest payments to Moscow under Article 10 would soon surpass the total reparation payments of 1,200 billion lei set in Article 11 of the Armistice. To make matters worse for Bucharest, Moscow had yet to set a date for Soviet troop withdrawal from Romania.[116]

However, while this was a pressing issue to the American delegation in Romania, Washington chose not to raise this question at Potsdam.

The State Department was far more concerned with reaching an agreement with the Soviets on the definition of war booty, than on protecting Bucharest from paying Moscow more lei. The Department wanted to make a distinction between material considered war booty, rightfully belonging to the Soviet Union, and American property, which should not be removed without compensation.[117]

Washington was also concerned about the recently concluded Sovrom agreements which gave the Soviets at least a dominant, if not exclusive, control over Romania's industry and trade. This exclusivity went counter to America's commercial interests and the United States wanted trade expansion on a multilateral, non discriminatory basis. Conceding that the Soviets had special security interests in Romania, the United States, however, opposed preferential economic arrangements which guaranteed Moscow monopolistic control of Bucharest's economy.[118] Moreover, Washington wanted free access for American businessmen into Romania in order to carry on commercial and governmental operations.[119]

The third issue involved Transylvania. Recalling the Wilsonian principle of self determination, the State Department wanted to revise the Romanian-Hungarian border so that lands with large Magyar populations would fall within Hungary's border. The Armistice had recognized that this boundary was subject to confirmation at the peace conference.[120]

Peace making was another concern. The British were very eager to make peace with Romania, and the other Balkan countries, assuming that such peace treaties would curtail Soviet influence. The United States did not share this view. To the contrary, they saw no reason to assume that the peace treaties would provide a panacea. If nothing else, the Armistice guaranteed continued Anglo-American presence, and some influence, through political representatives and membership on the Allied Control Commission.[121] On the other hand, the Armistice was not a long term solution. Washington was willing to end the Armistice and begin peace talks once there was a new government, freely elected and representative of all the people. The United States agreed that the Armistice terms caused undo problems for Romania. Nonetheless, Washington did not want to surrender her limited influence in Romania by replacing the Armistice with the present Soviet controlled government.[122]

The fifth issue concerned the withdrawal of Soviet troops from Romania as agreed upon in the Four Nation Declaration of Moscow on

October 30, 1943.[123] However, nothing could be done about this until there was peace. And the sixth and final issue renewed the call for reorganizing the Allied Control Commission to insure genuine three power decision making.

Anticipating that the Western Allies would want to address this last issue, Moscow announced a revision in the administrative operations of the Allied Control Commissions. In the Hungarian Allied Control Commission, the Soviets decided that Allied Control Commission directives to the Hungarian authorities would only be issued after "agreement" with the British and American representatives.[124] Four days later, on July 16, the Deputy Chairman of the Romanian Allied Control Commission, General Susaikov, announced similar revisions. There would be regularly called conferences of the Commission, at least every ten days, and directives would be issued to the Romanian authorities after tripartite "discussion." The Soviets guaranteed that the American and British representatives could travel freely throughout the country, provided the Commission was informed beforehand of time and destination. Finally, the British and Americans had the right to determine the size and composition of their delegations.[125]

The new directive read well. However, there was a glaring difference between the Hungarian and Romanian revisions. Tripartite discussion, was not tripartite agreement, and consequently, there was no reason to assume that there would be any difference in the conduct of affairs in Romania as a result of this new Soviet offer. Schuyler reminded the War Department that the Commission was the supreme authority in Romania; it was a policy making body and an executive agency as well. The Commission exercised complete and autocratic control over all phases of Romanian national life.[126] Therefore it was incumbent that at Potsdam, the Western Allies secure genuine equality in the Commission's decision making process.

The Conference opened on July 17, and quickly Truman suggested that the Big Three form a Council of Foreign Ministers which would draft treaties of peace with Italy, Romania, Bulgaria, Hungary, and Finland. Except for the issue of membership on the Council, the Big Three adopted the proposal.[127] As the European Advisory Council had served as the wartime problem-solving mechanism, the Council of Foreign Ministers, or CFM, could assume this function in peacetime, thereby enabling the Big Three to maintain at least the facade of unity.

With this structural organization approved, the American delegation raised the issue of recognizing the governments of Romania and Bulgaria. To implement the Yalta Declaration, the United States demanded that the present governments be reorganized through free elections to include representatives of all the significant democratic parties. Once this was done, Washington would recognize the new regimes and sign peace treaties with them. The Soviets rejected the American proposal. The United States had already recognized the Italian government,[128] why could it not recognize the governments in Romania and Bulgaria? Each of these countries had contributed ten to twelve divisions to defeat the enemies of the United Nations. Yet, the Western powers refused them diplomatic recognition. Legitimate governments already existed in Romania and Bulgaria, and they were at least as legitimate as the British controlled government in Greece and the Anglo-American controlled government in Italy.[129]

An impasse developed. The Americans argued that representatives of the world press ought to be able to enter the former Axis satellite countries, have freedom of movement and be able to send or broadcast their reports without interference. While discussions would continue for the next several days, the Soviets made only one concession. There would be greater freedom for the media in Romania, provided it did not interfere with internal security.[130] The Americans repeated their demand for free elections adding that they should be supervised by representatives of the Big Three. Molotov quickly dismissed the need for election supervisors. The only elections held to date in an ex-enemy country were in Finland. They were without supervision, and none of the Allied powers had any complaints. Consequently, there was no reason for supervised elections.[131] However, the debate went on. With America leading and Britain in support, the Western powers insisted on the need for representative governments in Romania and Bulgaria as the *sine qua non* for diplomatic recognition and subsequent peace treaties. At one point, when Churchill pointed out the restrictions imposed on the British representatives in Bucharest as an indication of the lack of freedom in Romania, Stalin retorted: "they are all fairy tales!"[132]

As the deadlock developed, the American Secretary of State, James Byrnes, found a middle ground. On July 24, he suggested to his foreign minister counterparts that following the conclusion of peace treaties with "recognized democratic governments" in Romania, Bulgaria, Hungary and Finland, the Big Three "support their application for membership in the United Nations."[133] Discussion ensued, especially over the definition of "democratic," which Byrnes had deliberately left vague. Finally, Molotov suggested that the ministers send Byrnes' proposal to the

Big Three, since they were "more reasonable people than we" and could find a solution.[134]

A couple of days later, Truman, Stalin, and Clement Attlee, Britain's new Prime Minister following Churchill's election defeat, issued a communique noting that the CFM would prepare treaties for Bulgaria, Finland, Hungary and Romania. "The conclusion of Peace Treaties with recognized democratic Governments in these States will also enable the three Governments [Big Three] to support application from them for membership in the United Nations."[135] The Big Three adopted the Byrnes resolution as a "quick fix" to a long term problem. The ambiguity of the proposal enabled Stalin, Truman and Attlee all to agree without anyone of them surrendering his position.

American economic concerns fared little better at Potsdam. Both Britain and the United States had concerns about the seizure of Allied property as "war booty" by the Soviets. There were only two articles in the Armistice which permitted property removal from Romania. The first, Article 11, dealt with reparations. But the Soviets did not claim that the oil equipment was removed for purposes of reparations. The second, Article 7, called upon Romania to hand over as war "trophies" material from Germany and her satellites. The problem was in distinguishing between German and non-German material, especially in the coveted area of oil equipment. The Soviets argued that the Germans owned most of the oil equipment and consequently, it was a legitimate war "trophy." The British and American representatives, encouraged by oil industry representatives, argued the contrary. Both of the Western powers wanted restitution of, or compensation for, Allied oil equipment already seized, and both wanted the Soviets to stop further removal of such equipment. On July 24, the British suggested a tripartite commission to investigate the origin of the oil equipment. The Soviets countered with the suggestion of two bilateral commissions, one with Britain and one with the United States.[136] The Western Allies agreed and the Potsdam Protocol called for the two commissions to begin work within ten days.[137]

The Americans postponed making a decision on their other economic concern, the resumption of commercial relations with Romania, pending recognition of a "responsible democratic government" in Bucharest. The Big Three sent the issue of Transylvania's border to the Council of Foreign Ministers as a treaty provision, along with the questions of continued Soviet occupation of Romania and the duration of the Armistice.

The last issue the American's wanted to address was equality in the decision-making process on the Allied Control Commission. Without question, the Soviet decision on July 16 to permit greater Anglo-American participation on the Control Commissions had its effect. The Hungarian resolution was welcomed by the Western Allies and, with the exception of General Schuyler, most of the American delegates accepted the Romanian offer as a genuine improvement.[138] Consequently, the Big Three adopted the Soviet proposal which called for tripartite discussion before the Commission sent directives to the Romanian authorities.[139] However, the final communique did not include the original Soviet language calling for "regular and frequent meetings" of the Allied representatives. Molotov argued the ambiguity of the words "regular" and "frequent" at such length that finally Byrnes, and Ernest Bevin, his British counterpart, accepted the deletion on the closing day of the conference.[140]

On August 9, President Truman told the American public that Romania, Bulgaria, and Hungary were not to be spheres of influence of any one power. They were governed by Allied Control Commissions composed of the representatives of the Big Three. "These Control Commissions, it is true, have not been functioning completely to our satisfaction; but improved procedures were agreed upon at Berlin."[141]

The Soviets Recognize the Groza Government

Coincidental with the opening of the Potsdam Conference, representatives of the National Liberal and National Peasant parties in Romania met with Prince Stirbei to organize political demonstrations against the Groza government. American sources maintain that the United States was deliberately kept in the dark so that the demonstration would not appear to be Anglo-American inspired. On July 18, Maniu stated categorically "the government must go." Two days later, Dinu Bratianu, also, called for an end to the FND government.[142] While Maniu would later admit that the activities were necessary to maintain party morale, he also believed that if free elections were held, the National Peasants "could confidently expect an overwhelming electoral majority." Maniu promised that his party would continue to organize nation wide opposition to the Groza regime.[143]

The essence of the Potsdam communique was that peace treaties would only be concluded with "recognized democratic governments." To facilitate the process, the Soviets recognized the Groza regime on

August 6, and resumed full diplomatic relations with Romania. Neither the United States nor Britain followed suit.[144] Washington notified its political representatives in Bucharest, that America hoped to see the Romanian government become more representative, but such a change would have to occur through Romanian efforts.[145] Berry and Melbourne urged the King to take action and to force the Groza regime to resign.[146] On August 16, Michael, who, ironically, had recently received the Soviet Order of Victory from Stalin,[147] met with representatives of the four parties to plan the coup. All but the Communists advised him to request the immediate resignation of the Groza government.[148]

On August 19, Michael asked Groza to resign, but he refused. Groza said that the Anglo-American position really had little significance since Moscow would sooner or later secure Anglo-American agreement to a peace treaty that would protect Romanian interests. On the following day the King repeated his request that Groza resign, and it was again refused. While Groza received assurances from Moscow,[149] Michael addressed identical letters to the American, British and Soviet representatives on the Allied Control Commission asking for their assistance to form a more representative government. The Soviets refused. The British and Americans did not respond because neither wanted to be blamed for the attempted coup. Shortly thereafter, Michael retired to his palace at Sinaia and refused to have further contact with members of the Groza government.[150] The Soviets had won the day. They were in no need of a peace treaty, and preferred control over Romania to Allied unity.

Ownership of Romania's Oil Equipment

The Potsdam Conference left the Big Three with several Romanian assignments. The Allies were first, to determine ownership of the oil equipment in Romania; second, to recognize a democratic government in Bucharest; and, third, to draft a peace treaty for the defeated nation. Without question, the oil equipment issue was the least significant, but the ensuing negotiations soon demonstrated the degree of mistrust which had developed among the victors within months of the war's end. On August 20, 1945, the Soviet-American Commission for the Study of Facts and Documents Concerned with the Removal of Oil Equipment from Romania held its first meeting. There would be eight more meetings extending through June 12, 1947.

The primary issue focused on ownership of the oil equipment in

Romania. The Romano-Americana oil company estimated the value of their lost equipment at about $2 million. While Berry believed this figure to be a bit high, he believed that the company had lost a substantial amount of money.[151] At the second meeting of the Commission on August 29, the Americans provided evidence of American ownership of Romano-Americana, and some files indicating removed equipment. The Americans suggested that the Soviets prepare similar lists in order to determine ownership of seized materials. The oil equipment belonged either to the Romano-Americana company or to the Germans, in which case, the Soviets had a perfect right to seize it as a war "trophy."

The third meeting proved critical. On September 6, The Soviets wanted the Americans to provide substantial documentation including the amount of oil equipment on hand in Romano-Americana properties as of January 1, 1942, and the amount, source and payment process of equipment received by the company between January 1, 1942, and October 1, 1944. Since the Soviets viewed all equipment as German property, the burden to prove ownership fell on the Romano-Americana company. This approach also meant that the Soviets did not have to provide any documentation. During the next four meetings, discussion focused on America's efforts to have the Soviets provide lists of specific items they considered German property. The Soviets refused, arguing that if a decision were made concerning a "part" of the equipment, it could prejudice decisions on the "whole" of the equipment. And since the Soviets viewed the "whole" as German property, there was no value in dealing with a selected "part."[152]

By the end of the seventh meeting, the American representatives agreed that they too were guilty of delaying tactics. The Americans hoped that their tardiness would convince the Soviets that their demand for complete documentation was foolhardy, and would hinder the overall work of the Commission. However, this tactic had not worked. Further, American efforts to have the CFM resolve the oil issued also failed.[153] Consequently, on April 8, 1946, the Americans decided to have the Romano-Americana company prepare extensive lists of materials on hand on January 1, 1942, receipts and consumption from January 1, 1942, through October 1, 1944, and stocks on hand on December 31, 1944. In essence, this fulfilled the Soviet request at the September 6, 1945 meeting.[154]

Roy Melbourne and C. Vaughan Ferguson, the American negotiators, presented the lists to the Soviets at the eighth meeting on October

8, 1946. The American team was frustrated. When they presented the lists, they told the Soviets that they were free to agree or disagree with the evidence. Whatever decision they made would be reviewed at a higher level. Melbourne and Ferguson had concluded that nothing could be gained through further meetings.

Efim Gurvich, the leading Soviet negotiator, wanted time to study the new materials. Reluctantly, Melbourne and Ferguson agreed to one more meeting. Eight months later, on June 12, 1947, the Commission reconvened. The Soviet position was unchanged. The oil equipment belonged to the Germans, and consequently the Soviet Union could seize it as war "trophies." Ferguson announced that in light of the fact that the Soviets had refused to present any documentation to prove that their seizures were legal, the American delegation refused to attend any more Commission meetings. The oil equipment issue ended as it had begun, without resolution and with the Soviets still using oil equipment confiscated from Romania.[155] Romano-Americana's parent company, Standard Oil, would wait until 1960 before receiving token compensation for its equipment.

American-British Recognition of the Groza Government

Unlike the oil issue, the other two tasks assigned the Big Three at Potsdam would reach resolution, but only after about 18 months of stressful negotiations. The Big Three had given the Council of Foreign Ministers the responsibility to draft a peace treaty with Romania, following Allied recognition of a democratic government in Bucharest. The issue of "democratic" nearly ended the Council talks. The CFM convened at Lancaster House, in St. James's Park, London, on September 11, 1945. Delegates from the United States, Great Britain, Soviet Union, France and China quickly agreed on the Council's procedure. All five Foreign Ministers could take part in preliminary discussions of each treaty, but when it came to voting on particular clauses, the state which had not signed the armistice would not be allowed to vote.[156] However, this agreement would prove to be the high point of the Fall meetings.

Moscow had recognized the Groza regime on August 6, before the Council convened. The United States had made no such determination. At the September 18 meeting, when the question of drafting a Romanian peace treaty came before the Council for discussion, the American Secretary of State made Washington's objections plainly known. The

Groza government did not represent the Romanian people and it was not democratic. Byrnes and Molotov quickly squared off. No longer inhibited by fear of forfeiting Western interests in Poland, and fortified by America's monopoly of the atomic bomb, Byrnes took a very strong position against the Soviets. Molotov was equally obstinate. America's unwillingness to share atomic secrets frightened Moscow, and Molotov decided to hide this fear behind a facade of belligerence. Further, Molotov was genuinely surprised that America refused to grant the Soviets a sphere of influence in the Balkans. Moscow had not interfered with Britain's move into Greece, and he assumed that Washington would act accordingly with respect to Soviet goals in Romania and Bulgaria. Molotov ignored the fact that America was not only not party to the "percentage" arrangements made in Moscow, but that Washington was appalled by the arrangement. Consequently, Byrnes' position caught Molotov off-guard and forced him to do everything he could to retain Soviet control in the Balkans.

Byrnes made it clear that Washington wanted first to discuss the representative nature of the Bucharest government, before America would begin any negotiations on a Romanian peace treaty. Molotov countered, noting that America was quick to support the Radescu government, which was hostile to the Soviet Union, but withdrew support from the Groza regime which was friendly to Moscow. Byrnes argued that America had no objections to a government friendly to the Soviets, provided it was "representative of all the democratic elements." He cited Poland as an example. At Potsdam the United States had agreed to a reorganization of the Polish government. Molotov rejected the analogy. Byrnes pressed on. The problem with the Groza government was that it was suspect in the eyes of America due to the role played by Vyshinsky. Further, Bucharest had restricted American press. Even in Greece, American correspondents were free to travel and report their findings. Molotov quickly retorted: "Apparently in Greece the correspondents are happy, but the people are not; whereas in Romania the people are happy, but the correspondents are not. The Soviet government attaches more importance to the feeling of the people."[157] The die was cast, and while further discussion ensued between Molotov and Byrnes, no progress was made on Romania.

The London meetings continued until October 2, and each day there seemed to be less and less agreement. Even the September 11 decision on Council procedure was rescinded. On September 22, Molotov wanted to eliminate France and China from most of the discussions. He implied that they were Western puppets. The most he would permit was for France to be consulted on West European problems and China on Far Eastern issues. When Bevin and Byrnes both refused, Molotov said that the Soviets would not be bound by the September 11 decision.[158] The Conference closed without even a communique, since Britain and America would not destroy the minutes of the September 11 meeting, and the Soviets refused to sign any joint statement.

Many members in the State Department were surprised that Byrnes was willing "to break up the conference on the issue of free elections in Romania and Bulgaria."[159] The Secretary's strong stance went counter to his nature. However, after the London meeting Byrnes returned to form. He thought of himself as a mediator. He also wanted to quickly conclude the peace treaties, so that America could reduce her substantial involvement in European affairs. As a result, he initiated several conciliatory moves. He extended diplomatic recognition to the provisional government of Austria on October 20, and to the provisional government of Hungary on November 2. In each case recognition was contingent on each country holding free elections. By the end of November, both nations held elections and the United States recognized both governments.[160]

The situation in Romania was not as easily resolved. Unrest continued in Bucharest. November 8 was the King's name day. The National Peasant and National Liberal parties had requested permission to assemble publicly to shout for the King. The Groza government consented and crowds gathered on the eighth. However, at the last minute the government withdrew its permission, and sent several truck loads of Communist workers into the demonstration taunting the crowd. Violence erupted and quickly government troops moved in to restore order. The Anglo-American representatives on the Allied Control Commission asked for a tripartite meeting, but the Soviet chairman refused. The Red Army was responsible for maintaining order in Bucharest, not the Commission. A few days later, the Communist newspapers blamed Maniu and Bratianu for the violence and deaths resulting from the demonstration.[161]

Reports from Bucharest bothered Byrnes. They consistently painted a bleak picture, portraying the Groza government as evil. Byrnes wanted more information on the internal situation in Bucharest. He apparently believed that a new set of eyes might see Romania in a different light. He called upon his old friend Mark Ethridge, publisher of the *Louisville Courier-Journal*, to visit Romania and Bulgaria.

Ethridge was liberal, and as such might show more understanding toward Communist tactics. State Department officials were somewhat chagrined by Byrnes's distrust of their observations. Nonetheless, Cyril Black of the State Department, and later professor of Russian History at Princeton, accompanied Ethridge. Black's specialty at the time was Bulgaria, and he would act as Ethridge's interpreter in that country.[162]

Ethridge arrived in Bucharest on November 19 and spent ten days in the capital. He met with King Michael, leading members of the Groza government, members of the opposition party, and foreign service people. Ethridge wrote Byrnes a 27 page report.[163] It reaffirmed "in every detail, the facts and conclusions reported. . . to the Department." Ethridge was convinced that the Groza government was in no sense representative, and that the two parties which did represent the majority of the people, the National Peasant and National Liberal parties, were not only without power, but their leaders were subject to constant harassment.[164] The report asserted that the Groza government was dominated by the Communist party which was controlled by Moscow. Ethridge concluded that "from past experience it is clear that measures short of free elections, such as broadening the base of the present government through Cabinet reconstructions, the withdrawal of Soviet occupation troops, etc. would provide no sound guarantee that Soviet policy had been altered."[165]

While Ethridge supported the findings of the American Mission in Bucharest, this did not minimize the State Departments embarrassment of having their views challenged by Byrnes. In an oral interview, John Campbell, then of the State Department, commented, "It didn't seem to me that he [Ethridge] could have come away with any other conclusion than those he reached. At any rate, somehow it satisfied Mr. Byrnes' questioning as to whether he was getting a totally unbiased situation report from his own diplomats in these countries."[166]

Even so, Byrnes yearned to renew negotiations with the Soviets. He genuinely believed he could find common ground with Molotov.[167] He had sent Harriman to meet Stalin at Gagra in the Crimea in October.[168] Direct dealings with Stalin might resolve the impasse the Secretary had had with Molotov in London. Harriman talked with Stalin and Molotov on numerous occasions during the next several weeks. The Soviets had a number of concerns including the atomic bomb, was it an American or Allied monopoly?, and Japan, was it tripartite, or an American bastion? In addition, there were American concerns about Allied controls in Eastern Europe, Iran, and Korea.[169] Byrnes also wanted to ease tensions in Soviet-American relations because the United Nations was scheduled to meet in January.

Truman's November talks with Clement Attlee concerning atomic energy controls provided Byrnes with an opportunity to resume talks with Molotov. Truman had agreed on November 15 to a multi-stage sharing of atomic energy secrets with Britain, which would leave the Soviets out in the cold. Without informing London, Byrnes wrote Molotov on November 23. He wanted to have a foreign ministers meeting in Moscow to discuss a number of items, including atomic energy controls.[170] On the 29th, Molotov agreed. The British were furious. They feared that Byrnes's unilateral decision to deal with the Soviets was indicative of a larger problem, namely, that America would solve issues with the Soviets independent of Britain's interests. However, if Britain chose not to go to Moscow, London would surrender her role as a major nation. Reluctantly, Bevin agreed on December 7 to attend the meeting.[171]

The Moscow Conference of Foreign Ministers opened at the Spiridonvka Palace on December 16. Byrnes presented his agenda which included establishing a government in Romania which the United States and Great Britain could recognize. This government had to include representatives of the National Liberal and National Peasant parties. Molotov replied that the Groza regime already had representatives from both of these parties. Further, he reminded his colleagues that the Yalta agreement permitted sovereign nations to settle their own internal affairs. In concluding, the Soviet minister noted that he found it strange that "the United States adopted a different attitude toward Greece than it did toward Bulgaria and Romania, even though the situation was much worse in the former country."[172]

Unable to convince Molotov, Byrnes sought out Stalin. The Soviet Premier was open to compromise and suggested that some changes in the Groza regime were quite possible. Further discussion established a commission composed of Harriman, Kerr, and Vyshinski. The three would go to Bucharest to encourage the Romanian government to include two new ministers, one each from the National Liberal and National Peasant parties. Stalin, however, placed one restriction. The ministers could not be Maniu, Bratianu or Nicolae Lupu, leader of the Democratic Peasant Party.[173] Byrnes and Bevin accepted the terms and all agreed that following the broadening of the government, "free and unfettered elections" would be held "as soon as possible on the basis of universal suffrage and secret ballot." All parties could participate in the election and the Romanian government would give "assurances" to grant freedom of the press, speech, religion, and association. In return, once the government was broadened and the assurances declared, Washington and London would officially recognize the Romanian regime.[174]

The Soviets had won the day. Byrnes's compromise did not alter the Groza government. Two additions to a cabinet of more than twenty ministers would make little difference, while, in return, the United States promised to recognize a Communist-dominated regime.[175] The Moscow Conference destroyed Byrnes's reputation. While Molotov was a frequent topic of nicknames, including "Stone Bottom,"[176] "Aunti Moll,"[177] and "balky mule,"[178] no one questioned his ability. In contrast, Sumner Welles, Roosevelt's Under Secretary of State, noted, in June, 1947, "that the greatest calamity in the United States was the appointment of Byrnes as Secretary of State."[179] In his memoirs, George Kennan described Byrnes's behavior at the Moscow Conference:

> He plays his negotiations by ear, going into them with no clear or fixed plan. . . . He relies entirely on his own agility and presence of mind and hopes to take advantage of tactical openings. In the present conference his weakness in dealing with the Russians is that his main purpose is to achieve some sort of an agreement. He doesn't much care what. The realities behind this agreement, since they concern only such people as Koreans, Romanians, and Iranians, about whom he knows nothing, do not concern him. He wants an agreement for its political effect at home. The Russians know this. They will see that for this superficial success, he pays a heavy price in the things that are real.[180]

President Truman, too, was unhappy with Byrnes's performance. He wrote the Secretary of State on Jan 5, 1946, severely chastising him for not keeping him informed of the Moscow negotiations. The President had seen neither a protocol nor a communique of the Conference. He wrote, "I'm tired of babying the Soviets." Further, he did not want to recognize the Romanian government until it satisfied America's requirements.[181] While part of Truman's writing was out of *angst*, he was genuinely disappointed by Byrnes's performance at Moscow.[182]

Harriman, Kerr and Vyshinski arrived in Bucharest on New Year's Day, 1946. They met King Michael and after several discussions, the King agreed to include Emil Hatieganu, a National Peasant, and Michael Romniceanu, a National Liberal, as ministers without portfolio in the Groza government.[183] On January 8, Groza announced that general elections would be held in the "shortest time possible" on the basis of universal suffrage and secret ballot with all democratic and anti-Fascist parties eligible to participate. Groza assured Harriman, Kerr and Vyshinski that under his regime the Romanian people were guaranteed freedom of the press, speech, religion and assembly. [184]

On the following day Kerr and Harriman asked Groza to further clarify the election process. Groza told them what they wanted to hear. All political parties in the present government could participate in the elections, monitor ballot counting, and have equal rights to broadcasting, printing and material distribution.[185] These assurances met the Moscow Conference requirement and on February 5, London and Washington recognized the Groza regime; a government the United States had earlier foresworn not to recognize until after Romania had held free elections.[186] Later Bucharest would appoint Mihai Ralea to represent its interests in Washington.[187]

Romanian Elections

Within a week of Washington's recognition of the Groza regime, Berry notified the State Department that according to a Communist source, Bucharest had no intention of fulfilling its promises.[188] The confidant added that "when you buy a horse from the Russians, you must always pay for it twice, first when you make the agreement, and second when you take delivery."[189]

Since Groza had promised elections, the Soviets wanted to ensure a Communist victory. To assist the Romanian Communist party, Moscow removed nearly 150,000 Soviet troops from Romania in early 1946,[190] and on April 15 agreed to extend Romania's reparations payment period under Article 11 from six to eight years. The Romanian Communists too worked to insure their victory. While the government claimed to be a coalition of all "democratic" parties, it was, in fact, controlled by the Communists. They held all key Cabinet posts including the Ministers of Interior, Justice and Propaganda. Communists also dominated the police, and all mayors and prefects in the provinces were Communist appointees. Further, the Communists frequently used Groza's Plowman's Front organization to facilitate their control in the villages.[191]

The major ideological opposition to the Communists was the Social Democratic Party led by Titel Petrescu. On March 10, the Communists urged the Social Democrats to join them in a common list of candidates. Petrescu refused. A power struggle ensued. The pro-

Communist wing of the party won and Petrescu led his Socialist followers out of the convention. The other opposition parties were the old "loyal opposition," the National Peasants and the National Liberals. Combined, the opposition parties only generated negative programs. They offered no positive platform, and American intelligence reports noted that the parties were even in disagreement as to whether or not to boycott the government elections.[192]

Washington's February 5, 1946, communique recognizing the Bucharest government had anticipated elections in April. However, by the middle of April the Groza government had announced neither election plans nor election procedures. Consequently, America's new Ambassador to the Soviet Union, Bedell Smith, asked the Soviets to join the United States and Great Britain in a tripartite effort to encourage the Romanians to live up to their assurances.[193] Three days later, on April 26, Moscow issued the first of a series of refusals, noting that Bucharest was carrying out its promises and that preparations were underway for upcoming elections.[194] Without Soviet cooperation, there would be no tripartite actions. Once again, the Western Allies were powerless to affect any change not supported by Moscow.

In May, Bucharest expelled the *Christian Science Monitor* correspondent, Reuben Markham, and Berry anticipated that with the recall of Frank O'Brien, the Associated Press correspondent, there would be no American news sources in Romania.[195] War criminal trials also began in May against Ion and Mihai Antonescu and 22 other war leaders. On May 17, the People's Tribunal condemned 13 to death. The Groza government used the trial as a weapon to implicate the National Peasants and National Liberals as Fascists and supporters of the Nazis.[196] Several days later the United States formally complained to the Groza government about election delays, press censorship, and harassment of opposition parties through government sponsored "bands of hooligans." Washington warned that Bucharest should be aware that it was creating a bad impression abroad, one that was in "reality circumventing commitments which it has made." The United States suggested that Romania should alter this impression by promulgating election laws, and implementing the terms of the Moscow agreement.[197] On June 5 the Romanian Foreign Minister replied that the Romanian government had violated no one's civil rights, and that the elections would be held once the people approved the laws, and the parties presented their list of candidates.[198]

While the United States continued to complain, the Romanian

Communists gained strength. ARLUS, the Romanian Society for Strengthening of Relations with the USSR, used its numerous local branches to disseminate pro-Soviet propaganda through weekly newspapers, radio broadcasts, public lectures, and concerts.[199] The marked increase in Soviet control even upset Groza. In frank conversations with Berry, the Prime Minister complained "of his inability to influence Government policy, claiming that the persons closer to quarters where political instructions are made decide everything."[200] In the words of a frustrated Burton Berry, "Romania was a Russian satellite, and the Groza government was a puppet government."[201]

During the summer, The Minister of Justice, Lucretiu Patrascanu drafted electoral laws which were passed by the Cabinet and approved by King Michael on July 13. They called for elections to establish an "Assembly of Deputies," a unicameral body, unlike the bicameral legislature provided for in the 1925 Constitution. While there was some debate as to whether the government could be reorganized by an electoral law, the arguments collapsed since the King had established a precedent when he approved such a process on September 2, 1944.[202]

During the next several months, the political parties prepared for the November elections. The electoral laws called for voter registration. The government quickly registered all Communists and known sympathizers, but delayed registering "unreliable" persons. The laws gave the right to vote to men and women 19 years of age or older.[203]

On November 19, 89% of the electorate, or nearly 7 million voters, cast their ballots. The Communist dominated leftist bloc received 348 of the 414 seats with 32 seats for the National Peasants, 3 for the National Liberals and 29 for the Hungarian Popular Union, a leftist Hungarian minority party in Transylvania.[204] Romniceanu and Hatieganu, the token opposition representatives resigned. On November 26, the United States and Great Britain sent a scathing letter of protest to Bucharest citing the corrupt and fraudulent tactics used during the election. Both powers refused to accept the election as fulfillment of the requirements of the Moscow Agreements.[205] Undeterred, the new assembly convened on December 1, 1946.

A Peace Treaty

The final Potsdam task required the Allies to draft a peace treaty for Romania. Washington saw the treaty as important since it would end the Armistice, end the Allied Control Commission, and hopefully open

Romania to American trade. The Moscow Conference in December, 1945, had established a treaty drafting procedure which called for the Council of Foreign Ministers to draft a treaty, a Plenary meeting of the 16 principal Allied powers to review the draft, and a final series of Council meetings to resolve problems and prepare the treaty for signature.[206]

The Foreign Ministers of the Big Three assigned the initial drafting task to their deputies who began work on the Romanian treaty on January 18, 1946. Progress was slow, in part because the deputies did not believe they had the power to make important decisions. Consequently, on April 25, Byrnes called a meeting of the Council of Foreign Ministers. Bevin and Molotov attended and the three agreed to participate directly in the treaty drafting procedure.[207]

The United States focused on several issues in the Romanian treaty, the most important of which were Transylvania, human rights, Soviet troop withdrawal from Romania, civil aviation, and the resumption of most-favored-nation trade relations between Washington and Bucharest. Since the Armistice, America had advocated changing the Hungarian-Transylvanian border to award Budapest some lands predominantly populated by Magyars. However, neither Britain nor the Soviets showed any enthusiasm. The United States maintained its position until May 7, 1946, when Byrnes accepted the Anglo-Soviet proposal, which retained the present border.[208] Campbell recalled talking to James Dunn, one of the American negotiators, about Byrnes' capitulation. Dunn retorted "We really don't care that much. We're not going to make an issue of it."[209] In August, during the Plenary session, the Hungarians arrived armed with maps, but to no avail.[210] Article 2 of the final treaty annulled the Vienna Decree and restored Northern Transylvania to Romania.

The CFM accepted the original American proposal on human rights which guaranteed all persons under Romanian jurisdiction, "without distinction as to race, sex, language or religion," human rights and the "fundamental freedoms including freedom of expression, of press and publications, of religious worship, of political opinion and of public meeting."[211] However, the Romanians objected to the article arguing that it was redundant. Article 5 of the Romanian Constitution guaranteed human rights, and they were equally guaranteed under the United Nations Charter, an organization which Romania hoped soon to join.[212] The Political and Territorial Commission for Romania, a subcommittee of the CFM, not only rejected the Romanian observations, but went further. The British delegation feared that Romania's historic anti-semitism could endanger her Jewish population. Therefore, the British proposed a second paragraph which emphasized non-discrimination. Romania could pass no law which discriminated between persons on the grounds of race, sex, language, or religion "in reference to their persons, property, business, professional or financial interests, status, political or civic rights." After considerable debate, the Plenary conference adopted the British proposal and incorporated it into Article 3 of the treaty.[213]

The issue of Soviet troop withdrawal was quickly solved, virtually without debate. The CFM agreed to withdraw all Allied forces from Romania within 90 days of the peace treaty coming into force, subject to the right of the Soviet Union to keep "such armed forces" as would be needed to maintain "lines of communication" with the Soviet Army in the Soviet zone of occupation in Austria.[214] The Anglo-American delegates assumed the Romanian occupation would be brief. Once there was an Austrian peace treaty, the need for occupation zones would end, and the Soviets would withdraw their forces from Austria and subsequently from Romania. However, as events unfolded, the Allies would not make peace with Austria until 1955, and the Soviets would not remove their troops from Romania until 1958.

In drafting the articles on the civil aviation section, the United States insisted that Romania grant "no exclusive or discriminatory right to any country" with regard to the operation of civil aircraft in international traffic, and that Bucharest provide equal opportunity to all countries to obtain international commercial aviation rights in Romania.[215] The British accepted the proposal, however, the Soviets did not.[216] Moscow argued against any mention of civil aviation. The Allies did not have the right to tell Romania how she should control her airspace, since this was a matter of national security.[217]

The aviation issue was not decided until the final session of the CFM in New York in December, 1946. Rather than be outvoted, the Soviets agreed that Romania had to afford all countries equal opportunity to secure commercial aviation rights. Further, Moscow accepted a French proposal that Bucharest permit civilian airplanes the right to fly over her airspace and to permit them to land for the purpose of refueling or repair.[218] However, these provisions were subject to reciprocal arrangements with other countries, and in no instance could Bucharest be forced to accept terms which would affect her national security interests.[219]

Economics was the final issue and without question it was the most important to the United States. Since early 1945, the State Department and the American Mission in Bucharest had studied the Romanian economy. The forecast was bleak. The economy was depressed, and the Soviets had seized control of many of Romania's assets through the Armistice terms, the Potsdam provisions, military occupation, control of the Allied Control Commission, and bilateral agreements with Bucharest.[220]

Three articles of the Armistice subjugated the Romanian economy to the demands of the Soviet Union. As discussed above, Article 10 required Romania to provide for the cost of maintaining Soviet troops in Romania. Article 11 prescribed terms for reparation payments. The Soviets decided to take much of their reparations through petroleum products. By so doing, Moscow reduced Bucharest's ability to trade oil for Western credits, and forced Romania to be more dependent on the Soviet economy.[221] Article 12 forced Romania to restore all property she had seized from the Soviets during the war. The Soviets set the original property value at 1 trillion lei, but on September 11, 1945, reduced the amount to 948 billion lei, of which some 300 billion lei remained outstanding in December, 1946.[222]

The Potsdam Declaration empowered Moscow to use former German assets in Romania to meet the $300 million reparation claims. As a result, the Soviets seized most anything they wanted, by labelling it German property.[223] The physical presence of the Red Army in Romania, coupled with Moscow's preeminent position on the Allied Control Commission enabled the Soviets to have their own way in Romania.

To insure control over Romania's economy after the war, Moscow signed a number of bilateral accords with Bucharest. They signed the first two agreements on May 8, 1945, the day the war ended in Europe. The first was a one year trade pact which provided for the mutual exchange of goods on a barter basis. The second was a five year economic collaboration accord, which permitted Moscow to establish Sovroms, a joint enterprise, in nearly every area of the Romanian economy.[224] The Sovroms had preferential status including lower tax rates than other foreign companies, foreign exchange privileges, and premiums on exports and imports. Through these devices, Sovrom products had a competitive edge over other privately owned enterprises.[225]

While Soviet control mechanisms made Western penetration of the Romanian economy difficult, American analysts had to consider the larger issue of the Romanian economy itself. Certainly there were markets in Romania for American goods, but could Bucharest pay for them? Two-way trade with Romania had nearly collapsed. In 1938, the United States exported over $6 million worth of goods to Bucharest, in contrast to $2 million in 1946. Imports were markedly worse. In 1938, Romanian exports to the United States exceeded $2.5 million, in contrast to a mere $33 thousand in 1946.[226] Economic reports from the United States Mission in Bucharest indicated that 1946 was a year fraught with problems. A currency inflation, which had first become noticeable in 1945, got out of hand in 1946; a serious drought in the northeastern part of the country caused widespread suffering, and disrupted the Government's plans for using its foodstuffs to exchange for imports of critically needed industrial equipment; the cost of living increased noticeably; shortages of food, fuel and other necessities of life became prevalent; and, the continued drain of the country's wealth in the form of reparations payments constituted one more burden on the Romanian economy. The situation by the end of 1946 was by far the worst in recent history.[227]

Reports from the American Mission in Bucharest emphasized another factor: a decline in the morale of the Romanian people. The Mission's observations were undoubtedly colored by the fact that it was a haven for dissidents who opposed the Groza regime and/or the Soviets. Nonetheless, the report noted that until the Autumn of 1946, there was a "rather airy optimism" among Romanian businessmen and industrialists generated by the belief that once the peace treaty was signed, Romania's economic difficulties would disappear. By late Fall, this attitude changed to "cynicism verging on despair" when these same people realized that the peace treaty would not alter the economy "one whit." As a result, many Romanians wanted to "get out" of business with as little financial loss as possible. There were numerous inquiries at the Mission as to whether American investors would like to purchase a business. These offers ranged from "large scale factories to swimming pools, restaurants, and mud bath spas." Conditions among the lower ranks of society were not better. Rising prices and drought brought about "a feeling of utter selfishness which automatically gives rise to hoarding."[228] The Mission's report concluded that there was little hope for improvement until at least 1948, and this would depend on a successful harvest.

While these reports were bleak, they did not at all deter American efforts to have all the peace treaties include an article guaranteeing most-favored-nation, or MFN, status. America's economy yearned for free and unrestricted world trade. In April, 1946, Byrnes told the Council of Foreign Ministers that America wanted "equal access" to trade, raw materials, and industry in the former Axis satellite states. Molotov agreed that Stalin, Truman and Churchill had accepted this language, but noted that all three stipulated that practical questions arising from this decision would be handled by diplomatic channels, rather than by articles in a peace treaty.[229] Several weeks later, with British and French support, the United States offered a draft article to the Romanian treaty. The proposal called for Romania to grant to the member states of the United Nations, for a period of 18 months after the treaty came into force, reciprocal MFN treatment "in all matters relating to commerce, industry, shipping and other forms of business activity within Romania," except for civil aviation. While opposed to the entire concept, the Soviets offered an amendment excluding arrangements

> customarily included in commercial treaties concluded by Romania before the war which relate to relations with neighboring countries. . . and the provisions with respect to reciprocity granted by each of the United Nations shall be understood to be subject to the exceptions customarily included in the commercial treaties concluded by that Power.

Romania was a "neighboring country" and the Soviets did not want their special arrangements with Bucharest undone by granting other nations equal economic opportunity. Molotov argued that his amendment simply articulated a common practice "indulged in by the United States in the cases of Cuba and the Philippines."[230] France, Britain and the United States quickly countered with their own proposal, which was nearly identical to the Soviet amendment except it excluded the phrase "which relate to relations with neighboring countries."[231]

Serious debate over the two amendments continued throughout the Summer. The Soviets accused the United States of wanting to use its economic power to "exploit" former enemy states. The Western powers parried that MFN was not designed by the strong to enslave the weak. Byrnes declared "Would anyone propose that an opposite intent be written into these treaties–that Italy or the Balkan countries should be free to discriminate?"[232] Molotov countered. If the most-favored-nation principle was so admirable, then why apply it for only eighteen months? In fact, if it were so worthwhile, why not make it compulsory for all nations?[233] The issue remained undecided until September 29 when it was voted on in the Economic Committee for the Balkans and Finland. The majority vote supported the French-British-American proposal and MFN became Article 31 of the final treaty. However, the State Depart-

ment noted that MFN did not apply to enterprises that were nationalized or entirely owned by the Romanian government.[234]

The final articles of the treaty stipulated the process for treaty implementation. Article 37 provided that the Heads of the Diplomatic
Missions in Bucharest of the United States, the United Kingdom and
the Soviet Union "acting in concert" would represent the Allied powers
in executing the treaty. Article 38 provided a process for resolving disputes including recourse to the United Nations.[235] The Plenary Conference adjourned October 15. The recommendations of the Conference
went to the CFM which met in New York from November 4 through
December 12. The CFM approved by simple majority the recommendations concerning Romania, and on February 10, 1947, representatives
of the Allies and Romania met at the Quai d'Orsay in Paris, and signed
a peace treaty.[236]

During the 29 months from the Romanian surrender to the signing
of the Peace Treaty, the United States had made few changes in the
Armistice terms. A comparison of the two documents reveals that there
were only two significant additions to the treaty: a guarantee of human
rights and a most-favored-nation clause. However, the implementation
articles of the treaty would prove sufficiently vague to insure Romania
much room for noncompliance.

Notes

The following abbreviations will be used throughout the notes in all the
chapters.

Archives and Presidential Libraries:

NA is the National Archives in Washington, D.C. and Suitland, Maryland.

HST Library is the Harry S. Truman Presidential Library in Independence,
Missouri.

DDE Library is the Dwight D. Eisenhower Presidential Library in Abeline,
Kansas.

JFK Library is the John F. Kennedy Presidential Library in Boston,
Massachusetts.

LBJ Library is the Lyndon B. Johnson Presidential Library in Austin, Texas.

NPMP is the Nixon Presidential Materials Project in Alexandria, Virginia.

GRF Library is the Gerald R. Ford Presidential Library in Ann Arbor,
Michigan.

JC Library is the Jimmy Carter Presidential Library in Atlanta, Georgia.

Collections within the Archives and Presidential Libraries:

DOS is Department of State
NSC is National Security Council Files
NSF is National Security Files
OSS R&A Reports are Office of Strategic Services Research and Analysis
  Reports
RG is Record Group
SMOF is Staff Memos and Office Files
WHCF is White House Central Files
WHSF is White House Subject Files

Newspaper abbreviations:

CSM is the Christian Science Monitor
NYT is the New York Times
WSJ is the Wall Street Journal

Other commons abbreviations:

CNN is Cable Network News
DOS Bulletin is the Department of State Bulletin
FBIS EEU is Foreign Broadcast Information Services, Eastern Europe
FRUS is Foreign Relations of the United States
RFE is Radio Free Europe

1. "Secret Supplemental Protocol of August 23, 1939." 800 General - 1946, Appendices, pp. 1-14, Box 19, RG84, Foreign Service Post of DOS - Bucharest: US Mission, Secret File, 1946, National Archives.
2. David Floyd, *Rumania: Russia's Dissident Ally* (New York: Frederick A. Praeger, 1965), pp. 8-10,
3. Report, German Policy Towards Romania, April 2, 1946, "Policy of Nazis" folder, Box 3, Harry Howard Papers, HST Library.
4. Robert Lee Wolff, *The Balkans in Our Time* (New York: W. W. Norton & Co., Inc., 1967), p. 235. The Romanian people also wanted to avenge their loss of Northern Transylvania to Hungary by the terms of the Vienna Decree of August 30, 1940, and the loss of Southern Dobrogea to Bulgaria through the Treaty of Craiova, September 7, 1940 (Vasile Netea, "Actions et ecrits contre le Diktat de Vienne," *Revue roumaine d'histoire*, Vol. XIII, Nos. 5-6 [1974], 765-788; Paul Quinlan (ed.), *Clash Over Romania: British and American Policies Toward Romania, 1938-1947,* [Los Angeles: Romanian Academy of Arts and Sciences, 1977], pp. 64-65).
5. W. Averell Harriman and Elie Abel, *Special Envoy to Churchill and Stalin, 1942-1946* (New York: Random House, 1975), pp. 121-122.

6. On August 14, 1941, Churchill and Roosevelt gave a press conference following their meeting in the North Atlantic and the statement is generally called the Atlantic Charter. It contains eight major points: both countries would support the principles of self-determination, plebiscites for territorial changes, free trade, economic prosperity, freedom of the seas and world disarmament; and both nations envisioned the destruction of Nazism (Joseph Harrington, *Masters of War , Makers of Peace* [Littleton, MA: Copley Publishing Group, 1987], p. 151). The Soviets accepted the Atlantic Charter through their Ambassador to London, Ivan Maisky (Herbert Feis, *Churchill, Roosevelt, Stalin: The War They Waged and the Peace They Sought* [New York: Princeton University Press, 1957], p. 24 n24).

7. Harriman and Abel, p. 122.

8. Winston S. Churchill, *The Second World War:* Vol. IV: *The Hinge of Fate* (Boston: Houghton, Mifflin Co., 1950), p. 332; Quinlan, *Clash Over Romania*, p. 79 n3.

9. John Lewis Gaddis, *The United States and the Origins of the Cold War, 1941-1947* (New York: Columbia University Press, 1972), p. 135.

10. Report, German Policy Towards Romania, April 2, 1946, "Policy of Nazis" folder, Box 3, Harry Howard Papers, HST Library.

11. [Cordell Hull], *The Memoirs of Cordell Hull* (New York: The Macmillan Co., 1948), II, 1176.

12. Francis L. Loewenheim, Harold D. Langley, and Manfred Jonas (eds.), *Roosevelt and Churchill: Their Secret Wartime Correspondence* (London: Barrie & Jenkins, 1979), p. 478.

13. Michael Shafir, *Romania: Politics, Economics and Society. Political Stagnation and Simulated Change* (Boulder, CO: Lynne Rienner Publishers, Inc., 1985), p. 29.

14. For more information see, *FRUS, The Conferences at Cairo and Tehran, 1943* (Washington, D.C.: U. S. U.S. Government Printing Office, 1961); also, Stephen Kertesz, *The Last European Peace Conference: Paris 1946, Conflict of Values*(New York: University Press of America Inc., 1985), pp. 8-10, and Hugh Seton-Watson, *The East European Revolution* (3rd ed.; New York : Frederick A. Praeger, 1956), pp. 89-90.

15. Stephen Fischer-Galati, *The New Rumania: From People's Democracy to Socialist Republic* (Cambridge, MA: The M.I.T. Press, 1967), pp. 19-20. For more information on America's role in the Romanian surrender see Ivor Porter's *Operation Autonomous: With S.O.E. in Wartime Romania* (London: Chatto and Windus, 1989).

16. Policy Paper, "Treatment of enemy and liberated states, Part C., The satellite states: Hungary, Rumania, and Bulgaria, July 5, 1944," pp. 1, 3-4, Folder 2, Box 4, Harry Howard Papers, HST Library.

17. The American representative was Ambassador Lincoln MacVeagh; the British Ambassador to Egypt was Lord Killearn.

18. John C. Campbell, "The American Outlook on the Balkans, 1944-1946," The AAASS Annual Conference (Honolulu, Hawaii, November 1988), pp. 12-

13; Policy Paper, "Treatment of enemy states. Part III, The satellite states: Hungary, Rumania, and Bulgaria, June 28, 1944," Folder 2, Box 4, Harry Howard Papers, HST Library; Wolff, *The Balkans in Our Time*, p. 239. For information as to how Hitler viewed Marshall Antonescu during this time see, Report, German Policy Towards Romania, April 2, 1946, "Policy of Nazis" folder, Box 3, Harry Howard Papers, HST Library.

19. For an in-depth study see, Lynn Etheridge Davis, *The Cold War Begins: Soviet-American Conflict over Eastern Europe* (Princeton, N.J.: Princeton University Press, 1974).

20. Oral interview of John C. Campbell by Richard McKinzie, June 24, 1974, p. 24, HST Library.

21. Campbell, "The American Outlook on the Balkans," p. 12.

22. John C. Campbell, "The European Territorial Settlement," *Foreign Affairs: An American Quarterly Review*, Vol. 26, No. 1 (October 1947), p. 200.

23. Oral interview of John C. Campbell by Richard McKinzie, June 24, 1974, p. 30, HST Library; see also, Campbell, "The European Territorial Settlement," 1947.

24. Oral interview of John C. Campbell by Richard McKinzie, June 24, 1974, p. 28, HST Library.

25. Policy Paper, "Treatment of enemy and liberated states; Proposed terms of surrender for Rumania, August 2, 1944," Folder 2, Box 4, Harry Howard Papers, HST Library; Geir Lundestad, *The American Non-Policy Towards Eastern Europe, 1943-1947: Universalism in an Area Not of Essential Interest to the United States* (New York: Humanities Press, 1975), pp. 226-227; Policy Paper, n.d., pp. 29, 51, 67, Summary of recommendations of policy towards East-Central Europe folder, Box 4, Harry Howard Papers, HST Library.

26. William Hardy McNeill, *America, Britain & Russia: Their Co-operation and Conflict, 1941-1946* (New York: Johnson Reprint Corp, 1970), p. 422.

27. Quinlan, *The United States and Romania*, pp. 94ff. The expression "tolerated opposition" meant that both the National Peasants and National Liberals, while officially forbidden to engage actively in politics under Marshal Antonescu, were, none the less, able to write memoranda to Antonescu expressing their views, which were often in sharp disagreement with those of the Marshal (Wolff, *The Balkans in Our Time*, p. 238).

28. McNeill, *America, Britain & Russia*, p. 422.

29. Loewenheim, Langley and, Jonas (eds.), *Roosevelt and Churchill*, pp. 502-503.

30. *Ibid.*, p. 527.

31. *Ibid.*, pp. 528-529; Winston S. Churchill, *The Second World War*, Vol VI: *Triumph and Tragedy* (Boston: Houghton, Mifflin, 1953), p. 76.

32. *Memoirs of Cordell Hull*, II, 1455-1456; Louis Fischer, *The Road to Yalta: Soviet Foreign Relations, 1941-1945* (New York: Harper & Row, 1972), p. 195; Oral interview of John C. Campbell by Richard McKinzie, June 24, 1974, p. 37, HST Library.

33. *Memoirs of Cordell Hull*, II, 1458.

34. Wolff, *The Balkans in Our Time*, p. 238.
35. See, Quinlan, *Clash Over Romania*, pp. 98ff.
36. *Ibid.*, p. 99.
37. Wolff, *The Balkans in Our Time*, p. 241.
38. Quinlan, *Clash Over Romania*, p. 102; Feis, *Churchill, Roosevelt, Stalin*, p, 413.
39. Quinlan, *Clash Over Romania*, p. 105.
40. Gabriel Kolko, *The Politics of War: The World and United States Foreign Policy, 1943-1945* (New York: Vintage Books, 1968), p. 130.
41. *Ibid.*; *Memoirs of Cordell Hill*, II, 1461; Quinlan, *Clash Over Romania*, pp. 107-108.
42. Oral interview of John C. Campbell by Richard McKinzie, June 24, 1974, pp. 1-4, HST Library.
43. *Ibid.*, p. 41. George Kennan was one of the few who correctly perceived Moscow's intentions toward Romania. In October he predicted that the Soviets would make Romania, "pay through the nose" (Hugh DeSantis, *The Diplomacy of Silence: The American Foreign Service, the Soviet Union, and the Cold War, 1933-1947* (Chicago: University of Chicago Press, 1979), p. 126.
44. Feis, *Churchill, Roosevelt, Stalin*, p. 416.
45. *FRUS, 1944* (Washington, D.C.: U.S. Government Printing Office, 1962), IV, 234-236.
46. Andrei Otetea (ed.), *The History of the Romanian People* (New York: Twayne Publishers, 1970), p. 567; Cristin Popisteanu and Petre Panzaru, *Romanian Historical Itinerary, 1944-1974* (Bucharest: Editura Enciclopedica Romana, 1974), p. 25.
47. Churchill, *Triumph and Tragedy*, p. 227.
48. Loewenheim, Langley, and Jonas (eds.), *Roosevelt and Churchill*, p. 585; see also, Adam B. Ulam, *Stalin, The Man and His Era* (New York: The Viking Press, 1973), p. 600.
49. Campbell, "The American Outlook on the Balkans," 1988, p. 15.
50. Wolff, *The Balkans in Our Time*, pp. 241-242.
51. J. F. Brown, *The New Eastern Europe: The Khrushchev Era and After* (New York: Frederick A. Praeger, 1966), p. 202.
52. Wolff, *The Balkans in Our Time*, pp. 278-279; Vladimir Tismaneanu, "Ceausescu's Socialism," *Problems of Communism*, Vol. XXXIV, No. 1 (January-February 1985), 54.
53. Quinlan, *Clash Over Romania*, p. 112.
54. Fischer-Galati, *The New Rumania*, pp. 24-25.
55. Eugene K. Keefe *et al.*, *Romania, A Country Study* (Washington, D.C.: U.S. Government Printing Office, 1979), p. 22; *Romania Yearbook, 1977* (3rd ed.; Bucharest, Editura stiintifica si enciclopedica, 1977), p. 157; Report, "'Front' Organizations in Balkan Countries: 1. Rumania," OIR Report No. 4654.1, p. 2, Box 1787, OSS-R&A Reports, DOS Decimal file, 1950-1954, National Archives.
56. *Romania Yearbook, 1977*, p. 147.

57. Seton-Watson, , p. 202. The Iron Guard was a native Fascist movement, begun by Corneliu Codreanu in 1927. Codreanu claimed direct inspiration from the Archangel Michael, and founded the spirit of the Guard on the standard triad of the far right: nationalism, the Orthodox religion, and anti-Semitism. Popular support for the Guard was significant. This was forcefully demonstrated when Codreanu was acquitted of a murder charge, in 1929, for killing the prefect of the city of Iasi. After this, King Carol supported Codreanu and the *Garda de Fier*, expecting to use their popularity for his own ends. Carol, however, was unwilling to allow the Guard to operate independent of his royal authority. He feared its power. In 1933, the king permitted Ion Duca, a Liberal, to form a government; Duca undertook a frontal attack on the organization, declared it illegal and imprisoned about 18,000 Guardists. He was assassinated, certainly on orders from Codreanu. King Carol retreated before this show of disregard for law or authority until November 1938, when again he attempted to crush the Guard. Again, thousands were arrested. Codreanu was shot "while trying to escape." (Ian M. Matley, *Romania, A Profile* [New York: Praeger Publishers, 1970], pp. 115-116.)

58. Wolff, *The Balkans in Our Time*, p. 280; Seton-Watson, *The East European Revolution*, p. 203. For additional information see Ghita Ionescu's *Communism in Rumania, 1944-1962* (London: Oxford University Press, 1964).

59. Report, "Some Basic Trends in Eastern Europe," p. 2, Box 1, Harry Howard Papers, HST Library.

60. *Ibid.*, pp. 3-4.

61. *Ibid.*, p. 6.

62. Report, "Regional Problems: The Problem of Balkan Union," November 28, 1944, pp. 2,6, Regional Problems folder, Box 3, Harry Howard Papers, HST Library.

63. Howard S. Piquet, "The Unconditional Most-Favored Nation Policy of the United States," p. 2, February 12, 1947, Legislative Reference Service, Library of Congress.

64. Kertesz, *The Last European Peace Conference*, pp. 57-58.

65. *FRUS, The Conferences at Malta and Yalta, 1945* (Washington, D.C.: U.S. Government Printing Office, 1955), p. 257.

66. The economic issue was foremost among many Washington thinkers (Harley Notter, *Postwar Foreign Policy Preparation, 1939-1945* [Washington, D.C.: Department of State, 1949], p. 359).

67. *FRUS, The Conferences at Malta and Yalta*, pp. 242-246.

68. Oral interview of John C. Campbell by Richard McKinzie, June 24, 1974, p. 41, HST Library.

69. Report, "To the President, A Report Upon Rumania from Burton Y. Berry," p. 5, November 19, 1946, President's Subject Files, File 186, Box 4, HST Library.

70. *FRUS, The Conferences at Malta and Yalta*, p. 248.

71. *Ibid.*, p. 972.

72. Quinlan, *Clash Over Romania*, p. 121.

73. *FRUS, The Conferences at Malta and Yalta*, p. 248.

74. Oral interview of John C. Campbell by Richard McKinzie, June 24, 1974, p. 43, HST Library.

75. Wolff, *The Balkans in Our Time*, p. 281.

76. *Ibid.*

77. Quinlan, *Clash Over Romania*, p. 123.

78. Seton-Watson, *The East European Revolution*, p. 206.

79. Report, "To the President, A Report Upon Rumania from Burton Y. Berry," p. 6, November 19, 1946, President's Subject Files, File 186, Box 4, HST Library.

80. James F. Byrnes, *Speaking Frankly* (New York: Harper & Brothers, 1947), p. 50.

81. U.S. Congress, House, Committee on Foreign Affairs, *Soviet Diplomacy and Negotiating Behavior: Emerging New Context For U.S. Diplomacy*, House Document 96-238, 96th Cong., 1st Sess., 1979, p. 217. Cited hereafter as House Committee on Foreign Affairs, *Soviet Diplomacy and Negotiating Behavior*, 1979.

82. Byrnes, *Speaking Frankly*, p. 51.

83. *Ibid.*

84. Radescu fled to Portugal (Dispatch, John C. Wiley to the Secretary of State, October 14, 1947, p. 3, Record Group 84, Foreign Service Post of DOS, Bucharest U.S. Mission, Secret Files, 1947, Box 30 National Archives).

85. Report, "To the President, A Report Upon Rumania from Burton Y. Berry." p. 7, November 19, 1946, President's Subject Files, File 186, Box 4, HST Library.

86. Churchill, *Triumph and Tragedy*, p. 420. See, Stephen Fischer-Galati, "The Communist Takeover of Rumania: A Function of Soviet Power," *Studies on the Soviet Union*, Vol. 11, No. 4. (1971), 281-291.

87. Stephen Fischer-Galati, *Twentieth Century Rumania* (New York: Columbia University Press, 1970), pp. 88-89,

88. Report, "To the President, A Report Upon Rumania from Burton Y. Berry," p. 8, President's Subject Files 186, Box 4, HST Library.

89. Oral interview of John C. Campbell by Richard McKinzie, June 24, 1974, p. 78, HST Library.

90. For more information see Henry Butterfield Ryan, *The Vision of Anglo-America: The US-UK Alliance and the Emerging Cold War of 1943-1946* (New York: Cambridge University Press, 1987).

91. Loewenheim, Langley, and Jonas, *Roosevelt and Churchill*, pp. 660-662; Churchill, *Triumph and Tragedy*, pp. 420-421.

92. Loewenheim, Langley, and Jonas, *Roosevelt and Churchill*, p. 668; *FRUS, 1945* (Washington, D.C.: U.S. Government Printing Office, 1967),V, 509-510.

93. Robert E. Sherwood, *Roosevelt and Hopkins, An Intimate History*(New York: Harper & Brothers, 1948), p. 875. Roosevelt's reluctance to press Moscow harder on the Romanian issue may have been influenced by the recently signed Declaration of Chapultepec on Reciprocal Assistance and

American Solidarity. This Declaration of March 3 restated the central notion of the Monroe Doctrine, claiming American control of the Western Hemisphere. The State Department wrote several reports on the implications of these decisions at Mexico City, noting in particular their function as models for Soviet claims to regional control of Eastern Europe (Report, "The Inter-American System and European Regional Arrangements," p. 3, March 15, 1945, Folder 4, Box 4, Harry Howard Papers, HST Library; Office Memorandum," pp. 1-2, March 6, 1945, Folder 4, Box 4, Harry Howard Papers, HST Library).

94. Harriman and Abel, *Special Envoy*, pp. 425-426; Oral interview of John C. Campbell by Richard McKinzie, June 24, 1974, p. 44, HST Library.

95. Report, "Problems Involved in the Rumanian Settlement," December 31, 1945, Report #3467, Part 1, p. 7, Box 1787, OSS-R&A Reports, DOS Decimal File, 1950-1954, National Archives.

96. Quinlan, *Clash Over Romania*, p. 129.

97. *Ibid.*, p. 21; Allied Control Commission, "The Rumanian Oil Industry," August 15, 1945, Record Group 84, Foreign Service Posts of DOS, Bucharest Legation, Misc. records, 1944-1949, Box 2, National Archives.

98. Report, "Problems Involved in the Rumanian settlement," December 31, 1945, Report #3467, Part 1, p. 69, Box 1787, OSS-R&A Reports, DOS Decimal File, 1950-1954, National Archives.

99. The $300 million (1,200 billion lei) reparations bill was, at face value, far less than the damage caused by the Romanian army in Russia. However, the Soviets shrewdly decided that the value of goods used to pay for reparations would be based on their 1938 world prices. This meant that the Soviets could extract between two and three times as much reparations than had they priced the goods at their 1944 value (Wolff, *The Balkans in our Time*, p. 344).

100. James L. Gormly, *The Collapse of the Grand Alliance, 1945-1948* (Baton Rouge: Louisiana State University Press, 1987), pp. 29-30.

101. Wolff, *The Balkans in Our Time*, p. 345;Report, " Problems Involved in the Rumanian Settlement," Report #3467, Part 1, p. 66, Box 1787, OSS-R&A Reports, DOS Decimal File, 1950-1954, National Archives.

102. *FRUS, 1945*, V, 647.

103. Memorandum for the President, "The Current Situation in Rumania," p. 1, May 3, 1945, George C. Marshall-War Department folder, President's Subject Files 183, HST Library; Kolko, *The Politics of War*, pp. 44-45.

104. *FRUS, Diplomatic Papers, 1945*, V, 201-203.

105. Quinlan, *Clash Over Romania*, p. 132.

106. Memorandum for the President, "The Current Situation in Rumania," p. 4, May 3 1945, George C. Marshall-War Department folder, President's Subject Files 183, HST Library; Memorandum, "The Situation in Rumania," p. 1, May 4, 1945, President's Subject Files, 186, HST Library.

107. War Department Intelligence Review No. 54, p. 43, February 27,1947, Box 18, Naval Aide Files, Alphabetical Files, Box 18, HST Library

108. The Soviets later claimed that U.S.S.R. had contributed 71% to the company and was entitled to 71% of the profits. Bucharest agreed.

(Memorandum, "Details in Connection with the Questions Raised in the U.S. State Department's Telegram RE:" Sovrompetrol." p. 2, January 31, 1947, Box 27, Record Group 84, Foreign Service Posts of DOS, Bucharest U.S. Mission Secret Files, National Archives).

109. Report, "Problems Involved in the Rumanian Settlement," December 31, 1945, Report #3467, Part 1, pp. 66-68, Box 1787, OSS-R&A Reports, DOS Decimal File, 1950-1954, National Archives.

110. *Ibid.*, p. 71; John C. Campbell, *American Policy Toward Communist Eastern Europe:The Choices Ahead* (Minneapolis: The University of Minnesota Press, 1965), p. 41.

111. Letter, "Personal and Secret from Premier J. V. Stalin to President H. S. Truman," May 27, 1945, Communications folder, Box 9, Naval Aide Files, Communications Files, HST Library.

112. Letter,"Number 280, Top Secret and Personal, From the President for Marshal Stalin," pp. 1-2, June 2, 1945, Communications folder, Box 9, Naval Aide Files, Communications Files, HST Library.

113. Letter, "Personal and Secret from Premier J. V. Stalin to President H. S. Truman," June 9, 1945, Communications folder, Box 9, Naval Aide Files, Communications Files, HST Library; *FRUS, The Conference of Berlin (The Potsdam Conference), 1945*, (Washington, D.C.: The U.S. Government Printing Office, 1960), I, 162.

114. Report, "Problems Involved in the Rumanian Settlement," December 31, 1945, Report #3467, Part 1, p. 15, Box 1787, OSS-R&A Reports, DOS Decimal File, 1950-1954, National Archives.

115. *FRUS, The Conference of Berlin*, I, 394-395.

116. *Ibid.*, pp. 390-391, 396.

117. Memorandum, Joseph Davies to President Truman, Berlin Conference, Volume XI, p, 9, Miscellaneous Papers, Conference Agendas, July 3, 1945, Box 4, Naval Aide File, HST Library.

118. *FRUS, The Conference of Berlin*, pp. 422-423.

119. Memorandum, DOS Agendas, Berlin Conference, Volume IV, p. 2, June 3, 1945, Box 1, Naval Aide File, HST Library.

120. *Ibid.*; DOS Recommendations, Berlin Conference, Volume IV, pp, 33-35, July 6, 1945, Box 1, Naval Aide File, HST Library.

121. *FRUS, The Conference of Berlin*, p. 380.

122. *Ibid.*, pp. 189, 390-391.

123. Memorandum, To the President from the Secretary of State, Berlin Conference, Volume XI, pp. 4-5, June 14, 1945, Box 4, Naval Aide File, HST Library.

124. *FRUS, The Conference of Berlin*, II, 1494.

125. *Ibid.*, pp. 690-691.

126. *Ibid.*, pp. 686-687.

127. Truman's original suggestion did not include Finland, but Byrnes added it. The Soviets objected to Truman's suggestion that China and France join the Big Three on the Council (*Ibid.*, p. 610).

128. For more information on American policy in Italy see, John Lamberton Harper, *America and the Reconstruction of Italy, 1945-1948* (New York: Cambridge University Press, 1986).

129. *FRUS. The Berlin Conference*, II, 644, 698-699.

130. *Ibid.*, pp. 646-649.

131. *Ibid.*, p. 250.

132. *Ibid.*, p. 371.

133. *Ibid.*, p. 327; Byrnes, *Speaking Frankly*, pp. 72-73.

134. *FRUS. The Berlin Conference*, II, 328.

135. *Ibid.*, pp. 1509-1510.

136. *Ibid.*, pp. 740-741; Byrnes, *Speaking Frankly*, pp. 75-76.

137. The Big Three agreed not to include this provision in the communique (*FRUS, The Berlin Conference*, II, 1496).

138. *Ibid.*, pp. 701-702,709-710, 720.

139. *Ibid.*, pp. 732, 1511.

140. *Ibid.*, pp. 554ff.

141. [Harry S. Truman] "Radio Report to the American People on Potsdam," *Public Papers of the Presidents of the United States. Harry S. Truman. Containing the Public Messages, Speeches, and Statements of the President, April 12 to December 31, 1945* (Washington, D.C.: U.S. Government Printing Office., 1961), pp. 203-207; U.S. Congress, Senate, Committee on Foreign Relations, *A Decade of American Foreign Policy: Basic Documents, 1941-1949*, Document No. 123, 81st Cong., 1st Sess., 1950, p. 1176.

142. *FRUS, The Berlin Conference*, II, 700-701.

143. *Ibid.*, pp. 714-715.

144. Memorandum, "Current Foreign Developments," p. 2, August 13, 1945, President's Subject Files, Box 186, HST Library.

145. *FRUS, 1945*, V, 565-566.

146. Gormly, *The Collapse of the Grand Alliance*, p.41.

147. *FRUS, The Berlin Conference*, I, 402-403.

148. Report, "To the President, A Report Upon Rumania from Burton Y. Berry", p. 10, November 19, 1945, President's Subject Files, File 86, Box 4, HST Library.

149. Wolff, *The Balkans in Our Time*, p. 285.

150. *FRUS, 1945*, V, 574-577; Lundestad, *American Non-Policy Towards Eastern Europe*, p. 239; Quinlan, *Clash Over Romania*, pp. 142ff.

151. Report, "Problems Involved in the Rumanian Settlement, " December 31, 1945, Report #3467, Part 1, p. 71, Box 1787, OSS-R&A Reports, DOS Decimal File, 1950-1954, National Archives.

152. Report, Reparations oil, Section XI, pp. 1-6. August 1945, File 711-9, Box 28, Record Group 84, Foreign Service Posts of DOS, Bucharest, U.S. Mission, Secret Files, 1947, National Archives.

153. Amelia C. Leiss (ed.), *European Peace Treaties After World War II: Negotiations and Texts of Treaties with Italy, Bulgaria, Hungary, Rumania, and Finland* (Milford, NY: World Peace Foundation, 1976), pp. 106-107.

154. Report, Reparations oil, Section XI, pp. 7-12, File 711-9, Box 28, Record Group 84, Foreign Service Posts of DOS, Bucharest, U.S. Mission, Secret Files, 1947, National Archives.

155. *Ibid.*, pp. 18-28; Correspondence, Romano-Americana, pp. 1-9, January 24, 1947, File 631, Box 27, Record Group 84, Foreign Service Posts of DOS, Bucharest, U.S. Mission, Secret Files, 1947, National Archives; Report, "Total Estimated War Losses," pp. 28-30, January 14, 1947, File 863.6, Box 32, Record Group 84, Foreign Service Posts of DOS, Bucharest, U..S. Mission, Secret Files, 1947, National Archives; Memorandum, "Problems of American Petroleum Interests in Rumania," pp, 1-8, June 11, 1947, Balkan Committee file, Box 29, Record Group 84, Foreign Service Posts of DOS, Bucharest, U.S. Mission, Secret Files, 1947, National Archives; *FRUS, 1947* (Washington D.C.: U.S. Government Printing Office, 1972), IV, p. 494.

156. McNeill, *America, Britain, & Russia*, p. 697.

157. Byrnes, *Speaking Frankly*, pp. 98-99. See also, C. L. Sulzberger, *A Long Row of Candles: Memoirs and Diaries (1934-1954)*(New York: The Macmillan Company, 1969), pp. 267-268.

158. James F. Byrnes, *All In One Lifetime* (New York: Harper & Brothers, 1958)p. 315-316.

159. Oral interview of John C. Campbell by Richard McKinzie, January 24, 1974, p. 57, HST Library.

160. McNeill, *America, Britain, & Russia*, p. 702.

161. Report, "To the President, A Report Upon Rumania from Burton Y. Berry," pp. 12-13, November 19, 1946, President's Subject Files, File 186, Box 4, HST Library.

162. Ethridge and Cyril Black wrote an account of this episode ("Negotiating on the Balkans, 1945-1947," *Negotiating with the Russians*, Raymond Dennet and Joseph E. Johnson(eds.), [Boston: World Peace Foundations, 1951], pp. 171-206).

163. Oral interview of Mark F. Ethridge by Richard D. McKinzie, June 4, 1974, pp. 13-21, HST Library.

164. Report, "To the President, A Report Upon Rumania from Burton Y. Berry," pp, 13-14, November 19, 1946, Presidential Subject Files, File 186, Box 4, HST Library.

165. *FRUS, 1945*, V, 633-637.

166. Oral interview of John C. Campbell by Richard McKinzie, January 24, 1974, p. 67, HST Library.

167. Oral interview of Mark F. Ethridge by Richard McKinzie, June 4, 1974, p. 12, HST Library.

168. *FRUS, 1945*(Washington, D.C.: U.S. Government Printing Office, 1967), II, pp.562-563.

169. Harriman and Abel, *Special Envoy to Churchill and Stalin*, pp. 513-520; Gormly, *The Collapse of the Grand Alliance*, p. 51; John C. Campbell *et al*, *The United States in World Affairs, 1945-1947* (New York: Harper & Brothers for the Council on Foreign Relations, 1947), p. 71.

170. Gormly, *The Collapse of the Grand Alliance*, p. 105.

171. *Ibid.*, p. 106; *FRUS, 1945*, II, 574-575, 599.

172. *Ibid.*, pp. 727-734.

173. For details see, *Quinlan, Clash Over Romania*, pp. 151ff; *FRUS, 1945*, II, 752-756; Byrnes, *All In One Lifetime*, pp. 338-339.

174. *FRUS, 1945*, II, 821-822.

175. Oral interview of Mark F. Ethridge by Richard McKinzie, June 4, 1974, pp. 21-22, HST Library. Mark Ethridge later noted that in selecting the two new cabinet members, "the Russians vetoed the first 22 names that were submitted and finally accepted the rector of the University of Cluj, who turned out to have been an underground Communist all his life. So we got royally hornswoggled on that."

176. House Committee on Foreign Affairs, *Soviet Diplomacy and Negotiating Behavior*, 1979, p. 50.

177. *Ibid.*, p. 89.

178. Robert H. Ferrell (ed.), *Off the Record: The Private Papers of Harry S. Truman* (New York: Harper & Row, 1980), p. 305.

179. Walter Millis (ed.), *The Forrestal Diaries* (New York: The Viking Press, 1951), p. 283.

180. George F. Kennan, *Memoirs, 1925-1950* (Boston: Little, Brown and Company, 1967), pp. 287-288.

181. Ferrell (ed,), *Off the Record*, pp. 78-80; Oral interview of Mark F. Ethridge by Richard McKinzie, June 4, 1974, p. 22, HST Library.

182. Byrnes uses Truman's statement to the New York Times in January 1946 as the President's approval of his decisions (NYT, January 9, 1946, p. 4).

183. Quinlan, *Clash Over Romania*, p. 152; also, *FRUS, 1946*, VI, 560.

184. Senate Committee on Foreign Relations, *A Decade of American Foreign Policy*, 1950, p. 1202; also, *FRUS, 1946*, VI, 562-568.

185. Senate Committee on Foreign Relations, *A Decade of American Foreign Policy*, 1950, p. 1203; also, *FRUS, 1946*, VI, 571.

186. Memorandum, "Memorandum for the President; Proposed Recognition of the Rumanian Government," January 23, 1946, Box 4, Office File 428, WHCF, HST Library; Senate Committee on Foreign Relations, *A Decade of American Foreign Policy*, 1950, p. 1203; *FRUS, 1946*, VI, 588.

187. Letter, Stanley Woodward to Matthew J. Connolly, September 25, 1946, pp. 1-4, Box 4, Office File 428, WHCF, HST Library.

188. Summary of Telegram, February 12, 1946, Box 20, Naval Aide files, State Department Briefs, HST Library.

189. Report, "To the President, A Report Upon Rumania from Burton Y. Berry," p, 16, November 19, 1946, President Subject files, Box 4, HST Library; Summary of Telegram, January 22, 1946, Box 20, Naval Aide Files, State Department Briefs, HST Library.

190. Intelligence Report No. 7, March 28, 1946, Box 16, War Department Intelligence Review (March 1946), Naval Aide Files, Alphabetical Files, HST Library.

191. Report, "Summary of the Major Industries and Estimate of the Political Situation: Rumania," p. 3, September 10, 1946, Office of Intelligence, Coordination, and Liaison Report No. 4125, Box 1787, DOS Decimal File 1950-1954, National Archives.

192. *Ibid.*, pp. 4-6.

193. Summary of Telegram, April 23, 1946, Box 20, State Department Briefs, HST Library.

194. Summary of Telegram, April 26, 1946, Box 20, State Department Briefs, HST Library.

195. Summary of Telegram, May 23, 1946, Box 20, State Department Briefs, HST Library; Report, "To the President, A Report Upon Rumania from Burton Y. Berry," p. 18, November 19, 1946, President's Subject Files, Box 4, HST Library.

196. Report, Intelligence Report No. 3642, July 16, 1946, pp., 22-23, Box 1787, OSS-R&A Reports, National Archives.

197. Senate Committee on Foreign Relations, *A Decade of American Foreign Policy*, 1950, pp. 1203-1204.

198. Report, Intelligence Report No. 3642, p. 9, July 16, 1946, Box, 1787, OSS R&A Reports, National Archives.

199. *Ibid.*, p. 2.

200. Report, "To the President, A Report Upon Rumania, by Burton Y. Berry," p. 18, November 19, 1946, Box 4, President's Subject Files, HST Library.

201. *Ibid.*, p. 19.

202. Report, Intelligence Report No. 3642, pp. 15-18, July 16, 1946, Box 1787, OSS R&A Reports, National Archives.

203. Seton-Watson, *The East European Revolution*, p. 208.

204. War Department Intelligence Review No. 42, pp. 17-18, November 27, 1946, Naval Aide Files, Alphabetical Files, Box 17, HST Library.

205. Senate Committee on Foreign Relations, *A Decade of American Foreign Policy*, 1950, p. 1206; Summary of Telegram, November 19, 1946, Box 20 State Department Briefs, HST Library; Telegram, Burton Y. Berry to Secretary of State, November 19, 1946, President's Subject Files, File 186, Box 4, HST Library. Berry advised the Department that though King Michael had accepted the results of the election, "if we can give him more than moral support, he might very well act differently" (Summary of Telegram, December 2, 1946, Box 20, State Department Briefs, HST Library).

206. *FRUS, 1945*, II, pp. 622-623, 640-641, 653, 723-724, 741-743. The sixteen additional Allied nations were Australia, Belgium, the Belorussian SSR, Brazil, Canada, Czechoslovakia, Ethiopia, Greece, India, Netherlands, New Zealand, Norway, Poland, the Ukrainian SSR, the Union of South Africa, and Yugoslavia.

207. Leiss (ed.), *European Peace Treaties After World War II*, p. 12.

208. Campbell, *Foreign Affairs*, Vol. 26, No. 1, pp. 196-218.

209. Oral interview of John C. Campbell by Richard McKinzie, June 24, 1974, p. 81.

210. *FRUS, 1946*, IV, 851.

211. *Ibid.*, p. 64.

212. *Ibid.*, p. 220.

213. *Ibid.*, pp. 432-433; Leiss (ed.), *European Peace Treaties After World War II*, p. 110.

214. *Ibid.*, p. 303.

215. *FRUS*, 1946, II, 297.

216. *FRUS, 1946*, IV, 77.

217. Memorandum, "Regarding the Implementation of the Article 31 of the Treaty of Peace with Rumania," pp. 41-42, May 9, 1947, Balkan Committee File, Box 29, Record Group 84, Foreign Service Posts of DOS, Bucharest, U.S. Mission, Secret Files 1947, National Archives; *FRUS, 1946*, II, 655-656.

218. "Regarding the Implementation of Article 31," p. 16, May 9, 1947, Balkan Committee File, Box 29, Record Group 84, Foreign Service Posts of DOS, Bucharest, U.S. Mission, Secret Files, 1947, National Archives.

219. *FRUS, 1946*, II, 1553-1554.

220. War Department Intelligence Review No. 3, pp. 4-5, February 28, 1946, Box 15, Naval Aide Files, Alphabetical Files, HST Library.

221. Report, "Problems Involved in the Rumanian Settlement," December 31, 1945, Report #3467, Part I, p. 45, Box 1787, OSS-R&A Reports, DOS Decimal File, 1950-1954, National Archives.

222. *Ibid.*, p. 104.

223. Report, July 17, 1947, Report #4456, pp. 27-31, Box 1787, OSS-R&A, DOS Decimal File 1950-1954, National Archives.

224. *Ibid.*, p. 36.

225. Report, "Problems Involved in the Rumanian Settlement," December 31, 1945, Report #3467, Part 1, p. 57, Box 1787, OSS-R&A reports, DOS Decimal File, 1950-1954, National Archives; Report, July 18, 1947, Report #4456, p. 37, Box 1787, OSS-R&A reports, DOS Decimal File, 1950-1954, National Archives.

226. U. S. Congress, House Committee on Foreign Affairs, *U. S. Foreign Policy and the East-West Confrontation*, Vol. XIV of *Selected Executive Session Hearings of the Committee, 1951-1956* (Washington, D.C.: U.S. Government Printing Office, 1980), pp. 46-47.

227. Report, "Economic Survey: Rumania, 1946-1947," p. 2, June 20, 1947, 850-Economics, Box 31, Record Group 84, Foreign Service Posts of DOS, Bucharest, U.S. Mission, Secret Files, 1947, National Archives.

228. *Ibid.*, pp. 3-4.

229. *FRUS, 1946*, II, 269;Dispatch, Secretary of State to the President, pp. 1-2, May 8, 1946, Council of Foreign Ministers [Bucharest] file, Box 9, Naval Aide Files, Communications Files, National Archives.

230. *Ibid.*, p. 2.

231. *FRUS, 1946*, IV, 77.

232. "Regarding the Implementation of Article 31," pp. 6-7, May 9, 1947, Balkan Committee File, Box 29, Record Group 84, Foreign Service Posts of

DOS Bucharest, U.S. Mission, Secret Files, 1947, National Archives.
    233. *Ibid.*, p. 9.
    234. *Ibid.*, pp. 33-35.
    235. Leiss, (ed.), *European Peace Treaties After World War II*, pp. 312-313.
    236. Sulzberger, *A Long Row of Candles*, p. 337.

CHAPTER II

AMERICA IN SEARCH OF
A ROMANIAN POLICY, 1947-1949

Initial Responses to the Peace Treaty

The Romanian government enthusiastically greeted publication of the Peace Treaty. Bucharest announced that the Treaty had "liquidated the shameful past," and enabled "democratic forces" to lead a new Romania. The Communist regime emphasized the role the Soviets had played to keep the punitive terms as mild as possible, noting that the only area in which Moscow was unsuccessful was in reparations. Despite Soviet efforts, the Western powers insisted upon fixing reparation payments at an amount greater than Romania could pay. Similarly, the Communist press attacked the most-favored-nation clause of the treaty, describing it as a means for the "rich" nations to dominate the "small" nations. The newspaper *Adevenil* carried Groza's assessment of the Treaty. "The Treaty provisions are our retribution for an absurd war and for a serious collapse. . . . What is more important however is that the essential factors were saved, i.e., the sovereignty and the frontiers, which make Romania a viable state."[1]

Immediately following the Treaty signing, the State Department told the American Mission in Bucharest to steadfastly pursue the implementation of Article 31, the MFN clause. The Department gave Berry two specific tasks: to actively work through diplomatic channels to eliminate "all cases of alleged discrimination against American interests," and to prepare detailed reports for the State Department on all cases of discrimination including privileges and benefits accorded to nationals and corporations of other countries. "Because this Article will remain in force only eighteen months, it is important that action on specific cases be initiated as soon as possible." The American Mission was authorized to present notes to the Groza government on each instance of discrimination. If the Romanian government did not act on a protest, "consideration should then be given to referring the matter in dispute to the Three Heads of Mission in accordance with Article 38 of the Treaty."[2] Washington authorized the American Mission to take action on its own in addressing issues with the Romanian government. Only if the matter were to be referred to the Three Heads of Mission would concurrence from the State Department be necessary. In addition, the Department wanted the Legation to begin to "stimulate" trade between the United States and Romania. Aware that these directives would be time consuming, the Department noted that it would try to find additional staff for the Legation.[3]

The reactive nature of the Department's directive indicated a major problem in Washington. Throughout World War II, America's foreign policy focused almost entirely on achieving military victory. However, once gained, the victory did not produce new foreign policy goals. Victory did end American isolation, and now Washington needed time to establish new foreign policy goals; goals consistent with the needs of a new world power in a divided world.

To help the Adminstration develop its new foreign policy, Congress passed the the National Security Act in July 1947, which established a National Security Council (NSC) as part of the Executive Office. Membership on the NSC included the President, the Secretaries of State, Defense, Army, Navy and Air force and the Chairman of the National Security Resources Board. The Director of the Central Intelligence Agency participated as an adviser. The duties of the NSC included considering policies dealing with national security and foreign affairs, and making recommendations on these issues to the President.

The NSC initially focused on developing a policy to contain the spread of communism, especially in Western Europe. The Soviet ideologue, Andrei Zhdanov had clearly acknowledged the existence of a bipolar world in his "two camps" speech of October, 1947. By this bifurcation, Romania lost her identify as an independent nation, and became part of the Soviet "camp." Consequently, guidelines for American-Romanian relations had to await NSC recommendations on American-East European relations, and the President did not receive these until

December, 1949. The primary cause for the delay was that America's policy toward Eastern Europe devolved from Washington's policies on national security and trade. Neither of which would be ready for two years. In the interim, America pursued a policy of protestation, protesting Treaty violations especially those involving human rights and such economic issues as compensation for lost property, equal opportunity in civil aviation and equitable access to the Danube River.

The Peace Treaty and the American Legation in Bucharest

In Bucharest, the American Legation focused much of its attention on Romania's implementation of Article 3, the human rights provisions of the Treaty. Berry was most disappointed in Washington's decision to sign the Peace. He was quite certain that the Groza government did not share the State Department's view that the Treaty did not invalidate the Allied declarations at Yalta, Potsdam and Moscow. He urged Washington to work to insure enforcement of the human rights provisions in Article 3. In addition, he asked to be transferred as soon as possible. He believed that a new person might be in a stronger position to implement American policy. He suggested that his replacement be a Charge d'Affaires with the title of Minister, rather than an Ambassador, to show America's disapproval of the recent elections.[4]

While Berry awaited his transfer, the Groza regime continued to repress political dissidents. The leaders of the opposition parties looked to the United States for help. Maniu wanted to oust the Groza government, but, to do so, he needed support from the Great Powers.[5] Six days later, on March 19, 1947, the State Department notified Berry that while it did not condone the dictatorial minority government in Romania, the "United States government cannot support or advocate attempt [of] violent overthrow with probable attendant consequences for [the] Romanian people."[6] The die was cast, as long as Soviet troops occupied Romania, Washington was not about to get involved in a revolution in Bucharest.[7]

Within weeks, the Groza government arrested hundreds of dissidents. May 4 began a second wave of mass arrests, resulting in more than 1,000 people imprisoned.[8] Washington protests fell on deaf ears. Berry reported that reliable sources indicated that Moscow was behind the arrests. The Soviets believed that Groza had permitted too much freedom thereby enabling the opposition parties to grow stronger. The arrests countered this growth and by accusing those arrested of membership in Fascist organizations, the arrests were justified by Article 5 of the Peace Treaty.[9]

Until May, Washington alone had protested the human rights violations. The British were tired of making futile protests, and did not think there was sufficient evidence of Soviet responsibility to raise the issue at the Allied Control Commission.[10] However, the renewed arrests spurred the British Foreign Office into action. London feared that continued inaction could eliminate all opposition in Romania,[11] and consequently Britain agreed to work with the United States to stop the arbitrary arrests.

Meanwhile, the United States Senate ratified the Peace Treaty with Romania with little debate. On the day of ratification, June 14, the President gave notice that American approval of the Treaty did not imply approval of the practices of the Groza government. Senate ratification simply terminated the state of war, and ended the Allied Control Commission.[12] Within a couple of days of Truman's speech, British and American representatives met to draft notes to Bucharest.[13] On June 24 and 25, the two governments sent similar notes to the Groza regime indicating their concern over the "drastic deprivation of civil liberties to which the Romanian people were being subjected, in particular the arbitrary arrest and detention of hundreds of opposition party and nonparty persons."[14] On July 12, the Romanian Foreign Minister, Gheorghe Tatarescu, replied that Bucharest saw no legal grounds for the Anglo-American protests. Further, he viewed these notes as efforts to interfere in Romania's internal affairs.[15] Two days later, Bucharest arrested Maniu.

Maniu's Arrest and Trial

His arrest culminated a long series of actions designed to eliminate the National Peasant Party. As early as the Antonescu trial in May, 1946, the Groza regime had inferred that Maniu was a Fascist. During the November, 1946, trials against alleged "terroristic" organizations, the prosecution tried to implicate members and leaders of the National Peasants Party.[16] In the Spring of 1947, Maniu did himself harm. He seriously thought about overthrowing the Groza regime. While he failed to secure American support, he did consider establishing a resistance government abroad. As the number of arrests increased, several members of the National Peasant Party tried to leave Romania illegally. They were arrested on July 14 along with Maniu. The Groza government quickly branded them as traitors. The government closed the party's newspaper, *Dreptatea*, and on July 30 the Council of Ministers outlawed the party. Those arrested would stand trial for conspiring to overthrow the government.[17]

Frustration mounted at the American legation in Bucharest. Rudolph Schoenfeld, who had replaced Berry on July 23 as America's new Minister to Romania, reported that for the past two months "virtually no, repeat no, Romanian national has dared enter the Mission" to discuss political matters. The fear of arbitrary arrest and the example of Maniu had frightened the Romanian people into silence. Schoenfeld wrote,

> Gestapo methods are being employed in questioning prisoners and it is reasonable to suppose some of the Missions' sources will be forced to make entirely false confessions giving sinister cast to their relations with the Mission, possibly involving acceptance of money. It is clear [that the Romanian] government is determined to implicate the United States in the forthcoming [trials].[18]

On August 18, the United States took the only punitive action it could take against Romania. Washington vetoed Romania's efforts to enter the United Nations. In June, the State Department and British Foreign Office shared ideas as to how to permit Italy, but not permit Romania and other Balkan states, to join the United Nations. Both agreed that the key word was "enabling." All five treaties with the ex-satellite states, had a common phrase that the peace treaty would settle questions still outstanding as a result of the war, thereby "enabling the Allied and Associated Powers to support" a country's application to become a member of the United Nations. London and Washington both agreed that the word "enabling" did not restrict any freedom of action. They could support Italy's request for membership, and deny Romania's.[19] Consequently, the United States voted against Romania's admission into the United Nations all five times Bucharest applied in 1947.[20]

Meanwhile, Romania ratified the Peace Treaty on August 23, and the Soviets did likewise a couple of weeks later. On September 15 the Big Three simultaneously deposited their ratified treaties in Moscow.[21] By this act, the articles of the Peace Treaty replaced the directives of the Control Commission as the primary Allied instrument to affect Romania's domestic policies. The American delegation to the Control Commission left Bucharest and by December 15, the only remaining American officials in Romania were those attached to the Legation.[22]

The much heralded Maniu trial opened on October 29. The government indicted Maniu, the National Peasant Party and the United States. Among the charges, Maniu allegedly conspired with "imperialist circles" in the United States and Great Britain to overthrow the government. Further, Maniu empowered Grigore Nicolescu-Buzesti to "draw up a plan under which a clandestine organization, supported by the Americans with equipment, arms, and funds was to be created in the country; and organs to direct the plot were to be created both in Romania and abroad under the supervision of American representatives." Nicolescu-Buzesti and his colleague, Constantin Visioanu, had left Romania with help from the American Military Mission to establish an espionage center outside Romania.[23] Finally, the indictments identified Major Thomas Hall and Lt. James Hamilton, both members of the United States staff for the Allied Control Commission, as collaborators assisting Maniu in his revolutionary activities.[24]

Washington was upset by the indictments, in part because there was evidence to prove that some of the allegations were correct. The National Peasant Party had not destroyed a large number of documents "confirming much of the indictment." Included in these materials was evidence that Maniu had talked with Hall and Hamilton about forming a resistance movement to overthrow the Groza government. During the trial, Maniu also admitted that he had communicated "subversive" documents to Washington and London.[25] The State Department decided to control damage, and it notified Schoenfeld in Bucharest to say nothing until after the close of the trial.[26]

As the Romanian Communists moved to consolidate their power, Groza looked to eliminate one of the few remaining centers of opposition to his government, Gheorghe Tartarescu. As leader of the Liberal Party and Romanian Foreign Minister, Tartarescu had some degree of independence. In May, he had criticized the police repression, and suggested that foreign credits were needed to improve Romania's industry. The Communist cabinet members countered, and blamed Taratescu and his followers for pursuing a policy of national discrimination against the Hungarians.

Tartarescu frequently spoke candidly to representatives of the American Legation. In September, he told Roy Melbourne, that if he or his colleagues deviated from Soviet policy, there would be "strong likelihood they would find themselves in the Lake Baikal region of Russia."[27] During the Maniu trial, several Foreign Ministry officials were indicted for anti-government activity. The Communists needed no further evidence. On November 5, they forced Tartarescu and his Liberal Party out of the government.[28]

On November 11, the Romanian court found Maniu and his colleague Ion Mihalache guilty and sentenced them to life imprisonment. The rest of the 19 co-defendants received sentences ranging from life to one year's confinement. Reaction was mixed. Moscow and the pro-government Bucharest press hailed the court findings as "stern but just." In London, Maniu's sentence strengthened the British Government's conviction that the Peace Treaty would probably not be honored by Romania. In Washington, while the American press railed at the sentence, the official State Department message was more restrained, largely because of the Hall-Hamilton affair. The State Department delivered an official note to the Romanian Foreign Ministry stating that the American Government noted the accusations made against it during the Maniu trials. However, the United States deemed it "unnecessary and inappropriate to dignify by specific refutation charges presented" alleging American efforts to overthrow the Romanian government.[29]

From Monarchy to Republic

The removal of Tartarescu and Maniu left the Communist party with only one remaining obstacle to total power, King Michael. The King symbolized traditional authority, and his opposition to the Groza government was well known. In November, 1947, he visited England to attend the wedding of Princess Elizabeth and the Duke of Edinburgh. In London, the American Ambassador, Lewis Douglas, met King Michael and urged him not to return to Bucharest.[30] A week later, on November 21, the two met again. The King was aware that he had lost power in Romania. In reality, he could not dissolve Parliament nor change the government. If he returned, he would be required to sign Communist decrees with which he did not agree, or to abdicate. He refused to do the former, while the latter would probably result in imprisonment. He asked if he could come to the United States to make a proclamation to the Romanian people explaining his departure. He owed his people an explanation.[31]

With instructions from Washington, Douglas met with King Michael on the twenty-fifth. He assured the King that there would be no problem with his coming to the United States, however, "it would be impracticable to issue a proclamation from the United States."[32] Britain, too, preferred he not make any statements from their soil.[33] However, the King wanted to talk to his people. He asked Douglas if the United States would "help get him out" if he returned to Bucharest, perhaps through asylum in the Legation. Douglas feared that due to the geographical location of Romania, the United States would be unable to do anything effective. After several days of wavering, the King decided on December 2 to return to Romania. He was upset by the cool reception he had received from both Washington and London,[34] and believed that his place was with his people.

The Groza regime was not pleased by his return. While in England, he had become engaged to Princess Anne of Bourbon-Parma. The new Foreign Minster, Ana Pauker, opposed the wedding, supposedly for financial reasons, but more likely because of the attention it would bring the King.[35] The Communists demanded his abdication. On December 30, Communist soldiers and secret police surrounded the Kyselef Palace and called upon the King to abdicate. Michael had no choice. Within hours he abdicated proclaiming that "I leave it to the Romanian people to choose the new form of state."[36] While King Michael packed to go to Switzerland, the Groza government proclaimed the Romanian People's Republic.

The new government called for new elections. The Communists worked quickly. On February 23 they merged with the Socialists to form the Romanian Workers' Party.[37] Four days later the Communists organized a new front organization, the People's Democratic Front, or FDP, which included members of the Romanian Workers' Party, the Plowman's Front, the National Popular Party, and the Hungarian' People's Union.[38] At the elections on March 28, 1948, the Communists and their allies won 405 of the 414 seats. The other nine seats went to the Democratic Peasant Party led by Dr. Lupu and the remnant of the Liberal Party led by Dinu Bratianu. The new government approved a new constitution on April 13 creating the Romanian People's Republic, which guaranteed minority and nationality rights, freedom of religion, press, opinion, assembly, processions, and demonstrations. The right of association and organization was prohibited to organizations that opposed the government. The new Constitution indicated that Romania was in transition from capitalism to socialism.[39]

The Mechanics of Implementing the Articles of the Peace Treaty

Meanwhile, in October, 1947, the Groza government had established an Interdepartmental Commission for the Application of the Peace Treaty. The Foreign Minister, Ana Pauker, chaired the Commission, but left the daily operations to Dr. Simion Oeriu. The Commission served as the machinery to deal with any alleged Treaty violations. Schoenfeld saw the Commission as nothing more than a "facade of correctness."[40] In his meetings with Oeriu, Schoenfeld could only discuss procedural matters. Oeriu repeatedly emphasized that he had no power to resolve Treaty matters until the entire Commission met, and that decision rested with the Foreign Minister.[41]

Frustrated, Schoenfeld sent a formal letter to the Romanian Foreign Ministry on February 2, protesting in great detail Bucharest's Treaty violations. He reviewed the entire history of broken promises since the Armistice. He focused on the recent trial of Iuliu Maniu as indicative of Romania's willful violation of the political and civil rights of the defendants. The government had intimidated witnesses, and, in the final analysis, had failed to substantiate the charge of treasonable activities, upon which the defendants were found guilty. Schoenfeld concluded that the "human rights and fundamental freedoms" which Bucharest agreed to implement when they signed the peace treaty did not exist in Romania.[42] The British sent an identical note the same day.

On February 6, the Soviet Embassy in Bucharest declared that it did not agree with these notes since their charges had no connection with the fulfillment of the Peace Treaty.[43] On March 3, Pauker's official response continued the government's normal line of argument. Bucharest had faithfully adhered to its guarantees of civil liberties consistent with the "necessities of national security;" the issues raised in the American and British notes were "entirely an internal concern of Romania," and did not permit foreign interference; and, finally, and most significantly, complaints concerning execution of the Treaty must come from the three Chiefs of Missions "acting in concert" and since the Soviets had not complained, Bucharest would not consider any complaints by the British and American representatives.[44] Pauker's response came as no surprise to Schoenfeld. He had earlier described her as a "most fiery Communist" who would "welcome nothing more at the outset of her term of office than [the] opportunity to give the United States a resounding rebuff." In his note to Washington, he concluded that "I hesitate to think of the propaganda possibilities inherent in the fact that she is a woman."[45] Schoenfeld in February decided that she was "ignorant of the problems involved and unacquainted with the substance of any case" involving Treaty violations. Her assistants were "uninformed and morally illiterate as well as stupid."[46] Pauker's "ignorance" obviously served her ends, enabling her to ignore treaty violations.

In her defense, she had far more serious problems to deal with than Treaty protests. Principal among them was the ouster of Lucretiu Patrascanu from his post as Minister of Justice. Long viewed as one of the party's most gifted and popular leaders,[47] Patrascanu was seen from the West as a moderate Communist. Some would later liken him to Tito, the maverick leader of Yugoslavia.[48] In 1946, Patrascanu had exhibited very strong nationalist sentiments, and urged the Romanian Communists to maintain Romania's patriotic values. This nationalist commitment upset the Soviets and Gheorghiu-Dej criticized Patrascanu at the Central Committee meeting of the Romanian Communist Party in November, 1946. Patrascanu continued to oppose Soviet influence in Romania. However, in February, his reputedly closest friend, Teohari Georgescu, denounced him as a "Menshevik who had befriended war criminals and capitalists." Gheorghiu-Dej justified Patrascanu's ouster since the latter had become a "victim of bourgeois ideology" and had "detached himself from the masses."[49] Avram Bunaciu, a "fanatical" Communist, replaced him as the Minister of Justice.[50]

This purge, coupled with the Communist's preoccupation with the upcoming elections, and Bucharest's normal indifference to Treaty violations, further frustrated Schoenfeld. He wrote to Washington that Treaty implementation promised to be "largely a unilateral task" involving "careful preparation of the legal record, long delays and eventual reference of most issues to disputes machinery provided by the Treaty."[51]

The "disputes machinery" involved Articles 37 and 38 of the Treaty. Ana Pauker's March 3 note to the Legation indicated that she was totally aware of these articles and saw them as protection from Anglo-American interference in Romanian politics. Article 37 stipulated that for the first 18 months after the Treaty came into force, questions concerning execution and interpretation of the treaty would be resolved by the three Heads of Mission in Bucharest "acting in concert." In the event agreement could not be reached within two months, Article 38 provided for the appointment of a three member Commission composed of the two disputing parties and a third party selected by mutual agreement. In the event there was no agreement as to the third member, the Secretary-General of the United Nations "may be requested by either party" to make the selection. The Commission's decision would be binding on both parties.[52]

Pauker's note stressed the significance of "acting in concert." The State Department was equally aware that Article 37 probably would never be invoked, because the Soviets would not "act in concert."[53] The only dispute resolving machinery left was Article 38 which was open to interpretation since, unlike Article 37, it did not require the Big Three to "act in concert." However, London did not share Washington's interest in enforcing Article 38. As early as December, 1947, the British indicated that they would not use Article 38 to address an "ideological" issue.[54] At times, London viewed human rights as an "ideological" issue, and was reluctant to press this as a Treaty matter because of the "bleak prospect" of success against Soviet opposition.[55]

By April, 1948, the State Department concluded that the United States could not effectively force Romania to live up to her obligations. Nonetheless, Washington decided to maintain its policy of protestation in order to "publicly condemn violations" of the Treaty. This tactic would show evidence of America's commitment to her Treaty obligations, and, at the same time, keep before world opinion Communism's indifference to human rights. [56]A couple of weeks later, the United States tried to invoke Article 37 on a non-ideological issue, Romania's fulfillment of the military articles in the Treaty. While the Romanian Armed Forces did not exceed the Treaty limitations, the police force, which was trained as a para-military unit, constituted a possible violation of the Treaty. Washington requested that Romania supply information on the police force. Bucharest agreed to compile the information but would only release it upon request by the three Heads of Missions. On May 4, Schoenfeld requested a meeting of the Heads of Missions. The British and Soviets agreed, and Schoenfeld suggested that the Soviet representative, Ambassador Kavtaradze select the date. He chose May 17. Members of the American Legation began to bet on how Kavtaradze would "wiggle out" of attending the meeting. On May 16, the Soviet Ambassador apologized to his colleagues. He had become ill and would be unable to attend the meeting. On May 26, he notified the American and British Legations that he saw no necessity for a meeting and would not attend one.[57] This ended Anglo-American efforts to challenge Romania's compliance with the Treaty's military provisions. The Western powers concluded that continued protests had little chance of accomplishing anything and might, in fact, have a "disadvantageous effect" by encouraging the Soviets to question the implementation of the military clauses in the Italian treaty.[58]

Schoenfeld's frustration and sense of helplessness was shared by American Ministers throughout Eastern Europe. Consequently, the State Department called a meeting in Rome of economic and military advisers from the Embassy in Rome, the Legations in Budapest, Bucharest and Sofia, economic advisers from the Missions in Belgrade, Trieste, Warsaw, Prague and Bern, and officials from Washington. The thirty-one representatives met in Rome on June 14, 1948.[59] After a week of discussion, the Conference decided that "Treaty implementation is not, and under existing conditions cannot be, a major element in the attainment of the political objectives of the United States in Eastern Europe." Rather, Treaty implementation would be treated as a moral issue, as an indication to the world of the nature of the ongoing political conflict between the United States and the Soviet Union. Continued protest against violations would not only show the world that the United States cared about the fate of Eastern Europe, but it might also "assist in the eventual alienation of the Balkan peoples from their own governments and from their Soviet overseers." Furthermore, continued protests would provide sufficient evidence for the United States to continue to oppose United Nations membership to these satellite states.[60]

The Conference decisions reflected the State Department's thinking in 1948. While policy development will be discussed later in this chapter, suffice to say that Washington saw the recent defection of Yugoslavia from Soviet control as a model for other Balkan states. Therefore, the Department recommended the United States use whatever means at hand to emphasize the unjust and immoral behavior of the Soviet Union. This involved a subtle shift of emphasis. Yugoslavia was still under Communist control, but it was independent of Moscow. Therefore, Washington wanted to focus on the evils inherent in Soviet influence, rather than to focus on the evils of Communism.

Returning from the Rome conference, Schoenfeld continued to send protests of Treaty violations to the Groza government, but he did so at a far slower rate. Washington's decision to stop elaborating violations of the military clauses of the Treaty had a general effect of curbing the enthusiasm of even the most zealous protesters.

In September, 1948, the Romanian government dissolved the Inter-departmental Commission for the Application of the Peace Treaty and transferred its functions to the Foreign Ministry. The dissolution "merely gave legal recognition to a condition already in existence," since the Commission had always been under the control of the Foreign Minister. Now Schoenfeld would simply direct his complaints about Treaty violations directly to Ana Pauker.[61]

Tito's break with Moscow persuaded the Soviets to increase Communist control in Romania. On January 12, 1949, the government passed a decree setting up "people's councils" in all the villages, towns and districts to bring the "socialist order" to the local level. In April, the government appointed representatives to the councils to insure Communist influence in all parts of the country. The councils took office in July, 1949.[62] The Communists also increased their control at the top levels of government. Groza expanded Vasile Luca's Ministry of Finance reponsibilities to include supervision of the State Bank, Bank for Credit, and all insurance and savings banks. On April 16, Groza promoted Pauker and Luca to Vice-Premiers, replacing two non-Communists.[63] Shortly thereafter, the government arrested Tartarescu, the leader of the dissident Liberal party and former Foreign Minister, and charged him with corrupt financial practices. By the end of 1949, the Communists had consolidated their control over Romania, and party membership numbered about 750,000.[64]

Human Rights and Treaty Implementation

March 15, 1949, ended the 18 month period stipulated in Article 37 of the Romanian Treaty for the Heads of Mission "acting in concert" to resolve problems. However, Article 38, which also involved Heads of Mission did not have a time limit. Early in 1949, there were a number of incidents involving religious persecution and other human rights violation in Hungary, Bulgaria, and Romania. On March 8, Llewellyn Thompson of the Office of European Affairs recommended that the State Department quickly invoke Treaty machinery in each of the three Balkan treaties, preferably prior to the opening of the United Nations General Assembly on April 1. Using Romania as the example, Thompson anticipated that Romania would reject America's complaints which would enable Washington to request a meeting of the three Heads of Mission in Bucharest. The Soviets would undoubtedly decline which would permit the United States to call for the appointment of a three member Commission, one representing Romania, one representing the United States, and one appointed by mutual agreement. Thompson expected that there would be no mutual agreement, therefore, under Article 38, the United States would ask the Secretary General of the United Nations to appoint the third member. Finally, Thompson noted that at any time, the United States could point out Romanian obstructionism and bring the entire issue to the United Nations.[65]

The Department accepted the recommendation and on March 29 sent a letter to the Romanian government. The note reviewed the past history of Romania's intransigence at implementing Article 3 of the Treaty. Romania's "flagrant conduct" in human rights affairs now forced Washington to call upon the Romanian Government "to adopt prompt remedial measures" in response to the noted violations. Further, the United States wanted Bucharest to "specify the steps" which it was prepared to take to implement fully the terms of Article 3 of the Treaty.[66]

As Thompson had anticipated the Romanian reply on April 18 denied all allegations labelling them as "inventions of the slanderous press of the imperialist monopolists." Bucharest rebutted the American criticism of the Maniu trial and described the defendants as "legionnaires, large landowners and great industrialists" who undoubtedly had received instructions from the United States Mission in Bucharest. Their sentencing constituted a "blow to the American Espionage services." In conclusion, the Romanian government rejected the American note as an attempt to interfere in the internal affairs of Romania.[67] On May 31, the State Department sent Bucharest another note. Since Romania refused to specify any measures to correct human rights violations, Washington concluded that a "dispute" existed "concerning the interpretation and execution of the Treaty." Since bilateral negotiations had failed to resolve the problem, the United States had decided to refer the issue to the British and Soviet representatives in Bucharest under the provisions of Article 38 of the Treaty.[68] The Article prescribed a two month period for the three Heads of Mission to solve the problem.

On June 11, the Soviets replied. From their viewpoint, Romania was fulfilling its Treaty obligations and there was no basis for any dispute. Therefore, there was no reason to convene a meeting of the Heads of Mission.[69] On June 30, Washington sent a further note to Moscow asking the Soviets to reconsider their position. The Soviet refusal on July 19 enabled Washington to implement the final part of its plan.[70] The American Legation in Bucharest delivered a note to the Romanian government on August 1 asking the Groza regime to join the United States in forming a Commission in accordance with Article 38 of the Peace Treaty.[71] At the same time, Washington appointed Edwin Dickinson as its representative to the Commission.[72] However, Bucharest remained steadfast in its opposition. Groza refused to appoint any representative to the Commission. After a month of delay, the American Secretary of State, Dean Acheson, denounced Romania at a press conference on September 14 noting that their refusal to appoint a delegate to the Commission was a "further illustration of their callous disregard of clear international obligations."[73]

Washington turned to the United Nations for help. Since December, 1948, the United Nations had concerned itself with human rights. Its Universal Declaration of Human Rights enumerated specific rights beginning with the concept that "all human beings are born free and equal in dignity and rights."[74] The General Assembly had discussed the observance of human rights in Bulgaria and Hungary in April, 1949, during its Third Regular Session.[75] On August 20, Australia asked the Secretary-General of the United Nations to include Romanian human rights on the agenda for the Fourth Regular Session.[76]

When the Session opened in September, 1949, Warren Austin, the United States representative to the United Nations reviewed the exchange of texts between Bucharest and Washington. On September 22, the General Assembly decided to refer the whole question of observance of human rights and fundamental freedoms in Bulgaria, Hungary and Romania to the Ad Hoc Political Committee for consideration and report. After considerable discussion and heated debate between Benjamin Cohen, America's alternate representative, and Andrei Vyshinsky, Moscow's representative and Foreign Minister, the General Assembly decided on October 22, 1949, to solicit an opinion from the International Court of Justice on the following issues: (1) Did the diplomatic exchange between the United States and Romania disclose a dispute as defined in Article 38 of the Peace Treaty?; (2) In the event of an affirmative answer, was Romania obligated to appoint a representative to a Commission?; (3) In the event of an affirmative reply, and in the event that Romania after 30 days did not appoint a representative, could the Secretary-General of the United Nations appoint a member to the Commission?; and (4) in the event of an affirmative reply, would this two member Commission be competent to make a definitive and binding decision to settle a dispute? The United Nations also announced its intention to retain the question of the observance of human rights and fundamental freedoms in Romania, Bulgaria and Hungary for its next session.[77] The Court would not render an opinion until March, 1950.

Economics and Treaty Implementation

In addition to complaints concerning human rights violations, Washington also criticized Bucharest for her reluctance to implement the economic clauses of the Treaty. In part, these complaints stemmed from Romania's efforts to centralize her economy. The goal of centralization supposedly was spelled out at a meeting between Soviet officials and Romanian Communists on March 7, 1945, one day after the Groza regime came into power. At the meeting, according to Dr. Herbert Silver, who was manager of the Romanian Economic Research Institute, Ana Pauker agreed to pass legislation which would collectivize agriculture, nationalize the banks, and eliminate Western business in Romania.[78]

Two weeks later, King Michael agreed to the Agrarian Reform Law which prohibited any one landowner from owning more than 50 hectares, or 123 acres, of land. Absentee landowners could own no more than 10 hectares. The state seized all the remaining lands for allocation to non-landowners, making it clear that there would be no compensation to former owners. Months later, however, the Romanian Ministry of Justice ruled that in accordance with Article 18 of the 1923 Constitution, foreign landowners could be reimbursed the "value" of appropriated lands.[79]

Initially the United States opposed the decision, and demanded restoration of the seized land. However, by September 1947, the State Department agreed to demand compensation rather than land restoration, since the latter was virtually impossible.[80] However, Washington wanted this compensation based on international law, rather than Article 24 of the Romanian Peace Treaty. For the Treaty clearly stipulated that compensation would be payable with local currency. In practice, this meant that a claimant would have to spend all the compensation in Romania. Claims under international law, on the other hand, could be paid for with currency exchangeable outside of Romania. Since most of the American claimants lived in the United States, this was obviously the preferred solution.[81]

Bucharest refused to accept the American interpretation. Negotiations continued until January, 1951, when the State Department decided that American claims would be compensated from Romania's assets in the United States frozen under the Trading With the Enemy Act. These assets totaled approximately $24.5 million,[82] and the claims issue would finally be resolved in 1960 through the terms of an American-Romanian agreement.[83]

Throughout 1947, the Groza regime continued to centralize the economy. On January 1, 1947, Bucharest nationalized the National Bank of Romania. Reaction at the American Legation was mixed. Unofficially, the Legation thought this was an appropriate action, for no government should have to depend on a private institution for its financial dealings. However, the Legation noted that "the present Romanian government has shown its intentions of using the bank for political purposes and the day is not far off when it will be the financial tool of Communist policy in Romania."[84]

In April, the government reorganized the Ministry of National Economy into the Ministry of Industry and Commerce with sweeping powers to organize, direct, supervise and control the activities of all industrial enterprises, except those coming under specific government departments.[85] One month later, on May 24, the government passed the Industrial Offices Bill which enabled them to interfere further in private enterprise. The following year, on June 11, 1948, the Romanian People's Republic completed the last major part of their reorganization. The government nationalized all industrial, transportation and mining enterprises along with all banks and insurance companies.[86] While these laws produced 55 claims by Americans for compensation, this number was small compared to the 400 American claims against Hungary.[87] American efforts to quickly resolve these property claims failed, and similar to the claims produced by the Agrarian Reform Law, the claimants had to wait until 1960 for a settlement.

Civil Aviation and Treaty Implementation

Another State Department concern was Romania's implementation of Article 31 of the Treaty, the guarantee of equal commercial aviation rights with Romania. As part of their effort to control the political and economic future of Romania, the Soviets had signed an agreement with Romania on August 8, 1945, creating TARS, an aviation Sovrom. This joint company insured that the Soviets would be the sole supplier of airplanes, and the principal supplier of aviation equipment to Romania. In return, Bucharest contributed her airports and the remainder of her civil aviation equipment to the Sovrom. TARS had the right to operate all airlines in Romania and to participate in international air traffic.[88] By February, 1947, the Soviets controlled all air traffic in Romania including crew selection and assignment, frequently supplying Soviet military crews for Romanian planes.

In May, 1947, the State Department opened negotiations with Bucharest to determine if Bucharest would permit an American commerical airliner to fly over Romania enroute to the Orient. The Pan American World Airways Company wanted to extend its service from Western Europe to Istanbul, Karachi and Calcutta. The most cost effective flight line to these eastern destinations was over Romania. In return, Washington agreed to grant Romania reciprocal arrangements to fly over American zones of occupation in Western Europe, and to assist Romania in developing air routes to the Near East.[89] The Romanians appeared interested, especially in establishing a Bucharest to Paris flight.[90] However, the Soviets had nothing to gain by opening Romania to the West, and consequently the negotiations collapsed before the Peace Treaty came into force. Similar American efforts to establish bilateral commercial aviation agreements with the Soviet Union and other East European countries also failed.

Washington's inability to conclude bilateral agreements in Eastern Europe was in part due to the fact that the State Department had not yet developed an aviation policy toward the Soviet Bloc. Work began on this project in the Fall of 1947. In June, 1948, the State Department sent its recommendations to the NSC. The Department believed that under no conditions would the Soviets permit the United States the right to fly into or fly over Soviet airspace including that of its satellites. Pan American World Airways did have flights to Prague. However, since the February, 1948, coup which gave the Soviets control of Czechoslovakia, patronage had declined to such an extent that its commercial advantages were no longer promising. The Department assumed that any Soviet interest in flying over Western territories would be purely for military and political purposes, not commercial.[91]

As a result, the Department recommended that the United States restrict the civil air operation of the Soviet Union and its satellites to their own territories until Moscow was willing to grant reciprocal aviation rights. Effective implementation required Washington to secure, on an informal basis, agreement among the Western allies to curtail all commercial air traffic with the Soviet Union and the satellites, including the use of their airspace. Further, the United States wanted her allies to agree not to supply spare parts or major maintenance to any Soviet or satellite aircraft. Since a large proportion of the planes operated by the satellite states were American built, they depended on Western spare parts. The National Security Council accepted the Department's recommendations on July 12, labelled the document NSC 15, and Truman approved it the following day.[92]

NSC 15 met stiff resistance from America's allies, most especially from Great Britain. The British refused to fully cooperate. London was willing to prevent the sale of equipment and to deny overhaul and maintenance facilities, but they did not want to curtail their air traffic. Britain operated a valuable military courier service to Warsaw, and had commercial service to Prague. If Great Britain prohibited Poland and Czechoslovakia air rights into the United Kingdom, Warsaw and Prague would immediately reciprocate. In December, 1948, London and Washington compromised. Both agreed not to grant permission for satellite services to their territory beyond what was absolutely necessary as a *quid pro quo* to obtain such services as they required; to deny all but the minimum facilities to satellite air services; to prevent the direct or indirect export of planes and air craft equipment to the satellites and the Soviet Union; and, to prevent Soviet and satellite aircraft the use of facilities for overhaul or major maintenance.[93]

The Anglo-American agreement departed from the provisions of NSC 15. The first provision in the joint statement permitted satellite flights into Britain provided reciprocal arrangements were possible. By April, 1949, the United States realized that they could not force their Allies to adopt the goals of NSC 15. When London supported a Netherland's decision to permit Hungarian planes to fly to Amsterdam in return for KLM flights to Budapest, the American Ambassador to Britain, Lewis Douglas, asked Washington to reconsider NSC 15.

Britain and the rest of Western Europe saw NSC 15 as an American attempt to curtail East-West European commercial aviation traffic until the United States was ready to participate. However, Washington refused to become involved until Moscow signed a reciprocal air traffic agreement. Since this development did not soon appear possible, London wanted Washington to change her policy. Douglas also included in his report the British Joint Chiefs of Staff position which challenged the American assumption that reciprocal air flights would produce additional security problems. London believed that satellite air transport service offered little, if any, significant intelligence information to Communist agents not already available through other means.[94]

Douglas's report stirred interest in Washington. On June 1, the State Department agreed to have the Joint Chiefs of Staff reconsider the military security aspects of NSC 15 now known as NSC 15/1.[95] On July 20, the American Joint Chiefs of Staff changed their position. America's efforts to isolate Eastern Europe and the Soviet Union could not work without the cooperation of America's Western allies. The Joint Chiefs accepted the British argument that there were military advantages to be gained through commercial air penetration behind the Iron Curtain. Therefore, the Joint Chiefs called for a review of NSC 15/1 to explore the feasibility of permitting bilateral reciprocal commercial aviation arrangements with Communist countries.[96]

In August, the NSC began the review. Because of Yugoslavia's break with Moscow, Yugoslavia was exempted from the restrictions of NSC 15/1.[97] Further discussion ensued and finally on December 28, the National Security Council produced NSC 15/2. This document, which the President approved as policy, continued to prohibit the sale of aircraft or airplane parts to the Soviet Union and its satellites, and to prevent the use of facilities for overhaul or major maintenance. Further, Washington did not want any arrangements made with the Soviet Union because Moscow would never permit commercial penetration of Soviet airspace. However, the satellites were a different issue. The NSC accepted the British arguments and agreed that the United States and its allies could make bilateral reciprocal commercial aviation agreements with East European countries provided there was a "balance of advantage" to the West.[98] Therefore Britain could retain her service to Prague and Warsaw, and other West European states could make reciprocal arrangements with satellite countries including Romania.

Free Navigation on the Danube

Another issue affecting American-Romanian relations at this time concerned free navigation of the Danube. At the close of the war, the Soviets controlled the Danube from Linz in Austria to the Black Sea. The United States wanted to establish a convention which would ensure free trade on the Danube and thereby reduce "Soviet economic and political domination of the Danube region." Due to American insistence, the peace treaties with Hungary, Romania and Bulgaria all contained articles calling for free and equal navigation of the river. Supplementing these agreements was the decision of the CFM in Moscow on December 6, 1946, that there should be a Danubian conference with representatives from France, Great Britain, the Soviet Union, the United States, the riparian nations: Bulgaria, Czechoslovakia, Hungary, Romania and

Yugoslavia, and the Ukrainian SSR. The Conference would convene within six months of the treaties coming into force.[99]

The three Balkan treaties came into force on September 15, 1947. The Soviets did not call for a conference since they had nothing to gain, while the British and French too remained silent accepting the reality of Soviet control of the Danube. However, the United States insisted on calling for the conference before the March 15, 1948, deadline. Washington believed that to do otherwise would forfeit future American influence on the Danube.

On February 27, 1948, the State Department notified Moscow of the need for a conference. On March 15, the Soviets agreed and suggested Belgrade, Yugoslavia, as the site. Washington approved and on July 30, the conference opened.[100] From the outset the State Department knew that the Soviets would control the conference. Decisions would be determined by majority vote and the Soviets had a 7 to 3 edge. The Department rationalized that the United States did not have to accept the results of the conference.[101] As for Romania's role at the Conference, Schoenfeld correctly predicted that Bucharest's policy would be "an abject reflection of whatever position the Soviets may take."[102]

The Conference quickly became a battle ground between Cavendish Cannon, the American representative and Andrei Vyshinsky, the Soviet delegate. However, the outcome of the battle was never in question. Everyone of the 28 Western amendments was defeated, while everyone of the 56 articles of the Soviet draft was approved. The voting was consistently 7 to 1, the United States the single nea since the British and French refused to vote.[103] On August 18, Vyshinsky and delegates from the riparian states and the Ukraine signed the Danube Convention. The three Western powers refused to sign the agreement. The Convention nullified all previous treaties governing the Danube and established a Commission to administer the Convention along the Danube from Linz to the Black Sea.[104]

On November 15, 1948, four days after the Commission's first meeting in Galatz, Romania, the United States advised the Soviet Union that it did not recognize the Danube Convention as internationally valid. The Convention disregarded the interests of non-riparian states, ignored the 1921 international agreement on the Danube, thereby denying the United Kingdom, France, Italy, Belgium and Greece their rights guaranteed by that accord, and separated the Danube Commission from any relationship with the United Nations. These factors clearly indicated that the Soviets intended to seal off the Danube from normal inter-course with the rest of the world.[105] The observation was correct, and the Soviets took no action to alter that perception.

America Adopts an East European Policy, NSC 58/2

Since signing the Peace Treaty with Bucharest, Washington had pur-sued a "tit for tat" policy toward Romania and Eastern Europe. America reacted to whatever Romania did or did not do. Treaty violations were protested for ideological reasons, not because any change could result. The protests aimed to portray Communism as immoral. George Ken-nan's "long telegram" from Moscow in February, 1946, provided the ra-tionale for this new approach. American had to contain the spread of Communism.[106] There was no value to be gained in negotiating with the Soviets; Moscow only understood firmness.[107] To many, Kennan's pro-posal meant that America had to draw a line, along which she would prevent the spread of Communism. One corollary to this approach was to accept those countries on the other side of the line as under Soviet control, and, as such, off limits to any American schemes to "liberate" them from Communism.[108]

While the Truman Doctrine and later the Marshall Plan seemed to reflect the State Department's adoption of the containment element in Kennan's policy, there was still considerable disagreement among gov-ernment officials about the non-liberation element. This group believed that the United States could not only contain Communism, but she could overturn Communism's recent conquests, especially in Eastern Europe.[109] This view was certainly apparent in May, 1947, when the State Department reviewed its Romanian policy.

The Department was still committed to "supporting" people who were "resisting attempted subjugation" by the Soviet Union.[110] Wash-ington knew that it would be "difficult" to restore democracy to Roma-nia in the foreseeable future. Nonetheless, the Department intended to pursue that goal. The principal means available was to protest all Treaty violations, with the hope of keeping alive the flame of democracy in Romania.[111] The Department recognized that this protesting tactic was not likely to "accomplish more than to retard the present momentum toward the consolidation of Soviet control of Romania." Optimists in the State Department believed that once the Treaty came into force, the United States could end its interim policy, and resume normal diplo-matic relations with Romania. Through Treaty implementation, the

United States would negotiate a bilateral MFN agreement with Bucharest enabling America to reduce Moscow's control over Romania.[112]

As the events of 1947 unfolded, Washington's ingenuous optimism eroded. The dissolution of the National Peasant Party, the trial and conviction of Maniu and other National Peasant Party leaders, the abdication of King Michael, and the establishment of the Romanian People's Republic, reflected the rapid consolidation of the Communist party's control in Romania. Meanwhile, Moscow increased her influence in Romania and Eastern Europe. Romania signed treaties of friendship and mutual assistance with the Soviet Union, Bulgaria, Czechoslovakia, Yugoslavia, Hungary, and Poland. Bucharest followed Moscow's lead in refusing Marshall Plan aid and, in September, 1947, Romania became a charter member of the Cominform. As the "two camp" mentality spread, the Soviet Ambassador to Romania addressed a Romanian Communist Party audience on the anniversary of the Bolshevik Revolution. He told them that the Soviet Union would "shake off the fetters now being prepared for us by imperialistic gangsters and warmongers. . . . No hand, not even one armed with the atomic bomb, will succeed in turning back the wheel of history."[113]

As the sides became drawn, the National Security Council reviewed America's policy toward the Soviet Union. On March 30, 1948, the Council approved NSC 7 which concluded that "the ultimate objectives of Soviet-directed world communism is the domination of the world."[114] Consequently, the United States could not depend on simply a "defensive policy" to check Soviet expansion. "A defensive policy by attempting to be strong everywhere runs the risk of being weak everywhere." America had to select areas most vital to her security, and to concentrate her forces to prevent Communism from spreading to them. NSC 7 also recommended that the United States work to undermine the strength of the Communist forces in the Soviet world. This would be done by developing, and, at the appropriate time, carrying out "a coordinated program to support underground resistance movements in countries behind the Iron Curtain."[115] NSC 7 was a reflection of the thinking of many Americans in 1947 who refused to accept as permanent Soviet control of Eastern Europe.

Three months later, the National Security Council's view received support form a most unlikely quarter, Yugoslavia. On June 28 the Cominform called for Tito's removal as the leader of Yugoslavia. Tito refused and the Yugoslavian Communists agreed to follow Tito and break from Moscow.[116] Without question, this event forced the State Department to review its policies toward the East European countries.

On January 14, 1949, the State Department completed its draft of a new policy for Romania which it sent to the American Legation in Bucharest for comment.[117] Unlike 1947 when the Department had viewed Romania as a direct object of American policy, this 1949 draft noted that Washington's policy toward Romania was a "derivative" of United States policy toward the Soviet Union. The success of any Romanian policy was "essentially dependent" on the success of Soviet-American relations. Nevertheless, the Department noted that Washington could still utilize local elements, such as anti-Soviet feelings among the Romanian people, to retard "communization" and eventually undermine Soviet control.[118]

The draft contained long-range and short-range objectives which the Chargé d'Affaires in Bucharest, C. Montague Pigott critiqued in his March 26 response. Ultimately Washington envisioned an independent free Romania which guaranteed human rights and fundamental freedoms to all peoples with equal commercial opportunity for all nations. The Department also saw Romania integrated into a well coordinated Balkan community of free states.[119] Pigott was surprised by Washington's idealism. These long-range goals were visionary and unrealistic. Romania had never experienced a democracy in the Western sense. Further, Romania was not like other Balkan countries. Her "peculiar geographic position" isolated her from the West, and made it far easier for the Communist regime to resist Western pressure concerning freedoms, human rights and equal economic opportunities.[120]

Washington's short-range goals included: protecting American interests in Romania; implementing the Treaty provisions; supporting the morale of the majority of the Romanian people by "keeping alive" their faith in the values of Western civilization; encouraging passive resistance against the Communist regime; and, developing trade.[121] While less critical of these proposals, Pigott noted that no one in the Legation had "little, if any, confidence in its ability to 'protect' American interests." Treaty violations would continue to be protested. Radio broadcasts by the Voice of America could reinforce Western values, however, the Legation added, the Romanians "themselves must work for their own deliverance and that liberation will not be handed them on a silver platter without effort on their part." The Chargé was cautious about expecting passive resistance and warned that America should do nothing in the way of support unless Washington was willing to make a serious commitment to carry through the effort. Finally, Pigott noted that even if trade were possible with the West, it would have no effect on the "stranglehold" the Soviets had on Romania.[122]

The State Department draft also speculated on some future issues. Foremost among them was if America's policy was successful, who would lead a liberated Romania? The question had relevance only in the immediate future for the longer the Soviets remained in control of Romania, the less chance there would be for a revolutionary change. The Department first considered King Michael. After his abdication in December, 1947, the King visited the United States and met the President on March 22, 1948. The Department had approved the meeting in part to confuse Moscow as to America's future designs on Romania.[123] While in Washington, the King met with Horace Nickels of the Department's Southern European Affairs Division. The King was frustrated by the Romanian exiles in America. Each of them was more interested in advancing personal goals than in working together for the good of Romania.[124] Nickels indicated that the Department was entirely neutral on the formation of a Romanian National Committee,[125] and thought it premature to establish a government-in-exile.

During the remainder of the year, the Department maintained limited contact with the King through his secretary, Mr. Ionnitiu. The Department's observation was that while the King had a large following, his popularity would diminish over time and if liberated, the Romanian people might not want to reestablish the Hohenzollern-Sigmaringen monarchy.[126] As for the exiles, the Department had reservations. They represented the old regime and offered "poor prospects of popular, effective leadership" for Romania.[127] While Pigott agreed with the Department's assessment of the exiles, he was more encouraging about the King. There was strong sentiment for Michael in Romania and if he demonstrated through words and deeds that he was doing everything in his power while in exile to liberate Romania, he could well return to power.[128]

After taking into consideration Pigott's comments along with those of his counterparts in the other East European capitals, the State Department's Policy Planning Staff prepared a draft proposal on American policy toward the East European satellites. The final draft, completed on August 25, went to the Under Secretary's Meeting on August 31, and arrived at the NSC on September where it was labelled NSC 58. The London Conference of United States Chiefs of Mission to the Satellite States endorsed the document on October 26 emphasizing especially America's efforts to foster Communist heresy, and to encourage non-Stalinist Communist regimes.[129] From the time it left the Policy Planning Staff in August, there were few revisions and the document arrived back at the NSC in November. As a second draft, the document became NSC 58/2, and the Council recommended it for the President's approval.[130]

The fundamental question which precipitated NSC 58/2 was identifying the courses of action available to the United States to reduce and eventually eliminate Soviet domination of Eastern Europe. In the recent months, the Soviets had shown some mettle. They had established an independent East Germany, set up the Council of Mutual Economic Assistance (CMEA), and exploded their first Atomic bomb. NSC 58/2 clearly noted that the satellites were in themselves "of secondary importance." In the bipolar struggle for power, the satellites had meaning as "adjuncts of Soviet power" which extended into Europe.[131]

However, Tito's rebellion seemed to indicate a tear in the seam of Soviet control in the satellites. Without question, Belgrade's break with Moscow encouraged the NSC to believe that the "time was ripe" for America to take the offensive to disrupt Soviet influence in Eastern Europe.[132] Washington conceded that its ultimate goal of an Eastern Europe without totalitarian regimes was impossible at the present time. Reminiscent of Pigott's critique of the State Department policy, the NSC noted that "democracy in the western sense is alien" to the satellites states, and democratic governments had "little chance of coming to power save through armed intervention from the West." If the United States intended to set up democratic governments in Eastern Europe, "an overwhelming portion of the task" would fall on Washington. NSC 58/2 favored a less belligerent approach, and called for the establishment of "schismatic communist regimes."[133] "However weak they now may appear, grounds do exist for heretical schisms and we can contribute to the widening of these rifts without assuming responsibility." The quarrel would be between the Kremlin and the heretical government, not Moscow and Washington. The NSC optimistically forecast that two camps could develop within the satellites, a Stalinist group and a non-conformist group. The United States could obviously exploit this situation and turn some of the satellite states towards the West.[134]

In reviewing the weapons available to Washington, two appeared as most practical: ideology and economics. The United States should attack Stalinist dogma as antithetical to political independence. Further, America should promote nationalism and constantly point out

Moscow's failures to adhere to the Charter of the United Nations.[135] However, the primary weapon at hand was economic. "All of the Soviet economic mechanisms of control, particularly those affecting the Council of Mutual Economic Assistance, are affected by the policies which we follow with regard to such matters as East-West trade, purchase of gold and export controls."[136] Truman approved NSC 58/2 on December 8, 1949.[137] Washington had taken nearly three years since it had signed a Peace Treaty with Romania to establish a policy toward the satellite states. Now the United States would promote Titoism as a first step toward the ultimate elimination of Soviet influence in Eastern Europe.

Notes

1. Letter, "Rumanian Reaction to the Peace Treaty," pp. 1-2, February 13, 1947, File 800 Peace Conference, Box 29, Record Group 84, Foreign Service Posts of DOS, Bucharest, U.S. Mission, Secret Files, National Archives.

2. "Regarding the Implementation of Article 31," p. 38, May 9, 1947, Balkan Committee File Box 29, Record Group 84, Foreign Service Posts, of DOS Bucharest, U. S. Mission, Secret Files, 1947, National Archives.

3. *Ibid.*, p. 39.

4. *FRUS, 1947,* IV, pp. 473-475.

5. *Ibid.*, pp. 477-478.

6. *Ibid.*, p. 479.

7. *Ibid.*, p. 481.

8. *Ibid.*

9. *Ibid.*, p. 482.

10. *Ibid.*, p. 480.

11. *Ibid.*, p. 488.

12. "Statement by the President on the Peace Treaties with Hungary, Rumania, and Bulgaria, June 14, 1947," *Public Papers of the Presidents of the United States, Harry S. Truman,* 1961, pp. 277-278.

13. *FRUS,1947,* IV, 490-491.

14. Senate Committee on Foreign Relations, *A Decade of American foreign Policy,* 1950, pp. 1206-1207; *FRUS, 1947,* IV, 492.

15. *Ibid.*

16. *FRUS, 1946,* VI, 658-662.

17. Report, "The Record of Iuliu Maniu and the Rumanian National Peasant Party," pp. 47-52, OIR Report No. 4544, November 17, 1947, File 800 Trials, Box 29, Record Group 84, Foreign Service Posts of DOS, Bucharest, U.S. Mission, Secret Files, National Archives.

18. Telegram, Melbourne to the Secretary of State, August 16, 1947, Box 1, Record Group 84, Foreign Service Posts of DOS, Rumania, Bucharest Legation, Top Secret Telegrams, 1947-1949, National Archives.

19. *FRUS,* 1947, I, 235-241.

20. These five votes occurred on August 18 and 21, on September 29 and 30, and on October 1 (*Ibid.*, IV, 500 n3).

21. *Ibid.*, III, 563-564.

22. *Ibid.*, IV, 50.

23. "The Record of Iuliu Maniu," OIR Report No. 4544, November 17, 1947, pp. 53-55.

24. *FRUS, 1947*, IV, 504 n2.

25. Memorandum, "H. P. Leverich to the Minister," pp. 1-2, November 13, 1947, File 800 Trials, Box 29, Record Group 84, Foreign Service Posts of DOS, Bucharest, U.S. Mission, Secret Files, 1947 National Archives.

26. *FRUS, 1947,* IV, 502-504. Romania's efforts to embarrass the United States inadvertently received support from the American Legation in Bucharest. Romanian authorities detained a member of the Legation, Charles Ferguson, for transporting a convicted Romanian smuggler following the latter's escape from prison (See, Telegram, "Schoenfeld to Secretary," December 13, 1947, Box 27, Record Group 84, Foreign Service Posts of DOS, Bucharest, U.S. Mission, Secret Files, 1947, National Archives).

27. *FRUS, 1947*, IV, 31.

28. Seton-Watson, *The East European Revolution*, p. 210.

29. *FRUS, 1947*, IV, 495-496, 503. Privately, the Department noted that although Maniu's patriotism was unquestioned, "his fanatical attitude in religious matters, his strong attachment for tradition, and his inordinate desire to avenge himself on those whom he thought had wronged him have been definite shortcomings" ("The Record of Iuliu Maniu," OIR Report No,. 4544, November 17, 1947, p. 57).

30. Summary of Telegrams, "Rumania," November 13, 1947, Sept-Dec 1947 File, Box 21, Naval Aide Files, State Department Briefs, HST Library.

31. *Ibid.*, November 24, 1947; *FRUS, 1947*, IV, 508-509.

32. Telegram, Personal for Lovett from Douglas, p. 1, November 29, 1947, Rumania File, Box 15 Naval Aide Files, Alphabetical Files, HST Library.

33. *Ibid.*, pp.. 1-2.

34. *Ibid.*, p. 2. "The British Foreign Office believes that King Michael has now decided to return to Rumania, partly because he has decided that the life of an exiled king is, after all, not too attractive" (Summary of of Telegram, "Rumania," December 4, 1947, Sept-Dec 1947 File, Box 21, Naval Aide Files, State Department Briefs, HST Library).

35. Wolff, *The Balkans in Our Time*, p. 291.

36. Press release, "Text of King Michael's abdication proclamation," December 30, 1947, Office File 428, WHCF, HST Library.

37. Report, "Chronology of Significant Events in Rumania, 1940-51," p. 12, OIR Report 5825, February 25, 1952, Box 1787, OSS R&A Reports, National Archives.

38. Report, "'Front' organizations' in Balkan Countries: 1. Rumania," OIR Report No. 46554.1, p. 3, box 1787, OSS-R&A Reports, DOS Decimal Files, 1950-1954, National Archives.

39. Ionescu, *Communism in Rumania*, p. 136.

40. Book, "Implementation of Peace Treaty with Rumania, May 28, 1948 - September 15, 1949," p. 1, Box 2, Record Group 84, Foreign Service Posts of DOS, Bucharest Legation, Misc. Records, 1944-1949. National Archives.

41. *Ibid.*

42. Senate Committee on Foreign Relations, *A Decade of American Foreign Policy*, 1950, pp. 1208-1212.

43. *FRUS, 1948*, IV, 291.

44. Book, "Implementation of Peace Treaty with Rumania," May 27, 1948, pp. 2-3, Box 2 Record Group 84, Foreign Service Posts of DOS, Bucharest Legation, Misc. Records, 1944-1949, National Archives.

45. *FRUS, 1947,* IV, 507.

46. *FRUS, 1948,* IV, 301.

47. Tismaneanu, *Problems of Communism*, XXXIV, No. 1, 56.

48. *Ibid.*

49. *Ibid.* Patrascanu would not be executed until 1954.

50. Wolff, *The Balkans in Our Time*, p. 292.

51. *FRUS, 1948*, IV. 302.

52. Leiss (ed.) *European Peace Treaties After World War II*, p. 313.

53. *FRUS, 1948*, IV. 323.

54. *FRUS, 1947,* IV, 513.

55. Book, "Implementation of Peace Treaty with Romania," May 27, 1948, p. 3, Box 2, Record Group 84, Foreign Service Posts of DOS, Bucharest Legation, Misc. Records, 1944-1949, National Archives.

56. Ibid., *FRUS, 1948*, IV, 325.

57. Book, "Implementation of Peace Treaty with Rumania,"May 28, 1948 - September 15, 1949, pp. 4-5, Box 2, Record Group 84, Foreign Service Posts of DOS, Bucharest Legation, Misc. Records, 1944-1949, National Archives; Report of the Committee on Foreign Affairs, pursuant to House Resolution 206, Background Information on the Soviet Union in International Relations, pp. 18, September 22, 1950, HST Library.

58. Policy Review, Violation of the Satellite Peace Treaties, p. 2, January 24, 1951, Box 125, Record Group 84, Foreign Service Posts of DOS, Bucharest Legation, U. S. Missions, National Archives.

59. *FRUS, 1948*, IV, 353, n1; Roy M. Melbourne, "Witness to the Start of the Cold War: The View from Romania," *The United States and Romania: American-Romanian Relations in the Twentieth Century*, ed. Paul D. Quinlan (Woodland Hills, California: American-Romanian Academy of Arts and Sciences, 1988), p. 104. The Treaty Committee was established on March 12, 1948, to facilitate the coordination of policy problems arising under the Treaties of Peace with Italy, Hungary, Bulgaria, and Romania. The committee was composed of representatives from the Offices of European Affairs, International Trade Policy, Financial and Development Policy, Legal Adviser, Transport and Communications, Information and Education Exchangee, Public Affairs , and the Special Assistant to the Secretary of State for Research and Intelligence,

United Nations Affairs (*FRUS, 1948*, IV, 310).

60. *FRUS, 1948*, IV, 361-363.

61. Book, "Implementation of the Peace Treaty with Rumania," May 28, 1948 - September 15, 1949, p. 1, Box 2, Record Group 84, Foreign Service Posts of DOS, Bucharest Legation, Misc. Records, 1944-1949, National Archives.

62. Wolff, *The Balkans in Our Time*, pp. 449-450; Stephen D. Kertesz (ed.), *The Fate of East Central Europe: Hopes and Failures of American Foreign Policy* (South Bend, IN: University of Notre Dame Press, 1956), p. 260.

63. Wolff, *The Balkans in Our Time*, p. 465.

64. *Ibid.*, p. 466.

65. *FRUS, 1949*, V, 233, 234-235.

66. Senate Committee on Foreign Relations, *A Decade of American Foreign Policy*, 1950, pp. 1163ff; Policy Review, Violation of the Satellite Peace Treaties, January 24, 1951, p. 4, Box 125, Record Group 84, Foreign Service Posts, Bucharest Legation, National Archives.

67. Senate Committee on Foreign Relations, *A Decade of American Foreign Policy*, 1950, pp. 1169-1170.

68. *Ibid.*, pp. 1171-1173; Policy Review, Violation of the Satellite Peace Treaties, January 24, 1951, p. 4, Box 125, Record Group 84, Foreign Service Posts, Bucharest Legation, National Archives.

69. *FRUS, 1949*, Vol. V. pp. 250-251.

70. Report of the Committee on Foreign Affairs, Pursuant to House Resolution 206, Background Information on the Soviet Union in International Relations, p. 19, September 22, 1950, HST Library.

71. Correspondence, Balkans Peace Treaties, - Human Rights Disputes, January 7, 1950, p. 2, Box 108, Record Group 84, Foreign Service Posts, Bucharest Legation, National Archives.

72. *Ibid.*

73. *FRUS, 1949*, V, 260; The United States would continue, without success, to send notes through February, 1950, requesting that Bucharest appoint a representative to the Commission (Correspondence, Balkans Peace Treaties, Human Rights Disputes, February 18, 1950, 5 pp. Box 108, Record Group 84, Foreign Service Posts, Bucharest Legation, National Archives).

74. Senate Committee on Foreign Relations, *A Decade of American Foreign Policy*, 1950, pp. 1156-1158.

75. *FRUS, 1949*, V, 243-246.

76. *Ibid.*, p. 266, Australia and Canada had joined the United States and Great Britain in their efforts to have Romania comply with its human rights obligations.

77. *Ibid.*, pp. 267-271; Senate Committee on Foreign Relations, *A Decade of American Foreign Policy*, 1950, pp. 1173-1175.

78. Report, July 17, 1947, Report #4456, pp. 27-31, Box 1787, OSS-R&A, DOS Decimal File, 1950-1954, National Archives.

79. Memorandum, American Claims in Rumania, p. 2, October 28, 1947, Balkan Committee File, Box 29, Record Group 84, Foreign Service Posts of

DOS, Bucharest, U.S. Mission, Secret Files, National Archives.

80. *Ibid.*, p. 3.

81. *Ibid.*

82. Policy Review, Violation of Satellite Peace Treaties, January 24, 1951, p. 3, Box 125, Record Group 84, Foreign Service Posts, Bucharest Legation, National Archives.

83. *Ibid.*, p. 2.

84. Report, "Economic Survey, Rumania, 1946-1947," Annex A, p. 2, June 20, 1947, 850-Economics, Box 31, Record Group 84, Foreign Service Posts of DOS, Bucharest, U.S. Mission, Secret Files, 1947, National Archives. The bank nationalization produced few claims, but for an exception see the case of Mrs. Kauffman-Cosla, whose funds in Romania were nationalized and whose accounts in America were frozen (Letter, September 24, 1947, File 711.2, B ox 27, Record Group 84, Foreign Service Posts of DOS, Bucharest, U. S. Mission, Secret Files, 1947, National Archives; *Ibid.*, November 13, 1947).

85. Transmitted translation, May 16, 1947, 5 pp., 804.4 Laws, Box 30, Record Group 84, Foreign Service Posts of DOS, Bucharest, U.S. Mission, Secret Files, 1947, National Archives; Report, "Economic Survey, Rumania, 1946-1947," Annex A p. 2, June 20, 1947, 850-Economics, Box 31, Record Group 84, Foreign Service Posts of DOS, Bucharest, U.S. Mission, Secret Files, 1947, National Archives. This law did exclude for a brief time the oil industry since it came under the government's Ministry of Mines and Petroleum. This gave Romano-Americana oil a lease on life (Report,[April 5, 1947], 2 pp., File 869,17-847 Confidential, Box 33, Record Group 84, Foreign Service Posts of the DOS, Bucharest, U.S. Mission, Secret Files, 1947, National Archives).

86. Report, "Economic Survey, Rumania, 1946-1947," Annex p. 3, June 20, 1947, 850-Economics, Box 31, Record Group 84, Foreign Service Posts of DOS, Bucharest, U.S. Mission, Secret Files, 1947, National Archives.

87. Memorandum, American Claims in Rumania, Balkan Committee File, p. 6, October, 28, 1947, Box 29, Record Group 84, Foreign Service Posts of DOS, Bucharest, U.S. Mission, Secret Files, 1947, National Archives.

88. Intelligence Review No. 38, October 31, 1946, War Department Intelligence Review, Box 17, Naval Aide Files, Alphabetical Files, HST Library.

89. Transmitted translation, Rumanian Civil Aviation Policy Toward the United States, p. 2, File 879.6, Vol. III, October 2, 1947, Box 33, Record Group 84, Foreign Service Posts of DOS, Bucharest, U. S. Mission, Secret Files, 1947, National Archives.

90. *Ibid.*, pp. 3-6.

91. Report, June 15, 1948, NSC Meeting No. 14, Box 204, NSC Meeting, President's Secretary's Files, HST Library Library.

92. *FRUS, 1948*, IV, 451 n1. There was one difference between the State Department recommendation and NSC 15. NSC 15 added that the United States would not terminate its bilateral agreement with Czechoslovakia, but would simply deny the Czechs a permit to operate trans-Atlantic flights to the United States (*Ibid.*, p. 455).

93. *FRUS, 1948*, IV, 286, 483-486; *FRUS, 1949*, V, 184. While the State Department worked to have Britain accept NSC 15, other Administration officials pursued policies in violation of NSC 15. In June, 1948, a regularly scheduled TARS flight from Arad to Bucharest landed in Salzburg, Austria, for emergency repairs. Lengthy negotiations and delays kept the plan down until March 31, 1949, whereupon a Romanian crew arrived to fly the DC-3 type aircraft back to Bucharest. The costs of the repairs was $3762.00, of which $144.00 was for parts. Much of the balance was for labor and fees. The parts cost suggests that the repairs were not "major maintenance" (Report, TARS, Salzburg, No. 543, 3 pp., February 18, 1949, Box 1, Record Group 84, Foreign Service Posts of DOS, Bucharest Legation, Misc. Records, 1944-1949, National Archives).

94. *FRUS, 1949*, V, 197.

95. *Ibid.*, p. 201.

96. Report, U.S. Civil Aviation Policy Toward the USSR and Its Satellites, pp. 2-3 December 28, 1949, NSC No. 51, Box 207, NSC Meetings 48-55, President's Secretary's Files, HST Library Library; *FRUS, 1949*, V, 206-207; Memorandum, U.S. Civil Aviation Policy Toward the USSR and its Satellites, NSC No. 14 8 pp., August 4, 1949, President's Secretary's Files, HST Library.

97. *FRUS, 1949*, V, 217; Memorandum, For the President, August 4, 1949, NSC No. 14, Box 204,NSC Meeting, President's Secretary's Files, HST Library.

98. Report, U. S. Civil Aviation Policy Toward The USSR and Its Satellites, NSC #51, pp.9-10, December 28, 1949, Box 207 President's Secretary's Files, HST Library.

99. *FRUS. 1948*, IV, 593.

100. *Ibid.*, pp. 608ff. In June the Soviets agreed to permit two Austrian representatives to attend as observers (*Ibid.*, p. 615).

101. John C. Campbell, "Diplomacy on the Danube," *Foreign Affairs: An American Quarterly Review*, Vol. 26, No. 2 (January 1949), 319.

102. *FRUS, 1948*, IV, p. 627.

103. Campbell, "Diplomacy on the Danube, January 1949, p. 326.

104. *FRUS, 1948*, IV, 719-721.

105. *FRUS, 1949*, V, 675-677.

106. John Lewis Gaddis, *Strategies of Containment: A Critical Appraisal of Postwar American National Security Policy* (New York: Oxford University Press, 1982), pp.30-31.

107. Gormly, *The Collapse of the Grand Alliance*, 1945-1948, p. 147.

108. Gaddis, *Strategies of Containment*, p. 21.

109. J. F. Brown, *Eastern Europe and Communist Rule* (Durham, N.C: Duke University Press, 1988), p. 107.

110. *FRUS, 1947*, IV, 482.

111. *Ibid.*, pp. 483-494.

112. *Ibid.*, p. 485.

113. Gormly, *The Collapse of the Grand Alliance*, 1945-1948, p. 166.

114. Report, "The Position of the United States with Respect to Soviet-

Directed World Communism," p. 1, March 30, 1948, NSC No. 12, Box 203, NSC
Meeting, President's Secretary's Files, HST Library.
115. *Ibid.*, pp. 5-8.
116. Campbell, *American Policy Toward Communist Eastern Europe*, pp. 11-
12.
117. *FRUS, 1949*, V, 521ff.   The State Department sent the policy to
Bucharest on February 16.
118. *Ibid.*, pp. 532-533.
119. *Ibid.*, p. 521.
120. *Ibid.*, p. 536.
121. *Ibid.*, p. 522.
122. *Ibid.*, pp. 538-539.
123. *FRUS, 1948*, IV, 407.
124. *Ibid.*, pp 408-412. Among the exiles were Alexander Cretzianu, former
Romanian Minister to Turkey; Grigore Niculescu-Buzesti, former Romanian
Foreign Minister; Constantin Visoianu, another Romanian Foreign Minister;
and, General Nicholas Radescu, former Prime Minister.
125. *FRUS, 1949*, V, 285 n1. On April 6, 1949, General Radescu, King
Michael's choice, had formed a Romanian National Committee including representatives from among the various exile groups.
126. *Ibid.*, pp. 534-535.
127. *Ibid.*, p. 535.
128. *Ibid.*, p. 543.
129. *Ibid.*, p. 33. The Chiefs of Mission met from October 24 to October 26.
130. *Ibid.*, p. 21.
131. Report, "United States Policy Toward the Soviet Satellite States in
Eastern Europe," p. 1, December 8, 1949, NSC No. 49, Box 207, NSC Meetings
48-55, President's Secretary's Files, HST Library.
132. *Ibid.*
133. *Ibid.*, p. 9.
134. *Ibid.*
135. *Ibid.*, p. 10.
136. *Ibid.*, p. 11.
137. *FRUS, 1949*, V, does not contain the results and determinations of NSC
58/2 since these were classified at the the time of publication. See NSC No. 49,
cited above nn. 131 to 136.

CHAPTER III

EXPORT CONTROLS AND SOCIALIZATION DECREES, 1947-1949

Commerce and State Departments' Views on Export Controls

NSC 58/2 promoted Titoism through ideological and economic warfare. Washington had already laid the groundwork for the former with its policy of protestation, which raised Treaty violations, especially those in the area of human rights, to a global level. The latter strand, economic warfare, was far more complex to implement and involved extensive export controls. Restrictive trade regulations were antithetical to many laissez-faire Americans. In addition, the controls were especially distasteful to Washington's European allies, who needed more trade, not less, in order to promote their own post-war economic recovery.

America's export control policy began on July 2, 1940. As World War II developed in Europe, Congress granted the President on July 2, 1940, sweeping export control powers to keep certain items of American manufacture from falling into the hands of aggressor nations. Congress continued the control system after the war, principally for items in short supply. The Commerce Department identified these items on Positive Lists.[1]

The expansion of the Cold War led Truman to conclude that Communism spread best where there was misery and want. To stem this development, the President authorized his new Secretary of State, George

Marshall, to announce an economic recovery program for Europe at the 1947 Harvard commencement. The June address extended help to the Soviet Union and to countries in Eastern Europe. However, Moscow refused and prohibited her satellites from participating in the American sponsored program. To implement the American offer, delegates from 16 European countries met on July 16, 1947, at the Chateau de la Meutte in Paris to discuss the recovery program and to form a Committee of European Economic Cooperation.[2] In September, the committee presented an outline for a European Recovery Program (ERP), a four year agenda for reconstruction which would form the basis of the Marshall Plan.[3] As a means to undermine the Marshall Plan, the Soviets resurrected the Comintern as the Cominform in the Fall of 1947, and instructed the Communist parties in France, Italy and Germany to frustrate the work of the Committee of European Economic Cooperation. Several days later, Zhdanov gave his famous "two camp" speech which, if nothing else, supported Kennan's view that the Soviets saw the world in hostile terms.

In viewing Moscow as hostile and pursuing a course of action for world domination, Washington sought and soon found a major weakness in the Soviet armor. Moscow's efforts to exploit her East European satellites through reparations, restitutions and war trophies, emphasized the degree of devastation that the war had wreaked upon the Soviet economy. More than 2,000 towns and cities had to be rebuilt, and Moscow lacked the capital and resources to do the reconstruction quickly.[4] By the Fall of 1947, both the Commerce and State Departments had each prepared studies on how America could best take advantage of this situation.

On November 12, the State Department's Eastern Europe Economic Working Party (EWP) presented a paper to the NSC entitled "Immediate U.S. Economic Policy toward Eastern Europe."[5] Two days later the Secretary of Commerce presented a paper to the NSC on the same subject. The Council referred both papers to the State Department's Policy Planning Staff for comment and recommendation. In reviewing the two papers the Staff took note of several factors. First, Soviet control over the satellites' economies was sufficient to view Eastern Europe and the Soviet Union as a single economic unit. Second, Moscow's main economic goal was to increase its military potential. And third, while American exports were not essential to the economic development of Moscow, they were important especially in critical areas such as diesel and electric locomotives, precision instruments, cranes, electrical generating equipment, and machinery for mines and refineries. In contrast, neither Soviet nor satellite exports were vital or of great importance to the United States. The only items of interest to Washington were manganese ore, chromium and iridium.[6] The Policy Planning Staff did note that the United States was prohibited by treaties and agreements from engaging in discriminatory trade practices. In fact, Washington was in the middle of discussions on the Draft Charter of the International Trade Organization in Havana which called for free trade.[7] However, the Staff added that Article 94 of the Draft Charter permitted members to take any action necessary "for the protection of its essential security interests."[8] Soviet hostility could easily be viewed by Washington as a threat to America's security.

The Policy Planning Staff also noted that the EWP proposals were far more moderate than those of the Commerce Department. According to the EWP paper, there should be no special controls applicable to Europe alone, and no controls at all on goods *not* in short supply going to the Soviet Union and her satellites.[9] The EWP was especially sensitive to free trade violations. The group argued that East-West trade would contract naturally as a result of implementing the European Recovery Program which emphasized West-West trade.[10]

In contrast, the Commerce Department proposal called for "the immediate termination, for an indefinite period, of shipments from the United States to the USSR and its satellites of all commodities which are critically short in the United States or which would contribute to the Soviet military potential." However the United States should avoid the appearance of "arbitrary discrimination" against the Soviet Bloc. To circumvent the discrimination issue, Commerce linked Europe to the Soviet Union and defined this combined area as "a recovery zone to which all exports should be controlled. Exports to any country in this zone should be permitted only when (a) the [importing] country furnishes adequate justification for its requirement, (b) European recovery and world peace are served thereby, and (c) the position of the United States is not adversely affected."[11]

After much discussion, on November 20, the Policy Planning Staff recommended the Commerce Department proposal. This meant that commercial shipments of all commodities to Europe would require individual validated licenses. The Staff further noted that if the NSC and President were to adopt their recommendation they should make a statement to the effect that the controls were only intended for a short time until the recovery period was over. Thereafter, normal trade practices would be restored immediately.[12]

On December 8, Acting Secretary of State Robert Lovett notified the Commerce Department that he was willing to accept the Staff recommendation provided that the State Department was involved in export control decisions, and that the clause requiring importing countries to provide adequate justification for each import be applied only where needed.[13] Commerce agreed and on December 17, 1947, the NSC recommended the revised proposal to the President requesting an effective date of March 1, 1948.[14]

On December 18, Truman approved the recommendation. Two weeks later the Commerce Department prepared a memorandum for all NSC members outlining the "framework of language" which would be used in the event they had to testify before Congress.[15] The Department did not want any more statements similar to the one made by the President on November 21. At a press conference, Mr. Truman announced that he saw no reason to stop shipment of machinery to the Soviet Union.[16] In addition the Department wanted to make sure that the public did not think that the export controls were "a subterfuge aimed at the USSR."[17] The memorandum defined the export controlled zone as Western Europe, Eastern Europe and the Soviet Union, and labelled this the "recovery" area. The Commerce Department intended to control all exports to this area through an "R" country procedure, the "R" representing "recovery." By including Western Europe in the "R" area, exports could be controlled to Eastern Europe and the Soviet Union "without apparent discrimination which might lead to retaliation," and kept open the door for imports from the Communist world.[18] On March 1, 1948, all American exports to the "R" zone would require individual validated licenses.

In contrast to the Administration's haste to restrict trade and halt the spread of Communism, Congress moved cautiously. The legislature did extend the 1940 export controls by passing the Second Decontrol Act on July 15, 1947. However, the House responded slowly to Truman's request for Marshall Plan funds. The catalyst which finally forced Congress to act was the February, 1948, Soviet-backed coup in Czechoslovakia. Four weeks later, the legislature passed the Foreign Assistance Act of 1948, which provided funds to implement the Marshall Plan. During the debate, House members received a study on the East European economy, which described in detail Moscow's intentions to make the satellite economies into Soviet centers of heavy industry.[19] Without question, East-West trade would be a great asset to implement this goal. On March 24, Karl Mundt of South Dakota proposed an amendment to the Act which called for the Administrator of the Marshall Plan to withhold aid to any nation which exported products to any non-participating Marshall Plan country, if those products could not receive an American export license. Congress adopted the amendment and it became Section 117(d) of the Foreign Assistance Act of 1948, passed by Congress on April 4.[20] This was the first time that the United States tied aid to trade.

Section 117(d) complemented a recent Cabinet decision. On March 26, Secretary of State Marshall brought a memorandum to his colleagues concerning the control of exports to the Soviet Bloc. He did not want to cut off all East-West trade, since it was an important factor in the European Recovery Program. However, American export controls alone could not effectively curtail the development of Soviet military power, as long as Western Europe and Canada supplied Moscow with many of the items embargoed by the United States. Marshall wanted Washington to persuade its allies to adopt similar export controls. This did not mean that there could be no trade between East and West, but it did mean that commodities which were identified as essential to the Soviet and satellite economies should be embargoed. Moreover, whatever trade continued should be designed to force the Soviet Bloc to continue to export strategic materials to the West in return for Western imports. This would mean that the United States and its allies would deal with the Soviets on a strictly *quid pro quo* basis with respect to significant trade items. The Cabinet approved the recommendation.[21]

The combined effect of Mundt's amendment and the Cabinet decision produced a far more aggressive Administrative attitude toward export controls. The White House wanted its allies to embargo a list of goods substantially parallel to those embargoed by the United States.[22] However, three problems quickly developed. First, discriminatory export controls were illegal. Second, the only "lists" which existed were the Positive Lists, which focused on items in short supply in the United States, rather than on items which had war potential. And third, Washington's West European allies wanted to increase, rather than limit, trade relations with the Soviet Bloc and were reluctant to adopt America's list of embargoed goods.

In May, the State Department reviewed America's treaty agreements with the countries of Eastern Europe and the Soviet Union. The Department wanted to find a loophole which would permit discriminatory export controls. Upon inspection, however, the Department realized

that the discriminatory nature of the "R" country export control procedure formally violated the MFN article in nearly every trade agreement
including the one with Romania.[23] The Department recommended that
Washington neither denounce any of the treaties, nor eliminate the
newly imposed March 1 licensing requirements.[24] In the event the Soviet Bloc countries did accuse the United States of trade violations, as
the Soviets had already done, the State Department suggested that no
reply be made. If pressed, the United States could delay its response,
thereby maintaining those parts of any trade agreement useful to
Washington. When there was finally no recourse remaining except to
terminate the treaty, the United States should accept this alternative
and do so with a number of countries, including Romania.[25]

In June, State Department officials gathered in Rome for the Conference on the Implementation of the Treaties of Peace and considered,
among other things, the Department's latest recommendation.[26] After a
week of discussion, the Treaty Committee agreed to the following: the
United States should not abrogate the East European Peace Treaties; in
the event of Communist criticism of America's export policy, Washington should point out that any country had the right to take such an action to protect its national defense; and finally, the United States should
counter Eastern Bloc propaganda with accusations of discrimination on
their part.[27]

The second problem involved designing lists of materials to be controlled on the basis of their war potential for Soviet Bloc countries.
Commerce Secretary Averell Harriman had organized an Ad Hoc
Committee to look into the issue in March, 1948.[28] On May 4, the
Committee reported that the United States had three major objectives
in trading with Eastern Europe: 1) to assist West European countries
obtain necessary imports from Eastern Europe, especially grain, timber,
coal and potash; 2) to prevent or delay further increases in the war potential of the Soviet Bloc; and 3) to insure an adequate flow of manganese and chromium and, to a lesser extent, the platinum group of
metals to the United States.

The Subcommittee recognized that the pursuit of the first and third
objectives were not compatible with the second. Nevertheless, the report attempted to address all three goals simultaneously with four export commodity classifications. Class 1 included commodities which by
their nature or because of easy convertibility, were of direct military
significance. These items should not be shipped from the United States
to any East European destination, except in extraordinary circum-

stances when a substantial gain could be made by the United States or its allies through a *quid pro quo* arrangement. Class 1-A included items of a military or semi-military nature which should ultimately be classified as munitions, and as such should only be exported under the terms of Class 1 items. Class 2 included items of important, though indirect, military significance or of considerable industrial potential to the Soviet Bloc. Class 3 included items which did not have any particular military significance, but were of some importance in maintaining the economic development of Eastern Europe. Class 4 included items with no military or economic significance. These were "non-essential items."[29] Export licenses could be granted for items in Classes 2 and 3 according to the degree to which a Soviet Bloc country was willing to make political or economic concessions, including exporting strategic materials to the United States. Class 4 items could be licensed relatively freely. The report concluded with the caution that American export controls would only be effective if the nations receiving European Recovery Program funds adopted similar controls.[30]

For the next two months, the State and Commerce Departments discussed the *Ad Hoc* Subcommittee's recommendations. State wanted a shorter list of items prohibited for export. Marshall was concerned about securing West Europe's support for the American plan and the shorter the list, the easier it would be to secure approval. Any list had to take into consideration that the welfare and development of the United States and her allies took precedence over efforts to weaken potential enemies.[31]

The Secretary of State was also opposed to relying on *quid pro quos* as the basis for trade. This was a complete reversal from his position at the March 26 Cabinet meeting where he endorsed a *quid pro quo* basis of trade with the Soviet Bloc. Marshall now believed that a *quid pro quo* process would favor those private exporting companies which could best work with the Soviets. Further, a *quid pro quo* would give Moscow a guide as to what to trade to secure strategic materials. He was opposed to any standardization of trade with the Soviet Bloc because Soviet-American relations were too unstable to suggest such regularity.[32] Marshall's export control list would include only those items whose export should be prohibited for security reasons. Therefore, he accepted the prohibitions on Class 1 and 1-A, but believed that items in Classes 2, 3 and 4 should be licensed freely provided immediate deliveries were possible.[33]

The Commerce Department largely accepted the latter of Marshall's ideas. On August 27, 1948, the Department established two lists, 1-A and 1-B. Class 1-A consisted of the items identified by the *Ad Hoc* Sub-committee as Classes 1 and 1-A. These included munitions, aircraft and equipment designed primarily to produce military or potentially military products in the Soviet Union and its satellites. Washington would pro-hibit the export of these items to Eastern Europe, and the Department wanted the ERP countries to voluntarily adopt these prohibitions.[34] Class 1-B, which was similar to the *Ad Hoc* Subcommittee's Class 2, listed additional items of great importance to Soviet war potential. These items were not subject to a complete embargo, but their export to Eastern Europe would be quantitatively limited. Commerce noted in its announcement that it would like to see some items moved from Class 1-B to Class 1-A.[35]

Export Controls and Western Europe

As the Administration became more interested in regulating trade, Congress began hearings in January, 1949 to discuss means to further extend the President's authority to control exports. Both houses de-signed identical bills authorizing the President to control the export of items in short supply in the United States, to implement foreign policy objectives, and to control exports which affected national security. The legislation authorized the President, or his designee, to prohibit or cur-tail exports of "any articles, materials, or supplies, including technical data" through June 30, 1951. There was little opposition in either house and on February 28, 1949, Congress approved the Export Control Act.[36] Few would have suspected that the legislation would continue in force until 1969.

While the Administration and Congress tightened America's export controls, the job of securing Western Europe's "voluntary" support for these controls fell on Paul Hoffman, the head of the European Cooper-ation Administration (ECA). The "voluntary" aspect was most impor-tant because the United States did not want any agreements in writing. The Administration knew that multilateral export controls were illegal, and America had signed the United Nations Charter thereby accepting the provisions of Article 102. This clearly stipulated that "every treaty and every international agreement entered into by any member of the United Nations" be registered with the Secretariat and published.[37]

Consequently, there could be no written agreements concerning illegal export controls. The State Department instructed Hoffman to begin secret bilateral negotiations with each of the ERP countries to encourage them to voluntarily cooperate.[38]

Hoffman worked from September, 1948 through May, 1949. The British and French led the European opposition, and refused to accept the American control lists. They were not opposed to controlling exports, but they did not want to control as many categories of items as did Washington. London and Paris designed their own list of controlled items, called the A-F lists.[39] In April, Hoffman notified Washington that Britain and France would make no further concessions. The A-F lists accepted 121 of America's 163 prohibited categories, and London and Paris agreed to monitor the other items.[40]

The NSC considered Hoffman's report on May 3, 1949. After a brief discussion, the Council agreed that the ERP countries could use the A-F lists to control exports, rather than the American ones.[41] However, this announcement did not produce the anticipated effect on America's allies. No European country, other than Britain or France, wanted to adopt the A-F list without knowing what the other countries intended to do. Consequently, in October, representatives from Britain, France, Italy, Belgium and the Netherlands met in Paris to discuss in secret the Anglo-French list. A month later they invited American representatives to attend these multilateral meetings, along with observers from Denmark and Norway. As a result of these secret discussions, the delegates from Britain, France, Italy, Belgium and the Netherlands agreed to adopt the Anglo-French lists. In addition, on November 22, 1949 they agreed to establish a Consultative Group, known as the CG, to work out classifications and clarify differences between the American 1-A and 1-B lists and the Anglo-French list.[42]

The CG held its first meeting in Paris on January 9, 1950, and decided to set up a permanent secretariat and a Coordinating Committee to oversee daily operations and resolve conflicts between the American and European representatives. This Coordinating Committee quickly became known as the COCOM and was responsible for implementing export controls on strategic items to the Soviet Bloc. All of these developments were done in secret because they were illegal, contradicted Western demands for free trade, and invited retaliation from Eastern Europe, an action which would impede Western Europe's economic recovery.[43]

Export Controls and American-Romanian Economic Relations

American-Romanian economic relations mirrored Washington's efforts to develop a restrictive export control policy between 1946 and 1949. At the outset, America promoted MFN status for Romania with the hope of using trade as a means to replace Soviet influence with Western values and culture. However, the Romanian government was not ready to establish a strong two-way trade. The great bulk of Romania's commerce consisted of reparation shipments to the Soviet Union. Bucharest had signed a number of trade agreements, many with the East European countries, as well as with France, and Switzerland. However, no substantial trade materialized because Bucharest could not live up to its commitments, especially in food exports, because of a two year drought.[44] In 1946, Bucharest did an economic self-analysis and concluded that trade had been hindered by limited funds, a shortage of long-term foreign credits, and a scarcity of merchandise.[45] The American Legation in Bucharest concluded in 1946, that Romania "today is in an economic mess that certainly rivals that of any other country in the world."[46]

Even so, some optimistic Romanian businessmen were eager to resume trade with the United States. Foremost among them was Nicolas Malaxa. His efforts to establish trade with American firms are worth noting since they reflected the deterioration of relations between Bucharest and Washington from April, 1946 through March of 1948.

In the 1920s, Nicolas Malaxa established a railroad car repair business called Malaxa and Company. He ingratiated himself with Maniu and became a major locomotive repair entrepreneur. In the 1930s, he befriended Madame Lupescu and quickly became one of King Carol's closest advisers. Malaxa gradually gained 30% control of the Methane Gas interests in Romania as well as the Reshita Iron Works. Malaxa mixed politics and business quite well, and in the process became the subject of numerous stories, which according to Burton Berry, were certainly exaggerated.[47] The new Groza regime had intended to send a commercial mission to the United States, but in April, 1946, Groza replaced it with an unofficial delegation from the American Chamber of Commerce in Bucharest. The Chairman of the Chamber, Max Ausnit, along with Malaxa, Jacques Bachori and Ionica Weiss, wanted to visit the United States to renew old trade connections and explore future commercial relations.[48] Berry saw Malaxa's inclusion in the mission as a sign that the Groza regime wanted to explore trade opportunities with Washington.[49] In June, the mission left with considerable fanfare in the local press, apparently generated by Malaxa, that suggested that the group would look for American investors to help build a great dye industry, and a large electric power station at the mouth of the Danube.[50]

By chance, Thomas Blaisdell of the Commerce Department met Malaxa in Zurich in July. The Romanian quickly assured him that the mission had the blessings of the Groza government, and was aimed principally at making arrangements for technical cooperation with some American corporations in the areas of motor cars, tractors and agricultural machinery.[51] Following Berry's advice, Washington granted visas to the Chamber of Commerce mission members. In December 1946, Ausnit and Malaxa met with members of the State Department. They reiterated their interest in encouraging American investment in Romania, but especially emphasized the growing famine conditions in Romania. This was the second year of the drought and both men urged the United States to make corn available for export to Romania.[52]

This was not the first time Romania had requested corn. On October 26, 1946, the Romanian Charge d'Affairs in Washington had asked to buy 1 million tons of corn from the United States. The State Department had referred the issue to the International Emergency Food Council which had the responsibility of allocating foodstuffs worldwide.[53] Within days of the Ausnit-Malaxa December visit, Berry cabled the State Department. He had met with the Minister of the National Economy, Gheorghiu-Dej concerning the drought. Through severe austerity, good supplies could last through January. After this time, there would be widespread starvation. Gheorghiu-Dej was willing to come to the United States to negotiate a purchase of corn or a loan of sufficient grain to tide Romania through the famine.[54] The State Department did not welcome a visit from Gheorghiu-Dej. On December 20, Brynes wrote to Berry that the visit would have no value for the United States. If Gheorghiu-Dej returned with corn, the Communists would take the credit, if he returned empty-handed, America would be blamed. Byrnes also believed that the visit was really designed to attract American investment capital. And in light of the poor treatment accorded American business interests in Bucharest, there was little hope for government support of private investment.[55] Until Romania resolved her outstanding claims issues with the United States, there would be no government support for American investment in Romania.

However, this lack of support did not extend to Romania's food problems. Following considerable discussion by the the Cabinet Committee on War Food Problems, President Truman announced on

February 17, 1947, that he had asked the American Red Cross to finance and supervise the distribution of 7,000 tons of foodstuffs to the
500,000 starving people in Moldavia. In addition, he authorized the sale
of additional grains and corn to prevent the recurrence of the famine.[56]
In truth, Truman had his doubts about this policy. He wrote that while
he was trying to solve the famine problem, it was "almost impossible to
do anything for the people" because they had "such a rotten government." He was particularly upset with the Romanian government for
sending 28,000 tons of foodstuffs to the Soviet Union, at the same time
that the United States was sending Moldavia 7,000 tons of emergency
grain.[57]

On March 9, the International Emergency Food Council agreed to
let Romania purchase about 95,000 tons of corn and oat. To facilitate
the sale, the United States government suggested that Romania deposit
$20.5 million worth of gold bullion into an American escrow account in
Switzerland. This money would be available to purchase food, underwrite credit and, pending Romania's concurrence, repay some of her
outstanding claims.

Bucharest agreed to set up the escrow account. Since Washington
had no objections to private organizations dealing with Romania, the
Chase National Bank of New York opened a $7.5 million line of credit
for Romanian food purchases. Humanitarian organizations also came to
the rescue. The American Jewish Joint Distribution Committee agreed
to advance Romania $2 million for food relief. The Committee made its
first payment of $420,000 on March 10, 1947, to purchase two boatloads
of grain made available by the United Nations Relief and Rehabilitation
Agency. The financial arrangement called for Romania to repay the
amount, less 10% which the American Jewish Joint Distribution Committee wanted Bucharest to use for additional relief work.[58]

Meanwhile, Malaxa continued to explore trade opportunities. He had
tried to gain control over the $7.5 million credit line, but without suc-
cess. However, Romania had begun new talks with the Chase National
Bank for a $50 million line of credit, and Malaxa was trying to become
part of the talks as a means to fund his purchases.[59] At the same time,
Malaxa met with Arthur Bunker and Stokely Morgan of Lehman Brothers and asked them to broker arrangements between himself and
several American corporations. Bunker and Morgan quickly met with
officials of the State Department for direction. Lehman Brothers had
lost money at the outbreak of World War II. They had expected to
make a commission of $10 a ton on the sale of 100,000 tons of potash to

Japan. However, the State Department had intervened and forced them to cancel the shipment. Lehman Brothers did not want to make a similar mistake. The State Department assured Bunker and Morgan that Washington favored East-West trade and anticipated that once the Romanian Peace Treaty came into force, normal commercial relations should resume between Washington and Bucharest on a most-favored-nation basis.[60]

During the summer of 1947, with support from the Lehman Brothers, Malaxa formed the American-Romanian Economic Corporation. In July, Malaxa visited the State Department and met with Messers Nickels, Hilton and Nitze to explore the possibility of expanded Romanian-American trade. He was interested in agricultural products primarily in order to do "something for [the] Romanian peasants." He believed that the "best antidote to Communism in Romania" was increased food production which could be achieved through fertilizer and equipment. Malaxa anticipated that his purchases would be financed out of the anticipated $50 million credit line then under negotiations between Bucharest and the Chase National Bank.[61] Malaxa would repay the credit through large exports of surplus foodstuffs to the West. The famine had ended, and the 1947 crop exceeded all expectations.[62] Malaxa raised questions on other purchases including pipe for a gas line from Ploesti to Bucharest. In closing, Malaxa made an "impassioned plea" for America to help Romania solve her problems. The problem was the "fight against Communism." As armies needed food, the Romanian peasants needed tractors and fertilizers to be "effective fighters against the growth of Communism."[63]

The Peace Treaty's coming into force did nothing to improve American-Romanian economic relations. Nonetheless, Malaxa continued to talk to and impress American industrial and banking concerns. He had convinced several oil equipment companies to bid for supplies needed in Romania. However, some of his American backers, especially Lehman Brothers heard rumors that Washington intended to restrict imports on certain items to Eastern Europe. On January 13, 1948, Frank Manheim of Lehman Brothers talked with Mr. Nickels and several colleagues about the future of Romanian-American trade. Without stating that export controls would take effect March 1, Nickels indicated that "certain export controls" might be put into place which would include oil equipment. Nickels noted that the political situation had rapidly deteriorated in Romania, and that there was a "substantial business risk" to be taken in trading with Bucharest. As he left, Manheim noted that Lehman Brothers were having second thoughts about continued involvement in the American-Romanian Economic Corporation.[64]

The March 1 export controls ended this phase of Malaxa's entrepreneurial efforts in America. He had arranged an $8 million contract for the International Derrick and Equipment Company, a subsidiary of the Dresser Industries, to supply oil field drilling equipment to Romania. Washington refused to export the equipment.[65] He had signed a contract with International Harvester to export farm equipment to Bucharest, and this venture too collapsed.[66] The Lehman Brothers soon severed their relations with Malaxa, bringing an end to the American-Romanian Economic Corporation.[67]

Romania's Socialization Decrees

The Malaxa episode reflected the rapid decline of American-Romanian economic relations during the immediate post-war period, and pointed to an even more rapid deterioration following America's imposition of export controls on Bucharest. In June, 1948, the Romanian government announced the nationalization of all industrial, transportation and mining enterprises. The government also tightened control over import trade by restricting import licenses to state owned corporations.[68] In August, the State Department retaliated. Washington made a list of items critical to Romania to insure that they would not be exported. These included agricultural machinery, machine tools, electrotechnical equipment, ballbearings, nonferrous metals, transportation equipment of all types, high grade steel, coke, rubber, asbestos, dyes, steel cable, communications equipment, carbon and graphite electrodes, refractory materials and power equipment including diesel and hydraulic.[69]

As retaliation became the currency of communication, the Soviet Bloc brought the matter of trade discrimination to world forums. In the General Assembly of the United Nations, Mr. Modzelewski of Poland accused the United States of discriminatory trade practices. The Commerce Department had denied 70 Polish requests for export licenses. Many of these items had no military purpose such as resin, radio lamps and ball bearings.[70] Quickly, the Polish delegation made a motion based on this November 2 speech condemning the United States for using trade discrimination for political ends. The General Assembly defeated the resolution on November 26, with only the Soviet Union and the East

European states voting in the affirmative.[71] Six months later, at a meeting of the General Agreement on Tariffs and Trade (GATT) the Czechoslovakian delegate, Mr. Augenthaler made a similar argument noting that the United States had refused to export $27 million worth of orders.[72]

Meanwhile, Romania worked on implementing its first and second One-Year plans, both of which called for placing the economy under strong state controls. The emphasis in both plans was on industry, especially heavy industry, while the goal of agriculture was collectivization. Neither plan had any place for private ownership, including private businesses. On July 28, 1949, the Romanian Presidium announced Decree No. 317, which regulated private import and export operations. The Decree required all Romanian private firms or individuals engaged in foreign trade to apply to the Ministry of Foreign Trade for permission to continue in business. By January, 1950, the American Legation reported that no application had been approved. For all intents and purposes, the Decree had abolished trade with private firms in Romania. All trade was controlled by the Ministry of Foreign Trade through a number of State import and export companies, such as Petrol-Export, Metal-Import, and Agro-Export.[73] On December 1 the Presidium passed Decree No. 444 which set up the Romanian Foreign Trade Chamber of Commerce as a subdivision of the Ministry of Foreign Trade. The principal duties of the new organization included supervising trade fairs, and arbitrating disputes concerning foreign trade transactions.[74] Schoenfeld cabled Washington on December 10 urging the Commerce Department to inform prospective businessmen that they should not expect any justice in the arbitration proceedings. A state owned company would probably not be found at fault in its dealings with foreign private enterprises.[75]

The effect of America's export regulations and Romania's socialization decrees was a dramatic reduction in Romanian-American trade. In 1947, the United States exported $15 million worth of goods to Romania; in 1948 $7.5 million; in 1949 $3 million; and, in 1950, $1.5 million. Romanian exports to the United States during the same years were $435,000 in 1947, $480,000 in 1948, $584,000 in 1949, and $120,000 in 1950.[76]Ironically, these statistics fulfilled the goals of both countries. In October, 1949, the United States Chiefs of Mission to the Satellite States met in London and urged the State Department to fully utilize export controls. The satellite economies were still suffering from the war and the Soviet Union was not in a position to supply these states with vital products now unavailable from the West.[77] In Bucharest, the Romanians were quoting the recent remarks of Hilary Minc, a Polish economist and leading theorist. In his November, 1949, article in the *Cominform Journal*, Minc announced that the goal of foreign trade was to make each East European country "more independent of the capitalist economy" and to hasten its socialist development.[78] The decreasing American-Romanian trade volume reflected successful implementation of policy in both Washington and Bucharest

Notes

1. Philip J. Funigiello, *American-Soviet Trade in the Cold War* (Chapel Hill: University of North Carolina Press, 1988), p. 33; Gary F. Bertsch (ed.), *Controlling East-West Trade and Technology Transfer* (Durham, N. C.: Duke University Press, 1988), p. 104.

2. The sixteen nations were Austria, Belgium, Denmark, France, Greece, Iceland, Italy, Luxembourg, the Netherlands, Norway, Portugal, Sweden, Switzerland, Turkey and the United Kingdom.

3. In April, 1948, the 16 nations formed the Organization for European Economic Cooperation, the OEEC, which would become the Organization for Economic Cooperation and Development, OECD, in September, 1961.

4. Norman A. Graebner, *The National Security: Its Theory and Practice, 1945-1960* (New York: Oxford University Press, 1986), p.13.

5. *FRUS, 1948*, IV, 489-490.

6. *Ibid.*, p. 490.

7. For Information on these discussions see *Foreign Relations of the United States, 1948*, Volume I. This was the World Conference on Trade and Employments held in Havana from November 1947 to March 1948.

8. *FRUS, 1948*, IV, 491.

9. Italics in original.

10. *FRUS, 1948*, IV, 492.

11. *Ibid.*, p. 506.

12. *Ibid.*, p. 507.

13. *Ibid.*, p. 508,

14. *Ibid.* Secretary of Commerce Harriman urged haste since a large amount of machinery was going to the Soviet Union for military purposes, and some of these exports created a shortage of commodities needed for the European recovery program (Report, NSC #4, 3 pp.,December 17, 1947, Box 203, President's Secretary Files, HST Library; NSC #2, 2pp., November 14, 1947, Box 203, President's Secretary Files, HST Library). Gunnar Adler-Karlsson suggests that the haste could have resulted from the Anglo- Soviet trade and financing agreement signed at Moscow on December 27. The United States had tried to discourage the British from signing the agreement, but without success. (Gunnar Adler-Karlsson, *Western Economic Warfare, 1947-1967: A Case Study in Foreign Economic Policy* [Stockholm: Almquist & Wiksell, 1968], p. 23).

15. Report, NSC #4, 2 pp. December 17, 1947, Box 203, President's Secretary Files, HST Library; *FRUS, 1948*, IV, 512 n1.

16. *Public Papers of the Presidents, Harry S. Truman, 1947*, pp. 500-502.

17. Report, NSC #4, 2 pp. December 17, 1947, Box 203, President's Secretary Files, HST Library.

18. *FRUS. 1948*, IV, 512-513.

19. U.S. Congress, House, Select Committee on Foreign Aid, *Preliminary Report Twenty Pursuant to H. Res. 296. The East European Economy in Relation to the European Recovery Program*, 80th Con., 2d Sess., 1948, pp. 4ff.

20. Report, "Understandings on Export Control in East-West Trade," pp. 1-2, NSC No. 46, May 3, 1949, Folder 206, President's Secretary Files, HST Library.

21. *FRUS, 1948*, IV, 527; Memorandum, JCS 1561/6 Appendix A, p. 39, Box 13, JCS 1946-1947, Central Document Files, National Archives. Marshall's recommendations stemmed from a report from his Department's Research and Development section entitled, "Trade as a Political Instrument in East-West Relations." This lengthy document analyzed the effects of a Soviet Bloc embargo on Western goods and a Western embargo on Soviet Bloc materials. The report concluded that neither embargo would have any significant political effect. The West would have considerable difficulty implementing a total embargo on the Soviet Bloc because of neutral countries, such as Switzerland and Sweden, which could provide capital, machinery, and technology to the East (Report, "Trade as a Political Instrument in East-West Relations," February 10, 1948, OIR Report No. 4520 (PV), R&A Reports, National Archives).

22. Report, "Understandings on Export Control in East-West Trade," p. 2, NSC No. 46, May 3, 1949, Folder 206, President's Secretary Files, HST Library; Funigiello, *American-Soviet Trade in the Cold War*, pp. 38-39, This action was certainly further than that envisioned by early proponents of export controls. Frederick Reinhardt, who was Chief of the Eastern European Affairs Division in the State Department in 1948, recalled that, when he was stationed in Moscow in 1947, he and several colleagues had cabled Washington recommending "some sort of trade control," but only for "truly strategic" items. What evolved was sort of an "Encyclopedia Britannica" control which included everything (Oral interview of G. Frederick Reinhardt by Theodore A. Wilson, June 13, 1970, HST Library).

23. "Implementation of Peace Treaty with Rumania," May 27, 1948, pp. 1-2, Box 2, Record Group 84, Foreign Service Posts of DOS, Bucharest legation, Misc. Records, 1944-1949, National Archives. Washington had not violated Bulgaria's trade agreement since the most-favored-nations clause only applied to American imports (*Ibid.*, p. 2).

24. *Ibid.*

25. *Ibid.*, pp. 3-5.

26. For the names of participants, see *supra* Chapter 2, n59.

27. *FRUS, 1948*, IV, 546-547.

28. *Ibid.*, 523 n.

29. *Ibid.*, pp. 536-540.

30. *Ibid.*, pp. 541-542.

31. *Ibid.*, p. 553. Edwin Martin later recalled one of Secretary Marshall's best observations, to the effect that, "more battles had been lost in worrying about the enemy's strength, rather than your own, than from any other cause" (Oral interview of Edwin McCammon Martin by Theodore A. Wilson, July 6, 1970, p. 11, HST Library).

32. *FRUS, 1948*, IV, 547-551.

33. *Ibid.*, p. 549.

34. Report, "Understandings on Export Control in East-West Trade," p. 3, NSC No. 46, May 3, 1949, Folder 206, President's Secretary File, HST Library. Italics in original.

35. *FRUS, 1948*, IV, 566.

36. U. S. Congress, House, Hearings before the Committee on Banking and Currency, *Export Control Act of 1949, H. R. 1661*, 81st Cong., 1st Sess., 1949; U. S. Congress, Senate, Hearing before the Subcommittee of the Committee on Banking and Currency, *Extension of Export Controls, S 548*, 81st Cong., 1st Sess., 1949.

37. Report, "Status of Controls Over Exports to the Soviet Union and its Satellites, April 17, 1950," p. 4, Box 19, Record Group 469, Special Representative, Paris, Trade and Finance Division Subsection Files 1949-1951, Trade E, National Archives.

38. *FRUS, 1948*, IV, 567.

39. Report, "Impact of Export controls on East-West European Trade," p. 3, May 5, 1950, OIR Report No. 5204, Box 116, Record Group 84, Foreign Service Posts of DOS; *FRUS, 1949*, V, 79.

40. Ibid.

41. Report, "Understandings on Export Control in East-West Trade." p. 4, NSC No. 46, May 3, 1949, Folder 206, President's Secretary Files, HST Library.

42. *Ibid.*, pp. 89-90; 67.

43. The West European countries wanted no official mention of export controls because of the problems this could cause in their legislatures. Under American pressure, they did agree to keep some form of secret minute of their commitment (*FRUS, 1950*, IV, 72).

44. Report, "Economic Survey of Rumania, 1946-1947," p. 42, June 20, 1947, 850-Economics, Box 31, Record Group 84, Foreign Service Posts of DOS, Bucharest, U.S. Mission, Secret Files, 1947, National Archives.

45. *Ibid.*, Annex B, p. 11.

46. *Ibid.*, Annex C, p. 2.

47. Report, "N. Malaxa's Methods of Operation," July 10, 1946, Box 23, Record Group 84, Foreign Service Posts of DOS, Bucharest, U. S. Mission, Secret Files, 1947, National Archives.

48. Telegram, April 19, 1946, File 611.713/4-1946, Box 2761, DOS Decimal File, 1945-1949, National Archives.

49. *Ibid.*

50. Telegram, June 7, 1946, File 611.713/6-746, Box 2761, DOS Decimal File, 1945-1949, National Archives.

51. Telegram, July 17, 1946, File 866.1-869.5, Box 23, Record Group 84, Foreign Service Posts of DOS, Bucharest, U. S. Mission, Secret Files, 1946, National Archives.

52. Telegram, December 19, 1946, File 611.713/12-1946, Box 2761, DOS Decimal File, 1945-1949, National Archives.

53. *FRUS, 1946*, VI, 645.

54. *Ibid.*, p. 669.

55. *Ibid.*, p. 672.

56. *FRUS, 1947*, IV. 476;"Statement by the President on the Famine in Rumania, February 17, 1947," *Public Papers of the Presidents of the United States, Harry S. Truman, 1947,* pp. 31-33.

57. *FRUS 1947*, IV, 476; Letter, Truman to Harriman, March 1, 1947, File No. 186, President's Secretary Files, HST Library.

58. Letter, Leavitt to Stilwell, March 12, 1947, pp. 1-2, File 871.5018/3-1247, Record Group LM 102, DOS Decimal File, Reel #10, Records of U.S. DOS Internal Affairs, Rumania, 1945-1949, National Archives.

59. Memorandum, "Trading Between the United States and Rumania," p. 2, May 7, 1947, File 611.713/5-747, Box 2761, DOS Decimal File, 1945-1949, National Archives; memorandum, "Private Credits to Rumania and Draft Note to Rumania," pp. 2-3, April 15, 1947, File 631- Rum-US, Box 27, Record Group 84, Foreign Service Posts of DOS, Bucharest, U. S. Mission, Secret Files, 1947, National Archives.

60. Memorandum, "Trading Between the United States and Rumania," pp. 1-2, May 7, 1947, File 611.713/5-747, Box 2761, DOS Decimal File, 1945-1949, National Archives.

61. Memorandum, "Rumanian Trade," p. 1, July 15, 1947, File 611.713/7-1547, Box 2761, DOS Decimal Files, 1945-1949, National Archives.

62. Montias, *Economic Development in Communist Rumania*, p. 23.

63. Memorandum, "Rumanian Trade," p. 2, July 15, 1947, File 611.713/12-1547, Box 2761, DOS Decimal Files, 1945-1949, National Archives.

64. Memorandum of conversation, January 13, 1948, File 611.713/1-1348, Box 2761, DOS Decimal Files, 1945-1949, National Archives.

65. Telegram, February 13, 1948, File 671-119/2-1348, Box 2899, DOS Decimal Files, 1945-1949, National Archives; telegram, April 10, 1948, File 671.119/4-1048, Box 2899, DOS Decimal Files, 1945-1949, National Archives.

66. Letter, March 16, 1948, File 611.713/3-1648, Box 2761, DOS Decimal Files, 1945-1949, National Archives.

67. After returning to Romania, Max Ausnit was arrested and tried on charges of setting up an espionage system with the United States. He was found guilty and imprisoned (U. S. Congress, Senate, Committee on Foreign Affairs, *Restrictions on Diplomatic Personnel By and From Iron Curtain Countries*, 83rd Cong., 1st Sess., 1953, p. 23). For additional information of subsequent Malaxa

schemes, including some involving Richard Nixon, see Roger Morris's *Richard Milhous Nixon: The Rise of an American Politician* (NY: Henry Holt and Co., 1990), pp. 648-649.

68. Airgram, p. 1, June 7, 1948, File 671.006/6-748, Box 2899, DOS Decimal Files, 1945-1949, National Archives. Some of the private American owned companies, such as Standard Fabrica de Telefoane si Radia, a subsidiary of I.T.&T., accepted state control in 1948 rather than be penalized by remaining in the private sector (*FRUS, 1948*, IV, 351). For a listing of American owned or controlled firms in Romania see, File 350 - American Interest in Rumania, 1946,2 pp., Box 15, Record Group 84. Foreign Service Posts of the DOS, Bucharest, U. S. Mission, Secret File, 1946, National Archives.

69. Telegram, August 25, 1948, File 671,519/8-2448, Box 2899, DOS Decimal Files, 1945-1949, National Archives; telegram, August 12, 1948, File 671.519/8-748, Box 2899, DOS Decimal Files, 1945-1949, National Archives; telegram, August 9, 1948, File 761.519/8-748, Box 2899, DOS Decimal File 1945-1949, National Archives.

70. Adler-Karlsson, *Western Economic Warfare, 1947-1967*, pp. 78-79.

71. *FRUS, 1948*, IV, 588.

72. Adler-Karlsson, *Western Economic Warfare, 1947-1967*, p. 79.

73. Letter, "State Control of Rumanian Foreign Trade Operations," January 17, 1950, 6 pp.,File 510, Box 115, Record Group 84, Foreign Service Posts of DOS, Bucharest, U. S. Missions, Secret Files, 1950, National Archives.

74. Letter, Formation of Rumanian Foreign Trade Chamber of Commerce, pp. 3-4, December 10, 1949, File 600.7117/12-1049, Box 2676, DOS Decimal Files, 1945-1949, National Archives.

75. *Ibid.*, pp. 1-2.

76. House Committee on Foreign Affairs, *U.S. Policy and the East-West Confrontation*, 1980, pp. 65, 478.

77. *FRUS, 1949*, V, 31-32.

78. Letter, State Control of Rumanian Foreign Trade Operations, p. 4, January 21, 1950, File 510, Box 115, Record Group 84, Foreign Service Posts of DOS, Bucharest, U.S. Missions, Secret Files, 1950, National Archives.

CHAPTER IV

LEGATION HARASSMENT AND EXPORT CONTROLS: THE TWIN PILLARS OF AMERICAN-ROMANIAN RELATIONS, 1949-1951

Bucharest and the American Legation

Increased Soviet influence in Romania was most felt by the staff at the American Legation in Bucharest. In September, 1948, Romanian authorities detained four members of the Legation staff for sixteen hours on charges of taking photographs in a forbidden zone.[1] Three months later, Bucharest requested that Washington recall Colonel Lovell, the Military Attache and Mr. Leverich, Counselor of the Legation, for attempted conspiracy. Without admitting involvement, Washington agreed and in turn requested that two members of the Romanian Legation in Washington be recalled.[2] This kind of reciprocal harassment continued throughout the first half of 1949. While Washington had the right to determine the size of the Legation staff, the State Department knew that, ultimately, Bucharest would control the number of American diplomatic personnel permitted into Romania. Consequently, in August, 1949, the Department reduced the staff to 53, and eliminated foreign personnel so that the Romanian government would not be able to intimidate or arrest Romanians working at the Legation.[3]

This staff reduction did not curb Bucharest's demands for further reductions. Time and time again, the Romanian government delayed issuing visas to replacement American personnel. The State Department asked Mihail Magheru, the new Romanian Minister to the United States, for assistance in November, but no changes ensued.[4] During the Spring, 1950, Bucharest stepped up its harassment of all Western Legations in an effort to eliminate, for all intents and purposes, Western diplomatic influence in Romania. On March 2, Bucharest demanded that the British and American Legations close their libraries and information offices.[5] Two weeks later, Bucharest refused to issue an exequatur to Murat W. Williams, a Second Secretary and Consul at the American Legation.[6] This refusal was part of Romania's "ratchcting" diplomacy toward the United States. Since 1946 requests from the American Legation in Bucharest for exequaturs had gone unanswered by the Romanian government. The Bucharest's refusal tightened the harassment ratchet one more notch.[7]

In April, Romanian officials arrested Nora Samuelli, a former Romanian employee of the United States Information Service (USIS) in Bucharest, Liviu Popescu-Nasta, the Romanian correspondent for the *New York Times*, and three former Romanian employees of the British Information Office (BIO) in Bucharest. The five were accused and convicted of conducting espionage for the American and British Missions in Romania, and were sentenced to various periods of imprisonment ranging from 15 years to life.[8] The local press portrayed the trial as cause for closing the USIS and BIO. Romanian officials also arrested Leonard Kirschen and Marcel Pohne, the last two independent correspondents for the Associated Press and United Press news agencies.[9] Schoenfeld notified Washington that the arrests left the Anglo-American Missions "virtually suspended in a vacuum" unable "to see, hear, or discuss" what was going on in the country.[10]

The harassment took its toll on Schoenfeld. The Minister asked for reassignment, but before the State Department could act, Bucharest moved the ratchet a notch tighter. On May 5, Bucharest restricted American travel to within 70 miles of the capital,[11] and five days later requested the American Legation to reduce its personnel to 11, including the Minister. In return, Bucharest would reduce its Mission staff in the United States to an equal number and accept travel restrictions.[12] Schoenfeld wanted to delay any response. However, the State Department feared that Romania would follow the Czechoslovakian example. Prague had initiated an identical campaign against the American

Embassy and demanded a two-thirds reduction of staff. When the State Department hesitated, Prague notified the Embassy that it had twenty-four hours to implement the staff reduction.[13] Rather than be confronted with this type of ultimatum, Washington notified Bucharest on May 22 that while retaining its right to staff its Legation, it would reduce its staff to ten people plus a Chief of Mission.[14] Two days later, Schoenfeld left Romania. He informed Ana Pauker that Murat Williams, the Third Secretary, would be in charge of the Legation, pending visa approval for James Gantenbein who would be the Chargé d'Affaires ad Interim.[15]

Schoenfeld's departure did not make life easier for the remaining members of the American Mission in Bucharest. In June, when several American military personnel assigned to the Legation were caught with a quantity of small arms ammunition at Lake Snagov, the Romanian press launched an explosive campaign depicting the Americans as terrorist enemies of the government. Two American enlisted men involved quickly left Romania. Bucharest demanded the departure of the Assistant Army Attache, Captain Herschel Hutsinpiller, whose residence bordered the Lake, and who the press too accused of being a terrorist. Williams, who was Acting Chargé d'Affaires, defended the Captain's innocence, but agreed to his departure on June 25 "in conformity with customary diplomatic practice."[16]

In July, Bucharest interrupted Washington's regular courier service to the Legation. On July 18, Williams saw Corneliu Bogdan, the Chief of the Western Affairs Section of the Romanian Foreign Ministry. The American Chargé argued that Washington had the right to control its own courier service. Bogdan disagreed. America's espionage activities over the years had forced Bucharest to request a reduction in Legation staff, and now it wanted Washington to reduce its courier schedule. To force this reduction, Bogdan announced that the government would issue visas to couriers, but at unspecified and irregular intervals.[17] In August, James Gantenbein received his visa and took charge of the Legation. His end-of-year report noted that by December, couriers arrived only once every two or three weeks.[18]

Bucharest's success in isolating the American Legation can best be measured by the fact that there were only a handful of dispatches from Romania throughout the entire year of 1951. The first, on April 20, described a visit by Corneliu Bogdan as the first visit at the Legation by a Romanian diplomat or Foreign Office official since 1948. Bogdan's visit was a courtesy call, to return John Campbell's visit to Bucharest earlier in the year. During the conversation, Bogdan noted his new appointment as temporary Chargé d'Affaires to the Romanian Mission in Washington. He would fill in for Magheru who intended to spend the summer in Bucharest.[19]

By 1951, America's prime sources of influence in Romania were Voice of America broadcasts and transmissions from the newly established Radio Free Europe. Gantenbein's September, 1951, report to the State Department indicated that Romanian propaganda continued to depict life in the United States as repressive, and vilified Washington's leaders including the President. While there was constant harassment, there was nothing out of the ordinary.[20]

However, during the last two months of 1951 harassment increased. In November, an American Air Force plane flying between Munich and Belgrade became lost and flew over Hungarian and Romanian airspace. Needless to say, Bucharest quickly identified the action as one of espionage and sabotage.[21] Several days later, the Romanian Foreign Ministry filed another complaint with Gantenbein, this time about Congress's recently passed Mutual Security Act.[22] One of the provisions of the Act allocated $100 million to organize refugees or escapees from the satellite states into military units to assist North Atlantic Treaty Organization forces, "or for other purposes."[23] Bucharest labelled the bill as an "aggressive act against the Romanian Peoples' Republic."[24] Later, the Foreign Ministry sent an official protest to the Legation describing the Act as one which "provided for the official subsidizing of criminal activities" against Romania. The "U. S. Government aims at forming mercenary gangs of traitors to the fatherland who have fled from Romania, Fascists and war criminals sheltered in the U.S. or other states – gangs which are to be used for aggressive purposes against the RPR."[25]

While government hostility had isolated the Legation and reduced the number of Americans living in Romania to less than 500, Gantenbein saw no reason for Washington to close the Legation. In spite of everything, the Mission performed a number of services which provided Washington with political, military and economic information otherwise unavailable. In addition, the Legation was a symbol of America's continued interest in the welfare of the Romanian people. Further, through its consular functions, the Legation assisted people who wanted to emigrate to the United States. In 1951, 32 people received such assistance. As a result, in January, 1952, Gantenbein recommended that Washing ton retain its Legation and maintain diplomatic relations with Bucharest.[26]

While Romania's behavior toward the American Legation was in part due to Soviet pressure, the harassment was also a direct reaction to several aspects of America's policy toward Eastern Europe. Bucharest was especially disturbed by Washington's continued protests concerning Romania's human rights violations, including raising the issue for debate in world forums. Further, Romania objected to America's unwillingness to export needed industrial products to Romania, and the United States' constant efforts to restrain the trade of West European countries with Romania and the Soviet Bloc.

Washington and Romanian Human Rights

America's efforts to draw world attention to Romania's human rights violations had resulted in the issue being debated at the United Nations. However, by October, 1949, the United Nations General Assembly needed help in interpreting Article 38 of the Romanian Peace Treaty which dealt with dispute resolution. The organization asked the International Court of Justice to interpret the article. Six months later, on March 30, 1950, the Court held that a dispute did exist between the Western Allies and Romania, and that the machinery of Article 38 should be implemented. The Court concluded that Romania was obligated to appoint a member to a Commission to resolve the dispute.[27] Bucharest denied the jurisdiction of the International Court, maintaining there was no dispute because there were no human rights violations. On July 18, the Court ruled that although Romania was in "willful disregard" of its Treaty obligations, Article 38 did not provide a contingency in the event one of the two parties refused to appoint a representative to a disputes commission. Therefore, the Court concluded that the Secretary General of the United Nations could not intervene and appoint a commissioner.[28]

Unable to use the Treaty machinery to keep Romanian human rights practices before the world, Washington decided to use the UN as its forum, an institution in which the United States had considerable influence. On October 2, 1950, at the Fifth Session of the UN General Assembly, the United States included an agenda item entitled: "Observance in Bulgaria, Hungary and Romania of Human Rights and Fundamental Freedom." The *Ad Hoc* Political Committee considered the item and on October 5 approved a resolution which condemned the three countries for refusing to fulfill their treaty obligations. The Committee also noted the continuance of serious human rights violations in the three countries, and invited member nations to submit evidence on such violations to the Secretary General. On November 3, the General Assembly approved the resolution.[29] Thirteen days later, Ambassador Warren Austin, the United States Representative to the United Nations, presented evidence of human rights violations in Romania to Trygve Lie, the UN Secretary General.[30]

In January, 1951, the State Department decided to continue to protest human rights violations in Romania. If nothing else, such protest would remind the world of the opinion of the International Court of Justice which stated that Romania was in "willful disregard" of her Treaty obligations.[31] At year's end, the Administration added further weight to the human rights issue. The White House encouraged towns and cities across America to sponsor festivals celebrating Human Rights Day. The December 10, 1951, commemoration honored the third anniversary of the UN Universal Declaration on Human Rights.[32]

The Effect of America's Export Controls on Romania

A second reason for Romania's harassment of the American Legation was America's export control policy. By the end of 1951 American-Romanian trade had nearly evaporated. Romania had nothing to gain economically by maintaining friendly relations with the United States. Moreover, Romania had centralized her foreign trade and essentially eliminated private enterprise. As a result, Romania's trade moved dramatically toward the Soviet Union and Eastern Europe. Her Second One Year Plan in 1950 called for 89% of her import and export trade to be with the Soviet Bloc.[33] Further, the goals of that plan and the following First Five Year Plan, 1951-1955, focused on increasing production of manufacturing items. Many of these items, such as machine tools and oil field equipment were on the American 1-A and 1-B lists.[34] The combined effect of Romanian and American legislation was that by June, 1950, there was not a single American firm operating in Romania,[35] and the Legation noted that for the entire year, only one American commercial traveler was known to have entered the country.[36]

The outbreak of the Korean War in June, 1950, reinforced America's Cold War mentality: the Communists were evil and were intent on conquering the free world. This attitude affected most government decisions including policy recommendations by the NSC, which will be discussed later, and Congressional legislation. By coincidence, the Trade Agreements Act of 1949 was due to expire on June 12, 1951.[37] Congress began hearings in January, 1951, and passed the Trade Agreements Extension Act on June 16 with several amendments, one of which had significant bearing on American-Romanian relations. Section 5 eliminated most-favored-nation status to imports from the Soviet Union and to imports from "any nation or area dominated or controlled by the foreign government or foreign organizations controlling the world Communist movement."[38] On June 27, Washington notified Bucharest that the United States intended to terminate the provisional commercial agreement signed on August 20, 1930.[39] On August 1, President Truman signed a proclamation suspending MFN for Romania effective August 31.[40]

Bucharest responded predictably. America's actions confirmed the "discriminatory" practices which she had pursed against Romania during the past few years, and Washington was responsible for the "further deterioration" of relations between the two countries.[41] However, as a matter of fact, the dollar value of American imports from Romania was relatively unaffected by the Trade Agreements Extension Act. The total annual value through most of the 1950s was about $375 thousand with caviar, beet pulp, goose feathers, and herbs being the principal imported products.[42]

America and COCOM

The third factor which provoked Romania to increase her harassment of the American Legation in Bucharest was Washington's persistent efforts to restrain West European trade with Romania and with the Soviet bloc. In January, 1950, COCOM opened its headquarters in Paris. Meetings were secret but information soon leaked that COCOM members met to discuss East-West trade controls. These leaks frightened the European representatives. On February 15 they demanded that no information or minutes of meetings be made available to anyone. If the public learned of the existence of multilateral arrangements to coordinate export controls, they would be forced to withdraw from COCOM.[43] In the Spring, COCOM replaced the Anglo-French List with an International List (IL) which reflected the participation of most of the European states. Like its predecessor, it did not mirror the American 1-A and 1-B list.

This disparity provoked considerable debate among officials in Washington, a debate which became exceedingly heated after June 25, 1950, when North Korean troops crossed the 38th parallel and attacked South Korea. Prior to the outbreak of the war, the State and Commerce Department squared off against one another on the issue of controls. The State Department saw trade as political, and, as such, Washington could only go so far in forcing her allies to adopt restrictions they opposed. Commerce, on the other hand, saw trade as an economic weapon, which, if properly used, could prevent, or at least inhibit, the growth of Communism.[44] The Korean War brought the two departments closer together on identifying items for export control, but did little to bring agreement as to the strategy the United States should use to force Western Europe into greater compliance with America's export control lists.

At its August 24 meeting, the NSC decided to establish an East-West trade policy. Commerce and State essentially agreed that in the light of the Korean War, the United States ought to impose restriction on any new items which would "significantly affect Soviet war potential or military activity" even if other nations did not follow suit. The State Department suggested that if the new items were strategically more important than some items currently on the IL lists, then the new items ought to replace the less strategic items. Commerce was more interested in adding items to the IL list than swapping.[45]

On the issue of how far the United States should go in insisting that Western Europe adopt America's controls, there was still significant difference between State and Commerce. The State Department opposed using any type of threat or sanction to compel compliance. Commerce wanted to use all means available, including threats and sanctions to force Western Europe to accept America's export controls.[46]

With the President attending the meeting, the NSC made several recommendations which reflected the impact of the Korean War and the more conservative views of the Commerce Department. The Council may also have been influenced by NSC 68. Though not formally approved by Truman until September 30,[47] the document estimated that the Soviet Union would have enough atomic bombs by 1954 to defeat the United States. To counter this development, NSC 68 recommended a massive military build up, so strong as to force the Soviets to abandon any plans for a surprise attack against the United States. Without question, this argument meant that military security was more important to America than Western Europe's economic recovery through continued

East-West trade.[48] Known as Action #347, the NSC agreed that the United States should use the upcoming Foreign Ministers' meeting and NATO committee meetings to influence Western Europe to conform "as close as possible," to American's export control policy. The NSC also agreed to deny shipments of strategic items to any West European state which shipped identical items to the Soviet Bloc.[49]

State Department officials notified their British and French counterparts of the decision to given them time to review their positions before the Foreign Ministers' meeting scheduled for September 18. As a result of this information, London and Paris modified their views. In the past, both had argued that severe export controls against the Soviet Bloc would impose severe economic hardship on Western Europe. Further, both countries believed that the only effective export control was an embargo. However, at the Foreign Ministers' meeting, both nations accepted two basic principles: (a) that strategic considerations should be predominant in selecting items for control; and (b) that controls should be extended to cover "selected items in key industrial areas contributing substantially to war potential."[50] Military security would outweigh economic recovery in determining items for export control.

While Britain and France agreed to prohibit exports of many goods on the American 1-A list, they were reluctant to adopt many of the items on the 1-B list. To reduce friction, the three countries agreed to prepare three categories of export goods. The first would be a list of goods prohibited for export to the Soviet Bloc. The second, would include items that should be quantitatively restricted for export. The third category of goods would be neither prohibited nor restricted, but information concerning their export to the Soviet bloc would be exchanged among the COCOM countries. The three countries also agreed that in making their recommendations on these categories, they would take into account the economic impact of these controls on Western Europe, especially in the area of "essential goods."[51]

As a result of this decision, representatives from the three countries met in London from October 17 to November 20 to establish three lists. Of the 318 original items proposed for possible export control, 74 were withdrawn, while the remaining 244 items were accepted for various types of control. Britain, France and the United States agreed to embargo 102 items, establish quantitative controls on 73 items, and exchange information on the remaining 69 items. At the close of the meeting, the delegates agreed to present these tripartite proposals to all the members of COCOM for their approval.[52]

Many Washington officials were unhappy with the results of the London meeting. Compliance, not compromise, was the goal of the NSC's August 24 directive. Even the State Department was disturbed. The Korean War threatened American security, and this, above all else, was the primary concern of the State Department. As a result, the Department asked the NSC to stiffen its policy in order to force Britain, France and the other COCOM countries to stop exporting items to the Soviet Bloc which could pose a threat to America's security.[53]

The NSC discussed the State Department recommendations and on November 24 the President approved NSC 91/1, a policy designed to persuade America's allies to adopt Washington's August 24 decisions. NSC 91/1 called for the United States to deny shipping COCOM members any items on the American 1-A list, which the West European countries refused to embargo to the Soviet Bloc. A similar stipulation dealt with items on the American 1-B list. Washington would send none of these commodites to COCOM countries unless they agreed that identical items would not be shipped to the Soviet Bloc in quantities considered excessive by the United States.[54]

The NSC recommendations of August 24 had urged Washington to use its influence in NATO, as well as at the Foreign Ministers' meetings, to persuade Western Europe to adopt more stringent export controls. On October 31, the former Secretary of State, George C. Marshall, began the offensive. He told his colleagues on the Defense Committee of NATO that embargoing items of direct military importance to the Soviet Bloc was not enough. Western Europe traded too many items of military potential with Eastern Europe. These were items which could be used to make military weapons. He noted especially Western Europe's persistent sale of such strategic materials as nickel, zinc, ball and roller bearings and precision instruments. This practice had to stop. He wanted his colleagues to inform their governments that the paramount concern in determining export controls to the Soviet Bloc had to be both an item's potential military and immediate military value. [55]

The Korean War had also made a dramatic impact on the American Congress. Prior to the outbreak of the war, Western Europe's noncompliance with Washington's export controls had disturbed only some Congressmen. For example, in January, 1950, Senator George Malone, from Nevada, had introduced a resolution prohibiting any American agency from granting financial aid to any foreign country which traded with the Communist world.[56] The resolution died with little debate.

However, as a result of the Korean War and a growing awareness that Western Europe was not cooperating with American efforts to control exports, Senator Kenneth Wherry of Nebraska revived the Malone resolution. On September 12, he proposed an amendment to the Internal Security Act of 1950 which would deny American assistance to any country exporting items of war potential to the Soviet Bloc. Wherry had bipartisan support from leading conservatives including Republican Senator James Kem of Missouri and the Virginia Democratic Senator, Harry Byrd.

On the fifteenth, Truman told the Cabinet that he would try to persuade the Democratic leadership to kill the amendment. Failing that, he would veto it. Truman knew that the Wherry Amendment would play havoc with America's diplomatic efforts to convince Western Europe to adopt Washington's export controls. Truman's personal intercession succeeded, and the Internal Security Act passed both houses without the Wherry amendment.[57]

However, debate on the Wherry amendment had raised Congressional consciousness about the issue of Western Europe's non-support of America's export controls. Consequently, the Wherry amendment backers quickly produced statistical evidence showing that in 1950 East-West trade was still 50% of what it had been in 1948.[58] Consequently, during the debate on the Supplemental Appropriations Act in late September, Representative Clarence Cannon of Missouri proposed an amendment. It stipulated that as long as the United States Armed Forces were involved in the Korean War, America would give no economic or financial assistance to any country whose trade with the Soviet Union or its satellites, including Communist China and North Korea, was found by the NSC to be contrary to the security interests of the United States. The Senate approved the Cannon Amendment and passed it on September 27, 1950 as part of the Supplemental Appropriations Act.[59]

Although the Cannon Amendment gave the NSC substantial discretionary power, the Council did not want to use it. NSC 91/1 was as far as the Council wanted to go in its arm-twisting approach toward Europe. Upon discussing the implications of the Cannon Amendment in December, 1950, the NSC decided that if a country did trade with the Soviet Bloc, this, of and by itself, would not be reason to terminate aid. In fact, the NSC urged that before any aid were withdrawn from an allied country, consideration had to be given to the goals of America's aid program, as well as to the relevant geographic, political and economic conditions that affected a particular country's trade with the Soviet Bloc.[60] In essence, the NSC did not want to use the sanctions granted it by Congress.

Meanwhile, the tripartite proposals emanating from the London Foreign Minister's meeting were circulated to the members of CO-COM. On January 16, 1951, agreement was reached on all but 47 items.[61] Armed with the threat of being able to employ the sanctions prescribed in Section 117D of the ECA Act, the Cannon Amendment and in NSC 91/1, the American negotiators were able to convince their European colleagues by January 26 to accept Washington's view on most of the items. A couple of weeks later the State Department notified the NSC that all of the major manufacturing and trading countries in Western Europe, with the exceptions of Switzerland and Sweden, had "voluntarily" agreed to expand their export controls on strategic shipments to the Soviet Bloc.[62]

American Export Controls: A 1951 Review

Escalation of the Korean War and Communist China's increased role in supporting North Korea, forced the NSC to continue to review its export control policy. Both the Commerce and the State Departments prepared recommendations for the NSC early in 1951. Once again the two departments differed with Commerce recommending a harder line. On January 17, Commerce presented a memo later labelled NSC 102. The Department wanted licenses required for all exports to the Soviet Bloc, including items "of little or no strategic significance."[63]

The State Department viewed the recommendation of NSC 102 as tantamount to an embargo, and the Department opposed an embargo by any name.[64] On February 12, it submitted a report to the NSC. This 40 page document, labelled NSC 104, argued against an embargo for several reasons. First, it would serve to orient the East European states more closely toward the Soviet Union. Second, many of America's West European allies would not cooperate. Some of the countries had large indigenous Communist parties, some had strong commitments toward neutrality, while others feared military reprisal. Third, many of the countries were dependent on Soviet Bloc trade. The Department believed that there could be an increase in the present controls provided that the concept of "economic defense" be maintained as distinct from "economic warfare." The West European powers were willing to take "economic defense" measures, but they would not participate in "economic warfare."[65]

Following the February 12 NSC meeting, both departments debated to what extent export controls to the Soviet Bloc should be increased. On February 21 they presented their compromise to the NSC. All items for trade to the Soviet Bloc would require a license. The current policy of denying export licenses to all items on the Positive List would continue. The Positive List would be expanded to include about 200 commodities under a newly created I-C list. Items on the I-C list would normally be denied export licenses if the shipment was in excess of a "minimum quantity" set by the Advisory Committee on Export Policy. All items not on the Positive List, and this was the essence of the compromise, should normally be granted export license for shipment to the Soviet Bloc.[66] The Council accepted the compromise as America's new export control policy toward the Soviet Union and its satellite states.[67] The President approved the policy as NSC 104/2 on April 12.[68]

From Cannon to Battle

Similar to the NSC, Congressional interest in trade sanctions took on a new urgency as reports on the fighting in Korea continued to dominate the front page of America's newspapers. By early 1951, conservative Congressmen came to the conclusion that the Administration was not implementing the Cannon Amendment. To solve this problem, they introduced two bills into the House, H.R. 1621 and H.R. 1939, both of which aimed to prohibit the export of goods from the United States to the Soviet Union, Eastern Europe and Communist China. The legislation would also deny economic or financial assistance to any country which did not likewise restrict its trade with these Communist states.[69] Neither of these bills permitted discretionary implementation of the sanctions. A special Foreign Affairs subcommittee under the chairmanship of Laurie C. Battle of Alabama began executive hearings on March 5, 1951, on both bills and on the entire issue of the effectiveness of America's export controls.

The subcommittee's work was long and arduous and it would not make recommendations until June. In the interim, many Congressmen wanted action, not the least of whom was James P. Kem, one of Secretary of State Acheson's most outspoken critics. Kem had visited wounded GIs at the Walter Reed Hospital, and on March 9 had written a scathing letter to the President, which subsequently appeared in the

Washington Star.[70] Kem attacked the British, Belgians, Italians and French for selling tools and products to the Soviet Bloc. The NSC knew about this, but refused to cut off aid as permitted by the Cannon Amendment.[71] Kem was not pleased with the official NSC response which noted that East-West trade was essential for West Europe's recovery.

On May 9 Kem introduced an amendment which would deny further economic and financial aid to any country which shipped war materials to the Soviet Bloc. Kem's proposal would plug a loophole in the Cannon amendment by removing the President's discretionary authority. To avoid Democratic attempts to kill the new amendment, as they had the Wherry proposal, Kem attached his to the Third Supplemental Appropriation Act for 1951, a bill that Congress had to pass. However, largely due to the lobbying efforts of ECA administrator Paul Hoffman, the amendment was modified to allow the President, on the advice of the NSC, the authority to make "exceptions" from the law's requirements in the interest of national security. On May 21, the new amendment received unanimous approval by both Houses and Truman signed it into law on June 2.[72]

The State Department was furious. The Kem amendment was another example of the intolerable Congressional encroachment upon Presidential authority in foreign policy matters. In essence the Amendment meant that the West European nations had to adopt American controls if they were to continue to receive economic aid. The major European states refused to accept the Kem requirement. The NSC shared the State Department's view and on June 14, with the President's approval, exempted all countries from the provision of the legislation pending further study.[73]

Meanwhile the Foreign Affairs subcommittee had released its report on June 7. It called for a new bill to replace House bills 1621 and 1939. The proposed legislation was quite similar to the two bills and to the original Kem Amendment. The major difference was that Battle's committee wanted the responsibility for the entire export control program placed under a single individual, rather than having it divided between the Commerce Department, State, the ECA and others.[74]

On the surface there appeared to be little difference between the Kem and Battle proposals. However, the White House was less upset with Battle's legislation, because Mr. Battle was willing to amend his bill to accommodate the Administration's need for discretionary power.[75] As a result, the new bill, formally called the Mutual Defense Assistance

Control Act of 1951, included an embargo on shipments of arms, munitions, atomic energy materials, transportation and petroleum materials of strategic value. Further, the legislation embargoed all items of primary strategic significance used to produce implements of war to any nation threatening the security of the United States including the Soviet Bloc. The Act extended these controls to all nations who wanted to continue to receive military, economic or financial assistance from the United States. Finally, the Act assigned supervisory reponsibility to a single individual called the Administrator, who would report all export violations to the President. The President could then decide whether or not to impose sanctions against the guilty country.[76]

On August 2, with White House support, the House unanimously approved the Mutual Defense Control Act, which subsequently became known as the Battle Act. On August 16, the Senate Foreign Relations Committee recommended the Act for Senate approval. The Kem supporters waged heated debated, but without success. The final vote was 55 in favor of the Battle Act and 16 opposed, with 25 Senators not voting. On October 26, Truman signed the legislation into law.[77] The Battle Act superceded the provisions of section 117d of the Foreign Assistance Act of 1948 and the Kem Amendment.

The Battle Act placed the Administrator within the State Department and provided him with an advisory board, the Economic Defense Advisory Committee, which had representatives from 11 government agencies. Truman appointed Averell Harriman as the Battle Act Administrator and under Section 103 of the Act, he had 30 days to prepare a list of items that were subject to export controls.[78] On November 25, Harriman established the list and sent copies to the COCOM countries. The secret list focused on primary strategic items in two categories. Category A covered arms, munitions and war materials, and if any country sent these to the Soviet Bloc, the United States would immediately terminate all assistance. Category B included some strategic materials and items of strategic military potential. Exports of these items to the Soviet Bloc mandated cessation of American aid, unless the President made a determination to the contrary. The lists became effective January 24, 1952.[79]

America's East European Policy: A 1951 Review

American export control policy was not the only American foreign policy to be reexamined at this time. The strength of the Communist resistance in North Korea challenged the underlying assumptions of America's policy toward Eastern Europe. Since accepting NSC 58/2 in December, 1949, the world had changed. The idea that the United States could successfully encourage Titoism proved short lived. In fact, Washington's changing perceptions about the strength and resilience of the Communist movement in Eastern Europe was reflected in the State Department progress reports concerning the implementation of NSC 58/2.

The first progress report, in February, 1950, promoted cautious optimism. The Department did not know what success it was having in promoting schismatic regimes in Eastern Europe. The report did indicate that the Department believed that in light of recent purges involving Communists and non-Communists in the satellite states, that some "cracks" might be opening in the Soviet control apparatus which the United States might exploit.[80]

The second report, a scant three months later, noted that the "Soviets have been successful in warding off any trend which would start one or more of the satellite countries along the road which Yugoslavia has taken." Nonetheless, the State Department wanted to continue to try to implement the long term goal of NSC 58/2. The Department would continue to provide moral support to the democratic majorities in the satellite states in order to bring about the ultimate goal of a free and independent Eastern Europe.[81]

The State Department presented its third progress report a year later, in May, 1951. The Korean War had made an impact on American thinking. Soviet control over their satellites was so strong that it could use them as surrogate warriors against the United States. The Kremlin willingly committed North Korea to military action. Further, while American propaganda through Voice of America might promote Titoism, Washington's economic policies, either through embargo or assistance, could not enable a satellite state to break away from Soviet control.[82] In reviewing the degree of control Moscow exercised over the Bloc countries, the State Department concluded that Romania was the "most Sovietized of all the satellites."[83] Since the promotion of Titoism no longer appeared to be a viable short range goal for the United States, the State Department asked the NSC to reappraise America's satellite policy. The NSC agreed, but the reappraisal would not be completed until December, 1953.

Notes

1. *FRUS, 1948*, IV, 369. The Four were Wayne Fisher, Third Secretary and Vice Counsul, Paul Green, Attache, and Ruth Garr and Peggy Maggard, clerks.

2. *Ibid.*, pp. 392-393.

3. *FRUS, 1949*, V, 19-20.

4. *Ibid.*, pp. 543-544. Magheru presented his credentials to President Truman on September 26, 1949.

5. Report, "Romania in 1950," p. 1, January 11, 1951, Box 120, Record Group 84, Foreign Service Posts of DOS, Bucharest, U. S. Missions, 1950-1951; *FRUS, 1950*, IV, 1052.

6. An exequatur is a document indicating that the host nation permits the person named on the document to carry out the functions of a consul. A consul can perform consular functions without an exequatur, provided the consul presents credentials to the host country. This in fact had been the situation between Washington and Bucharest for over two years. However, Romania's refusal to grant an exequatur meant that Williams could only conduct consular business within the Legation, and could deal only with the Romanian Foreign Ministry and not with local officials (March 18, 1950, File 611.6641/3-1850, Box 2342, Record Group 59, NND832920, National Archives).

7. *Ibid.*, p. 1. Romania had already reduced the support staff at its Legation in Washington, and the only two officers left were Minister Magheru and a Third Secretary, Ion Nitescu (*FRUS, 1950*, IV, 1057). Washington had not issued exequators to Romanian Consuls in the United States since 1946, but had never refused Romanian requests (*Ibid.*, p. 1059).

8. *Ibid.*, p. 1061 n1; Report, "Rumania in 1950," p. 1, January 11, 1951, Box 120, Record Group 84, Foreign Service Posts of DOS, Bucharest, U. S. Missions, 1950-1951, National Archives.

9. *Ibid.*, p. 2.

10. *FRUS, 1950*, IV, 1062.

11. Senate Special Subcommittee on Security Affairs, *Restrictions on Diplomatic Personnel*, 1953, p. 22; *FRUS, 1950*, IV, 1066-1067.

12. Report, "Rumania in 1950," p. 2, January 11, 1951, Box 120, Record Group 84, Foreign Service Posts of DOS, Bucharest, U. S. Missions, 1950-1951, National Archives; *FRUS, 1950*, IV, 1063. The American Legation was not the only one asked to reduce staff. Bucharest requested the French Mission to reduce its staff to three persons, making it equal to the Romanian Legation in Paris (Circular, "Bureau of European Affairs, Weekly Review, June 28, 1950," p. 2, Box 109, Record Group 84, Foreign Service Posts of DOS, Bucharest, U. S. Mission, 1950, National Archives.

13. *FRUS, 1950*, IV. 550-557.

14. *Ibid.*, pp. 1065-1066.

15. *Ibid.*, p. 1067 n4.

16. *Ibid.* pp. 1068-1069.

17. Circular, "Bureau of European Affairs-Weekly Review," p.2, June 28, 1950, Box 109, Record Group 84, Foreign Service Posts of DOS, Bucharest, U. S. Mission, 1950, National Archives.

18. Report, "Rumania in 1950," p. 4, January 11, 1951, Box 120, Record Group 84, Foreign Service Posts of DOS, Bucharest, U. S. Mission, 1950-1951, National Archives.

19. Deptel No. 276, 2pp. February 27, 1951, Box 120, Record Group 84, Foreign Service Posts of DOS, Bucharest, U.S. Mission, 1950-1951, National Archives.

20. *FRUS, 1951*, IV, 1512-1515.

21. *Ibid.*, p. 1519. The plane was forced down in Hungary and the crew was interned there until December 28, when the United States reluctantly paid fines for the release of the plane's crew (Ibid., pp. 1468-4181; Verbal Notes, 4 pp. November 21, 1951, 3 pp. November 23, 1951, 2 pp. November 26, 1951, "Dispatches, Notes, Etc.," Box 3, Record Group 84, Foreign Service Posts of DOS, Bucharest legation, Misc. Records, 1951-1952).

22. This act established the Mutual Security Agency which replaced the Economic Cooperation Administration effective December 30, 1951. The Act aimed at providing military and other assistance to countries friendly to the United States. Congress appropriated nearly $7.5 billion to fund the Agency's operations. The President approved the bill on October 10, 1951. See, *FRUS 1951*, I, 389.

23. Bennett Kovrig, *The Myth of Liberation: East-Central Europe in U.S. Diplomacy and Politics Since 1941* (Baltimore: The Johns Hopkins University Press, 1973), pp. 102-103.

24. December 5, 1951, File 611.66/12-551, Box 2342, Record Group 59, NND 832920, National Archives; *FRUS, 1951*, IV, 1518-1520.

25. Verbal note, 2 pp. November 28, 1951, "Dispatches, Notes, Etc.," Box 3, Record Group 84, Foreign Service Posts of DOS, Bucharest legation, Misc. Records, 1951-1952, National Archives.

26. Deptel No. 161, pp. 1-3, January 30, 1952, "Misc. Cables Jan-Feb 52," Box 3, Record Group 84, Foreign Service Posts of DOS, Bucharest legation, Misc. Records, 1951-1952, National Archives.

27. Policy Review, Violation of Satellite Peace Treaties, p. 5, January 24, 1951, Box 125, Record Group 84, Foreign Service Posts of DOS, Bucharest legation, U. S. Missions, National Archives.

28. *Ibid.*, p. 6.

29. *FRUS, 1950*, IV, 59; Policy Review, Violation of Satellite Peace Treaties, p. 6, January 24, 1951, Box 125, Record Group 84, Foreign Service Posts of DOS, Bucharest, U.S. Missions, National Archives.

30. *FRUS, 1951*, IV, 1307. See also, *Trygve Lie, 1946-1953*, Vol. 1 of *Public Papers of the Secretaries-General of the United Nations*, eds. Andrew W. Cordier and Wilder Foote (New York: Columbia University Press, 1969), pp. 254, 405.

31. Policy Review, Violation of Satellite Peace Treaties, pp. 10-11, January 24, 1951, Box 125, Record Group 84, Foreign Service Posts of DOS, Bucharest

legation, U.S. Missions, National Archives; Circular, "Bureau of European Affairs - Weekly Review," p. 3, March 14, 1951, Box 125, Record Group 84, Foreign Service Posts of DOS, Bucharest legation, U. S. Missions, National Archives. In March, Britain notified Washington that she would no longer protest human rights violations in Romania, nor in any of the Balkan states. London believed that more could be gained by treating the Balkans in a wider context, and hoped in this way to get get concessions from the Soviets at the Four Power Talks in Paris.

32. Circular, December 5, 1951, p. 2, "350 - Policy Review," Box 125, Record Group 84, Foreign Service Posts of DOS, Bucharest legation, U.S. Missions, National Archives.

33. Telegram, "Purported Foreign Trade Program of Rumania for 1950," p. 1, November 15, 1949, 671.0031/11-1549, Box 2899, DOS Decimal File 1945-1949, National Archives.

34. Report, pp. 1-2, 21 January, 1950, "510 East-West Trade II," Box 116, Record Group 84, Foreign Service Posts of DOS, Bucharest legation, U. S. Missions, National Archives.

35. America's export control lists had produced severe shortages of industrial goods, and Bucharest invented a variety of ways to circumvent the controls. In June, 1950, Bucharest tried to trade people for spare parts. The IBM World Trade Corporation had a subsidiary in Bucharest, the Compania Internationala De Masini Electrocontabile S.A. The managers of the company, Mssrs, Berindie and Hauser wanted to leave Romania. Bucharest agreed provided IBM furnish $20 thousand in spare parts to overhaul the worn out machines. When informed, the State Department approved the concept, provided IBM could get the necessary export licenses from the Commerce Department (Correspondence, March 8, 1950, June 28, 1950, June 29, 1950, File 411.66/6-2850, Box 1854, Record Group 59, NND862903, National Archives).

36. Report, "Rumania in 1950," p. 4, January 11, 1951, Box 120, Record Group 84, Foreign Service Posts of DOS, Bucharest, U. S. Missions, 1950-1951, National Archives; Telegram, Rumanian Trade with the United States, 2pp. April 21, 1950, 611.6631/4-2850, Box 1854, Record Group 59, NND802903, National Archives. The lone businessman was Russel Singleton who represented Deak and Company, an exporting and importing company based in New York. Singleton had visited Romania in 1949 and met with officials for Romano-Export with the purpose of purchasing precious stones and antique jewelry (Memorandum of Conversation, 2pp, June 20, 1950, File 411.669/6-2050, Box 1854, Record Group 59, NND862903, National Archives).

37. This Act stemmed from the 1934 Trade Agreements Act which established an unlimited and unconditional MFN policy for the United States.

38. FRUS, 1951, I, 1376.

39. Press Release, p. 2, July 6, 1951, Box 123, Record Group 84, Foreign Service Posts of DOS, Bucharest, U.S. Missions, National Archives.

40. FRUS, 1951, I, 1382 n2.

41. Telegram, Termination of US-Rumanian Commercial Agreement of

August 20, 1930, 3 pp., September 19, 1951, File 411.6631/9-1951, Box 1854, Record Group 59, NND862903, National Archives.

42. Export Control Quarterly Report, 3rd Quarter, 1959, p. 29, Office file 149-B, Box 767, WHCF, DDE Library; Letter, Trade with Rumania, May 22, 1951, Box 125, Record Group 84, Foreign Service Posts of DOS, Bucharest, U.S. Missions, National Archives.

43. *FRUS, 1950*, IV, 76.

44. On March 1, Washington gave the State Department the East-West trade responsibilities previously administered by the ECA(*Ibid.*, p. 82.);Report, Export Controls and Security Policy, April 26, 1950, p. 1, NSC Meeting No. 56, Box 208, NSC Meetings 56-64, May 4 - August 10, 1950, President's Secretary's Files, HST Library; *FRUS, 1950*, IV,151.

45. Report, Export Controls and Security Policy, pp. 1-3, August 21, 1950, NSC Meeting No. 66, Box 209, NSC Meetings, President's Secretary's Files, HST Library.

46. *Ibid.*, pp. 4-5.

47. *FRUS, 1950*, I, 400.

48. *FRUS, 1950*, IV. 171.

49. *Ibid.*, pp. 179-180.

50. *Ibid.*, p. 204.

51. *Ibid.*, pp. 187-188.

52. *FRUS, 1951*, I, 1012.

53. Memorandum for the President, Revised Draft Statement of Policy on East-West Trade, p. 1, November 24, 1950, NSC Meeting No. 72, Box 210, NSC Meetings 71-79, November 9, 1950 - January 12, 1951, President's Secretary's Files, HST Library.

54. "Identical" meant items falling within a particular United States 1, 1-A, or 1-B listing (*Ibid.*, pp. 1-3).

55. Memorandum for the NSC, East-West Trade, November 1, 1950, NSC Meeting No. 70, Box 209, NSC Meetings, President's Secretary's Files, HST Library.

56. Adler-Karlsson, *Western Economic Warfare, 1947-1967*, pp. 25-26.

57. *FRUS, 1950*, IV, 189 n1; Funigiello, *American-Soviet Trade in the Cold War*, pp. 52-53.

58. Adler-Karlsson, *Western Economic Warfare, 1947-1967*, p. 26.

59. *FRUS, 1950*, IV, 193, 189 n2.

60. *Ibid.*, pp. 251-255.

61. *FRUS, 1951*, I, 1012.

62. Memorandum for the NSC, East-West Trade, pp.1-2, February 19, 1951, NSC Meeting No. 84, Box 211, NSC Meetings, President's Secretary's Files, HST Library.

63. Report, Export Control Policy Toward the Soviet Bloc, pp. 1-4, January 19, 1951, NSC Meeting No. 83, Box 211, NSC Meetings, President's Secretary's Files, HST Library.

64. *Ibid.*, p. 7.

65. Report to the NSC, U.S. Politics and Programs in the Economic Field which May Affect the War Potential of the Soviet Bloc, pp. 1-3, February 12, 1951, NSC Meeting No. 84, Box 211, NSC Meetings, President's Secretary's Files, HST Library.

66. Report to the NSC, Export Control Policy Toward the Soviet Union and Its Eastern European Satellites, p. 3, February 21, 1951, NSC Meeting No. 84, Box 211, NSC Meetings, President's Secretary's Files, HST Library; *FRUS, 1951*, I, 1049; Memorandum for the NSC, U.S. Policies and Programs in the Economic Field which may Affect the War Potential of the Soviet Bloc, 11 pp., February 20, 1951, NSC Meeting No. 84, Box 211, NSC Meetings, President's Secretary's Files, HST Library.

67. Memorandum for the NSC, Export Control Policy Toward the Soviet Bloc, 2 pp., February 26, 1951, NSC Meeting No. 84, Box 211, NSC Meetings, President's Secretary's Files, HST Library.

68. For details and recommendations see, *FRUS, 1951*, I, 1059-1069.

69. Senate Special Subcommittee on Foreign Affairs, *Control of Exports to Soviet Bloc*, 1951, p. 1.

70. See *The Washington Star*, March 11, 1951.

71. Funigiello, *American-Soviet Trade in the Cold War*, p. 65.

72. *FRUS, 1951*, I, 1073.

73. *Ibid.*, pp. 1121-1122.

74. Senate Special Subcommittee on Foreign Affairs, *Control of Exports to Soviet Bloc, 1951*, pp. 16-17.

75. *FRUS, 1951*, I, 1125.

76. U. S. Congress, Senate, *Executive Sessions of the Senate Foreign Relations Committee (Historical Series)*, Volume II, Part 2, 82nd Cong., 1st Sess., 1951 (Washington: U. S. Government Printing Office, 1976), pp. 684ff.

77. *FRUS, 1951*, I, 1176-1177.

78. *Ibid.*, p. 1213.

79. [Battle Act Administrator] *Mutual Defense Assistance Control Act of 1951, Public Law 213, 82d Congress. First Report to Congress* (Washington, D.C.: U. S. Government Printing Office, 1952), pp. 12-13.

80. Report to the NSC, United States Policy Toward the Soviet Satellite States in Eastern Europe, pp. 1-2, February 3, 1950, NSC Meeting No. 51, Box 207, NSC Meetings 48-55, November 17, 1949 - April 20, 1950, President's Secretary's Files, HST Library.

81. *FRUS, 1950*, IV. 31-32.

82. Report to the NSC, United States Policy Toward the Soviet Satellite States in Eastern Europe, p. 4, May 22, 1951, NSC Meeting No. 93, Box 212, NSC Meetings 86-93, March 14 - June 6, 1951, President's Secretary's Files, HST Library.

83. *FRUS, 1951*, IV, 1230.

CHAPTER V

A NEW LOOK AND A NEW COURSE

Export Controls Revisited

From the last year of the Truman Administration through the end of Eisenhower's first term, Washington did considerable rethinking about its export and security policies made in the context of a Korean War and the Senate Committee on Un-American Activities Hearings chaired by Joseph McCarthy. During this period, Europe became more independent of the United States through the development of the European Coal and Steel Community and the West European Union, which would pave the way for the European Economic Community. American also endured three years of war in Korea which ended in a cease fire, rather than a victorious peace treaty. The Soviet Union had not collapsed, Tito's deviation had not been copied in Eastern Europe and, to make matter worse, Moscow had exploded the world's first air-dropped hydrogen bomb in August, 1953. Combined, these events forced the United States to reconsider its various export control policies, including NSC 104/2, which regulated exports to the Soviet Bloc, NSC 91/1 which regulated exports to COCOM countries, and the Battle Act, which regulated exports to both the Communist world and COCOM. In addition, Washington rethought its basic national security policy laid out in NSC 68, and its special policy toward the East European satellites stated in NSC 58/2. The results of this rethinking coupled with internal developments in Romania changed Washington's views toward Bucharest. In 1952, America considered severing relations with Romania, in 1956 Washington was willing to begin talks with Bucharest to settle outstanding claims issues.

From the outset there were difficulties in trying to coordinate the efforts of the different agencies responsible for export controls. In November, 1951 Truman directed that the Secretary of State, who was responsible for implementing NSC 104/2 work with the Battle Act Director to "establish and maintain arrangements which would assure the effective accomplishment of their respective duties."[1] However, this directive did not provide for any coordination with the Commerce Department, which worked with its Office of International Trade to implement NSC 91/1. To make matters worse, Truman's orders did not really facilitate implementation. NSC 104/2 and the Battle Act had separate, and, at times, different lists of items controlled for export.

In an effort to circumvent Western export controls and increase East- West trade, Moscow sponsored a major Economic Conference on April 3, 1952. It was attended by 471 delegates representing 49 countries, including 13 American businessmen. The Soviets offered Western representatives a variety of trade opportunities. The French and British representatives were treated especially well. In the weeks following the conference, there was widespread concern among Western governments that Soviet propaganda efforts to drive a wedge between West European and American business people were successful. West European businessmen resented the Battle Act. To stem this tide of antagonism, the West European governments urged a Consultative Group meeting at the earliest possible moment.

The Consultative Group met on June 24-25 in Paris. The meeting focused on America's right to threaten sanctions against COCOM countries for agreements made prior to the Battle Act, some of which involved sales of strategic items to the Soviet Bloc. Britain, France and Italy combined had already shipped $2.5 million worth of such materials. Harriman struck a deal with the delegates. If they would eliminate subsequent shipments of materials contracted earlier, he would urge the President not to employ sanctions for the violations.[2] The COCOM members reluctantly agreed. However, this reluctance forced Washington to take even stiffer measures. In October, 1952, the United States forced the West European states to adopt a full import certificate, delivery verification program (IC/DV). In short, before the United States would grant a friendly country an export license, Washington wanted to know the ultimate destination of the exported product. "In this way it was hoped to have full control over the commodity from the moment of export to the final use in a friendly nation."[3]

As could be expected, the January, 1953, progress report on NSC 104/2 indicated that future COCOM discussions would be "lengthy and controversial." In the report Harriman suggested that the United States ought to consider new tactics and approaches to secure greater Western adherence to the Battle Act controls.[4]

In May, the new Eisenhower Administration followed Harriman's advice and had the Planning Board of the NSC respond to four options concerning America's export control policy: (1) to maintain the present policy, (2) to abandon the trade control program, (3) to intensify the scope and force of the program, and, (4) to establish the program on a narrower basis by concentrating on commodities and services of major importance to Soviet war potential.[5]

The NSC report of May 25, 1953, labelled NSC 152, analyzed each option. The present policy was a near embargo on all shipments to the Bloc. In addition, the United States frequently refused to ship goods to friendly countries which had less restrictive controls. The NSC noted that maintenance of this policy would probably slow down the growth of the Bloc's war potential for a short period of time.[6] The second option, to abandon all trade controls, would probably make an important contribution to Soviet war potential as well as to their entire economy. This option would be difficult to implement, since it would require Congressional approval which probably was not forthcoming. This option, the report concluded, was only viable if war with the Soviet Union were not likely in the foreseeable future. The third option, to strive for complete parallelism within the Free World of America's export controls, would have "some adverse impact" on the Soviet Bloc, but it would be resisted by NATO. Moreover, such an alternative should only be contemplated if the threat of war were imminent. The fourth option, to reduce the number of items controlled to only those that were directly strategic, rather than potentially strategic, would have had little impact on the Soviet Union. Moscow already secured most marginally strategic items through normal and illegal trade routes. This option would be welcomed by Western Europe and also by American businessmen who would like to compete for the Soviet markets. Congress and the public would probably object to this option, but it could be done without changes in legislation.[7]

The NSC discussed the recommendations for two months and on July 31, four days after the cease fire in Korea, adopted NSC 152/2 which superseded NSC 104/2 and NSC 91/1. The new policy reflected a change in American thinking, which was partly due to the recent death of Stalin, and an obvious effort by Moscow to change the West's image of the Soviet Union from one of hostility to one of trust. The underlying assumption of NSC 152/2 was that war with the Soviet Union was no longer imminent. Rather, Soviet-American relations would remain strained and tense for a long period of time. Consequently, the NSC chose option four. American efforts should be devoted to establishing an export control system on a narrower and more flexible basis, by focusing on items which contributed significantly to the war potential of the Soviet Bloc.[8] NSC 152/2 called for a "gradual and moderate relaxation" of export controls of shipments to Eastern Europe provided that "in the pace and timing of such relaxation due consideration is given to the effects on the total economic defense effort."[9]

NSC 152/2 addressed Harriman's concerns about the COCOM negotiations, noting that the United States should not use export controls as a substitute for negotiations with friendly countries. Washington should adopt a flexible approach to export controls, and take into consideration the "impact of the control system on the economic, political and financial situation of our allies."[10] Finally, the report recommended that the United States should reduce its tariff barriers to facilitate greater trade in the free world.[11] This view clearly reflected a growing concern of the new Republican Administration. President Eisenhower was committed to a balanced budget, therefore the United States had to reduce trade barriers and export controls in an effort to increase trade, not only with the West but also with the Soviet Bloc. In November, the NSC reviewed this report and after making one change concerning trade with Communist China, reaffirmed their support for NSC 152/3.[12]

Emergence of a New Look

The change in export control policy reflected a changing mood in Washington, which was equally apparent in the NSC's deliberations about American security issues. NSC 20, approved in 1948, addressed the issue of a Soviet-American war, and the aftermath of an American victory. NSC 68, approved in 1950, was founded on a far greater fear of the world's second nuclear armed country, the Soviet Union. The policy concerned itself with Soviet war capabilities, and assumed that the Soviets would be in a position to attack the United States by 1954. However, in the early 1950s, Washington's perception of the Soviet Union changed. The Korean War had forced the United States to dramatically increase her defense budget, and in the process increased the confidence of the Washington defense community. At the same time, however, the Soviet Union had continued to grow stronger and by the end of 1952 both superpowers would have hydrogen bombs.

As an ongoing responsibility, the NSC had continued to review American national security objectives and programs. A Steering Committee of the Senior Staff of the NSC began a major review in October, 1951. The Committee produced two studies, the first report, labelled NSC 135, was a collection of eight documents which focused on various issues of America's preparedness against a Soviet attack. The second report, designated NSC 135/1, was a series of draft conclusions which the NSC accepted on August 12, 1952. NSC 135/1 described the Soviets as hostile to the non-Communist world but suggested that the Soviets would only attack the West if they perceived that an attack by the West was imminent.[13] The NSC suggested that the strongest deterrent to war would be the "achievement and maintenance" of an overall position of strength by the free world.[14] Ten days later, on September 3, President Truman notified the NSC to postpone its review until the new Administration took office the following year.[15]

The new American President, Dwight D. Eisenhower, chose John Foster Dulles to be his Secretary of State, primarily to accommodate the right wing of the Republican party.[16] Dulles had been one of the proponents of "roll back," which proposed that through the threat of nuclear retaliation, the United States could free the "captive peoples" of Eastern Europe and "roll back" the areas controlled by the Soviets.[17] While Dulles was not alone in his views, other's in the Administration still supported containment. Consequently, the President set up a separate task force in May, called Project Solarium, named for the meeting room in the White House. The group was to consider three alternative policies toward the Soviet Union: continuing containment, which meant opposing Communist expansion without risking a general war; "drawing a line" between the Soviet Bloc and the non-Communist world, which meant that if any nation succumbed to Communism on America's side of the line, the United States might consider this cause for an offensive war; and, third, initiating "roll back", which meant that the United States would promote unrest and divisiveness in the Soviet Bloc to ultimately force the Communists to lose control of certain areas.[18]

On September 30, Project Solarium presented its recommendations to the NSC. Labelled NSC 162, the report was discussed throughout October, with particular emphasis on equating Eisenhower's desire to maintain a balanced budget with the economic costs of a strong military defense.[19] On October 30, the Council adopted and the President approved NSC 162/2, as America's basic national security policy. Of the three alternatives, the NSC decided to continue containment. The concept of "drawing a line" was rejected because it eliminated the possibility of negotiations with the Soviets, and because the uncommitted areas of the world could not be easily labelled "communist" or "free world."[20] As for "roll back", the report noted that the West was unable to detach any European state from Soviet control, unless Moscow acquiesced.[21]

NSC 162/2 became known as the New Look. It saw the Soviet Union as hostile, but unwilling to deliberately begin a war, at least through 1955, the period covered by the recommendation. The New Look also called for America's defense to be based on nuclear power. Only by stockpiling sufficient atomic weapons and delivery systems could the free world remain free. A "massive atomic capability" provided the balance between security and economics, for atomic weapons were less expensive to build than were conventional weapons.[22]

The New Look saw the world as divided, but stable. The means to maintain that stability were nuclear weapons and negotiations. The reasons that NSC 162/2 included the possibility of negotiating with the Soviets were numerous. Some of the more important need mentioning because combined they produced new thinking in American foreign policy. Western Europe's growing reluctance to adopt more constraints toward the Soviet Bloc was certainly an important issue. The victory of the Republican Party, with its traditional disdain of the Communist world, gave Eisenhower greater room to move to the Left. He could open a door for Soviet talks, and still maintain an anti-Communist rhetoric which reverberated with terms like "massive retaliation" and a "bigger bang for the buck."[23] Had the Democrats won the election, they could not have moved Left without being labelled "Commies" or "pinkos." Developments in the Communist world also played a role. Stalin's death, the cease-fire in the Korean War, and the new Soviet peace offensive under Malenkov, all contributed to making a New Look possible.[24] Finally, without minimizing the importance of the New Look, it must be noted that not everything was "new." In its conclusions, NSC 162/2 called for the United States to continue to use propaganda and covert actions to create problems for the Soviets, retard their economic and military growth, and complicate their control in the satellites.

America's New East European Policy

As Washington altered its policies on export control and national security, it also reconsidered its policy toward Eastern Europe. In May, 1951, the State Department called for a revision of NSC 58/2, Washington's policy toward the satellite states. The revision took nearly 30 months, and during that time, whenever the NSC considered America's basic national security policy, it usually included a paragraph on Eastern Europe. In the summer and fall of 1952, the United States believed that through economic controls, it was possible to create rifts between Moscow and her satellites. However, the hopes of encouraging Titoist-like rifts apparent in earlier years were quieted. The most that America could now accomplish was to force the Soviets to spend more time and money for internal security in the Bloc.[25]

Early in the following year, there was considerable discussion by the NSC about forming a Volunteer Freedom Corps (VFC) similar to that envisioned by Charles Kersten in his amendment to the Mutual Security Act of 1951. On May 20, the NSC accepted NSC 143/2 which called for setting up a VFC in West Germany. Units would be made from volunteers who had escaped from the Iron Curtain countries, excluding Germans. These units would later be formed into battalions, and used to implement America's psychological warfare against the Soviet Union.[26]

The VFC appealed to some American Congressmen, but it did not appeal to the West German Chancellor, Konrad Adenauer. On June 26, the Chancellor refused to host the VFC. He believed that the Soviets, as well as many West Germans, would view the action as provocative and aggressive.[27] While the NSC would continue to discuss the psychological value of a VFC, the idea never came to fruition.[28]

Finally, in December, 1953, the NSC completed its revision of NSC 58/2. The Council was especially influenced in its thinking by the recent uprising in East Germany. The fact that the uprising occurred at all, supported Washington's hope that nationalism was still alive in Eastern Europe. However, America's failure to affect the uprising and the speed with which the Soviets restored order forced the United States to conclude that the "detachment of any major European satellite from the Soviet Bloc does not now appear feasible except by Soviet acquiescence or by war."[29] While NSC 58/2 had raised Titoism as a model, NSC 174 regarded the Yugoslavian experience as unique. Tito was successful because of all the satellite leaders in Eastern Europe, he alone had a military and political organization that was personally loyal to him. His organization had been forged in combat during World War II, and he was able to impose his will on the Yugoslav peoples after the war without substantial Soviet aid. All the other Communist regimes were from the very beginning dependent on Soviet support, and had remained dependent.[30] Finally, the Tito model was successful because of Yugoslavia's geography. The country did not border the Soviet Union as did Romania, Poland, Czechoslovakia and Hungary, and Yugoslavia's long coastline gave her easy access to American naval support.

NSC 174 called for America to support nationalistic movements in the satellites, for this was the "strongest leverage available for strengthening the morale of the satellite people." Nevertheless, the new policy cautioned that such a tactic could be counterproductive. Nationalism was a double edged sword which in addition to arousing anti-Soviet feelings, also created divisions among the satellite peoples themselves. Magyars opposed Slavs and Romanians, Slovaks opposed Czechs, while Poles opposed Germans. These conflicts could raise a number of operational problems for American propaganda efforts. Too much nationalism could "interfere with United States post-liberation objectives."[31]

NSC 174 accepted the reality of Soviet military domination over the satellites, and so did not expect the East European peoples to successfully rise up and overthrow Communism.[32] Instead, NSC 174 called for the United States to make the Soviets spend more money and expend more energy to maintain their control in the satellites. This tactic would reduce the amount of money and energy that Moscow could spend on advancing Communism globally. Consequently, NSC 174 called on Washington to "maintain flexibility in United States economic policies toward the Soviet bloc, and toward individual satellites, in order to gain maximum advantage with the limited economic weapons at hand."[33]

In anticipating outcomes of the new policy, NSC 174 did not hold out great hope for success in Romania. Geographically, it was the "key to Soviet control of the Danube basin and the Balkan peninsula." The Soviets had troops stationed in Romania to maintain control, although nominally serving as line-of-communication troops for Soviet forces in Austria. Unlike other satellite regimes, the Romanian Communist party had undergone no Soviet-backed purges during its first seven post-war years. The only significant purge, which will be discussed below, was in 1952, and it resulted in a new concentration of party and state power in the hands of Gheorghe Gheorghiu-Dej. While there was some dissatisfaction among Romanians, there was "virtually no attempt to conduct organized resistance or evasion. . . . Popular disaffection is expressed mainly through individual acts of evasion or economic sabotage, listening to Western radio broadcasts, and occasional individual flights abroad."[34] Eisenhower accepted NSC 174 as America's new policy toward Eastern Europe on December 23, 1953, and in the process insured that Romania retained her image of being the "most Sovietized" of the satellite states.

Romanian-American Propaganda Wars

The evolutionary process that produced the New Look in Washington was mirrored by events in Bucharest. Romanian-American relations markedly improved from a low point of harassment in 1951 to thoughts of improved trade by the end of 1953. During the first six months of 1952, Bucharest and Washington maintained a "tolerable relationship," with two focal points of antagonism.[35] The first concerned the February publication of a Romanian Foreign Office white book entitled *The Aggressive Policy and Machinations of American Imperialism Against the Romanian People's Republic.* The polemic attacked Washington for accepting the testimony of "lamentable wrecks" and "scurrilous tools" of Fascism as being representative of the Romanian people. It labelled nearly all of the Legation personnel from Burton Berry, the Minister, to Robert Shea, the Legation Secretary, as American espionage agents and "warmongers' cat's-paws."[36] The lengthy attack concluded that America's behavior toward the Romanian People's Republic was indicative of its efforts to employ "criminal war" tactics in its plans for world hegemony.[37] In order to insure that most Romanians were aware of the evils of America and the Legation, Bucharest devoted a lengthy review of the book in *Scinteia*, the Romanian Communist party newspaper.[38]

Bucharest's purpose in the publication was to offset an increase in Voice Of America's propaganda broadcasts. The long term objective of the propaganda was "to bring about Romania's release from Soviet control and effect her return to the family of free and democratic nations." In the interim, Washington hoped the propaganda would "stimulate passive resistance to communist ideology and Kremlin control." To accomplish these goals the propaganda was designed to assure the Romanian people that America was still concerned about their future, their freedom and their economic well-being. At the same time, the propaganda sought to convince the Romanian people that the retro-gressive influence of the Soviet Union was the only obstacle to a pros-perous and free Romania.[39]

The second issue which increased tension in the Legation occured in May when Bucharest announced that the United States was guilty of using germ and chemical warfare during the Korean War, especially on prisoners of war encamped on Koje Island and Fusan. The *Agerpres* ar-ticle linked America's alleged behavior with that of Hitler, and sug-gested that a Nuremberg type trial was appropriate for American officials guilty of these crimes.[40]

To be sure, the American press countered with anti-Romanian sto-ries of its own. In addition to defection stories and reports of human rights violations,[41] the *New York Times* carried a statement by President Truman decrying the mass deportations of Romanian people to Soviet labor camps. Another story, this one released by the Vatican, accused Romania of treating Catholic clergy as "slave laborers."[42] In March, Bucharest added fuel to the fire when it stopped Jewish emigration from Romania. The principle means of emigration was via the ship "Transylvania," which sailed from Constanza, Romania, to the Israeli port of Haifa. At the end of March, Romania removed the ship from service, placed it in drydock for repairs and provided no substitute ves-sel.[43] The American press soon jumped on this development and in the ensuing months, articles frequently appeared describing the anti-semetic attitude of the Romanian government.[44] Romania curtailed Jewish emigration until 1956. This fact coupled with Washington's political designs, insured that the propaganda war would continue throughout 1952 and for the next several years.

Gheorghe Gheorghiu-Dej Comes to Power

Meanwhile, there were significant internal developments in the Ro-manian government. On May 26-27, 1952, the Plenum of the Central Committee of the Romanian Workers' Party agreed to remove Vasile Luca and Teohari Georgescu from their party posts and Ana Pauker from the Politburo and Secretariat.[45] The man responsible for the purge was Gheorghe Gheorghiu-Dej, who emerged victorious from a party power struggle which first surfaced in the spring of 1950.[46] At that time Gheorghiu-Dej called for a verification of the party's membership. By using this time-honored device, Gheorghiu-Dej purged 192,000 mem-bers leaving him with a majority of supporters in the party. On June 23,

1950, he attacked the recruitment policy of the immediate post war years, for bringing "hostile elements" into the party. These "hostile elements" were non-Romanians. Gheorghiu-Dej wanted the Romanian Workers' Party to be a party of Romanian workers.[47] The 1950 purge clearly indicated a split between two power groups, the "natives" led by Gheorghiu-Dej and the "Moscovites" led by Pauker, Luca, and, to a lesser degree, Georgescu.[48]

The struggle for control of the party bureaucracy continued for the next two years. Pauker, Luca and Georgescu tried to win support from the peasantry who were dissatisfied by Gheorghiu-Dej's rapid collectivization. They encouraged kulak production and a slowing down of the collectivization drive. In August, 1951, the "Moscovites" blamed the "natives" for shortfalls in agriculture and industry. Gheorghiu-Dej struck back, calling for doctrinal purity. The 1949 agricultural guidelines did not permit continued kulak production, but they did allow the peasants to form into voluntary agricultural associations, similar to the Soviet TOZ. He further called for another currency reform which was designed to wipe out the kulaks and urban speculators. By championing Stalinist orthodoxy and Romanian interests, Gheorghiu-Dej undermined his opposition.[49]

In February, 1952, Gheorghiu-Dej accused the "Moscovites" of "deviationism" at the Plenum of the Central Committee. At a second plenum, held in May he succeeded in removing Luca and Georgescu from their party positions and in reducing the power of Ana Pauker.[50] Years later, the three would be identified as promoters of Stalin's cult of personality.[51] By May 29, 1952, Gheorghiu-Dej was the leader of the Romanian Worker's Party, and on June 2 he became Premier of Romania. The following day he promised the Grand National Assembly that he would correct the abuses made by Luca and Georgescu, and he would strengthen Bucharest's ties with Moscow.[52]

Historians continue to debate whether Gheorghiu-Dej had a grand design for Romania, or whether he seized power for purely personal reasons.[53] While there is no conclusive evidence, historians appear to lean more toward the view that he favored a brand of national communism committed to having a Romanian led party lead Romania into socialism.[54]

Although a Romanian nationalist, Gheorghiu-Dej knew that his continued success rested on maintaining close relations with Moscow. On August 30, *Agerpres* carried an article celebrating the 8th anniversary of Romania's liberation from Fascism and credited the Soviet Army with

the overthrow of the Fascist dictators.[55] The new Constitution of
September 24 also acknowledged the role played by Moscow in establishing the new democratic state. The document was designed to assist
Romania through its transition to socialism, whereupon there would be
a new constitution. The document established the Grand National Assembly as the sole legislative body with representatives elected every
four years. All workers' organizations had the right to present candidates for election, but the only political party which could propose candidates was the Romanian Workers' Party. Chapter 2 reorganized the
state by reducing the 28 regions provided by a September, 1950, decree
into 18, each containing an industrial cite as a nucleus.[56]

As these events unfolded, they passed almost without comment by
the American Legation in Bucharest. Government harassment had so
isolated the Legation from information, that Gheorghiu-Dej's purge and
seizure of power came as a surprise to America's Chargé d'Affaires ad
Interim Gantenbein. He wrote on June 21, 1952, that neither he nor the
other Western Legations in Bucharest had any indication that a purge
was imminent. In fact, he did not know that Pauker had been in charge
of agriculture, nor that she had been falling from power since 1950.[57] As
for the constitution, the Legation simply forwarded a copy to the State
Department without comment. Romanian harassment and American
restrictions had curtailed many of the functions of the Legation to the
point that there was even talk about the logic of retaining the facility. In
fact the only correspondence of any substance between the Legation
and Washington concerned Romania's efforts to circumvent America's
export controls.

Italian-Romanian trade proved to be the major topic of the communiques. In December, 1950, the two countries signed a one year trade
agreement which was automatically renewed. During the post war years,
the two-way trade averaged between two and three million dollars. Of
prime importance to Italy was Romania's export of 20,000 tons of
wheat. In return, the Italians provided manufactured products, including, on occasion, items on the COCOM list. In February, 1952, the
Legation sent a detailed report on Italian export control violations.
However, the note recommended that Washington be tolerant and not
invoke the sanctions called for in the Battle Act. The Legation suggested that the reason for Italy's agreement to trade wheat for rolling
mills, threading machines and a centerless grinder was to facilitate release of a member of the Italian Legation imprisoned in Bucharest.[58] As
noted above, the President accepted the Legation's argument and re-

fused to impose the Battle Act sanctions on Italy.[59] Romania also tried to convince other Western nations to trade industrial material with her. In January, 1952, Romania published a slick new journal, *Romanian Foreign Trade*. The leading article emphasized the value that Romania's raw materials could have for the economies of Great Britain and West Germany.[60] The irregularly issued journal offered significant amounts of petroleum, grain and timber to Western traders, even though these items were in short supply in the Eastern Bloc.[61] Direct contacts were made with the Belgian Chargé and the British Legation both of whom indicated that they would strictly adhere to Western export controls.[62]

While the American Legation received no direct trade overtures, they did notice a decline in harassment. The Legation believed it was due to the appointment of a new Minister, Harold Shantz on September 27, 1952.[63] Shantz arrived on November 20 to replace Gantenbein, and his first dispatch to Washington suggested that Bucharest's attitude had changed, but the change was mercurial, and did not mean that the Legation had any further access to information.[64] Consequently, there was no correspondence of substance from Bucharest for the next six months.

The New Course in Moscow and Bucharest

Changes in Moscow in 1953, promoted continued change in Romania. Stalin's death followed by the uprising in East Germany, encouraged Georgi Malenkov, Stalin's successor, to create a new Soviet image. The "New Course" as it was labelled by the West, aimed to reduce Cold War tensions and portray Moscow as an advocate of peace and understanding. Gheorghiu-Dej was eager to capitalize on this new image. Shortly after Stalin's death in March, 1953, Nikita Khrushchev visited Bucharest. While there he met an "Old Bolshevik" comrade, Emil Bodnaras, the Romanian Defense Minister. During their conversation, according to Khrushchev, Bodnaras raised the question, "What would you think about pulling your troops out of Romania?" Gheorghiu-Dej was clearly trying to reduce Soviet influence, but the "New Course" was not yet that accommodating. Khrushchev admitted that he was taken back by the question, and replied with a rather elusive response that the Soviet Union had to keep troops stationed in Romania because of a possible Turkish offensive.[65]

Moscow's announcement of the New Course was greeted enthusiastically in Romania. However, Gheorghiu-Dej willingness to adopt a similar program was not simply a slavish-satellite response to Soviet leadership. Rather, Gheorghiu-Dej needed to find a solution to a collapsing Romanian economy. The goals of the First Five Year Plan, begun in 1951, were not being met. Excessive emphasis on heavy industrialization had produced sharp declines in consumer goods and food products. Collectivization had been poorly handled and consequently, the burden of agricultural production had fallen on the private farmers who received little government support. The result was that Romania's 1953 farm production was less than the pre-war levels.[66] These trends were apparent in 1952, and consequently when Malenkov introduced his economic reforms in March, 1953, Gheorghiu-Dej saw them as a means to reverse the downward trend in Romania's economy.

Leaders of the Romanian Worker's Party met at a Party Plenum on August 19-20 to discuss economic reforms for Romania. On August 23, the ninth anniversary of Romania's "liberation," Gheorghiu-Dej announced the New Course. The new plan focused on manufacturing consumer products rather than heavy industrial goods. Forced collectivization gave way to monetary incentives to induce private farmers to join agricultural associations. Romania would reduce her agricultural exports to provide more foodstuffs for domestic consumption.[67]

The New Course provided a breathing space so that Bucharest could review its industrial growth, and distinguish between projects worth continuing and postponing. Emphasis on increased foodstuffs and consumer products also undermined a growing passive resistance among laborers and farmers to the forced collectivization and heavy industrialization policies of the Five Year Plan. The New Course appeared to give the consumer some of the fruits promised by the socialist transformation, and this was especially important to Gheorghiu-Dej who pursued a Stalinist model in Romania. By adopting the New Course, he could undermine resistance, both by non-communists as well as by party members, to his personal style of leadership.[68] Finally, the New Course gave Gheorghiu-Dej an opportunity to continue to promote national Communism. At the 19th Congress of the CPSU in Moscow the previous October, he had announced the "one family feeling" of all Romanians.[69] At the announcement on August 23 he noted that the Romanian Workers' Party was the party of all Romanians, and it was dedicated to the construction of socialism in Romania for the benefit of all Romanians. "The party's historical goal and Romania's national goal were proclaimed to be the one and the same."[70]

The New Course announcements further alleviated hostility between the American Legation and the Bucharest regime. A changed attitude had first been noticed in the Fall of 1952, and dispatches from the Legation in early 1953 indicated hopes for even greater improvements. In April, the State Department and the Legation worked on plans to produce a weekly publication for distribution in Romania similar to the *Romanian News*, which was distributed by the Romanian Legation in Washington. However, while the Legation's discussions with the State Department continued into the Summer, the first issue of *U.S. News*, as the publication was tentatively named, never reached the streets of Bucharest.[71] Gheorghiu-Dej's New Course did not include the distribution of American propaganda.

However, the changing attitude did permit American reporters access to Romania for the first time in three years. The occasion was the World Festival of Youth and Students for Peace and Friendship hosted by Gheorghiu-Dej in August, just prior to the Party Plenum. While the American Congress passed a resolution encouraging the "valiant struggle" for freedom of the "captive peoples" in Eastern Europe,[72] correspondents from the *New York Times* and *Christian Science Monitor* wandered around Bucharest. Their reports indicated that while the Romanian people disliked Communism, they accepted it. As the *New York Times* reported "no people dislike Communism more than the Romanians, and none do less against it."[73]

Gheorghiu-Dej's announcement of the New Course prompted Shantz, the American Minister in Romania, to suggest that Washington consider increasing its trade of consumer goods with Bucharest. The State Department was not especially receptive to the idea. Romania had continued to circumvent America's export controls. The most recent infraction was a shipment of 100 Willys Universal jeeps, which were built in the United States, shipped to Syria and transshipped on the Italian vessel, "S.S. San Piero" to Costanza, Romania.[74] In addition, Romania continued its efforts to embarrass the United States. On October 9, Bucharest began a trial allegedly involving a group of spies and terrorists who were parachuted into Romania by American espionage agents. All sixteen were found guilty and received sentences from three years of hard labor to death.[75]

This kind of activity affected Washington. When the State Department reviewed Shantz's request, it noted that while recent NSC decisions and export control regulation revisions permitted flexibility in dealing with the satellite states, there was no reason to sell the Romanians consumer goods. The State Department interpreted the New Course as a sign that the satellite economies were in trouble. Therefore, it would be inappropriate for the United States to "help the Commies out of their predicaments." Furthermore, there was no easy mechanism available for trade. The government was not ready to engage in bilateral negotiations, while the private sector was wary of trading with the Soviet Bloc.[76]

On the other hand, Washington was not totally negative toward Romania. NSC 174, adopted in December, 1953, called for the United States to continue diplomatic relations with Romania, in spite of their limited value. If nothing else, the presence of the American Legation served several purposes. It was a source of information, a vehicle to monitor the effectiveness of American propaganda, a visible reminder that America was concerned about the welfare of the Romanian people, and a means to maintain contact with the Bucharest regime.[77] Therefore, while Washington was not ready to reestablish trade relations with Romania, it was equally unwilling to sever political relations.

Notes

1. Report, On the Implementation of U. S. Policies and Programs in the Economic Field Which May Affect the War Potential of the Soviet Bloc, April 23, 1952, p. 1,NSC Meeting No. 117, Box 217, NSC Meetings 116-120, April 30 - June 25, 1952, President's Secretary's Files, HST Library.

2. *FRUS, 1952-1954*, I, 914.

3. Adler-Karlsson, *Western Economic Warfare, 1947-1967*, p. 65.

4. *FRUS, 1952-1954*, I, 915-916.

5. Report, Review of Economic Defense Policy, May 25, 1953, p. 1, NSC 152/3, Box 5, Special Assistant NSC, White House Office, DDE Library.

6. Western Europe's reluctance to adopt American export controls was in part due to the fact that the United States had four different lists. List I had 260 listings and List II had 85, and COCOM agreed to control all of the items on these lists. List IA had 25 listings and IIB, 168, most of which COCOM refused to control. Each listing could contain hundreds of specific items, for example, list number 112 consisted of all "military electronic computing devices." U. S. Congress, *Mutual Defense Assistance Control Act of 1951*, Public Law 213, 82d Cong. 1st Sess., 1951, p. 713.

7. Report, Review of Economic Defense Policy, May 25, 1953, 29pp., NSC 152/3, Box 5, Special Assistant NSC, White House Office, DDE Library.

8. Report, On Economic Defense, July 31, 1953, p. 1, NSC 152/3, Box 5, Special Assistant NSC, White House Office, DDE Library.

9. *Ibid.*, p. 3.

10. *Ibid.*, p. 7.

11. *Ibid.*

12. Report, On Economic Defense, November 6, 1953, p. 4, NSC 152/3, Box 5, Special Assistant NSC, White House Office, DDE Library.

13. *FRUS, 1952-1954*, II, 89ff.

14. *Ibid.*, p. 152.

15. *Ibid.*, p. 125.

16. Gaddis, *Strategies of Containment*, p. 129.

17. Cecil V. Crabb, Jr. and Kevin V. Mulcahy, *Presidents and Foreign Policy Making From FDR To Reagan* (Baton Rouge: Louisiana State University, 1986), p. 161. The early years of the first Eisenhower administration were particularly rich in "fantastic" suggestions on how to roll back the Red tide in east-central Europe and in the Balkans. H. Freeman Matthews was a thirty year veteran of the State Department in 1953, and he later recorded one proposal suggested for the case of Albania. "When they first came in," Matthews told Richard McKinzie, "they had the idea you could roll back Communism by wishful thinking, or sending balloons over into Czechoslovakia, that sort of thing. They had to learn and it took a while. For instance, I received a visit from one of the younger men who came in and of whom I thought very highly – a good friend of mine – and he had been instructed to find out ways to roll back the Communists. It seemed that the best thing, the weakest link to the Communist curtain, was Albania. Therefore, we must get Albania into proper hands. He came to me and said, 'We're thinking of sending a battleship, a couple destroyers in near the harbor in the Adriatic and fire a few shots.'

And I said, 'Well, that isn't political warfare, that is active warfare. What is the demarkation line?

'Well,' he said, 'if the shots just landed in the water that would be political warfare; but if they landed in the country, that would be real warfare.'

I burst out laughing, I said, 'You'll have to do better than that if you expect to get any acquiescence from me.' But it was fantastic the ideas they would get.

(Oral interview of H. Freeman Matthews by Richad McKinzie, June 7, 1973, p. 34, HST Library

18. *FRUS, 1952-1954*, II, 325-326.

19. For a discussion of the point see, *FRUS 1952-1954*, II, 491-534.

20. *FRUS, 1952-1954*, II, 587.

21. *Ibid.*, p. 580.

22. *Ibid.*, p. 581. This emphasis on atomic weapons was a major change from past policy, including the policy formulated in the lastest NSC 153 series (Report, Restatement of Basic National Security Policy, June 10, 1953, 14pp., NSC 153/1, Box 5, Special Assistant NSC, White House Office,DDE Library.

23. Gaddis, *Strategies of Containment*, p. 159; John Newhouse, *War and Peace in the Nuclear Age* (New York: Alfred a. Knopf, 1989), p. 93.

24. *FRUS, 1952-1954*, II, 584-585.

25. *Ibid.*, p. 155.

26. *FRUS, 1952-1954*, VIII, 218-220.

27. *Ibid.*, p. 224.

28. Note by the Acting Executive Secretary to the National Security Council, United States Objectives and Actions to Exploit the Unrest in the Satellite States, June 29, 1953, p. 2, President's Papers 1953, Box 7, White House Office; Allen W. Dulles to Sherman Adams, August 6, 1954, encs., 11pp., File 116-1954, Box 571,Official Files, WHCF DDE Library. Labor Service Organizations eventually replaced the VFC. Membership consisted of refugees from the East European satellites and performed non-combat duties (*FRUS, 1952-1954*, VIII, 232ff).

29. Report, United States Policy Toward the Soviet Satellites in Eastern Europe, December 11, 1953, p. 5, NSC 174, Record Group 273 5W1, NSC,Policy Papers, DDE Library.

30. *Ibid.*, pp. 13-15.

31. *Ibid.*, p. 8.

32. *Ibid.*, p. 12.

33. *Ibid.*, pp. 19, 9.

34. *Ibid.*, pp. 32-33.

35. Telegram, Report on the First Six Months of 1952, June 27, 1952, p. 16, Box 4, Record Group 84, Foreign Service Posts of DOS, Bucharest legation, Misc. Records, 1952, National Archives.

36. Ministry of Foreign Affairs of the Rumanian People's Republic, *The Enemies of Peace and of the Peoples' Liberty: The Aggressive Policy and Machinations of American Imperialism Against The Rumanian People's Republic* (Bucharest, 1952), pp. 1-3.

37. *Ibid.*, p 38.

38. Telegram, February 8, 1952, File Misc. Cables, Jan-Feb 52, Box 3, Record Group 84, Foreign Service Posts of DOS, Bucharest legation, Misc. Records 1951-1952, National Archives.

39. Policy Review, April 17, 1952, 4pp.,File SW Economic Plans; IIA Plan for Rumania, Box 132, Record Group 84, Foreign Service Posts of DOS, Bucharest legation, National Archives.

40. "Against the Atrocities of American Imperialists," *Agerpres,*May 31, 1952, p. 2.

41. NYT, March 15, 1952, p. 3; March 19, 1952 p. 14; March 20, 1952, p. 28; CSM, March 15, 1952, p. 18; see also, Joseph Harrington and Bruce Courtney, "Romania's Changing Image: Bucharest and the American Press, 1952-1975," *The United States and Romania,* edited by Paul D. Quinlan.

42. NYT, March 1, 1952, p.3; May 29, 1952, p. 10.

43. Dispatch, April 30, 1952, 2 pp.,File 301 Rum-Israel Relations, Box 129, Record Group 84, Foreign Service Posts of DOS, Bucharest legation, National Archives.

44. NYT, October 8, 1953, p. 8;CSM, June 18, 1952, p. 1; October 3, 1953, p. 6.

45. Fischer-Galati, *The New Rumania*, pp. 41-42.

46. The first person purged from the party's Central Committee was Nicolae Radovanovici on January 24, 1950. See, Dispatch, Changes in Composition of

Central Committee of Rumanian Workers' Party, File 766.00/1-2850, Rumanian Internal Affairs, Decimal File, U.S. DOS 1950-1954, Record Group LM103 Reel No. 1, National Archives.

47. Fischer-Galati, *The New Rumania*, p. 37.

48. Stephen Fischer-Galati, "Rumania and the Sino-Soviet Conflict," *Eastern Europe in Transition*, ed. Kurt London (Baltimore: The Johns Hopkins Press, 1966), p. 263.

49. Fischer-Galati, *The New Rumania*, pp. 40-41.

50. Wolff, *The Balkans in Our Time*, pp. 468ff; Dispatch, Economic Conditions on the Eve of the Second Party Congress as Highlighted by the Sentencing of Vasile Luca, August 31, 1954, File 766.00/10-1354, Rumanian Internal Affairs, Decimal File 1950-1954, Record Group LM103 Reel No. 2, National Archives. In July, Pauker would step down as Foreign Minister.

51. "Report of the Delegation of the Rumanian Workers Party to the 22nd Congress of the C.P.S.U. Delivered by Gheorghe Gheorghiu-Dej at the Plenary Meeting of the C.C. of the R.W.P. Held Over November 30-December 5, 1961," *Agerpres*, December 10, 1961.

52. Fischer-Galati, *The New Rumania*, pp. 41-42; Fischer-Galati, *Twentieth Century Rumania*, pp. 123-125.

53. Kenneth Jowitt, *Revolutionary Breakthroughs and National Development: The Case of Romania, 1944-1965* (Berkeley: University of California Press, 1971), pp. 127ff.

54. Fischer-Galati, "Rumania and the Sino-Soviet Conflict," p. 264; Keefe *et al.*, *Romania, A Country Study*, p. 25; Matley, *Romania: A Profile*, p. 129. For a different view see, Vladimir Tismaneanu, "The Tragicomedy of Romanian Communism," *Eastern European Politics and Societies*, Vol. 3, No. 2 (Spring 1989), pp. 329ff.

55. "Celebration of Eighth Anniversary of Rumania's Liberation," *Agerpres*, August 30, 1952, pp. 1,4,9.

56. Translated transcripts, "Gheorghe Gheorghiu-Dej's Report on the Draft Constitution of the Rumanian People's Republic" [*Scinteia*, September 24, 1952], "The Constitution of the Roumanian People's Republic" [*Scinteia*, September 26, 1952], 38 pp., File Unarranged Misc. Sept-Nov 1952, Box 5, Record Group 84, Foreign Service Posts of DOS, Bucharest legation, Misc. Records, 1952-1953, National Archives. One of the eighteen was an "autonomous Magyar region," modelled on a Soviet device, the "autonomous oblast." This design enabled the Hungarians to retain their culture and customs and thereby reduced their animosity toward Bucharest (Wolff, *The Balkans in Our Time*, p. 452). The region's boundaries were redrawn in 1960 and renamed the Mures–Autonomous Magyar Region. In 1967, the Mures would be abolished.

57. Dispatch, Further Comments on Recent Political Developments in Rumania, June 21, 1952, File June-August 1952, Box 4, Record Group 84, Foreign Service Posts of DOS, Bucharest legation, Misc.Records 1952, National Archives.

58. Dispatch, Analysis Report for Battle Act Cases – Italy vis-a-vis Rumania, February 12, 1952, 9pp., File 466.659/4-1052. Box 2162, NND 862910, Record Group 59, National Archives.

59. Following the release of the Italian Legation officer in Bucharest, the Italian Legation promised its American counterpart that it would inform Rome as to the, "the necessity of preventing further occurrences" of such shipments (Memorandum of Conversation, Battle Act Exception for Italian Shipment to Rumania, June 13, 1952, p. 2, File 466.659/6-1352, Box 2162, NND862910, Record Group 59, National Archives).

60. Telegram, Issue of *Rumanian Foreign Trade*, February 27, 1952, p. 1, File Telegrams - February 1952, Box 3, Record Group 84, Foreign Service Posts of DOS, Bucharest legation, Misc. Records 1951-1952, National Archives.

61. Dispatch, Transmission of "Rumanian Foreign Trade," December 24, 1952, p. 1., File 40.66/12-2452, Box 1787, Decimal File 1950-1954, DOS, National Archives.

62. Dispatch, Reactions of Western Representatives in Bucharest to Rumanian Foreign Trade Propaganda, May 7, 1952, 2pp., File 466.00/5-752, Box 2162, NND862910, Record Group 59, National Archives.

63. Telegram, [Information from Trieste on Bucharest], November 12, 1952, 1p., File 611.66/11-1252, Box 2342, NND832920, Record Group 59, National Archives.

64. Telegram, November 20, 1952, 1p., File 611.66/11-2052, Box 2342, NND832920, Record Group 59, National Archives.

65. [Nikita Khrushchev] *Khurshchev Remembers: The Last Testament*, Translated and edited by Strobe Talbott (Boston: Little, Brown & Co., 1974), pp. 227-229. This conversation later acquired the look of a turn in the road of Romanian independence of Moscow; some Romanians, in fact, made false claims to having "been there." Summerscale places Bodnaras in Moscow, for example, and Pacepa, in his polemic, denies Ceausescu's version in which he, not Gheorghiu-Dej, was the patriot who put the question of troop withdrawal to Khrushchev (Peter Summerscale, *The East European Predicament: Changing Patterns in Poland, Czechoslovakia and Romania* [London: Gower for Royal Institute of International Affairs, 1982], p. 20; Ion Mihai Pacepa, *Red Horizons: Chronicles of a Communist Spy Chief* [Washington, D.C.: Regnery Gateway, 1987], p. 255-257).

66. Daniel Norman, "'New Course' in Rumanian Agriculture," *Problems of Communism*, Vol. IV, No. 4 (July-August 1955), p., 36; Montias, *Economic Development in Communist Rumania*, p. 40; Godfrey Lias, "Satellite States in the Post-Stalin Era," *International Affairs*, Vol. 30, No. 1 (January 1954), p. 45.

67. Montias, *Economic Development in Communist Rumania*, p. 41; Wolff, *The Balkans in Our Time*, p. 504.

68. Fischer-Galati, *Twentieth Century Rumania*, pp. 129ff.

69. "At the Bookshop Windows," *Agerpres*, October 15, 1952, p. 5.

70. Fischer-Galati, *The New Rumania*, p. 53.

71. Memorandum, Distribution of a U.S. Publication in Rumania, April 16,

1953, 3pp., Box 133, Record Group 84, Foreign Service Posts of DOS, Bucharest legation, General Records 1953-1955, National Archives; DOS to Bucharest, June 29, 1953, 3 pp., File 125.1-125.3, Box 133, Record Group 84, Foreign Service Posts of DOS, Bucharest legation, General Records 1953-1955, National Archives; Authors' interview with Ambassador Corneliu Bogdan, March 19, 1987, New York City.

72. House Committee on Foreign Affairs, *U.S. Foreign Policy and the East-West Confrontation*, 1980, pp. 522-523.

73. NYT, August 16, 1953, p. 5.

74. Dispatch, Transshipment of 100 Jeeps from the United States to Rumania, November 5, 1953, 4pp., File 466,119/11-553, Box 2162, NND862910, Record Group 59, National Archives.

75. "Trial of a Group of Spies and Terrorists Parachuted by the American Espionage Service," *Agerpres*, October 13, 1953, p. 9.

76. Dispatch, DOS to Bucharest, November 2, 1953, File 350 Political Affairs - Rumania, pp. 1-3, Box 134, Record Group 84, Foreign Service Posts of DOS, Bucharest legation, General Records 1953-1955, National Archives.

77. Report, United States Policy Toward the Soviet Satellites in Eastern Europe, December 11, 1953, p. 18, File NSC 174 Policy toward East Europe, Office for Special Assistant for NSC, White House Office, DDE Library.

CHAPTER VI

THE MIRROR EFFECT: A SOVIET-AMERICAN THAW PRODUCES BUCHAREST-WASHINGTON TALKS

Commission on Foreign Economic Policy

During its first year, the Eisenhower Administration had certainly defined its foreign policy toward the Soviet Bloc. NSC 152/3 relaxed export controls, NSC 162/2 established the New Look and NSC 174 called for disrupting Soviet-satellite relations. In addition, both the President and Congress tried to determine which agency or department was responsible for American foreign economic policy. With encouragment from the White House, Congress passed Public Law 215 on August 7, 1953, which established a Commission on Foreign Economic Policy. Eisenhower appointed Clarence B. Randall, head of the giant Inland Steel Company, chair of the Commission.[1]

East-West trade was among the issues the Commission had to address. Randall noted that one of the major problems was the inability of government officials to view the Soviet Union objectively. McCarthyism frightened everyone. Randall concluded that the people who compiled the Battle Act lists of strategic materials believed it was "much safer politically to say that an item could not be shipped, than to take the responsibility for letting normal trade develop."[2] This prejudice existed even among Commission members, including his Vice Chairman, Lamar Fleming. On December 12, Randall wrote Fleming noting that his latest draft on East-West trade was focused entirely on using trade for its psychological advantage in penetrating the Iron Curtain. He chided that nothing was mentioned about the historical importance and signficance of East-West trade to many of America's allies.[3] Randall wanted to increase East-West trade, and worked diligently for five months to convince his colleagues that increased trade was beneficial to the free world.[4]

On January 23, 1954, the Commission presented its report to the President and to Congress. The nearly 100 page document contained four pages on East-West trade. The report noted the historical importance of East-West trade to America's West European allies. Further, the report recognized that the post-war Western trade restrictions had "weakened the economies of friendly countries and increased their need for our aid." Therefore, the Commission recommended that so far as could be done without jeopardizing military security, the United States should "acquiesce in more trade in peaceful goods between Western Europe and the Soviet Bloc." Finally, the Commission offered the hope that "more trade in goods for peaceful purposes would in itself serve to penetrate the Iron Curtain and advance the day when normal relationships with the peoples of Eastern Europe" could be resumed.[5]

The United States and the Consultative Group(CG) Nations

While the report stirred criticism from the Defense Department,[6] it was well received in Western Europe. The COCOM countries endorsed Randall's call for a more flexible trade posture in Washington for a number of reasons. First, American aid had dramatically declined in recent years. In 1950, Washington provided France with $700 million in foreign assistance funds, Germany with $733 million, Italy with $401 million and the United Kingdom with $955 million. However, by the end of 1952 those figures had dropped to $262 million for France, $107 million for Germany, $170 million for Italy, and $350 for the United Kingdom.[7] Second, the European Recovery Program had worked, and Western Europe's productivity had increased sufficiently to need more export markets. Third, the United States was in the middle of a mild recession following the cease fire in Korea, and this produced fears in Western Europe of a decline in trans-Atlantic trade. Fourth, the Soviet "peace offensive" along with Malenkov's efforts to stimulate East-West trade had won some supporters.[8] Fifth, Europe realized that the United States would not implement the sanctions prescribed in the Battle Act for trade with Eastern Europe. The President had made twice the number of exceptions for Battle Act trade violations in 1953 than in 1952. In fact, by 1954, Washington had not imposed sanctions on any country violating the Battle Act.[9] Sixth, West Europe was aware that there was a growing market for consumer products in Eastern Europe, especially in the areas of woolen clothing and shoes.[10] And seventh, the existence of COCOM was no longer a secret, and a number of newspapers in 1953 had noted the existence of export control lists. On November 12, 1953, the President of the Board of Trade in the United Kingdom made the first public announcement of COCOM to the British Parliament, but noted that the group was an informal consulative body without executive power.[11]

There was also some interest in the United States to expand trade with the Soviet Bloc. NSC 152/3 had called for a gradual and moderate relaxation of controls toward the Bloc. Washington was especially eager to get rid of its huge agricultural surplus and saw Eastern Europe as a perfect market. However, the American public learned of Washington's efforts to sell surplus butter and cottonseed oil to the Soviet Bloc at prices below what the American consumer paid. Therefore on February 10, 1954, the Cabinet decided to deny export licenses for cash sales of United States Government owned surplus agricultural goods.[12] Nonetheless, the United States did not close the door on the possibility of barter. This was quickly noted in West European capitals. On February 25, the British Prime Minister, Winston Churchill, called for a substantial increase in East-West trade. Further, he demanded that there be a "substantial relaxation of the regulations" affecting manufactured goods and raw materials. The Prime Minster further announced that his government was willing to examine the strategic lists with his "American friends."[13]

The cat was out of the bag. In early March, Churchill formally notified Washington as to the degree of the "substantial relaxation" Britain anticipated. France soon joined Britain in calling for major changes in the COCOM lists.[14] Initial discussions quickly bogged down over the issue of equipment and raw materials that were not used directly in the manufacture of munitions, but which still had an indirect and potential impact on the military capabilities of the Sovet Bloc. The United States pressed the issue of security, while Britain focused on lost trade opportunities. As criticism of America's position mounted in the House of Commons, Washington agreed to a tripartite meeting in London. Harold Stassen, the Battle Act Director joined Peter Thorneycroft of

Great Britain and Maurice Schumann of France for a two day conference on March 29-30, 1954.[15]

In preparation for the meeting, Washington considered the implications of relaxing trade with the Soviet Bloc. The National Intelligence Estimate of March 16 concluded that any anticipated modifications of export controls would "not greatly advance the rate of growth of the Bloc's military potential," nor would it "significantly affect the political cohesion" of the Bloc.[16] On March 29 Stassen arrived in London. At the outset, the negotiations were difficult. Thorneycroft demanded rapid and drastic decreases in controls. However, due to the intervention of Churchill and Foreign Secretary Eden, the impasse was solved. The British withdrew their demand and called for a rapid and orderly review of the items on the COCOM, or International Lists. Churchill noted that the the leftist Labor party wanted more trade with the Soviet Union as did the Conservative party businessmen.[17] On March 30, the three governments issued a joint communique announcing that the 15 members of the Consultative Group should meet and review each item on the International List to determine those that were genuinely strategic.[18] On April 2, Stassen presented a summary of the meeting to the NSC. The Council supported Stassen and agreed that the United States had to accept a relaxation of controls on less strategic items.[19] The CG met on April 13-14 for the first time in eleven months. The members agreed to make a comprehensive review of all goods on the three IL lists, embargo, quantitative control and surveillance, with the aim of substantially reducing the number of controlled items.[20]

The COCOM review process forced the NSC to reconsider America's export control policy embodied in NSC 152/3. On June 11, the NSC agreed that the COCOM meetings had produced a new criterion with which to determine an item's exportability. While the United States used the "war potential" of an item, the other nations used its "military capability" as the criterion.[21] As a result, the West European countries had a much shorter list of embargoed items than did the United States. The NSC faced a choice. It could restructure America's export control policy to resemble COCOM policy, and allow American businessmen to sell items considered strategic by the "war potential" standard of NSC 152/3. Or the NSC could maintain the current American export control policy, and handicap American businessmen in their global competition for export markets.[22]

In considering solutions to the dilemna, the NSC favored maintaining controls over all commodities considered strategic by COCOM, and additional items which the United States alone produced and considered as contributing to the "war potential" of the Soviet Bloc.[23] On June 18 the NSC resumed discussion on export controls. Eisenhower was opposed to establishing any policy that the United States could not enforce. He believed that America should make concessions "to allow our allies to make a living. But beyond that, the United States itself does not want to make profits out of commerce with the Soviet Bloc."[24]

Further discussion produced consensus. The NSC agreed to amend its policy. America would decontrol a substantial number of items which were already freely traded by Western Europe which Washington had formerly embargoed because of their "war potential."[25]

Meanwhile, the COCOM discussions had produced agreement. On July 21, the same day that delegates met in Geneva to sign a cease-fire for Indochina, the CG agreed to put revised COCOM control lists into effect beginning August 16. There were no changes made in prohibiting the exports of munitions or atomic energy items. However, the International Lists of embargoed items, quantitative controls and surveillance were significantly reduced by more than 50%.[26]

The magnitude of these reductions, forced the United States to revise its Battle Act lists. On August 25, Washington announced new lists. Title I, replaced the 1 and 1A lists, and reduced the number of embargoed item categories from 297 to 217. The Title II list, formerly I-B, was reduced and made similiar to the COCOM quantitative and surveillance lists. Several days later, Commerce Department Secretary Weeks announced that in spite of the revision, America's lists were still more extensive than COCOM's since Washington controlled some strategic items made solely in the United States.[27] What the Secretary did not elaborate upon was that all American exports to the Soviet Bloc still required export licenses. And, that this licensing procedure remained largely at the discretion of the Commerce Department, which was notorious for its restrictive practices.

The Council on Foreign Economic Policy (CFEP)

While the NSC had come to a decision in June, it had not done so easily. There was a wide range of opinion within the Administration. The State, Commerce and Defense Departments held strikingly disparate views on East-West trade forcing endless debate among government leaders. The COCOM review reminded the President of this problem, and on July 12 he asked Rowland Hughes, Director of the

Bureau Of the Budget and Nelson Rockefeller, Chairman of the President's Advisory Committee on Government Organization, to make recommendations concerning the machinery needed to implement an effective foreign economic policy.[28] Hughes and Rockefeller recommended that Joseph Dodge, former Director of the Bureau of the Budget, make the actual study. Dodge agreed and after three months of work submitted his final report to the President recommending the creation of a White House staff organization devoted exclusively to developing foreign economic policy.

Eisenhower accepted the recommendation and asked Dodge to stay on and organize the committee. He agreed and on December 11, 1954, the President appointed Dodge Chairman of the Council on Foreign Economic Policy, or the CFEP. Members of the Council included representatives from the Departments of State, Treasury, Commerce and Agriculture, the Director of the Foreign Operations Administration, the President's Administrative Assistant for Economic Affairs, the Presidents National Security Affairs Advisor and a member of the Council of Economic Advisers.[29]

Following its organizational meeting on December 22, 1954, the CFEP met at least once every two weeks commencing January 4, 1955. One of the major issues of controversy was East-West trade. On January 20, the Council identified the problem: the exportability of dual purpose items, those which had both military and civilian uses, unlike munitions and weapons. This problem produced nearly irreconcilable views as to the purpose of increasing East-West trade.[30] To complicate the issue, there was not only the COCOM lists, but there were CHINCOM lists. The CG had established a China Committee, or CHINCOM, to consider export controls for Communist China.[31] The COCOM revision did not reduce the CHINCOM controls and consequently, there was a fear among some of the CFEP members that dual use items shipped to the Soviet Bloc could arrive in Beijing or Hanoi. Therefore the CFEP initially accepted the concept of the "bloc-as-a-whole," thereby preventing it from singling single out a particular East European satellite state for special treatment.[32] In April, 1955, the CFEP agreed to maintain the recommendations in NSC 152/3.[33] In January, 1956, Congress accepted a Foreign Economic Policy report that recommended no change in America's export control policy.[34] A month later, Eisenhower and Prime Minister Eden of Great Britain issued a joint statement indicating that export controls should be maintained, but periodically reviewed.[35]

As the months passed, Dodge indicated that he would like to return to the private sector. He had not anticipated the amount of time involved in overseeing the work of the CFEP. The President accepted his resignation in June, 1956, and appointed Clarence Randall as the new Chairman of the CFEP.[36] Randall was familiar with America's foreign economic policy. At his first meeting as Chairman, he told the CFEP to initiate a new review of East-West trade with an eye to relaxing export controls.[37]

Security and Trade

The gradual relaxation of export controls was made possible by America's changing self image. The New Look policy resulted from a feeling of security. America was no longer frightened by the specter of a Soviet attack as she had been in the early 1950s. In fact, when Secretary of State Dulles revealed the new policy at the National Press Club in Washington, D.C. on December 22, 1953, he called it a doctrine of "massive retaliation."[38] America would defend herself and her allies with massive nuclear power. Dulles did not mean that America would take the offensive. To the contrary, "massive retaliation" was a policy for peace. Since any military conflict initiated by the Soviets would result in the destruction of the Soviet Union, Moscow would be deterred from aggression.

NSC 162/2, or the New Look, remained America's basic security policy until January 7, 1955, when President Eisenhower adopted NSC 5501.[39] This policy was originally drafted in December,[40] and like its predecessor, was founded on America's confidence in her own strength. However, the policy did recognize that continued Soviet atomic missile development over the next several years would, by the early 1960s, provide Moscow the means to deliver a massive nuclear strike to American soil. NSC 5501 foresaw that the result of total war in the forthcoming intercontinental ballistic missile age "would bring about such extensive destruction as to threaten the survival of both Western civilization and the Soviet system." Washington predicted that nuclear parity would produce nuclear deterrence, and NSC 5501 anticipated what later became known as mutual assured destruction, or MAD. The result was that Washington had to seek greater flexibility in its response to Soviet aggression. As for Eastern Europe, NSC 5501 saw no reduction in Soviet control. The new policy continued the view of its predecessor: through a flexible combination of military, political, and economic instruments coupled with propaganda and covert actions, the United States could develop rifts between the satellite states and Moscow.[41]

NSC 5501 was a watershed.[42] It was the last time American policy focused on the view that the world consisted of two irreconcilable hostile camps. The Soviets mounted a peace offensive to alter its world image. This movement included reconciliation with Yugoslavia, a peace treaty with Austria, an offer to dismantle NATO and the newly formed Warsaw Pact, and Nikita Khrushchev's participation in the Geneva summit meeting with representatives from Britain, France and the United States, the first such gathering since Yalta. Soviet efforts were successful and America's West European allies demanded greater contact with Eastern Europe.[43]

As a result, when the NSC reviewed its basic national security policy in March, 1956, it called for a change. The new policy, NSC 5602/1, retained most of the language of its predecessor, but called for the United States to "sponsor proposals for a select expansion of free world-Communist bloc contacts." While one of the purposes was to gain greater information about the satellite states, the process involved reducing trade barriers for peaceful purposes. Further, the new policy urged the United States and its allies to be ready to establish reciprocal concessions with Moscow and Eastern Europe, provided that such contacts did not reduce the security of the free world.[44] NSC 5602/1 pointed to Washington's later acceptance of peaceful coexistence as the basis of East-West relations.

Eastern Europe

This change in America's basic national security policy did not produce change in Washington's policy toward the East European satellites. The first review of NSC 174 in July, 1954, indicated some major implementation problems. The long range goal of the policy, and all American policies toward Eastern Europe, was to restore freedom to the satellites. Short term objectives, included support to nationalist movements, and the disruption of Soviet-satellite relations. However, the Soviets had effectively frustrated Washington's efforts to implement either set of goals. Since NSC 174 prohibited the use of any means that could lead to war, the United States had relied, to a large measure, on covert operations. But these too failed. The satellites had intensified their border patrols, effectively jammed Voice of America and Radio Free Europe broadcasts, and tightened internal police controls. As a result, Washington had made little headway in implementing the policy objectives.[45] However, lacking any attractive alternatives, the NSC made no recommenations to change NSC 174.

However, no change did not mean no action. During much of the next year, the White House focused on the upcoming Geneva summit meeting as an means to influence developments in the satellites. The Senate Foreign Relations Committee held hearings in June, 1955, on the same issue and resolved that Communist domination in the satellite states should be an agenda item at the July 18 summit.[46] At the same time, Nelson Rockefeller, Special Assistant to the President, appointed a task force of academicians and businessmen to explore the available means of exploiting Communist Bloc vulnerability. The 11 member panel met at Quantico, Virginia, under the chairmanship of Walter Rostow from June 5-10. Their report indicated that the United States enjoyed a significant, but transitory period of overall strength vis-a-vis the Soviet Union.[47] Consequently, Washington should move quickly to capitalize on this position. The panel suggested that at Geneva, the United States should make a series of proposals calling for a greater exchange of persons, information and goods between East and West.[48] On July 11, the NSC urged the Administration to use the summit as a means to publicly call attention to the need for greater freedom in the satellites. America should demand Soviet withdrawal of troops from Hungary and Romania. These forces were no longer needed to maintain "lines of communication" with troops in the Soviet occupation zone in Austria in light of the peace treaty signed with Vienna on May 14, 1955. [49]

On July 18 representatives from Britain, France, the United States and the Soviet Union met in Geneva. The Soviets were not about to permit the Western delegates to use the issue of the satellites for propaganda. The Communist negotiators refused to discuss the issue as an agenda item. The Soviets were far more interested in German reunification and this became the focus of the summit. The satellite issue was included in statements by the United States, but only discussed with the Soviets in informal sessions, without success.[50]

This failure was clearly noted at the NSC's February 29, 1956, meeting which reviewed the progress of NSC 174. While there was more optimism expressed in the effectiveness of the broadcasts of Radio Free Europe and the Voice of America, NSC members were ready to revise the policy. NSC 174 did not sufficiently emphasize the differences among the satellite states and the February review called for a new policy "with specific adaptations" for each of the countries.[51] In March the President concurred and called for a revision of NSC 174.[52]

After four months of work, the National Security Council adopted NSC 5608/1 on July 18, 1956. The new policy reasserted America's long range goal of freeing the satellite states from Soviet control. However, the document also responded to recent developments in the Soviet Bloc. Khrushchev's reconciliation with Tito meant that Moscow accepted "different paths to Socialism." This view was reinforced at the historic 20th Party Congress held in Moscow from February 14-25, 1956. Khrushchev attacked Stalin for his "crimes" and "cult of personality." The United States wanted to take advantage of this new spirit of moderation. Moscow's apparent acceptance of many paths to socialism permitted some innovation in the satellite states, and the NSC wanted to use this new development to promote independence and nationalism in Eastern Europe.[53] NSC 5608/1 urged the Administration to seek new legislation through Congress "to provide the flexibility required to utilize increased trade [with Eastern Europe] as an incentive to promote the objectives of U.S. policy toward the satellites." NSC 5601/1 expressed frustration with "legislative restrictions" which denied all Soviet Bloc nations most-favored-nation treatment and which did not "permit individual treatment" to each East European nation "as circumstances may warrant."[54]

The NSC analyzed the degree to which American activities could help each satellite gain independence from Moscow. Romania was viewed as the least likely, for while Romania's cultural heritage was oriented toward the West, and while her people harbored a tradition of "Russophobia," there was no popular movement for change that could not easily be destroyed by the police.[55] On the other hand, Romania was "pressing the United States in an unprecedented manner for trade development as well as for increased cultural exchanges."[56] NSC 5608/1 cautioned that these efforts undoubtedly had the approval of Moscow, but urged Washington to treat them as opportunities for exploitation. In the final analysis, however, Romania still retained its image of being the "most Sovietized" of all the satellite states. Consequently, the NSC held out little hope for change in Romania.[57]

America and Romania, 1954-1956

As could be expected, American-Romanian relations from 1954 to 1956 reflected Washington's changing attitude toward East-West trade and the Soviet Bloc. However, Bucharest-Washington relations would prove far more productive than anticipated by the NSC. Throughout most of 1954 and 1955, the American press continued to print stories depicting Romania in negative tones.[58] Foremost among these stories was the Georgescu affair. At the close of World War II, Mr. Georgescu, an official of the Standard Oil Company, and his wife were visiting the United States. When they tried to return to Romania to join their two sons, the Romanian government refused them entry. Over the years, the Georgescus sought the release of their children, who lived with their grandmother. In May, 1953, Christache Zambeti, the first Secretary of the Romanian Legation in Washington offered Mr. Georgescu a deal. If he would spy for the Romanian government in Washington, Bucharest would release his two sons. Georgescu notified the State Department, and on May 27, 1953 the United States expelled Zambeti.[59] Two weeks later, Georgescu wrote to Eisenhower explaining that he would not turn against the United States, his adopted homeland, even to secure the release of his two sons. However, he would be most appreciative if the President could intercede. World press had called attention to the Romanian calumny, and Georgescu believed that Bucharest could be induced to release his children.[60]

Various groups gave public support to Georgescu including the City Council of the City of New York which passed a resolution in June, noting the courage of the Georgescus and urging the President to do everything in his power to have the boys released. The Voice of America frequently carried reports on the story and entrusted the safety of the boys to the Romanian people.[61] After a year of negotiations, Bucharest released the two boys, Constantin, age 20, and Peter, age 15. They met their father in Munich and together they returned to meet their mother in New York on April 13, 1954.[62] On May 1, the Georgescus visited the White House to personally thank the President accompanied by a horde of reporters and photographers.[63]

The press carried many other stories about Romania, including reports of human rights violations, accounts of Jewish persecution, and interviews with defectors.[64] However, the most bizarre account appeared in the New York Times on May 8, 1954. The House Committee on Communist Aggression had begun hearings concerning the Soviet seizure of power in Romania. The purpose was to gather documentation for presentation to the United Nations concerning human rights violations.[65] The Romanian Princess Ileana, sister of the late King Carol, testified that "the faith of Romanians in liberation is so great that during a severe snow storm last winter, a rumor was widespread that the oversized snow flakes were the result of United States scientific experiments that would eventually paralyze the Communist regime."[66]

Gheorghiu-Dej was the principal architect of improved American-Romanian relations in the mid-1950s. The Romanian leader's desire to promote national Communism in Romanian occurred coincidentally with Washington's interest in pursuing a more flexible policy toward Eastern Europe. Gheorghiu-Dej recognized the coincidence and knew that improved relations with the United States could help him secure a degree of independence from Moscow.

Although Gheorghiu-Dej followed Moscow's lead in adopting a "New Course" policy in August 1953, he did not intend to mirror Moscow. He indicated this through a series of small overtures to the West in the Fall of 1953. Gheorghiu-Dej permitted Western newspapermen greater access to Romania, and he relaxed travel restrictions on Western diplomats permitting them to travel up to 20 miles outside the city limits of Bucharest.[67] On February 14, 1954, he announced that the principles agreed to by Beijing and Moscow concerning their future relationship should become the basic principles for all intra-socialist state relationships. Gheorghiu-Dej especially endorsed the principle of "complete equality of rights, mutual respect of national interests, [and] a common desire for peace."[68] The following month Bucharest opened discussions with Moscow to end the Sovroms. On March 31, both countries signed the first of two secret treaties which would close 14 of the 16 Sovroms by the end of the year.

During the Spring, Moscow urged the satellites to adopt a collective leadership model which Gheorghiu-Dej reluctantly accepted. He knew that he was not in total control of the Romanian Workers' Party. In addition, the Soviets appeared willing to rehabilitate leaders earlier purged. Gheorghiu-Dej was especially concerned that such rehabilitation could reinstate Lucretiu Patrascanu, imprisoned since 1948. Consequently, in April, Gheorghiu-Dej had Patrascanu executed.[69] Several days later he stepped down as Secretary-General of the Party, and appointed his old friend Gheorghe Apostol as First Secretary and Nicolae Ceausescu, Mihai Dalea and Ianos Fazekas as secretaries. Ceausescu, a protege of Gheorghiu-Dej, became a candidate-member of the Politburo along with the Minister of Internal Affairs, Alexandru Draghici.[70] While Gheorghiu-Dej accepted Moscow's collective leader ship, he did not intend to have it mean that he would lose control of Romania.

Continuing his drive to make Bucharest more independent of Moscow, Gheorghiu-Dej embraced Beijing's recent Sino-Indian trade and travel agreement which included a pledge of non-aggression in the form of the "Five Principles of Peaceful Coexistence." These included mutual respect for each other's territorial integrity and sovereignty, mutual non-aggression, mutual noninterference in each other's internal affairs, equality and mutual benefit and peaceful coexistence.[71] Gheorghiu-Dej saw these principles as ideal for his present goals and heralded them as a basis for Romania's relations with Communist and non-Communist countries.

On August 23, at the tenth anniversary of Romania's liberation, Gheorghiu-Dej continued his move toward nationalist Communism. For the first time, Romania did not give the Soviet Union the lion's share of the credit for liberating Romania. Rather, Gheorghiu-Dej announced that the Fascists were ousted by the "patriotic forces led by the Romanian Communist Party." Moscow's role in the liberation was limited to the Soviet offensive against Iasi, which created the opportunity for the Romanian Communist Party to defeat the German Fascists.[72]

Three weeks later, Gheorghiu-Dej signed a second treaty with Moscow which confirmed the fact that all but two of the Sovroms would close at the end of the year.[73] In November, Apostol, the new First Secretary of the Party, noted that the dissolution of the Sovroms conformed to Moscow's support of peaceful coexistence, especially with respect to the principles of equality of rights and non-interference in the internal affairs of other countries.[74]

Meanwhile, reports from Shantz at the American Legation in Bucharest coupled with Gheorghiu-Dej's pubic announcements, forced Washington to reassess its view toward Romania. Without question, Gheorghiu-Dej was trying to open trade initiatives with the West. He had contacted the British early in 1954 about opening talks to resolve outstanding claims issues.[75] However, the British were reluctant to respond until they completed the COCOM revisions. Gheorghiu-Dej made similar overtures to Washington, but received no response. In August, he used the occasion of the 10th anniversary of Romania's liberation to call for expanded trade with the West. He also appealed to Western countries to abolish their export control policies.[76]

Washington slowly responded. In July, 1954, the United States established the Foreign Claims Settlement Commission which replaced both the War Claims Commission and the International Claims Commission. The new Commission was designed to resolve claims for property and other losses of American nationals in Communist countries.[77] In December, London notified the State Department that Britain had agreed to open talks with the Romanians to resolve outstanding financial issues including claims stemming from Bucharest's 1948 nationalization decrees.[78]

On February 9, 1955, the Supreme Soviet of the U.S.S.R announced that Moscow would adhere to the principles of equality, non-intervention in the internal affairs of other nations, and respect for the territorial integrity, independence and sovereignty of other states. Within two weeks, Gheorghiu-Dej enthusiastically endorsed the Soviet declaration.[79] Peaceful coexistence and the principle of non-interference became the slogans of the Communist world, and were even embraced in Bandung, Java, at the Afro-Asian People's Solidarity Conference in April, 1955. Bucharest continued to watch Moscow's peace offensive with an eye to using Soviet actions to further Gheorghiu-Dej's goals. In May, the new Soviet team of Party Secretary, Nikita Khrushchev and Prime Minister Nikolai Bulganin, who replaced Malenkov on February 8, 1955, visited Belgrade, Yugoslavia to seek reconciliation with Tito. Khrushchev surprised his Yugoslavian audience when he unexpectedly declared that the blame for the Soviet-Yugoslavian break rested on Lavrenty Beria, former head of the Soviet secret police. Yugoslavia had never left the fold of Marxist-Leninism, so there was no reason for further disagreement between the two states.[80] Khrushchev's endorsement of socialist pluralism encouraged Gheorghiu-Dej ito continue his pursuit of a Romanian road to socialism.

Gheorghiu-Dej's behavior had not passed unnoticed in Moscow. Khrushchev did not like Gheorghiu-Dej. The Romanian was nothing but a Stalinist who supported China's efforts to challenge Soviet control of the world Communist movement, especially in Africa and Asia. The Soviet Party leader visited Romania on the occasion of the eleventh anniversary of Romania's liberation from Fascism. While it is unclear as to whether Khrushchev intended to try to replace Gheorghiu-Dej, it is known that the Soviet leader insisted on keeping a division of function between the party and the state to prevent Gheorghiu-Dej from having too much power. Gheorghiu-Dej defiantly struck back. He quickly defended the inalienability of the sovereign rights of all nations regardless of their socioeconomic or political organization.[81] Amidst the festivities honoring Soviet-Romanian friendship month,[82] the Romanian leader announced in October that he would assume the position of First Secretary of the Party. He then removed the pro-Moscow Miron Constantinescu as head of the State Planning Commission and appointed Chivu Stoica, his staunchest ally, as Premier.[83]

Meanwhile, the United States began to process Romanian claims, the bulk of which originated from war damage and nationalization decrees.[84] The President had authorized that the assets previously vested under the Trading with the Enemy Act could be used to pay the claimants.[85] There were over 1,000 claimants with requests in excess of $60 million. Since Romania's frozen assets totaled only about $20 million, the claims settlement process would take nearly five years.

In October, Romania again indicated that she wanted to open talks with the United States.[86] The American Legation notified the State Department that it should expect requests from Romania for technical assistance especially in the area of agriculture. The Legation also reported an increase in the number of requests from American citizens and firms to do business with Bucharest.[87] In November, Eisenhower appointed Robert Thayer as America's new minister to Bucharest replacing Shantz. Thayer was personally committed to increasing Romanian-American contacts in the hope of "driving a wedge between the Romanians and the Soviets."[88] Thayer believed that the Romanians wanted to "get out from under [the Soviet Union], but they needed some help from us in the way of business, trade. . . because they're now completely dependent on the Soviets."[89] Gheorghiu-Dej could not have agreed more. However, not all officials in Washington shared Thayer's enthusiasm. Gheorghiu-Dej's defiance to Moscow was not recognized in Washington. Many State Department officials were still locked into the Cold War view of Romania's complete subordination to Moscow. All events in Bucharest were thought to be directed from the Kremlin. A common line of thinking was "we just gotta hold these fellows down and contain them, and any sign of letting up is going to hurt."[90]

Nonetheless, Thayer's persistence and events in Bucharest gradually had their effect in Washington. In November, 1955, the first delegation from the Romanian Peoples' Republic arrived in the United States. The three men, Dr. Virgio Gligor, who was the Deputy Minister of Agriculture, along with Professor Grigore Obrejeanu and Silviu Brucan came at the behest of Roswell Garst of Garst and Thomas Hybrid Corn Company. Garst had visited the Soviet Union and Romania and invited each country to send representatives to his plant to purchase corn.[91]

The officials liked what they saw, and later Bucharest purchased hybrid corn from the company.

Increased demand for trade and normalization of relations were not the only sources of Romanian pressure on the United States. Bucharest still wanted membership in the United Nations and the Soviet peace offensive called for the inclusion of five satellite states into the peace-keeping body. The Cold War had divided the world into two camps, and since the United States controlled most of the votes in the United Nations, Washington saw no reason to extend membership to Moscow's allies. Through the use of the Security Council veto, the United States and the Soviet Union had prohibited any new state from joining since 1950. However, the Soviet's New Course had won supporters, and even America's Western allies conceded that the two superpowers should accord membership to the nearly 20 nations whose membership applications had been repeatedly denied. Feeling pressure from Moscow as well as from Paris and London, America reviewed her United Nations membership policy in March, 1955.

Since the end of World War II, the United States had maintained that the Soviet satellite states did not meet the qualifications of Article 4 of the UN Charter which required new members to be able to carry out their obligations as independent peace-loving states. Washington had consistently argued that the satellite states lacked independence of action.[92] The recent Ninth Session of the General Assembly asked the Security Council to reconsider the pending applications and make positive recommendations to the next session of the General Assembly.[93] In April, 1955, the United States began to discuss a "package" deal with the Soviets. Moscow had earlier offered to admit 14 countries to the United Nations including Austria, Ceylon, Finland, Ireland, Italy, Jordan, Libya, Nepal, Portugal and their five satellite states: Albania, Bulgaria, Hungary, Romania, and the Mongolian People's Republic. However, the United States wanted Japan included and the Mongolian People's Republic excluded due to Washington's support of Chiang Kai-Shek's claim that Mongolia was part of China.[94]

Soviet opposition to the inclusion of Japan, and America's refusal to accept the Mongolian People's Republic stalled all hopes of a "package" deal. The upcoming Geneva summit further delayed American-Soviet efforts in the United Nations since both saw the summit as means of resolving the impasse.[95] However, the summit provided no solutions. The matter was again the sole province of the UN, but since the Spring, a new climate of opinion had developed. The Bandung Conference, the

San Francisco Commemorative Meetings in honor of the 10th anniversary of the United Nations, and the "spirit" of the Geneva summit provided an atmosphere of compromise, and the Secretary General of the United Nations, Dag Hammarskjold, wanted the membership issue resolved at the 10th Session of the General Assembly.[96]

In late September, 1955, the Vice Chairman of the Soviet Delegation to the United Nations, Vasili Kuznetsov, remarked to the American representative, Henry Cabot Lodge, that he had a new membership "package" involving 16 of the new applicants, which now numbered 22. The Soviets would not support membership applications from Japan, Spain, North Korea, South Korea, North Vietnam and South Vietnam.[97] Kuznetsov's offer, and the overwhelming desire of most members of the General Assembly to increase membership in the United Nations forced Washington to resume the membership negotiations. By November, the United States agreed to accept 17 new members including the four East European satellite states, and Japan, but excluding the Mongolian People's Republic. Aware that the American Congress would object to satellite entry into the United Nations, the State Department attempted to sooth Congressional leaders by emphasizing that a 77 member United Nations would be more heavily weighted in favor of the free world, than the current 60 member organization.[98]

However, the Administration had to sooth more than Congress. The Soviets wanted the Mongolian People's Republic included. To resolve the deadlock, Dag Hammarskjold asked Canada to offer a compromise. Much to Washington's chagrin, the Ottawa list numbered 18 states, including the Mongolian People's Republic.[99] The Canadian list gathered rapid support, and on December 1, the Special Political Committee of the United Nations asked the Security Council to award membership to all 18 applicants.[100]

On December 8, the General Assembly supported this recommendation by a vote of 52 to 2, with five abstentions. Cuba and Nationalist China had voted no, and the latter threatened to do the same at the Security Council if the Mongolian People's Republic were recommended for admission to the UN. Eisenhower realized that a Nationalist Chinese veto would anger the majority of the members of the United Nations, and thereby provide greater support to Moscow's efforts to have Beijing be the new representative of China. To avert this from happening, the President wrote twice to Chiang Kai-shek asking him not to veto the Mongolian People's Republic application.[101]

As the Security Council prepared to vote on the 18 states, the United

States and the Soviet Union pledged not to use their veto against any membership application. On December 13, the Security Council voted on each of the applicants. The second country recommended was the Mongolian People's Republic, and despite American pressure Nationalist China vetoed its application. The "package" arrangement was destroyed, so the Soviets vetoed the remaining non-Communist applicants. Following the debacle, the Soviets requested a meeting with the Americans. During the night the two countries worked out a new package of 16 states, excluding Japan and the Mongolian People's Republic. On December 14, the Security Council accepted all 16 members.[102] After nine years of trying, Romania was a member of the United Nations.

Gheorghiu-Dej had little time for celebration since he was preparing for the Second Party Congress scheduled to open on December 23. He had postponed this Congress twice in 1954 while he strengthened his control over the party. Gheorghiu-Dej used the Congress to announce his message of national Communism. Romania's national goal was still its transformation to socialism, but this would now be done by developing her own national interests, rather than by subordinating them to the goals of the socialist world. Romania would cooperate with other socialist states, but that cooperation would be based on mutual respect, equality of rights, and respect for each other's national characteristics. Relations with non-socialist countries would also be based on the principles of non-interference in internal affairs, respect for national sovereignty, equality of rights, and peaceful coexistence.[103] At the close of his five hour speech, he announced that Nicolae Ceausescu and Alexandru Draghici were now full members of the Politburo.[104]

Gheorghiu-Dej's assertion of national goals was clearly misunderstood in Washington. The State Department's Research and Intelligence Office presented a detailed analysis of the Second Party Congress to the Department on Feburary 27, 1956. The report consistently noted that the most important part of the Congress was Gheorghiu-Dej's policy speech. However, the report interpreted his emphasis on "non-intervention" as meaning that the West should not interfere in Romania's internal affairs. Later, analysts would realize that the Kremlin was the target of Gheorghiu-Dej's remarks.[105]

The Second Congress also focused on economics. Gheorghiu-Dej called for expanded relations with the West. He especially targeted the United States urging them to rid themselves of "reactionary circles" and accept the realities of the post-war world.[106] Chivu Stoica outlined specific economic changes. Romania had not met the goals of the First

Five Year Plan. This failure was partly due to the New Course, and partly due to Romania's debts to the Soviet Union. When Moscow agreed to end the Sovroms, they did so with the understanding that Romania would buy back the Soviet share of the Sovroms over the next several years. This provision upset Bucharest's balance of payments, and reduced her capital investment ability.[107] In addition, in 1954 Romania had to increase its grain shipments to the Soviet Union to compensate for Moscow's poor harvests.[108] Consequently, the goals of the Second Five Year Plan, 1956-1960, called for Romania to continue her rapid heavy industrialization, and to double the amount of land collectivized from 26.5% to 50% by 1960.[109]

While the Second Congress strengthened Gheorghiu-Dej's hold over Romania, his position was severely jolted by announcements made at the 20th Party Congress of the CPSU in Moscow. Khrushchev publicly denounced Stalin as a criminal, guilty of the "cult of personality" which meant that he placed his interest above those of the party. Of all the satellite leaders, not one was as Stalinist as Gheorghiu-Dej. He was a Romanian Stalinist whose political and economic policies were based on those of the former Soviet leader. His pledges of friendship and brotherhood between Bucharest and Moscow made at the 20th Party Congress[110] would do little to deter his enemies in Romania, who wanted to use the de-Stalinization program to curb his power.

When he returned from Moscow, Gheorghiu-Dej said nothing about the de-Stalinization. He waited until March 23, 1956, before he presented his official report of the Congress to the Romanian party's Central Committee. At this meeting, he noted Khurshchev's indictment of Stalin and attributed it to Stalin's departure from the Marxist-Leninist concept of the role of personality. Stalin's actions had produced a "negative influence."[111] Gheorghiu-Dej pretended that Khrushchev's remarks came as old news to his party colleagues, since Romania had already undergone de-Stalinization in the 1952 purges of Ana Pauker and Vasile Luca.[112] However, neither Miron Constantinescu nor Iosif Chisinevski accepted the party leader's rationale. Both men wanted to liberalize Romania and looked to Khrushchev as the model for change. Constantinescu was the only person who could have replaced Gheorghiu-Dej as party leader, while Chisinevski was the major spokesman for Moscow in the party.[113]

While Gheorghiu-Dej would survive this challenge, he had to take steps to appease the liberals. He permitted more worker transfers, released some political prisoners, and reduced the number of secret police.[114] However, there were no significant changes, and this was made clear to all in the report published in the May 23, 1956, issue of *Scinteia*. Gheorghiu-Dej announced that there was no problem of personality cult in Romania. The only mistake the party leadership had made was its neglect to report the "Pauker clique's" deviations in greater detail to the public. That failure accounted for the few manifestations still remaining of the obnoxious cult, and these would be soon uprooted.[115] As for the liberal challengers, Constantinescu and Chisinevski would pay for their views in the purge of 1957, described in the next chapter.

Meanwhile, Gheorghiu-Dej had continued to send overtures to the West for increased exchanges in goods and information. On March 7, 1956, he notified Washington that Romania wanted to begin negotiations to resolve unsettled economic and financial problems including claims of American citizens to former properties in Romania, and the status of blocked Romanian funds in the United States. Further, he wanted to resume commercial exchanges between the two countries.[116] To facilitate developments, Gheorghiu-Dej appointed Silviu Brucan as the new Romanian Minister to the United States. Brucan was one of the three men who had visited the the United States the previous November to look into the purchase of corn and farm equipment. He met with Secretary of State Dulles and on April 28 Washington notified Bucharest that the United States was willing to discuss some of the items mentioned in the Romanian note of March 7. In addition, the State Department wanted to talk about the status of American citizens in Romania, and the Department was interested in establishing a library in Bucharest, open to the public.[117]

On April 30, Brucan met with Eisenhower in the White House and upon leaving was questioned by reporters. Brucan told them that his government had invited an American delegation to come to Bucharest to resolve all outstanding issues.[118] Soon stories appeared in the *New York Times* describing Romania's willingness to settle her outstanding debts with the United States.[119]

Brucan's White House meeting sparked further American-Romanian contacts. On June 12, Bucharest proposed that the two countries establish a joint commission to meet in Romania around September 1 to discuss claims and trade. Gheorghiu-Dej was also willing to have American books and publications available in Romania, and wanted to open consulates on a reciprocal basis in several cities in the United States and in the Romanian Peoples' Republic.[120]

Through July and August, Romania continued to press for trade talks. The State Department noted that they had received an "unprccedented" number of requests for commercial transactions between the two countries.[121] *Agerpres* maintained a steady stream of stories about American visitors to Romania,[122] while the NSC noted that more than 600 Romanians had visited the United States in 1956.[123] Bucharest permitted the United States Information Agency to hold an architectural exhibit in Bucharest, entitled "Built in USA," and the Romanians had agreed to purchase hybrid corn seed, called Pioneer 301, from the Garst company.[124] The Romanian offensive finally paid off. During the first week of September, the State Department announced that it was willing to open talks with Bucharest on October 15.[125]

Notes

1. Commission on Foreign Economic Policy, *Report to the President and the Congress* [U. S. Government Printing Office, January 23, 1954], p. iii, File 115-M 1954, Box 588, Office File, WHCF, DDE Library.

2. Journal entry, December 2, 1953, p. 8, File November 20-December 23, 1953, Box 1, Clarence B. Randall Journal, 1953-1961, DDE Library.

3. Clarence B. Randall to Lamar Fleming, December 12, 1953, File Herrings Discussions, Box 3, (Randall Commission) CFEP: Records, 1953-1954, DDE Library.

4. Journal Entry, January 9, 1954, File January 6 - 26, 1954, Box 1, Clarence B. Randall Journal, 1953-1961, DDE Library; Lamar Fleming to CFEP, December 11, 1953, 3pp., File Draft No. 1 of Commission's Report, Box 37, Memos of Reports (Randall Commission), CFEP: Records, 1953-1954, DDE Library; Lamar Fleming to CFEP, December 30, 1953, 4pp., File Draft No. 2 of Commission's Report, Box 37, Memos of Reports (Randall Commission), CFEP Records, 1953-1954, DDE Library; Lamar Fleming to CFEP, January 6, 1954, 2pp., File Draft No. 3 of Commission's Report, Box 37, Memos of Reports (Randall Commission), CFEP Records, 1953-1954, DDE Library.

5. Commission on Foreign Economic Policy, *Report to the President and the Congress* [U. S. Government Printing Office, January 23, 1954], pp. 65-66, File 116-M 1954, Box 588, Office File,WHCF, DDE Library.

6. C. E. Wilson to Gabriel Hauge [encs.], February 12, 1954, pp. 581-582, File CCS 091.31(9.28.45) Sec. 27, Box 11, Central Decimal File, JCS 1954-1956, National Archives.

7. Adler-Karlsson, *Western Economic Warfare, 1947-1967*, p. 45.

8.]Battle Act Administrator] *The Strategic Trade Control System, 1948-1956. Ninth Report to congress* (Washington: U. S. Government Printing Office, 1956), p. 23.

9. *FRUS, 1952-1954*, I, 1254; U. S. Congress, Senate, Permanent Subcommittee on Investigations, *Report of the Committee on Government Operations*, Report No. 2621, 84th Cong., 2d Sess., 1956, pp. 46ff.

10. Report, Availability of Consumers' Goods in the Eastern European Satellites, October 9, 1953, p. 4, File Russia, Box 62, Subject Series, Confidential Files, WHCF. DDE Library.

11. Adler-Karlsson, *Western Economic Warfare*, 1947-1967, pp. 90ff.

12. Adler-Karlsson, *Western Economic Warfare*, 1947-1967, pp. 90ff.

13. Report, United States Policy on Economic Defense, August 30, 1954, pp. 6-7, NSC152/3,U.S. Economic Defense Policy File, Box 5, Special Assistant NSC. White House Office, DDE Library.

14. *Strategic Trade Control System*, 1948-1956, p. 26.

15. Senate, *Committee on Government Operations*, 1956, p. 8; *Strategic Trade Control System, 1948-1956*, p. 26.

16. Senate, *Committee on Government Operations*, 1956, p. 9.

17. *FRUS, 1952-1954*, I, 1128-1129.

18. Memorandum, US-UK-France Consultation on East-West Trade, April 1, 1954, p. 8, 191st Meeting NSC, Box 5, NSC Series, Ann Whitman Files, DDE Library.

19. [Battle Act Administration] *The Revision of Strategic Trade Controls: Fifth Report to Congress* (Washington: U.S. Goverment Printing Office, 1954), pp. 13-14.

20. Memorandum, US-UK-France Consultation on East-West Trade, 1 April 1954, p. 9, 191st Meeting NSC, Box 5, NSC Series, Ann Whitman Files, DDE Library.

21. *The Revision of Strategic Trade Controls, Fifth Report to Congress*, p. 17.

22. Memorandum, United States Security Export Controls, June 11, 1954, p. 2, File NSC 152/3, Box 5, Special Assistant NSC, White House Office, DDE Library.

23. *Ibid*., pp. 4-5.

24. *Ibid*., p. 7.

25. Memorandum, Discussion at the 202nd Meeting of the National Security Council, June 17, 1954, June 18, 1954, p. 5, File 202nd Meeting, Box 5, NSC Series, Ann Whitman Files, DDE Library.

26. *Ibid*., p. 7.

27. T*he Revision of Strategic Trade Controls, Fifth Report to Congress*, p.21; Memorandum, Discussion at the 207th Meeting of the National Security Council, Thursday, July 22, 1954, July 23, 1954, p. 3, NSC Series, Box 5, AnnWhitman Files, DDE Library.

28. "The Council on Foreign Economic Policy: An Introductory Briefing Paper for the Incoming Administration," by Clarence B. Randall, January 20, 1961, p. 1, Randall's Briefing Folder, Box 272, NSF, JFK; History of the CFEP, n.d., p. 2, Joseph Rand Records 1954-1961, Box 17, Q-S, Finding Aids of Personal Papers & Archives, DDE Library; Letter, Eisenhower to Rowland R. Hughes and Nelson A. Rockefeller, July 12, 1954, 2pp., File CFEP, Box 18, Subject Series, Confidential Files, WHCF, DDE Library; Memorandum, Sherman Adams to the Cabinet, July 15, 1954, 13pp., File CFEP, Box 18, Subject Series, Confidential Files, WHCF, DDE Library.

29. "The Council on Foreign Economic Policy: An Introductory Briefing Paper for the Incoming Administration," by Clarence B. Randall. January 20, 1961, Randall's briefing folder, Box 277, NSF, JFK; History of CFEP, n.d., Joseph Rand Records 1954-1961, Box 17, Q-S, Finding Aids of Personal Papers & Archives, DDE Library.
30. Memorandum, Summary Review of Economic Defense Policy and Program, January 20, 1955, p. 2, File CFEP 501- East-West Trade, Box 1, Policy Papers Series, US CFEP Records, DDE Library.
31. U.S. Congress, Senate, Committee on Foreign Relations, *A Background Study on East-West Trade Prepared for the Committee by the Legislative Reference Service of the Library of Congress*, 89th Cong., 1st Sess., 1965, p. 5.
32. Memorandum, Interim Report on the Review of Economic Defense Policy, March 23, 1955, File CFEP 501-East-West Trade, Box 1, Policy Papers Series, US CFEP Records, DDE Library.
33. Report by the Joint Strategic Survey Committee to the Joint Chiefs of Staff on Economic Defense Policy with Respect to Trade with the Communist Bloc, April 29, 1955, p. 602, CCS 091.31 (9.28.45) Sec. 28, Box 11, Central Decimal Files, JCS 1954-1956, DDE Library.
34. U. S. Congress, Senate, Joint Committee on the Economic Report, *Foreign Economy Policy*, Report No. 1312, 84th Cong., 2d Sess., 1956, p. 31.
35. Handbook on the Foreign Economic Policy of the United States As Expressed in Legislation and Statements of the President, Volume II, November 12, 1956, File 116-EE CFEP, Box 592, Office Files, Central Files, DDE Library.
36. Report Appendix, CFEP Personnel, n.d., 2pp., Joseph Rand Records 1954-1961, Box 17, Q-S, Finding aids of Personal Papers and Archives, DDE Library.
37. Journal Entry, March 2, 1956, Folder Aug 2-Sept 25 1956, Box 3, Clarence B. Randall Journal, 1953-1961, DDE Library. *Idem.*, August 1, 1956.
38. *FRUS, 1952-1954*, II, 609.
39. *Ibid.*, p. 844 n.11.
40. The policy was originally designated NSC 5440.
41. Policy Statement, Basic National Security Policy, December 13, 1954, p. 9, File NSC 5440/1, Box 14, Office for Special Assistant for NSC, White House Office, DDE Library.
42. Marc Trachtenberg, "A 'Wasting Asset': American Strategy and the Shifting Nuclear Balance, 1949-1954," *International Security*, Vol. 13, No. 3 (Winter 1988/89), p. 43.
43. House Committee on Foreign Affairs, *Soviet Diplomacy and Negotiating Behavior*, 1955, p. 325; Alvin Z. Rubinstein, *Soviet Foreign Policy Since World War II: Imperial and Global* (2nd ed.; Boston: Little, Brown & Co., 1985), pp. 85-86. Hereafter, Rubinstein, *Soviet Foreign Policy Since World War II.*
44. Policy Statement, Basic National Security Policy, March 15, 1956, pp. 12-14, File NSC 5602/1, Box 17, Office for Special Assistant for NSC, White House Office, DDE Library.
45. Progress Report on NSC 174, July 15, 1954, p. 2, File NSC 174-Policy

toward East Europe, Box 8, Office for Special Assistant for NSC, White House Office, DDE Library.

46. U. S. Congress, Senate, Committee on Foreign Relations, *Hearing on S. Res. 116 Favoring Discussion at the Coming Geneva Conference of the Status of Nations Under Communist Control*, 84th Cong., 1st Sess., 1955.

47. W. W. Rostow to Nelson A. Rockefeller, June 10, 1955, p. 2, File Russia, Box 63, Subject Series, Confidential Files, WHCF, DDE Library.

48. Summary of Recommendations, Quantico Vulnerabilities Panel, June 10, 1955, p. 2, File Russia, Box 63, Subject Series, Confidential Files, WHCF, DDE Library.

49. Note to the NSC on Basic U.S. Policy in Relation to Four-Power Negotiations, July 11, 1955, p. 12, File Four-Power Negotiations, Box 17, Office for Special Assistant for NSC, White House Office, DDE Library.

50. Report, United States Policy Toward the soviet Satellites in Eastern Europe, February 29, 1955, p. 4, File NSC Progress Report 2/29/56, Record Group 273 5W1, NSC Policy Papers, National Archives.

51. *Ibid*.

52. Minutes, 280th Meeting of the NSC, March 22, 1956, p. 2, National Archives.

53. Report, U.S. Policy Toward the Soviet Satellites in Eastern Euroope, July 3, 1956, pp. 1-3, File NSC 5608 - 7/3/56, Record Group 273 5W1, NSC Policy Papers, National Archives; *Idem*. July 18, 1956,NSC 5608/1 - 7/18/56, 6pp.

54. U.S. Policy Toward the Soviet Satellites in Eastern Europe, July 3, 1956, p. 11, File NSC 5608 -7/3/56, Record Group 273 5W1, NSC Policy Papers, National Archives.

55. *Ibid*., p. 42.

56. *Ibid*., p. 43.

57. *Ibid*., pp. 41-44.

58. For more see, Harrington and Courtney, "Romania's Changing Image."

59. NYT, May 27, 1953, p. 1.

60. V. C. Georgescu to Eisenhower, June 12, 1953, 4pp., Folder Alpha Cases-Georgescu, Papers of Charles W. Thayer, DDE Library.

61. Wolff, *The Balkans in Our Time*, p. 473;Rudolph Halley to Eisenshower, July 21, 1953, File Georgescu Case 215-A, Box 886, Office Files, WHCF, DDE Library.

62. Thayer to Lurton, September 20, 1954, Folder Alpha Cases-Georgescu, Papers of Charles W. Thayer, DDE Library.

63. Press clipping, May 1, 1954, File Georgescu Case 215-A, Box 886, Office Files, WHCF, DDE Library.

64. CSM, April 18, 1954 p. 16; NYT, March 26, 1954, p. 5 April 19, 1954, p. 3; May 19, 1954, p. 10; May 29, 1954, p. 14.

65. NYT, May 7, 1954, p. 13.

66. NYT, May 8, 1954, p. 9.

67. NYT, August 11, 1953 p. 9; October 18, 1953, p. 37.
68. Fischer-Galati, *The New Rumania*, p. 50.
69. Tismaneanu, "Ceausescu's Socialism," 1985, pp. 56-57.
70. Fischer-Galati, *The New Rumania*, p. 50.
71. Harold C. Hinton, *Communist China in World Politics* (Boston: Houghton Mifflin Company, 1966), p. 283.
72. "Tenth Anniversary of Rumania's Liberation," *Agerpres*, August 10, 1954, p. 2.
73. NYT, October 3, 1954, p. 5. Sovrompetrol lasted until December, 1955, and Sovromcvart, the uranium-mining enterprise ended in November, 1956 (Montias, *Economic Development in Communist Rumania*, p. 50). However, in October, 1956, a Romanian-Soviet accord obliged Bucharest to send 85% of her uranium production to the Soviet Union (George Cioranesco *et al.*, *Aspects de relations russo-roumaines: Retrospectives et orientations* [Paris: Minard, 1967], 1970), p. 197.
74. Fischer-Galati, *The New Rumania*, p. 51.
75. Telegram, London to Secretary of State, December 15, 1954, File 411.6631/12-1554, Box 1854, Record Group 59, NND862903, National Archives.
76. Foreign Trade of the RPR in the Ten Years Since Liberation," *Agerpres*, August 10, 1954, pp. 14-15.
77. U. S. Congress, House Committee on International Relations, *Hearings Before the Subcommittee on International Trade and Commerce. Status of Claims Settlements with Nonmarket Countries: East German Claims Bill (H.R. 14642)*, 94th Cong., 2d Sess., 1976, p. 3.
78. Telegram, London to Washington, Deember 15, 1954, File 510 Rumania - Other Countries, Box 134, Record Group 84, Foreign Service Posts of DOS, Bucharest legation General Records, 1953-1955, National Archives.
79. Gheorghe Gheorghiu-Dej, *Concerning the Foreign Policy of the Government of the Rumanian People's Republic. Speech Delivered at the 5th Session of the Grand National Assembly, February 22, 1955*, (Bucharest: Rumanian Institute for Cultural Relations with Foreign Countries, 1955), 1.
80. Francois Fejto, *A History of the People's Democracies: Eastern Europe Since Stalin* trans. Daniel Weissbort (New York: Praeger, 1971), p. 35; Otto Pick, "Problems of Adjustment: The Gorbachev Effect in Eastern Europe," *SAIS Review*, Vol. 8, No. 1, (Winter-Spring 1988), p. 57.
81. Fischer-Galati, *Twentieth Century Rumania*, p. 141.
82. NYT, October 16, 1955, p. 33.
83. Fischer-Galati, *Twentieth Century Rumania*, p. 141.
84. House Subcommittee on International Trade, *East German Claims Bill*, 1976, p. 9.
85. Press Release, November 7, 1955, p. 1, File Education III-C 1954, Box 544, Office Files, WHCF. DDE Library.
86. NYT, October 12, 1955, p. 2.
87. Memorandum, Outstanding Problems-Political Section, October 29,

1955, p. 2, File 350, Political Affairs-Rumanian Government, Box 134, Record Group 84 Foreign Service Posts of DOS, Bucharest legation, General Records 1953-1955, National Archives.

88. Oral interview of Robert Thayer by John Luter, June 17, 1972, p. 27, DDE Library.

89. *Ibid.*

90. *Ibid.*, p. 28.

91. NYT, November 28, 1955, p. 3; *Scinteia*, January 3, 1956, p. 3.

92. *FRUS, 1955-1957*, Vol. XI, *United Nations and General International Matters*, pp. 284, 268.

93. *Ibid.*, p. 264.

94. *Ibid.*, pp. 268-269.

95. *Ibid.*, pp. 283ff.

96. *Public Papers of the Secretaries-General of the United Nations*, Vol. II: *Dag Hammarskjold, 1953-1956*, Andrew W. Cordier and Wilder Foote, eds. (New York: Columbia University Press, 1972), pp. 629-630.

97. *FRUS, 1955-1957*, XI, 305.

98. *Ibid.*, pp. 310-311, 322.

99. *Dag Hammarskjold*, p. 630; *FRUS, 1955-1957*, XI, 326.

100. *Ibid.*

101. *FRUS, 1955-1957*, XI, 427.

102. *Dag Hammarskjold*, p. 631.

103. Fischer-Galati, "The Sino-Soviet Conflict," 1966, p. 265; *Idem.*, *The New Rumania*, p. 55.

104. Report, Political Significance of Rumanian Workers' Party Congress, December 1955, February 27, 1956, File Report 7189 2/27/56, Box 1787, OSS R&A, Reports, National Archives.

105. *Ibid.*, p. 2.

106. *Ibid.*

107. Montias, *Economic Development of Communist Rumania*, pp. 43, 50.

108. Norman, "'New Course' in Rumanian Agriculture," 1955, p. 41.

109. Ronald Haly Linden, *Bear and Foxes: The International Relations of The Eastern European States, 1965-1969* (Boulder, CO: East European Monographs, Columbia University Press, 1979), pp. 177-179; CIA Report, Communism in Eastern Europe: Post-Stalin Developments in the Satellites, August 28, 1958, p. 1, File Communism in Eastern Europe, Box 5, Subject Series, NSC Series, Briefing Notes, Office of the Special Assistant for National Security Affairs, White House Office, DDE Library.

110. [Gheorghe Gheorghiu-Dej] "Rede Auf Dem XX. Parteitag Der Kommunistischen Partei Der Sowjetunion, 17 Februar 1956," *Gh. Gheorghiu-Dej: Artikel und Reden: Dezember 1955 - Juli 1959* (Bukarest, Politischer Verlag, 1959), p. 193.

111. CIA Report, Communism in Eastern Europe: Post-Stalin Developments in the Satellites, August 28, 1958, p. 4, File Communism in Eastern Europe, Box 5, Subject Series, NSC Series, Briefing Notes, Office of the Special

Assistant for National Security Affairs, White House Office, DDE Library.

112 *Ibid.*; Fischer-Galati, *Twentieth Century Rumania*, p. 145.

113. *Ibid.*, p. 59.

114. CIA Report, Communism in Eastern Europe: Post-Stalin Developments in the Satellites, August 28, 1958, pp. 5-9, File Communism in Eastern Europe, Box 5, Subject Series, NSC Series, Briefing Notes, Office of the Special Assistant for National Security Affairs, White House OFfice, DDE Library.

115. *Ibid.*, p. 8.

116. "In the Interest of Improving and Developing Relations Between the Rumanian People's Republic and the United States of America," *Agerpres*, July 20, 1956, p. 10.

117. *Ibid.*;Transcript of News Conference, Silviu Brucan, April 30, 1956, p. 1, File 215-Rumanian Government, Box 886, Office Files, WHCF, DDE Library.

118. *Ibid.*, pp. 1-2.

119. NYT, May 1, 1956, p. 23; May 2, 1956, p. 1; May 5, 1956, p. 2.

120. "Improving Relations Between the Rumanian People's Republic and the United States of America," 1956, p. 11.

121. Report, U.S. Policy Toward the Soviet Satellites in Eastern Europe, July 3, 1956, p.43, File NSC 5608-7/3/56, Record Group 273 5W1, NSC Policy Papers, National Archives.

122. "Foreign Guests Visiting Rumania," *Agerpres*, August 20, 1956, pp. 14-15.

123. Report, U.S. Policy toward the Soviet Satellites in Eastern Europe, November 20, 1957, p. 3, File NSC 5608/1, Box 17, Office for Special Assistant for NSC, White House Office, DDE Library.

124. *Ibid*,; NYT, September 26, 1957, p. 1,

125. NYT, September 7, 1956, p. 10.

CHAPTER VII

FROM A FALSE START TO A CLAIMS SETTLEMENT, 1956-1960

An Hungarian Uprising

After nearly a decade of bickering, America and Romania appeared ready to put the past behind them. Bilateral negotiations were compatible with NSC 5602/1 which permitted trade. They were also a means to implement NSC 5608/1 which encouraged differentiation, and which saw commerce as a form of wedge to split the Romanian satellite from Moscow. On October 15, 1956, American and Romanian delegates began their scheduled talks in Bucharest. Nine days later, at the request of Washington, Romania sent three representatives to the United States to observe the upcoming Presidential elections. This was the first part of a reciprocal arrangement whereby the United States would send observers to the February, 1957 elections.[1]

However, these auspicious beginnings were soon derailed. The success of Wladislav Gomulka and the anti-Stalinists in Poland on October 19-20, encouraged many Hungarians to believe that Budapest could do likewise. Students took to the streets on October 23 demanding the evacuation of Soviet troops, new governmental elections, and a new economic system. The Hungarian leader, Ernest Gero, appeared unable to restore order. Soviet tanks appeared in Budapest. Soviet intervention replaced Gero with Imre Nagy and Janos Kadar, both moderates and anti-Stalinists. Nagy and Kadar were unable to restore order because the rebels saw them as advocates of even greater change. Nagy was sympathetic to their demands including dismantling the Warsaw Pact and establishing a multi-party political system. Moscow could not afford to permit this sort of revolutionary change in Hungary; the Polish model was the limit of Khrushchev's liberalism. On November 4, tanks reappeared in Budapest and opened fire on the insurgents. Kadar broke from Nagy and called for a new government similar to that of Gomulka in Poland. The Soviet tanks restored order and Nagy fell from power.[2]

The world was shocked by the fact that the Soviets had used tanks to kill civilians and students. Bucharest too was stunned. At the outset of the revolution in October, liberal forces in Romania were excited by the developments in Hungary. They viewed the uprisings as the means for countries to develop their own paths to socialism.[3] However, as the Soviets began to play a larger role in suppressing the revolution, Gheorghiu-Dej took steps to make sure that the spirit of revolt did not spread to Romania. He feared Soviet support of anti-Stalinist leaders. Gomulka's ascendency in Poland combined with Mathias Rakosi's fall in Hungary meant that if an uprising were to break out in Romania, he would probably be replaced. To counter any revolutionary moves, Gheorghiu-Dej announced some liberal reforms on October 30 including increases in the minimum wage, family allowances and pensions.[4]

Reverberations from the Hungarian revolution were felt in a number of places. Satellite governments learned that Soviet support did not automatically extend to the leaders of satellite states.[5] Anti-communist forces learned not to look to the United States for revolutionary support. Romania learned that national Communism could be pursued within limits without Soviet intervention.[6] Gheorghiu-Dej also learned that Moscow rewarded satellite states which maintained order during the October uprisings. In December, Moscow agreed to lend Romania 450,000 tons of wheat and 60,000 tons of fodder to compensate for her poor harvest. In addition, the Soviets agreed to postpone debt payments until 1959.[7] Finally, Moscow agreed to open talks about reducing Soviet troop levels in Romania. This led to a status of forces agreement in April, 1957, which contained the written assurance that the temporary stationing of troops in Romania in no way affected her sovereignty.[8]

However, the events of October did little for the Romanian-American economic and financial talks in Bucharest. By early November the talks had collapsed.[9] Two months later, on January 24, 1957, the State Department announced that Bucharest was unwilling to fulfill its commitment to let three American political science professors observe Romania's February elections.[10]

CFEP, COCOM, Congress and Foreign Economic Policy

The CFEP, meanwhile, had initiated a review of America's economic policy. The major problem was the international export control lists. The CHINCOM list continued about 450 items more than did the COCOM list. The United Kingdom and other members of the CG had pressed to eliminate the China differential. The Europeans argued that through transshipment China could receive all of the embargoed items from the Soviet Bloc.[11]

On February 5, the CFEP adopted new guidelines for America's foreign economic policy. The major change was the recommendation that the CHINCOM list be reduced. The rationale was that unless the United States made a substantial concession to her allies, the entire multilateral export control mechanism could collapse. The new policy did not eliminate America's unilateral embargo on certain items to all Communist countries. But the policy did provide for trade differentiation among the East European satellite states through "adjustments of both unilateral and multilateral controls over trade with selected satellites to encourage their national self-determination and independence."[12] The report specifically noted that there were advantages to maintaining personal, cultural, and commercial contacts between the free world and the satellite states.[13] Significantly, this report indicated a slight change in American thinking. Trade was more possible with the Soviet satellite states than with the Soviet Union. This change would become more apparent in the next several months as Washington considered a variety of means to dispose of huge agricultural surpluses.

Meanwhile, CG negotiations continued in Paris. Since the latest CFEP recommendations did not call for any significant changes in the CHINCOM list, Britain told her colleagues on June 5, that henceforth she would only use the COCOM list to embargo items to the Communist world. Several days later, all of the other European members of CHINCOM accepted the British proposal, isolating the United States. Washington alone retained the CHINCOM list.[14]

Washington's trade policy with the Communist world appeared strange at times, especially in 1957. While Congress showed little interest in trading with Communist China, the legislature was willing to trade with the Communist countries of Eastern Europe, especially to sell them surplus American food products. As early as February, 1954, the United States had tried to dispose of surplus agricultural products purchased by the government as a form of subsidy to the American farmer. However, since they tried to sell the surplus below the price paid by the American consumer, the public cried out in disbelief. Nonetheless, the continued increase in government owned surplus food, nearly $400 million worth by March, 1954, spurred the NSC to look for alternative solutions. On April 1, the NSC decided that foodstuffs could be bartered for strategic materials, such as manganese, chrome and nickel, from the Soviet Union and Eastern Europe.[15]

While the Administration began secret negotiations with Moscow to work out barter arrangements, the United States Congress passed Public Law 480 (PL 480), the Agricultural Trade Development and Assistance Act of 1954, on July 10. This legislation would quickly kill the Moscow-Washington talks. Congress was far more anti-Communist than the Executive Branch. McCarthyism lived in Congress. Many legislators were also opposed to the President's discretionary power in foreign economic trade, which enabled the President to ignore the intent of legislation. The fact that the White House had not imposed sanctions against nations violating the Battle Act infuriated some Congressmen. In addition, the President could make so called "executive agreements" with countries, which circumvented the intent of Congress.

In 1952, Senator John Bricker of Ohio had introduced a resolution calling for a Constitutional Amendment to limit executive agreements, and in the process give Congress greater control over the execution of foreign policy.[16] The White House had fought this "Bricker Amendment" since its inception, and was still doing so in 1954. The antipathies generated by the anti-Communist elements in Congress, combined with those members who resented the President's apparent cavalier approach to their concerns in foreign policy, produced PL 480. Section 304 of the law stated that the President could dispose of surplus agricultural products "to assist friendly nations to be independent of trade with the Union of Soviet Socialist Republics and with nations dominated or controlled by the Union of Soviet Socialist Republics and to assure that agricultural commodities sold or transferred thereunder do not result in increased availability of those or like commodities to unfriendly nations."[17] This stipulation ended the State Department's secret negotiations with Moscow.

PL 480 ran counter to the NSC recommendations supporting barter with the Soviet Bloc. After considerable debate by the Cabinet and the NSC, Eisenhower asked the Justice Department to determine whether there was any "legal prohibition against direct or indirect trading with or sales to the Soviet Bloc." On February 21, 1955, Assistant Attorney General Lee Rankin responded that such transactions were illegal.[18] In a supplementary memorandum dated February 28, 1955, Rankin reconsidered his advice noting that he did not think that PL 480 limited the discretionary power of the President in relation to money transactions. However, he urged the President not to exercise that discretionary power without giving consideration to the policy Congress established through PL 480.[19]

While PL 480 did enable the United States to reduce its surplus food, the law was not in concert with the NSC and CFEP desires to use trade, including food, as a means to affect change in the Soviet Bloc. However, Eisenhower's heart attack on September 24 sharply curtailed the White House's ability to influence Congress. Eisenhower had to wait until January 9, 1956, before he could renew his appeal and he did so in his annual farm message. Eisenhower asked the legislature to repeal section 304 of PL 480 prohibiting the sale of surplus farm products to the Soviet Bloc. Although the 84th Congress discussed surplus disposal, it did not repeal Section 304.[20]

Eisenhower was furious and referred to the restrictions in PL 480 as "damned foolishness." He wanted legislation drafted that linked the disposal of surplus farm products to foreign policy, so that Congress would have to repeal Section 304 or be responsible for compromising America's national security objectives.[21] While various agencies and departments began drafting the requested legislation, the President and many Congressmen prepared for the upcoming Presidential election.

Following his easy victory, Eisenhower renewed his efforts. In his budget message to Congress on January 16, 1957, he repeated his request that legislation be enacted authorizing the barter of non-strategic government agricultural surpluses to the nations of Eastern Europe.[22] The 85th Congress was far more receptive to the President. The widely publicized events in Poland and Hungary had shown that change was possible in the Soviet Bloc. Further, the President's reelection gave him a mandate that forced Congress to respond. After considerable debate, Congress amended Section 304 of PL 480 to permit barter transactions with the East European satellites. However, the August 13 vote did not remove the prohibition against Moscow or Beijing.[23]

Eisenhower's victory in 1956 gave continuity to American policy. The NSC decisions made during the first administration, were continued with few modifications during the second administration. In September, 1957, the NSC approved NSC 5704/3 as American's new economic defense policy. The new policy maintained much of the export control policy of NSC 152/3, but added provisions for more flexibility. The document encouraged Washington to view the countries of Eastern Europe as individual states, rather than as a monolithic bloc. Specifically, the new policy called upon the Commerce Department to permit shipments of commodities not under export control to Eastern Europe and, "where appropriate, to remove the requirement of specific licenses for such shipments to the entire European Soviet Bloc." Further, NSC 5704/3 urged Washington to "make appropriate and timely unilateral adjustments . . . in the scope and severity of controls . . . to encourage and support" Eastern Europe's "progress toward national self-determination and independence."[24]

Although the United States was reducing its restrictions on East-West trade, it was not doing so fast enough for most of her COCOM partners. Sputnik's successful flight in October, 1957, seemed to indicate to many West Europeans that export controls had failed to prevent the Soviets from achieving a great scientific and technological triumph. Early in 1958 the British called for another significant revision of the COCOM lists. London wanted to remove 150 items from the embargo list and eliminate entirely the quantity and surveillance lists.[25] The British wanted to embargo only items which "would be required to prepare Soviet forces for fighting a short violent war." London opposed the present criteria which was to embargo items which would "hinder the general industrial development of the Bloc."[26]

The British demand again produced debate among Administration officials. However, sustained European pressure forced Washington to compromise. On July 18-19, 1958, the American representative agreed with his CG colleagues to sharply reduce the COCOM embargo list, and to replace the quantitative and surveillance lists with a new "watch" list. This list would monitor certain exports according to their quantity and technological development, and make recommendations for their control when necessary.[27] On August 14, Secretary of Commerce Weeks announced that the United States would make "significant changes" in its export controls as a result of the recent COCOM meetings.[28] Weeks noted that America would still prohibit the export of more items than those restricted by the International Lists, but the net effect would be a significant reduction. In September, the State Department announced it had adjusted the Battle Act to conform to the recent COCOM decisions. Two months later, the Commerce Department announced that over 250 items no longer required an export license for shipment to a friendly country.[29]

Washington and Eastern Europe

The ongoing battle between the United States and the other COCOM members indicated a major transition in America's foreign policy. In spite of McCarthyism and the Korean War, the Eisenhower Administration was slowly changing its perception of the Communist world. The White House no longer viewed Eastern Europe simply as an extension of the Soviet Union. Rather, the Administration began to see Eastern Europe as an entity composed of different parts, each of which warranted specific attention. Eisenhower's reelection in 1956 permitted this transition to continue. While America had little or nothing to do with the events in Poland and Hungary in 1956, Washington did see these changes as transformational. The United States believed that changes would evolve in the satellite states, and America ought to maintain contact with the Eastern Bloc in order to capitalize on these developments. NSC 5810/1, which became America's basic security policy on May 5, 1958, continued to view the Soviet Union's drive for world Communism as the basic threat to American security, however, it urged Washington to "encourage expansion of U.S.-Soviet Bloc exchanges" in order to "foster evolutionary trends within the Bloc."[30]

Four days later, on May 9, the NSC reviewed America's policy toward Eastern Europe outlined in NSC 5608/1. The NSC agreed that the United States should continue to "drive a wedge" between the satellite states and Moscow. The NSC recognized that the past policy of "ostracizing the [Soviet] dominated regimes has had the concurrent effect of inhibiting increased direct U.S. contacts with the people of the dominated nations." The Polish and Hungarian uprisings provided clear evidence that "party and popular unrest" in Eastern Europe seriously challenged Soviet control. America should "exploit" the individual differences between states. A major means to do this was increased contacts between the United States and the individual satellite nations.[31]

For the first time, the NSC viewed Romania as a target for such contacts. While the Communists still had a strong hold in Romania, the NSC noted that the Romanian leadership had tried to increase contacts with Washington to secure technology and to "give substance to its claims of legitimacy and permanence in the eyes of its own people." The new NSC policy, labelled NSC 5811, concluded that Bucharest was "therefore exceptionally receptive to increased contacts with the West."[32]

Bucharest-Moscow-Washington

Meanwhile in Bucharest, the Hungarian uprising had abruptly ended the American-Romanian economic talks in November, 1956. Washington's efforts to use Soviet intervention in Budapest as a propaganda ploy did not improve matters. In February, the United States representative to the United Nations criticized the Soviets for interfering in the internal affairs of Hungary. In return, the Romanian delegation denounced America for its attack on Moscow.[33] However, the Romanian statement was made more for form than substance. For, Chivu Stoica, the chairman of the Romanian Council, made a speech several weeks later to the Grand National Assembly in which he used a theme which would frequently reappear. He told the assembled delegates that Romania wanted to develop cultural relations with France and Italy "with whom we are linked by traditions of friendship and cooperation, and with the other Latin peoples of Europe and South America, with whom we share a common cultural background."[34]

Although Romania appeared open to resume talks with Washington, the United States was slow to respond. Bucharest wanted to talk about future trade, while the State Department wanted to resolve past problems, including claims, the dollar value of which was three times the amount of available Romanian assets in the United States. In addition, the State Department wanted to establish an American library, or reading room, in Bucharest, but the Gheorghiu-Dej government was not ready to take this step.

Gheorghiu-Dej, however, was interested in continuing his drive for greater independence from Moscow. In May and June, the *New York Times* and *Christian Science Monitor* carried several reports indicating changes in Romania. Elie Abel noted that a recent art exhibit in Bucharest emphasized individual styles rather than "socialist realism," the traditional hallmark of communist art.[35] The press also reported that Romania no longer required students to learn the Russian language in school.[36] Major newspapers also carried interviews with Dr. Rosen, the Chief Jewish Rabbi in Romania, who said there were no Zionists imprisoned in Romania. To the contrary, the Gheorghiu-Dej government had given a great deal of support to the 250,000 Jewish Romanians.[37]

While some of these liberal measures could be interpreted as implementing Moscow's "thaw" in Romania, Gheorghiu-Dej dispelled all thoughts of that in July when he purged Miron Constantinescu and Iosif Chisinevski, the leading Kremlinologist, from the Romanian Worker's Party.[38] Initial reports of the purge appeared confusing because of similar activities in Moscow. On July 3, the Soviets announced the purge of the "anti-Party" group including Lazar Kaganovich, Georgi Malenkov, Vyacheslav Molotov and Dimitri Shepilov. On the following day, the Romanian press reported the purge of Chisinevski and Constantinescu.[39] The party accused the two men of "fractionalist activities" and "of disseminating the cult of personality. . . especially the glorification of Ana Pauker."[40]

However, the purges were not at all similar. In Moscow, Khrushchev eliminated Stalinists, while in Bucharest, Gheorghiu-Dej eliminated Khrushchevites. What the West was slow to learn, was that Gheorghiu-Dej only mimicked the Soviets when such mimicking advanced the cause of Romania's national Communism. Gheorghiu-Dej completed his reorganization and appointed Ion Gheorghe Maurer as Minister of Foreign Affairs and gave Nicolae Ceausescu greater party responsibilities.[41] Finally, the purge enabled Gheorghiu-Dej to reinforce his campaign to build a Romanian road to socialism on neo-Stalinist lines.[42]

In November, 1957, leaders of the twelve Communist parties in power met in Moscow to celebrate the 40th anniversary of the Bolshevik Revolution. The meeting was not without serious debate. Mao Zedong, the leader of the People's Republic of China, viewed Khrushchev's peace offensive as revisionist. Since the Bandung Conference, Beijing had challenged Moscow for leadership of the world Communist movement. The 20th Party Congress in 1956 appeared to be an attack against Mao who was a Stalinist, and who embraced the cult of personality. Sputnik too contributed to the Sino-Soviet split. The orbiting satellite gave Moscow a sense of confidence, and encouraged the Soviets to pursue a program for peaceful coexistence. To Mao, Sputnik was evidence of Communist superiority over capitalism. He believed the Soviets were foolish not to exploit their space accomplishment. This division of opinion was apparent at the 40th anniversary meeting, and in order to save face and present a united front, the Soviets announced on November 22, 1957, the Moscow Declaration which included the passage:

Socialist countries base their relations on the principles of complete equality, respect for territorial integrity, state independence and sovereignty, and non-interference in one another's affairs. . . . The socialist states also advocate the general expansion of economic and cultural relations with all other countries. . . on the basis of equality, mutual benefit and non-interference in internal affairs.[43]

Few people could have been happier with this declaration than Gheorghiu-Dej. It enabled him to pursue his Stalinist path to Romanian socialism. Soon after his return to Bucharest, he told the Party members on December 17 that Romania endorsed the Moscow Declaration. He also told the assembled delegates that he would tolerate no "liberalism" when it concerned the Party line, Party unity, and Party leadership.[44] Romanian Stalinism was the guideline for the Romanian Worker's Party.

The Moscow Declaration also implicitly approved Romania's recent efforts to renew contacts with the West, including those with the United States. In December, Gheorghiu-Dej decided to revive his relations with Washington. He notified the State Department that he would permit the United States to send three representatives to observe the next Romanian election. He also invited members of the United States Society of Editors and Commentators, who were visiting the Soviet Union and Eastern Europe, to visit Romania.[45] The Romanian leader continued his outreach to the United States in 1958. On February 27, the *New York Times* interviewed Chivu Stoica, the new Chairman of the Council of Ministers. This was the first time an American newspaper interviewed a Romanian leader. Stoica announced that Romania wanted to buy $100 million worth of industrial equipment from the United States. However, due to export restrictions, Bucharest would probably have to divert this trade to Western Europe.[46] Washington did not respond to Stoica's overture, primarily because Romania had not agreed to resolve the claims issue.

Gheorghiu-Dej continued his drive for greater independence. He wanted the Soviets to withdraw their troops from Romania. He sent Stoica, Bodnaras and the new Foreign Minister, Avram Bunaciu, to Hanoi and Beijing in March, 1958. They used the developing Sino-Soviet rift as background to tell their audiences about the inherent contradictions in Moscow's foreign policy. The Soviets preached peaceful coexistence, but maintained troops in foreign lands.[47] Gheorghiu-Dej continued to press the Soviets to withdraw its troops, and on May 24 Moscow finally agreed to do so.[48]

The reasons the Soviets agreed remain unclear, however there are a number of explanations. The withdrawal did not reduce Soviet national security, nor did it reduce Soviet ability to militarily intervene in Romania. At the same time, the withdrawal gave Moscow's peace offensive greater credibility in the West. Perhaps Khrushchev's acquiescence was designed as a gesture of friendship to Bucharest to keep her loyal to Moscow and preempt Chinese influence in Eastern Europe.[49] Another argument was that Moscow believed that a troop withdrawal would give the Romanian Communist party and government greater legitimacy in the eyes of the people. This in turn would reduce the type of hostility which prompted the Hungarian uprising.[50] A third possibility, offered by America's first Ambassador to the Romanian People's Republic, William Crawford, was that the withdrawal was a reward for Romanian support during the Hungarian uprising. Crawford further argued that this withdrawal coupled with the 1952 purge and the end of the Sovroms in 1956, were three telltale signs of change in Bucharest which were missed by the United States.[51] A fourth, and least likely explanation, was provided by Ion Pacepa in his *Red Horizons*. He suggests that Gheorghiu-Dej traded blueprints for a rolling mill which produced ultra-hard alloys needed for space rockets to Khrushchev for the troop withdrawal.[52] Regardless of the reason, the last of the Soviet troops left Romania at the end of July, 1958.[53]

The Soviet troop withdrawal gave Gheorghiu-Dej the psychological lift needed to further develop his plans for Romania's economic autonomy. According to Montias, Gheorghiu-Dej probably used the occasion of the November, 1958, Party Plenum to announce a major reorientation of Romania's trade away from the Soviet Bloc and toward the West.[54] The Second Five Year Plan had been modified within a year of its inception. At the Central Committee Plenum which met from December 27-29, 1956, Gheorghiu-Dej had revised the focus of the Five Year Plan and channeled funds previously allocated to heavy industry into consumer products.[55] At the 1958 Party Plenum, he announced the guidelines for a Six Year Plan covering the period 1960-1965. The goals called for accelerated industrialization. The Party leaders agreed to "aggrandize the iron and steel industry and to press forward with the development of a complex machine building industry."[56] Gheorghiu-Dej intended to end Romania's role as breadbasket for the CMEA countries, and embark on a road toward economic independence through industrialization and Western trade.

A Claims Settlement and a Cultural Exchange

Within days of the Plenum, Stoica granted an interview to the *Washington Post*. The Chairman of the Council of Ministers indicated that Romania was willing to trade with the West. As evidence, in 1957, 25% of Romania's trade was with Western countries in contrast to 13% in 1953. The total value of Romania's Western trade in 1957 exceeded $200 million, but little of it was with the United States although Romania's markets were open to American trade. However, Washington only exported a "campaign of calumny" to Romania through the radio broadcasts of Voice of America and Radio Free Europe. Yet, in spite of this, Stoica announced that Romania still wanted to develop greater trade with the United States.[57]

Bucharest's efforts to woo the United States did not go unnoticed. In January, 1959, in reviewing its East European policy, the NSC noted Romania's interests in expanding trade relations and entering into limited and controlled cultural, technical and educational exchanges with America.[58] However, there were problems especially in placing Romanian exhibits in the United States. Bucharest's insistence upon literal reciprocity restricted contacts, because few Americans wanted to visit Romania while large numbers of Romanians wanted to visit the United States. The State Department had arranged for a Romanian Folk Art exhibit in Washington and New York, and the Department encouraged Americans to visit Bucharest.[59] However, few people responded.

However, the future of trade relations between Washington and Bucharest depended not on exhibitions, but on the two countries settling the claims issue, and the Foreign Claims Settlement Commission had not yet completed its work. In addition, Romanian-American relations were also sidetracked by Nikita Khrushchev's June 2, 1958, letter to Dwight Eisenhower. The Soviet leader wanted to massively expand United States-Soviet Union trade in "non-strategic" goods. He wanted to trade manganese, chrome, asbestos, lumber and furs for industrial equipment, especially the kind needed to produce synthetic materials and consumer goods.[60] The request surprised the Administration. America was not ready to trade with the Soviet Union. Moscow could not receive most-favored-nation treatment on its exports, it was ineligible for long term credits, and Congress would have to draft legislation to alter existing export controls. These problems affected America's response to an offer the State Department viewed as genuine and not intended for propaganda purposes.[61] As a result, most Washington agencies involved in trade with the Communist world spent considerable time and energy over the next year discussing Khrushchev's proposal.[62] In consequence, Romania's trade overtures fell a bit by the wayside. In fact, on March 4, 1959, Eisenhower appeared to dampen hopes for all East-West trade, when he announced that "I do not believe that at this moment we are ready for any radical change in policy with respect to trade" with the Communist world.[63]

Nonetheless, Romanian officials were aware that the Foreign Claims Settlement Commission was about to complete its work on Romania's claims. With this in mind, Bucharest notified Washington in mid-April that it was willing to begin discussions on war damage and nationalization issues.[64] A couple of months later, Gheorghiu-Dej sent a trade delegation led by Vice Premier Alexandru Birladeanu and the President of the State Planning Commission, Gheorghe Gaston-Marin, for a unofficial visit to Western Europe. During their stay, the delegation secured about $60 million worth of contracts, the most important being a nearly $20 million contract with Rustyfa, an Anglo-American concern based in Britain, to construct a tire plant in Romania.[65]

Meanwhile, the United States completed its work on Romania's claims and on August 9 announced that the total money awarded to claimants amounted to nearly $60 million, however America had only a little over $20 million in frozen Romanian assets. Washington wanted to begin talks with Bucharest to resolve this problem, before any negotiations began on trade.[66] Romania appointed a new minister to Washington, George Macovescu,[67] and the claims negotiations began on November 16, 1959.[68]

Meanwhile, the White House continued to prod Congress to liberalize America's trade laws, especially the Battle Act. Eastern Europe was open for business in non-strategic items, and the only sellers were West Europeans. This upset the American business community and they began to urge Congress to amend the present legislation. Foreign pressure too mounted. Poland wanted more trade, while Romania wanted to begin trade. And then there was Mr. Khrushchev's letter of June, 1958, which exposed the crippling restrictions imposed on the Executive Branch by the Battle Act. Consequently, on April 15, 1959, Senators John F. Kennedy of Massachusetts and George D. Aiken of Vermont introduced S. 1697 which would amend the act, and give the President authority to approve economic aid to certain Communist dominated countries if he deemed it important to national security. The President had indicated that it was necessary for the United States to be in a position to aid Communist satellites that were "resisting Soviet domination."[69]

The Senate Foreign Relations Committee recommended the bill to the Senate on August 3. After heated debate, the Senate approved the amendment on September 12 by a 49-40 roll call vote.[70] Three days later, Nikita Khrushchev arrived in the United States to visit the President at Camp David.[71] While the legislation still limited trade between the United States and the Soviet Union, its passage indicated a changing mood in America which Khrushchev wanted to foster.[72]

The amended Battle Act spurred Romania to quickly resolve the claims issue. The new legislation would permit the United States to help Bucharest fulfill the goals of its new Six Year Plan. The negotiations themselves remain classified, but unlike Romania's claims settlement discussions with other countries which extended over several years, these talks were completed in only five months.[73] On March 20, 1960, the United States and the Romanian People's Republic signed a Settlement of Claims agreement in Washington, D.C. The total amount of compensation for claims amounted to $24,526,370. The value of Romania's frozen assets was put at $22,026,370, leaving a balance of $2.5 million. Romania agreed to pay this sum in five installments, each of $500,000 through July 1, 1964. In return for payment, the United States agreed that it would no longer pursue claims arising from events in Romania which occurred before September 16, 1947.[74] Of the more than 1,000 original claimants, 498 received compensation amounting to approximately $1,000 per claim plus 38% of their entitlement.[75] Following the signing, the Romanians hosted a cocktail party attended by East Coast financial and business leaders. Also attending were representatives of the Administration including the Secretary of Commerce, Frederick Mueller.[76] Bucharest intended to waste little time in laying the ground work for future trade negotiations. In the meantime, Romania began talks with State Department officials concerning cultural and technical exchanges.[77]

In May, 1960, the Central Committee of the Party approved a long term economic program which included the Six Year Plan, as outlined in 1958, and a Sixteen Year Plan, from 1960-1975. As a result of these two plans, the Party envisioned a 500% increase in industrial production, and a 200% increase in agriculture. This was not a variation of the Chinese "leap forward" program, rather the plans called for a steady increase over a 16 year period.[78] The Central Committee recommended that the plans be approved at the next Party Congress.

During the week of June 20, 1960, Communist party delegates gathered in Bucharest for the Romanian Worker's Third Party Congress. This would prove to be an historic meeting. Khrushchev apparently intended to use the Congress as a forum to force the Chinese into accepting Moscow's leadership of the world Communist movement. The Soviet leader attacked the Chinese from the opening moment of the convocation. Beijing was not following Marxist-Leninist teaching because Mao was unable to apply Marxist doctrine "creatively." Khrushchev's personal attack on Mao was rebutted by the leader of the Chinese delegation, Peng Zhen. The public display of personal animosity indicated the degree of ill will between the two leaders. Khrushchev and Mao not only differed over theoretical and practical issues, they also disliked one another immensely.[79]

Khrushchev's willingness to make the Sino-Soviet split a Communist issue, gave Gheorghiu-Dej an opportunity to further his goals. Moscow had shown little support for Romania's Six Year Plan. In December, 1959, a Soviet report on the Twelfth session of CMEA, which met in Sofia, gave no indication that Moscow approved the rapid industrialization called for in the Romanian plan. In fact, the list of CMEA countries that were expected to expand their steel output between 1961 and 1965 did not include Romania. In March and April, 1960, Birladeanu went to Moscow to seek Soviet support of the Six Year Plan. No official statements flowed from these discussions.[80] Therefore, Gheorghiu-Dej used the Third Congress to announce to all the delegates, including the Soviet contingent, the goals of Romania's new Six Year Plan. According to Montias, Gheorghiu-Dej's keynote address indicated that Moscow supported the Plan, and had agreed to aid in the construction of a steel mill in Galati enabling Romania to produce 4 million tons of steel a year. Moscow economists were surprised at this statement.[81] There is no evidence to indicate that Khrushchev agreed to this aid. If the Soviet leader did not make the commitment, Gheorghiu-Dej decided to capitalize on the Sino-Soviet rift and have Moscow pay for Bucharest's loyalty. Soviet efforts to control the world Communist movement could afford a split with China and with Albania, but it could not lose the support of other East European satellites without losing leadership credibility in the Communist world. Gheorghiu-Dej apparently realized this and used the Congress to publicly accept Soviet aid. At the close of the Third Congress, the Romanian delegates unanimously approved the Six Year and Sixteen Year Plans.[82]

The furor caused by the Sino-Soviet split forced Khrushchev to call a meeting in November, 1960, of Communist party leaders from 81 countries. The Romanian delegation arrived early, and on November 11 signed a trade pact with Moscow implementing Khrushchev's aid offer. The pact included Soviet technical support in constructing the Galati mill as well as a five year commercial agreement calling for Moscow to ship raw materials to Bucharest in return for finished products.[83] During the Moscow meeting, Romania supported the Soviet Union in its fight against Beijing for leadership of the world Communist movement.

Meanwhile, America and Romania had continued their talks about developing cultural and technical exchanges. Finally, on December 9, 1960, Foy Kohler, the Assistant Secretary of State for European Affairs, and George Macovescu, the Romanian Minister, exchanged diplomatic notes which provided for visits and exchanges between the two countries through 1962. Included were opportunities for exchanges of art exhibits, theater performances, books and publications, and radio and television programs.[84] This agreement proved to be the final development in the Eisenhower Administration's policy toward Romania. The significance of the treaty should not be minimized. It was the first such agreement Washington signed with an East European country. The accord also indicated the great distance that both countries had covered during the eight years of the Eisenhower Presidency. Romania had finally shed its image, long held in Washington, of being the "most Sovietized" of all the satellite states. Finally, the agreement foreshadowed the direction that the newly elected American President, John F. Kennedy, would take in his relations with Bucharest.

Notes

1. *American Foreign Relations, Current Documents, 1957* (Washington, D.C.: U.S. Government Printing Office, 1961), p. 720.

2. See, Fejto, *A History of the People's Democracies,* pp. 66ff.

3. NYT, October 27, 1956, p. 4.

4. CIA Report, Communism in Eastern Europe; Post-Stalin Developments in the Satellites, August 28, 1958, p. 12, Communism in Eastern Europe File, Box 5, Subject Series, NSC Series, Briefing Notes, Office of the Special Assistant for National Security Affairs, White House Office, DDE Library.

5. Summerscale, *The East European Predicament*, p. 35.

6. Campbell, *American Policy Toward Communist Eastern Europe*, p. 33.

7. Ionescu, *Communism in Rumania, 1944-1962*, p. 272; CIA Report, Communism in Eastern Europe; Post-Stalin Developments in the Satellites, August 28, 1958, p. 13, Communism in Eastern Europe File, Box 5, Subject Series, NSC Series, Briefing Notes, Office of the Special Assistant for National Security Affairs, White House Office, DDE Library.

8. Ibid., p. 17; NYT October 31, 1956, p. 1; "Signing of Agreement Between the Governments of the RPR and the USSR on the Legal Status of the Soviet Troops Temporarily Stationed in the RPR," *Agerpres*, April 25, 1957, p. 15.

9. NYT, November 4, 1956, p. 34.

10. *Current Documents, 1957*, p. 720.

11. Report, On Foreign Economic Policy Discussions Between United States Officials in Europe and Clarence B. Randall and Associates, September 1956, p. 10, File Council on Foreign Economic Relations, Box 18, Subject Series, Confidential Files, WHCF, DDE Library.

12. Memorandum, For Robert H. Cutler, February 7, 1957, pp. 1-2, File CFEP 501 East- West Trade, Working Papers 1957, Box 1, Policy Paper Series, USCFEP, DDE Library.

13. Minutes, 53rd Meeting, February 5, 1957, p. 2, File CFEP 501 East- West Trade, Working Papers 1957, Box 1, Policy Paper Series, USCFEP, DDE Library.

14. Adler, Karlsson, *Western Economic Warfare, 1947-1967*, pp. 94-95; Bertsch, *Controlling East-West Trade and Technology Transfer*, p. 245.

15. Report, United States Policy on Economic Defense, August 30, 1954, p. 7, NSC152/3 U.S. Economic Defense Policy File, Box 5, Special Assistant NSC, White House Office, DDE Library;Working Group Report, Disposal Abroad of Government-Owned Agricultural Surpluses, March 9, 1954, p. 7, CCS091.31, 9.28.45.Sec 24, Box 10, Decimal File 1954-1956, Joint Chiefs of Staff, National Archives.

16. See, Duane Tananbaum, *The Bricker Amendment Controversy: A Test Case of Eisenhower's Political Leadership* (Ithaca, N.Y.: Cornell University Press, 1988).

17. U. S. Congress, Senate, Committee on Government Operations, *Hearings Before the Subcommittee on Foreign Aid Expenditures*, 89th Cong., 2d Sess., 1966, p. 16.

18. Memorandum, For Gerald D. Morgan, February 21, 1955, 10pp., East-West Trade File, Box 2, Subject Series, Dodge Series, Records 1954-1961, Office of the Chairman, USCFEP, DDE Library.

19. Memorandum, For Gerald D. Morgan, March 1958, p. 4, CFEP 502 File, Box 3, CFEP Paper Series, Records, Office of the Chairman, USCFEP, DDE Library.

20. Letter, J. Lee Rankin to James S. Lay, Jr., April 17, 1955, 2pp., East-West Trade File, Box 2, Subject Subseries, Dodge Series, Records 1954-1961, Office of the Chairman, USCFEP, DDE Library.

21. Memorandum, Discussion at the 282nd Meeting NSC, April 26, 1956, pp; 4-7, 282nd Meeting File, Box 7, NSC Series, Ann Whitman Files, DDE Library.

22. Handbook on U.S. Foreign Economic Policy, September 30, 1957, I, 103a, Box 5, CFEP Paper Series, Records, Office of the Chairman, USCFEP, DDE Library.

23. U. S. Congress, House, *Extension of Public Law 480, Conference Report [To Accompany S.1314]* , Report No. 683, 85th Cong., 1st Sess., 1957, p. 3; Summary, Significant Actions in CFEP, p. 4, CFEP File, Box 4, Staff Series, Office of the Chairman: 1954-1961, CFEP, DDE Library.

24. Report, U.S. Economic Defense Policy, September 16, 1957, pp. 1-2, NSC5704/3 File, Box 20, Office of the Special Assistant, White House Office, DDE Library.

25. Memorandum, CFEP 566 - U. S. Economic Defense Policy, February 13, 1958, 2pp., NSC5704/3 U. S. Economic Defense Policy [Controls on East-West Trade] File, Box 20, Office of Special Assistant for NSC, White House Office, DDE Library.

26. Memorandum, CFEP 566 - U.S. Economic Defense Policy, February 14, 1958, p. 1, NSC Misc. File, Box 3, Agency Subseries, Office of the Chairman, CFEP, DDE Library.

27. [Battle Act Administrator] *A Survey of the Strategic Trade Control Program, 1957-1960: Fourteenth Report to Congress* (Washington, D.C.: U. S. Government Printing Office, 1961), pp. 1-4;[*Idem.*] *The 1958 Revision of East-West Trade controls: Twelfth Report to Congress* (Washington, D.C.: U. S. Government Printing Office), p. 3; Adler-Karlsson, *Western Economic Warfare*, 1947-1967, p. 97.

28. *State Department Bulletin,* September 8, 1958, p. 392. Hereafter cited as *DOS Bulletin.*

29. *The 1958 Revision of East-West Trade Controls*, p. 4 n5.

30. Report, Basic National Security Policy, May 5, 1958, pp. 17-18, NSC5810 File, Box 20, Office of the Special Assistant, White House Office, DDE Library.

31. Report, U. S. Policy Toward the Soviet-Dominated Nations in Eastern Europe, May 9, 1958, pp. 4-5, 7, NSC5811 File, Record Group 573 5W1, Policy Papers, NSC, National Archives.

32. *Ibid.,* p. 14.

33. *Scinteia*, February 28, 1957, p. 1.

34. Fejto, *A History of the People's Democracies*, p. 87.

35. NYT, May 19, 1957, p. 34.

36. CSM, June 27, 1957, p. 4.

37. NYT, May 22, 1957, p. 3.

38. Fischer-Galati, *The New Rumania,* pp. 68-69; Lawrence S. Graham, *Romania, A Developing Socialist State* (Boulder, CO: Westview Press, 1982), p. 60.

39. CIA Report, Communism, in Eastern Europe; Post-Stalin Developments in the Satellites, August 28, 1958, p. 18, Communism in Eastern Europe File, Box 5, Subject Series, NSC Series, Briefing Notes, Office of the Special Assistant for National Security Affairs, White House Office, DDE Library.

Gheorghiu-Dej removed Constantinescu and Chisinevski from the Political Bureau and the latter from his position as Secretary of the Central Committee.

40. *Ibid.*, p. 19.
41. Paul Lendavi, *Eagles in Cobwebs*, (New York: Anchor Books, 1969), p. 362.
42. Stephen Fischer-Galati, "Romania's Development as a Communist State," *Romania in the 1980s*, ed. Daniel N. Nelson (Boulder, CO: Westview Press, 1981), p. 10.
43. Floyd, *Rumania: Russia's Dissident Ally*, p. 42.
44. CIA Report, Communism, in Eastern Europe; Post-Stalin Developments in the Satellites, August 28, 1958, p. 28, Communism in Eastern Europe File, Box 5, Subject Series, NSC Series, Briefing Notes, Office of the Special Assistant for National Security Affairs, White House Office, DDE Library.
45. DOS Report, Current Status of East-West Exchanges: Report No. 10, February 15, 1958, pp. 44-45, Department of State: Jan-May 1958 File, Box 75, Subject Series, WHCF, DDE Library.
46. NYT, February 27, 1958, p. 2. Stoica was known to the West principally because of his earlier suggestion for a nuclear free zone in the Balkans. Hans E. Tutsch, "Eastern Europe and the Non-Communist World," *Eastern Europe in the Sixties*, ed. Stephen Fischer-Galati [New York: Frederick A. Praeger, 1963], pp. 221-224.
47. Fischer-Galati, *The New Rumania*, p. 70.
48. Ionescu, *Communism in Rumania, 1944-1962*, p. 288.
49. Robert L. Hutchings, *Soviet-East European Relations: Consolidation and Conflict* (Madison: University of Wisconsin Press, 1987), p. 31.
50. Christopher D. Jones, *Soviet Influence in Eastern Europe* (New York: Frederick A. Praeger, 1981), p. 84.
51. Interview of William A. Crawford by William A. Moss, March 12, 1971. p. 1, JFK Library; Mary Ellen Fischer, "Political Leadership in Rumania under the Communists," *International Journal of Rumanian Studies*, Vol. V, No. 1 (1987), p. 9.
52. Pacepa, *Red Horizons*, pp. 309-310.
53. "Departure of the Last Units of Soviet Troops Stationed in the Rumanian People's Republic Under the Warsaw Treaty," *Agerpres*, August 1, 1958, p. 16.
54. Montias, *Economic Development in Communist Rumania*, p. 201.
55. CIA Report, Communism, in Eastern Europe; Post-Stalin Developments in the Satellites, August 28, 1958, p. 14, Communism in Eastern Europe File, Box 5, Subject Series, NSC Series, Briefing Notes, Office of the Special Assistant for National Security Affairs, White House Office, DDE Library.
56. Montias, *Economic Development in Communist Rumania*, pp. 53, 101ff. See also, R. V. Burks, "The Rumanian National Deviation: An Accounting," *Eastern Europe in Transition*, ed. Kurt London (1966), p. 101, and Linden, *Bear and Foxes*, p. 180.
57. "Interview of the Chairman of the RPR Council of Ministers, Chivu Sto-

ica, Granted to the Correspondent of Washington Post," Murray Marder, *Ager-pres (Supplement)*, November 24, 1958, pp. 3, 7.

58. Report, U. S. Policy Toward the Soviet-Dominated Nations in Eastern Europe, January 7, 1959, p. 3, NSC5811/1 File, Record Group 273 5W1, Policy Papers, NSC. National Archives.

59. *Ibid.*, pp. 4-5.

60. Memorandum, On the Expansion of US-USSR Trade, June 16, 1958, p. 1, Khrushchev Letter File, Box 2, CFEP Paper Series, Records, Office of the Chairman, USCFEP, DDE Library.

61. *Ibid.*, pp. 1-5.

62. For an example of this activity see, Letter, Paul H. Cullen to CFEP (encs.), April 7, 1959, 5pp, Subject File-Communist Trade, Areeda Papers, DDE Library.

63. [Dwight D. Eisenhower] *Public Papers of the Presidents of the United States, 1959* (Washington, D.C.: U.S. Government Printing Office, 1960), p. 231.

64. CSM, April 20, 1959, p. 10.

65. Ionescu, *Communism in Rumania, 1944-1962*, p. 301.

66. *DOS Bulletin*, November 23, 1959, p. 764.

67. *Scinteia*, August 23, 1959, p. 4.

68. *American Foreign Relations: Current Documents, 1959* (Washinton, D.C.: U. S. Government Printing Office, 1963), pp. 849-850.

69. *Congressional Quarterly, Almanac,1959*, Volume XV,(Washington, D.C.: Congressional Quarterly Inc., 1960), p. 196.

70. *Ibid.*, pp. 196-197.

71. Franklin Roosevelt created this presidential retreat, near Thurmont, Maryland, from what had been originally a CCC camp. He, named it Shangri-La, but Eisenhower renamed the place for his grandson (David Brinkley, *Washington Goes to War* [Alfred A. Knopf, 1988], p. 202).

72. On the Camp David meeting see, Dwight D. Eisenhower, *The White House Years: Waging Peace, 1956-1961* (Garden City, N.Y.: Doubleday & Co., 1965), pp. 434ff. and, *Khrushchev Remembers*, trans. & ed. Strobe Talbott, pp. 406ff. See also, Talking Paper, Major Themes of Khrushchev's Public and Private Statements and U. S. Counter-Arguments, September 8, 1959, 15pp., Russia (18) File, Box 64, Subject Series, Confidential File, WHCF, DDE Library; *DOS Bulletin*, October 19, 1959, pp. 549-59.

73. Talks between the United Kingdom and Romania which had opened in 1954 were still underway when Romanian talks with the United States began in November 1959 (Report, Patterns of Rumanian claims Settlements with Western Countries, October, 30, 1959, pp.1-4, [Bureau of Intelligence and Research] Report 8143, Box 1787, OSS R&A Reports, National Archives).

74. [Department of State] *Settlement of Claims of United States Nationals and Other Financial Matters: Agreement Between the United States and Rumania. Signed at Washington March 30, 1960 with Exchanges of Notes* (Washington, D.C.: U. S. Government Printing Office, 1960), pp. 1-3; *Scinteia*, March 31, 1960, p. 4.

75. Senate Subcommittee on International Trade and Commerce, *Status of Claims Settlements with Nonmarket Countries*, 1976, p. 9.

76. *Scinteia*, March 31, 1960, p. 4.

77. Report, U. S. Policy Toward the Soviet-Dominated Nations in Eastern Europe, July 27, 1960, p. 4, NSC5811/1 File, Record Group 273 5W1, NSC Policy Papers, National Archives.

78. Report, Rumanian Long-Range Economic Plans, July 13, 1960, p. 4, [Bureau of Intelligence and Research] Report 8300 File, Box 1787, OSS R&A Reports, National Archives.

79. Donald S. Zagoria, *The Sino-Soviet Conflict, 1956-1961* (Princeton, NJ: Princeton University Press, 1962), pp. 325ff; O. B. Borisov and B. T. Koloskov, *Sino-Soviet Relations, 1945-1973: A Brief History* (Moscow: Progress Publishers, 1975) p. 164; *Khrushchev Remembers*, trans. & ed. Strobe Talbott, pp. 475ff.

80. Montias, *Economic Development in Communist Rumania*, pp. 203-204.

81. *Ibid.*, p. 204.

82. Gheorghiu-Dej Reports to the Central Committee of the Romanian Workers' Party, *Agerpres*, June 25, 1960, pp. 10-11; Ghita Ionescu, *The Reluctant Ally: A Study of Communist Neo-Colonialism* (London: Ampersand Ltd., 1965), 33; Fischer-Galati, *Twentieth-Century Rumania*, pp. 161ff; Campbell, *American Policy Toward Communist Eastern Europe*, p. 50; Fischer-Galati, *The New Rumania*, p. 80 n6.

83. Montias, *Economic Development in Communist Rumania*, pp. 204-205; Floyd, Rumania: *Russia's Dissident Ally*, pp. 59, 62; Jens Hacker, *Der Ostblock: Entstehung, Entwicklung und Strucktur, 1939-1980* (Baden-Baden: Nomos Verlagsgesellschaft, 1983), pp. 645-648. Hereafter, *Der Ostblock, 1939-1980*.

84. [Department of State] "Rumania; Cultural Relations," No. 4642, *Treaties and Other International Acts* (Washington, D.C.: U.S. Government Printing Office, 1961); *DOS Bulletin*, December 26, 1960, pp, 968-971.

CHAPTER VIII

FROM CLAIMS SETTLEMENT TO TRADE AGREEMENT

The years from 1961 through 1964 focused on three major developments: first, the struggle between the White House and Congress over export regulations concerning West-West trade and East-West trade; second, Bucharest's clash with Moscow concerning Romanian independence and her role in CMEA; and, third, the success of Kennedy's policy of penetration and Gheorghiu-Dej's policy of leaning to the West culminating in the June, 1964, commercial accord between Romania and the United States.

Kennedy's Foreign Economic Policy, 1961-1962

Following his election in November, 1960, President-elect Kennedy received a report on foreign economic policy from one of his transition task forces chaired by George Ball. The Ball Report called for America to establish an "open competitive Free World economy in which the forces of economic growth. . . will bring about the most efficient use of our resources. . . ."[1] The growing balance of payments deficit was the most significant problem the new Administration would face. The solution was to expand international trade by reducing world trade barriers. This goal would require "a commitment to common action on the part of the industrialized countries."[2]

The Ball Report also called for America to change its views toward East-West trade. The "Communist bloc trade now threatens to become [a] new disruptive force in [Western] commercial relations," because "we persist in regarding trade with the Communist bloc as immoral," while our Western European allies do not. Further, the United States had based its East-West trade policies on the "unrealistic assumptions that: 1, the Soviets need Western trade items to build a military potential and; 2, we can induce, or force, our allies and the less-developed areas to concur in our views." What were needed, according to the report, were "mutually acceptable standards for expanded Western trade with the Communist bloc." The Ball report urged Kennedy to have Congress amend the Trade Agreement Extension Act, the Battle Act and the Export Control Act in such a way as to provide greater trade flexibility with the Communist world, and increased economic power for the President. The result would enable the White House to work with Western Europe to establish a common trade policy toward the Communist Bloc.[3] The President accepted the Ball Report and it became the blueprint for his foreign economic policy.

When he arrived in the White House, the new President made some significant organizational changes. Unlike Eisenhower, who preferred a pyramid management structure, Kennedy used a spoked wheel structure with himself at the hub. Kennedy wanted a mechanism for change and believed that the pyramid model prevented innovation. He reduced the power of the NSC, nearly eliminated Cabinet meetings, and abolished the CFEP. He surrounded himself with generalists, most of whom had the title of Special Assistant to the President. Kennedy wanted personal control of the government and a spoked wheel model suited his style.[4]

In his State of the Union address to Congress, on January 30, 1961, President Kennedy clearly indicated his interest in Eastern Europe. He asked Congress "for increased discretion to use economic tools" to help him reestablish "historic ties of friendship" with the Soviet Bloc. Precisely, he wanted Congress to amend the Battle Act.[5] As a Senator, Kennedy had introduced S. 2828 in August, 1959, which gave the President discretionary power to deal with the Soviet Bloc overriding the provisions of the Battle Act, Mutual Security Act, and PL 480.[6] The bill passed the Senate, but was not considered in the House. Consequently on February 6, 1961, Kennedy asked Secretary of State Dean Rusk to have legislation introduced in the Senate to amend the Battle Act.[7] S. 1215 introduced on February 21 provided the needed amendment language.[8]

In addition to amending the Battle Act, Kennedy also had to change the Export Control Act. Kennedy had replaced Eisenhower's CFEP with a new organization to monitor export controls, the Export Control Review Board, or ECRB. This was a scaled down model of the CFEP in so far as it had only three members, the Secretaries of Commerce, State and Defense. The Chairman was the Secretary of Commerce, and the ECRB functioned as his advisory board making recommendations concerning export licenses in relation to national security issues. The ECRB began operating on May 24, 1961, and within a few days began to review all of the items on the control lists with an eye to liberalizing the licensing process.[9]

While the ECRB maintained the preeminence of the Commerce Department's role in export controls, this development did not preclude the State Department from continuing its efforts to reduce America's export barriers. On May 25, the Department sent a lengthy review of Washington's economic relations with the Soviet Bloc to McGeorge Bundy, Kennedy's Special Assistant for National Security. The review reiterated many of the points of the Ball Report plus the personal philosophy of the new Secretary of State. Unlike his predecessor, John Foster Dulles, who believed in a "rollback" approach to Eastern Europe, Dean Rusk wanted to inject Western ideas of freedom behind the Iron Curtain through increased contacts and trade with the Soviet Bloc states.[10]

The May 25 review emphasized that America's economic relations with the countries of Eastern Europe should be designed to aid individual satellite states in their efforts to secure greater independence from the Soviet Union. Specifically, the review suggested that Section 5 of the Trade Agreements Extension Act of 1951 be amended to give the President discretionary powers to grant MFN treatment to imports from particular Bloc states. Without MFN, import duties were based on the Smoot-Hawley Tariff of June 15, 1930, which was notorious for its prohibitive rates. Turning to exports, the review urged a reduction in the Commerce Department's embargo lists to make them identical to those of COCOM. Commerce could still deny export licenses for equipment which could contribute to Moscow's military strength. As for the Battle Act, which was under the control of the State Department, the review recommended that no changes be made other than those in the Battle Act amendment presently under Congressional consideration. Approval of this amendment would provide the President with sufficient discretionary power to permit economic and financial assistance to Bloc countries.[11]

The State Department recommendations were ill timed. The new President was already in the midsts of his first foreign policy disaster, the infamous Bay of Pigs invasion of Cuba in April, 1961. Two months later, he met Premier Khrushchev in Vienna. The Soviet leader viewed

Kennedy as naive and irresolute. He bullied Kennedy and threatened to curtail Western right of access to West Berlin. While Kennedy made it clear that the United States had a vital interest in West Berlin, the damage was done. Few Congressmen wanted to relax trade with the Soviet Bloc in light of Khrushchev's threats. Moreover, even fewer Congressmen wanted to surrender the legislature's control over foreign policy to a President who authorized the Bay of Pigs invasion.

Congressional opposition to the new Administration's efforts to liberalize East-West trade was apparent in June. On the 22nd, The Commerce Department announced that it would lift its ban against exporting subsidized surplus agricultural products to the Soviet Bloc. The Department wanted to sell the food for American dollars or convertible currency.[12] Congress retaliated. Delbert Latta of Ohio proposed an amendment to the Agricultural Act of 1961 which prohibited the export of any subsidized agricultural commodity to any nation "other than friendly nations." "Friendly nations" included all countries other than the Soviet Union and states dominated or controlled by the world Communist movement.[13] Congress approved the Latta Amendment, and Commerce suspended its plans. Congressional unwillingness to expand East-West trade extended to the Battle Act amendment as well. Although approved by the Senate, conservative House Democrats did not allow the amendment to emerge from the House Foreign Affairs Committee.[14]

Further Administration efforts in 1961 to implement recommendations in the Ball Report abruptly ended when East Germany erected the Berlin Wall. To many, the Wall symbolized the restrictive nature of the Communist world which could not be easily affected by increased East-West trade. Conservative Congressmen, still distrustful of the Administration, established a House Select Committee on Export Control on September 17 to investigate American exports to the Soviet Union.[15] The Select Committee's investigation lasted over six months.

Meanwhile, on January 25, Kennedy submitted the Trade Expansion Act of 1962 to Congress. Since Congress was unwilling to increase trade with the Soviet Bloc, the Administration's proposal did not include liberalized East-West trade provisions. In fact, the bill was anti-Communist in nature. The bill noted that the Soviet Bloc had nearly tripled its trade with 41 Third World nations in recent years, in its effort to "penetrate, encircle, and divide the Free World." The most effective way the United States could aid less-developed countries was to help open new markets for their exports. The bill called for an expansion of

America's trade with the Common Market to reduce Washington's balance of payments deficit and to stimulate economic growth. The bill proposed that Congress increase the President's negotiating authority so that the Administration could reduce trade barriers especially between the United States and the Common Market. By so doing, "Communist hopes for a trade war between these two great economic giants would be frustrated, and Communist efforts to split the West would be doomed to failure."[16]

Although Kennedy did not mention trade with Communist countries in the Trade Expansion Act of 1962, he continued to oppose efforts on Capitol Hill to restrict the President's "flexibility" in East-West trade. During a June 7 news conference Kennedy reminded the press that as a Senator, he had supported President Eisenhower's efforts at maintaining this flexibility. Kennedy explained that because of circumstances in the Soviet Bloc he hoped that the legislature would give him the flexibility to provide "assistance to a country which was following an independent policy."[17]

Meanwhile, the House Select Committee on Export Control had completed its investigation of America's export practices with the Soviet Union. The committee was extremely critical of the Administration's unwillingness to punish countries which violated export controls and Battle Act provisions. On April 9, the President had asked for a permanent extension of the Export Control Act scheduled to expire on June 30, 1962. The Select Committee's findings fueled conservative Congressmen in both houses. In the Senate, Wayne Morse from Oregon attacked the State Department, blaming it for its lack of cooperation with Congress. He asserted that "the State Department did not want any restrictions" on trade, and he suggested that Congress should "exercise checks against the State Department in the field of foreign policy."[18] The situation was no better in the House. Representative Kitchen of North Carolina, who had chaired the Select Committee, submitted four amendments which would have required the Commerce Department to deny the export of any item whose economic significance could affect America's national security. Further, he wanted to change the penalty for violating the Export Control Act from a misdemeanor to a felony.[19]

As Congress vented its wrath against the Administration and other liberal elements which wanted to expand all trade, including East-West commerce, time was running out on renewing the legislation. The Senate had approved three amendments to the renewal, while the House approved four. Conference deliberations were unable to work out all the details as the clock ran down toward June 30. On the final day, the House and Senate approved a three year extension of an amended version of the Export Control Act. The significant amendments dealt with a broadening of the criteria used to deny items export licenses. The legislation of 1949 was designed to stop the export of "strategic" items. Such items were primarily defined as those which contributed to the military potential of the Communist world. However, the amended act broadened the control system to take into account the "economic significance" of exports to the Communist Bloc. While the tone of the amendment was severe, it did not dramatically alter present practice. The amendment simply justified the denial of export licenses to items not labelled "military," but which were considered to be a threat to America's national security. Since the amendments did not eliminate presidential discretion, Kennedy signed the renewal on July 1, 1962.[20]

Meanwhile, Congress continued to discuss the President's key trade legislation, the Trade Expansion Act of 1962. The furor heard during the Export Control Act debates was again voiced by members in both Houses. Despite the Administration's efforts to retain discretionary power in dealing with the Soviet Bloc, Congress passed the Trade Expansion Act of 1962 with Section 231(a) prohibiting the President from granting most-favored-nation treatment to Communist countries. This section also meant that MFN had to be withdrawn from Poland and Yugoslavia. The new legislation extended the President's authority to enter into trade agreements for five years and authorized him to reduce import duties up to 50% on items which the United States and Common Market countries together accounted for 80% of the free world market. Section 241 of the act created a special representative for trade negotiations, the STR, which worked out of the Executive Office of the President and assumed responsibility for America's multilateral tariff negotiations, formerly a duty of the State Department.[21] On October 11, 1962, Kennedy signed the Act. As a footnote, Kennedy delayed implementing the withdrawal of MFN from Poland and Yugoslavia until December, 1963, when the law was amended by the Foreign Assistance Act of 1963. This permitted any country which at the time of the enactment of the Trade Expansion Act had MFN status, to retain it provided the President determined that such continuance was in the national interest.[22]

Three days after Kennedy signed the Trade Expansion Act, the White House learned that the Soviets were building missile launching sites in Cuba. The ensuing crisis brought the Soviet Union and the

United States to the "brink" of nuclear disaster and encouraged both superpowers to embark on a course of peaceful coexistence. On December 19, 1962, Nikita Khrushchev sent a note to the President reviving the idea of a test ban, first raised by Prime Minister Macmillan of Great Britain and President Eisenhower. Khrushchev noted that the Cuban crisis had made it possible "to solve a far simpler question – that of cessation of experimental explosions of nuclear weapons. . . ."[23] A week later, Kennedy responded and in January representatives from the two countries began negotiations on what would become a Nuclear Test Ban Treaty.

As these talks continued, Kennedy made numerous announcements of his willingness to establish an understanding with the Soviets. In the process, the President indicated also that he wanted to expand East-West contacts. On May 16, 1963, he notified the ECRB that he wanted them to examine the entire question of East-West trade, including the possibility of significantly broadening that trade, while remaining consistent with America's security interests.[24] Shortly thereafter, he asked the Policy Planning Council of the State Department to consider the same question.[25]

Bucharest and Washington

Meanwhile, the climate generated by the Bay of Pigs, the Vienna Summit and the Berlin Wall, affected not only the President's relations with Congress, but also America's relations with Romania. The momentum for negotiations generated during the last year of the Eisenhower Administration did not carry over into Kennedy's first years in office. World developments in 1961 and 1962 revived the fear of Communism that was so evident in the early days of the Cold War. Communists were bogeymen, who could not be trusted. Gheorghiu-Dej tried to maintain the momentum of the Eisenhower period but without success. In the Summer of 1961, he sent a high powered delegation to the United States headed by Alexandru Moghioros. Allegedly, the group was interested in studying advanced agricultural techniques, but in truth the purpose of the mission was to secure long term American economic assistance.[26] In August, Gheorghiu-Dej invited representatives from Allis Chalmers, a major American manufacturer of heavy industrial equipment, to visit Bucharest.[27] Neither of these attempts produced immediate results.

Romania's overtures included a marked change in the treatment of

Americans in Bucharest. In October, the American Legation noted that unlike other East European countries, there had been no harassment of Western missions, no *persona-non-grata* actions and virtually no anti-Western actions for several years.[28] Nonetheless, the United States showed little response to Bucharest's new attitude. In December, Gheorghiu-Dej appointed Petre Balaceanu as Romania's new minister to the United States. He met the President on December 12, 1961, and during their talk, Kennedy mentioned that the United States was interested in trade development. However, existing political tensions, symbolized by the Berlin War, restricted his ability to make any measurable changes in Romanian-American trade.[29]

In January, 1962, the President appointed William Crawford as America's new Minister to Romania with the unambitious mission "to keep us from having problems. . . keep the flag flying, keep the lid on."[30] Nevertheless, Crawford was committed to improving relations between Bucharest and Washington. Crawford's years of experience in East European and Communist affairs would enable him to do far more than simply "keep the lid on."[31]

Shortly after Crawford's arrival, Bucharest hosted a State Department sponsored "Plastics USA" exhibit,[32] and in February *Agerpres* carried an interview with a team of American experts visiting Romania's cellulose and paper industry. Speaking for the American team, Dr. John McGovern praised Romania for her use of modern equipment and hoped that technical exchanges between the two countries would continue.[33] In March, American newspapers published glowing reports of Romania's continued economic growth. Bucharest's foreign trade had increased about 60% since 1958, and much of that increase had been with Western countries.[34] At the same time, Gheorghiu-Dej had the Romanian Minister in Washington meet with Commerce Secretary Luther Hodges and his Assistant, Jack Behrman. Balaceanu wanted to buy $200 million worth of equipment to construct 10 factories in Romania. He needed the Commerce Department to approve export licenses for the needed machinery, including materials to build two synthetic rubber plants.[35]

Balaceanu could not have picked a worse month to approach the Commerce Department. On March 19, Hodges had submitted a memo to the President requesting that the Treasury Department assume responsibility for administering the Export Control Act. The Commerce Department was tired of being maligned and criticized by other government agencies as well as by Congress.[36] On April 3, Secretary of the

Treasury, Douglas Dillon rejected the idea and Kennedy agreed to keep export controls within the Commerce Department's jurisdiction.[37] Since he could not get rid of the responsibility for export controls, Hodges decided to reduce the amount of criticism his Department received, especially from the anti-Communist groups. The Department would be far more restrictive in granting export licenses to Soviet Bloc countries than in the past.[38] As a result, in May, the Commerce Department refused Romania's export license requests for nine of the ten factories and demanded additional information on the tenth. Balaceanu withdrew the proposal and this ended Romania's first serious effort to dramatically increase trade with the United States.[39]

Bucharest and Moscow

In addition to trying to establish trade relations with the United States and other Western nations, Gheorghiu-Dej focused much of his energies on increasing Romania's economic independence from the Soviet Union. The November-December, 1960, Moscow meeting of representatives from 81 Communist parties, not only gave Gheorghiu-Dej the opportunity to secure Soviet aid for his Galati steel complex, but the meeting also provided the Romanian leader with a theoretical framework for national communism. The Moscow Declaration which ended the meeting on December 6 proved to be a watershed. The Soviets accepted the principal that their model was not necessarily the appropriate model for each socialist nation.[40] Gheorghiu-Dej would frequently cite the Moscow Declaration to support his independence from the Soviet Union.

Spurred by the economic success of the Common Market, Khrushchev called for greater Soviet control over CMEA. He opposed the centrifugal tendencies in CMEA, and wanted Moscow to oversee and approve the national plans of each of the satellites states. Khrushchev's designs ran absolutely counter to those of Gheorghiu-Dej. If Moscow had its way, Romania would focus her economy on filling the agricultural needs of CMEA members, rather than on implementing an economic program designed to meet Romania's national goal of industrialization. Bucharest strongly resisted Moscow's efforts to centralize CMEA, in contrast to East Germany and Czechoslovakia who saw the Moscow plan as a means for them to concentrate on heavy industry. Gheorghiu-Dej was determined to resist. He rejected Khrushchev's demand for economic integration proposed to Romanian delegations in

March and again in July, 1961.[41] In August, when Khrushchev suggested greater military and economic integration to the Warsaw Pact nations, Romania again refused, citing the Moscow Declaration[42]

Upon his return from the 22nd Party Congress of the CPSU in Moscow, Gheorghiu-Dej reported to the Central Committee of the Romanian Workers' Party. From the opening address on November 30, to the closing ceremonies on December 5, two themes became apparent: de-Stalinization and Romanian independence. The de-Stalinization included not only attacks against Pauker and Luca, but led to the destruction of Stalin edifices in Romania. Statues of Stalin disappeared and street names changed. Stalin Boulevard and Stalin Square were renamed "Aviatorilor" after a nearby monument to World War I aviators.[43]

Gheorghiu-Dej's de-Stalinization program had an added advantage. Not only did it appease Moscow, but it helped to promote Romanian independence. De-Stalinization implicitly enabled Romania to disassociate herself from a Stalinized Soviet past. At the Central Committee meeting, Gheorghiu-Dej continued to rewrite Romania's role in the August 23, 1944, defeat of Fascism. In 1954 Gheorghiu-Dej had been bold enough to declare that the Romanian Communist Party and the Soviet army were co-liberators of Romania. Now, Gheorghiu-Dej announced that the lion's share of responsibility and credit for defeating Hitler's forces belonged to the Romanian army and the Romanian people, and implicitly, not to the Soviet Union. By identifying Pauker, Luca, Georgescu, Chisinevski and Constantinescu with Stalin and the anti-Party group, Gheorghiu-Dej justified his purges and blamed all of Romania's problems on the Stalin-Molotov clique.[44] Conversely, all of Romania's successes were due to the Romanian Worker's Party which was committed to the national interests of Romania.[45]

At the Central Committee meeting, Gheorghiu-Dej reiterated his opposition to "erroneous theories" which denied each socialized country the right to build its own heavy industry. He described the Soviet interpretation of the "principles of specialization and cooperation within the framework of the socialist international division of labor" as "distorted."[46] By these remarks, Gheorghiu-Dej put Moscow on notice that he intended to continue to oppose any attempt to force Romania to abandon her national economic goal of heavy industrialization.

Within six weeks of the Central Committee meeting, Bucharest signed a number of trade agreements which indicated that Gheorghiu-Dej intended to pursue Romania's national economic plans without breaking from the Soviet Union. In the middle of January, Romania signed multi-year agreements with France, Italy and Austria in which the Western countries agreed to provide Romania with metallurgical and industrial equipment.[47] At the end of the month, Romania signed a pact with Moscow which exchanged Romanian oil for Soviet manufactures. However, within a few months, Gheorghiu-Dej complained that Moscow was sending inferior products and forcing Bucharest to sell its oil products below world prices.[48]

Romania's eagerness to trade with the West attracted some attention in the United States. American newspapers began to carry stories of Bucharest's booming economy. The *New York Times* noted that Romania had tripled her industrial output three fold since 1950.[49] A few weeks later, another article indicated that 1961 was the "second successive year" that Romania was "the most dynamic economy in Eastern Europe."[50] By May, the *Wall Street Journal* carried an article on Mamaia, a Romanian vacation site on the Black Sea, where communists could "enjoy a merry-go-round of night clubbing, sailing and opera recitals" without having to think that "he is slipping into the pleasure loving ways of capitalism."[51] The tone of these articles indicated, albeit small, a change in America's perception of Romania. The American business community would take note that trade opportunities could exist in Bucharest. However, the time was not yet right to develop these opportunities. Neither the American Congress, nor the majority of American people were ready to trade with a Soviet satellite in view of the prevailing anti-Communist sentiment.

Romania's Western overtures attracted far more attention in Moscow than in Washington. Bucharest's blatant efforts to pursue an independent course, prompted Khrushchev to call a CMEA summit conference. Since its inception in 1949, CMEA had functioned primarily as a propaganda device to counter the Marshall Plan and the Common Market.[52] Now, the Soviet leader wanted to make CMEA a supranational economic organization. As a first step toward implementing this vision, Khrushchev introduced "The Basic Principles of the International Socialist Division of the Labor" on June 6 to the delegates assembled in Moscow. The Romanians opposed all forms of forced supranationalism, especially a model which would promote Romanian agriculture at the expense of industry. Bucharest's persistent opposition forced the Soviets to moderate their demands due to the provisions of the CMEA charter. This 1960 document stipulated that recommendations and decisions could only be adopted "with the consent of the member countries concerned." Consequently, no country could be forced into some cooperative venture against its will.[53]

To accommodate the defiant Romanians, the June 7 "Basic Principles" document included a statement recognizing that CMEA was a community of "free, sovereign nations" who were involved in a "voluntary effort" to coordinate national economic plans.[54] The summit also agreed to establish an Executive Committee with the powers of a "united planning organ" to coordinate member states' national economic plans into a unified CMEA plan.[55] Although Bucharest had accepted the concept of an Executive Committee, Gheorghiu-Dej did not intend to let this Committee interfere with Romania's national economic goals.

After the Romanian delegation returned to Bucharest, a *Scinteia* editorial on June 11 summarized the Moscow meeting noting that the summit decisions did not abrogate any of the resolutions made at the party's Third Congress. Romania was free to determine her own economic plans, which implicitly meant that Gheorghiu-Dej had rejected the functions of an Executive Committee.[56] Unlike a statement in the Moscow Declaration of 1960, Romanians did not "cherish the unity of the socialist camp like the apple of their eye."[57]

Khrushchev was angry and visited Romania on June 17. Gheorghiu-Dej brought the Soviet leader to see some of Romania's new factories. Khrushchev did not like what he saw and warned the "Romanians in pretty abusive language that they were on the wrong track and shouldn't be going ahead with this kind of thing."[58] Gheorghiu-Dej defended Romania's industrialization and based its development on Marxism which required heavy industrialization as a precondition for socialism. Furthermore, he was tired "of sending corn to Poland so Poland could raise hogs to sell to the West for industrial goods." Romania should trade her foodstuffs directly with the West for manufactured products.[59] The exchange deteriorated into what the French call a "*dialogue des sourds*," a conversation between deaf men.[60]

In August, 1962, Khrushchev revealed his true purpose in convening the CMEA summit. In an article in *Kommunist*, the policy journal of the Soviet Communist Party, Khrushchev said that his goal was to make the economies of the socialist camp into a "single entity." The article also implied that satellite states which were unwilling to accept his plan for "international specialization" could lose Soviet financial aid.[61] This threat affected Gheorghiu-Dej because he could not implement Romania's industrial program without foreign assistance. Consequently, Khrushchev's position forced Gheorghiu-Dej to look for alternative sources of technological and economic help.

William Crawford, America's Minister to Romania, urged the United States to help Gheorghiu-Dej. The Administration was receptive, but Congress was not. In July, President Kennedy had again called for increased trade with Eastern Europe as a means to stimulate democracy in the Soviet bloc.[62] Two months later, William Tyler, the Assistant Secretary of State, testified before the European Subcommittee of the House Committee on Foreign Affairs, that America should establish "normal and active relations with the Eastern European governments of the Soviet Bloc."[63] However, the American Congress remained steadfastly opposed to dealing with the Communists. In October, Congress passed the Trade Expansion Act which prohibited the government from granting MFN to East European countries. Congress's attitude had restricted Romanian-American trade to $3 million between August, 1961 and June, 1962.[64]

In spite of these developments, Bucharest continued to keep a door open for improved relations with Washington. *Agerpres* carried articles on the successful eleven week tour of "Romanian Rhapsody," a Romanian music ensemble which gave 56 performances in towns across the United States from Seattle to New York City.[65] Crawford, too, tried to maintain good relations between the two countries. In November, he prepared a draft treaty to expand the American-Romanian cultural exchange program, which was responsible for the "Romanian Rhapsody" tour. His proposal, which was later accepted, called for increased exchanges of students, tourists, publications, and films.[66]

In addition to looking to America for increased trade, Gheorghiu-Dej looked to the Third World and Western Europe. In September, he and Prime Minister Ion Gheorghe Maurer visited Indonesia and India, where they signed a pact with New Delhi to ship iron ore to Romania.[67] Gheorghiu-Dej also began negotiations with England and France for aid in building the Galati steel mill, since the Soviets had reneged on their earlier promise of assistance. On November 25, 1962, Bucharest signed an agreement with an Anglo-French consortium.

The October Cuban Missile Crisis prompted Romania to accelerate her independence. Khrushchev's willingness to bring Romania, and the rest of the Soviet Bloc, to the brink of nuclear disaster without informing Bucharest infuriated Gheorghiu-Dej.[68] Furthermore, in the aftermath of the crisis, the Soviets appeared weak in contrast to the United States, and this weakness encouraged China to be more critical of Soviet behavior. The growing Sino-Soviet split forced Moscow to tolerate Romania's independence in exchange for Bucharest's support in the struggle against Beijing.[69]

Romania's obstructionism in CMEA enraged Khrushchev. In his November, 1962, report to the Central Committee of the CPSU, he blamed Bucharest for CMEA shortcomings.[70] However, Gheorghiu-Dej would not be threatened. On December 29, he told the delegates at the Grand National Assembly that he had no intention of abandoning his fight to implement Romania's national economic plans.[71] This "tit for tat" continued. At the February, 1963, CMEA meeting, Khrushchev demanded that Romania abandon its industrial expansion and concentrate on petroleum products, fertilizers and agriculture. Alexandru Birladeanu, the Romanian representative, refused. When notified of Khrushchev's statements Gheorghiu-Dej wrote the Soviet leader a note indicating that he would withdraw Romania from CMEA unless CMEA altered its demands.[72]

When Birladeanu returned, he was given a hero's welcome by party leaders. The Romanian Workers' Party Central Committee hastily convened a plenum on March 5 and overwhelmingly endorsed Birladeanu's stand. The Committee announced that the principal means of developing the division of labor was "the coordination of national economic plans" based on the 1960 Moscow statement "of observance of national independence and sovereignty, of full equality of rights, comradely mutual aid and mutual benefit."[73] The real significance of this meeting was that the Romanians openly voiced their disagreement with the Soviet Union.[74]

To emphasize its position, the Romanian Workers' Party held a series of closed meetings throughout the country to explain its new policy. The discussions at the meetings brought out nationalist sentiments, and revived latent anti-Russian feelings.[75] What J. F. Brown calls the "Romanian deviation"[76] clearly reflected a split not only between Bucharest and Moscow, but among CMEA members themselves. There were two blocs, the industrially developed Northern Tier, and the underdeveloped Southern Tier. Romania's position was simple: she refused to forfeit her industrial future in order to be the food supplier for East Germany and Czechoslovakia.

Gheorghiu-Dej continued his policy of *tous azimuts*.[77] He made friendly gestures toward the Tirana-Beijing Axis. He began diplomatic talks to normalize relations with Albania in March, and signed a commercial agreement with China in April, 1963.[78] CMEA conferences in April and May did not reduce the tension between Moscow and

Bucharest. Gheorghiu-Dej grew in confidence. In April, he sent a trading mission to Italy and Switzerland. In a marked departure from past practices, the May Day parade in Bucharest did not include a single picture of a living Soviet leader.[79] In May, Khrushchev sent a high level delegation to Bucharest led by Nikolai Podgorny, a member of the CPSU Presidium. The 13 day visit was apparently designed to pressure Romania to change its mind. However, speeches by Gheorghiu-Dej and Politburo member, Nicolae Ceausescu, indicated that Bucharest had no intention of budging from its anti-supranational CMEA position. The speeches stressed Romania's desire to industrialize, the indispensability of "equalization of level of development" in the Bloc, and the view that intrabloc cooperation was to help "bolster the progress of each socialist country and thus the system as a whole."[80] Khrushchev had again failed to alter Romania's drive for independence.

On June 14, Peking issued a 24 point letter entitled "Proposal Concerning the General Line of the International Communist Movement" criticizing Soviet leadership of world Communism.[81] Moscow asked the CMEA nations not to publish the critique. Romania refused, and on June 20 *Scinteia* published a summary of the article[82] because it reaffirmed Bucharest's position on economic independence. Needless to say, Khrushchev was embarrassed, and there is a report that he may have made a secret visit to Romania on June 24-25. If the meeting took place, nothing is known of the discussion except that Khrushchev was unable to change Gheorghiu-Dej's views.[83]

Khrushchev called for another CMEA conference in Moscow. The delegates met on July 24-26. At the meeting, the Romanians won a surprising victory. Confronted with a growing split with China, a maverick Albania, and a weakened public image resulting from the Cuban Missile crisis, Khrushchev was unable to force the Romanians to change their position. Since unanimity was needed to effect a single unified economic plan for CMEA, Khrushchev conceded and agreed to postpone Bloc integration until 1966. On July 28, *Scinteia* carried an article on the CMEA summit indicating a clear victory for the Romanian position.[84] Gheorghiu-Dej's persistence cleared the road for Romania to pursue her own path to socialist construction.

Crawford and Kennedy Open Doors for Romania

Crawford had watched these events intently. Due to Congress's mood, America had signed but two agreements with Romania in the past year. One concerned visa issuance,[85] and the other was a two year cultural exchange agreement.[86] In March, 1963, Crawford asked the State Department to review its policy with Romania in light of Gheorghiu-Dej's independent course. He related his request to the State Department's "Guidelines On The Bloc Countries of Eastern Europe" developed the previous month. This called for liberalizing America's trade relations with the satellite states. However, nothing came of his request.[87] On June 26, President Kennedy addressed the students at the Free University of Berlin, and for the first time the President referred to Romania as an example of "economic and political variation and dissent" that was appearing in the Soviet Bloc.[88]

Three days later Crawford sent a lengthy report to the State Department renewing his request that Washington help Romania develop greater independence from Moscow. Bucharest already was trading with Western Europe, and the volume constituted about 35% of Romania's total trade. This was money and trade that could easily be earned by American businesses. Crawford specifically urged the Commerce Department to grant export licenses to the H.K. Ferguson Company of Cleveland, Ohio, and Air Products and Chemicals Incorporated of Allentown Pennsylvania for the export of equipment and technical data needed for the construction of the Galati steel mill. Crawford asked Washington to begin informal conversations with medium-level Romanian officials to indicate that trade restrictions could be reduced in return for improved consular relations in Bucharest. Finally, Crawford suggested that at a later date, Romania and the United States ought to begin trade talks.[89]

In Washington, numerous government agencies prepared reports on East-West trade and specific country studies in response to the President's requests for information in May, 1963. The first response came from the Central Intelligence Agency on July 15 entitled "Romania's Vulnerability to Soviet Economic Pressure." The CIA report noted the "striking progress" Romania had made in industrial production, which grew at an average annual rate of 15% during 1960-1962. Agricultural production was also at an historically high level for several years. As a result, Romania could withstand Soviet economic sanctions.[90] While a total Soviet embargo on Romania would cause some serious losses, Bucharest could readily shift her trade to Western Europe. In fact, this shift had already begun. West Germany, France and the United Kingdom supplied Romania with much of her needed industrial equipment.[91]

The second response arrived on July 26 from the Policy Planning Council of the State Department. This 69 page report addressed several issues involving trade with the Soviet Union and Eastern Europe. At the outset, the report indicated that any trade expansion would be of minor economic significance. Rather, the rationale behind trading with Eastern Europe was to reduce Soviet control over its satellite states. Present restrictions, including American export controls and COCOM lists, served as "obstacles" to those satellite states wanting greater economic independence from Moscow.[92] Further, the restrictions limited America's ability to influence "the forces which are now making for unrest in Eastern Europe."[93] The State Department urged Washington to begin bilateral negotiations with satellite states to establish agreements requiring annual review, so that the "United States would be in a position quietly to reward or punish a regime in accordance with its political attitudes and conduct."[94] If Washington demonstrated a willingness to trade, some East European countries such as

> Hungary and possibly Romania, would be prepared to go as far as Poland from the first. . . . Thus, the effect of a change in trade relations with the United States could well prove a significant factor in preserving the national identity of the satellite countries and the Western orientation of the satellite peoples.[95]

In conclusion, the State Department recommended that the President use all the discretionary power available to him to facilitate trade with Eastern Europe, and ask Congress to pass legislation reducing America's trade restrictions toward the Soviet Bloc.[96]

Three days later, on July 29, the State Department responded to Crawford's telegrams. While agreeing that Moscow-Bucharest relations were fragile, the State Department wanted to wait for further developments before sending a high level trade delegation to Romania. In the interim, the Department would recommend that the Commerce Department approve export licenses for the Galati project. Moreover, the State Department did agree that Washington should "take limited action" to indicate America's "readiness to support Romanian determination to follow an independent course."[97]

On August 4, Secretary of Agriculture, Orville Freeman, became the first American cabinet member to visit Romania since World War II. The Secretary was enthusiastically welcomed throughout his one day tour of dairy farms, chicken hatcheries, and industrial cites.[98] Moreover, in anticipation of his visit, Bucharest suspended radio jamming of the broadcasts of Voice of America and Radio Free Europe.[99]

In the evening, Gheorghiu-Dej hosted a high level dinner for Freeman at a villa in Eforie. Gheorghiu-Dej used the occasion to discuss the methods available to improve economic relations between the two countries. He described the balanced nature of the Romanian economy which was making rapid progress toward industrialization. At the close of World War II, 80% of the population worked in agriculture, now 65% did. Farm productivity had significantly increased, and Romania exported food to "earn dollars to invest in factories."[100] Gheorghiu-Dej wanted to increase trade with the United States. He wanted to buy industrial installations, specifically a synthetic rubber plant. American businesses, including Phillips Petroleum, had indicated an interest in building the facility but were restricted because of America's export licensing system. Gheorghiu-Dej knew that the President's discretionary power could facilitate export licensing. The Romanian leader wanted President Kennedy to know that Romania was eager to buy from the United States, and would find the money to pay for its purchases. Bucharest did not need American aid or credit to finance its dealings.[101] Gheorghiu-Dej also used the dinner to reassure Freeman that Romania was independent of the Soviet Union. Although Romania was part of CMEA, this did not restrict Bucharest's economic freedom of action, including freedom to trade with the United States. He noted that "others" must recognize that "we Romanians have our own road."[102]

Following dinner, Crawford and Deputy Foreign Minister Malita talked on their way back to their quarters. During the conversation, each learned that the other was going to Washington on August 7. Both men thought that the Freeman-Gheorghiu-Dej meeting had gone well, and Malita hoped that America would think about raising the level of Romania's diplomatic Mission in the United States to an Embassy. In return, Crawford suggested that Romanian-American relations could best be improved were Bucharest to let more people emigrate, especially those seeking family reunification.[103] In addition, he asked if Romania could lift its travel restrictions on Legation personnel imposed in 1956.[104] Two days later, Malita informed Crawford that Bucharest would end travel restrictions for Legation personnel as of August 20, provided the United States did the same for the members of the Bucharest Legation in Washington and the Romanian delegation to the United Nations.[105]

Back in Washington, Crawford and Malita met with Averell Harriman on August 8. The Undersecretary had just returned from Moscow.

Crawford and he were old friends and the Minister would later say, that Harriman's willingness to support his views enabled American-Romanian relations to progress rapidly during the next year.[106] During the meeting, Malita stressed Romania's desire for immediate improvement in economic relations with Washington. He wanted export licenses for equipment and technology in six fields: chemistry, oil, rubber, cellulose, television and radio. While Romania would normally send individual delegations to negotiate each of these areas, Malita preferred sending Gheorghe Gaston-Marin, Chairman of the State Planning Committee, to Washington to negotiate an entire trade agreement.

Harriman supported Malita. Kennedy had called for a major review of America's policy toward Eastern Europe, and certainly Romania's drive for greater independence from Moscow would be a subject for discussion. Harriman wanted to begin talks with Gaston-Marin at the earliest possible date, but to do so "would require considerable consultations within the United States government." The review was not complete, and Washington had not yet decided on a new policy toward the Soviet Bloc. Harriman assured Malita that Crawford would keep him informed of future developments.[107]

On August 9, Crawford joined Malita and Petre Balaceanu, the Romanian Minister, for lunch at the Romanian Legation in Washington. During the discussions, Crawford indicated that Washington had agreed to reduce travel restrictions for Romanian delegations assigned to the Legation and to the United Nations. Crawford also indicated that he would continue to press the Administration for improved relations with Romania.[108]

A couple of weeks later Crawford met with the President. While there are no transcripts of the meeting, Crawford recalled that he summarized recent Romanian developments and mentioned particularly the failure of the United States to act on Balaceanu's request for $200 million in contracts. Kennedy was "very anxious to document this whole picture." He was "strongly in favor of some action, but he was cautious about congressional reaction." He believed the trade issue could best be addressed by emphasizing the business opportunities America was losing to West Germany, France, Italy and Britain.[109] The President wanted Crawford to share his ideas with the Commerce Department, and he arranged a meeting for Crawford with Franklin Delano Roosevelt, Jr., the Under Secretary of Commerce.[110]

Crawford told Roosevelt about recent developments in Romania, including her relations with CMEA. He emphasized Bucharest's desire to trade with the West, but noted that due to America's export licensing practices, most of this trade went to Western Europe and not to American businesses. Roosevelt indicated that Washington was presently reviewing its policies toward Eastern Europe. However, the Under Secretary indicated that the Commerce Department was not about to move quickly toward improving trade relations with Romania. Roosevelt pointed out the difficulties involved in making significant changes in America's licensing procedures. Major changes could break down the COCOM system of controls, and American businessmen were not yet ready to trade with Eastern Europe.[111]

Crawford's frustrations with the Commerce Department were no worse than his frustrations toward the State Department.

> It seems to me that about two-thirds of my work was really negotiating with the State Department, and about one-third with the Romanians. . . . My main problem was to convince the Department that things really were changing, and that the Romanians really were carrying on this kind of resistance to Soviet pressures and attempting to assert their own independence, at least in the economic field, and that somebody wasn't just pulling marionettes by a string for optical effect.[112]

In analyzing the causes of this problem, Crawford believed that the people who worked on the Romanian desk in the State Department had "old ideas of how it used to be." In addition, the Department was accustomed to change occurring slowly in a Communist country, and was not able to adjust to the rapid pace of events in Romania.[113]

Meanwhile, on August 9, the ECRB completed its review of East-West trade requested by Kennedy on May 16. Much of the report focused on American-Soviet relations. However, those elements pertaining to satellite trade reiterated many of the same points made by the State Department's Policy Planning Council document of July 26. The ECRB recommended that it should be authorized to "prepare guidelines for a less restrictive, step-by-step expansion in trade with individual nations of Eastern Europe within the present legal structure." In addition, the ECRB recommended that the Departments of State and Commerce determine the content of a new East-West Trade Act which would then be proposed to Congress. This Act would give the President "all the administrative authority he needs to use trade as an effective political instrument for dealing with the USSR and its satellites."[114] The ECRB supported its call for modified bilateral trade pacts because they would encourage satellite independence and, give America an instrument to implement an effective "carrot and stick" policy.[115] In the meantime, working under the present legal structure, the ECRB suggested that depending on political circumstances, Washington could increase trade on a step-by-step basis by approving items for export from a "shopping list" submitted in advance, similar to that offered by the Romanians in March, 1962. This process would be mutually attractive since the United States could react quickly to changes in the political climate, and the satellite state could be guaranteed shipment of approved products.

On September 19, the President notified the ECRB that while he liked their recommendations, "I am strongly in favor of pressing forward more energetically than this report and its recommendations imply in our trade with the Soviet and Eastern Bloc." Kennedy was motivated by the new spirit of cooperation evidenced by the Moscow Test Ban Treaty, and by the increased trade between Western Europe and the Soviet Bloc. The President specifically noted that he wanted the ECRB to quickly prepare less restrictive guidelines for a "step-by-step" trade expansion with individual East European countries. In the interim, he wanted all agencies to know that the "spirit" of this comment should immediately be reflected in the export licensing process.[116]

Formal American-Romanian relations were put on the back burner while the ECRB drafted new trade guidelines. During this interlude, *Scinteia* carried several stories of Washington's changing attitude toward East European trade, including a press release of the President's September 19 instructions to the ECRB.[117] In October, the paper reported Secretary of Commerce Hodges' speech in Houston on the twenty-fourth which reaffirmed America's ongoing review of its trade policies.[118] American newspapers countered with a bevy of stories about Romania, focusing especially on her eagerness for Western trade. The *New York Times* reported that in order to "catch up" Romania needed to "purchase the most modern equipment – meaning Western equipment."[119] Eric Bourne in the *Christian Science Monitor* noted that Romania had made "immense, impressive strides" in industrialization but she had "scarcely begun."[120] In "Romania: Another Split in Communist Ranks," Philip Ben wrote in the *New Republic* that "Romania has become a country of great opportunities for the West."[121]

The American press also carried articles indicating Bucharest's independent stance from Moscow. Especially noteworthy was Romania's break from the Soviet Union in the United Nations. On November 19, for the first time, Romania opposed the Soviets and supported a Latin

American resolution calling for a study to denuclearize Latin America.[122] In addition, Bucharest replaced the *Timpuri Noi*, which was a Romanian language edition of the Soviet *New Times*, a foreign affairs propaganda journal, with *Lumea*, written in Romanian by Romanian editors.[123]

Meanwhile, President Kennedy used his discretionary power to increase East-West trade. After the Test Ban Treaty, Moscow indicated that she was willing to purchase surplus wheat from the United States. The Commerce Department had already indicated its support for this type of program in June, 1961.[124] Kennedy asked the Attorney General's office if they were any legislative impediments to such a sale. The reply indicated that they were no Congressional restrictions on selling surplus wheat to Moscow for cash.[125] Armed with this information, the President informed Congress on October 10 that the preceding day he had authorized the sale of wheat to the Soviet Union and other East European countries. The sales would be concluded by private America grain dealers for American dollars or gold, either cash on delivery or under normal commercial credit terms.[126] As an aside, Kennedy's decision prompted the AFL-CIO to demand that 50% of all the wheat sold to the Soviet Union and Eastern Europe had to be transported on American flag ships. The Commerce Department agreed citing the precedent of the Cargo Preference Act, PL 664, passed by the 83rd Congress in the early 1950s. This 50/50 shipping requirement would play havoc with East-West trade during the next decade.[127]

Kennedy's announcement infuriated the conservative members of Congress. Senator Karl Mundt, the author of Section 117(d) of the Foreign Assistance Act of 1948, introduced a bill to prevent the Export-Import Bank from guaranteeing private financing of wheat sales to the Soviet Union. The Export-Import Bank, or Eximbank, was first established by President Roosevelt on February 2, 1934, ironically, to promote commercial relations between the Soviet Union and the United States. The bank's function was to help finance and facilitate export and import trade between the United States and other nations. The Mundt bill would impede the wheat sales and deny the President discretionary authority to deal with the Communist world.

On November 15, the President wrote, what proved to be his last letter on trade, to Senator Mike Mansfield. Kennedy urged Mansfield to stop the bill. The legislation would not hurt the Communists, but it would damage American producers and exporters. The Eximbank believed that the "state credit of the Soviet Union and other Communist countries is sufficiently reliable to justify a guarantee in support of U.S. exports." Kennedy anticipated that the wheat sales would be made for payment in gold or dollars, or on short term credit not exceeding 18 months. The proposed sale still depended on negotiations between the Soviet government and private traders and the availability of Eximbank credit would be central to the talks. Finally, Kennedy warned that the Mundt bill would "be an act against the national interest."[128]

The Senate Banking and Currency Committee began hearings on the bill on November 20 and 21. The question of financing was crucial since the Soviets had made the availability of credits a condition of the sale. Kennedy's assassination postponed the hearings, but the new President, Lyndon B. Johnson, continued Kennedy's policy and assured the defeat of the Mundt bill on November 26.[129] This represented the first legislative victory of the new Administration, and cleared the way for the Soviets to purchase $140 million worth of wheat. [130]

From Kennedy to Johnson

While Kennedy's death was mourned world wide, including Romania where *Scinteia* featured a picture of the deceased President, America's efforts to improve relations with Bucharest and Eastern Europe continued without interruption.[131] There were two major threads of East-West trade policy that continued throughout the Johnson Administration. The first was to encourage non-strategic trade by removing specific licensing requirements and simplifying the export licensing procedures. The second was to make full use of discretionary Presidential authority in existing legislation and to seek Congressional approval for additional Presidential authority to respond to changing conditions in Eastern Europe.[132]

On December 18, the ECRB submitted two papers to the White House, one entitled "Policy Guidelines on Trade with Eastern Europe" and the other, an "Action Program for Romania," the only country study brief prepared.[133] The first paper set forth general principles and a scenario for the use of expanded trade as a means of countering Soviet influence in Eastern Europe. The second gave a specific set of proposals for negotiating with Romania on commercial and related matters.[134] Johnson approved the recommendations in February, 1964, and decided to use Romania as his test case for negotiating with individual satellite states. Gheorghiu-Dej's drive for economic independence fit precisely into the East-West paradigm suggested by both the ECRB and the State Department.

Meanwhile, Karl Mundt had renewed his efforts to limit the role of the Eximbank in trade with Eastern Europe. He filed an amendment to the Foreign Assistance and Related Agencies Appropriation Act of 1964. This amendment would have prohibited the Eximbank from financing commercial exports to Eastern Europe. The Administration fought the amendment, and Congress agreed to modify the legislation to provide for a Presidential waiver. Title III of the Act as amended on January 6, 1964, prohibited the Eximbank from financing exports to Communist countries unless the President issued a determination that such support was in the national interest. On February 4, President Johnson made a determination that the Eximbank could issue guarantees for financing agricultural sales to several East European countries, including Romania.[135] On February 25, Secretary of State Dean Rusk addressed the Full Citizenship and World Affairs Council in Washington, D.C.[136] His topic was "Why We Treat Different Communist Countries Differently." In his address, Rusk announced that America's policy was to "encourage evolution in the Communist world toward national independence." The Secretary of State indicated that Romania had "asserted a more independent attitude. . . [and]. . . we are responding accordingly."[137]

Romania had watched these developments in Washington with great interest. The new President appeared equally supportive of trade with Bucharest. *Scinteia* reported Congressional debate about the extension of Eximbank credits to Eastern Europe.[138] On December 30, Gheorghiu-Dej submitted a long list of agricultural equipment to the Commerce Department for export licensing valued at about $330 thousand.[139] Two days later, Gheorghiu-Dej received Crawford at the Palace in Bucharest. The Romanian President expressed satisfaction with the progress of Romanian-American relations. He said that they had progressed on a "step by step basis" and efforts on both sides were beginning to show useful results. He anticipated that through continued effort, patience and diligence, 1964 could be an even more successful year.[140]

Gheorghiu-Dej's overtures to the United States impressed the American press. Throughout the last half of January, 1964, the *New York Times* carried a glowing article about Romania nearly every day. On January 19, Romania was praised for its independence,[141] on the

20th, a pleasant looking picture of Gheorghiu-Dej appeared with an article indicating that he was in charge of the "de-Russification" of Romania,[142] on the 22nd, Romania was declared a "former satellite"[143] and on the 25th, David Binder wrote, "a Latin gleam has replaced the hangdog look" among Romanians and their "talk is wittier and gaier."[144] On February 4, Gheorghiu-Dej himself, may have had a "Latin gleam" when he learned that President Johnson had approved Eximbank credits to finance agricultural sales to Romania. Even if Bucharest did not need to import American surplus food, the approval indicated that Romanian-American relations were moving forward.

Romanian Independence, April, 1964

In keeping with his centrifugal foreign policy, Gheorghiu-Dej decided to try to act as a mediator to resolve the growing Sino-Soviet split. Rather than take sides, Romania hoped to become a "third force" in the international Communist movement.[145] On March 3, Premier Ion Gheorghe Maurer led a delegation to Beijing to talk with Mao Zedong and Zhou Enlai. The week long meeting failed to resolve any differences, and Maurer returned to Bucharest via Moscow.[146] He informed Khrushchev that the rift remained, and as the Soviet leader later recalled, Maurer added that the "Chinese said you took Bessarabia away from us." Khrushchev recalled that this "left a nasty taste in our mouths. We began to suspect that maybe the Romanians still held a grudge against us for returning Bessarabia to the Soviet Union after the war."[147] Unable to become a "third force" and unwilling to be led by either Moscow or Beijing, Gheorghiu-Dej scheduled an eight day Plenum of the Central Committee which would become an historic meeting. The Plenum convened on April 15, two days before Khrushchev's 70th birthday, thereby preventing Gheorghiu-Dej from attending the massive celebrations. At the Plenum, Gheorghiu-Dej announced the "Statement on the Stand of the Romanian Workers' Party on the Problems of the International Communist and Working Class Movement," which became known as the Romanian Declaration of Independence. The entire statement appeared in *Scinteia* on April 26, following its adoption by the plenum on April 22.

The importance of the Statement was its public nature. Essentially, it was a summation of Gheorghiu-Dej's efforts to give Romania greater independence from Moscow. Among other issues, the Statement noted the Sino-Soviet rift and the Moscow Treaty, and called for peaceful coexistence, Balkan denuclearization, and world disarmament. Supported by quotes from Marx and Lenin, Romania reaffirmed its support of the principles in the Moscow Declaration of 1960, frequently chanting the virtues of "the principles of national independence and sovereignty, equal rights, mutual advantage, comradely assistance, noninterference in internal affairs, and the observance of territorial integrity." Romania criticized the efforts of those who wanted to make CMEA into a supranational organization. "The sovereignty of the socialist state requires" that it hold "in its hands all the levers of managing economic and social life. Transmitting such levers to the competence of superstate or extrastate bodies would make of sovereignty an idea without any content." Romania was also eager to expand its trade and develop "economic links with all states irrespective of their social systems."[148]

In its Statement, Romania was careful not to threaten the Soviet Union. The document did not include the issue of Bessarabia, so recently discussed, nor did it blame Moscow for the split in the world Communist movement. Rather, the Statement was a public declaration of Romania's independence as a sovereign socialist state, under the leadership of the Romanian Workers' Party.[149] Equally important the Statement announced that Romania intended to lead its own economic life by establishing ties with Western markets without breaking relations with CMEA.

An American-Romanian Trade Agreement

Meanwhile in Washington, the Senate Foreign Relations Committee had begun hearings on the whole issue of East-West trade. Testifying before the House Subcommittee on Europe, on March 10, 1964, Averell Harriman explained that America needed a policy of differentiation to capitalize on the changing atmosphere in Eastern Europe. "Our policy is to encourage the evolution now in progress by using every kind of peaceful contact available."[150] Three days later, Dean Rusk told the Senate Foreign Relations Committee that America's policy toward the Communist world had three objectives: (a) to prevent the Communists from expanding; (b), to reduce the dangers of war; and (c), to encourage independence movements. He added that one of the prime instruments available to America to influence developments in Communist countries was trade.[151]

In keeping with Johnson's decision to use Romania as a test case for negotiating with a Soviet satellite, the State Department sent a lengthy note to Crawford on April 7. Washington was ready to receive a Romanian delegation led by Gheorghe Gaston-Marin as suggested by Malita the previous August. The agenda was wide-ranging including special licensing procedures for Romania, financing arrangements, levels of diplomatic missions, reciprocal publication opportunities, and consular affairs. The invitation included one condition, that Romania submit a "shopping list" of commodities which it was interested in purchasing so that the Department of Commerce could evaluate each item in the light of export control criteria before negotiations began.[152]

Crawford immediately conveyed the invitation to Gheorghiu-Dej. The Romanian was delighted, however, some members of the party had misgivings about dealing with the United States. They were concerned that the agenda for the upcoming party Plenum would certainly upset the Soviets, and the United States could do nothing in the event of a major split between Bucharest and Moscow. A development such as this could lead to Romanian isolation within Eastern Europe. Other opposition focused on the effects of Romania's exposure to "bourgeoisie decadence." However, Gheorghiu-Dej had the support of Maurer and Gaston-Marin, as well as other party leaders including Ceausescu, Birladenau, Stoica and Bodnaras.[153] By the end of April, Gaston-Marin had compiled a "shopping list" of installations which the Romanians wanted to purchase. While the list was kept secret from the public, it included two rubber manufacturing plants, three glass making plants, as well as facilities which could produce synthetic glycerine, ammonia, and synthetic leather, as well turbines, oil collection treatment equipment and a nuclear electric power station. This last item was more in the order of a "wish list" item, and the Romanians agreed that discussion on that item could be postponed until a later date.[154]

On May 18, the negotiations began. Under Secretary of State Averell Harriman led the American delegation which included William Crawford, America's Minister to Romania, Jack Behrman, the Assistant Secretary of Commerce for Domestic and International Business, and Richard Davis, the Acting Assistant Secretary of State for European Affairs. Gheorghe Gaston-Marin, Chairman of the Romanian State Planning Committee, led the delegation from Bucharest which included Mihai Florescu, the Minister of Petroleum and Chemical Industries, George Macovescu, the First Deputy Minister for Foreign Affairs, Mihai Petri, the Deputy Minister for Foreign Affairs, and Petru Balaceanu, the Romanian Minister to the United States.[155] The negotiations were secret and lasted until the end of May.

Five days after the negotiations began, the President made a memorable address in Lexington, Virginia. Johnson told the audience at the dedication of the George C. Marshall Research Library that the United States would "build bridges across the gulf which has divided us from Eastern Europe." They would be bridges of increased trade, of ideas, of visitors, and of humanitarian aid. America's motives were clear: first,

> to open new relationships to countries seeking increased independence yet unable to risk isolation; second, to open the minds of a new generation to the values and the visions of the Western civilization from which they come and to which they belong; third to give freer play to the powerful forces of legitimate national pride; [and] fourth, to demonstrate that identity of interest and the prospects of progress for Eastern Europe lie in a wider relationship with the West.[156]

The President's speech certainly explained the logic behind the ongoing talks in Washington. In addition, the negotiations addressed the radically new demands of the United States Chamber of Commerce announced at their annual convention. On April 29, the Chamber called on Washington to reduce the number of embargoed items to the Soviet Union and Eastern Europe, and urged parity in America's level of trade with both East and West Europe. This resolution represented a "major policy change" by the Chamber of Commerce. For the first time a major business organization made a resolution on East-West trade which "went beyond generalities to specific policy recommendations."[157] The Chamber wanted increased trade with the Soviet Bloc and in the process undermined the traditional argument of the Commerce Department that American businessmen were not ready to trade with the Communists.

Meanwhile the American-Romanian negotiations progressed and quickly focused on four areas: long term credits, most-favored-nation status, ambassadorial representation and export license regulations. The issue of credits was the most cumbersome, and within two days both sides agreed that the Romanians should establish a subcommittee to hold parallel talks with Eximbank officials. On May 21, Mihai Petri, Petre Balaceanu, along with Romulus Petrescu, the Director of the Foreign Department of the Romanian State Bank, met with Walter Sauer and other officials of the Eximbank. Sauer described the role of the Eximbank and noted that at present the bank could only authorize Romania credits for eighteen months, and only on agricultural products. However, he anticipated that the President would authorize the bank to grant credits for non-agricultural products in the near future. Petri reviewed Romania's relations with Western Europe over the past six years indicating that Bucharest had used credits for about 60% of her $480 million worth of imports. He expected to request between $20 and $80 million in credits from the United States. He also wanted long term credits, up to 10 years, for some agricultural products. Sauer countered that the bank normally did not give a large line of credit, but examined specific projects on an individual basis. Further, the bank would not extend credit over a ten year period.[158]

Following this initial encounter, the delegates resumed their credit negotiations later in the week. On May 26, the Romanian learned that export licenses could be issued for 11 of the 15 plants on their shopping list. Before discussing the possible purchase of these plants from American firms, Petri wanted to know the kind of financing that was available from the Eximbank. The total purchase price was approximately $275 million. Sauer suggested that assuming that Romania's financial position was secure, Romania should begin preliminary discussions with American private suppliers and then present an outline of the proposed transactions. The Eximbank would consider each transaction on a case by case basis. If Eximbank decided to participate in the transaction it would enter an agreement with the State Bank of Romania and work out the specific terms, including interest rates, not to exceed five years. Petri tried to negotiate for terms in excess of five years, but without success.[159]

Gaston-Marin argued strongly for the United States to grant most-favored-nation treatment to Romania. Bucharest wanted Romanian exports to the United States to be treated no differently than were exports from Poland and Yugoslavia. Although Harriman sympathized with the request, his hands were tied by Congress. Section 231A of the 1962 Trade Expansion Act directed the President to withdraw MFN from all Communist or Communist-dominated countries. Congress was not about to award MFN to Romania. The broadest statement Harriman could make was to promise that the United States would give "continuing consideration to means of increasing trade" and this phrase became Article Six of the final agreement.[160]

The third topic concerned elevating the diplomatic Mission from a Legation to an Embassy. Romania was especially interested in this, both as another manifestation of Romania's independence from Moscow, and as a means to compete with the Soviets who had an Embassy in Washington.[161] The Administration agreed to the request. Romania appointed Petre Balanceanu as Ambassador to the United States in August, but the American implementation proved a bit slower. Johnson did not want to make Eastern Europe a campaign issue, so he waited until after his November reelection to appoint William Crawford as America's first Ambassador to the Romanian People's Republic.[162]

The last major issue, export licensing, was the most important. Washington had agreed to license 11 of the 15 plants on Romania's "shopping list."[163] To facilitate the export licensing process, the United States agreed to establish a general license procedure for exports to Romania, similar to that accorded to Poland earlier. The procedure enabled Romania to import most American commodities without applying for individual export licenses. The Commerce Department would publish a list around July 1 indicating items which were prohibited for shipment due to America's national security needs and COCOM requirements. Both nations agreed to protect each other's industrial rights and processes and not to reexport each other's technology.[164]

Having resolved these major issues, Harriman and Gaston-Marin issued a joint communique on June 1 indicating the major settlements. The communique also indicated that both countries had agreed to resolve outstanding consular problems and to negotiate a new consular convention. Both agreed to expand cultural and informational exchange programs, establish trade offices in Bucharest and New York City, and open tourist promotion facilities in the two countries. In addition, Gaston-Marin gave oral assurances that Romania would begin to permit dual nationals to leave for the United States, as well as Romanians who were separated from their families in America.[165] In assessing the importance of the agreement, McGeorge Bundy wrote to the President on May 29, "perhaps the single most significant aspect of these talks was Romania's determination to succeed in establishing a new and substantial relationship with the United States – an important factor in Romania's drive for independence from Moscow."[166]

The success of this new agreement was contingent on Romania receiving non-agricultural credits from the Eximbank. While Bucharest wanted MFN, Gheorghiu-Dej realized that this was dependent on the American Congress, and would not be possible for some time. On the other hand, the availability of Eximbank credits was solely dependent on the White House. The Romanian request for long term credit was flatly denied. However, during the negotiations, Harriman had led Gaston-Marin to believe that short term credits would be forthcoming. On June 15, President Johnson sent a letter to Congress indicating that in compliance with Title III of the Foreign Aid and Related Agencies Appropriations Act of 1964, he had made a determination that it was in the national interest for the Eximbank "to issue guarantees in connection with the sale of United States products and services to Romania." Johnson noted that this determination was in addition to that made in February concerning agricultural products. This June 15 determination was "to cover all types of United States products and services."[167]

Moscow and Bucharest's Statement of Independence

As negotiations progressed in Washington, Gheorghiu-Dej continued his drive for greater independence from Moscow. The April "Declaration of Independence" prompted numerous anti-Soviet meetings throughout Bucharest. In early May, the Romanian Workers' Party sponsored indoctrination campaigns in government agencies, places of work, and even in high schools. The main theme was the Soviet's exploitation of Romania's economy for the past twenty years.[168] By the end of the month, Radio Bucharest and Radio Moscow exchanged propaganda barbs. The polemical broadcasts continued into the first week in June.[169]

On June 5, Romania increased its criticism of Moscow. Mr. Murgescu, the Editor of *Viata Economica*, Romania's leading economic journal, published an article entitled "Conceptions Contrary to Basic Principles of Economic Relations Between Socialist States." The twelve thousand word treatise was a polemic "replete with invective and heavy sarcasm" directed against Soviet economists and especially against the geographer, E.B. Valev. In February, Valev had published an article in the Moscow University journal *Vestnik* entitled "Problems of Economic Development of Danube Regions of Romania, Bulgaria and the USSR."[170] Valev called for establishing an "interstate production complex" in the lower Danube in order to improve the area's economy. Romania would contribute 72 per cent of the land needed to form this complex, while Bulgaria supplied 21 per cent and the Soviets, 7 per cent.[171] Murgescu's article accused Valev of trying to "truncate" Romania and violate her national sovereignty. In addition, the Valev proposal was a thinly veiled attempt to remove Transylvania from Romania's control by assigning that area to the production complex.[172] Finally, Murgescu attacked Valev's article as an indication of the true purpose of CMEA. Murgescu declared that Romania would not participate in any "interstate complex," in any form of "superstate" collaboration, or in any "socialist integration" scheme proposed by CMEA.[173]

The Soviets were shocked by the sharpness of the Romanian attack. However, the Kremlin did not want to further alienate Romania, especially after her successful negotiations with Washington. Consequently, on July 3 *Izvestia* carried an article by Mr. Bogomolov, one of the Soviet's top CMEA economists, which repudiated Valev's article. Bogomolov wrote that Valev's approach "was fundamentally wrong and not in line with Soviet Communist policy."[174] A couple of weeks later, the *World Marxist Review* published the April 22 Romanian Workers' Party Statement without comment.[175]

The first six months of 1964 had been a productive time for Gheorghiu-Dej. He had secured an arrangement with the United States that enabled Romania to purchase much needed industrial equipment. At the same time, he had successfully separated Romania's national economic goals from CMEA's ventures. Finally, through the April Statement, he had made public Romania's claim to national sovereignty, and thereby gained the support of Western opinion to buttress his efforts to distance Bucharest from Moscow's control.

Notes

1. Report to John F. Kennedy by the Task Force on Foreign Economic Policy, December 31, 1960, p. 1, Task Force Reports: Foreign Affairs - Transition Files, Prepresidential Papers, Box 1073, JFK Library.

2. *Ibid.*, pp. 12-13.

3. *Ibid.*, pp. 13, 14, 43, 47, 49-50.

4. Stephen Hess, *Organizing the Presidency* (rev. ed. Washington, D.C.: The Brookings Institution, 1988), pp. 74-75; History of the CFEP, n.d., Joseph Rand Records 1954-1961, Box 17, Q-S, finding Aids of Personal Papers & Archives, DDE Library.

5. [John F. Kennedy] *Public Papers of the Presidents of the United States, 1961*(Washington, D.C.: U. S. Government Printing Office, 1962), p. 26.

6. U. S. Congress, Senate, S.2828, *A Bill To Authorize the President Under Certain Conditions to Permit the Entering into a Loan, Grant, or Other Aid Agreements with Certain Nations*, 85th Cong., 1st Sess., 1957, 4pp; Report on U.S. Policy toward the Soviet Satellites in Eastern Europe, November 20, 1957, p. 6, NSC5608/1 File, Box 17, Office of the Special Assistant for National Security Affairs, White House Office, DDE Library.

7. Memorandum for Secretary of State, February 6, 1961, NSAM No. 8 File, NSF Box 328, JFK Library.

8. Samuel F. Clabaugh and Richard V. Allen, *East-West Trade: Its Strategic Implications, Analysis, and Inventory of Congressional Documents, 1959-1963* (Washington, D.C.: Georgetown University, The Center for Strategic Studies,

1964), p. 51; *DOS Bulletin*, March 27, 1961, p. 444.

9. File Memorandum on Meeting Held Re: Export control, White House, May 18, 1961, 3-3-3 Folder, Box 241, WHCF, JFK Library; Executive Order 10945; Memorandum, To Secretary Hodges, Export Control Policy Criteria, May 18, 1961, East-West Negotiation, Box 296, NSF, JFK Library.

10. Thomas J. Schoenbaum, *Waging Peace and War: Dean Rusk in the Truman, Kennedy, and Johnson Years* (New York: Simon and Schuster, 1988), p. 266.

11. Memorandum, DOS to McGeorge Bundy, May 25, 1961, 21pp., File Economic Relations with Soviet Bloc - May 25, 1961, Box 176, Country Files, USSR General, NSF, JFK Library; Funigiello, *American-Soviet Trade in the Cold War*, p. 129.

12. *Ibid.*, p. 131; Report, p. 63, Sec. G, "East-West Trade"," Vol. I, Chap, 3; Box 1, State Department Administrative History, LBJ Library.

13. Samuel F. Clabaugh and Edwin J. Feulner, Jr., *Trading With the Communists* (Washington, D.C.: Georgetown University, The Center for Strategic Studies, 1968), p. 30.

14. Funigiello, *American-Soviet Trade in the Cold War*, p. 131.

15. *Ibid.*, p. 132.

16. [John F. Kennedy] *Public Papers of the Presidents of the United States, John F. Kennedy, 1962* (Washington, D.C.: U. S. Government Printing Office, 1963), pp. 14-15; 68ff.

17. [Department of State] *American Foreign Policy, Current Documents, 1962* (Washington,D.C.: U..S. Government Printing Office, 1966), p. 642.

18. *Congressional Record*, June 28, 1962, p. 111351.

19. *Ibid.*, p. 11491; William J. Long, *U.S. Export Control Policy: Executive Autonomy vs. Congressional Reform* (New York: Columbia University Press, 1989), p. 25.

20. *Congressional Record*, June 28, 1962, p. 11492; Senate, Committee on Foreign Relations, *A Background Study on East-West Trade*, 1965, p. 13.

21. U.S. Congress, House, *Hearings Before the Committee on Ways and Means on H.R. 9900*, 87th Cong., 2d Sess., 1962, pp. 1-9; *Idem.*, Senate, *Hearings Before the Committee on Finance on H.R. 11970*, 87th Cong., 2d Sess., 1962, pp., 1-2; I. M. Destler, *Making Foreign Economic Policy* (Washington, D.C.: The Brookings Institution, 1980), p. 134.

22. Vladimir N. Pregelj, "Most-Favored Nation Treatment of Foreign Trading Partners by the United States: A Summary," January 28, 1986, Congressional Research Service, The Library of Congress, p. 5; Memorandum, DOS to McGeorge Bundy, January 5, 1963, 4pp., NSAM No. 12, Box 339, NSF, JFK Library.

23. *Public Papers of the Presidents, 1963*, p. 55 n.

24. Memorandum, President to Export Control Review Board, May 16, 1963, 2pp., File East-West Trade, September 17, 1963-October 7, 1963, Box 296, NSF JFK Library.

25. Report, U.S. Policy on Trade with the European Soviet Bloc, July 26,

1963, p. 1, File, East-West Trade, Box 310, Subject Files, NSF, JFK Library.
26. Fischer-Galati, *The New Rumania*, p. 83.
27. Telegram, Bucharest to Department of State, August 25, 1961, File January 1961-December 1961, Box 155, Rumania, NSF. JFK Library.
28. *Idem.*, October 25, 1961.
29. *Idem.*, November 12, 1961.
30. Oral interview of William A. Crawford by William A. Moss, March 12, 1971, p. 10.
31. *Ibid.*, p. 6.
32. Telegram, Bucharest to Department of State, December, 1961, File January 1961-December 1961, Box 155, Rumania, NSF. JFK Library.
33. "Statements by American Experts who Visited Rumania," *Agerpres*, February 10, 1962, p. 10.
34. NYT, March 25, 1962, p. 24.
35. Oral interview of William A. Crawford by William A. Moss, March 12, 1971, p. 12.
36. Draft Order, Hodges to Kennedy, March 19, 1962, Box 200 Subject File, FG 651, WHCF, JFK Library.
37. *Idem.*, Douglas Dillon to Kennedy, April 3, 1962.
38. Funigiello, *American-Soviet Trade in the Cold War*, p. 136.
39. Oral interview of William A. Crawford by William A. Moss, March 12, 1971, p. 12.
40. Philip E. Mosely (ed.), *The Soviet Union, 1922-1962: A Foreign Affairs Reader* (New York: Frederick A. Praeger, 1963), 442; Robert H. McNeal (ed.), *International Relations Among the Communists* (Englewood Cliffs, NJ: Prentice-Hall, Inc., 1967), pp. 108-112.
41. Floyd, *Rumania: Russia's Dissident Ally*, p. 67.
42. Fischer-Galati, *The New Rumania*, p. 83.
43. G. M. Razi, "Rumania: Don't Rock the Boat!," *Problems of Communism*, Vol. XI, No. 3 (May-June 1962), p. 21; Report of the Delegation of the Rumanian Workers' Party to the 22nd Congress of the C.P.S.U.," *Agerpres*, December 10, 1961, pp. 13ff.
44. *Ibid.*
45. Lendavi, *Eagles in Cobwebs*, p. 363; Corneliu Vasilescu, *Romania in International Life* (Bucharest: Meridane, 1969), pp. 30,32;Ionescu, *Communism in Rumania*, p. 383; Robert Fowler, "Romanian Foreign Policy," *Problems in Communism*, Vol. XX, No. 6 (Nov-Dec 1971), p. 62; Oral interview of William A. Crawford by William A. Moss, March 12, 1971, p. 62; George Gross, "Rumania: The Fruits of Autonomy," *Problems of Communism*, Vol. XV, No. 1 (Jan-Feb 1966), p. 17.
46. Montias, *Economic Development in Communist Rumania*, p. 207; Gross, "Rumania: The Fruits of Autonomy," 1966, p. 2.
47. NYT, January 21, 1962, p. 23.
48. Cioranesco *et al.*, *Aspects de relations russo-roumaines*, p. 200.
49. NYT, December 12, 1961, p. 65.

50. NYT, January 9, 1962, p. 60.

51. WSJ, May 17, 1962, p. 16.

52. Aurel Braun, *Romanian Foreign Policy Since 1965: The Political and Military Limits of Autonomy* (New York: Frederick A. Praeger, 1978), p. 29.

53. Hutchings, *Soviet-East European Relations*, p. 24.

54. McNeal (ed.), *International Relations Among the Communists*, pp. 125-127; Brown, *Eastern Europe and Communist Rule*, pp. 146-147.

55. Hutchings, *Soviet-East European Relations*, p. 25.

56. Fischer-Galati, *The New Rumania*, p. 88.

57. McNeal (ed.), *International Relations Among the Communists*, p. 109.

58. Oral interview of William A. Crawford by William A. Moss, March 12, 1971, p. 13.

59. *Ibid.*, p. 14.

60. Ionescu, *The Reluctant Ally*, p. 161. For further information on this meeting see, Montias, *Economic Development in Communist Rumania*, p. 212; Jowitt, *Revolutionary Breakthroughs and National Development*, pp. 198ff; Floyd *Rumania: Russia's Dissident Ally*, pp. 70-77; Burks, "The Rumanian National Deviation: An Accounting," 1966, p. 98.

61. Floyd, *Rumania: Russia's Dissident Ally*, pp. 71-72.

62. *Public Papers of the Presidents*, 1962, p. 572.

63. Report, p. 6, Sec. F, "Eastern Europe," Vol. I, Chap. 3; Box 1, State Department Administrative History, LBJ Library.

64. Report, p. 2, Folder "Outstanding Validated licenses by expiration date and by value, Dept. of Commerce, Soviet Bloc Licensing data, 7/3/61-8/22/61," Box 270A-273, Department of Defense, Bureau of the Budget 12/31/61, Departments and Agencies, NSF Files, JFK Library.

65. "Successful tour of the 'Rumanian Rhapsody' Ensemble in the U.S.A.," *Agerpres*, October 15, 1962, p. 11; "Rumanian Rhapsody," *Agerpres*, December 25, 1962, p. 22.

66. Telegram, Bucharest to DOS, November 16, 1962, 3pp., Folder Rumania 1/1/62-12/30/62, Box 155A, NSF, JFK Library.

67. Fischer-Galati, *The New Rumania*, p. 90.

68. Oral interview of William A. Crawford by William A. Moss, March 12, 1971, p. 33.

69. Fischer-Galati, *The New Rumania*, p. 91; Floyd, *Rumania: Russia's Dissident Ally*, p. 72.

70. Ionescu, *The Reluctant Ally*, pp. 68-69.

71. Floyd, *Rumania, Russia's Dissident Ally*, p. 76.

72. Telegram, Bucharest to DOS, April 20, 1963, Folder Romania 1/1/63-6/30/63, Box 155A, NSF, JFK Library.

73. Gross, "Rumania: The Fruits of Autonomy," 1966, p. 18; Montias, *Economic Development in Communist Rumania*, p. 214.

74. Telegram, Bucharest to DOS, June 29, 1963, p.5, Folder Romania 1/1/63-6/30/63, Box 155A, NSF, JFK Library.

75. Gross, "Rumania: The Fruits of Autonomy," 1966, pp. 18-19.

76. Brown, *Eastern Europe and Communist Rule*, p. 140.

77. Jean-Anne Chalet, *La Roumanie, alliee rebelle* (Paris: Casterman, 1972), p. 127.

78. Ionescu, *The Reluctant Ally*, pp. 99-100; Telegram, Bucharest, to DOS, July 1, 1963, 4pp., Folder Romania General 7/1/63-8/6/63, Box 155, NSF, JFK Library; Telegram, Bucharest to DOS, May 11, 1963, 3pp., Folder Romania General 1/1/62-6/30/63, Box 155, NSF, JFK Library.

79. *Ibid.*, p.2.

80. Intelligence report, Director of Intelligence and Research to Secretary, June 7, 1963, 2pp. Folder Rumnia General, 1/1/61-6/30/63, Box 155, NSC, JFK Library.

81. Floyd, *Rumania: Russia's Dissident Ally*, p. 87.

82. Telegram, Bucharest to DOS, June 29, 1963, p. 7, Folder Rumania 1/1/64-6/30/63, Box 155A, NSF, JFK Library.

83. Telegram, Bucharest to DOS, July 3, 1963, 2pp., Folder Rumania General 7/1/63-8/6/63, Box 155, NSF:CO. JFK Library; Oral interview of William A. Crawford by William A. Moss, March 12, 1971, p. 15.

84. Telegram, Bucharest to DOS, July 31, 1963, Folder Rumania General,7/1/63-8/6/63, Box 155, NSF:CO, JFK Library; *Khrushchev Remembers*, trans. & ed. Strobe Talbott, p. 216.

85. [U.S. Department of State] "Agreement Between the United States of America and Rumania," [No. 5063] *Treaties and Other International Acts* (Washington, D.C.: U.S. Government Printing Office, 1962), pp, 2-5.

86. [U.S. Department of State] "Rumania, Cultural Relations ," [No. 5325] *Treaties and Other International Acts* (Washington, D.C.: U.S. Government Printing Office, 1963), pp, 1-3.

87. Telegram, Bucharest to DOS, June 29, 1963, p. 3, Folder Rumania 1/1/63-6/30/63, Box 155A, NSF. JFK Library.

88. *Public Papers of the Presidents*, 1963, p. 528.

89. Telegram, Bucharest to DOS, June 29, 1963, 10 pp., Folder Rumania 1/1/63-6/30/63, Box 155A, NSF. JFK Library.

90. Economic Intelligence Memorandum, Rumania's Vulnerability to Soviet Economic Pressure, July 1963, p. 3, Folder Rumania General 7/63, Box 155, NSF:CO, JFK Library.

91. *Ibid.*, p. 8-11.

92. Report, U.S. Policy on Trade with the European Soviet Bloc, July 26, 1963, p. 5, File, East-West Trade, Box 310, Subject Files, NSF, JFK Library.

93. *Ibid.*, p. 8.

94. *Ibid.*, p. 63.

95. *Ibid.*, p. 42.

96. *Ibid.*, p. 10.

97. Telegram, DOS to Bucharest, July 31, 1963, pp. 1-3, Folder Rumania General 7/1/63-8/6/63, Box 155, NSF:CO, JFK Library.

98. Report, p. 79, Trip to Communists Countries, Notes 3, Box 8, Freeman Collection, JFK Library.

99. Oral interview of William A. Crawford by William A. Moss, March 12, 1971, p. 17.

100. Report, p. 2, Notes on meeting at Eforie, August 4, 1963, Notes 5 Box 8, Freeman Collection, JFK Library. Included among the guests were Minister Crawford, Ion Gheorghe Maurer, Vice President of the State Council, Alexandru Moghioros, First Deputy Chairman of the Council of Ministers, Gheorghe Gaston-Marin, Vice Chairman of the Council of Ministers, Mircea Malita, the Deputy Foreign Minister, as well as representatives from the Higher Council of Agriculture.

101. *Ibid.*, pp. 1-3; Telegram, Bucharest to DOS, August 6, 1963, pp. 1-7; Intelligence report, Director of Intelligence and Research to Acting Secretary, August 10, 1963, Folder Rumania 8/6/63-8/22/63, Box 155, NSF, JFK Library.

102. Intelligence report, Director of Intelligence and Research to Acting Secretary, August 10, 1963, p. 2, Folder Rumania 8/6/63-8/22/63, Box 155, NSF:CO, JFK Library.

103. Authors' interview of William A. Crawford, Washington, D.C., April 18, 1979.

104. Telegram, Bucharest to DOS, August 6, 1963, p, 8.

105. *Ibid.*, p. 9.

106. Authors' interview of William A. Crawford, Washington, D.C., April 18, 1979; oral interview of William A. Crawford by William A. Moss, March 12, 1971, p. 23.

107. Intelligence report, Director of Intelligence and Research to Acting Secretary, August 10, 1963, p. 2, Folder Rumania 8/6/63-8/22/63, Box 155, NSF:CO, JFK Library.

108. *Ibid.*

109. Oral interview of William A. Crawford by William A. Moss, March 12, 1971, p. 21; Authors' interview of William A. Crawford, Washington, D.C., April 18, 1979.

110. Also present at this interview between Crawford and Roosevelt were George Donat, the Deputy Director of the Bureau of International Commerce, Leon Lewins, working for the Bureau as an expert in international economics, and Peter Warker, a specialist in Eastern Europe.

111. Memorandum of Conversation, Liberalization of the US Export Controls for Rumania, August 23, 1963, 3pp., Folder Rumania 9/11/63-11/22/63, Box 155, NSF, JFK Library.

112. Oral interview with William A. Crawford by William A. Moss, March 12, 1971, p. 16.

113. *Ibid.*

114. Memorandum for the President, August 9, 1963, pp. 5-7, Folder East-West Trade, Box 1, NSC Meetings, NSF, LBJ Library.

115. *Ibid.*, p. 15.

116. Memorandum from the President, For the Export Control Review Board, September 19, 1963, Folder East-West Trade, Box 1, NSC Meetings, NSF, LBJ Library.

117. *Scinteia*, September 19, 1963, p. 6; September 21, 1963, p. 6.

118. *Scinteia*, October 26, 1963, p. 6.

119. NYT, September 15, 1963, p. 31.

120. CSM, September 25, 1963, p. 2.

121. *New Republic*, October 19, 1963, pp. 12-13.

122. CSM, November 21, 1963; Intelligence report, Director of Intelligence and Research to Acting Secretary, November 20, 1963, 2pp., Rumania Breaks Soviet Bloc Ranks in the UN, Folder Romania 9/11/63-11/22/63, Box 155, NSF:CO, JFK Library; Bucharest to DOS, 21 November 1963, Folder Rumania General 9/11/63-11/22/63, Box 155, NSF, LBJ Library.

123. Floyd, *Rumania: Russia's Dissident Ally*, p. 97.

124. Report, p. 1, Sec. G, "East-West Trade," Vol. I, Chap. 3; Box 1, State Department Administrative History, LBJ Library.

125. Memorandum to Theodore C. Sorensen, Commercial Sales of Agricultural Products to the USSR or other Soviet-Bloc Nations, October 14, 1963, Folder NSC Meeting No. 518, October 1, 1963, Box 314, NSF, JFK Library.

126. U. S. Congress, Senate, Committee on Foreign Relations, *Background Documents on East-West Trade*, 89 Cong., 1st Sess., 1965, p. 274; Circular, DOS to Bucharest, October 14, 1963, p. 1, Folder East-West Trade, Box 310, NSF, JFK Library.

127. Memorandum, Assistant Secretary of Commerce to Assistant to the President, July 13, 1971, 3pp., Folder EX.TA 3/CO Exports, Box 17, TA, WHCF, NPMP.

128. Letter, John F. Kennedy to Mike Mansfield, November 15, 1963, 2pp., Folder East-West Trade, Box 310, NSF, JFK Library.

129. Report, pp. 1-2, Sec. G, "East-West Trade," Vol. I, Chap. 3; Box 1, State Department Administrative History, LBJ Library.

130. The Soviets did not use Eximbank credits to make the purchase.

131. *Scinteia*, November 23, 1963, p. 4.

132. Report, p. 13, Sec. G, "East-West Trade," Vol. I, Chap. 3; Box 1, State Department Administrative History, LBJ Library.

133. Oral interview of William A. Crawford by William A. Moss, March 19, 1971, p. 35.

134. Report, pp. 13-14 Sec. G, "East-West Trade," Vol. I, Chap. 3; Box 1, State Department Administrative History, LBJ Library.

135. *Ibid*., pp. 8-9; U. S. Congress, Senate, Committee on Banking, Housing and Urban Affairs, *Hearing before the Subcommittee on International Finance. The Role of the Export-Import Bank and Export Controls in U.S. International Economic Policy*, 93rd Cong., 2n Sess., 1974, p. 53. Hereafter, Senate Subcommittee on International Finance, *The Export-Import Bank and Export Controls in U.S. International Economic Policy*, 1974.

136. *DOS Bulletin*, March 16, 1964, p. 394.

137. Campbell, *American Policy Toward Communist Eastern Europe*, pp. 120-122.

138. *Scinteia*, December 25, 1963, p. 4.

139. List of Pending Bloc Applications Relating to Fertilizer Plants and Agricultural Equipment, March 18, 1964, Folder East-West Trade, Box 1, NSC Meetings, NSF, JFK Library.

140. Telegram, Bucharest to DOS, January 1, 1964, p. 1, Folder Romania, Volume I, Cables, Container No. 203-204, NSC Country File, LBJ Library.

141. NYT, January 19, 1964, p. 18.

142. NYT, January 20, 1964, p. 8.

143. NYT, January 22, 1964, p. 36.

144. NYT, January 25, 1964, p. 5.

145. Fischer-Galati, "The Sino-Soviet Conflict," 1966, p. 241.

146. Randolph L. Braham, "Rumania: Onto the Separate Path," *Problems of Communism*, Vol. XIIII, No. 3 (May-June 1964), p. 18.

147. *Khrushchev Remembers*, trans & ed. Strobe Talbott, p. 232.

148. *Agerpres*, April 26, 1964, Supplement, 4pp.

149. For diverse opinions on the meaning of the document see, Fischer-Galati, *The New Rumania*, pp. 101-102; Vladimir Socor, "The Limits of National Independence in the Soviet Bloc," *Orbis*, Fall, 1976, pp. 702-704; Floyd, *Rumania: Russia's Dissident Ally*, pp. viii ff; Mary Ellen Fischer, "Political Leadership in Rumania Under the Communists," 1987, p. 12.

150. [Department of State] *American Foreign Policy: Current Documents, 1964* (Washington, D.C.: U. S. Government Printing Office, 1965), p. 620.

151. *Ibid.*, p. 621; Richard P. Stebbins, *The United States in World Affairs, 1964* (New York: Harper & Row, 1965), p. 94; U. S. Congress, Senate, Committee on Foreign Relations, *East-West Trade, Part I*, 88th Cong., 2d Sess., 1965, p. 3.

152. Memorandum, George Ball to the President, "Extension of Export-Import Bank Guarantees on Sales of Non-Agricultural Products to Rumania and Poland," May 13, 1964, McGeorge Bundy Files, vol. 4, 5/1-27/64, Memos to President, Box 1, NSF Aides Files, LBJ Library.

153. Fischer-Galati, *The New Rumania*, p. 104.

154. Memorandum, James L. Greenfield to McGeorge Bundy, Rumania Talks, June 2, 1964, p. 2, Rumania, Volume 1, Cables, Container No. 203-204, NSC, Country File, LBJ Library.

155. *DOS Bulletin*, June 15, 1964, p. 924.

156. *Public Papers of the Presidents of the United States. Lyndon B. Johnson, 1963-1964*(Washington, D.C.: U.S. Government Printing Office, 1965), I, 709. Zbigniew Brzezinski was the author of the "building bridges" idea (J. F. Brown, *Eastern Europe and Communist Rule*, p. 108).

157. Jules Davids, *The United States in World Affairs, 1964* (New York: Harper & Row, 1965), p. 95. The Chambers may have been motivated by the recent arrival of a large British delegation in Moscow which promised long terms credits in exchange for increased Soviet trade.

158. Memorandum of conversation, May 21, 1964, 3pp., Folder Rumania, Volume I, Cables, Container No. 203-204, NSC Country File, LBJ Library.

159. Memorandum, Export-Import Bank Financing for Rumania, May 27,

1964, 4pp., Folder Rumania, Volume 1, Cables, Container No. 203-204, NSC Country File, LBJ Library. Sauer was on firm ground with his five year maximum and Petri was undoubtedly aware of the Berne Union formula. Organized in 1934 by twenty-three public and private export credit insurance institutions, the Berne Union operated on what it called the "five year understanding." This required that insurance institutions not insure credit extensions beyond five years (Senate, Committee on Foreign Relations, *East-West Trade, Part I*, 88th Cong., 2d Sess., 1965, p. 186).

160. *American Foreign Policy: Current Documents, 1964*, p. 628.

161. Oral interview of William A. Crawford by William A. Moss, March 12, 1971, p. 24.

162. Memorandum, Ralph A. Dungan to the President, July 15, 1964, Folder Rumania, Volume 1, Cables, Container No. 203-204, NSC Country File, LBJ Library; Oral interview of William A. Crawford by William A. Moss, March 12, 1971, p. 26; Memorandum, Benjamin H. Read to McGeorge Bundy, August 11, 1964, Folder Rumania, Volume 1, Cables, Container No. 203-204, NSC Country File, LBJ Library.

163. The National Security Council even considered Romania's request for a nuclear electric power station.   However, the Atomic Energy Commission would not authorize the sale of this plant until July 31, 1968 (Report, p. 47, Sec. F, "Eastern Europe," Vol. I, Chap. 3; Box 1, State Department Administrative History, LBJ Library; Memorandum, John P. Trevithick to Charles E. Johnson, May 27, 1964, p.2, Folder Rumania, Volume 1, Cables, Container No. 203-204, NSC Country File, LBJ Library.

164. Memorandum, McGeorge Bundy to the President, May 29, 1964, 2pp., volume 5, NSF Aides Files, LBJ Library.

165. *Idem.*, Attachment, "Joint Communique," 2pp; U.S. Congress, House, Hearings Before the Subcommittee on Trade of the Committee on Ways and Means, *United States-Romanian Trade Agreement*, 94th Cong., 1st Sess., 1975, p. 164; Transcript of News Briefing, June 1, 1964 (Department of State), 26pp., Folder Rumania, Volume 1, Cables, Container No. 203-204, NSC Country File, LBJ Library. *Agerpres* published the Communique on June 15.

166. Memorandum, McGeorge Bundy to the President, May 29, 1964, p.2, volume 5, NSF Aides Files, LBJ Library. Bogdan concurred that the treaty was useful to Romania in its drive for independence (Authors' interview of Corneliu Bogdan, New York City, March 19, 1987).

167. U. S. Congress, Senate, Committee on Foreign Relations, *Background Documents on East-West Trade*, 89th Cong., 1st Sess., 1965, p. 280.

168. Telegram, Bucharest to DOS, May 18, 1964, pp. 1-2, McGeorge Bundy Files, vol. 4; 5/1-27/64, Memos to President, Box 1, NSF Aides Files, LBJ Library.

169. Telegram, Bucharest to DOS, June 14, 1964, p. 2., Folder Rumania, Volume 1, Cables, Container No. 203-204, NSC Country File, LBJ Library.

170. *Ibid.*, pp 2-3.

171. *Idem.*, June 12, p. 1.

172. Cioranesco et al., *Aspects des relations russo-roumaines*, p. 205.

173. Telegram, Bucharest to DOS, June 14, 1964, p. 2., Folder Rumania, Volume 1, Cables, Container No. 203-204, NSC Country File, LBJ Library.

174. Montias, *Economic Development in Communist Rumania*, p. 233.

175. "Rumania and Russia Stonewalling," *The Economist* (Vol. 212), July 18, 1964, pp. 236-236.

CHAPTER IX

PROMISES POSTPONED

A Fragile Beginning and the Miller Committee

The promises made in the June communique would take more than a decade to be fulfilled. The Johnson administration's East-West trade agenda, including efforts to grant Romania MFN trade status, would be paralyzed because of Congressional concerns over the escalating conflict in Vietnam.

The June communique provided a mechanism whereby Romanian representatives could make commercial arrangements with private American businesses. When arrangements required short term credit, the Romanians could now apply for them through the Eximbank. Throughout the Summer, Romanian delegates met with various American firms to arrange purchases for some of the plants already approved for export licensing by the Commerce Department. The Firestone Rubber Company of Akron, Ohio, showed interest in building two synthetic rubber plants in Romania, while Universal Oil Products of Des Plaines, Illinois, was willing to talk about building a catalytic petroleum cracking plant.[1]

At the same time, government officials from both countries began negotiations to renew their cultural exchange accord, and to establish ground work for a consular convention. Although American Presidential elections loomed in November, both countries tried to maintain momentum to expand relations. In September, Secretary of State Rusk told the Economics Club of Detroit, that although Romania remained a Communist country, it was showing a strong spirit of independence.[2] Matthew Mestrovic in *Commonwealth* noted the new availability of American books in Bucharest including works by Steinbeck,

Hemingway, and Faulkner.[3] *Time* Magazine and the *New York Times* both carried articles describing Romania's search for American markets.[4] In November, the Senate Foreign Relations Committee held hearings on East West Trade. 105 of the 125 businessmen who testified before the Committee favored an expansion of trade with Eastern Europe.[5] At the same time, Gaston-Marin told the American publisher William Randolph Hearst that Romania welcomed Western "capitalist" investment, and was interested in establishing joint ventures with Western companies.[6]

Neither Khrushchev's fall from power nor the American Presidential election had any significant impact on American-Romanian relations. Johnson won by a comfortable majority, which insured continuity in America's foreign and economic policies. The men who made these policies met with the President for lunch on Tuesdays, and soon became known as the "Tuesday Cabinet." Those attending the meeting normally included the Secretaries of State and Defense, the Director of the CIA, the Chairman of the Joint Chiefs of Staff, and the Special Assistant for National Security Affairs.[7] The "Tuesday Cabinet" grew in importance as the Vietnam War escalated. In essence, America had a six person war cabinet.[8] In addition to bypassing the regular Cabinet and the NSC, the President frequently looked beyond government to seek advice through, what he called, Outside Task Forces. Following his election, he organized one such group to examine America's foreign economic policy which gave him its recommendations on November 25, 1964.

The report noted that United States policy toward trade with Communist countries normally reflected American-Communist political relations. Experience showed that America's restrictive trade policies had not significantly affected the Communist world. The Task Force recommended that "in the years to come United States policy should actively encourage" two-way trade with the Soviet Union and Eastern Europe. To do so, Washington should be "ready to guarantee export credits" that were competitive with those granted by other industrial countries. Further, the Administration should propose a new East-West Trade Act to Congress which would give the President discretionary power to grant MFN and negotiate trade agreements with Communist countries "whenever he finds such an agreement to be in the public interest."[9]

Johnson agreed with the recommendation and indicated this in his address to the officers of Radio Free Europe on December 2. He announced that "history is on the march in Eastern Europe and on the march toward increased freedom." Many of the people and some of the rulers "long for deeper, steadier, and more natural relations with the West. We understand this longing and we intend to respond to it in every way open to us."[10] On December 21, William Crawford presented his Ambassadorial credentials to Gheorghiu-Dej and emphasized Johnson's "building bridges" theme. [11] Two days later, the United States and Romania completed negotiations on the second renewal of the cultural relations accord, first signed in 1960. This two year extension provided a framework for arranging visits and exchanges between the two countries through December, 1966.[12] By the close of 1964, the Johnson Administration could point with pride to the initial results of their June agreement with Romania. Total two-way trade with Romania tripled from 1963 to 1964 from $2 million to over $6 million.[13]

1965 began auspiciously. In his State of the Union Address, Johnson announced that "in Eastern Europe restless nations are slowing beginning to assert their identity. Your government, assisted by the leaders in American labor and business is now exploring ways to increase peaceful trade with these countries. . . ."[14] On the same day, Dean Rusk told the press that Firestone Tire and Rubber Company and Universal Oil Products had initialed agreements with Romania to construct a synthetic rubber plant and a catalytic petroleum cracking unit.[15] A couple of weeks later, a nine man Romanian delegation came to Washington to negotiate credit arrangements with the Eximbank for purchasing the two installations.[16] At the same time, Bucharest sent another group of delegates to the United States to negotiate a consular convention as suggested in the June communique.[17]

Meanwhile, Johnson decided to review the entire issue of East-West trade. William Blackie, President of Caterpillar Tractor Company, had just returned from the first government sanctioned business trip to the Soviet Union since World War II. Blackie reported that Moscow wanted to trade with America. However, unless the United States modified its export regulations, the Soviet Union would continue to obtain what it needed from other Western powers.[18] Blackie's report added to the vast amount of data collected on East-West trade during the Kennedy-Johnson years. The President decided he needed action recommendations. Confronted with a lack of consensus among his top advisors on East-West trade, Johnson looked to the private sector, particularly to leaders of major corporations who were highly involved in international commerce. In late January, he asked J. Irwin Miller, Chairman of the Board of Cummins Engine Company, to head up a blue ribbon panel whose members were drawn from the corporate sector. This group soon became known as the Miller Committee.[19]

The degree of disagreement among Johnson's Cabinet quickly became apparent as the Miller Committee began its investigation through a series of interviews with key members of the Administration. Secretary of State Dean Rusk and Secretary of Defense Robert McNamara favored trade expansion, without any *quid pro quos*. In their opinion trade was not so essential to Eastern Europe and the Soviet Union as to make it contingent on political concessions. McNamara believed that "past restrictions on trade" with the Soviet Bloc had been "unrealistic." Unlike his predecessors, the Secretary of Defense wanted America to trade anything that was "not clearly related to military use."[20] Secretary of the Treasury Douglas Dillon was neutral on the issue. While he believed that the present export regulations were too restrictive, he saw the real problem of trading with the Soviet Bloc as a domestic issue. The American public had to be educated so as not to perceive such trade as treason.[21] At the other end of the spectrum were the Secretaries of Agriculture[22] and Commerce. Both agreed that American trade with the Communist world should be limited to "anything they can eat, drink or smoke." Further, they agreed that all trade with the Communist world should be conducted on a *quid pro quo* basis.[23]

The disagreement within the Administration hindered Romania's efforts to secure Eximbank credits. Part of the problem rested with Bucharest. In the May, 1964, negotiations, Romania indicated that she would need credits in the range of $40 to $50 million. However, when Romania began talks with the Eximbank, she asked for credits in excess of $80 million. To compound matters, because several of the transactions were turn-key contracts, export licenses and credits once committed would have to be honored by the Eximbank regardless of whatever changes might occur in Romanian-American relations. Otherwise, businesses would risk considerable loss. Few companies would want to begin construction to later discover that either needed materials could not receive export licenses or that the Eximbank refused to underwrite the project.[24]

On February 15, 1965, Crawford talked with Gaston-Marin in Bucharest. The Romanian was upset by the lack of progress in talks with the Eximbank as well as with Firestone and Universal Oil Products. Firestone appeared to be reneging on assurances the company had earlier given regarding the quality of the product that the rubber plant would produce. Gaston-Marin indicated that Romania did not need to deal with Firestone and if delays continued, Romania would withdraw its negotiating team from the United States. As usual, Crawford was sensitive to the Romanian position and urged the State Department to do what it could to influence the negotiations. He realized that it was "entirely a business proposition," and as such was outside the normal purview of the Department. Nonetheless, he hoped something could be done because were the project to collapse, "as a partial consequence of official US attitudes," the example set would have "unfortunate results" for "expanding links" with Romania and the rest of Eastern Europe.[25]

Not only were commercial relations bogged down between Washington and Bucharest, but so too were negotiations to establish a consular convention. The major stumbling block was the issue of Romanian emigration practices concerning dual nationals and Romanians seeking unification with their families living outside the country. The talks would continue until May, 1965, when they were "recessed" *sine die*.[26] Romania and the United States would finally sign a consular convention in 1972.

On February 24, 1965, President Johnson took the first major step in escalating America's involvement in the Vietnam War. He approved "Operation Rolling Thunder," the sustained bombing of North Vietnam. Except for a break at Christmas, this would continue unabated throughout 1965. The escalation had little opposition from the legislature since Congress had overwhelmingly endorsed greater American involvement in the war by their vote on the Tonkin Gulf resolution on August 7, 1964. However, Johnson's February decision would soon pose a problem for American-Romanian relations. Increasingly, members of Congress opposed American trade with Eastern Europe because they were concerned that American exports might be transshipped from Eastern Europe to North Vietnam to strengthen America's Southeast Asian enemy. This problem would continue to plague Johnson's East-West trade agenda for the remainder of his Presidency.

As American public opinion once again focused on the evils of Communism, progress in American-Romanian relations slowed to a halt. In December, 1964, Goodyear rubber company began an attack on Firestone for negotiating with the Communists. The company's newspaper, *The Wingfoot Clan*, urged consumers to switch from Firestone to Goodyear products. [27] In the following months, Firestone came under attack from the Young Americans for Freedom (YAF), a Philadelphia based conservative organization. The YAF distributed literature throughout the country indicting Firestone for its willingness to do business with the Communists.[28]

To make matters worse, on March 19, 1965, Gheorghiu-Dej died of lung cancer. His successor, Nicolae Ceausescu, recalled the Romanian negotiating team from Washington. The talks with Firestone and the Eximbank had become so involved that the original terms discussed in the Summer of 1964 were no longer valid.[29] The halt in negotiations coupled with increased propaganda against their company, forced Firestone to end their talks with Romania on April 19. Crawford wrote several strong letters to the State Department explaining the adverse affects this termination would have on the future of Romanian-American relations, and on Johnson's "building bridges" program. East European countries would be suspect of America's intentions. Even though the American government was willing to open doors to the Soviet Bloc, bilateral agreements between private American companies and East European governments did not necessarily follow.[30] Furthermore, by agreeing to deal with the United States, an East European country revealed its industrial and technological weaknesses, and at the same time risked punitive sanctions from Moscow for following too independent a course. Crawford's remarks fell on deaf ears.

The State Department talked with Firestone officials and expressed the Department's concerns. However, the rubber company reiterated that under present conditions, Firestone was not prepared to renew negotiations. The company's officials conceded that if the climate improved in the next six months to a year, Firestone "might be prepared to reconsider."[31]

Universal Oil Products' talks with Bucharest were successful. On April 1, the ECRB met to make a final determination as to whether or not the United States would provide export licenses for petroleum equipment. The Departments of Commerce, Interior and Defense had opposed granting export licenses, while the State Department urged immediate approval. Debate was heated, but Rusk won the day.[32] Secretary of the Interior, Stewart Udall was impressed by Gheorghiu-Dej's efforts toward independence. Udall supported Rusk. The Interior Secretary was willing to sell Romania petroleum equipment to "enhance their ability to be politically independent."[33] Udall indicated that he was going against the wishes of his department and those of the petroleum industry, but he "would defer to State." Several days later, the ECRB recommended that the Commerce Department grant the needed export licenses to enable Universal Oil Products to build a catalytic cracking plant in Romania. With this approval, the Eximbank, on April 26, authorized a guarantee of $20 million in credit for the construction of the facility.[34]

Meanwhile, the Miller Committee had continued to study the entire East-West trade issue. The group met for five two-day sessions throughout March and April.[35] It had full access to government sources of information, and the benefit of material submitted by interested private organizations. Also the Committee made considerable use of a March 17 report from the Council for Economic Development (CED), on which Miller had served as a member of its subcommittee on East-West trade.[36]

The Miller Committee labored until April 29 when it submitted its findings and recommendations to the President. The Committee concluded that "political, not commercial or economic, considerations should determine the formation and execution" of American trade policies toward European Communist countries. The main goals of American trade policies were to encourage the European Communist countries to seek independence from the Soviet Union, while bringing their trade practices "into line" with "normal" world trade practices. To do so, the Committee recommended that the United States should continue its policy of differentiation. Washington should adapt its trade policies to the political circumstances and opportunities that presented themselves in individual East European countries.

The Committee noted that the United States should maintain its controls on "strategic items that could significantly enhance Communist military capabilities." However, with respect to non-strategic trade, the United States should actively engage in trade negotiations with individual Communist countries and be prepared to remove trade restrictions on a selective basis. While the Committee believed that the current American policy regarding Eximbank commercial credit was adequate, the Committee called for a more "flexible and selective" policy for export licensing. The Committee favored a relaxation of export controls on a country by country basis in exchange for concessions and improved relations. Interestingly, the Committee believed that the language of the Export Control Act of 1962, even with the restrictive amendment, was ambiguous enough to allow export licensing for constructive purposes.

The Committee found that the most "serious barrier" in the way of expanding peaceful trade with European Communist countries, was the prohibition on granting them MFN. The Committee declared that "vesting discretionary authority in the President to grant as well as with draw such tariff treatment would be the single most important step in permitting the government to use trade more effectively as an instrument for shaping our relations with these countries." The Committee emphasized that there should be a "distinction" between this MFN tariff treatment and the MFN tariff treatment granted by statute to "Free World" countries. "It should be granted to Communist countries only for the duration of the agreement of which it is a part, and it should be subject to periodic review." In conclusion, the report noted that "trade is one of the few channels available to us for constructive contacts with nations with whom we find frequent hostility. In the long run, selected trade, intelligently negotiated and wisely administered, may turn out to have been one of our most powerful tools of national policy."[37]

Attached to the twenty-seven page report was a minority report by the AFL-CIO representative Nathaniel Goldfinger. His comments focused on greater control over technology exports, greater emphasis on *quid pro quo* trade agreements, a position the Miller report did not adopt, protection from "dumping" of products made by "slave labor," and a stronger emphasis on national security as the criterion for East-West trade.[38] However, in spite of these reservations, Goldfinger signed the Miller report.

Miller's committee had made some bold recommendations. Although Johnson personally agreed with them, he was cautious to embrace them publicly. Enthusiastic endorsement of expanded East-West trade would have few supporters. The press had carried too many stories about the failed Firestone negotiations, while Congress showed little enthusiasm for expanding trade with Communist countries in view of Vietnam. However, McGeorge Bundy noted that while the report called for change, it was "carefully designed to protect both you and the committee from charges of softness of any sort."[39] Francis Bator, Deputy Special Assistant to the President urged Johnson to make the report public to avoid the embarrassment that might result were the report leaked to the press.[40] On May 6, the President released the Miller report and the following day at a speech commemorating the twentieth anniversary of the Allied victory in Europe, he reiterated his "building bridges" theme noting that he intended to recommend measures to Congress to increase East-West trade.[41]

Meanwhile, a Congressional committee headed by Wright Patman, a Texan like the President, was working on legislation to renew the Export Control Act. Johnson asked Secretary of Commerce John Connor and J. Irwin Miller to meet with Patman to promote the recommendations of the Miller Report. The President also asked Miller to see Mike Mansfield and Wilbur Mills, Senate and House leaders, and discuss the need for discretionary MFN authority for the President.[42] On May 11, Johnson sent Patman's Committee on Banking and Currency a formal proposal to implement the Miller report. However, the committee was more concerned with an Arab boycott amendment than it was with East-West trade. The Arab League had tried to induce American businessmen to join them in a boycott of Israeli products. Congress wanted to retaliate and impose trade restrictions on the Arab League. In the process, however, Congress also appeared to be restricting the President's discretionary authority in implementing the Export Control Act. Consequently, White House personnel were forced to throw their efforts into maintaining the present discretionary authority of the President, rather than extending it. Their efforts were successful. In June, Congress passed the Export Control Act with an Arab boycott amendment that did not interfere with the President's regular discretionary authority.[43] The Arab boycott had muddied the waters. The Administration agreed to set aside the President's MFN proposal until specific East-West trade legislation was addressed on Capitol Hill.[44] Though the President believed this would occur in the Fall, no East-West legislation would reach Congress until May, 1966.

From Gheorghiu-Dej to Ceausescu

Following the April, 1964, "Declaration on the Stand of the Romanian Workers' Party Concerning the Problems of the International Communist and Working Class Movement" and the subsequent repudiation by *Izvestia* of the Valev thesis to remake the lower Danube, Bucharest continued to pursue a strongly anti-Soviet position. In July, 1964, Moscow proposed that a preliminary conference of representatives from 26 Communist parties meet in Moscow in December, 1964. The purpose was to prepare for a world conference at which the Soviets hoped to expel the Chinese Communist party from the World Communist movement. In spite of visits by Nikolai Podgorny, soon to be President of the Soviet Union, the Romanians refused to attend.[45]

Romania's confrontational approach to Moscow continued even after Khrushchev's ouster in October. Without question, Gheorghiu-Dej was pleased by the change in Soviet leadership since his struggle with Khrushchev went beyond the realm of ideology and politics to a personal dislike. Khrushchev's fall bought Moscow time to prepare for the the upcoming preliminary party conference. The new Soviet leaders, Leonid Brezhnev and Aleksei Kosygin rescheduled the meeting for March, 1965. However, when the conference opened Romania was conspicuously absent.[46]

Khrushchev's fall seemed to fuel Gheorghiu-Dej's drive for "desatellization." On October 31, 1964, Romania unilaterally cut its armed forces from 240,000 men to 200,000 and reduced the length of conscription from 24 months to 18 months.[47] This saved Romania money and gave substance to her call for peaceful coexistence. Bucharest went further and argued that its share of the Warsaw Pact budget was excessive. Her complaints managed to have the Soviets significantly reduce the size of their military liaison mission to Bucharest. To further reduce Soviet influence in Romania, Gheorghiu-Dej refused to permit further Warsaw Pact military maneuvers on Romanian soil.[48]

At a meeting of the Central Committee of the Romanian Workers Party on November 30, Gheorghiu-Dej announced his intention to continue to look beyond CMEA for trade and industrial equipment.[49] Bucharest was in the process of negotiating with Firestone and Universal Oil Products in the United States and with firms in France for industrial equipment.[50] A couple of weeks later, copies of *Notes on the Romanians*, by Karl Marx appeared in bookstalls across Romania. Edited by the prominent Marxist historians, Otetea and Zane, the book included four hitherto unpublished documents by Marx condemning Tsarist Russia's seizure of Bessarabia. The publication was designed to revive anti-Soviet sentiment in Romania, and within forty-eight hours, 30,000 copies of the book were sold.[51]

In February, 1965, Gheorghiu-Dej's efforts to reach out to the United States met dual setbacks. The much heralded Firestone negotiations were breaking down and the United States appeared ready to increase its participation in Vietnam. These setbacks effectively limited Gheorghiu-Dej's freedom of action *vis a vis* the United States. Bucharest was in an awkward position. Gheorghiu-Dej sent Gaston-Marin to Moscow, and on February 17 the two countries signed a trade protocol.[52] The accord indicated that socialist brotherhood had to be maintained when capitalist countries threatened to topple a Communist regime.

Lung cancer ended Gheorghiu-Dej's life on March 19, 1965, but it did not end Romania's "de-satellization" program. In fact, those attending the funeral reflected the success of Romania's independent path, for among the delegates were Anastas Ivonovich Mikoyan from the Soviet Union and Zhou Enlai from Communist China.[53] The new party leader, Nicolae Ceausescu, wasted little time in indicating that Romania would continue along her own road to socialism.[54] Ceausescu continued to prohibit Warsaw Pact forces from holding maneuvers on Romanian territory, and, in May, at the Central Committee Plenum he suggested that the party change its name from the Romanian Worker's Party to the Romanian Communist Party.[55] The name change not only indicated the "revolutionary" nature of the party, but it raised the Communist Party of Romania to the same level as the party of the Soviet Union. Ceausescu further suggested that Party membership criteria be broadened to encourage greater participation.

1,566 delegates assembled in Bucharest on July 19 for the opening of the 9th Congress of the Romanian Communist Party.[56] Among them were Deng Xiaoping of China and Leonid Brezhnev of the Soviet Union.[57] The five day conclave would prove to be historic.[58] The Congress addressed the issue of political and economic reform in Romania. The delegates adopted a new Constitution which changed the country's name from a People's Republic, which frequently indicated a satellite status, to the Socialist Republic of Romania. In addition, the Constitution replaced the Politburo with a small Standing Presidium, which would later be called the Permanent Bureau, and added an Executive Committee as an intermediate body between this new echelon and the Central Committee. This reorganization enabled Ceausescu to place his followers in the new Executive Committee. Gaston-Marin was among those who lost power. While blamed for agricultural failures, the former head of the State Planning Council was also removed because of his pro-American views, and his identification with Gheorghiu-Dej, who came under mild criticism at the Congress for his "cult of personality."[59] As one prominent American daily noted in an editorial, the new Constitution did not mention the Soviet Union, and for the first time, not a single portrait of Lenin, Marx or Engels hung from the walls of the meeting hall.[60]

The 9th Congress also called for economic reform. In his opening remarks, Ceausescu announced a new program labelled the "consolidation of the socialist society." This was a transition period which would lead to the "multilateral" development of Romania's economy. During the transition, Ceausescu wanted Romania to increase her national income and trade volume by 40% by 1970.[61] Throughout the Congress, speakers noted the importance of laying the groundwork for

Romania's multilateral development. This development included a number of vital economic concepts such as sustained industrialization, agricultural growth, expansion of domestic raw materials, increased foreign trade on the basis of "mutual advantage," increased literacy, and central planning.[62]

Without question, the 9th Party Congress and Romania's new Constitution bolstered Ceausescu's sense of leadership. In the annual August 23 celebrations, *Agerpres* carried an article indicating that the victory over Hitlerism in 1944 was "initiated, organized and led by the Romanian Communist Party." The Soviet army was not even mentioned in passing.[63] However, Ceausescu could not be quite as independent of Moscow as had Gheorghiu-Dej. The new Romanian leader did not have the same degree of leverage against the Soviets. The Sino-Soviet rift in 1965 was not nearly as intense as it had been several years earlier. And the "American card" was not as useful as it had been prior to Washington's increased involvement in the Vietnam War. At the 9th Party Congress, Ceausescu had limited his condemnation of America to a few sentences.[64] However, Johnson's announcement in July to send an additional 44 combat battalions to Vietnam, coupled with Congress's unwillingness to adopt new East-West trade legislation reduced Ceausescu's Western leverage against Moscow. As a result, in September, Ceausescu visited the Soviet Union and indicated that he would no longer raise the issue of Romanian claims to Bessarabia. In turn, the Kremlin agreed to ignore Hungarian demands for a greater voice in Transylvanian affairs.[65]

East-West Trade and the Vietnam War, 1966

The same factors which reduced Ceausescu's leverage with Moscow, curtailed Crawford's effectiveness in Bucharest. The American Ambassador asked for reassignment. On September 6, the White House announced that Richard Davis of New York, a career Foreign Service Officer, would succeed Crawford as Ambassador to Bucharest.[66] Two weeks later, the first American trade expansion mission visited Romania. Under the leadership of Paul Pauley, the Director of the Office of International Trade Promotion in the Department of Commerce, the seven man team spent ten days at the end of September meeting with Romanian representatives from the fields of metallurgy, electrical and agricultural equipment and petrochemicals.[67] Upon their return, the team informed the President that Romania was still "a fertile field" for trade. However, three old concerns remained: the lack of MFN for Romanian products, American export restrictions and limited Eximbank credits.[68]

The Administration was well aware of Ceausescu's complaints, but Congress was not willing to pass new legislation. Having failed in his efforts to have Patman amend the Export Control Act, Johnson asked Senators Long, Fulbright and Mansfield to support a new East-West Trade bill.[69] Again concerns about transshipment from Eastern Europe to North Vietnam crippled the President's efforts. This negativism was especially true among Congressmen with ethnic East European constituencies. These voters strongly opposed all American trade with Eastern Europe since they viewed all such traffic as helping the Soviets. Other Congressmen wanted to tie an East-West trade package to Soviet political concessions. Still others were simply opposed to aiding any nation which supported North Vietnam in any way. Leaders of this group included Senate Minority Leader, Everett Dirksen from Illinois, and House Minority Leader, Gerald Ford from Michigan. Both men announced that Republican Congressional leaders had endorsed a "no concessions-no deal" policy towards Communist countries.[70] Faced with this substantial opposition, Mansfield and Fulbright decided not to bring the East-West trade bill to the floor during the first session of the 89th Congress.[71]

While most of Johnson's advisors supported the Miller Committee's recommendations, a new dispute arose within the Administration. Dean Rusk led a group who advised against pushing for an East-West trade package. Rusk recognized the slim chance the bill would have given current Congressional sentiment. McGeorge Bundy disagreed. Bundy believed the Administration could win the support of Wilbur Mills and William Fulbright, and these two men would push the bill through Congress.[72] Johnson accepted Bundy's advise and on January 12, 1966, asked Congress to grant the Executive discretionary authority to increase East-West trade so that he could "build bridges" to Eastern Europe.[73]

It soon became apparent that Johnson had followed the wrong advise.[74] In April, 1966, Congressional leaders warned him not to press for East-West trade legislation. Even his supporters told him that it would not have a "ghost of a chance" because of Vietnam and the 1966 Congressional elections. Few Congressmen wanted to support a bill which could be identified as "pro-Communist" by a campaign opponent.[75] Nonetheless, Johnson persisted. On May 3, at a ceremony commemorating the Polish Christian Millennium, Johnson announced that he would instruct Secretary of State Rusk to send Congress legislation to "expand trade between the United States and Eastern Europe."[76]

Sure enough, Rusk sent Congress an East-West trade bill the following week. Known as the East-West Trade Relations Act of 1966, the bill was designed to give the President authority to negotiate commercial agreements with East European countries. The bill would also give the President the authority to grant MFN treatment to individual Communist countries for a limited period of time.[77]

Nicolae Ceausescu's Romanian Nationalism

As Johnson pressed for his trade bill, Ceausescu worked to distance himself from Gheorghiu-Dej while maintaining most of his predecessor's goals. He replaced some of Gheorghiu-Dej's people, and raised questions concerning the trial of Lucretiu Patrascanu, suggesting that his execution did not result from any wrong doing on his part.[78] Later, in April, 1968, Ceausescu would rehabilitate Patrascanu as a national Communist alleging that his arrest, trial and execution were based on "gross fabrication," and that he had been "prooflessly branded as an agent of the Anglo-American espionage services."[79]

During the first half of 1966, Ceausescu travelled extensively throughout the country emphasizing the importance of industrialization for Romania's national independence and sovereignty. On May 7, he made a major address commemorating the 45th anniversary of the founding of the Romanian Communist Party. He praised the role the party had played in the development of the Socialist Republic. He attacked the Comintern for interfering in the establishment of the Romanian Communist Party,[80] and by its forcing the appointment of party cadre who were unfamiliar with Romanian ways.[81] These actions "promoted the dismemberment of the national state and the Romanian people's disintegration."[82] In his 60 page address, he mentioned Gheorghiu-Dej only once, revived Romania's claims to Bessarabia in light of recent Soviet support to Hungarian interests in Transylvania, condemned military alliances as anachronistic, and noted that Romanian-American relations were developing slowly, but "not because of Romania's restraint."[83] All in all, the speech was a *tour de force* for Romanian nationalism.

America's continued escalation of the war in Vietnam forced Ceausescu to lean more toward Moscow to symbolize Communist unity and support for the North Vietnamese. As a result, Ceausescu wanted to avoid taking sides in the Sino-Soviet rift. When Zhou Enlai visited Bucharest for eight days in June, 1966, Ceausescu refused to permit the Chinese leader to use Romania as a podium for another Beijing attack against Moscow. Ceausescu censored Zhou Enlai's prepared remarks, limited him to a few impromptu public statements and issued no official communiques of the Chinese leader's visit.[84]

On June 28, four days after Zhou's departure, Ceausescu urged the party's Central Committee to approve the new five year plan, 1966-1970, drafted at the 9th Party Congress in July, 1965. The approved plan was more ambitious than the draft and called for an annual growth rate of 11.6 per cent, a full percentage point higher than originally expected. The party leader saw the plan as a means to produce an economy of abundance, a new stage of socialist development that would enable the "wealth of society" to "gush forth more quickly."[85]

During the next several months, Ceausescu continued Gheorghiu-Dej's *tous azimuts* foreign policy. Ceausescu's Western press image soared. The *Christian Science Monitor* called him a "political acrobat," the *Economist* described him as the "de Gaulle of Eastern Europe."[86] In early 1967, he broke Eastern Bloc policy and recognized Bonn on January 31. In the process, West Germany abandoned the Hallstein Doctrine which prohibited Bonn from having diplomatic relations with any country recognizing East Germany.

Also in February, Ceausescu addressed a specially convened conference on Foreign Trade. In his speech on the 23rd, he exhorted the delegates to make efficiency the goal in foreign trade. Trade was "not being done for the love of trade. We do not sell for the sake of selling."[87] The current five year plan called for a 55% increase in the volume of foreign trade. He cited several countries as the sources for this increase, and conspicuously omitted the United States. In conclusion, he called for the Ministry of Foreign Trade to permit some decentralization to facilitate trade expansion, and called on the diplomatic service to spend most of their time improving economic relations with foreign countries.[88]

Vietnam, Congress and East-West Trade, 1967

Ceausescu's omission of the United States as a vigorous trade partner was partly due to the Johnson Administration's failure to get an East-West trade package through Congress. On May 11, 1966, the President had delivered the East-West Trade Act of 1966 to Capitol

Hill in spite of Congressional advice to the contrary. On the following day, Wilbur Mills, Chairman of the House Way and Means Committee, killed the bill. He told the President that he did not support the measure and would not hold hearings on it. Since tariff laws originated in Mills' committee, the House would not get to vote on the East-West trade bill in 1966. In the Senate, Majority Leader Mike Mansfield introduced the Administration's East-West trade bill on May 17. Although he called the bill a symbol of peace, he privately confided that there was little hope for its passage. This prediction proved correct and the bill did not leave the Senate Finance Committee.[89]

Johnson failed to appreciate the effects that the Vietnam War had on American public opinion. The most rabid anti-Communists in America were given new legitimacy. One group, calling itself the "Committee to Warn of the Arrival of Communist Merchandise on the Local Scene," organized boycotts of Polish hams and Yugoslavian tobacco.[90] Additional opposition appeared when the Eximbank agreed to extend credits to enable Romania to process pork for export to the United States.[91] Stubbornly, the Administration persisted. In a major foreign policy address to the National Conference of Editorial Writers in New York City on October 7, Johnson vowed to continue to "press" for his MFN legislation. He declared that America had to "shift from the narrow concept of coexistence to the broader vision of peaceful engagement" with the peoples in Eastern Europe. The President announced his intentions to reduce export controls on East-West trade with respect to hundreds of non-strategic items; to permit the Eximbank to extend credit to four East European countries – Poland, Czechoslovakia, Hungary and Bulgaria; and to further liberalize travel regulations to Eastern Europe.[92] The Administration moved quickly to implement Johnson's announcement. On October 12, the Commerce Department relaxed export licensing requirements on about 400 non-strategic items for shipment to the Soviet Union and Eastern Europe.[93]

Congressional opposition to improved relations with Communist countries hardened. Congressmen of all political persuasions found it difficult to support legislation which would risk the transshipment of American exports to North Vietnam. And there were transshipments. Romania made them at the same time she was willing to assume the role of mediator between the United States and the forces of Ho Chi Minh.[94] As a further hindrance to the Administration, United States commerce with Eastern Europe totaled less than 1% of America's exports.[95] Many Congressmen had a difficult time trying to understand why the White House would jeopardize its relationship with the legislature, especially during a war, for such a paltry gain. However, Johnson's East-West trade program did not stem from economic concerns. He had accepted the recommendations of the Miller Report. For the time being, East-West trade was pursued primarily for political reasons. The President believed that trade could be used as a "carrot or stick" to affect change in Eastern Europe. Unfortunately for him, he failed to realize that Congress was more eager to fund weapons to destroy Communism in Southeast Asia, than it was to sanction economic weapons to affect Communist policies in Eastern Europe.

As 1966 came to a close, Johnson's escalation policies had placed about 400,000 American troops in Vietnam. Yet, victory did not appear any closer. Defense Secretary McNamara used "systems analysis" specialists to evaluate the war and they concluded that it could take generations before North Vietnam would surrender. America's bombing strategy was not working.[96] Confronted with this data, Johnson agreed to seek a peaceful solution to Vietnam.

On October 22, 1966, the American Ambassador to the United Nations, Arthur Goldberg, talked with the Romanian Foreign Minister Corneliu Manescu in New York. Romania had earlier indicated a willingness to mediate between Washington and Hanoi, and Manescu reaffirmed this commitment.[97] However, he stressed that no talks could begin with Hanoi until the United States ceased its bombing of North Vietnam. Goldberg was willing to discuss that issue and wanted to know what Hanoi would do in return for a halt to the bombing.[98] So began Romania's role as mediator between the United States and North Vietnam, a role she would continue to hold through early 1968. The question of bombing remained the focal point throughout the negotiations. The United States insisted on a *quid pro quo* from Hanoi before she stopped bombing, while North Vietnam wanted the bombing to stop before she made any commitments.[99]

As the mediation talks continued, Johnson decided to, once again, resubmit his East-West trade bill to Congress. He notified the legislature in January, 1967, of his intent. His legislative liaisons negotiated with Wilbur Mills but failed to secure his support. The most that Mills would concede was a promise that he would "make a major effort" to at least hold hearings on the bill at some point in the session.[100]

General Westmoreland returned to the Capitol in April. While informing the President that the "war could go on indefinitely," he agreed to Johnson's request to be optimistic in public. On the following day,

April 28, the General spoke to Congress. He reassured the legislature that all the evidence pointed to a "steady and encouraging success."[101] Westmoreland's remarks shored up support for continuing the war effort, and consequently doomed the East-West trade bill for another session. In May, the Republican congressional leadership took a stand against increased trade with the Soviet Bloc. Unaware of Romania's mediation role, Senate Republican leader Everett Dirksen and Gerald Ford, the House Republican leader, opposed any increase in economic aid to the Soviet Bloc until the Communist countries indicated that "they seek peace in Vietnam." Ford could not understand how "the Johnson-Humphrey Administration continues to urge that we trade with the enemy by 'building bridges' between us and these Communist dealers in death."[102] With this opposition, Mills refused to begin hearings on the East-West trade bill.[103] In June, the Six Day war between Israel and Egypt broke out. The Soviets threw their support to Egypt, and ended any lingering hope for hearings on the East-West trade bill in 1967.

Bucharest and Washington

Meanwhile in Bucharest, Ceausescu continued to consolidate his power. His February, 1967, speech on foreign trade was only the first of a series of addresses which indicated that he intended to rule Romania single-handedly. On May 7 he wrote an article in *Scinteia* which repeated the themes of the April, 1964, Declaration and emphasized the "leading role of the party" in building socialism. He asserted Romania's right to follow her own revolutionary path and rejected the "mechanical copying" of "foreign systems."[104]

Within the next few weeks, Ceausescu gave ample proof that Romania would continue its independent development. In May, he met with American businessmen who were part of the first privately organized trade mission approved by the United States government. This was one of the first groups to visit Romania under her new travel regulations which no longer required tourists to have visas. All that a person needed was a passport and a tourist document provided by Romanian authorities.[105] During their visit, the delegates explored new trade opportunities in light of the Commerce Department's recent decision to relax the export licensing restrictions on about 400 non-strategic items.[106] Several days later, Ceausescu won more support in America when Romania became the only Warsaw Pact nation not to sign the June 9 Moscow note condemning Israel for its actions in the Six Day War.[107]

Since Congress refused to deal with his East-West trade bill, the President tried to build his own bridges to the East. He met Soviet Premier Kosygin in June at Glassboro, New Jersey, and on the following day, the 26th, met the Romanian Prime Minister, Ion Gheorghe Maurer, at the White House. Maurer's visit gained little press attention because of the Glassboro meeting, but his visit marked only the second time the head of a Communist government was honored at the White House. According to a Romanian diplomat, Maurer made a "powerful impression" on Johnson.[108] Johnson's view may well have been affected by his briefing papers. Walter Rostow, Johnson's National Security Advisor, indicated that Romania was following a course "exceedingly independent of Moscow." He added, that Johnson would probably like Maurer because he was a "somewhat off-beat Communist leader."[109] In addition to talking about expanding trade, Johnson apparently told Maurer that the United States would support the Romanian Foreign Minister Corneliu Manescu's candidacy for President of the United Nations.[110]

Maurer's visit sparked a series of events which, when combined, indicated that Romanian-American relations were on a solid footing. In March, Ceausescu gave Mr. Richard Nixon, the former Vice President of the United States, a welcome fit for a state dignitary. Nixon was overwhelmed. He wrote in his memoirs, "everywhere we were greeted with outbursts of friendship from the people."[111] On July 24, Ceausescu told the Grand National Assembly about the recent progress in relations between Washington and Bucharest. Romania wanted to develop a greater friendship with the United States and to expand relations on "mutually advantageous grounds, in the interest of cooperation and peace the world over."[112] Three days later Corneliu Bogdan met President Johnson in the White House. Bogdan was Romania's new Ambassador to the United States replacing Petre Balaceanu who returned to Bucharest for reassignment.[113] Bogdan had prepared a protocol type of speech, but when he met the President, he threw the prepared remarks aside, and the two men talked about MFN for Romania, and about Bucharest's on-going role as a secret mediator between Hanoi and Washington. For the next several months, Bogdan became a major conduit for this mediation.[114]

In August, Romania publicly admitted that she was providing military aid to Hanoi.[115] Nevertheless this did not affect Bucharest-Washington relations. In September, the State Department permitted the Romanian vessel, the *Sinaia*, to visit a number of ports in the United States normally not open to East European ships.[116] In October, Ceausescu sent Johnson a message through Anghel Rugina, a Professor at Northeastern University, who was visiting Bucharest. The note asked "where the are those bridges to the East? We here in Romania are looking for real bridges of doing business with the United States. But up to now not even one single pillar of those desirable bridges has come to the surface."[117] The message only reinforced Johnson's frustrations with Congress.

Meanwhile, Ceausescu continued to make his own mark on Romania. In July, he secretly experimented with some economic reforms involving the transfer of 71 state controlled enterprises to a decentralized management system. Ceausescu announced the success of the experiment at a Central Committee meeting in October, whereupon he introduced an outline for economic reform called the "Directives of the Central Committee of the Romanian Communist Party on the Perfecting of Management and Planning the National Economy." While described as a method of decentralization, the reforms really aimed at de-bureaucratization. The reforms removed the ministry officials from the daily operations of enterprises and set up a profit incentive program to stimulate production at the local level. Simply put, the reforms were designed to establish more direct ties between producers and clients. One industry that was particularly affected was the Ministry of Foreign Trade which Ceausescu especially wanted to make more efficient. The reforms in this area called for Romania to establish foreign trade organizations (FTO) to facilitate Romanian exports.[118]

In December, Ceausescu consolidated his power. He called a National Party Conference on the sixth. In addition to approving the economic reforms introduced in October, the Party also approved Ceausescu's reorganization proposals which reunited the positions of Secretary-General of the party and President of the State Council. This had been the case under Gheorghiu-Dej, but following his death, the positions were separated as a symbol of the end of the personality cult. Chivu Stoica, the former President of the State Council, urged the merger of the two positions to insure unity of the state and party at the international level.[119] Ceausescu accepted, and was without peer in Romania.

Meanwhile, the negotiations between Washington and Hanoi had reached a new level of intensity. On September 29, 1967, Johnson announced in a speech in San Antonio that American would halt the bombing of North Vietnam in return for "productive discussions." In other words, if the bombing stopped, would Hanoi agree not to take military advantage of the halt? Romania agreed to relay the message to Hanoi. Once Bucharest established direct contact with the North Vietnamese government, Harriman flew to Romania and met with Maurer on November 28. For the next several months, Ceausescu's government was America's premier conduit to North Vietnam. The code name for the Romanian channel was "Packers," named after the successful professional football team, the Green Bay Packers.[120]

Romania's role as intermediary ended abruptly in February, 1968, when the North Vietnamese unleashed a highly successful offensive at Tet against South Vietnamese and American troops. This ended the Romanian channel, and indicated that perhaps Hanoi had only intended to use Bucharest to conceal the Vietcong's true intentions from the United States. Following the Tet attack, President Johnson sent Ceausescu a personal note of gratitude, thanking him for his peacemaking efforts.[121]

Congress and East-West Trade, 1968

Meanwhile, Congressional opposition to the East-West trade bill remained a thorn in Johnson's side. On December 12, 1967, Wilbur Mills told the Administration that East-West trade was the last item on his agenda for the second session of the 90th Congress.[122] Nonetheless, in his economic message to Congress in January, 1968, the President repeated his request for Congress to pass his East-West trade bill. Congress responded. On January 30, the House Committee on Foreign Affairs' Subcommittee on Europe began hearings which would take two months reviewing the entire spectrum of legislation and issues involved in East-West trade.[123] At the outset, the Committee Chair, Edna Kelly, announced that since this was a Presidential election year, the current session of Congress would be shorter than usual. "Consequently," she explained, "the prospects of any major legislative breakthrough in the field of East-West trade are rather slim for 1968."[124]

Since 1968 was a Presidential election year, Republican candidates made trading with the Communists a campaign issue. Remembered for his strident anti-Communism in the late 1940s, Richard Nixon capitalized on this image. In November, 1967, he told the *U. S. News and World Report* that "it makes no sense to build bridges to Eastern Europe ... and to close our eyes to the fact that they are ... supporting our enemies in Vietnam." In February, 1968, he told some followers in Hillsboro, New Hampshire, that Communists did not understand trade without a *quid pro quo*. "We should use this tremendous leverage that of peaceful trade . . . as a device to liberalize the policies of the Eastern European countries."[125]

Meanwhile, Edna Kelly's Subcommittee continued its hearings. One of the early speakers was Paul Findley of Illinois, who urged granting Romania MFN status as a reward for her taking positions independent of the Soviet Union and other Eastern Bloc countries.[126] While Findley's position was more pro-trade than others, most speakers at the hearings viewed Romania as an exception when talking about East-West relations. Myron Kratzer of the U.S. Atomic Energy Commission testified that Romania was being considered for a heavy water plant to help her build a nuclear power reactor.[127] Other testimony indicated that Romania, along with Poland and Yugoslavia, were receiving American agricultural exports under the barter program.[128]

While the Subcommittee on Europe held hearings on East-West trade, the House and Senate debated bills to permit the Eximbank to make higher risk loans. During the discussion, the question was raised as to whether the Johnson Act of 1934 limited the bank from extending credits to governments in default of their payments to the United States. In fact, the Soviet Union and all East European countries were in default of their payments. However, on May 9, 1967, the Attorney General had made a finding and determined that the Johnson Act did not prohibit banks, including the Eximbank, from extending credits to Communist countries.[129] As a result, Paul Fino of New York, proposed an amendment to do what the Johnson Act could not do. The Fino Amendment prohibited the Eximbank from extending credits to "any country furnishing goods, supplies, military assistance or advisers to a nation engaged in armed conflict with with the United States." This included the Soviet Union and all Eastern Bloc countries except Yugoslavia. The Senate passed the amendment along with an extension of the Eximbank for five years on February 21, 1968, and six days later the House did the same. Confronted by overwhelming support for the amendment, Johnson signed the bill into law on March 13. This act ended Eximbank credits for Romania.[130]

On March 31, President Johnson stunned the American people when he announced on television that he would not seek reelection. He wanted to use his remaining months in office to resolve the Vietnam conflict. Consequently, other issues including East-West trade were put on a back burner. In an April 26 review of America's policy toward Eastern Europe, Dean Rusk expressed regret that Congress had refused to move on East-West trade legislation.[131]

Meanwhile, having consolidated his power at the December, 1967, National Party Conference, Ceausescu finally agreed to attend an international Communist meeting in Budapest on February 26, 1968. Romania had refused to participate in the Moscow Consultative Conference in 1965 and in the April, 1967, meeting of the European Communist parties at Karlovy Vary. However, on February 14, Ceausescu announced that Romania would attend the Budapest meeting to exchange views and have a "broad and fruitful exchange of opinions."[132]

Paul Niculescu-Mizel led the Romanian delegation which attended the opening ceremonies on February 26. Two days later, the Romanians walked out of the conference and returned home. Niculescu-Mizel initially objected to the Soviet delegate's criticism of China. However, when Khalid Bakdash of Syria criticized Romania's independent policy, Niculescu-Mizel insisted that all the delegates from the 66 parties attending denounce Syria's attack on a fraternal socialist state. The conference members refused, and the Romanians went home.[133]

Within a week, Romania again exhibited her independence. Ceausescu attended a Warsaw Pact meeting in Sofia, Bulgaria, to discuss a proposed nuclear non-proliferation treaty. He opposed the treaty because it provided no guarantees that nuclear weapons could not be used against non-nuclear countries.[134] His refusal to compromise finally forced the Warsaw Pact to issue its first communique without a unanimous endorsement.[135] Ceausescu's obstinacy was a deliberate move to give greater recognition to Romania's independence. Because three months later, with little fanfare, Romania supported the non-proliferation treaty.[136]

Romania's continued rejection of Soviet leadership impressed a few liberal Congressmen in Washington. In May, 1968, Walter Mondale of Minnesota, and twelve other Senators sponsored a joint resolution, S. 169, which proposed that the "Export Control Act regulations and the Export-Import Bank financing restrictions should be examined and modified to promote" trade in peaceful goods between the United States and the nations of Eastern Europe. In his remarks, Mondale noted that the "winds of change are blowing across Eastern Europe, but the breezes rarely enter Congress." To help implement his resolution, Mondale announced that as Chairman of the International Finance Subcommittee of the Senate Banking and Currency Committee, he intended to begin hearings on East-West trade.[137] On June 4, the hearings began and extended through July 25, 1968. Mondale heard testimony from conservatives, such as John Davis Lodge of the Committee to End Aid to the Soviet Enemy and W. B. Hicks, Jr. of the Liberty Lobby, both of whom called for Congress to further restrict trade with the Communist world. On the other hand, members of the Johnson Administration used the opportunity to promote East-West trade and, to again, propose discretionary authority for the President to grant MFN to individual East European countries.[138] The hearings did not lead to legislation because Congress adjourned in October in preparation for the upcoming Presidential elections.

While developments in Vietnam consumed most of the Administration's attention, the cultural relations accords signed biannually with Romania provided a means to keep American-Romanian relations warm. Dr. Donald Hornig, the President's Special Assistant for Science and Technology, invited a delegation of Romanian scientists to come to the United States for several weeks and meet with their American counterparts. Romania agreed and on June 18, Alexandru Birladeanu, the Deputy Chairman of the Council of Ministers and Chairman of the Romanian National Council of Scientific Research, brought a team of six scientists to the United States. The Romanians visited industries and universities in New York, Chicago, Los Angeles and Cape Kennedy.[139]

On July 8, the United States and Romania signed an agreement to broaden contacts in science and technology. Unlike other exchange agreements, which were typically vague, this document broke new ground. Both governments agreed to exchange industrial knowledge and technology "including arrangements in the field of patent licenses and know-how with adequate protection for industrial rights." This was a new step forward because it addressed an issue that had long been a deep concern of American firms interested in trade with Romania.[140]

During the three week visit, Birladeanu made contacts with private American firms to purchase computers and, ironically, with Goodyear Tire to build a synthetic rubber plant in Romania. In addition, the Administration indicated that it would approve the purchase of a heavy water plant from an American company, but would make no official announcement of this agreement until after Congress adjourned.[141] Before leaving, delegates from both countries agreed to increase professional exchanges especially in the fields of transportation, coal research, and wildlife preservation.[142] Following the joint communique to the press, the *New York Times* picked up Johnson's "building bridges" theme and described the new scientific exchange agreement as a "breakthrough" to "unlocking many doors now closed in Eastern Europe."[143]

Ceausescu and the Czechoslovakian Invasion

Romania's strides toward independence received a sharp rebuff on August 21, 1968, when troops from five socialist states marched into Czechoslovakia, bringing an end to the "Prague Spring." In January, 1968, a group of disgruntled Stalinists and reformers ousted Antonin Novotny as General Secretary of the Czechoslovak Communist party and brought in Alexander Dubcek. Novotny had been viewed as Moscow's pawn, while Dubcek was a rallying figure for liberal reform and greater autonomy in domestic affairs. A free press symbolized the changes which appeared during the Spring of 1968. The secret police was linked to the Soviet KGB, and consequently lost much of its power. Prague did not tell Moscow about the anticipated reforms, and Soviet leaders feared that continued change could reduce the power of the Communist party in Czechoslovakia.[144]

In contrast, Ceausescu refuted rumors that continued reform in Czechoslovakia might provoke retaliation from Moscow. On July 15, Ceausescu announced that "not for a moment" can anyone conceive that the Warsaw Treaty could be a reason "for justifying an interference in the domestic affairs of other states." Romania had "full confidence in the Communist Party of Czechoslovakia" to build socialism in their country in accordance with "their hopes and aspirations."[145] On August 16, Ceausescu signed a treaty of friendship, cooperation and mutual assistance with Czechoslovakia.[146] Five days later, troops from the Soviet Union, East Germany, Poland, Hungary and Bulgaria marched into Prague, Czechoslovakia.

Within hours, Ceausescu spoke to throngs of people assembled in front of the party headquarters in the Republic Palace Square. Describing the Czech invasion as "a great mistake," Ceausescu announced the immediate formation of "armed patriotic detachments of workers, peasants and intellectuals" to defend the Romanian homeland. "The entire Romanian people will not allow anybody to violate the territory of our Homeland."[147] This was Ceausescu's finest hour. It was also the point of no return for Romanian independence.[148] Romania's foreign policy never appeared to be more independent of the Soviet Union than it did in August of 1968. For not only did Ceausescu refuse to participate in the invasion, he, in the most public way, announced his opposition to the world. No doubt, the intensity of Ceausescu's reaction to the Czech invasion derived from his fear that Romania was next in line. He was frightened because he had never believed that the Soviets would attack a satellite country which had a single party political system and which had remained in the Warsaw Pact. However, Czechoslovakia fulfilled both of these criteria, and had been far less antagonistic toward Moscow than had Bucharest.[149]

The Soviets appointed Gustav Husak to replace Dubcek, who disappeared from political life until November, 1989. Rumors ran rampant of an impending invasion of Romania. The UPI reported that the Soviets told Bucharest that unless Ceausescu resigned, they would invade.[150] The Western press promoted this opinion. Cartoons appeared showing a large Soviet boot crushing Hungary in 1956 and Czechoslovakia in 1968, with a caption indicating that Romania was next.[151]

On August 30, the United States notified Moscow that "we don't know what will occur" if Soviet forces move against Romania.[152] The American threat quickly ended rumors of a possible Soviet attack. On the following day Soviet Ambassadors visited officials in most Western capitals to assure them that Moscow did not intend to invade Romania. Ambassador Anatoly Dobrynin visited Rusk to assure the United States that "rumors of a possible Soviet move against Romania were without foundation."[153]

By mid-September, the fear of a Soviet invasion of Romania had passed, but the events of August had a lasting impression. Soviet justification became known as the Brezhnev Doctrine, first articulated on November 12, 1968, to the 5th Congress of the Polish United Workers' Party. After noting that socialist states "stand for strict respect for the sovereignty of all countries," Brezhnev declared that "when external and internal forces to socialism" threaten to destroy socialism, "this is no longer merely a problem for that country's people, but a common problem, the concern of all socialist countries."[154]

The Brezhnev Doctrine indicated the limits of Soviet tolerance of independence, and the lengths that Moscow was willing to go to insure hegemony in the Bloc. Further, it showed the world and the West that no significant changes would occur in Eastern Europe without Soviet approval. Therefore, an effective "building bridges" program could not bypass Moscow. Finally, the Soviet invasion forced Czechoslovakia to turn away from political and economic reform, and convinced Romania to not push her maverick foreign policy too far.[155] In late September, Marshal Yakubovski, the Soviet Commander of the Warsaw Pact forces, visited Bucharest. Following his meeting with Ceausescu, Romania agreed to end her boycott of the Warsaw Pact Defense Minister's meetings, and to participate in Warsaw Pact maneuvers.[156] However, Ceausescu refused to surrender Romanian sovereignty. On November 29 he told the National Assembly that the Soviets had no right to intervene in the internal affairs of Czechoslovakia, and that Romania had "the right and duty to take all the measures it deems necessary to defend its unity and cohesion."[157]

As the scare passed, Romania resumed her moderate position toward the United States. Ceausescu, no doubt, appreciated Washington's August 30 warning to Moscow.[158] Prior to the Czech crisis, Romania described America's involvement in Vietnam as a "typically imperialist, brutal and barbarous" act.[159] On October 7, Ceausescu urged the "United States to end at least the bombing" of North Vietnam in order to "create conditions for positive results" in the peace talks in Paris, which had begun the previous May.[160] In November, negotiations began between Washington and Bucharest to renew their cultural relation and exchange agreement. On November 26, John Leddy of the State Department and Romanian Ambassador Corneliu Bogdan signed a new agreement extending and expanding their exchange program through 1970.[161]

This agreement proved to be the final act of Johnson's efforts to "build bridges" to Romania. Though his East-West bill floundered, Johnson managed a degree of success in expanding Romanian-American relations. From 1963 through 1967, trade volume increased 924 per cent,[162] in spite of Congressional opposition to East-West trade, in spite of the Vietnam war, and in spite of the lack of MFN trade status. In fact, no President since World War II had done more for East-West trade than had Lyndon B. Johnson.

Notes

1. U. S. Congress, House Committee on Foreign Affairs, Hearings before the Subcommittee on Europe, *East-West Trade*, 90th Cong., 2d Sess., 1968, p. 150.

2. *DOS Bulletin*, October 5, 1964, p. 465.

3. Matthew M. Mestrovic, "Rumania Looks West," *Commonweal*, September 25, 1964, p. 12.

4. NYT, December 21, 1964, p. 8; "Romania: The Independent Satellite," *Time*, July 22, 1964, p. 31.

5. U.S. Congress, Senate, Committee on Foreign Relations, *A Compilation of Views of Businessmen, Bankers, and Academic Experts*, 88th Cong., 2d Sess., 1964, p. 3.

6. Floyd, *Rumania: Russia's Dissident Ally*, p. 132.

7. Memorandum for the President-Elect, Proposal for a New National Security Council System from Henry Kissinger [December 1968], p. 1, Alphabetical Subject File 1970, Box 19, Ehrlichman, White House Special Files, NPMP.

8. Hess, *Organizing the Presidency*, rev. ed., pp. 100-101; Crabb and Mulcahy, *Presidents and Foreign Policy Making*, p. 215.

9. Memorandum for the President, Task Force on Foreign Economic Policy, November 25, 1964, pp.22-24, Box 1, Outside Task Forces, 1964, LBJ Library.

10. *DOS Bulletin*, December 21, 1964, p. 876.

11. Telegram, Bucharest to DOS, December 21, 1964, 2pp., Folder Rumania, Volume 2, Cables, Box No. 203-204, NSC Country File, LBJ Library.

12. [Department of State] "Rumania: Cultural Relations," [No. 5739] *Treaties and Other International Acts* (Washington, D.C.: U.S. Government Printing Office, 1965), pp. 1-3.

13. Much of this increase was counted in the large quantities of bituminous coal and raw cotton exported from the United States to Romania (U.S. Congress, Senate, Hearing Before the Subcommittee on International Finance of the Committee on Banking and Currency, *East-West Trade*, 90 Cong., 2d Sess., 1968, p. 109). Hereafter, Senate Subcommittee on International Finance, *Hearings on East-West Trade*, 1968.

14. *Public Papers of the Presidents, Lyndon B. Johnson,1965*, I, 3.

15. NYT, January 5, 1965, p. 10.

16. Memorandum on Guarantees of Supplier Credits to Rumania, January 4, 1965, 3pp., Folder Rumania, Volume 2, Memos, Box No. 203-204, NSC Country File, LBJ Library.

17. Report, p. 50, Sec. F., "Eastern Europe," Vol. I, chap. 3; Box 1, State Department Administrative History, LBJ Library.

18. *Public Papers of the Presidents, Lyndon B. Johnson* (1965), I, pp. 11-12.

19. Memorandum, McGeorge Bundy to J. Irwin Miller, February 2, 1965, 2pp., McGeorge Bundy Files, Vol. 8, Memos, NSF Aides Files, LBJ Library. In addition to William Blackie, the committee members included Eugene Black, Chairman, Brookings Institution, George Brown, Chairman of the Board, Brown and Root Inc., Charles Engelhard, Jr., Chairman, Engelhard Industries, James Fisk, President, Bell Telephone Laboratories, Nathaniel Goldfinger, Director of Research, AFL-CIO, Crawford Greenwalt, Chairman of the Board of E. I. DuPont de Nemours and Co., William Hewitt, Chairman of the Board, Deere and Company, Max Millikan, Professor of Economics, Massachusetts Institute of Technology, Charles Mortimor, Chairman, General Foods Corporation, and Herman Wells, Chancellor, Indiana University. The Committee also had the secretarial services of Edward Fried, a member of the State Department's Policy Planning Council (Joseph Harrington and Bruce Courtney, "Romanian-American Relations During the Johnson Administration," East

European Quarterly, Vol. XXII, No. 2 [June 1988], pp. 220-221). The only member of the group who was appointed primarily for political reasons was Nathaniel Goldfinger, the official representative of the AFL-CIO. George Meany, head of the union, was diametrically opposed to dealing with the Communists, and if any such bargain had to be struck, the Communists would have to make political concessions in order to trade with the United States (U.S. Congress, Senate, Hearings Before the Committee on Foreign Relations, *East-West Trade*, 89th Cong., 1st Sess., 1965, p. 235). As a sop to Meany, the White House appointed Goldfinger (Memorandum for the President from McGeorge Bundy, March 3, 1965, Bundy File, Memos to President, Box 3, NSF Aides Files, LBJ Library).

20. Summary of Conversation, February 18, 1965, 2pp., Folder Miller Conversations, Box 23 Miller Committee, NSF Committee Files, LBJ Library.

21. *Idem.*, March 3, 1965, 2pp.

22. *Idem.*, n.d., 2 pp.

23. *Idem.*, February 16, 1965, 1p.

24. Memorandum on Guarantees of Supplier Credits to Rumania, January 4, 1965, 3pp., Folder Rumania, Volume 2, Memos, Box No. 203-204, NSC Country File, LBJ Library. A "turn-key contract" was one where Romania bought an industrial plant from the blue-prints to completion so that they had only to turn the key, open the door, and begin production.

25. Telegram, Bucharest to DOS, February 16, 1965, 3pp., Folder Rumania, Volume 2, Memos, Box No. 203-204, NSC Country File, LBJ Library.

26. Report, p. 50, Sec. F., "Eastern Europe," Vol. I, chap. 3; Box 1, State Department Administrative History, LBJ Library.

27. Report, Termination of Firestone Negotiations for Sale of Two Synthetic Rubber Plants in Rumania, April 24, 1965, 2pp.. Firestone File, Box 22, Miller Committee, NSF Committee Files, LBJ Library.

28. *Idem.*, Telegram, DOS to Bucharest, April 22, 1965, p. 5.

29. *Ibid.*

30. *Idem.*, Telegram, Bucharest to DOS, April 19, 1965, 3pp.; Telegram, Bucharest to DOS, April 23, 1965, 2pp.

31. *Idem.*, Telegram, DOS to Bucharest, April 22, 1965, p. 3.

32. *Idem.*, Memorandum, Determination of Policy Regarding Proposed Exports of Petroleum Exploration and Refining Equipment and Technology to Rumania, April 1, 1965, p, 1.

33. Summary of Conversation, March 3, 1965, 3pp., Folder Miller Conversations, Box 23, Miller Committee, NSF Committee Files, LBJ Library.

34. U. S. Congress, House, Committee on Foreign Relations, Hearings Before the Subcommittee on Europe, *East-West Trade*, 90th Cong., 2d Sess., 1968, p. 150.

35. Administrative Details, and List of Specific Issues, n.d., 4pp., Chronological File, Box 21, Miller Committee, NSF Committee Files, LBJ Library.

36. Letter, Alfred C. Neal to J. Irwin Miller, March 17, 1965, Correspondence, General III, Box 21, Miller Committee, NSF Committee Files, LBJ Li-

brary. The CED report, which emanated from lengthy discussions with French, German, Italian and Japanese economic organizations advocated an increase in East West trade (Voting Copy, East-West Trade: A Common Policy for the West, March 18, 1965, p. 1, Chronological File, Miller Committee, Box 21, NSF Committee Files, LBJ Library). The CED recommended that East-West trade policies be based on four criteria: realism – seeing conditions as they are; selectivity-differentiating Western policy according to the specifics of each Eastern Bloc country; flexibility – establishing no permanent Western policy; and, cooperation – having all Western trading countries work together (*Ibid.*, pp. 11-12).

37. Report to the President, April 29, 1965, 27pp., Miller Committee, Box 25, NSF Committee Files, LBJ Library.

38. *Idem.*, Statement of Comment by Mr. Goldfinger.

39. Memorandum for the President from McGeorge Bundy, On the Draft Report of the Committee on East-West Trade, April 26, 1965, 2pp., Bundy Files, Vol. 10, Memos, Memos to the President, NSF Aides Files, LBJ Library.

40. Memorandum, From Ed Fried to Francis Bator, Status Report on the Miller Committee, April 23, 1965, 2pp., Chronological File, Miller Committee, Box 21, NSF Committee Files, LBJ Library; *Idem.*, Further Information, April 30, 1965, 2pp.

41. *Public Papers of the Presidents, Lyndon B. Johnson, 1965*, I, 508.

42. Memorandum, Ed Fried to Francis Bator, Further Information, April 30, 1965, 2pp., Chronological File, Miller Committee, Box 21, NSF Committee Files, LBJ Library.

43. U. S. Congress, Senate, Hearing Before the Committee on Banking and Currency, *Extend and Amend the Export Control Act of 1949*, 89th Cong., 1st Sess., 1965, pp. 33-35;Memorandum, Francis Bator to McGeorge Bundy, June 30, 1965, Bator Memos, Note No. 100, Box 1-2, NSF Name File, LBJ Library.

44. Memorandum, Francis Bator to the President, East-West Trade Legislation, August 5, 1965, Bundy Files, Memos to the President, Box 4, NSF Aides Files, LBJ Library.

45. George Gross, *Rumania, The Fruits of Autonomy* (1966), p. 22.

46. *Ibid.*

47. *Ibid.*, p. 23.

48. Dale R. Herspring, "The Soviet Union and the East European Militaries: The Diminishing Asset," *Soviet Foreign Policy in a Changing World*, eds. Robin F. Laird and Erik P. Hoffmann (New York: Aldine Publishing Company, 1986), p. 555; A. Ross Johnson, "The Warsaw Pact: Soviet Military Policy in Eastern Europe," *Soviet Policy in Eastern Europe*, ed. Sarah Meiklejohn Terry (New Haven: Yale University Press, 1984), p. 263.

49. Fischer-Galati, *The New Rumania*, p. 110.

50. Alexander Werth, "Russia's Satellites in New Orbits," *The Nation*, January 11, 1965, p. 29.

51. Cioranesco, *et al.*, *Aspects des relations russo-roumaines*, pp. 218-226; Fischer-Galati, "The Sino-Soviet Conflict" (1966), p. 275 n17.

52. Fischer-Galati, *The New Republic*, pp. 111-112.

53. "Rumania's Leaders: Three Hands on the Mantle," *The Economist*, April 3, 1965, pp. 32-33.

54. *Scinteia*, March 25, 1965, p. 1.

55. Aurel Braun, *Romanian Foreign Policy Since 1965: The Political and Military Limits of Autonomy* (New York: Praeger Publishers, 1978), p. 105.

56. Gheorghe Surpat, "Romania in epoca inaugurata de Congresul al IX-1ea al P.C.R. Consolidarea societatii (1966-1970)," *Anale de istorie*, Vol. XXXII, No. 5 (Summer 1986), p. 80.

57. Telegram, Bucharest to DOS, July 25, 1965, Folder Rumania, Volume 2, Cables, Box 203-204, Country File, NSC, LBJ Library.

58. *Romanian News*, December 2, 1988, p. 6.

59. Brown, *Eastern Europe and Communist Rule*, p. 277; Fischer-Galati, *The New Rumania*, p. 105 n2; Nicolae Ceausescu, *Romania On the Way of Completing Socialist Construction: Reports, Speeches, Articles,*(Bucharest, Meridiane Publishing House, 1969),I, p. 101. Hereafter cited as Ceausescu, *On the Way*.

60. CSM, July 27, 1965.

61. Ceausescu, *On the Way*, I, 45; Shafir, *Romania: Politics, Economics and Society*, p. 39.

62. Trond Gilberg, *Modernization in Romania since World War II* (New York: Praeger Publishers, 1975) pp. 15-21. For quantitative goals see, The Chamber of Commerce of the Socialist Republic of Romania, *Romania's Economic Development Over 1966-1970* (Bucharest, 1966), pp. 35-38, and Kinnell (ed.), *Communism in the World Since 1945*, p. 178.

63. *Agerpres*, August 20, 1965, p. 1.

64. Ceausescu, *On the Way*, I, 101.

65. Fischer-Galati, *The New Rumania*, pp. 114-115 n29.

66. Press release, September 6, 1965, Folder Rumania, Volume 2, Cables, Box 203-204, Country File, NSC, LBJ Library.

67. Press release, U.S. Trade Expansion Mission Going to Poland and Rumania, March 25, 1965, 2pp., Folder, Correspondence General III, Box 21, Miller Committee, NSF Committee Files, LBJ Library; *DOS Bulletin*, October 4, 1965, p. 553.

68. Telegram, Hayes Redmon to Bill Moyers, November 8, 1965, Folder CO251, Box 65, Countries File, WHCF, LBJ Library; *American Foreign Policy, Current Documents*, (1965), II, 538; NYT, December 2 1965, p. 58.

69. Memorandum, Francis Bator to the President, East-West Trade Legislation, August 5, 1965, Bundy Files, Memos to the President, Box 4, NSF Aides Files, LBJ Library. Senator Russell Long came from Louisiana, William Fulbright came from Arkansas, and Michael Mansfield from Montana.

70. Lyndon Baines Johnson, *The Vantage Point: Perspectives of the Presidency, 1963-1969* (New York: Hold, Rinehart and Winston, 1971), p. 472; *Congressional Quarterly, Almanac, 1965*, Volume XXI, p. 503.

71. Memorandum, Francis Bator to the President, East-West Trade Legislation, August 5, 1965, Bundy Files, Memos to the President, Box 4, NSF Aides Files, LBJ Library.

72. Memorandum, McGeorge Bundy to the President, January 8, 1966, Bundy Files, Vol. 18, Memos, Memos to the President, Box 6, NSF Aides Files, LBJ Library.

73. *Public Papers of the Presidents, Lyndon B. Johnson, 1966,* I, 3

74. McGeorge Bundy resigned on February 28, and was replaced by Walt Rostow on April 1.

75. *Congressional Quarterly, Almanac, 1966,* Volume XXII, p. 438.

76. *Ibid*. It is interesting to note that the American press reflected the American public's renewed anti-Communist sentiments. Communist countries were once again described as "Red" nations; and it was smugly reported that at the Great Market Hall in Bucharest, "dung smeared chicken eggs [sold] at a dollar a dozen" (WSJ, January 27, 1966, p. 14).

77. Department of State [Reprint], *East-West Trade Relations Act of 1966* (Washington, D.C.: U.S. Government Printing Office, 1966), pp. 6-7.

78. CSM, December 21, 1965, p. 10; Keefe et al., *Romania: A Country Study,* pp. 65-67.

79. *Agerpres,* April 26, 1968, pp. 12-13. In rehabilitating Patrascanu, Ceausescu removed one of his sharpest critics, Alexandru Draghici. Because Draghici was in charge of internal security at the time of Patrascanu's arrest, Ceausescu removed him from the Standing Presidium and from all his other posts (*Ibid.*).

80. Ceausescu, On the Way, I, 332.

81. *Ibid.,* p. 336.

82. *Ibid.,* p. 338.

83. *Ibid.,* p. 387; Fischer-Galati, *The New Rumania,* p. 115.

84. Lendavi, *Eagles in Cobwebs,* p. 406; Milorad M. Drachkovitch (ed.), *Yearbook on International Communist Affairs, 1966* (Stanford, CA: The Hoover Institution on War, Revolution and Peace, 1967), p. 72.

85. Ceausescu, *On the Way,* I, 11.

86. CSM, July 8, 1966; *The Economist,* August 27, 1966, p. 814.

87. Ceausescu, *On the Way,* II, 205.

88. *Ibid.,* p. 217.

89. *Congressional Quarterly, Almanac,* 1966, Vol. XXII, 439.

90. *DOS Bulletin,* September 26, 1966, pp. 446ff; Memorandum, Francis Bator to the President, A New Attack on Your Bridge-Building Policy, September 29, 1965, 2pp., Bundy Files, Vol. 15, Memos to the President, Box 5, NSF Aides Files, LBJ Library.

91. The White House received a letter dated July 26 from Don F. Magdanz, the Executive Secretary of the National Livestock Feeders Association (Omaha, Nebraska). The letter was forwarded to the Secretary of Agriculture early in August, marked for "suitable acknowledgement or other appropriate handling" (Referral, August 2, 1966, Folder CO051, Romania, Box 65, Countries File, WHCF, LBJ Library.

92. *Public Papers of the Presidents, Lyndon B. Johnson,1966,* II, 1128-1129; *Congressional Quarterly, Almanac,* 1966, Vol. XXII, 439.

93. By the end of the Johnson Administration, the Commercial Department

would have relaxed export requirements on nearly 700 items (Report, pp. 1-2, "Export Control" Vol. I, Part III, Department of Commerce, Administrative History. LBJ Library). A coalition of enraged conservative Congressmen united in an effort to block Eximbank credits to Eastern Europe countries. On October 18, Republicans and southern Democrats attached an amendment to the fiscal 1967 Supplemental Appropriation Bill banning Eximbank credits (*Congressional Quarterly, Almanac*, 1966, Vol. XXII, 440).

94. Authors' interview of Corneliu Bogdan, March 19, 1987.

95. Report, p 10, "Export Control." Vol. I, Part III, Department of Commerce, Administrative History. LBJ Library.

96. Gaddis, *Strategies of Containment*, p. 263.

97. *The Pentagon Papers: The Defense Department History of the United States Decisionmaking on Vietnam. The Senator Gravel Edition* (Boston: Beacon Press, 1975), IV, p. 95.

98. *The Secret Diplomacy of the Vietnam War: The Negotiating Volumes of the Pentagon Papers*, ed. George C. Herring (Austin: University of Texas Press, 1983), p. 773; Lyndon B. Johnson, *The Vantage Point*, p. 590.

99. *Secret Diplomacy of the Vietnam War*, 1983, pp. 773ff; also, Marvin Kalb and Elie Abel, *Roots of Involvement: The U.S. in Asia, 1784-1971* (New York: W. W. Norton & Co., Inc., 1971), pp. 223-225.

100. Memorandum, Francis Bator to the President, March 24, 1967, Folder Bator Memos, Box 1,2, NSF Name Files, LBJ Library.

101. Stanley Karnow, *Vietnam, A History* (New York: The Viking Press, 1983), p. 504.

102. *Los Angeles Times*, May 26, 1967, p. I28.

103. Joan Edelman Spero (ed.), *The Politics of International Economic Relations* (New York: St Martin's Press, 1985), p. 369.

104. Richard V. Allen (ed.), *Yearbook on International Communist Affairs, 1968* (Stanford, CA: Hooer Institution Press, 1969), p. 508.

105. WSJ, April 12, 1967, p. 2.

106. *DOS Bulletin*, June 12, 1967, p. 88.

107. Jeffrey Simon, *Cohesion and Dissension in Eastern Europe* (New York: Praeger Publishers, 1983), p. 208.

108. Authors' interview of Corneliu Bogdan, March 19, 1987.

109. Memorandum, W. W. Rostow to the President, June 26, 1967, Folder Rumania, Volume 3, Memos, Box 203-204, NSC Country File, LBJ Library.

110. Background Paper, President's meeting with Romanian Premier, June 1967, 2pp., *Idem*; "The Mavericks in Bucharest," *Newsweek*, July 21, 1967, pp. 36-37.

111. Richard Nixon, *The Memoirs of Richard Nixon* (New York: Grosset & Dunlop, 1978), pp. 281-282,

112. Ceausescu, *On the Way*, II, 411.

113. Memorandum, Francis Bator to the President, May 19, 1967, Folder Rumania, Volume 3, Memos, Box 203-204, NSC Country File, LBJ Library.

114. Memorandum, Benjamin H. Read to W. W. Rostow, August 1, 1967,

Idem; Authors' interview of Corneliu Bogdan March 19, 1987.

115. Allen (ed.), *Yearbook on International Communist Affairs, 1968*, p. 516.

116. Memorandum, Benjamin H. Read to W. W. Rostow, August 18, 1967, Folder Rumania, Volume 3, Memos, Box 203-204, NSC Country File, LBJ Library.

117. Memorandum, W. W. Rostow to the President, October 24, 1967, *Idem*.

118. U. S. Congress, A Compendium of Papers Submitted to the Joint Economic Committee, *East European Economies: Post-Helsinki*, 95th Cong., 1st. Sess., 1977, pp. 1264ff; Valerie J. Assetto, *The Soviet Bloc in the IMF and the IBRD* (Boulder, CO: Westview Press, 1988), pp. 141ff; Iancu Spigler, *Economic Reform in Rumanian Industry* (London: Oxford University Press, 1973), pp. 3-4.

119. Allen (ed.), *Yearbook on International Communist Affairs, 1968*, p. 509; J. F. Brown,"Romania Today: Towards Integration," *Problems of Communism*, Vol. XVIII (Jan-Feb 1969), 3-16.

120. Herring (ed.), *The Secret Diplomacy of the Vietnam War*, pp. 522-523; *Senator Gravel Edition of The Pentagon Papers*, IV, 228; Lyndon B. Johnson, *The Vantage Point*, p. 268.

121. Herring (ed.), *The Secret Diplomacy of the Vietnam War*, pp. 802ff; Memorandum, Ray Wotring to W. W. Rostow, January 1, 1968, Folder Rumania, Volume 3, Memos, Box 203-204, NSC Country File, LBJ Library.

122. Memorandum, Joseph Califano, December 12, 1966, Folder Foreign Trade, Box 15, Interagency Task Force, 1966, LBJ Library.

123. U. S. Congress, House, Committee on Foreign Affairs, Hearings Before the Subcommittee on Europe, *East-West Trade*, 90th Cong., 2d Sess., 1968, p. 1.

124. *Ibid*, pp. 1-2.

125. Trade with Communists, Folder East-West Trade (1966-1968), Box 25, Martin Anderson Issue Files-Subject, Nixon Presidential Materials Project. Nixon's remarks fueled Republican opposition to any sort of expanded trade with the Communist world. As Republican leader in the House, Gerald Ford would constantly respond to constituent mail that, "this was not the time to 'build bridges' between the East and West through trade" (Letter, Gerald R. Ford to Mr. Josiah Hamilton, July 16, 1968, Folder 131-1, Box 131, Ford Legislative Files, GRF).

126. U. S. Congress, House, Committee on Foreign Affairs, Hearings Before the Subcommittee on Europe, *East-West Trade*, 89th Con., 2d Sess., 1968, pp. 255ff.

127. *Ibid*., pp. 219-220.

128. *Ibid*., p. 162.

129. *Ibid*., p. 199.

130. The amendment eliminated the President's discretionary power that had permitted him to make a determination that it was in America's national interest to permit the Eximbank to grant credits to a Communist country (U. S. Congress, House, Committee on Banking, Currency and Housing, Hearings Before the Subcommittee on International Trade, Investment and Monetary Policy, *Oversight Hearings on the Export-Import Bank. Staff Report and Recom-*

mendations. The Export-Import Bank of the United States: Selected Issues Before the Congress, 94th Cong., 2d Sess., 1976, p. 15 ; Senate Subcommittee on International Finance, *The Export-Import Bank and Export Controls in U.S. International Economic Policy*, 1974, p. 52).

131. Minutes, NSC Meeting of April 24, Eastern Europe, April 26, 1968, 4pp., Vol. 5, Box 2, NSF Meetings File, LBJ Library.

132. Richard F. Staar (ed.), *Yearbook on International Communist Affairs 1969* (Stanford, CA: Hoover Institution Press, 1970), p. 721.

133. *Ibid.*; *Agerpres*, March 2, 1968, pp. 2,6; *Agerpres*, March 11, 1968, pp. 49-50.

134. *Agerpres*, April 29, 1968, p. 27.

135. Raymond L. Garthoff, *Detente and Confrontation: American-Soviet Relations from Nixon to Reagan* (Washington, D.C.: The Brookings Institution, 1985), p. 112.

136. Memorandum, Keeny to W. W. Rostow, March 18, 1968, Folder Rumania, Volume 3, Cables, Box No. 203-204, NSC Country File, LBJ Library.

137. Philip D. Grub and Karel Holbik, *American-East European Trade: Controversy, Progress, Prospects* (Washington, D.C.: The National Press, Inc., 1969), pp. 23-26.

138. *Congressional Quarterly, Almanac 1968.* p. 736; Senate Subcommittee on International Finance, *Hearings on East-West Trade*, 1968, p. 87.

139. Memorandum, Donald Hornig to the President, July 2, 1968, p. 1, Folder Rumania Volume 3, Cables , Box 203-204, NSC Country File, LBJ Library.

140. *Ibid.*, 2.

141. *Ibid.*, p. 2; *Idem.*, Memorandum, W. W. Rostow to the President, April 26, 1968.

142. *Idem.*, Press Release and Joint Statement, June 28, 1968, p. 4.

143. See, *Idem.*, Memorandum, Donald Hornig to the President, July 12, 1968.

144. Rubinstein, *Soviet Foreign Policy Since World War II*, p. 94; Peter Summerscale, "Is Eastern Europe a Liability to the Soviet Union?," International Affairs, Vol. 57, No. 4 (Autumn 1981), p. 587.

145. Ceausescu, *On the Way*, III, pp. 300-301.

146. *Ibid.*, p. 359.

147. *Ibid.*, pp. 383-384.

148. Hacker, *Der Ostblock, 1939-1980*, p. 815.

149. J.F. Brown, "Rumania Today: The Strategy of Defiance," *Problems of Communism*, Vol. XVIII (March-April 1969), pp. 32-38.

150. Note, W.W. Rostow to the President, August 23, 1968, Folder Rumania, Volume 3, Cables , Box 203-204, NSC Country File, LBJ Library.

151. NYT, September 8, 1968, p. 15.

152. Author's interview of W. W. Rostow, Boston, April 11, 1988.

153. Memorandum, Lou Schwartz to W. W. Rostow, September 3, 1968, Folder Rumania Volume 3, Cables , Box 203-204, NSC Country File, LBJ

Library; *Idem.*, Paris to DOS, September 2, 1968.
154. Hutchings, *Soviet-East European Relations*, p. 43.
155. Laird and Hoffmann, *Soviet Foreign Policy in a Changing World*, p. 537; Marion Mushkat, "Kann ein kleiner Staat sich selbst verteidigen? Die rumanische Version," Berichte Des Bundesinstituts fur Ostwissenschaftliche und Internationale Studien [Bonn, Bundesrepublik Deutschland], June, 1979.
156. Brown, "Rumania Today: The Strategy of Defiance," 1969, p. 36.
157. Staar (ed.), *Yearbook on International Communist Affairs, 1969*, p. 725.
158. C. L. Sulzberger, *An Age of Mediocrity: Memoirs and Diaries, 1963-1972* (Macmillan Publishing Co., Inc., 1973), p. 471.
159. *Agerpres*, February 21, 1968, p. 3.
160. *Agerpres*, October 7, 1968, p. 12.
161. *DOS Bulletin*, December 23, 1968, p. 680.
162. Report, p. 3, "Export Control." Vol. I, Part III, Department of Commerce, Administrative History, LBJ Library.

CHAPTER X

THE NIXON-CEAUSESCU VISITS

East-West Trade and a Visit to Bucharest

Shortly after his November, 1968, victory, President-elect Richard M. Nixon met Henry Kissinger at the Pierre Hotel in New York. Unlike his predecessor, who used a "Tuesday Lunch" meeting with principal advisors to formulate America's international policies, Nixon fully intended to be the principal architect of America's foreign policy.[1] He told Kissinger that he had little confidence in the State Department, distrusted the Foreign Service, and saw no role in foreign policy for the CIA because it was staffed by Ivy League liberals who had opposed him politically.[2] Rather, foreign policy would be run from the White House, with advice from the NSC, and he wanted Kissinger to be his National Security Adviser.[3] Kissinger agreed and Nixon announced the appointment on December 2, at a press conference at the Pierre.

During the presidential transition, Nixon's advisors drafted a memo indicating major areas requiring immediate policy decisions. Foremost was Vietnam, and this would become the prime focus during the early days of the Nixon Administration. As with the end of the Johnson administration, all other issues including Eastern Europe and East-West trade slid into the background.[4]

Meanwhile, as Nixon prepared to begin his first term in the White House, Ceausescu continued Romania's independent path. At CMEA's 20th anniversary meeting in January, 1969, Ceausescu's continued opposition to Bloc integration forced the Council to table all decisions until its April meeting.[5] A few days later, Ceausescu met Tito in the Romanian town of Timisoara. Both men denounced the doctrine of "limited sovereignty," a euphemism for the Brezhnev Doctrine, and on February 8, Ceausescu categorically repudiated the doctrine as incompatible with Marxism-Leninism.[6] Ceausescu also maintained his neutralism in the Sino-Soviet conflict, even when Soviet forces engaged Chinese troops on Damansky Island in the Ussuri River. In March, Moscow asked the Warsaw Pact to condemn China for its encroachment on Soviet territory. Romania refused and blocked Warsaw Pact involvement in the conflict.[7]

However, despite her opposition to the Brezhnev Doctrine, Romania felt the impact of the Czechoslovakian invasion. Moscow had made it clear that she did not intend to permit significant deviation from what she perceived as a correct socialist course. While Romania continued to pursue a foreign policy independent of the Soviet Union, the independence was measured by a degree of caution as Romania adopted a more moderate opposition policy toward CMEA and the Warsaw Pact. At the 23rd CMEA Council session in April, the members adopted a new program involving "interestedness" and "voluntarism." States "interested" in "voluntarily" participating in cooperative ventures with other CMEA members were free to do so. Now decisions on some issues no longer required unanimity. This program ended Romania's veto over CMEA actions while still allowing nonconformity.[8] As for the Warsaw Pact, while Romania did not permit Pact maneuvers on Romanian soil, Bucharest did agree to send troops to participate in the May, 1969, war games in sub-Carpathian Russia.[9]

Romania continued her omnidirectional foreign policy with the non-communist world. In February, 1969, Ceausescu made an historic gesture. He was aware that Nixon had a "soft spot" for Romania as a result of the thunderous welcome he received during his 1967 visit to Bucharest.[10] In February, Ceausescu instructed Ambassador Bogdan to invite President Nixon to visit Bucharest. The invitation was not in writing. In fact, since the Czechoslovakian invasion, Bogdan had implemented a "think aloud" communication system with Washington. Bogdan urged the President to visit Romania before going to Moscow.[11] For the next several months, Bogdan renewed the invitation. He was "persistent, but not noisy, because," he recognized, "Romania is not the center of the world."[12]

Nixon ignored the Romanian invitation. His energies were focused first on his eight day working visit to America's European allies at the end of February, and then, upon his return, on luring the Soviet Union into a "peacemaking role in the Middle East and even possibly in

Vietnam." The President explained in his March 4 press conference that he wanted to work with Moscow to defuse situations which otherwise could lead to superpower confrontation. He explained, "let's face it . . . without the Soviet Union's cooperation, it may be difficult to move as fast as we would like in settling the war in Vietnam."[13] This was part of Nixon's doctrine of "linkage." The President was willing to negotiate with the Soviets on a broad range of topics. However, developments in one area would affect negotiations in another. Kissinger had told the Soviets on December 18, 1968, that the new President was willing to talk about limiting strategic weapons, a Soviet goal, in return for help in solving problems in the Middle East and Southeast Asia.[14]

Two months after his inauguration, Nixon asked Soviet Premier Alexei Kosygin for help to end the Vietnam War. Kissinger followed up the request meeting frequently with Soviet Ambassador Anatoly Dobrynin. In their discussions, Kissinger implied a link between Soviet support in resolving Vietnam, and American help in the Middle East. However, both Nixon and Kissinger failed at this early attempt at linkage. On May 27, Kosygin rejected the proposal noting that "taking into account the complexity of each of these problems. . . it is hardly worthwhile to attempt somehow to link one with another."[15]

Meanwhile, the new Administration had a number of other issues to address, including America's foreign trade policy. A Nixon appointed Task Force submitted its findings to the President on January 31, 1969. The report essentially recommended little change. While the Administration might want to liberalize trade, domestic pressures for protection were quite strong. Increasing inflation, and a growing balance of payments deficit made it difficult to further reduce trade barriers to imports. However, the report recognized that the new Administration had to make some statement indicating a "fresh approach" to foreign trade. The Task Force suggested that the President make a strong statement indicating his interest in reducing barriers to international trade. The report paid little attention to East-West trade save that it would develop subsequent to future foreign policy decisions. In the meantime, the President ought to urge Congress to pass legislation giving the White House greater trade flexibility than it presently had.[16]

In April, the entire issue of East-West trade came before Senator Walter Mondale's Subcommittee on International Finance, which held hearings to renew the Export Control Act of 1949, due to expire on June 30. The Administration asked for a simple four year extension of the 1949 act. However, the Senate proposed S. 1940 which called for expanded trade with the Communist Bloc. The Nixon Administration quickly voiced its opposition. Various Administration officials trooped before the Subcommittee explaining that expanded East-West trade would produce only modest economic gains, but pose significant political problems.[17] In contrast, business representatives argued that America was losing substantial trade to West European competitors due to the restrictive nature of the 1949 act. Specifically, the Export Control Act restricted 1,200 items for East-West trade, and all but 200 were readily available from other Western suppliers.[18] During the hearings, Chairman Mondale remarked that a French official told him that he was very grateful for America's unilateral restrictions on trade. "You're giving us 5 to 10 years that we desperately need to gain the markets where we cannot now effectively compete with you . . . I think you are being very foolish, but, I hope you will continue."[19]

As the hearings continued, leaders of big business continued to call for expanded trade. Among the advocates were representatives from Control Data Corporation, Raytheon Company, International Telephone and Telegraph, Eastman Kodak, Allied Chemical Corporation, General Electric Company and the U. S. Chamber of Commerce.[20] Slowly a groundswell developed for expanded trade, including some Administration officials. The NSC called for increased trade along with the Departments of State and Commerce. Even some Republican hardliners, such as Senators John Tower and Karl Mundt, could agree to legislation which gave the President more tools with which to expand trade with the East, provided that the legislation itself did not liberalize such trade.[21] Included among these tools was the right to award MFN treatment to Communist countries, as long as this action would not compromise America's national security.[22]

Five days later on May 21, Kissinger sent Nixon his recommendations on foreign trade. He too suggested that the President support legislation granting the Executive greater discretionary authority. Such power would enable him to use trade as a *quid pro quo* for political concessions from Moscow and the Eastern Bloc.[23] Within hours, Nixon met with the NSC. Moscow's consistent refusal to intervene in the Vietnam war, angered the President. In spite of Kissinger's advice, and the recommendations of most of the NSC members, Nixon opposed any and all legislation which would liberalize trade with the Soviets and Eastern Europe.[24]

Nixon missed the point of his advisors. By accepting discretionary authority to grant MFN to Communist countries, Nixon could have vented his anger at Moscow by not granting MFN to the Soviet Union, and by granting it to East European nations as a reward for their insubordination to the Kremlin. At the same time, by holding MFN like a carrot in front of Moscow, he could have induced Moscow into accepting his doctrine of "linkage" – MFN for substantive Soviet participation in the Vietnamese peace settlement. What Lyndon Johnson had fought for five years to obtain, was Richard Nixon's for the asking within six months of taking office, and yet, he turned it down in a fit of anger. This was a decision Nixon would later regret when the legislative and executive branches once again switched sides.[25]

Nixon's frustration with Moscow reached new heights on May 27 when Kosygin told him that the Kremlin would not help Washington resolve the Vietnam War. Nixon decided to "needle" Moscow and accept Ceausescu's long standing offer to visit Bucharest.[26] He mentioned the idea to Bob Haldeman, his Chief of Staff, on June 9.[27] The President fondly recalled the warm welcome he had received during his 1967 visit to Romania. As word leaked out among Administration officials, few supported the President's idea. The State Department was thoroughly opposed to a Romanian visit.[28] Overtures to Bucharest at this time could only hurt Soviet-American relations, which were the Department's paramount concern. If nothing else, the Department's opposition further convinced the President to go forward with his idea. As Ehrlichman noted, the Romanian visit was Nixon's own idea. He wanted to do something "bold."[29] As Bogdan would later say, the President wanted to "tweak the nose of the Russians."[30]

The suddenness of Nixon's decision surprised everyone, including Ambassador Bogdan. "Out of the blue" he received a call that Kissinger wanted him to come to the White House to talk about a visit to Bucharest. The Ambassador was in Canada, but quickly returned to Washington and met Kissinger on June 21.[31] Bogdan learned that the President intended to make an around-the-world trip following the Apollo 11 splashdown in the Pacific, and wanted to include Bucharest on the schedule.[32]

Forty-eight hours later, Romania approved Nixon's visit.[33] To accommodate the President, Ceausescu had to postpone the much heralded 10th Party Congress and consequently, postpone the arrival of the Soviet delegation to the Congress. Ceausescu was well aware of a changing climate in America. Congress and American businessmen were calling for increased trade, even including MFN treatment to certain East European countries. He did not want to miss an opportunity to influence their thinking. Nixon would be well received in Bucharest, and in the process Ceausescu would use the visit as further evidence of Romania's independence from Moscow.

On June 28, the President made public his intention to visit Romania. The announcement sent mixed signals. Nixon's opposition to liberalizing East-West trade placed him in the anti-Communist camp, yet, he deliberately chose to be the first American President to pay a state visit to a Communist country. His doctrine of linkage called for a reduction of political tensions between the "superpowers," yet, he chose to visit the East European Communist country which was most obstructionist to Soviet demands.

During the months of June and July, more sophisticated reasons developed to explain the Romanian visit.[34] Principal among these was that Romania was a path to China. Bucharest had frequently championed China's right to dissent from the Kremlin's designs.[35] While in many ways this was self serving, Romania, nonetheless, had the best relations with China of any major Communist country. Since Washington did not recognize the Beijing regime, Nixon needed an interlocutor to talk with the Chinese. Romania appeared to be a prime candidate. As Nixon explained to Kissinger, "by the time we get through with this trip they [the Soviets] are going to be out of their minds that we are playing a Chinese game."[36] A Beijing-Washington Axis would give Nixon leverage in his efforts to induce Moscow into accepting "linkage" as part of American-Soviet relations. Further, improved relations with China could eventually lead to a resolution of the Vietnam conflict, either directly through Beijing or by prompting the Soviets to get involved in the peace process.

Throughout July, both Romania and the United States prepared for the President's departure. On July 4, Ceausescu permitted the American Chargé d'Affaires to appear on television and inform the Romanian people of Nixon's upcoming visit. Later, the Romanians, for the first time ever, aired a fifty minute television program commemorating America's Independence day.[37] Two days later, *Scinteia* explained Nixon's visit as another indication that Romania was "determined to reach out even farther to explore any possibilities of stepping up international collaboration."[38] By the middle of the month, an *Agerpres* release noted that there were "no direct litigious issues" between Washington and Bucharest, and that Romania looked forward to improved economic, technical and scientific relations with the United States.[39] The American press also promoted the up coming visit. The

Christian Science Monitor called Romania "a country of open doors."[40] The *U.S. News and World Report* suggested that when Nixon arrived in Romania he would "find a smiling dictator, a surprised and delighted people."[41]

In preparation for Nixon's Romanian visit, Kissinger met with two experts on Romanian affairs, economics professor John Montias from Yale and history professor Stephen Fischer-Galati, from the University of Colorado.[42] Fisher-Galati spent several hours with Kissinger briefing him on contemporary developments in Romania's domestic and foreign policies. Before leaving, Kissinger asked if there were any special advice Fisher-Galati might have for himself and the President. The historian replied with a quip made by his daughter earlier, "don't drink the water."[43]

On July 24, Nixon watched the splashdown of the Apollo 11. On the following day, he began the Asian leg of his around-the-world trip and stopped in Guam on his way to Manila. Surrounded by reporters, the President agreed to an informal press conference at which he enunciated what became known as the "Nixon Doctrine." The central thesis was while the United States would continue to honor its commitments to its friends and allies, America would look to the threatened nation to assume the primary responsible of providing manpower for its own defense. America would no longer shoulder the entire responsibility for the defense of the free world.[44]

Nixon landed in Pakistan on August 1, to talk with President Yahya Khan about being a conduit between America and China.[45] On the following day, Ceausescu welcomed Nixon to Romania complete with an Honor Guard and a 21 gun salute.[46] At the airport, both speakers addressed the hundreds of thousands of people gathered. Nixon emphasized that this was the first state visit by an American President to a socialist country. He wasted little time in notifying China, Eastern Europe and the Soviet Union that he was open to change. "Every nation, of whatever size, and whatever region of the world will find us receptive to realistic new departures in the path to peace."[47]

Following their speeches, Nixon and Ceausescu got into the Presidential limousine and slowly drove past seemingly endless lines of cheering people the ten miles into town. At one point, for the first time in motorcade history in Romania, but in typical Nixon style, the Presidential car stopped. Both Presidents jumped out, reached into the crowds, shook hands, and waved to those in the distance.[48] Finally, the

President drove to the Council of State, a romanesque building in downtown Bucharest which served as the Presidential residence. There the two men met for three hours to discuss numerous bilateral issues.[49]

For Nixon, the major issues were China and Vietnam. Ceausescu willingly agreed to act as a channel between Washington and Beijing. He also agreed to resume his efforts to mediate the Vietnam conflict.[50] In return, he wanted to secure MFN treatment for Romanian exports to the United States. Nixon was willing to talk about the issue, but indicated that ultimately the decision was in the hands of Congress. Evidence indicates that Nixon made no promise or guarantee of MFN for Romania, but he did agree to work to liberalize trade regulations with Bucharest.[51]

That evening, the President and Mrs. Nixon attended a gala reception. Romania, along with Yugoslavia, had been the only East European countries to carry the Apollo moon mission live on television. Ceausescu toasted Nixon for America's success. In response, the President reiterated his primary message: the United States was willing "to reciprocate the efforts of any country that seeks normal relations with us" regardless of its domestic system. America wanted "the substance of detente, not its mere atmosphere."[52]

On August 3, while Nixon and Ceausescu toured housing developments and open air markets, negotiators for both countries worked out an arrangement to establish a library in each other's country. The Romanian Library in New York City and the American Library in Bucharest would make available reference books, periodicals, films and tapes to the public. They would also host concerts, recitals, lectures and sponsor language courses. Ambassador Richard Davis and the Deputy Minister of Foreign Affairs of Romania, Vasile Gliga, signed the understanding on August 3.[53] This accord along with an earlier agreement reciprocally abolishing certain visa fees, maintained the spirit of exchange and reciprocity envisioned in the first cultural exchange arrangement signed in 1960.

Following an American hosted lunch, Nixon and his entourage left on Air Force One for Andrews Air Force Base, outside of Washington, D.C. His Romanian visit had received extensive press coverage in the United States, most of it quite positive. One enthusiastic commentator explained that "for the citizens of Bucharest, [the Nixon visit] was like receiving a visitor from another planet – an unreal event preceded and followed by unchanging reality."[54] Even the President was taken by his visit. He told the *New York Times*, that "this was the most moving experience I have had in traveling to over 60 countries. . . People were out by the hundreds of thousands, not ordered by their government, but cheering and shouting."[55]

Congressional Reaction to the Visit

The excitement surrounding the visit extended to Congress as well. Due to continued debate, the legislature had been forced to extend the 1949 Export Control Act beyond its expiration date of June 30.[56] Hearings before the Senate and House Banking and Currency Committees had produced a number of liberalizing amendments to the Export Control Act. Congress noted that Administration officials appeared confused as to what position they should take. Before Congressional subcommittees, representatives of the State and Commerce Departments supported the President's position which called for a simple four year extension of the 1949 act, without amendment. This was the position Nixon had taken at the May 21 NSC meeting over the objections of most of his advisors, including Kissinger. However, in implementing trade regulations, the Commerce Department and, to a lesser degree, the State Department used all the legislative power at their command to increase East-West relations. State wanted to expand trade for political reasons, while Commerce wanted to accommodate the increasing demands of big business.[57]

The success of Nixon's visit to Romania prompted some Congressmen to press for MFN for Romania. In the House, Congressman Paul Findley of Illinois introduced H.R. 13305 on August 4 which called for Congress to give the President the authority to grant MFN treatment to Romania. Findley argued that Romania deserved MFN because of her desire for friendship with the United States, and as a reward for her independence from Moscow. In addition, MFN trade status would enable Romania to increase her exports to the United States and thereby earn more dollars with which they could purchase more American products.[58] His colleague in the Senate, Walter Mondale, introduced a parallel bill, S. 2775 on August 5.[59] Mondale was long known for his efforts to expand trade with Eastern Europe. In May, 1968, he had introduced a bill to extend MFN treatment to products from Czechoslovakia.[60] As events unfolded neither bill would make it out of committee.[61] Nevertheless, even though Nixon had nothing to do with either bill, their introduction gave credence to his assurances to Ceausescu, and encouraged the Romanian leader to maintain friendly relations with the White House.

Meanwhile, Ceausescu convened the 10th Party Congress on August 6. Brezhnev and Kosygin deliberately boycotted the Congress to show the Kremlin's displeasure over Ceausescu's decision to postpone it in order to accommodate President Nixon.[62] The Congress was an indication of Ceausescu's growing power. The Congress increased the size of the Central Committee and elected a nine man Standing Presidium, which included only three hold-overs from the Gheorghiu-Dej regime: Ceausescu, Prime Minister Maurer, and Vice Chairman of the Council of State, Emil Bodnaras. Further, for the first time, the Congress, rather than the Central Committee, elected Ceausescu as Party Secretary.[63]

The Congress also announced the new Five Year Plan, from 1971-1975, which began Romania's "multilateral development," a program designed to have Romania join the ranks of "developed" socialist states by 1990.[64] Both the directives for the Five Year Plan and the guidelines for economic development through 1980 called for expanded trade "with all states" regardless of their social systems.[65] The Five Year plan envisioned a 40-45% increase in the volume of foreign trade over the goals of the 1966-1970 plan.[66] This was significant since Romania had a 4.9% growth rate from 1965 to 1970, second only to Bulgaria among Eastern Bloc countries.[67] America was to play a role in this foreign trade growth, for exports to the United States had increased 500% from 1965 to 1970, and Bucharest anticipated even greater growth during the early 1970s.[68]

As to how America would increase her role in Romania's economy was still a question. Bogdan made sure that Washington did not forget Bucharest, while *Agerpres* carried a brief note on August 31 recalling Nixon's visit and indicating that his visit had "been a positive fact" toward peace and security.[69] At the same time, Congress continued to consider the Administration's request to renew the Export Control Act. The hearings had ended and following a Summer recess, the House approved the President's recommendation for a simple four year extension of the 1949 act, despite strong opposition from a large liberal minority.

However, the Senate appeared more open to the calls for liberalization heard at the Banking and Currency Subcommittee hearings. In October, Senators Edmund Muskie, from Maine, and Mondale proposed replacing the Export Control Act, then under Senate considera tion, with an Export Administration bill. The new legislation would expand East-West trade by limiting export controls to items which increased only the "military" potential of another nation. This language would eliminate the restriction in the 1962 Export Control Act which also prohibited the export of items on the basis of their "economic" significance. The Mondale-Muskie proposal also called upon the Commerce Department to grant export licenses to items which were readily available to the Communist world through other Western nations. In short, the Export Administration bill urged the President to bring America's export control policy in line with COCOM regulations.[70]

Kissinger and Nixon fought back. In an effort to defuse support for liberal trade expansion, they offered to remove 135 items from America's export control list thereby bringing it more closely into line with the COCOM lists.[71] The ploy failed. Senate liberals acknowledged the Administration's move as a step in the right direction, and continued to move forward with the new legislation. With Senate approval secure, Senate and House conferees met on two occasions and hammered out a bill which was approved by both houses on December 23. The Export Administration Act tied export regulations primarily to national security. The government could restrict goods and technology which could make a significant contribution to the military potential of another nation. Some non-military goods could be restricted if the President determined that their export would threaten America's national security. However, the President had to inform Congress as to the reasons for his decision. The legislation called for a complete review of all controlled items with a view of reducing the number of items prohibited for export on the American lists. One of the considerations for reducing the list was the availability of a product from other non-Communist countries. The Act included a policy statement pointing out the importance of exports for America's balance of payments, and the growth and stability of the domestic economy. On December 29, the President reluctantly signed the new legislation.[72]

While Congress worked to help America become more involved in East European affairs, so too did Dr. Lee DuBridge, Nixon's Science Adviser. Before Nixon's visit to Bucharest, DuBridge had asked the President to expand America's scientific cooperation with Romania.[73] During their meeting in Bucharest, both Ceausescu and Nixon agreed to cooperate in the fields of science and technology. Consequently, on September 17, Nixon reminded Ceausescu of their conversations and asked if Lee DuBridge could visit Bucharest during a scheduled trip to Europe.[74] Ceausescu agreed. On September 24 DuBridge and a team of technology and science specialists arrived in Bucharest and spent three days meeting with their Romanian counterparts.[75]

The President was also willing to try other means to improve American-Romanian relations. In September, he invited the Romanian Davis Cup team to the White House following their match with the United States in Cleveland on September 19-21, 1969.[76] He encouraged big business to deal with Romania, and several American firms established contracts with Bucharest.[77] Badger Company, a subsidiary of Raytheon Company, built an acrilonitrile plant at Pitesti to make synthetic fibers, and Corning Glass International was building a factory to make glass bulbs for TV picture tubes. American firms had also participated in a handful of joint ventures with West European firms doing business with Romania.[78] As business increased, and America's image of Romania changed, American tourism in Romania increased 50% from 1967 to 1969.[79]

In the meantime, the underlying purpose of Nixon's overtures to Romania did not come to fruition. Ceausescu's efforts to become a channel connecting Washington to Beijing failed. Despite warm Sino-Romanian relations, China did not trust any East European satellite. Beijing believed they were all controlled by the Kremlin including Romania, in spite of its apparent independence.[80] In September, 1969, Nixon and Kissinger decided to try direct talks through the Chinese and American Embassies in Warsaw. This channel proved successful when several months later American Ambassador Walter Stoessel literally chased after the Chinese delegation in Warsaw to give them a message. Eight days later, on December 11, Stoessel received an invitation to the Chinese Embassy in Warsaw and direct talks began.[81]

Though the Romanian gambit failed, American-Romanian relations continued to progress. Lee DuBridge had thoroughly enjoyed his September visit to Bucharest. The academicians and business people who accompanied DuBridge enthusiastically endorsed a policy of increased technological and scientific cooperation between the two countries. On November 20, DuBridge asked the Department of Commerce to consider easing the restrictions on trade with Romania. Specifically, he wanted the Department to alter its export licensing practices to permit American firms to enter joint venture agreements with Romania.[82] On December 15, Secretary of Commerce Stans responded indicating that at present his Department was considering a State Department recommendation to liberalize export controls to Romania. The action, if approved, would place under general license to Romania a number of commodities whose export, at present, required individually validated license. The proposal would give Romania an export control status nearly as liberal as Yugoslavia's, and better than that of Poland.[83] Kissinger sent a note to the Commerce Department on December 29, 1969, supporting the proposal and encouraging prompt action. He added that the President had a "strong interest in taking all acceptable administrative measures to ensure the expansion of U.S.-Romanian trade."[84]

By years end, American-Romanian relations were quickly moving forward. However, further progress depended on the White House making a decision on a comprehensive East-West trade policy. Throughout 1970, Administration officials labored without success to establish such a policy. The principle road block was the lack of a centralized agency responsible for America's foreign economic policy. In July, 1969, the President's Advisory Council on Executive Organizations, PACEO, presented a detailed report which included a brief history of post-World War II efforts to coordinate Washington's foreign economic policy. Kennedy discontinued Eisenhower's Council on Foreign Economic Policy, and for the next eight years the NSC assumed the responsibility, through the Office of Deputy to the Assistant to the President for National Security Affairs. The Deputy was Francis Bator. Assisted by a small staff, he became the "President's man" on foreign economic policy. However, during this period, other White House officials with access to the President challenged Bator's exclusive right to formulate policy. The Assistant Secretary of State and the STR played increasingly strong roles. In 1968-1969, the title of Deputy was abolished and the job was divided between two men, with assignment of foreign aid to one, and trade and monetary affairs to the other. Foreign economic policy was no longer coordinated by one group.[85]

By 1969, the report noted, there were a myriad of agencies involved in either formulating or implementing America's foreign economic policy. Among the groups were the Cabinet Committee on Economic Policy, the NSC, the Office of the Special Representative for Trade Negotiations, the Office of Management and Budget, the Cabinet Committee on Export Expansion, the National Advisory Committee on International Monetary and Financial Affairs, the Trade Expansion Advisory Committee, the Export Control Review Board, and the Economic Defense Advisory Committee.[86] Faced with this byzantine structure, PACEO recommended on August 17, 1969, that the President establish a Council on International Economic Policy.[87] Substantial bureaucratic infighting slowed its implementation until January, 1971. In the meantime, America adopted an *ad hoc* approach to foreign economic policy.

On February 18, the President sent Congress a message on foreign relations entitled "A New Strategy for Peace." In it, he indicated that the United States did not view Eastern Europe as monolithic. While recognizing the primacy of Soviet interests in the Eastern Bloc, Washington was willing to work toward the "gradual normalization of relations" with the individual East European countries. The President specifically cited Romania in his report. He recalled his visit to Bucharest "which will remain unforgettable for me in human terms" and the progress being made in relations between the two countries.[88]

Nonetheless, the report did not mention East-West trade. The confusion continued. Even Peter Flanigan, the President's economic adviser, was not in a position to recommend policy. In February, Kissinger assured him that a policy regulating exports to countries behind the Iron Curtain "will be forthcoming."[89] But, while this was an important issue to Flanigan, it was not among Kissinger's priorities. The war in Vietnam, relations with China and the Soviet Union, and on-going developments in Western Europe, especially those relating to Georges Pompidou's ascendency to power in France, and Willi Brandt's *Ostpolitik* in the Federal Republic of Germany, all ranked higher than trade relations with Eastern Europe.

On March 2, the President sent a memo to Haldeman, Ehrlichman and Kissinger. He decided that as the principal architect of America's foreign policy, he was "spreading" his "time too thin." He wanted to focus only on five issues in foreign policy: East-West relations, the Soviet Union, Communist China, Eastern Europe, but only if it really affected East-West relations "at the highest level," and Western Europe. All other issues would be dealt with through brief semiannual reports.[90] Except for Nixon's personal interest in Romania, Bucharest would have been treated as were the other East European countries, as meaningful only in the broader context of Soviet-American relations. However, due to this interest, Nixon separated Romania from other Communist countries and placed it in a new and special country group for export controls, Group Q, which meant that Romania had special licensing treatment for items unilaterally controlled by the United States.[91]

Ceausescu Visits America

Meanwhile the Kremlin took another step to end Romania's obstructionist policies in CMEA. At the 24th Council session in May, 1970, CMEA agreed to establish an International Investment Bank, the IIB. According to Article 19 of the Bank's Charter, all issues, other than those concerning the Charter, would be decided by a majority of not less than 3/4 of the votes. Again, the unanimity role was abandoned in favor of majority voting. Romania protested and initially refused to join the IIB. However, Romania needed investment funds. If she continued to boycott the bank, she would have no influence in East European banking matters. Faced with this reality Bucharest joined the bank in January, 1971.[92]

Also in May of 1970, Romania was deluged by torrential rains which caused disastrous flooding destroying millions of acres of agricultural land. The United States quickly sent $11.5 million to Romania in relief funds. Other nations joined the relief effort and this assistance, coupled with an energetic and immediate response by the Romanian government, considerably alleviated suffering. However, it would take several years for Romania's economy to recover the losses incurred.[93]

Moscow was quick to capitalize on Romania's economic woes. Brezhnev and Kosygin called Ceausescu to Moscow in May. During the meeting, Ceausescu agreed to sign the long delayed Romanian-Soviet Treaty of Friendship, Cooperation and Mutual Assistance in Bucharest in early July. Radio Free Europe reports suggested that the Soviets pressured Ceausescu by threatening to cut off needed iron ore shipments to Romania.[94] On July 6, a Soviet delegation visited Bucharest. Although Brezhnev was notably absent, representatives from both countries signed a 20 year pact, which unlike a similar agreement between Prague and Moscow, contained no mention of the Brezhnev Doctrine. In fact, the treaty clearly emphasized Romania's traditional view of international relations which was based on national independence, equality and non-interference in internal affairs.[95] The Romanian Council of State ratified the treaty on September 30, 1970.

As usual, Ceausescu's relations with Moscow did not diminish his efforts to improve commercial relations with Washington. Romania had consistently worked to impress Nixon's Science Adviser Lee DuBridge. Bucharest was interested in technology, and wanted to learn about computers and petroleum cracking plants. Romanian officials expressed their interest in purchasing high technology equipment. DuBridge lobbied for Ceausescu. He managed to secure $75,000 from the National

Science Foundation to help technology exchanges. He also urged the White House staff people to promote greater collaboration between Washington and Bucharest.[96] On June 25, Foreign Minister Corneliu Manescu met with Nixon.[97] While no documents have yet been declassified on their meeting, subsequent developments suggest that Manescu talked to the President about Ceausescu's plan to visit the United Nations in October in honor of the organization's 25th anniversary. Ceausescu wanted to spend additional time touring the United States to meet with various business leaders.

Nixon suggested that the Romanian leader come to the White House on October 26, at the close of his American visit.[98] Nixon's graciousness was prompted not only by his desire to reciprocate for his August, 1969, visit to Romania, but also to renew the Romanian channel to Beijing. The initial talks in Poland had stalled. Mao Zedong refused to move toward a Sino-American rapprochement until the United States withdrew its military presence from Taiwan. He indicated this three times in discussions with his old friend Edgar Snow, the leftist American journalist, whom he invited on several occasions to China in late 1969. Mao permitted Snow and his wife to appear on the reviewing stand in Tienanmen Square on October 1, China's National Day. Their appearance on the stand was unprecedented, and Mao was trying to send an encouraging signal to the United States. However, the White House did not trust Snow, due to his leftist leanings and his strong support for Mao in the 1930s. Consequently, the Administration failed to understand the importance of Mao's gesture to Snow. The message was simple. Mao would personally sponsor the Sino-American detente.[99] Kissinger later noted in his memoirs, that the "excessive subtlety had produced a failure of communication."[100] On October 5, 1970, Nixon sent a far from subtle message to Beijing. He told *Time* magazine that "if there is anything I want to do before I die, it is to go to China."[101]

On October 13, Ceausescu arrived in New York. He spent two weeks visiting California, Detroit and Williamsburg. He met with executives from Intercontinental Hotels, Dow Chemical, Caterpillar Tractor and Combustion Engineering. His message was straight forward: he wanted to establish joint ventures with American companies.[102] On October 22, he addressed the Foreign Policy Association of New York. He told them he wanted to expand Romanian-American trade and relations, but significant expansion was contingent on Romania receiving MFN treatment for her exports to America.[103] His message did not not go unnoticed. Several members of the Administration shared Ceausescu's desire for expanded Romanian-American trade. Both the Secretaries of State and Commerce had called for greater commercial ties with Eastern Europe and Romania, and they tried to capitalize on Ceausescu's visit to the White House. Both Secretaries Rogers and Stans sent notes to the President asking him to publicly endorse expanded commerce between Bucharest and Washington. Such a statement would not only please Ceausescu, but it would reassure American businessmen that they had White House approval in their dealings with the Communist Bloc.[104]

On October 26, Ceausescu and Nixon met at the White House at 11 a.m. Nixon wanted Ceausescu to let the Chinese know that he viewed Taiwan as an "internal" affair of Beijing. This meant that the United States would not interfere in any solution Beijing thought appropriate for Taiwan. This was the same message he had given to Yahya Khan, the Pakistani President who also recently visited the White House.[105] For his part, Ceausescu wanted to expand American-Romanian relations and secure MFN for Romania's products.

That night, Nixon hosted a dinner for Ceausescu at the White House. Among the guests were executives from DuPont de Nemours, Sun Oil, Motorola, Marriott, Ford, and 20th Century Fox.[106] Nixon congratulated Ceausescu on being the first President of Romania to visit America. During the exchange of toasts and cordialities, Nixon noted that Ceausescu headed a government which was one of the few in the world which had good relations with the Soviet Union and the People's Republic of China. This was a significant statement, for it was the first time Nixon had ever referred to the Beijing government by that name[107]

The President's discussions with Yahya Khan and Ceausescu concerning China would produce results. On December 8, Pakistan notified the White House that Zhou Enlai would welcome a special envoy from the United States to discuss American military withdrawal from Taiwan. On January 11, 1971, the Romanians sent along a similar message to the White House, which also included an invitation to the President to come to China.[108]

On the morning after the Ceausescu dinner, the Secretaries of State and Commerce tried again to promote trade with Eastern Europe. They both urged that MFN treatment and Eximbank credits be made available to Communist countries.[109] However, Peter Flanigan, the President's economic adviser, discouraged the idea. On October 28 he wrote to NSC economist Fred Bergsten that in principle it would be desirable to reduce trade barriers with the Communist world, in practice this would not be a good move. Communist countries needed foreign credits to trade, and as a result most sales would be financed by the American taxpayer.[110]

Commerce Secretary Maurice Stans was not to be put off so easily. He decided to deal directly with the President. On November 19, he, Peter Flanigan, and Undersecretary of Commerce Siciliano went to the Oval Office. During the discussion on East-West trade, Nixon indicated that for the present, he was opposed to liberalizing trade with Moscow. He was silent on the issue of extending MFN treatment and granting Eximbank credits to Communist countries. However, he did tell Stans that he was free "to encourage sales" to any of the East European countries.[111]

Meanwhile, Ceausescu continued his efforts to expand relations with the United States. In Bucharest, America's new Ambassador, Leonard Meeker,[112] and Vasile Gliga, the Romanian Deputy Foreign Minister, renewed the Romanian-American cultural, educational, and scientific exchange program for another two years on November 27. The agreement broadened the areas of exchange, especially in the field of medicine, and, for the first time, permitted undergraduate university students to participate in the exchange program.[113] A week later, Gheorghe Ionita, of the Romanian Embassy, met with members of the President's Council of Economic Advisers in Washington. Ionita wanted to know if members of the Economic Council of Romania could meet with members of the Council of Economic Advisers in the Spring. The Chairman of the Romanian council was Professor Manea Manescu, a distinguished economist, and a person close to Ceausescu.[114] On December 22, Bogdan repeated the request to Helmut Sonnenfeldt of the NSC, and added that in the spirit of the recent Romanian-American agreement, there could be an exchange of visits by the two economic councils.[115] Two days later, Kissinger agreed. He notified Paul McCracken, Chairman of the Council of Economic Advisers that this type of exchange would "be well in line with the President's interest in promoting closer contacts with Romania."[116]

However, "closer contacts" did not mean MFN for Romania. On December 23, the Under Secretaries Committee, composed of the Under Secretaries of Commerce, State and Defense, completed its review of American-Romanian economic relations as requested by Kissinger. Their recommendation was that MFN and Eximbank credits should not be sought for Romania alone. These actions "should be sought in the larger framework," which included the Soviet Union and the other East European countries. Bucharest should not be singled out for special treatment, because such an act "would be highly embarrassing to the Romanians *vis-a-vis* the Soviets."[117] This thought would persist for the next four years and stifle the efforts of Ceausescu and Bogdan to secure MFN for Romania.

Notes

1. Memorandum for the President-Elect, Proposal for a New National Security Council System from Henry Kissinger [December 1968], pp. 1-2, Alphabetical Subject Files 1970, Box 19, Ehrlichman, White House Special Files, Nixon Presidential Materials Project.

2. Henry Kissinger, *White House Years* (Boston: Little, Brown and Co., 1979), p. 11.

3. Tad Szulc, *The Illusion of Peace: Foreign Policy in the Nixon Years* (New York: The Viking Press, 1978), p. 22, Memorandum for the President-Elect, Proposal for a New National Security Council System from Henry Kissinger [December 1968], pp. 1-2, Alphabetical Subject Files 1970, Box 19, Ehrlichman, White House Special Files, Nixon Presidential Materials Project.

4. *Ibid.*, p. 7.

5. Hutchings, *Soviet-European Relations,* pp. 7-9.

6. *Agerpres*, February 10, 1969, p. 31.

7. Kissinger, *White House Years*, p. 173; *Agerpres*, March 3, 1969, p. 22.

8. Hutchings, *Soviet-European Relations,* pp. 80-83.

9. *Ibid.*, p. 157.

10. Author's interview of Corneliu Bogdan, March 19, 1987.

11. *Ibid.*

12. *Ibid.*

13. Szulc, *The Illusion of Peace*, p. 68.

14. Kissinger, *White House Years*, p. 127.

15. *Ibid.*, p. 144.

16. Report of the Task force on Foreign Trade Policy, January 31, 1969, 6pp., Folder Foreign Trade (1969-70), Box 45, Martin Anderson Task Force, Subject Files, Nixon Presidential Materials Project.

17. U.S. Congress, Senate, Committee on Banking and Currency, Hearings Before the Subcommittee on International Finance, *Export Expansion and Regulation*, 91st Cong., 1st Sess., 1969, p. 271.

18. *Ibid.*, pp, 190ff; *Congress and the Nation* (Washington, D.C.: Congressional Quarterly Services, 1973), III, 120.

19. Senate Committee on Banking and Currency, *Export Expansion and Regulation*, 1969, p. 190.

20. *Ibid.*, p. iii.

21. Memorandum, Lamar Alexander to Bryce N. Harlow, May 15, 1969, 2pp.,Folder Ex TA Trade [December 1968-August 1969], Box 1, Subject Files (TA)Trade, WHCF, Nixon Presidential Materials Project.

22. Garthoff, *Detente and Confrontation*, p. 91; Kissinger, *White House Years*, p. 173.

23. *Ibid.*, p. 153.

24. *Ibid.*, p. 154.

25. *Ibid.*, p. 155.

26. *Ibid.*, p. 156.

27. Haldeman Notes, Folder (May-June 69) Part II, Box 40, H.R. Haldeman, Staff Members & Officers Files, WHSF, Nixon Presidential Materials Project.

28. Later the Department would deny that there was any opposition (*DOS Bulletin*, September 8, 1969, p. 207).

29. Ehrlichman Notes, Folder 4, p. 2, Box 9, Ehrlichman, 1969 JDE Notes of Meetings, WHSF, Nixon Presidential Materials Project.

30. Author's interview of Corneliu Bogdan, April 11, 1987

31. *Idem.*, March 19.

32. Kissinger, *White House Years*, p. 156.

33. *Ibid.*

34. Henry Gemmill in the WSJ, August 8, reported that "some informed officials" had characterized these new reasons as "rationalizations served up . . . by a Dr. Kissinger turned short-order cook."

35. Henry Kissinger, Massachusetts Bay Community College, March 28, 1988.

36. Kissinger, *White House Years*, p. 156.

37. NYT, July 5, 1969, p. 3.

38. *Scinteia*, 7 September, 1969, p. 10

39. *Agerpres*, July 14, 1969, p. 1.

40. CSM, August 2, 1969, p. 5.

41. "Rumania's Red Carpet for a U.S. President," *U.S. News & World Report*, August 4, 1969, pp. 40-41.

42. Henry Kissinger to Professor John Montias, July 22, 1969, Folder Gen Co 125 Romania Begin 12/31/69, Box 64, Subject Files Co, WHCF. Nixon Presidential Materials Project; Idem., Henry Kissinger to Professor Stephen Fisher-Galati, July 22, 1969.

43. Author's conversation with Stephen Fisher-Galati, March 27, 1987.

44. Memorandum, Alexander Haig to Tod Hullin, December 2, 1970, Folder 11/1/70-12/31/70, Box 2, Subject Files FO, WHCF, Nixon Presidential Materials Project; Gaddis, *Strategies of Containment*, p. 298.

45. Garthoff, *Detente and Confrontation*, p. 218.

46. *Scinteia*, August 2, 1969, p. 1.

47. *Public Papers of the Presidents of the United States,Richard Nixon,1969* (Washington, D.C.: U. S. Government Printing Office, 1970), p. 604.

48. Transcript, CBS News-Special Reports "The President Abroad," August 2, 1969, p. 3, Folder TR25 8/1/69-8/6/69, Box 28, TR [Trips] Subject Files, WHCF, Nixon Presidential Materials Project.

49. *Ibid.*, p. 4.

50. Szulc, *The Illusion of Peace*, p. 133.

51. Author's interview of H. R. Haldeman November 11, 1987; Author's interview of John Ehrlichman November 11, 1987, Later, a perception developed among officials of the American government that Nixon had promised Ceausescu MFN status, but there is no evidence to support this view (U. S. Congress, House, Hearings Before the Committee on Ways and Means, *Trade Reform*, 93rd Cong., 1st Sess., 1973, p. 3528, and U. S. Congress, House, Committee on Ways and Means, Hearings Before the Subcommittee on Trade, *United States-Romanian Trade Agreement*, 94th Cong., 1st Sess., 1975, pp. 33).

52. Szulc, *The Illusion of Peace*, p. 34;

53. *DOS Bulletin*, September 1, 1969, pp. 196-198.

54. Julian Hale, *Ceausescu's Romania: A Political Documentary* (London: George Harrap and Co., Ltd., 1971), p, 152.

55. NYT, August 4, 1969, p. 1; Memorandum, P. J. Buchanan to the President, August 27, 1969, EX CO125 Romania (1969-70), Box 63, Subject Files CO, WHCF, Nixon Presidential Materials Project. Haldeman Notes, August 5, 1969, 8pp., Folder (July-September 69), Box 40, H.R. Haldeman, Staff Members & Officers Files, WHSF, Nixon Presidential Materials Project; *Idem*., September 5, 1969, 2pp.

56. NYT, August 4, 1969, p. 1.

57. Memorandum, Henry Kissinger to Bryce Harlow, June 23, 1969, 3pp., Folder Ex TA Trade [December 1968-August 1969], Box 1, Subject Files (TA) Trade, WHCF, Nixon Presidential Materials Project; Memorandum, William E. Timmons to Glenard P. Lipscomb, June 13, 1969, 2pp., Gen TA3 Exports (1969-1970), Box 16, Subject Files TA-Trade, WHCF, Nixon Presidential Materials Project; Letter, Richard I. Phillips to A. J. Rademacher, October 7, 1969, 2pp., Folder Gen TA Trade October 69-February 70, Box 8, Subject Files TA Trade, WHCF, Nixon Presidential Materials Project.

58. U. S., *Congressional Record, House*, August 4, 1969, pp. 22104, 22151.

59. U. S., *Congressional Record, Senate*, August 5, 1969, p 22300.

60. Report, p. 19, "Export Control," Vol. I, Part III, Department of Commerce, Administrative History. LBJ Library. In reply to a query from the authors, Mondale wrote (March 2, 1989) that he persistently introduced and supported legislation to give Romania MFN status because he wanted to help the Socialist Republic to become more independent from the Soviet Union. In addition, he thought that if Congress agreed to grant MFN to Romania, it "might lead to more domestic liberalization." Finally, he believed that through MFN, Romania would be led to liberalize her emigration policies, and permit Jews to leave the country.

61. Mondale's persistence over the next few years in his effort to get MFN treatment for Romania earned him the name "Mondalescu" among officials in Bucharest (Authors' interview of Corneliu Bogdan, November 1, 1989.)

62. Kissinger, *White House Years*, p. 157.

63. Shafir, *Romania: Politics, Economics and Society*, p. 72; Richard F. Staar (ed.), *Yearbook on International Communist Affairs 1970* (Stanford, CA: Hoover Institution Press, 1971), p. 75; *Scinteia*, August 13, 1969, p. 1.

64. *Scinteia*, August 7, 1969, p. 10; Antonin J. Liehm, "East Central Europe and the Soviet Model," *Problems of Communism*, Vol. XXX (September-October 1981), p. 53 nn. 8,9.

65. *Expansion of Romanian Economy Over 1971-1980*, ed. The Chamber of Commerce of the Socialist Republic of Romania (Bucharest: 1969), p. 33.

66. *Directives of the Tenth Congress of the Romanian Communist Party Concerning the 1971-1975 Five Year Plan, And the Guidelines for the Development of the National Economy in the 1976-1980 Period (Bucharest, 1969)*, p. 69.

67. Lincoln Gordon *et al.*, *Eroding Empire: Western Relations with Eastern Europe* (Washington, D.C.: The Brookings Institution, 1987), p. 331.

68. Andreas C. Tsantis, Roy Pepper *et al.*, *Romania: The Industrialization of an Agrarian Economy Under Socialist Planning* (Washington, D.C.: The World Bank, 1979), p. 575; Alexandru Zamfir and Constantine I. Rapcea, *Strategia competitivitajii in comertul international* (Bucharest: Editura politica, 1976), p. 135.

69. *Agerpres*, August 31, 1969, p. 23.

70. Walter F. Mondale, "East-West Trade: A Congressional Perspective," *New York University Center for International Studies Policy Papers*, Vol. 3, No. 3, (1970), p. 9; Steven Elliott, "The Distribution of Power and the U. S. Politics of East-West Energy Trade Controls," *Controlling East-West Trade and Technology Transfer*, ed. Gary K. Bertsch, pp. 70-71.

71. Memorandum, Maurice H. Stans to Henry Kissinger, October 31, 1969, 3pp., Folder Foreign Economic Policy 1969, Box 45, Subject Files, Martin Anderson Task Force, Nixon Presidential Materials Project.

72. Memorandum, Henry Kissinger to the President, December 29, 1969, 2pp., Folder Ex TA3 Exports, Box TA12, TA Trade, Subject Files, WHCF, Nixon Presidential Materials Project; "Fifteenth Annual Report of the President of the United States on Trade," December 6, 1971, p.29, Folder Ex TA5 Trade exports, Box 65, TA Trade, Subject Files, WHCF, Nixon Presidential Materials Project.

73. Memorandum, Henry Kissinger to the President, July 22, 1969, Folder Ex CO Romania (1969-1970), Box 63, Subject Files CO, WHCF, Nixon Presidential Materials Project.

74. *Idem.*, Memorandum, Henry Kissinger to the President, September 17, 1969.

75. *DOS Bulletin*, October 20, 1969, p. 338-339.

76. Schedule, September 22, 1969, Folder Ex CO125 Romania (1969-1970), Box 63, Subject Files, CO, WHCF, Nixon Presidential Materials Project.

77. Ehrlichman Notes, Folder 4, p. 2, Box 9, Ehrlichman, 1969 JDE Notes of Meetings, WHSF, Nixon Presidential Materials Project.

78. "Rumania tries the hard sell on trade," *Business Week*, July 26, 1969, pp. 74-75.

79. Alan M. Jones (ed.), *United States Foreign Policy in a Changing World*, p. 131.

80. Henry Kissinger, Hofstra University, January 19, 1987.

81. Szulc, *The Illusion of Peace*, p. 122; Garthoff, *Detente and Confrontation*, p. 221.

82. Letter, Maurice Stans to Lee A. DuBridge, December 15, 1969, 3pp., Folder Ex TA3 CO Exports, Box 18, Subject Files, Trade, WHCF, Nixon Presidential Materials Project.

83. *Idem.*, Memorandum, Helmut Sonnenfeldt to Henry Kissinger, December 23, 1969, 2pp. This proposal of course did not include the offer of MFN. Therefore the overall commercial relations of Yugoslavia and Poland *vis a vis* the United States would continue to be far better than Romania's, which had still to face the Smoot-Hawley tariffs.

84. *Idem.*, Henry Kissinger to Acting Secretary of Commerce, December 19, 1969.

85. Organization Chart, "Coordinating Groups in Foreign Economic Policy," July 17, 1969, Appendix C, pp.4-5, Folder, FECOM 8-3 Reports For Economic Policy, Box 72, PACEA, WHCF, Nixon Presidential Materials Project. The Export Control Review Board was later named the Export Administration Review Board and charged with implementing the Export Administration Act of 1969.

86. *Ibid.*

87. Memorandum, August 17, 1969, 35pp., Folder Subject Category FECOM, Foreign Econ Policy, Box 71, President's Advisory Commission on Executive Organizations [PACEO], WHCF, Nixon Presidential Materials Project.

88. U. S. Congress, House, *Message from the President of the United States. United States Foreign Policy for the 1970's: A New Strategy for Peace*, House Document No. 91-258, 91st Cong., 2d Sess., 1970, pp. 138-139.

89. Memorandum, Peter M. Flanigan to Maurice Stans, February 3, 1970, Folder EX FG21, Dept of Commerce 2/1/70-2/28/70, box 19, Subject Files, WHCF, Nixon Presidential Materials Project.

90. Memorandum, The President to Haldeman, Ehrlichman, and Kissinger, March 2, 1970, 3pp, Folder President's Memos, Box 229, SM of H. R. Haldeman, WHSF, Nixon Presidential Materials Project.

91. Pompiliu Verzariu, Jr., and Jay A. Burgess, *Joint Venture Agreements in Romania: Background for Implementation* (Washington, D.C.: U. S. Department of Commerce, 1977), p. 11.

92. Hutchings, Soviet-East European Relations, pp. 80-81.

93. CSM, July 16, 1970, p. 3; *Agerpres*, June 15, 1970, p. 1; Richard F. Staar (ed.), *Yearbook on International Communist Affairs, 1971* (Stanford, CA: Hoover Institution Press, 1971), p. 75.

94. Staar, *Yearbook on International Communist Affairs, 1971*, pp. 79-80.

95. *Ibid.*; Hutchings, *Soviet-East European Relations*, pp. 162-163; Georges Cioranesco et al., *Aspects des relations sovieto-roumaines, 1967-1971* (Paris: Minard, 1971), p. 114.

96. Memorandum, Lee DuBridge to Bob Finch, June 9, 1970, 6pp., Folder EX FO 5-2 6/1/70-9/30/70, Box 55, F.O. Foreign Affairs, Subject Files, WHCF, Nixon Presidential Materials Project.

97. Memorandum, Kissinger to the President, 25 June, 1970, Folder CO125 Romania 1969-1970, Box 63, CO Subject Files, WHCF, Nixon Presidential Materials Project.

98. *Idem.*, Memorandum, Hugh W. Sloan to Henry Kissinger, September 30, 1970.

99. Garthoff, *Detente and Confrontation*, pp. 225-226.

100. Kissinger, *White House Years*, pp. 698-699.

101. *Time*, October 5, 1970, p. 12.

102. "Suggested Remarks at the Arrival of President Ceausescu," October 25, 1970, 2pp., Folder EX CO125 Romania 1969-1970, Box 63, CO Subject Files, WHCF, Nixon Presidential Materials Project; "A Communist comes to talk business," *Business Week*, October 31, 1970, p. 28.

103. Ceausescu, *On the Way*, V, 89-90.

104. Memorandum, Maurice Stans to the President, October 15, 1970, Folder Ex CO125 Romania, 1969-1970, box 63, CO Subject Files, WHCF, Nixon Presidential Materials Project.

105. Kissinger, *White House Years*, p. 699; Garthoff, *Detente and Confrontation*, p. 227.

106. Guest list, October 26, 1970, Folder EX FG21 Commerce 10/1/70-10/30/70, Box 20, Subject Files, WHCF, WHSF, Nixon Presidential Materials Project.

107. *DOS Bulletin*, November 23, 1970, p. 649.

108. Garthoff, *Detente and Confrontation*, pp. 227-228.

109. Memorandum, C. Fred Bergsten to Paul McCracken, October 27, 1970, Folder Trade East-West, Box 48, Staff Members & Officers Files, WHCF, Nixon Presidential Materials Project.

110. Memorandum, Peter Flanigan to Fred Bergsten, October 28, 1970, Folder Ex TA Trade, Box 1, (TA) Trade, Subject Files, WHCF, Nixon Presidential Materials Project.

111. Memorandum, Peter Flanigan to Henry Kissinger, November 23, 1970, Folder Ex TA Trade 11/17/70-12/31/70, Box 2, (TA) Trade, Subject Files, WHCF, Nixon Presidential Materials Project; Idem., Memorandum, Peter Flanigan to the President, November 19, 1970, 2pp.

112. Leonard Meeker replaced Richard Davis in August of 1969. Apparently Nixon did not like Davis who was a Johnson appointee. Bogdan, too, had some reservations, noting that Davis was "a little bit lazy" (Authors' interview with Corneliu Bogdan, April 11, 1987).

113. *DOS Bulletin*, January 25, 1971, pp. 126-130.

114. Memorandum, Hendrik S. Houthakker to Henry Kissinger, December 8, 1970, Folder EX FO 5-2 10/1/70-12/31/70, Box 55 F.O. Foreign Affairs, Subject Files, WHCF, Nixon Presidential Materials Project.

115. Memorandum, Helmut Sonnenfeldt to Henry Kissinger, December 22, 1970, Folder EX CO 125 Romania 1969-1970, Box 63, CO, Subject Files, WHCF, Nixon Presidential Materials Project.

116. *Idem.*, Memorandum, Henry Kissinger to Paul McCracken, December 24, 1970.

117. *Idem.*, Memorandum, C. Fred Bergsten to Henry Kissinger, December 23, 1970.

CHAPTER XI

MFN MISSED

The CIEP

During its first two years in office, the Nixon Administration had failed to establish an effective trade program. The principal problem was that no one agency was responsible for overseeing America's foreign trade program. Nixon had known of the problem since 1969, but did nothing to resolve it until January 18, 1971, when the President established the Council on International Economic Policy (CIEP). In addition to himself, CIEP members included the Secretaries of State, Treasury, Agriculture, Commerce, Labor, the Director of the Office of Management and Budget, the Chairman of the Council of Economic Advisers, the Assistant to the President for National Security Affairs, the Executive Director of the Domestic Council and the Special Representative for Trade Negotiations. The purposes of the Council were threefold: (a), to achieve consistency between domestic and foreign economic policy; (b), to provide a clear top level focus for the full range of international economic policy issues including trade, investment, balance of payments, finance, foreign aid, and defense; and (c), to maintain close coordination with basic foreign policy objectives.[1] To oversee the daily operations of the Council, Nixon appointed Peter G. Peterson, Chairman of the Board and Chief Executive Officer of Bell and Howell Company, as Executive Director of the CIEP.[2]

Since Peterson would report directly to the President, the CIEP was analogous to the NSC. The former would handle all international economic affairs, while the latter controlled political-military affairs. However, neither the CIEP nor Peterson ever attained the influence held by

Kissinger and the NSC. Nonetheless, the CIEP was a significant step forward toward establishing a coherent international economic policy.[3]

While the CIEP would spend nearly two years in drafting a comprehensive trade reform bill, its establishment came none too soon. Heated debate over trade issues was waged from one end of Pennsylvania Avenue to the other. The AFL-CIO maintained its demand for greater protection from foreign imports, while the State and Commerce Departments called for expanded trade.[4] In Congress, Senator Mondale continued to demand greater East-West trade. He asked his colleagues to think about amending the Export Administration Act of 1969, due to expire on June 30, 1971.[5] To complicate matters, the Overseas Private Investment Corporation, OPIC, began operations in January. Approved by Congress in December, 1969, this government owned corporation provided Americans investing in friendly developing countries insurance protection against political and commercial risks including expropriation, currency inconvertibility, and damage from war and revolution.[6]

As discussion grew Peterson advised the President on February 27, 1971, that this was "not the opportune moment" to increase East-West trade. He urged the President to have Administration officials "soft-pedal" discussions of expanded trade until the CIEP could determine the economic advantages and the best political *quid pro quos* that could be exchanged for trade concessions with the East European states.[7]

The confusion in trade policy was but one of the Administration's problems. As Nixon recounted in his memoirs, "the first six months of 1971 were the lowest point of my first term as President." Unemployment was at 6%, the highest since 1961, the February Laotian operation was a military success but a "public relations disaster" and the dollar fell on the foreign exchange markets to its lowest point since 1949.[8]

Washington and Romanian MFN: Round I

This inhospitable atmosphere did not deter Romanian efforts to secure MFN treatment for her exports to America. On January 4, Washington announced the recent signing of a textile agreement with Romania, and three weeks later, Leonard Meeker, America's Ambassador to Bucharest, urged the State Department to award Romania MFN for its products.[9] However, Kissinger supported Peterson's "soft-pedal" policy and cautioned Meeker against making any promises of MFN to Romania.[10] Meanwhile, Bogdan continued to be a shuttle for messages to Beijing. The Ambassador planned to return to Bucharest in early February, and agreed to convey Kissinger's oral message to Chinese officials that America was still willing to discuss the issue of Taiwan.[11]

In February, 1971, Nixon announced his intentions to ask Congress to give him the authority to guarantee American private investment in Romania.[12] As though on cue, Ceausescu responded. On March 17, Bucharest enacted Law No. 1 which enabled Romania to become the first CMEA country to consider establishing joint ventures with foreign firms. Article 57 permitted foreign companies to build joint projects in Romania, and Article 58, permitted Romania to do the same in foreign lands.[13] While many of the details of joint ventures were left to Law 424 in November, 1972, Law No. 1 emphatically declared Romania's willingness to trade with the West. The legislation allowed firms to open commercial offices in Romania or be represented there through special Romanian organizations. Further, Bucharest agreed to establish "free zones," similar to those in the West. Such zones allowed import storage, processing and assembling without full custom formalities. Also goods reexported abroad from such zones would not be subject to Romanian custom duties, and those destined for Romanian markets could be assessed only the lowest duties.[14]

Ceausescu had several reasons for announcing Law No. 1. He needed foreign technology, management, marketing expertise and capital. Long term joint ventures could fulfill all of these needs, and at the same time insure that technology was kept current and responsive to world market demands. He also wanted to improve Romania's trade position in order to implement his latest five year plan, 1971-1975, which called for significant trade expansion.[15] Further, joint ventures could enable Romania to gain access to the much needed marketing networks of Western trading partners.

No sooner had Bucharest announced Law No. 1, than Senator Mondale, renewed his efforts to secure MFN for Romania. On March 29 the Senator, along with his colleague from Massachusetts, Edward Brooke, introduced S. 1389 which, if approved, would authorize the President to negotiate a commercial agreement including a provision for MFN with Romania.[16] Mondale hoped the MFN proposal would not only encourage trade, but that it would permit a greater emigration of Jews from Romania.[17] This issue of Jewish emigration had been primarily viewed by Washington as a Soviet issue, and this was still the situation in 1971. However, various Congressmen were aware that in the years following the Czechoslovakian invasion, pressure had increased on Jewish populations not only in the Soviet Union but also in Eastern Europe.[18]

However, since Romania had maintained relations with Israel during the Six Day War, and in January, 1971, had signed a five year renewal of its trade and cooperation agreement with Israel, the issue of Jewish emigration did not affect the Administration's relations with Romania at this time.[19] In fact, in the year preceding Mondale's MFN proposal, the State Department had received only one complaint involving Jewish emigration from Romania which warranted considerable discussion. In January, Rabbi Anton Silver went to the American Embassy in Bucharest and requested assistance to emigrate from Romania. He had been trying to leave since 1951 without success. Upon investigation, the State Department learned that the Rabbi was the only ritual slaughterer of veal in Bucharest, and Rabbi Rosen, Romania's Chief Rabbi, did not want him to leave. The Romanian government supported Rabbi Rosen. While Israel was willing to approve Rabbi Silver for immigration, it did not want to antagonize the Chief Rabbi by pressing for Rabbi Silber's departure. When informed of this situation by the State Department, Kissinger decided that the issue could best be resolved between Israel and Romania. Washington already had its hands full in trying to "prod" the Romanian government to approve travel documents for some 2,000 dual nationals who wished to emigrate to the United States.[20]

Mondale's MFN proposal reflected growing Congressional support for expanded East-West trade, but it did not reflect the mood at the White House. Peterson and Kissinger had urged caution in February, and in March, the Under Secretaries agreed to "oppose in low key" any changes in America's trade relations with Eastern Europe.[21] However, the Senate wanted change. In April, it passed by a vote of 66-1 a bill which, among other provisions, repealed the 1968 Fino Amendment. Two months later, the House Banking Committee would report out a similar proposal. However, Congress would not act on this legislation until August, as described below.

In the meantime, Commerce Secretary, Maurice Stans, made a two week trip to Europe and the Middle East. He visited Bucharest in early May and told the Romanians that if Congress granted MFN treatment to Eastern Europe, "Romania would be first in line."[22] Without question, Stan's statement went against the Administration's line toward East-West trade. However, his remarks certainly reflected the intention of the Mondale legislation. Further, Stans facilitated the work of Bogdan. In addition to his work as a conduit to China, Bogdan had also worked vigorously to promote Romanian MFN. Bogdan described his

MFN efforts with the White House and Congress as analogous to working with "two heads of a hydra, you don't want to offend either."[23] His goal was to "build bridges" with both branches of government without playing one against the other.[24] He labored discreetly and tirelessly, and his efforts produced results.

On May 17, NSC members Helmut Sonnenfeldt and Ernest Johnston, suggested to Kissinger that the President ought to reconsider his "low key" opposition to MFN treatment for Romania. They argued that it would be "hard for the Romanians to understand Administration opposition to a bill [Mondale-Brooke] directed solely at them" in light of the President's public statements supporting greater economic relations with Bucharest. Further, Bogdan laid to rest the concerns raised by the Under Secretaries Committee the previous December, when he assured Mondale staff members that Ceausescu did not think that such support would aggravate Romania's relations with Moscow.[25] Kissinger supported the recommendation and relayed the suggestion to the President. While the Administration normally opposed legislation for a specific country, Kissinger saw more advantages than disadvantages to Nixon supporting the Mondale-Brooke bill. The President had frequently noted his particular relationship with Bucharest. By refusing to support the bill, he would undermine the credibility of his previous statements, and call into question America's current support for Romania's application to the GATT.[26]

Following a meeting with Secretary of Commerce Stans on June 3, Nixon agreed to alter his position toward Romania.[27] On June 10 he told Kissinger that the Administration would no longer object to legislative proposals providing discretionary authority to the President to extend MFN treatment to Romania.[28] The efforts of Bogdan, Mondale and Stans had paid off. The White House was no longer an obstacle to Romanian MFN. The decision now rested solely with Congress.

Bogdan turned his full attention toward lobbying legislators for support. The person most responsible for moving MFN legislation through Congress was the Chairman of the House Ways and Means Committee, Wilbur Mills. Within days of Nixon's decision, Bogdan asked to see Mills. However, the Chairman denied his request.[29] The Ambassador tried a different tact. He enlisted the support of a Washington lobbyist, Robert B. Anderson. As the former Secretary of the Treasury under Eisenhower, Anderson was a familiar figure on Capitol Hill.[30] In addition, he had a vested interest in supporting Romanian MFN. His firm, Robert B. Anderson and Co., Ltd., of New York, was the first American enterprise to establish a joint corporation with Romania in May, 1971. The Romanda Corporation was a 50/50 arrangement between Anderson's company and the Romanian state agency, Terra. The corporation's purpose was to develop ventures in which Romania could obtain an equity position.[31]

Nixon's decision on Romania was part of a shift in his commercial and political policies with the Communist world. On June 10, the same day that he made his decision on Romania, the White House lifted the trade embargo on China, and published a list of items withdrawn from export controls for Beijing.[32] This action, coupled with his earlier decisions to eliminate travel restrictions to China, and to refer in writing to the People's Republic of China, reflected the success of the initial round of indirect Sino-American negotiations, primarily through Pakistani channels. The President was now eager to have direct talks with the Chinese leaders in Beijing.[33]

June 10 was also the date that Nixon ended America's 50/50 cargo preference restriction on grain exports to Communist countries.[34] In October, 1963, President Kennedy had authorized the sale of American wheat, flour, and other surplus agricultural commodities to the Soviet Union and Eastern Europe. In implementing this decision, the Commerce Department had used the provisions of the Cargo Preference Act, passed by the 83rd Congress, which regulated government to government transactions. The provisions required that at least 50% of all such shipments had to be made on American flag ships. After the large initial Bloc purchases in 1963-1964, the trade dried up. No East European country was willing to pay the additional freight rate of $14.00 per ton for grain shipped on American flag ships. American exporters were unable to bid competitively against foreign suppliers. Consequently, after 1964, no shipments whatsoever were made on American flag ships.

By 1971, the Agriculture Department estimated that the 50/50 shipping requirement had lost American farmers over $565 million in potential wheat sales alone between 1965 and 1970. During the same period, the Department concluded that America lost sales of $23 million of corn, $44 million of barley and $10 million of oats and rye. Not only did the 50/50 cargo preference not help the American shipping industry and the ocean-going labor force, for which it was intended, but worse still, it injured American farmers, grain dealers, and the domestic transportation industry, while exacerbating America's balance of payments deficit.[35]

With this in mind, Nixon suspended the 50/50 cargo preference restriction and opened America's granaries to foreign markets. In his eagerness to promote detente, the President also ended the requirement for suppliers to obtain Commerce Department approval to export wheat, grain and flour to China, the Soviet Union and Eastern Europe.[36]

Bucharest-Moscow-Beijing

Meanwhile in Bucharest, Ceausescu had altered the goals of the 1971 economic plan. The Polish uprisings in December, 1970, sent a strong message throughout the Bloc countries, and Ceausescu decided to reduce the severe housing cutbacks called for in the original plan.[37] In March, 1971, he postponed sending the Romanian Economic Council to Washington. Ceausescu wanted the White House to know that he was annoyed by the President's refusal to press for Romanian MFN.

The Romanian leader, however, made no changes in his relations with Moscow. On April 1, Ceausescu reiterated Romania's independence at the Soviet Union's 24th Party Conference. Ceausescu boldly reminded the Soviet leaders that Romania was willing to have relations with all countries, regardless of their economic or social systems on the principles of national sovereignty, independence, equal rights and non-interference in internal affairs.[38] Shortly thereafter, Brezhnev showed his displeasure with Ceausescu's remarks by refusing to attend ceremonies in Bucharest commemorating the 50th anniversary of the founding of the Romanian Communist Party.

Ceausescu escalated tensions with the Kremlin even further on June 1, when he became the first East European party chief to visit Beijing since the beginning of the Sino-Soviet split. Zhou Enlai met him at the airport and praised Romania for "opposing big-power chauvinism," a euphemism for the Soviet Union.[39] Ceausescu's week long visit to China prompted a flood of criticism in the East European press.[40] The Soviet press warned of the danger of a Balkan triangle consisting of Romania, Yugoslavia and Albania under the tutelage of China.[41] In addition, the Kremlin beamed broadcasts into Romania warning that Beijing's policies undermined Communist unity.[42] Further, while Ceausescu was still in China, Moscow held military maneuvers in the southern part of the Soviet Union near Odessa, close to the Romanian frontier. The maneuvers, labelled "Operation Yug71," focused on the type of tactics essential for an invasion of Romania, including night attacks, river crossings, and air and amphibious assault.[43]

After China, Ceausescu visited Kim Il Sung in North Korea. The six day visit made a lasting impression on Ceausescu. Authoritarianism greatly appealed to the Romanian leader and the Korean cult of personality fit Ceausescu's temperament.[44] Upon returning to Bucharest, he wasted little time in implementing internal changes modelled after the Chinese and Korean regimes. On July 6, he presented what one writer called, his "July Thesis" to the Executive Committee of the Romanian Communist Party.[45] He wanted to improve the "political-ideological activity and Marxist-Leninist education" of the party cadre and of the Romanian people. His proposals rested on the preeminent position of the party; a program of education and, where necessary, reeducation, to insure conformity with Ceausescu's interpretation of Marxist-Leninist thought; and, fidelity to a Romanian nationalism, which recognized no other nationalisms in Romania.[46] While the proposals appeared to be designed to strengthen the role of the party, their real role was to increase the party leader's ideological control over the masses. The "July Theses" was a bridge to the authoritarian model which so impressed him in North Korea and China. Moreover, the proposals would further develop Ceausescu's cult of personality, a goal which surfaced clearly at the 10th Party Congress.

At the end of July, Bucharest hosted the 25th Session of the CMEA Council. Originally scheduled for adoption in 1970 and delayed again in early 1971, CMEA approved its "Comprehensive Program for the Further Extension and Improvement of Cooperation and the Development of Socialist Integration." The 100 page document reflected Ceausescu's success in preventing CMEA from becoming a supranational organization, since all cooperation was clearly stated as "voluntary." However, Romania could no longer veto CMEA actions. Her persistent opposition to socialist economic integration forced the other CMEA members to eliminate the need for unanimity in the decision making process. The "Comprehensive Program" gave guidelines for two five year programs extending through 1980. The Plan established a framework for bilateral and multilateral talks between "interested countries," joint ventures, especially with Moscow, and procedures for economic cooperation. The plan was a compromise between Khrushchev's goals for 1962 and Ceausescu's demands for independent national socialist economic programs.[47]

Ceausescu's courtship of Beijing along with President Nixon's July 15 announcement of his forthcoming visit to China caused alarm in the Kremlin. Moscow talked of the Washington-Bucharest-Beijing axis, while the East European press, especially Hungary, pointed to an emerging "Tirana-Belgrade-Bucharest line" as the Western end of an anti-Soviet axis stemming from China. Within this atmosphere, Soviet and East European party leaders, minus Ceausescu, met in the Crimea in the first day of August. The official summary of the conference indicated unanimity on a variety of topics including the Comprehensive Plan. However, the issue of Romania was obviously a major topic of discussion. The Romanian press complained of pressure and blackmail from unnamed sources. Tensions mounted. Bucharest brought several of its military divisions to full strength to prepare for war games, but no games were held. As talk of possible Soviet intervention in Romania increased, the Kremlin sent Vice Premier Mikhail Lesechko to Bucharest in August to calm the waters. Two months later, Romanian and Soviet defense ministers exchanged military missions, and toasts in both capitals indicated that the crises had passed.[48]

Washington and Romanian MFN: Round II

Meanwhile in Washington, Nixon's June 10, 1971, decision not to interfere with Romanian MFN prompted Representative Paul Findley of Illinois to introduce two bills to the House on July 26. The first authorized the President to negotiate a commercial accord with Romania, and, the second, a general bill, would give the President the authority to extend MFN to any country which was a member of the GATT and had diplomatic relations with the United States. Findley told Congress that America should reward Romania for its independent foreign policy. MFN would make Bucharest less economically dependent on Moscow.[49] However, in spite of his statements, neither of Findley's bills clearly stipulated MFN for Romania as did the Mondale-Brooke legislation.

While Congress discussed various proposals for expanding trade with the Communist world, the Administration worked to resolve America's first trade deficit since 1893 as well as a rapidly increasing balance of payments deficit.[50] In July, Nixon decided to take some drastic measures to improve the economy. He told his Assistant for Domestic Affairs, John Ehrlichman, that America's international trade policy could no longer be designed primarily with an eye to implementing foreign policy. Foreign trade was now an instrument of domestic policy.[51] On August 15 the President presented his New Economic Policy on national television. Without consulting other members of the international monetary system, and without discussion with his own State Department, the President announced that the dollar would no longer be convertible into gold, and that the United States would impose a 10% surcharge on all imports.[52] Removing the gold backing from the dollar allowed the dollar to float according to the supply and demand of international markets. This had the effect of devaluing the dollar and thereby reducing America's foreign trade disadvantage. Simply put, American exports would sell cheaper overseas, while foreign imports would be more expensive in America.[53]

Two days later, Nixon signed into law the Export Expansion Finance Act of 1971, which repealed the Fino Amendment's prohibition on extending Eximbank credits to countries which aided nations at war with the United States. The history of this bill reflected the change in the Administration's approach to trade with the Communist world. At the outset, Senate and House committee versions of the bill encountered little opposition. However, when the bill came to the House floor, Representative Chalmers Wylie of Ohio proposed an amendment to retain the Fino Amendment. On July 8, the House adopted the amendment by a vote of 207 to 158. Support for the bill came principally from representatives who believed that the Administration was adamantly opposed to trading with Communist countries. Once the Administration indicated that this was no longer the case, the House reconsidered the measure and quickly repealed the Fino language.[54] Once again the President could determine whether or not it was in America's national interest to extend Eximbank credits to East European countries, including Romania.

The Administration's sudden support for trade expansion spurred the Romanian Embassy to action. In early August, Bogdan met with Wilbur Mills and pressed his case for MFN.[55] Three weeks later, Gheorghe Ionita, Counselor at the Embassy, had lunch with Arthur Downey, one of Sonnenfeldt's assistants. Ionita wanted the President to extend Eximbank credits to Romania. On September 15, Bogdan had lunch with Sonnenfeldt, and two days later met Nixon in the Oval Office. While no information is available concerning their discussion, Bogdan certainly talked about Eximbank credits and MFN. The Ambassador could point to a number of successful ventures between American businesses and Romania. Corning Glass and a subsidiary of International Telephone and Telegraph had already built factories in Romania, while negotiations were underway with Boeing aircraft for a fleet of commercial jets, and with Gulf Energy and Environmental

Systems for a nuclear reactor.[56] These types of projects could easily multiply with MFN and Eximbank credits.

By the end of the month, efforts to expand East-West trade resumed on Capitol Hill. Senator Magnuson, from Washington, along with 24 co-sponsors, introduced bill S. 2620 which called for expanding America's exchange program with nonmarket economies. The bill also provided the President the authority to negotiate commercial agreements, including MFN, with these nations.[57] Three weeks later, a delegation of Governors, representing the United States National Governors Conference, visited Romania from October 19-22. They met with government officials in an effort to find ways their individual states could profit from trade with Bucharest.[58]

On November 4, Ionita invited Herbert Stein, a member of the Council of Economic Advisers, to lunch at the Romanian Embassy. Ionita apologized for the most recent postponement of Manea Manescu's visit to the United States, and indicated that the Chairman of Romania's Economic Council would like to meet with Stein's colleagues sometime in March 1972. Ionita also used the occasion to ask Stein to persuade the President to extend Eximbank credits to Romania.[59]

The hard work of the Romanian Embassy staff was nearly undermined by Ceausescu's domestic policies. American newspapers began to carry stories of Ceausescu's efforts to establish a personality cult in Romania. The *Christian Science Monitor* reported that each issue of *Scinteia* printed Ceausescu's speeches which numbered over 5,000 words daily.[60] In contrast, Romanian intellectuals, especially those who disagreed with the government, were forced to send their writings to the West for publication.[61] To institutionalize his control, Ceausescu repeated the main themes of his "July Thesis" at a November Plenum of the Central Committee. He reminded the delegates that "every personality can assert itself only in close connection with the Party" and the Party comes "under the guidance of the Secretariat."[62] In other words, the political-ideological orientation of Romania would conform to the thoughts of Nicolae Ceausescu, Secretary-General of the Party.

Bogdan and Ionita effectively limited the damage caused in America by the press and Ceausescu's statements. On November 22 Nixon rewarded their efforts. The President announced that he had determined that it was in America's national interest for the Eximbank to guarantee, insure and extend credit for the purchase or lease of any product or service to Romania.[63] During the next year Romania would negotiate over $11 million worth of transactions with the Eximbank.[64] The

President's determination also helped Bucharest in its application for GATT membership. Although the United States could not formally support Romania's application to GATT since America had not accorded Bucharest MFN, Washington did act as an "honest broker" and through "informal consultations" assisted Romania in joining the trade and tariff agreement on November 14, 1971.[65]

In December, after nearly a year of work, Peterson submitted the CIEP's recommendations on a new foreign economic policy to the White House. The report called for the President to develop an aggressive new American trade policy. A policy which would reduce import and export controls, and establish new arrangements for expanding trade with Eastern Europe, including the discretionary award of MFN status.[66]

While the Administration agreed with Peterson that it should submit a bold trade package to Congress, there was considerable debate over the timing of the package. Should it be introduced in 1972 or, assuming reelection, in 1973? On December 20, Peterson met with a group of economists, most of whom had worked as consultants to various government economic agencies. While there was unanimous agreement that America needed a new and bold trade program, seven out of twelve were pessimistic about the chances for its passage in 1972. Time was needed to negotiate new parameters for export controls with America's West European allies. Time was also needed to educate the American public as well as key members of Congress as to the need for a policy which included trade with Communist nations.[67]

Peterson's report coupled with the recommendations for postponing a trade package until 1973 fit well with the President's new list of priorities. Beijing and Moscow were uppermost in Nixon's mind. Administration officials worked vigorously to complete preparations for the President's departure to China on February 17. At the same time, the NSC and CIEP turned their attention toward trade talks with Moscow.[68] The Commerce Department also worked on Soviet-American trade proposals. Prior to his resignation in January, 1972, Secretary of Commerce Stans gave the President a memo on unfinished business. He indicated that the Soviets were eager for MFN, and were willing to negotiate a settlement of their lend-lease debt, incurred during World War II, to facilitate MFN treatment. In addition, they wanted to purchase about $1 billion worth of corn and grain feed over the next five years.[69]

On January 27, 1972, the President announced Stans' resignation and his intention to replace him with Pete Peterson.[70] The new CIEP head would be Peter Flanigan, whom Ehrlichman described as a person who would "do the President's will."[71] Flanigan also assumed Peterson's other job as Assistant to the President for International Economic Affairs.

At his first meeting as Director of the CIEP Flanigan indicated that he intended to continue the policies of Peterson. There would be no Administration trade package this year. Protectionist Congressmen had already rallied behind the Foreign Trade and Investment Act of 1972. Known as the Burke-Hartke bill, this legislation increased the possibility of protective tariffs and mandated extensive import quotas.[72] Flanigan saw no need to give the protectionists another podium for their views. In addition, 1972 was a Presidential election year, and he did not believe that this was the best time to introduce bold new legislation. The CIEP would focus its efforts throughout 1972 on developing trade legislation for the following year as well as on forming strategies for trade negotiations with the Soviets.[73]

Washington and Romanian MFN: Round III – The Lost Round

The Administration's efforts to move from a bipolar to a multipolar foreign policy meant that Washington's attention would be focused on developments in Moscow and Beijing, making Bucharest appear relatively unimportant. Bogdan was aware of this development and worked assiduously to keep Romania's request for MFN before Washington officials. The need for MFN had grown over the past two years because of the rapidly expanding trade between Washington and Bucharest. As Romania's exports to the United States increased, more and more items were subject to discriminatory tariffs. In 1970, 42% of Romania's exports to America were taxed at a rate much higher than the same products from an MFN country. In 1972, the figure was 75%. The increase was partly due to the fact that Romania's exports were largely in products which fell into the discriminatory rate categories. The other main cause of the increase was the result of the recently completed Kennedy Round of the GATT talks. The GATT nations agreed to further reduce tariffs between MFN countries. This reduction increased the differential between MFN and non-MFN rates. For example, Romania's prime export to the United States was fuel. Without MFN, the tariff was 5 cents per gallon, with MFN, the tariff was 1.25 cents per gallon.[74]

On January 4, 1972, Bogdan saw Herb Stein of the Council of

Economic Advisers, to arrange for Manea Manescu's long postponed visit to the United States. As Chairman of the Economic Council of Romania, Manescu wanted to meet with his counterparts, primarily to lobby for MFN and to discuss a variety of economic topics. Stein agreed to send the request forward for consideration.[75]

Meanwhile, Bogdan tried to deal with Wilbur Mills, but without much success. According to the Ambassador, the Chairman of the House Ways and Means Committee did not "know where Romania was." Further as an "Arkansas Congressman, he did not know what MFN was, he thought it was preferential treatment." Bogdan had to convince him that in spite of the name, most-favored-nation, the term only provided equality of trade opportunity.[76] Since direct talks with Mills produced little, Bogdan enlisted the support of David Abshire, Assistant Secretary for Congressional Relations. He lobbied Mills to support Romanian MFN, but, also without success.[77] Mills wanted Nixon to personally call him requesting support for Romanian MFN. This would sooth his ego and give him a Presidential IOU.[78] However, the President had no intention of calling Mills personally; if IOUs were involved, they would concern significant issues, and Romanian MFN was not a significant issue. Nixon's priorities were with his trip to Beijing and his summit in Moscow, not to mention his own reelection.[79]

In the meantime, the Council of Economic Advisers agreed to meet with Manescu.[80] However, Bogdan wanted the Romanian economist to meet the President.[81] Perhaps through direct conversation, Nixon would agree to call Mills and request that the Mondale-Brooke bill be brought to the House floor for discussion. While Nixon had publicly stated his support for the bill, he did not want to do anything that would interfere with the growing sense of "detente" developing between Washington and Moscow. The President had already interrupted Moscow-Washington relations with his visit to Romania in 1969. He had no intention of doing this again. Detente with the Soviet Union was too important to be jeopardize by overtly supporting MFN to Romania, Moscow's most maverick satellite. However, Bogdan's persistence prevailed and the President agreed to see Manescu on March 21.

On March 18, Ion St. Ion, Ion Stoichici and Manea Manescu, three representatives of the Economic Council of Romania, arrived at Dulles International Airport. Met by Herb Stein, they proceeded to the Embassy Row Hotel in Washington, D.C. to begin their eleven day visit to the United States. Their itinerary included meetings with the Council of Economic Advisers, and representatives from the Treasury, State and

Agriculture Departments, as well as visits to IBM, Manufacturers-Hanover Trust, Standard Oil, Control Data and the Standard Research Institute in San Fransisco.[82] At 4:15 on March 21 Manescu and Bogdan met with Nixon in the Oval Office.[83] While the President gave no indications that he would personally intervene to facilitate Romanian MFN, he did agree to extend OPIC insurance guarantees to Bucharest.[84] He expected that this measure would encourage more businesses to enter into joint ventures with Romania.

Aware that the moment for Romania to secure MFN was quickly passing, Bogdan tried yet another approach. He asked Secretary of State Rogers for assistance. Rogers agreed and on March 22 wrote Mills a note indicating that the Administration "would welcome and support legislation" giving the President the authority to negotiate an MFN agreement with Romania.[85] However, Rogers was not Nixon and Mills refused to move. To make matters worse for Bogdan, on March 23, Peterson notified Flanigan that until the President designed his trade reform legislation, the Commerce Department would not take a position on MFN. Furthermore, conversations with members of the House Ways and Means Committee indicated that Chairman Mills had no inclination to hold hearings on MFN or East-West trade until he received the Administration's package.[86]

By April 1, the opportunity for Romanian MFN had passed. Bogdan prepared to return to Bucharest. But before he left, he was interviewed by Clifford Evans, the Washington Correspondent of RKO General Broadcasting Corporation. The Ambassador told Evans that he hoped that action on Romanian MFN would be "taken very quickly." Romania was "not asking for any hand-out or philanthropy. We are asking for just a mutual advantageous relationship."[87] Several days later, Bogdan landed in Bucharest for a well deserved vacation. The Ambassador could not foresee that it would take three more years before Romania would receive MFN; a three year delay precipitated by Mills' ego and Nixon's preoccupation with detente.

The Administration and Moscow

Without question, superpower relations was the focus of the Nixon Administration during the first six months of 1972. Americans everywhere saw the President walking on the Great Wall of China. Some Americans also understood the significance of the Shanghai Communique released on February 28 which recognized Taiwan as "part" of

China, thereby ending America's "two-China" policy. However, long before the hoopla over China began, the Administration had concentrated its energies on Soviet-American relations and the summit in Moscow. Progress in the Strategic Arms Limitation Talks promoted other Soviet-American negotiations, especially those concerning the sale of grain to the Soviet Union. Unknown to the West, the Soviet Union confronted a disastrous grain failure in 1972. Moscow absolutely needed to purchase massive amounts of grain to avoid widespread famine. In April, Secretary of Agriculture Earl Butz led a trade mission to Moscow, unaware of the degree of the predicted Soviet shortfall.[88] In conversations with Secretary General Brezhnev and Soviet Agricultural Minister Matskevich, Butz learned that the Soviets were interested in a three year agreement to purchase substantial amounts of feed grains and soybeans. When Butz departed on April 12, he left behind the trade mission to continue the grain negotiations. He did not anticipate any agreement prior to the Moscow summit.[89]

On May 20, Richard Nixon arrived at Moscow's Vnukovo Airport. The President hoped that his meeting with Brezhnev would lead to a Soviet- American trade agreement which would include provisions for MFN treatment for Soviet exports.[90] The highpoint of the summit was the signing of the SALT agreement on May 26.[91] While the Summit is remembered for the SALT agreement and the statement of Basic Principles which obligated both sides to do their utmost to avoid military confrontations, there was substantial headway made on commercial issues.[92] Soviet Foreign Trade Minister Patolichev and Commerce Secretary Peterson discussed MFN, credit, and business facilities. At the same time, separate negotiations took place for a bilateral maritime accord, an agreement on grain sales and a solution to Moscow's outstanding Lend Lease obligations from World War II.

By the time the summit ended, both sides agreed to establish a Joint Commercial Commission to negotiate a trade agreement. The United States offered to work out an arrangement so that the Soviets could purchase at least $750 million worth of grain over a three year period. In a note to Kissinger, Peterson indicated that there were only two unresolved issues hindering the resumption of American-Soviet trade: legislation allowing the extension of MFN to the Soviet Union and a Presidential determination of Soviet eligibility for credits.[93]

By far the easier of the two issues was credit eligibility. There was little question as to Soviet ability to pay. Since June 10, 1971, when the White House announced that Moscow no longer needed Department of

Commerce permission to buy wheat, flour and other grains, Moscow had made substantial cash purchases of feed grains from private American companies. Nixon wanted to encourage further sales and on July 8 announced that the Commodity Credit Corporation would supply credit for the Soviets to buy a minimum of $750 million in grain over the next three years.[94] However, unknown to the Administration, Soviet buyers had quietly contracted with the Continental Grain Company on July 5 to supply them 4 million tons of wheat as well as 4.5 million tons of corn. Moscow used cash thereby avoiding unnecessary publicity about the enormity of the purchase. As information leaked out about the size of the sale, the Soviets quickly bought an additional 7.8 million tons of grain from Continental and several other granaries. In one year the Soviets purchased nearly $1 billion worth of grain which represented nearly all of America's stored surplus. As America's grain supply became scarce American food prices soared. Some bakeries were forced to close because of the high price of flour. With the increased food prices, American consumers paid more for the grain than did the Soviets. In essence, American taxpayers subsidized the Soviet purchases at a time when the Soviets would have had to have paid at least world market price or faced catastrophic food shortages.[95] As this fact emerged through the press, it would affect the thinking of a number of Congressmen when they had to consider granting MFN treatment to the Soviet Union.

Meanwhile on Capitol Hill, the House and Senate completed hearings on the extension of the Export Administration Act of 1969 with a section legislatively creating a Council on International Economic Policy. If passed, this would end the informal nature of the CIEP and provide statutory authority for the Council thereby giving greater legitimacy to its undertakings.[96] Discussion focused on the length of the extension and the relationship between the CIEP and Congress. The Administration pressed for an extension to 1975, and wanted the CIEP to have virtually no accountability to the legislature. Congress refused on both points principally because the legislature wanted more influence in foreign policy. Meanwhile the *Washington Post* reported a break in at the Democratic National Committee's headquarters in the Watergate apartment complex on June 17. As the story developed, it appeared to be more than normal campaign shenanigans. The *Washington Post* began to point the finger at some government officials, and while the Oval Office remained above suspicion, the Administration came under attack.[97] Consequently, Congress was able to exert its power and it limited the extension of the Export Administration Act until June 30, 1974. The legislature approved the CIEP and exempted the Executive Director for having to testify before Congress. However, both houses required the CIEP to submit an annual report as a means of keeping Congress informed about America's foreign economic plans.[98] On August 29, Nixon signed the legislation into law.

Bucharest Between Moscow and Washington

Meanwhile in Bucharest, Ceausescu continued his *tous azimuts* foreign policy, but he chose to exercise more restraint than he had in the past. He did not want to repeat the crisis of the previous Summer, for alienation from Moscow could easily result in Romanian isolation. Soviet-American detente reduced the effectiveness of Bucharest's maverick foreign policy in America. As Soviet-American relations improved, Washington became more reluctant to encourage Romania's disruptive ways. Ceausescu also learned that Romania's bid for American MFN was not going as well as expected. One of Ceausescu's top priorities in 1972 was improving Romania's balance of trade. The country was slipping into debt and owed the West substantial money for earlier credit arrangements. One way to remedy the situation would be to expand exports and reduce imports. To implement his new trade program, Ceausescu labelled Romania a "developing country." This identification meant that Romania was eligible for trade preferences with many Western nations including the United States. In addition, as a "developing country" Romania would have greater access to Third World markets, a trading zone Ceausescu had just begun to explore.[99] While his ventures into Africa would bring him into competition with Moscow, his request in March to secure preferential treatment from the EEC was the first such effort made by any Communist country. During the next several months, Ceausescu used the "developing label" wherever it was advantageous.[100]

Ceausescu looked with suspicion upon the Nixon-Brezhnev summit. The Romanian leader feared that Bucharest could become an expendable pawn in Soviet-American relations. Nixon's interest in Beijing-Moscow-Washington diplomacy jeopardized the recent progress Romania had struggled to achieve in her relations with the United States. The Moscow summit eliminated Ceausescu's hope of receiving MFN from Washington in the near future. Wilbur Mills refused White House requests to introduce any MFN legislation for the Soviet Union. He did not want MFN to be "Christmas-treed" to protectionist measures presently under consideration by Congress.[101] If Mills was unwilling to respond to White House pressure for Moscow, the Congressman would certainly be far less responsive to pressure for Romanian MFN.

Aware that Ceausescu was probably disappointed by recent events, Nixon sent Secretary of State Rogers to Bucharest during the first week in July. The President wanted to assure the Romanian leader that American-Soviet relations would not improve at the expense of American-Romanian relations. However, Rogers did tell Ceausescu that there would be no Romanian MFN this year. Mills would not budge on the issue.[102] While in Bucharest, Rogers signed a new Consular Convention replacing the one signed in 1881. This new agreement insured unhindered communication between a citizen and his consul, and facilitated prompt visits to citizens who were detained.[103] In his farewell remarks, Rogers endorsed the long held Romanian position that all countries were equally sovereign and had the right to determine their own affairs without outside interference. Rogers closed with a message from Nixon. The United States placed a "high value" on her relations with Romania and would do "all it could to make those relations prosper" in the future.[104]

Two weeks later, Ceausescu addressed the National Party Conference. He explained that Romania was no longer an underdeveloped country, as she was when she first adopted socialism. Now, she was a "developing country" with the goal of becoming a multilaterally developed socialist state within the next 15 to 20 years.[105] To reach this end, Romania had to improve her export production. The quality of the products had to "become more competitive" and production had to be "permanently adapted to the requirements of the foreign market." Increased exports were absolutely essential for Romania to balance its foreign payments.[106]

Following the Conference, Ceausescu flew to Moscow for the 26th session of the CMEA Council. As in February, when he had attended the Warsaw Pact meeting in Prague, Ceausescu avoided controversy.[107] Following the CMEA meeting, Ceausescu joined the meetings of the Soviet-Romanian Commission on Economic Cooperation. Both sides agreed to begin coordinating their 1976-1980 economic plans much earlier than normal. Ceausescu agreed to invest with other members of CMEA to build a cellulose plant and a metallurgical complex in the Soviet Union. Bucharest and Moscow also agreed to work together to construct an hydroelectric and irrigation plant on the river Pruth, which served as part of their common border.[108]

In August, Ceausescu received more assurance from Washington that Nixon did not intend to scrap Romanian-American relations. During Roger's visit to Bucharest, Ceausescu had asked if America would support Romania's application for membership in the International Monetary Fund, or IMF. The White House told Bogdan that America would not oppose Romania's membership application. However, Washington would not be an advocate, since there were still some monetary issues unresolved between the two countries, especially the issue of defaulted bonds owed to the United States.[109]

During the next two months, Romania applied for membership in the IMF, sent a delegation to tour the United States in exchange for the American Governor's trip the preceding year, and agreed to let the United States Information Agency set up an exhibit at the Bucharest trade fair.[110] However, in spite of these efforts, Ceausescu's worst fears were about to come true. Through no fault of her own, Romania's relations with the United States would be absorbed by the larger issue of Soviet-American relations. Senator Henry "Scoop" Jackson, an outspoken conservative Democrat from the state of Washington, began a battle with the White House that would soon blur the distinction between American-Soviet relations and America's relations with individual satellite states.

Congress and Moscow

The Moscow summit, the SALT treaty and the ensuing trade and commercial negotiations acted as red flags to conservative Congressmen and Senators. No one was more upset by the negotiations than "Scoop" Jackson. The Senator opposed Soviet-American detente, and he would do all he could for the next several years to undermine Nixon's designs. In February, 1972, he had introduced a bill in the Senate to provide financial assistance to Jews who wished to leave the Soviet Union.[111] In May, Jackson's bid for the Democratic presidential nomination came to an abrupt end following poor showings in the Florida, Ohio, and Wisconsin primaries. He soon turned his attention back to Soviet-American relations. During the Summer, Jackson developed his own version of "linkage." Nixon and Kissinger's doctrine of linkage tied Soviet foreign policy to improved American-Soviet relations. Jackson's went a step further. His doctrine of linkage tied improved Soviet-American relations to Soviet internal policies, especially those concerning Jewish emigration.[112] If the Soviets concurred, then conservative Congressmen would drop their opposition to improved relations with the Communist world. If the Soviets refused, then the detested "Era of Detente" would come to an end. Either way, Jackson would be satisfied.

On August 3, the Soviet Union played directly into Jackson's hand. For reasons as yet undetermined, Moscow announced an "exit tax" on all emigrants. Theoretically the tax was to refund the Soviet state for the subsidized educational expenses incurred by the state for the emigrants. In practice, the tax varied widely in amount, and produced a significant reduction in emigration.[113] The Soviet action gave Jackson the opportunity he awaited. Jackson's staff, led by Richard Perle, together with the staff of Senator Ribicoff of Connecticut, led by Morris Amitay, had already designed a "Jackson Amendment" linking Jewish emigration from the Soviet Union to Soviet-American trade. Moscow's August 3 announcement provided a perfect rationale for introducing the proposal.[114]

On September 12, Ribicoff told the press that the Administration should stop trying to grant trade concessions to the Soviet Union if Moscow implemented its "education tax" on Jewish emigrants to Israel. Ribicoff described the fees, which ranged from $5,000 to $25,000, as "a totally reprehensible form of extortion."[115] The Jewish lobby, in the form of the National Council of Soviet Jewry, quickly rallied behind Ribicoff and Jackson. Constituent letters decrying the plight of the Jews in the Soviet Union increased ten fold.[116] In the House on September 22, Charles Vanik of Ohio proposed an amendment to the Foreign Assistance Bill that would deny Eximbank credits and loans to any nation which charged more than $50 for an exit visa. While the amended bill would pass the House on a voice vote, the amendment was later dropped in conference.[117]

On October 4, Jackson sponsored an amendment to Magnuson's East West Trade Relations Act, S. 2620, which would deny MFN treatment and participation in various American credit programs to non-market economy countries which denied their citizens the right to emigrate, or imposed prohibitive taxes on such emigration.[118] Jackson's amendment had 72 cosponsors which even included such long time supporters of East-West trade as Walter Mondale.[119]

The White House did not challenge the amendment. With Presidential elections only a month away, Nixon had no intention of opposing a politically popular movement. Furthermore, he knew that the Jackson amendment would never become law. The Ninety-Second Congress was due to adjourn on October 18, and the adjournment would kill the amendment. However, the overwhelming groundswell of support for the measure prompted the President to discuss the exit tax with the Soviets. Andrei Gromyko indicated that Moscow might lift the tax, but he could not assure the White House that this would occur.[120]

On October 11, the Soviet commercial delegation arrived in Washington to take up the problems left unresolved by the Joint Commercial Commission in July. Three days later, the Soviets and the United States signed a new maritime agreement facilitating grain shipments to Moscow. On October 18, the two countries signed a trade and Lend-Lease agreements. These documents ended a twenty-five year hiatus in normal commercial relations between the two countries. Both accords contained several provisions which required MFN reciprocity for implementation.[121]

In recognition of the signing, President Nixon made a determination that it was in the best interest of the United States to permit the Eximbank to extend credits to the Soviet Union.[122] In return, Moscow announced that exit fees would be waived for a number of emigrating families. Several days later the Soviet Council of Ministers agreed that as a matter of policy, fees would be waived for any "justifiable" reason.[123] However, this decision did not eliminate the possibility of excessive fees for some Jewish emigrants. Consequently, Jackson and his supporters, which now numbered three-fourths of the Senate, prepared to reintroduce their amendment once Congress reconvened on January 3. Congressional debate over linking trade to emigration practices as the *sine qua non* for approving the Soviet-American commercial arrangements totally dwarfed Bucharest's efforts to secure MFN. Bogdan and Ceausescu would work in vain over the next two years to separate Romanian MFN from the larger issue of Soviet-American relations.

Notes

1. Memorandum, Richard Nixon to Secretaries of State, Treasury, Agriculture, Commerce, and Labor; the Director, Office of Management and Budget, the Chairman, Council of Economic Advisers, the Assistant to the President for National Security Affairs, the Executive Director of the Domestic Council, the Special Representative for Trade Negotiations, January 18, 1971, 3 pp., Folder EX F6-11 1/1/71-1/31/71, Box 3 F6-11 (State Dept), Subject Files, WHCF, Nixon Presidential Materials Project.

2. Press Release, The White House, January 19, 1971, 2pp., Folder FECOM 7-2 Press Releases, Box 71, PACEO, WHCF, Nixon Presidential Materials Project.

3. I. M. Destler, *Making Foreign Economic Policy*, p. 138.

4. U. S. Congress, Senate Committee on Finance, Hearings Before the Subcommittee on International Trade, *Foreign Trade*, 92nd Cong., 1st Sess., 1971, p. 7; Legislative Referral Memorandum, March 11, 1971, 4 pp., Folder EX TA Trade March-April 1971, Box 2, (TA) Trade, Subject Files WHCF, Nixon Presidential Materials Project; *Idem.*, Budget Restraints & Export Credit, March 19, 1971, 4pp., Appendix; *Idem*, Export Expansion and Export Promotion, March 26, 1971, 8pp.; *Idem.*, The Multinational Corporation Threat, March 29, 1971, 7pp., 3 Tables.

5. U.S., *Congressional Record*, 92d Cong., 1st Sess., 1971, CXVII, 386-389.

6. [Department of Commerce] *Report of the President on Export Promotion Functions and Potential Export Disincentives*, September 1980, pp. 6.14-6.16; U. S. Congress, House Committee on Foreign Affairs, Hearings Before the Subcommittee on Foreign Economic Policy, *Overseas Private Investment Corporation*, 93rd Cong., 1st Sess., 1973, p. 431.

7. Memorandum, Peter Peterson to the President, February 27, 1971, Folder Joint Committees of Congress, March-Sept 1971, Box 36, EX FG Subject Files, WHCF, Nixon Presidential Materials Project.

8. Nixon, *Memoirs*, p. 497.

9. *DOS Bulletin*, February 8, 1971, p. 186; NSC Correspondence Routing and Control Profile, February 11, 1971, Folder CF CO-125 Rumania, 1971-74, Box 8, Confidential Files 69-74, Subject Files, WHCF, Nixon Presidential Materials Project.

10. Ibid.

11. Kissinger, *White House Years*, p. 704.

12. *DOS Bulletin*, March 22, 1971, p. 357.

13. Verzariu and Burgess, *Joint Venture Agreements in Romania*, p. 34; Petru Buzescu, "Foreign Investments and the Taxation of Foreign Enterprises and Persons in Romania," Law Library, Library of Congress (1986), pp. 4-5.

14. David Granick, *Enterprise Guidance in Eastern Europe: A Comparison of Four Socialist Economies* (Princeton, NJ: Princeton University Press, 1975), p. 79.

15. Academia de Stiinte sociale si politice a Republicii Socialiste Romania, *Eficienta si Crestere Economica* (Bucharest: Editura Academiei Republicii Socialiste Romania, 1972), pp. 362ff.

16. U.S., *Congressional Record*, 92d Cong., 1st Sess., 1971, CXVII, p. 8316

17. *Supra.*, Chap X, n61.

18. Letter, Williams Timmons to Senator Robert Dole, January 23, 1971, Folder EX CO158 USSR 1/1/71-4/30/71, Box 71, CO 158 USSR, Subject Files, WHCF, Nixon Presidential Materials Project.

19. *Facts on File*, January 30, 1971.

20. Memorandum, Henry Kissinger to Arthur Burns, February 27, 1971, Folder Ex CO 125 Romania, Box 63, CO, Subject Files, WHCF, Nixon Presidential Materials Project.

21. Memorandum, Maurice Stans to the President, July 13, 1971, Folder Ex

F621 Dept of Commerce 6/1/71-7/30/71, Box 21, Subject Files 1969-74, WHSF:WHCF, Nixon Presidential Materials Project.

22. *Idem.*, Memorandum, Ernest Johnston to Henry Kissinger, June 2, 1971; Memorandum, Robert C. Brewster to Henry Kissinger, April 14, 1971, Folder Ex FG11 4/1/71-4/30/71, Box 4, F611 (State Dept) Subject Files, WHCF, Nixon Presidential Materials Project.

23. Author's interview of Corneliu Bogdan, April 11, 1987.

24. *Idem.*, March 19, 1987.

25. Memorandum, Ernest Johnston and Helmut Sonnenfeldt to Henry Kissinger, May 17, 1971, Folder Ex Co 125 Romania, Box 63, Co, Subject Files, WHCF, Nixon Presidential Materials Project.

26. *Idem.*, Draft memorandum, Henry Kissinger to the President, [June 1971].

27. Memorandum, Maurice Stans to the President, July 13, 1971, Folder Ex F621 Dept of Commerce 6/1/71-7/30/71, Box 21, Subject Files 1969-74, WHCF, Nixon Presidential Materials Project.

28. Memorandum, Henry Kissinger to Chairman, NSC Under Secretaries Committee, June 10, 1971, Folder Ex Co 125 Romania, Box 63, Co, Subject Files, WHCF, Nixon Presidential Materials Project.

29. Memorandum, William Timmons to Henry Kissinger and Peter Peterson, August 13, 1971, Folder Ex F621 Dept of Commerce, 8/1/71-8/31/71, Box 21, Subject Files 1969-74, WHSF:WHCF, Nixon Presidential Materials Project.

30. Memorandum, William Timmons to Henry Kissinger, June 14, 1971, Folder Ex Co 25 Romania, Box 63, CO, WHCF, Nixon Presidential Materials Project; *Idem.*, Memorandum, Helmut Sonnenfeldt To Henry Kissinger, June 15, 1971; *Idem.*, Memorandum, Henry Kissinger to William Timmons, June 16, 1971.

31. Braun, *Romanian Foreign Policy Since 1965*, p. 26.

32. Memorandum, Henry Kissinger to the President, April 27, 1971, Folder Presidential Memos, 1971, Box 230, SMOF Haldeman, WHSF, Nixon Presidential Materials Project; Kissinger, *White House Years*, 732.

33. *Ibid.*, pp. 707ff.

34. Letter, Richard Nixon to John W. Scott, June 29, 1971, Folder Ex(TA) Trade June 8-29, 1971, Box 3, (TA) Trade, Subject Files, WHCF, Nixon Presidential Materials Project.

35. Memorandum, Robert McLellan to Peter Flanigan, July 13, 1971, 3pp. Folder EX TA 3/CO Exports, Box 17, TA, WHCF, Nixon Presidential Materials Project; *Idem.*, Memorandum, Peter Flanigan to Jim Loken, July 17, 1971; Background of Department of Commerce Shipping Restrictions on Grain to Eastern Europe, July 12, 1969, folder EX TA Exports, Box TA12, TA Trade, Subject Files, WHCF, Nixon Presidential Materials Project.

36. Destler, *Making Foreign Economic Policy*, p. 37.

37. Richard F. Staar (ed.), *Yearbook on International Communist Affairs, 1972* (Stanford, CA: Hoover Institution Press, 1972), p. 69.

38. NYT, April 2, 1971, p. 1; Ceausescu, *Romania On the Way*, V, 884.

39. *Facts on File*, 1971, p. 448.

40. Staar (ed.), *Yearbook on International Communist Affairs*, 1972, p. 73.

41. Braun, *Romanian Foreign Policy Since 1965*, p. 118.

42. Simon, *Cohesion and Dissension in Eastern Europe*, pp. 219-220.

43. Braun, *Romanian Foreign Policy Since 1965*, pp. 133-134.

44. Author interview of Corneliu Bogdan, April 11, 1987. For a consideration of Ceausescu's thought and technique of authoritarianism see, Mary Ellen Fischer, *Nicolae Ceausescu: A Study of Leadership* (Boulder, CO: Lynn Reinner Publishers, 1989).

45. Tismaneanu, "Ceausescu's Socialism," 1985, p. 61.

46. Ceausescu, *Romania On the Way*, VI, 174-177; Fischer, *Ceausescu*, p. 180,

47. Hutchings, *Soviet-East European Relations*, pp. 83ff; *Agerpres*, September 15, 1971, pp. 2-3; Brown, *Eastern Europe and Communist Rule*, pp. 147ff; Franklyn D. Holzman, *The Economics of Soviet Bloc Trade and Finance* (Boulder, CO: Westview Press, 1987), p. 21.Vladimir Sobell, "The Evolution of COMECON Institutions," *The Soviet Union and Eastern Europe* (New York: Facts on File Publications, 1986), p. 417.

48. Hutchings, *Soviet-East European Relations*, p. 99.

49. U. S., *Congressional Record*, 92nd Cong., 1st Sess., 1971, CXVII, 27199.

50. *Congress and the Nation* (Washington, D.C.: Congressional Quarterly Services, 1973), III, 127.

51. Notes, July 27, 1971, Folder JDE notes 4/23/71-8/21/71, Box 11, Ehrlichman Papers, Nixon Presidential Materials Project.

52. Spero, *The Politics of International Economic Relations*, p. 54.

53. *Congress and the Nation, III: 1969-1972* (Washington, D.C.: Congressional Quarterly Services, 1973), p. 128.

54. Memorandum, Maurice Stans to the President, July 13, 1971, Folder EX FG21 Commerce, 6/1/71-7/30/71, Box 21, Subject File 1969-1974, WHSF, Nixon Presidential Materials Project; Memorandum, William J. Mazzocco to Juan J. Gallegos, February 7, 1972, 3pp.,Folder Gen TA3 Exports, March-June 13, 1972, Box 16, TA Trade, Subject Files, WHCF, Nixon Presidential Materials Project.

55. Memorandum, William Timmons to Henry Kissinger and Peter Peterson, August 13, 1971, Folder, Ex CO 125 Rumania, Box 63, CO, Subject Files, WHCF, Nixon Presidential Materials Project.

56. NSC Correspondence Profile, August 30, 1971, Folder Ex F6 6-6; 7/1/71-8/31/71, Box 2, F6 6-6, Subject Files, WHCF, Nixon Presidential Materials Project; Memorandum of Information for the File, Secretary of Commerce to the President, September 7, 1971, Folder Ex F6-21, Dept of Commerce; 9/1/71-9/30/71, Box 21, Subject File, WHSF: WHCF, Nixon Presidential Materials Project; Memorandum, Helmut Sonnenfeldt to Henry Kissinger, September 10, 1971, Folder Ex F6 6-6; 7/1/71-8/31/71, Box 2, F6 6-6, Subject Files, WHCF, Nixon Presidential Materials Project; Memorandum, Dwight L. Chapin to Henry Kissinger, September 14, 1971, Box 8, Confidential

Files 69-74, Subject Files, WHSF: WHCF, Nixon Presidential Materials Project; Memorandum, Henry Kissinger to James R. Schlesinger, October 4, 1971, Folder Ex TA3/CO Exports; CO 100-CO 150 1969-1972, Box 18 Subject Files, Trade, WHCF, Nixon Presidential Materials Project.

57. Legislative Referral Memorandum, November 5, 1971, 15pp., Folder Ex TA Trade; Oct-Nov 1971, Box 3, (TA) Trade, Subject Files, WHCF, Nixon Presidential Materials Project; U. S. Congress, *Congressional Record*, 92d Cong., 1st Sess., CXVII, 34104.

58. *DOS Bulletin*, October 11, 1971, p. 384.

59. Memorandum, Herbert Stein to Henry Kissinger, November 5, 1971, Folder, White House Staff Memos; Henry Kissinger, Box 3, Ezra Solomon Staff Member and Officer Files, WHCF, Nixon Presidential Materials Project.

60. CSM, November 10, 1971, p. 7.

61. CSM, November 15, 1971, p. 8.

62. Ceausescu, *Romania On the Way*, VI, 595, 625.

63. Memoranda of Information for the File, November 22, 1971, Folder Ex Fo 4-2, Box 46, Foreign Affairs FO, Subject files, WHCF, Nixon Presidential Materials Project; Senate Subcommittee on International Finance, *The Export-Import Bank and Export Controls in U.S. International Economic Policy*, 1974, p. 58.

64. *Ibid.*, p. 59.

65. Background Paper, Romania and the GATT, July 10, 1976, 2pp., Folder Rom 6/24/76, Box 315, Seidman, GRF Library.

66. Peter G. Peterson, *The United States in the Changing World Economy*, Vol. I, *A Foreign Economic Perspective* (Washington, D.C.: U.S. Government Printing Office, December 27, 1971), pp. iii, 28, 43.

67. Letter, William Timmons to Warren Magnuson, Abraham Ribicoff, and others, December 20, 1971, Folder Ex TA Trade; December 1-20, 1971, Box 3, (TA) Trade, Subject files, WHCF, Nixon Presidential Materials Project.

68. Memorandum of Information for the File, January 17, 1972, Folder Ex F621 Dept of Commerce; 1/1/72-1/31/72, Box 21, Subject file 1969-1974, WHSF, Nixon Presidential Materials Project.

69. Memorandum, Maurice Stans to the President, January 17, 1972, 4pp., Folder Ex F6 21 Dept of Commerce; 1/1/72-1/31/72, box 21, Subject Files 1969-1974, WHSF: WHCF, Nixon Presidential Materials Project.

70. *Idem.*, Memorandum, Alexander Butterfield to the President, January 27, 1972, 2pp.

71. Notes, February 19. 1971, Folder JDE Notes 1/5/71-9/21/71, Box 11, Ehrlichman Papers, Nixon Presidential Materials Project.

72. U. S. Congress, *Congressional Record*, 92d Cong., 2d Sess., CXVIII, 20602.

73. Council Meeting Scenaria, n.d., 6pp., Folder U.S.-U.S.S.R. Trade; April 1970-March 1972, Box 12, Flanigan Papers, Nixon Presidential Materials Project.

74. John E. Jelacic, *Impact of Granting Most Favored Nation Treatment to the Countries of Eastern Europe and the People's Republic of China.* Staff Research Studies, No. 6 (Washington, D.C.: United States Tariff Commission, 1974) pp. 25-28.

75. Memorandum, Herbert Stein to Henry Kissinger, January 4, 1972, Folder, White House Staff Memos; Henry Kissinger, Box 3, Ezra Solomon Staff Member and Officer Files, WHCF, Nixon Presidential Materials Project.

76. Author interview of Corneliu Bogdan, March 19, 1987.

77. Author interview of Corneliu Bogdan, April 11, 1987

78. *Ibid.*; According to Herb Stein, another reason that Mills hesitated to support MFN for Romania was his intention to run for the presidency in 1972, and his conviction, no doubt well grounded, that advocating MFN for a Communist country would get him little popular approval and win him few votes. (Author interview of Herbert Stein, November 20, 1987).

79. Author interview of Corneliu Bogdan, April 11, 1987.

80. Memorandum, Peter Flanigan to Herbert Stein, March 1, 1972, Folder Ex CO 125 Romania, Box 63, CO, Subject Files, WHCF, Nixon Presidential Materials Project.

81. Memorandum, Herbert Stein to David Parker, March 1, 1972, 2pp., Folder CF CO 125 Romania 69-70, Box 8, Confidential Files 69-74, Subject Files, WHSP:WHCF, Nixon Presidential Materials Project.

82. Itinerary, March 17, 1972, 5pp., Folder Romania Visit, Mar 20-21, 1972, Box 16, Marina Whitman,SMOF, WHCF, Nixon Presidential Materials Project.

83. Memorandum, Jeanne W. Davis to Steve Bull, March 21, 1972, Folder Ex F6 6-6; 1/1/72-2/29/72, Box 3, F6 6-6 NSC, Subject Files, WHCF, Nixon Presidential Materials Project.

84. Letter, Ronald Ziegler to George W. Stamm, April 7, 1972, Folder (Gen) CO 1-4 Communist Bloc 1/1/71-, Box 5, CO, Subject Categories, WHCF, Nixon Presidential Materials Project; WSJ, March 22, 1972, p. 3.

85. *DOS Bulletin*, April 10, 1972, p. 552.

86. Abstract of Secretarial Correspondence, Peter Peterson to Peter Flanigan, March 23, 1972, Folder Ex TA Trade; February-March 1972, Box 4, TA Trade, Subject Files, WHCF, Nixon Presidential Materials Project.

87. Transcript, Oral interview of Corneliu Bogdan by Clifford Evans, April 6 and 7, 1972, 9pp., Folder Gen CO Romania 1/1/71, box 64, CO, Subject Files, WHCF, Nixon Presidential Materials Project.

88. Funigiello, *American-Soviet Trade in the Cold War*, p. 184.

89. Transcript, Press Conference, Earl Butz to Henry Kissinger, April 17, 1972, 12pp., Folder U.S.-U.S.S.R. Trade April 1970-March 1972.

90. Possible Scenario for Development of US-USSR Economic Relations, n.d., 8pp., Folder U.S.-U.S.S.R. Trade; April 1970-March 1972, Box 12, Flanigan Papers, Nixon Presidential Materials Project.

91. On this event see, Nixon, *Memoirs*, pp. 609ff.

92. See, Gaddis, *Strategies of Containment*, pp. 318ff.

93. Memorandum, Peter Peterson to Henry Kissinger, May 17, 1972, 6pp., Folder CO 158 5/16/72-5/31/72, Box 72, CO, Subject Files, WHCF, Nixon Presidential Materials Project.

94. Destler, *Making Foreign Economic Policy*, pp. 38-40; Funigiello, *American-Soviet Trade in the Cold War*, p. 184. The CCC began in 1948.

95. *Ibid.*, Destler, *Making Foreign Economic Policy*, pp. 40-41; Henry Kissinger, *Years of Upheaval* (Boston: Little, Brown and Company, 1982), p. 247.

96. U. S. Congress, House Committee on Banking and Currency, Hearing Before the Subcommittee on International Trade, *Extension of the Export Administration Act of 1969*, 92nd Cong., 2d Sess., 1972, p.3; U. S. Congress, Hearing Before the Senate Committee on Foreign Relations, Export Administration Act Amendments, 92nd Cong., 2d Sess., 1972, pp. 1-6.

97. For an extended account see, Carl Bernstein and Bob Woodward, *All the President's Men* (New York: Simon and Schuster, 1974).

98. Memorandum, Peter Flanigan to Wilfred Rommel, August 22, 1972, Folder Ex TA Exports TS August 1-22, 1972, box 14, Trade, WHCF, Nixon Presidential Materials Project; *The Battle Act Report 1972; Twenty-Fifth Report to Congress* (Washington, D.C.: U.S. Government Printing Office, 1972), p. 21.

99. Christopher Coker, "Adventurism and Pragmatism: The Soviet Union, Comecon, and Relations with African States," *International Affairs*, Vol. 57, No. 4 (Autumn 1981), pp. 613-633; Colin Lawson, "The Soviet Union and Eastern Europe in Southern Africa: Is There a Conflict of Interest," *International Affairs*, Vol. 59, No. 1 (Winter 1982/1983), pp. 32-40.

100. One of the more important places where he made this pronouncement was at Santiago, Chile, where he was among the delegates gathered for the Third UNCTAD Conference in April and May 1972 (Edgar Rafael, *Entwicklungsland Rumaenien* [Munich: R. Oldenbourg, 1977], p. 54).

101. Memorandum, Peter Flanigan to the President, May 19, 1972, Folder Ex TA Trade; May-June 1972, Box 4, TA Trade, Subject Files, WHCF, Nixon Presidential Materials Project.

102. Memorandum, Larry Brady to Bob McDermott, July 10, 1972, Folder ExCo 125 Romania 1/1/71, Box 63, CO, Subject Files, WHCF, Nixon Presidential Materials Project.

103. *DOS Bulletin*, October 16, 1972, p. 449; Letter, Department of State to the President, September 6, 1972, 4pp., Folder ExCo 125 Romania 1/1/73, Box 64, CO, Subject Files, WHCF, Nixon Presidential Materials Project.

104. *DOS Bulletin*, August 7, 1972, p. 168.

105. Ceausescu, *Romania On the Way*, VII, 423ff,

106. Nicolae Ceausescu, *Report Presented at the National Conference of the R.C. P. , July 19, 1972* (Bucharest: Meridiane Publishing House, 1972), pp. 13ff; See, *Societatea socialista multilateral dezvoltata. Documente ala Partidului Communist Roman* (Bucharest: Editura politica. 1972).

107. Hutchings, *Soviet-East European Relations*, pp. 172-173.

108. Richard F. Staar (ED.), *Yearbook on International Communist Affairs*,

1973 (Stanford, CA: Hoover Institution Press, 1973), pp. 65-66.

109. Memorandum, Richard D. Erb to Peter Flanigan, July 26, 1972, Folder Ex CO 125 Romania; 1/1/71, Box 63, CO, Subject Files, WHCF, Nixon Presidential Materials Project. The bonds in question were those issued during the 1920s and which were defaulted several years later. Now, Ceausescu agreed that Romania would negotiate a settlement with the American bondholders before the close of 1976 (U.S. Congress, House Committee on Ways and Means, Hearings Before the Subcommittee on Trade, *United States-Romanian Trade Agreement*, 94th Cong., 1st Sess., 1975, pp. 46-49, hereafter, House Subcommittee on Trade, *Romanian Trade Agreement*, 1975).

110. WSJ, September 22, 1972, p. 16; *DOS Bulletin*, September 25, 1972, p. 342; Memorandum, Jeanne W. Davis to Henry Loomis, April 26, 1972, Folder Ex F6 6-6 3/1/72-4/31/72, Box 3, FG 6-6 NSC, Subject Files, WHCF, Nixon Presidential Materials Project.

111. Letter, Henry M. Jackson to the President, February 6, 1972, Folder Ex CO 158; 2/1/72-2/29/72, Box 71, CO, Subject Files, WHCF, Nixon Presidential Materials Project.

112. Paula Stern, *Water's Edge: Domestic Politics and the Making of American Foreign Policy* (Westport, CT: Greenwood Press, 1979), p. 28.

113. Kissinger, *Years of Upheaval*, p. 250.

114. Stern, *Water's Edge*, p. 23.

115. See, Correspondence Profile, Peter Peterson to Henry Kissinger, September 13, 1972, Folder Ex CO 158; 9/1/72-9/30/72, Box 73, CO, Subject Files, WHCF, Nixon Presidential Materials Project.

116. Folder CO 158; 3/1/72-3/30/72, Box 72, CO 158-USSR, Subject file, WHCF, Nixon Presidential Materials Project; Memorandum, Roland L. Elliott to Jeanne Davis, September 25, 1972, Folder Ex CO 158; 9/1/72-9/30/72, Box 73, CO, Subject Files, WHCF, Nixon Presidential Materials Project.

117. Funigiello, *American-Soviet Trade in the Cold War*, p. 184.

118. U.S., *Congressional Record*, 92d Cong., 2d Sess., 1972, CXVII, 33660.

119. *Ibid.*, p. 33664; Stern, *Water's Edge*, p. 34; Vladimir M. Pregelj, "Most-Favored-Nation Policy Toward Communist Countries: Updated June 30, 1987," Economic Division, Congressional Research Service , p. 5.

120. Stern *Water's Edge*, p. 44.

121. See texts of agreements, Folder EX TA; October 1972, Box 5, TA Trade, Subject Files, WHCF, Nixon Presidential Materials Project.

122. *Idem.*, Presidential Determination, October 18, 1972.

123. Pregelj, "Most-Favored-Nation Policy Toward Communist Countries," 1987, p. 5.

CHAPTER XII

LINKAGE GONE AWRY: THE JACKSON-VANIK AMENDMENT

Romania's Omnidirectional Foreign Policy

The fanfare accompanying the Soviet trade agreement along with the Administration's announcement in late October, that the war in Vietnam would end within days,[1] completely suppressed the impact of the Senate's "preliminary inquiry" into the Watergate affair.[2] Consequently, on November 7, millions of Americans went to the polls and gave Richard Nixon 60.8% of the vote, the second largest plurality ever achieved by a Presidential candidate. Nixon's reelection meant that America would continue to forge a multipolar foreign policy designed by Nixon and implemented by Kissinger.

The President's first concern following his reelection was Vietnam.[3] The war did not end as promised by the Adminstration, and critics were quick to suggest that the announcement was made solely for reelection purposes. While there was some truth to this criticism, the intent of the announcement was sincere. Kissinger and Le Duc Tho, who represented North Vietnam, thought they had ended their three year talks with resolutions to all of the substantive issues. Both men failed to see that Nguyen Van Thieu, the head of South Vietnam, would not accept an American-North Vietnam solution to a problem involving South Vietnam. On November 20, Thieu presented 69 objections to the settlement.[4] The Kissinger-Le Duc Tho talks collapsed on December

13, and five days later Nixon ordered "Operation Linebacker II," the resumption of heavy bombing in North Vietnam.[5]

The strategy worked and on January 2, 1973, talks resumed in Paris. The breakthrough came on January 9 when Kissinger and Le Duc Tho again reached agreement. Kissinger feared President Thieu's reactions but Nixon was determined to prevail. He told Kissinger, "brutality is nothing. You have never seen it if this son-of-a-bitch doesn't go along, believe me."[6] Reluctantly, Thieu accepted the agreement and on January 27, Nixon signed a peace agreement ending the Vietnam War. On March 29, North Vietnam released American POWs and the United States began to withdraw its troops from Vietnam.

In addition to Vietnam, the President intended to recommend East-West trade legislation in 1973.[7] Few people were happier with this decision than Bogdan and Ceausescu. While Congress's adjournment had killed the Mondale-Brooks and Findley legislation, Bucharest anticipated that the MFN bills would be reintroduced early in the next legislative session. To make trade with Romania more appealing to the West, Ceausescu's government passed two decrees on November 2. Decree No. 424 permitted the formation of joint companies in Romania especially in the fields of industry, agriculture, construction, tourism, transportation, and technology.[8] Decree No. 425 dealt with the tax on profits of joint companies, and had provisions for tax exemptions during early years of development.[9] On November 20, Ceausescu told the delegates at the Central Committee Plenum, that Romania's 1973 economic plans called for a 21.5% increase in foreign trade over 1972.[10]

As Romania prepared for increased trade with the West, the CIEP wrestled with the question of how to package the Communist country trade bill. Should it be separate from a comprehensive trade act, or should the issues of MFN for Romania and the Soviet Union be combined within a single legislative proposal.[11] While the CIEP debated, Wilbur Mills made a decision. He told the Administration on November 21 that if the President so requested, he would be "agreeable to give top priority to trade legislation." However, he believed that MFN for the Soviet Union and Romania had to be part of the trade legislation, not separate.[12]

Meanwhile, American-Romanian relations continued to grow. On December 2, Washington sent the "Educational Technology–USA" exhibit to Cluj, where in sixteen days it was seen by some 70,000 Romanians.[13] On December 15, Romania became the first Bloc nation to join the International Monetary Fund and the International Bank for

Reconstruction and Development, or World Bank. Membership in the IMF automatically exempted Romania from the American sanctions imposed by the amended Johnson Debt Default Act of 1934. The original legislation prohibited loans to any country which owed the United States money, including World War I debts. The amendment exempted all member nations of the IMF.[14] On the same day, the United States and Romania signed a two year accord providing for exchanges and cooperation in the areas of education, culture, science and technology through 1974. The new agreement was the most comprehensive since the beginning of the exchange program in 1960 and included provisions for government, social, professional and civic exchanges between the two countries.[15] One institution which especially profited by the increased cordiality between the United States and Romania was the American Library in Bucharest. By the end of its first year, in December, 1972, more than 4,000 people had visited the facility. The library had 7,000 books, 180 maps and three daily newspapers, the *New York Times*, the *Washington Star-News*, and the *Christian Science Monitor*. Especially important was the fact that the library operated outside the grounds of the American Embassy, the only such facility in the Soviet Bloc.[16]

Romania's *tous azimuts* foreign policy continued. As she increased her dealings with the United States, including $1.6 million of Eximbank credits, Romania also worked to improve relations with the Soviet Union. In December, 1972, Ceausescu visited Moscow to celebrate the 50th anniversary of the creation of the USSR. In private talks with Brezhnev he reassured the Soviet leader that Romania would continue to provide economic support for the joint projects agreed to in July.[17] However, this rapprochement did nothing to alter Romania's recently passed Defense Law, which called for a "War of the Entire People" in the event of foreign attack. The Soviet invasion of Czechoslovakia had left its impact in the Balkans. Both Yugoslavia and Romania modernized their territorial defense systems which called upon the populace to participate in disobedience, sabotage, demonstrations, strikes and espionage against any country which tried to occupy the homeland.[18]

The Trade Reform Bill of 1973

In Washington, 1973 began with resumed Vietnam negotiations, the appointment of Senator Sam Ervin of North Carolina to head a Senate Investigating Committee on Watergate, and new legislative proposals to link trade to emigration. On January 3, Representative Dominick Daniels of New Jersey introduced H.R. 151, an "Act for Freedom of Emigration in East West Trade."[19] The bill was similar to the October Jackson bill, and was precipitated by Moscow's refusal to eliminate the education tax.

On December 26, *Novosti*, a Soviet press agency, interviewed Soviet Deputy Minister of Internal Affairs, Boris Shumilin on the issue of the education tax. He explained that the tax applied to all citizens, regardless of nationality. The Soviet state did "not intend to act as a philanthropist toward persons leaving for capitalist countries on whose education the State had spent considerable sums." Shumilin noted that the elderly and handicapped would be exempted from paying the fee, and there would be a decreasing percentage required of all emigrants depending on their years of work. If a man had worked 25 years, he would only have to pay 25% of the tax. If he worked 8 years, he would have to pay 75% of the tax.[20] On the following day, the Soviet government published the decree of the Presidium of the Supreme Soviet concerning the education tax, implicity indicating that it had no intention of eliminating it. The boldness of the Soviet move infuriated conservative Congressmen as well as the American Jewish community. The American Israel Public Affairs Committee called upon Jewish leaders across the country to support a new Jackson amendment.[21]

Meanwhile on January 3, Mills told the Administration that he was still firm on his position that MFN to Communist countries should be part of the trade bill. He believed that the trade legislation would be the "hardest piece" of legislation to pass that would come before the House Ways and Means Committee throughout 1973. But, he did believe that a bill would emerge after about six weeks of hearings.[22]

Secure that Mills would support a trade bill, the Administration intensified its work to develop a comprehensive package. Unlike Mills, the Administration still had not decided whether or not to include Communist MFN in the legislation, to include it for all Communist countries, or to include it for all but the Soviet Union and leave Moscow a separate issue. By January 8, all agencies with the exception of the Commerce Department agreed to include MFN treatment for all Communist countries as part of the Comprehensive Trade Bill. Commerce, which viewed trade from an economic rather than a political viewpoint, feared that the trade-emigration linkage issue could kill MFN for all Communist countries, not just the Soviet Union.[23] By January 17, the CIEP had drafted a Trade Reform Bill of 1973 which would increase the President's power to provide flexibility for either bold liberalizations or necessary restrictions. The authority suggested would enable the President to implement a system of temporary generalized preferences for developing countries, provide for bilateral and multilateral negotiations with traditional trading partners, and make MFN trade agreements with Communist countries.[24]

With the Administration's decision to include MFN for all Communist countries, Bogdan and several Congressmen stepped up their efforts to keep Romanian MFN a separate entity. On January 18, Findley introduced the Romanian Trade Relations Act of 1973 with seven cosponsors, all from the House Ways and Means Committee. The bill, H.R. 2304, contained no language linking trade to emigration or human rights.[25] However, the bill never reached the floor of the House. According to Bogdan, Nixon's decision to look for "global solutions," ended the Romanian "differentiation." In spite of Nixon's personal feelings toward Romania, Bucharest was simply one more Communist country from the viewpoint of the new trade legislation. Bogdan later believed that if Romania had "spent more money to lobby Congress, they could have received MFN."[26]

Meanwhile, the trade-emigration forces continued to grow. On January 23, Senator Jacob Javits of New York held a press conference indicating that the Jackson amendment would be reintroduced in Congress.[27] In the House, Vanik rounded up a majority of the Ways and Means Committee members as cosponsors of a Jackson-Vanik amendment, but without Chairman Mills' endorsement. On February 5, Vanik asked Mills to take charge of the Jackson-Vanik amendment. On the sixth, Mills agreed and on the following day, he introduced H.R. 3910. The bill prohibited MFN treatment and commercial and guarantee agreements with any non-market economy country which denied its citizens the right to emigrate, or which imposed more than nominal fees upon its citizens as a condition to emigrate.[28]

Although the Mills-Vanik bill was independent of any Administration trade package, the handwriting was on the wall. Congress planned to link the issue of emigration to any White House trade bill granting MFN to the Soviet Union. One question that confronted the Administration was who should do the linking, Congress or the President.[29] Nixon wanted to make sure that the White House retained control of the legislation. He recognized that the CIEP had failed to take charge of America's foreign economic policy. Consequently, he appointed the new Secretary of the Treasury, George Shultz, as "super-counsellor" for all economic policy, including international economic policy.[30] Within a few weeks, the President made Shultz America's chief representative to the United States-USSR Joint Commercial Commission, and placed him in charge of the newly formed East-West Trade Policy Committee. Shultz was the "economic Czar," in charge of all aspects of America's foreign economic policy, including Congressional legislation. Under Shultz was Peter Flanigan, who still chaired the CIEP, and Frederick Dent, who had replaced Pete Peterson as Commerce Secretary.[31]

Meanwhile the President met with the AFL-CIO executive council in Bal Harbour, Florida. Labor opposed trading with the Communists, and especially opposed giving Communist made products MFN treatment. The wage scales of American workers prohibited their products from competing favorably against cheaply produced products from the Communist Bloc. Nixon tried to calm labor's fears noting that the trade bill would contain restrictive and, if necessary, retaliatory provisions to protect American labor from unfair foreign competition. After the meeting, Shultz and Meany played golf and the Treasury Secretary promised to keep the AFL-CIO leader informed of the Administration's thinking on the trade bill.[32]

On March 15, Senator Jackson introduced an amendment to an East-West Trade Relations Bill tying the rate of Jewish emigration to the awarding of MFN treatment for Soviet products. His amendment had 73 cosponsors and essentially challenged the Administration to force the Soviets to eliminate their excessive emigration taxes.[33] Jackson told Flanigan that he fully intended to tie his amendment to the trade bill. He was fed up with the Soviets. Some time ago he had sent a letter to Ambassador Dobrynin which called for a reply. But, to date he had received nothing. Flanigan immediately told Sonnenfeldt to have Dobrynin reply to Jackson, "given Jackson's importance in this problem."[34]

Anticipating Jackson's amendment, Nixon sent Shultz to Moscow to see Brezhnev. While no documents are available on their talks, Shultz apparently convinced the Soviets that unless they lifted their tax on exit visas, Congress would never pass their bilateral trade agreement of October, 1972. On March 22, Moscow informed the White House that they would soon resolve the tax issue.[35]

Meanwhile, in an effort to win Wilbur Mills' support for the Administration trade bill, Peter Flanigan visited the Congressman at his home in Arkansas in February. After several hours of discussion, Flanigan realized that the key to Mills' support was a personal phone call from the President requesting the Congressman's help.[36] By early March, Mills had not heard from the President and he began to waffle on some of his earlier promises to the Administration. He told Shultz and the *New York Times* that he would take up trade legislation only in an emergency. Tax reform legislation was now his primary concern.[37] On March 15, Flanigan again saw Mills, and asked him about the timing of the Trade Bill and the extension of MFN to the Soviet Union. Mills remained steadfast. If the President called him, he would be happy to set up trade hearings around April 30, right after Congress returned from its recess.

The issue of MFN was more complicated. Mills was concerned about the Soviet tax on exit visas. Flanigan tried to deflect the issue. He urged the Ways and Means Chairman to accept legislation introduced by Jacob Javits, which would give the President the right to grant MFN to countries behind the Iron Curtain, subject to Congressional veto. This process would remove the issue of Soviet MFN from the trade bill and buy time to negotiate the emigration tax with Moscow. Mills objected. He did not want to grant Congress veto power since it violated the Constitutional right of the Executive to act. Further discussion proved uneventful, and Flanigan and Mills agreed to see what actions the Soviets would take concerning the exit visa tax.[38]

On March 17 the President personally asked Mills to move from taxes to trade. Mills agreed and promised to begin hearings on the trade package on May 1.[39] On March 19, Nixon appointed the Special Trade Representative, Ambassador William Pearce, to manage the Administration's trade bill through Congress. Pearce would report to Flanigan who reported to Shultz.[40] Two days later, Mills told Congress that Nixon would be asking for more trade and tariff authority than given any other President, but it was "essential if we are to move forward."[41]

On March 30, Dobrynin gave Kissinger a note labeled "confidential for the President." It stated that Moscow's emigration policy was solely and exclusively a Soviet issue. However, the note indicated that the tax would be lifted. The tax had intended to be discretionary, and it would be applied only in "unusual" circumstances of state security. This was just the news that Jackson needed to hear. But, Dobrynin would not give Kissinger or Nixon the right to communicate this information to Congress.[42] Moscow did not want her reconsideration of the tax issue viewed as a sign of weakness by the American press, an outcome which would surely follow were Congressmen told of the decision.

The secretness of the communication tied the Administration's hands. Further, Dobrynin's involvement brought Kissinger into the trade bill. He and the President saw the trade bill with its MFN provisions as issues of foreign rather than domestic policy.[43] Consequently, Flanigan recommended to Kissinger on April 2 that the President's trade package include the Javits formula giving either house of Congress three months to veto a Presidential grant of MFN to a Communist country. Flanigan was aware of Dobrynin's note, but realized that there was no time to alter the attitude of the Jewish leaders in Congress. If nothing else, this approach would enable the President to "meet his personal commitment to Brezhnev" to secure a Soviet trade agreement including MFN, and it would "protect detente."[44] Kissinger agreed and on April 6, Flanigan again asked Mills to support the Javits formula. Mills said he "understood," and would support the bill the "way the President wants it." Several hours later the bill went to press for release on April 10.[45]

Romanian MFN

Meanwhile Bogdan continued to work for Romanian MFN. He had succeeded in establishing contacts with even the most conservative Congressmen, but not with the AFL-CIO.[46] The union became his main opposition and wanted to keep Romanian exports at a discriminatory rate. The difference between MFN and non-MFN rates had continued to increase. By 1973, for example, non-MFN tariff on footwear was 20%, the MFN tariff was 5%; on woven woolen fabrics, the non-MFN tariff was 75%, the MFN tariff was 15%; the non-MFN tariff on ball bearings, generators and switchgear was 35%, while the MFN tariff was less than 9% on each item.[47] Bogdan's efforts received support from David Rockefeller, Walter Mondale, and Edward Brooke. Rockefeller reported to the *New York Times* in late February that he thoroughly enjoyed his recent tour to Bucharest, and noted that Romania was ready for trade and credits.[48] Four days later, Senators Mondale and Brooke cosponsored a new bill, S. 1085, authorizing the President to negotiate a commercial agreement extending MFN treatment to Romania. Similar to Findley's bill in the House, the Mondale-Brooke bill contained no language linking trade to emigration or human rights.[49]

In spite of these proposals, Bogdan knew that Romanian MFN legislation had little chance of passage. Consequently, he tried a new approach. He asked to meet with Kissinger to discuss a long-term trade agreement.[50] Known as LTAs, these bilateral accords provided a set of regulatory provisions on trade, and a legal framework for continuing negotiations and consultations on problems which arose between the two countries. Western businessmen liked LTAs because the agreements indicated that both countries were committed to closer commercial relations, and the accords provided legal protection for doing business with state-trading monopolies in Communist countries. To centrally planned economies, LTAs fit well into their five year plans, frequently coinciding with them, and supported the East European system of centralized control over commercial relations with foreign enterprises. All in all, the LTAs met the needs of both partners in East-West trade.[51] While Bogdan and Kissinger did meet, there are no minutes available. However, since Romania and the United States would not sign an LTA until 1976, Kissinger apparently told the Ambassador that a separate Romanian agreement was inappropriate at this time.

Meanwhile, Senator Mondale's interest in supporting Romanian MFN had some tangible results for his Minnesota constituents, especially those at Control Data Corporation. Since 1968 the computer firm had tried to market its products in Romania. However, the company was unable to secure export licenses for computer equipment from the Commerce Department. As the climate of opinion toward East-West trade improved, Control Data resumed discussions with Romania over a variety of projects including turn-key plants and joint ventures. The talks continued over the next two years. Technical teams exchanged visits between Control Data and Bucharest. Finally, the Commerce Department indicated that it was willing to approve export licenses for the required technology. On April 4, 1973, representatives from Control Data and the Romanian Machine Building Ministry signed a joint venture agreement in Bucharest.[52] Ceausescu approved the new organization, called RomControl Data, in July, 1973, and six months later the United States followed suit. The purpose of the joint venture was to build and equip a factory for the production of peripheral computer and data processing equipment, and to manufacture and market computer hardware. Production began in October, 1974.[53]

On April 5, Romania signed an agreement with another American firm. After nearly 18 months of negotiations, General Tire agreed to build a $75 million radial tire factory in Floresti, Romania. This was not a joint venture, but the negotiations were nearly as complicated as those with Control Data. The Romanians insisted on penalty clauses. If the plant did not "work," they would not pay for the construction. Further, Bucharest insisted the plant be equipped with state-of-the-art technology, a concept which proved difficult to implement because of the time delay between signing an agreement and completing construction. In the interim, "state-of-the-art" technology frequently changed. Finally, after numerous visits by Romanian experts to the General Tire headquarters in Akron, the negotiations closed on a successful note.[54]

The Jackson Amendment

On April 2, 1973, John Dean began to testify before Sam Ervin's Senate Investigating Committee on Watergate. Eight days later, the President sent his trade reform package to Congress. The proposal increased Presidential authority to negotiate changes in tariff and non-tariff barriers, to provide relief and assistance to import-impacted industries and workers, to establish a generalized system of tariff preferences for developing countries, and, to extend most-favored-nation treatment to Communist countries. On this latter point, the President specifically noted that such authority would permit him to implement the trade agreement with the Soviet Union and it "would also enable us to fulfill our commitment to Romania."[55]

The same day the President sent his 124 page trade bill to Congress, Senator Jackson and 76 cosponsors introduced an amendment to the legislation prohibiting the award of MFN treatment to any nonmarket country that restricted emigration.[56] The Administration moved quickly. Kissinger spoke with Dobrynin asking for Soviet permission to inform Congress that Moscow only intended to deny emigration "for reasons of state security," and that the Soviet Union would only collect "normal and insignificant duties" from those approved for emigration.[57] Dobrynin agreed to the release on April 16. He was undoubtedly instructed to do so by Brezhnev who expected to announce to the Central Committee on April 26 that he wanted their approval to expand relations with the West.[58] On April 18, Nixon called several Congressional leaders, including Senator Jackson, to the White House to inform them of the Soviet note.

In better days this meeting would have decoupled MFN from emigration. However, Dean's recent testimony at the Watergate hearings implicated most of the Presidents advisers including Robert Haldeman, his Chief of Staff, John Ehrlichman, his domestic adviser and John Mitchell, the Attorney General. Congress saw an opportunity to take advantage of a stricken Executive. Jackson would not be placated by the Soviet promise to suspend the education tax. He wanted more. Moscow had to guarantee a minimum number of annual exit visas, and ease emigration restrictions for all nationalities.[59]

The Trade Reform Bill and the Jackson Amendment effectively ended Romania's independent bid for MFN. Trade terms for Bucharest were the same as those for Moscow. However, Romania was not threatened by the trade and emigration linkage. Bucharest permitted Jews to emigrate. In fact, the government's policy upset Romania's Chief Rabbi, Rabbi Rosen. He was opposed to Jewish emigration. According to Harry Barnes, the American Ambassador to Romania, Rosen saw a "paradox." "The Jewish culture was in serious danger of disappearing in proportion to emigration."[60] Consequently, Romania had to wait on the sidelines for the legislation to pass, before it could apply for MFN consideration. Neither the Findley and Mondale-Brooks proposals nor the persistent efforts of Bogdan could separate Romania from the ensuing eighteen month Congressional debate. A debate which focused primarily on Moscow's eligibility for MFN, but implicitly included all other Communist countries.

Jackson's amendment infuriated Nixon. Upon learning of it, he confided to Ehrlichman that Jackson's supporters were "professional Jews. . . . I'm not a professional Quaker and they hate me for it." Nixon wanted to deal with the Soviets through "quiet diplomacy," and he was aware that Moscow could not permit the wholesale emigration of all Russian minorities without their having "to change their system." He also feared that Jackson's position could "jeopardize disarmament possibilities" with the Soviets.[61]

While Jackson and Vanik had support from a majority of Congressmen, the AFL-CIO, and some of the Jewish community, they no longer had the unqualified support of Wilbur Mills. Mills was impressed by the Soviet note. Moscow had delivered on its end of the bargain, and on April 19 the Ways and Means chairman told the *Washington Post* that he supported the President's request to grant MFN to the Soviet Union.[62] While Mills would later waffle on the issue, the Administration saw his support as sufficient to guarantee passage of the trade package. With Mills's backing the House would pass the requested MFN authority, and even if this provision were rejected by the Senate, Mills was "convinced that the conference committee on the trade bill would restore" MFN. That being the case, the Adminstration saw little need to cooperate or compromise with the anti-MFN Congressmen. The Administration's strategy assumed that "Mills' attitude on MFN is far more important from a legislative standpoint than Jackson, Ribicoff and Javits combined."[63]

On April 29, Ehrlichman and Haldeman resigned their White House posts in the wake of John Dean's testimony. Two weeks later, on May 9, the House Ways and Means Committee began hearings on the Trade Reform Act of 1973 with its Jackson-Vanik language. The provisions prohibited MFN treatment to any nonmarket economy country which denied its citizens the right to emigration, or which imposed more than nominal fees as a condition to emigration. The Administration presented its testimony at the outset of the hearings in support of the bill including granting the President MFN authority, without the restrictions called for in the Jackson-Vanik amendment.[64] As the hearings continued into June, a number of witnesses appeared representing special interests. Several of them spoke specifically in support of granting Romanian products MFN treatment. Foremost among them were the National Confederation of American Ethnic Groups, the League of Free Romanians, the Sculptured Tubing Company of Chicago, and the BAP Distributing Company, an importer of children's furniture from Romania.[65]

The hearings ended on Friday, June 15, and on the next Monday, the Ways and Means Committee moved to deliberate the bill's substance. The markup would take four months, but two weeks after the process began, Wilbur Mills was hospitalized and did not return to resume the Chairmanship until early November. His absence was particularly significant because many members of the Ways and Means Committee depended on Mills' expertise in trade matters to direct their thinking.[66]

On July 24, Nixon met with Mills in the Oval Office. In spite of earlier agreement, the Chairman had not supported the Javits formula permitting Congress to veto a Presidential award of MFN to a nonmarket country. Mills was still opposed to giving Congress veto power over a Presidential determination. Nixon suggested an alternative. If he awarded a country MFN and it subsequently imposed new exit fees, he would withdraw the MFN. He explained that the Administration would publicly oppose this proposal, but would privately "urge our friends to support it." If this strategy failed, Nixon wanted Mills to consider separating the entire issue of MFN to non-market economies, known initially as Title V of the bill, from the remainder of the trade legislation.[67]

Ceausescu Seeks a Washington Invitation

Meanwhile, developments in Romania had made little impact in Washington. On occasion some supporter of Romanian MFN would mention the recent business arrangements between Bucharest and Control Data or General Tire, but little else. Nonetheless, Ceausescu continued to reorganize his bureaucracy in a manner reminiscent of musical chairs. In April, he transferred Paul Niculescu-Mizel from his post as Secretary for International Relations to that of Deputy Chairman of the Council of Ministers. Stefan Andrei became the new International Relations Secretary, while Gheorghe Macovescu replaced Corneliu Manescu as Foreign Minister. In June, Ceausescu increased the size of the Central Committee to 41 members, including two women, one being his wife Elena.

In foreign policy, he continued to try to play West against East. He established joint ventures with Italy and West Germany, bought Boeing 707s from the United States and purchased several IL-62 aircraft from Moscow. In June, the Common Market granted generalized preferences to Romanian exports, the first Warsaw Pact state to receive this concession. A month later, Ceausescu attended the annual Crimea meeting of the Warsaw Pact states. He agreed to permit map exercises in Romania, and later held private talks with Brezhnev. One topic discussed concerned Romania's interest in importing oil and gas from the Soviet Union.[68]

However, the Romanian President also wanted to increase trade with Washington. Bogdan's reports indicated that the movement for a separate resolution granting Romania MFN was quickly eroding. To complicate matters, Leonard Meeker resigned as Ambassador to Romania and left his post on May 10. His replacement Harry Barnes would not arrive for ten months. As a result, Ceausescu decided to deal directly with Washington. Earlier in the year, President Nixon had indicated that if the Romanian President wanted to visit the United States, he was most welcome.[69] In light of the MFN situation, Ceausescu notified the President during the Summer that he was interested in meeting with him in the White House.[70]

Congress, Trade and the Yom Kippur War

Meanwhile, Congress returned from its August recess. With Mills still out of action, the Administration sought a meeting with the acting Chairman of the Ways and Means Committee Al Ullman, a Democrat from Oregon. The Committee had completed its markup of the first half of the bill, but still had to finish Title V, which was MFN for Communist countries and Title VI, generalized tariff preferences for developing nations. The President wanted to talk with Ullman and his assistant, Herman Schneebeli, a Republican Congressman from Pennsylvania, before they completed the markup of Title V.[71]

At this September 12 meeting, Nixon explained to the Congressmen his concerns about the present legislation. Through private conversations with Brezhnev, he had managed to have the Soviets suspend the education tax and give assurances "that emigration would continue at a substantial rate." Nixon emphasized that "it would be a major foreign policy setback, endangering the search for peace and the reduction of arms, and likely to produce greater repression in the USSR, if I were prevented from extending MFN by impossible legislative requirements." He understood the position of Congress, and was willing to consider a reasonable compromise, something less extreme than the Jackson-Vanik amendment. In conclusion, Nixon told Ullman and Schneebeli that his staff was "ready to work with you along those lines."[72]

Presidential pressure failed to change the mood of the Ways and Means Committee. On Wednesday, September 26, the Committee attached a Jackson-Vanik type amendment to Title V. The only consolation the White House had was that credits were deleted from the restrictions. On Thursday, Nixon met with Republican leaders of the House. He wanted them to eliminate the amendment, otherwise he would not be able to implement the Soviet-American trade agreement nor would he be able to fulfill his commitment to Romania.[73]

Several hours later, the Ways and Means Committee considered exempting Romania from the emigration amendment.[74] However, the discussion was short lived. An exemption would only be given if Romania was not violating the amendment, but if Bucharest was not in violation, then the exemption was not necessary. There was a growing interest in human rights on Capitol Hill. In 1973, the Subcommittee on International Organizations and Movements of the House Committee on Foreign Affairs noted that "the human rights factor is not accorded the high priority it deserves in our country's foreign policy. . ."[75] To address this situation, Congress drew up the first human rights legislation and made it Section 32 of the Foreign Assistance Act of 1973. Both houses would approve the legislation in December which expressed the "sense of Congress that the President should deny any economic or military assistance to the government of any foreign country which practices the interment or imprisonment of that country's citizens for political purposes."[76] Some of the supporters of the Jackson-Vanik amendment reflected that "sense of Congress," and viewed excessive emigration taxes as an infringement on human rights. Consequently, there was little support to exempt a country such as Romania from legislation which promoted human rights.

Meanwhile the Soviets took steps which improved their image in Congress. On September 26 they ratified two international covenants on human rights adopted by the United Nations in 1966, including a provision on free emigration. Two days later, Nixon met Gromyko in the White House. The Soviet Foreign Minister believed the President when Nixon assured him that he would prevail on the issue of MFN and the Soviet trade agreement.[77] On October 1, Shultz arrived in Moscow to attend the Soviet-American Trade Commission meeting. The Soviets warned him that the Kremlin would make no further concessions on emigration.[78]

Meanwhile, the Ways and Means Committee had delayed its final vote hoping that Kissinger would testify before it. However, his confirmation hearings as Secretary of State, replacing Rogers, took longer than anticipated, and he was unable to appear. While some have suggested that his testimony would have altered the Jackson-Vanik amendment, there is little evidence to support this. Kissinger and Nixon believed that the amendment was primarily the product of the Jewish lobby. Neither saw that the Jackson-Vanik amendment had support from the AFL-CIO, anti-detente Congressmen and a growing number of human rights activists.

On October 3, the Committee forwarded the bill to the floor of the House. Generally speaking, the Administration should have been pleased with the bill since most of its proposals were adopted. The Executive Branch received more authority to negotiate trade and tariffs than ever before, but the Legislature could use veto procedures to balance the President's power. The bill enabled the United States to dramatically expand trade, especially with market economies. Only on the issue of MFN to nonmarket economies were Administration desires frustrated. The bill, as voted out of the Committee, included the Jackson-Vanik amendment as Title IV. The only exemption to the amendment was on credits, and this failed inclusion by a tie vote. Therefore it could be restored by a vote of the full House.[79]

The House expected to act on the trade bill around October 17 or 18. However, on October 6 Syrian and Egyptian forces attacked Israel and the Yom Kippur War began. Kissinger asked Congress to postpone debate on the bill since any action would undercut efforts to work with Moscow to end the Mideast War. This became the first of a series of

Presidential requests for delay which would postpone House debate on the bill until December.[80]

Ceausescu Visits Washington

While the Yom Kippur War stalled the trade bill, the conflict gave Ceausescu an opportunity to improve Romania's image in America, and to insure him an invitation to the White House. Breaking ranks with the Warsaw Pact nations, Ceausescu declared Romania neutral in the Middle East War. Bogdan emphasized this position sufficiently that on October 12, Kissinger asked General Haig, Haldeman's replacement, to find a convenient time for Ceausescu to visit the President.[81]

Haig needed nearly a month to secure Nixon's approval, but the delay was understandable. The White House was mired in the Watergate scandal. Foremost among the problems was ownership of the notorious tapes, first mentioned by Alexander Butterfield during his July 16 testimony before the Senate Watergate Committee. By October, the tape battle focused on the infamous 18 1/2 minutes of missing conversation. The taped silence produced a veritable flock of Congressional resolutions concerning Watergate, twenty-two of which called for Nixon's impeachment or for an investigation of impeachment proceedings.[82] Meanwhile, the Vice President, Spiro Agnew, resigned his position and pleaded no contest to one count of tax invasion. In return, the Federal government dropped its indictments against him for violations involving bribery and conspiracy when he was Governor of Maryland.

Finally, in early November, Nixon invited Ceausescu to come to Washington on December 4. The Romanian President's primary objective was to lobby for Romanian MFN. He indicated that he also wanted to talk further about the possibility of a long-term agreement with the United States. On November 14, the East West Trade Policy Committee Working Group of the State Department discussed the Romanian request for an LTA. Ceausescu wanted to sign LTAs on economic, industrial and technological cooperation, similar to what he had negotiated with West Germany in June. The Committee saw the LTA as Ceausescu's best trade option failing MFN. Through an LTA, Bucharest could attract more American business investment in Romanian industry, and preferably in a manner that would pay for itself. However, the Committee recognized that the conclusion of an LTA with Romania would "impact directly on any future U.S.-Soviet discussions of a similar accord. Moscow would be likely to interpret a long-term economic agreement with Romania as a calculated affront and expression of dis-interest in US-Soviet economic relations." Consequently the Committee recommended that the United States limit itself to signing a Joint Statement with Romania which would endorse joint equity ventures, in-dustrial cooperation, and, if necessary, a future long-term agreement.[83]

Unaware of this recommendation, which Nixon would later adopt, Ceausescu told the Central Committee and the Supreme Council of Economic and Social Development on November 28 that the 1974 eco-nomic plan provided for equilibrium in the balance of foreign payments for the first time since the Communists took office in August, 1944. He also indicated that Romania's long term goal was to eliminate foreign debt by 1980.[84] However, both targets meant a substantial increase in exports, and Ceausescu expected 1974 exports to increase by more than 140% over those of 1973.[85] Ceausescu wanted as much of that growth as possible to come from increased sales of Romanian products to America.

On December 4, Ceausescu arrived in Washington bearing gifts for President Nixon. In keeping with the tradition begun when Nixon visited Romania in 1969, the two leaders and their wives exchanged presents. Ceausescu gave the Nixons a Romanian made Chinese tea service while the the President and his wife gave a set of Tiffany vermeil demi-tasse spoons to the Ceausescus.[86] After the exchange, Ceausescu and his eco-nomic and foreign policy advisers met with their American counterparts for the next three days. Following his meeting with Nixon, Ceausescu visited the Board of Trade. He told those assembled that he was de-lighted to hear that they too "would act for a most rapid solution" to the problem of Romanian MFN.[87] Ceausescu's lobbying efforts inspired Representative Peter Frelinghuysen from New Jersey, to announce on the House floor that Romania "was entitled" to MFN.[88] However, not everyone was impressed by the Romanian President. Bogdan arranged a meeting between Ceausescu and Senator Jackson at the Blair House. The Ambassador warned Ceausescu not "to dwell on little issues, like visas. Talk about broader issues." However, the President refused to follow Bogdan's advice, and the meeting "did not go very well." Ceausescu "had too much confidence in Nixon and would not listen to anyone who told him Nixon was in danger of impeachment."[89]

Meanwhile, members of the Romanian and American staffs man-aged to prepare four agreements for signature by the end of the first day of Ceausescu's visit. The first was an income tax convention that insured that citizens or businesses of one nation would not be subject to discriminatory taxation in the other country. The second regulated fisheries in the western region of the Middle Atlantic, and granted Romanian fishing vessels the right to call at the ports of Baltimore, Philadelphia and New York for repairs or rest. The third bilateral agreement provided for the continuation and possible expansion of Pan American World Airways services to Bucharest and, for the first time, permitted TAROM, the Romanian airline, to begin service to New York using the recently purchased Boeing 707s.[90] The final accord was between the United States Chamber of Commerce and the Chamber of Commerce and Industry of Romania. This agreement established a U.S.-Romanian Economic Council designed to resolve problems arising from business transactions between the two countries. The Council would meet annually and alternate the meeting site between Romania and the United States.[91]

Ceausescu ended his first day in the United States with a formal dinner at the White House. Those attending included Kissinger and Commerce Secretary Dent as well as four Senators and five Representatives, including two on the Ways and Means Committee.[92] At the close of the dinner, Nixon spoke of the close relationship that existed between he and President Ceausescu. He praised the Romanian President for his staunch support of the principle that every nation, large or small, had the right to its independence and freedom. While toasting Ceausescu as the leader of a "great and friendly nation," the President discreetly avoided any mention of MFN or an LTA.[93]

On the following morning, Ceausescu and Nixon met in the Cabinet Room of the White House at 11 a.m., where they signed a Joint Statement of Principles which clearly reflected the recommendation of the East West Trade Policy Committee. The statement affirmed that the relations between the two countries would be based on the purposes and principles of the United Nations Charter. Both countries agreed to "encourage trade expansion as well as industrial, scientific and technical cooperation, in particular, such forms of collaboration as joint ventures and joint research."[94] Both Presidents also signed a Joint Statement on Economic, Industrial and Technical Cooperation which established a Romanian-American Economic Commission.[95] This body facilitated government-to-government economic communication, unlike the United States-Romanian Economic Council established the preceding day, which focused on business-to-business relationships.

Following the ceremonies, Ceausescu went to Capitol Hill and spoke to members of Congress. He urged them to grant Romania MFN because it would give Romanian products an "equal footing" in the American market. He noted Romania's increased imports of American goods, but added that "at the same time, we are supposed to export to the United States." Free trade was not only an economic issue, it was also a means to promote "peace all over the world."[96] After lunch, Ceausescu spoke with reporters at the National Press Club in Washington. He mentioned that he had received assurances of support for Romanian MFN from various Congressmen as well as from the President. When asked if he had spoken with Senator Jackson, Ceausescu said yes and tried to move onto other issues. In response to questions about the Jackson-Vanik amendment, he rhetorically proposed: "What would you and the American people say, if other countries were to introduce amendments to their laws which would condition the relations with the United States on the solving of some internal problems of the USA?"[97]

Ceausescu spent the rest of the day meeting with representatives of major American firms including General Electric, Singer Sewing Machine, International Telephone and Telegraph, Pratt Whitney, White Motor Company and Manufacturers Hanover Trust.[98] That evening he held a reception for the Nixons at the Romanian Embassy.[99] Ceausescu toasted the President speaking in flattering terms about Nixon's role in international relations, and envisioned the future as a period of friendship and cooperation between the United States and Romania.[100] Ceausescu spent his last two days in the United States visiting businessmen in North Carolina, Ohio, Connecticut and New York. On December 7, he returned to Bucharest.[101]

The Trade Reform Bill from House to Senate

As the Mideast War came under control, the White House had to take a position on the Trade Reform Bill. Kissinger had tried to make a deal with Jackson in late November, but failed. He wanted the Senator to use his influence to accept the Trade Reform Bill without Title IV, which included the Jackson-Vanik language. Jackson refused, but indicated that when the bill came to the Senate he would be open to some sort of compromise on the present language.[102] As a result, Kissinger urged the President to continue to delay a House vote on the basis that the delay was "required . . . to achieve a settlement in the Middle East."[103]

However, other Administration officials, especially Shultz and

Flanigan, urged the President to move the bill through the House. Although it would pass with the Jackson-Vanik amendment, the President could indicate that this was unacceptable to him, and put pressure on the Senate to remove the emigration language. In private, the President could reassure the Soviets that if the Senate refused to uncouple MFN and emigration, he would veto the bill. Nixon's economic advisors recognized that passage of the Trade Reform Bill was necessary for the United States to improve its trade competitiveness with Western Europe and Japan. Further, American negotiators needed the additional authority requested in the bill for upcoming GATT talks. Finally, the President might just as well recognize the fact that further postponement of the trade bill would not prohibit Congress from amending other legislation with Jackson-Vanik language. In short, though the Jackson-Vanik amendment was undesirable, the bill's passage was more important.[104]

On December 3, Nixon notified Speaker of the House, Carl Albert, to schedule floor action on the Trade Reform Bill before Christmas. In his letter, he urged the House to remove Title IV and approve the legislation.[105] On December 11, the House voted 319 to 80 to approve the Vanik amendment, including a provision linking credit availability to emigration practices. The House then voted 272-140 to pass the amended Trade Reform Bill. Liberals and conservatives had banded together to deny the White House an easy road to detente. The bill now headed for the Senate, and Mr. Jackson.

The new year started with a new Vice President, Gerald Ford, whom Nixon had appointed on December 6. The new year also brought a rash of trade related hearings including those to extend the Eximbank and the Export Administration Act as well as those scheduled for the Trade Reform Act. On January 5, Nixon appointed STR Ambassador William Eberle to replace Ambassador Pearce as the trade bill's new manager. Eberle was supposed to be responsible for overall strategy as well as for day-to-day tactics to ensure that Congress passed an Administration oriented Trade Reform Bill.[106] However, Eberle's role was quickly seized by Kissinger.

The Secretary of State was annoyed that his advice had not been taken in December. He had been too busy with confirmation hearings, and mediating the Yom Kippur War to spend much time on the trade bill while it was in the House. He had asked Nixon to continue to delay the House vote, but was overruled. With the Mideast War behind him, he gave the trade bill greater priority. He saw Eberle and the office of the Special Trade Representative as his assistants. They were to provide information, and not get involved with strategy for moving the bill through the Senate.[107]

Kissinger's special concern was Section 402 of the House approved bill which he saw as a threat to Soviet-American detente and to the Nixon-Kissinger goal of a multipolar foreign policy. Section 402, otherwise known as the Jackson-Vanik Amendment, stipulated that no country would be eligible to receive nondiscriminatory tariff treatment or government credits, credit guarantees or investment guarantees if the President determined that such a country (a) denied its citizens the right or opportunity to emigrate; (b) imposed more than a nominal tax for emigration or on visas or on other documents required for emigration; and (c) imposed more than a nominal tax, levy or fee on any citizen as a consequence of the desire of such citizen to emigrate to the country of his choice. Section 402 further provided that the President had to submit a report to Congress that none of these provisions had been violated.[108]

On March 4, the Senate Finance Committee began hearings on the trade bill. The Chairman of the Committee was Russell Long, who had been chair since 1966 and was viewed as one of the Senate's most astute and powerful figures.[109] At the same time that Long opened hearings, Eberle sent Kissinger a memo on issues and approaches the Secretary of State might take to affect a compromise with Jackson. Kissinger was eager to talk with the Senator, and believed that a compromise acceptable to people on both sides of the issue could be reached. The Eberle report stated that while a number of the cosponsors of the Jackson-Vanik language would like to find a compromise, "no one suggests that anyone but Senator Jackson will be able to agree to a compromise." Some of the issues that were important to Jackson were Soviet performance in emigration. If the Soviets maintained their current rate of emigration, which was about 40,000 annually, this might suffice. In addition, the Soviets would have to stop harassing people applying for exit visas, and provide some sense of "place in line" so that emigrant applicants would generally know when they would be approved for departure. Jackson might be open to a "private understanding" that would permit some language changes.[110] Eberle concluded by enclosing a note from Jackson enumerating specific questions which he wanted the Soviets to answer. Among them were the rules and procedures used by the Soviets to determine emigration approval, the length of processing time for an application's approval or denial, disposition of special cases referred to Moscow by Washington, and the form in which any Soviet undertakings with respect to Title IV would be communicated.[111]

Kissinger met with Dobrynin. The Soviet Ambassador had told him in 1973 that the Soviets would try to maintain an emigration level of about 35,000. However, there had been a decline of about 28% during the last quarter of 1973, compared with the similar period in 1972. Dobrynin explained that the number of applicants declined sharply in view of the Yom Kippur War. Dobrynin also filled in Kissinger on the number of "hardship cases" brought to the Soviet's attention. Of the 738 cases, 268 either had or were about to receive exit permits, 177 had not applied and 149 were refused, but their cases were presently under review.[112]

Armed with this information Kissinger met Jackson on March 6. The initial encounter left Kissinger empty-handed. He described Jackson as a "fierce negotiator" who tied him up in a "Catch-22 proposition." Jackson saw the results in the "hardship cases" as proof positive that the more you demanded, the more the Soviets would concede. Consequently, he was not easily disposed toward compromise.[113] Kissinger did suggest that the Senate could grant the Soviets MFN treatment, and review their emigration practice every two years. Jackson refused. He wanted a written guarantee that Moscow would substantially increase its number of emigrants.[114]

On the following day, the Secretary of State testified before the Senate Finance Committee. His testimony did not reflect an interest in compromise that he had indicated to Jackson the previous day. He told the Finance Committee that the trade bill was absolutely essential to give the President flexibility to reduce trade barriers, and to normalize relations between the United States and the countries of Eastern Europe and the Soviet Union. In light of the energy crisis, produced by the Arab oil embargo, Kissinger wanted the President to have the power to restore international economics to a multilateral level, and end the bilateral negotiating that resulted from the embargo.[115]

He was totally opposed to Title IV. He understood the issue of human rights, but he did not believe that America's foreign policy should "be made dependent on the transformation of the Soviet domestic structure," which was the intent of the emigration language. When asked by Chairman Long whether he would recommend that the President sign the bill in its present form, Kissinger said "I would think very seriously about recommending a veto."[116]

Kissinger's answer indicated a new development in the Administration which Jackson failed to see. When the trade bill was in the House, Jackson saw that the Administration's priority was to have a bill passed, and therefore he could hold the bill hostage, as it were, to secure his emigration language.[117] However, if Kissinger's answer correctly reflected present White House thinking, then no bill was better than a measure linking emigration to trade. In that situation, Jackson would lose his leverage. Further, his persistence would only incur the wrath of many Congressmen who wanted to end America's trade deficit by giving the President the tools to access broader markets.

On March 15, Kissinger met with Jackson and Ribicoff. Jackson wanted a written guarantee from Moscow of 100,000 exit visas annually. Kissinger knew that the Soviets would never make this guarantee, and further they would never submit their internal policies to the United States for approval. However, Kissinger saw a solution. If the Soviets verbally explained their position to the United States, the Administration could send a note to the Soviets stating Washington's understanding of Soviet practices. This would involve no written commitment by Moscow and accomplish the same purpose. Kissinger decided to suggest this to Gromyko when the two met in Moscow in April to prepare for the third Nixon-Brezhnev summit.[118]

Washington and Bucharest, 1974

American-Romanian relations continued without stress, but without much progress. Following his confirmation as Ambassador to Romania in December, 1973, Harry Barnes arrived at his post on March 14, 1974, three days after the Eximbank decided to temporarily suspend credits to Romania. This action, which also affected Yugoslavia, Poland and the Soviet Union, was triggered by the bank's intention to approve about $250 million worth of loan applications to Moscow, including one for $49.5 million to finance natural gas exploration in Yakutsk Province. The irony of Washington helping the Soviets develop more energy sources, at the same time Americans were paying quadruple the price for gasoline than they had a year earlier, irritated Senator Richard Schweiker of Pennsylvania. On March 8, he asked the General Accounting Office (GAO) to investigate the legality of the loans.[119]

On the following day, the GAO determined that the Eximbank could not grant loans without the President approving each individual project. The GAO based its decision on a 1945 Congressional Act amended in 1968 prohibiting the extension of credits to any Communist country, unless the President decided that such credits were in America's national interest and so indicated to Congress. The Eximbank argued that such determinations had been made by the President for loans to Yugoslavia in 1967, to Poland and Romania in 1971 and to the Soviet Union on October 18, 1972. The GAO's finding forced the Eximbank to suspend credits to the Communist countries on March 11 pending a decision by the Attorney General.[120]

On March 15, J. E. Corette III, General Counsel to the Eximbank, took the position that the Bank had acted legally, and that the President had the authority to grant exemptions based on national interest on a country-by-country basis, rather than by individual project. On March 21, Attorney General Saxbe upheld Corette's position and within hours, William Casey, Chairman and President of the Eximbank, released the suspended credits. With this decision, the Eximbank released two lines of credit for firms doing business with Romania. One was for $785,000 to help finance DAB Industries' sale of equipment to build an engine bearing and bushing production line. The other was for $368,000 to underwrite Wean United of Pittsburgh's sale of welding machines and spare parts to Bucharest.[121]

Meanwhile, Ceausescu continued to reorganize the Party leadership. The March, 1974, Plenum of the Central Committee abolished the Permanent Presidium, which was the most powerful body in the party, and replaced it with a Permanent Bureau. The Permanent Bureau did not report to the Central Committee, and by November, the Bureau had only five members including Ceausescu, Premier Manea Manescu, Deputy Premier Gheorghe Oprea, Minister of Foreign Trade Ion Patan, and Foreign Minister Stefan Andrei.[122] Ceausescu used the reorganization to remove several people from their posts, the most important being Ion Gheorghe Maurer, a prominent statesman since 1961. He was the most influential spokesman in Romania calling for Ceausescu to moderate his radical policies. Maurer "gave to the regimes of both Gheorghiu-Dej and Ceausescu what many would call a touch of class."[123] Maurer's leadership ability coupled with his popularity in Western circles threatened Ceausescu, who suffered from an "inferiority complex,"[124] and forced the President to remove Maurer for reasons of health.[125]

Ceausescu also spent time promoting an image of Romania as champion of equality and human rights. He told the delegates meeting at the Conference on Security and Cooperation in Europe (CSCE) that Romania wanted to abolish all restriction in international trade and called for the Conference to adopt universal MFN.[126] Ceausescu was also aware that human rights was a growing concern in the United States. Consequently, in March he told reporters in Argentina about Romania's religious diversity and the fact that the state recognized 14 different religious cults.[127] A month later he told an audience of German and Magyars, that "injustice, be it done to a Romanian, a German or a Magyar is all the same . . . abuse is nothing but abuse!"[128]

Meanwhile, Secretary of Commerce Dent arrived in Bucharest on April 12 leading an American delegation to the first meeting of the Romanian-American Economic Commission. In his opening remarks, Dent indicated that the American delegation was committed to working for Romanian MFN. However, without MFN little of substance could be negotiated. Nonetheless, both sides agreed to set a level of $1 billion as their goal for bilateral trade by 1980. The meeting ended on April 13, and all agreed that the next session would convene in Washington in 1975.[129]

Four days later, an American exhibit opened in Bucharest on "Progress and the Environment." During the next three weeks, over 140,000 visitors came to the American pavilion. On May 25 the exhibit moved to Brasov which attracted more than 100,000 onlookers, many of whom were Romanian scientists and educators.[130] As the exhibit toured Romania, American business representatives of the United States-Romanian Economic Council arrived in Bucharest for a two day meeting. Following the December 4, 1973, decision to establish a Council, several business men held a founders meeting in Washington in January. They elected a six man Executive Committee headed by Gabriel Hauge, Chairman of Manufacturers Hanover Trust. Membership soon grew to include representatives from 25 American firms chosen to become charter members because of their "actual or potential" involvement in Romania.[131] On May 31, Hauge led a 44 member delegation to Romania. During the course of the proceedings, both sides agreed to exchange commercial traineeships, and to establish a commission of experts to facilitate the prearbitral resolution of commercial disputes. Following a closing session with President Ceausescu at the presidential palace, the American delegation returned to the United States on June 1.[132]

Meanwhile in Washington, the Senate Finance Committee had held hearings on the Trade Reform Bill. Several witnesses presented testimony specifically supporting Romanian MFN. Both Max Berry, a member of the Board of Directors of the East-West Trade Council, a business organization, and G. W. Fincher of General Tire International promoted Romanian MFN. Support also came from ethnic organizations, such as the League of Free Romanians. Secretary General of the League, Barbu Niculescu, urged MFN for Romania as a means to "stimulate" liberal reforms within the country.[133]

On April 10, the Finance Committee completed its public hearings on the trade bill. Realizing that nothing was going to be accomplished until Kissinger and Jackson reached a compromise, Chairman Long did not schedule the Finance Committee to begin markups on the bill for nearly two months.[134] While this bought time for Kissinger, it did little good for the President. On March 1, a Federal grand jury indicted Nixon's closest advisers, Ehrlichman, Haldeman and Charles Colson along with the former Attorney General John Mitchell for attempting to cover up the Watergate investigation and for lying to the FBI. On May 9, the House Judiciary Committee began hearings to determine if there was sufficient evidence to impeach the President.

Meanwhile, Kissinger had talked to Gromyko in Moscow during the last week of March. The Soviet Foreign Minister indicated that he was willing to go along with Kissinger's scheme to placate Jackson. Gromyko agreed that following consultation between the two countries, the United States could send the Soviets a note indicating their understanding of Soviet emigration practices. This would require no response or affirmation by Moscow, and at the same time it could accommodate Jackson. Kissinger returned home and in early April offered the compromise to Jackson, Javits and Ribicoff. Jackson was not satisfied. He still wanted to talk about 100,000 exit visas a year, and wanted them to be given preferentially to Jews living outside the urban areas.[135]

Kissinger met Gromyko again, this time in Geneva on April 28. During their two day discussions, the Foreign Minister gave Kissinger permission to give assurances that there was no legal bar to emigration from the Soviet Union, except for those holding security clearances. In addition, Gromyko agreed that the Secretary could tell Jackson that emigration figures could reach about 45,000 annually, but this could not be in writing since the Soviets did not know how many applicants there would be.[136]

Following the meeting, Kissinger expected to return to Washington within ten days. However, his efforts to bring peace to the Middle East took most of his time for the next month. He did not return to Washington until June 4, one day after the Senate Finance Committee began markups of the trade bill.[137] While Kissinger would note in his memoirs that the Mideast negotiations gave Jackson time to mobilize his forces,[138] the Secretary was unwilling to let anyone else deal with the Soviets over the emigration issue. According to an "anonymous top trade official," Dobrynin and Kissinger made an agreement that "neither side was to carry on conversations, and that there would be no channels of conversation except when they designate."[139] As a result, progress toward a Jackson-Kissinger compromise had to wait until the Secretary of State returned to Washington at the end of the first week in June.

Kissinger met Jackson, Javits and Ribicoff and told them of the Soviet offer. Jackson was still unmoved. On June 24, the Senator announced that he was going to put forward "new, unspecified conditions" on emigration. The timing was deliberate. Nixon left for Moscow on June 26, and Jackson's announcement would interrupt any Presidential effort to reach a compromise with the Soviets.[140] During his private sessions with Brezhnev, Nixon pressed the Soviet leader to "make some sort of gesture on Jewish emigration, if only to pull the rug out from Jackson."[141] While Brezhnev later said he would "let all the Jews go," he did not give Nixon any specific assurances.[142]

Aware of the developing impasse over Soviet emigration and trade, Bogdan and Ceausescu tried to resurrect Romanian MFN. In late May, the Ambassador had lunch with Mike Dunn, the Assistant Secretary of Commerce for International Affairs, and reminded him of the importance of MFN to Romania.[143] A few days later, Claude Brineger, the Secretary of Transportation, visited Bucharest and met Ceausescu. The President emphasized the importance of MFN for expanded trade between the two countries.[144] However, some Congressmen and Administration officials heard some unsettling stories about Romania. In July, the House Committee on Foreign Affairs' Subcommittee on Europe held hearings on Detente. Among the documents entered as evidence was a State Department report on Romanian emigration practices. Visas cost about $300. However, the Office of Passports in Bucharest requested the payment of $50 additional in hard currency, i.e. American dollars. This posed a problem for all Romanians, because private possession of foreign currency was illegal and punishable up to five years in prison. Consequently, passports could only be obtained for a fee, and the market rate in 1974 was approximately $5000.[145] While this evidence did not become common knowledge, it certainly suggested that Romanian emigration practices were not terribly different from those of Moscow. This was undoubtedly the reason why Ceausescu refused to answer reporters questions about Romanian visa and passport issues, noting that they were exclusively issues of internal policy and not subject to public discussion.[146]

President Ford and the Trade Reform Bill

Throughout the summer, Watergate took control of America. Russell Long had called for a second session to markup the trade bill on July 29, but it lasted only five days. The House Judiciary Committee passed its third and final article of impeachment on July 30. Ten days later, on August 9, Richard M. Nixon resigned as President of the United States. At noontime, Chief Justice Warren Burger swore in Gerald Ford as America's 38th President.

Five days later, Ford became emersed in the Administrative side of the trade bill. He met with Dobrynin for the first time. The Ambassador assured him that his government could orally guarantee 55,000 Jewish emigrants annually, but Moscow could not put this in writing.[147] A few hours later, the President talked with Russell Long and indicated that he wanted the trade bill moved along.[148] On August 15 Ford had breakfast with Kissinger, Jackson, Javits and Ribicoff and urged them to resolve their differences and reach agreement soon.[149] Following the Congressional recess, Long resumed the markup of the trade bill. On September 20, Ford told Jackson about Dobrynin's guarantee. Jackson wanted it in writing.[150] Ford urged him to work out a compromise and for the next month Kissinger, Ford, Jackson and Dobrynin tried to work out a process acceptable to both the Senator and the Soviets.[151]

By early October Jackson and Kissinger reached a compromise, or at least Kissinger thought they had. Through an exchange of letters, the Soviets assured Jackson that Moscow would not reimpose the education tax, would not geographically discriminate against emigrant applicants, and, depending upon the number of applicants, would issue up to 60,000 Jewish visas annually.[152] On October 18, Kissinger and Jackson met with Vanik, Javits and the President in the Oval Office. Kissinger and Jackson signed the letters and the compromise was done. Jackson would change his amendment to stipulate that the President could grant MFN status to the Soviet Union for eighteen months, if he received assurances that Soviet practices would lead "substantially" to free emigration. Thereafter, the President could annually renew Soviet MFN subject to Congressional veto.[153]

Following the meeting Jackson held a press conference and announced that he understood that there would be an annual emigration of 60,000 Jews from the Soviet Union and he considered that a "benchmark" of minimal compliance with the amendment provisions.[154] Kissinger was furious. Both Gromyko and Dobrynin had insisted that total numbers were not to be made public. On October 26, Gromyko wrote Kissinger a private note critizing the Jackson-Kissinger letters as a "distorted picture of our position." Gromyko called the entire emigration issue a domestic one, and expected a decrease rather than an increase in the number of persons wishing to emigrate.[155]

Meanwhile, the Administration's efforts to expand Soviet-American detente received another setback, this time from Senator Adlai Stevenson, Chairman of the Senate Banking Subcommittee on International Finance. Stevenson did not approve of the Attorney General's March, 1974, decision in behalf of the Eximbank.[156] He and Jackson both wanted to put a ceiling on credits available to Moscow, especially for those earmarked for energy research. On September 19, Stevenson amended the Export-Import Bank bill to limit Soviet credits to $300 million. He further proposed that for the Eximbank to loan, guarantee or extend credits to any Communist country, in excess of $40 million, later amended to $50 million, the President had to make a determination that such action was in America's national interest. On December 19, both houses approved the amended Export-Import Bank bill extending the bank's authority through June 30, 1978.[157] The Stevenson provision, although directed at Moscow, affected Romania. The amendment overturned Nixon's 1971 Eximbank determination and shut Bucharest off from the bank's funds pending a new Presidential determination.[158]

As Congressional animosity against the Soviets increased, Bogdan and Ceausescu became alarmed. The Ambassador had already met the new President in August. Bogdan brought Vasile Pungan, a "special envoy of Ceausescu" to the White House to discuss Ford's view of American-Romanian relations.[159] During the August 27 meeting, the President accepted Ceausescu's invitation to visit Bucharest, and assured the Romanians that he too wanted to increase and improve relations between the two countries.[160]

Ford's words sufficed for a while. However, by November, Ceausescu needed reassurance that all was well between Washington and Bucharest. To allay his fears, Kissinger visited Romania on November 3-4. He told the Romanian press that he was hopeful that once the trade bill was passed, Romania could receive MFN. He talked with Ceausescu and on November 4 the two issued a joint communique, which was nearly a requirement in Romania, recounting the recent successes in Romanian-American relations, and predicting that the future would bring even greater development and understanding.[161]

Back in Washington, the Finance Committee had completed its markup of the Trade Reform bill and on November 20 agreed to report the bill with the understanding that it would not be brought to a vote until Kissinger appeared before the Committee to answer questions.[162] Kissinger met with the Committee on December 3. The Secretary of State did not mention his October 26 letter from Gromyko. Rather, he tried to salvage detente. He told the Committee that he had received assurances from the Soviets that they would place no unreasonable impediment before anyone wanting to emigrate, except those holding security clearances; there would be no harassment to emigration applicants; there would be no discriminatory criteria applied to those desiring to leave; and, the emigration tax suspended in 1973 would remain suspended. However, the Soviets did not make any commitment to numbers, "if any number was used in regard to Soviet emigration, this would be wholly our responsibility; that is, the Soviet Government could not be held accountable for or bound by any such figure."[163] He noted that in Jackson's letter, which was released to the press, "contained certain interpretations and elaborations . . . which were never stated to us by Soviet officials."[164]

Kissinger's testimony helped Congress accept the new Jackson language which was added to Title IV. Simply stated, the compromise allowed the President to waive the freedom-of-emigration requirement, if he (a) determined that the waiver would substantially promote the objectives of the requirement, and (b) if he had received assurances from the applicant country that its emigration practices would lead substantially to the achievement of free emigration.[165]

As the Senate began to debate the bill, Senator Mondale made an amendment to Title V, the generalized system of tariff preferences, or GSP.[166] This system legalized discriminatory tariff rates for less developed nations, or, as they were sometimes called, beneficiary developing countries. The discrimination gave some of these country's exports duty free status when imported by a cooperating developed country. The Finance Committee had reported the bill out with some changes, one of which would preclude any Communist country from receiving GSP. Mondale asked that the Senate amend the bill to exempt Yugoslavia and Romania from the prohibition. Both countries were LDCs, lesser developed nations, and consequently eligible for GSP treatment.[167] On the following day, December 13, Mondale renewed his request, adding that his amendment would only provide GSP to those Communist countries which were members of the GATT and the IMF, held MFN status, and were not controlled by international Communism. The Senate approved the amendment.[168] While it did not immediately affect Romania, it would later when Romania received MFN. Since she was a "developing country," Bucharest would be eligible for GSP treatment.

On December 13, the Senate passed the Trade Reform Bill by a 77-4 vote. There were a host of amendments which forced the bill to a House and Senate conference which met on December 18. As the discussions began, Moscow released a text of the private note it had sent Kissinger on October 26. The note was accompanied by a TASS commentary stating clearly that the Soviet Union would "flatly reject as unacceptable any attempts . . . to interfere in internal affairs that are entirely the concern of the Soviet state and no one else."[169] The Soviets obviously did not want to have anyone assume they had permitted the United States to restrict their internal policies, and they did not mind embarrassing Mr. Kissinger in the process.

On December 20 both houses adopted the major provisions of the bill, including the Jackson compromise language, and Mondale's GSP amendment. Congress renamed the legislation the Trade Act of 1974, and on January 3, 1975, President Ford signed the bill into law. Seven days later, Moscow notified Washington that it could not accept the waiver provisions of the Jackson-Vanik amendment, and therefore could not comply with the provisions of the 1972 trade agreement. On January 14, Kissinger made a public statement indicating the Soviet position.

While the Trade Reform Bill did not become the vehicle for Soviet-American detente as originally intended, it would provide a means for Romania to receive MFN. For all Bucharest had to do was to first, negotiate a bilateral agreement with Washington, and second, fulfill the requirements of the Jackson-Vanik amendment. This meant that Romania had to give oral assurances to the President of the United States that its policies led substantially toward free emigration. In return, the President could waive the freedom-of-emigration requirements in the Trade Act of 1974, subject to Congressional approval, and grant Romanian exports to America MFN treatment. The initial waiver would be for eighteen months. Thereafter, MFN could be annually renewed following new Romanian assurances, a Presidential determination to waiver the requirements, and no Congressional action of disapproval. Bogdan and Ceausescu could finally see a light at the end of the tunnel, and it spotlighted the letters MFN.

Notes

1. Kissinger, *White House Years*, p. 1360ff.
2. The Staff of The New York Times, *The End of a Presidency* (New York: Holt, Rinehart, and Winston, 1973), p. 157.
3. Nixon, *Memoirs*, p. 717.
4. Kissinger, *White House Years*, pp. 1417ff.
5. Stern, *Water's Edge*, p. 49.
6. Kissinger, *White House Years*, p. 1469.
7. Notes, November 17, 1972, Folder JDE Notes-Meeting with President August 7-December 13, 1972, Ehrlichman Notes, Nixon Presidential Materials Project; Memorandum, Deane R. Hinton to the Members of the CIEP Legislative Steering Group, November 20, 1972, Folder Ex CO 125 Romania; 1/1/171, Box 63, CO, Subject Files, WHCF, Nixon Presidential Materials Project.
8. Verzariu and Burgess, *Joint Venture Agreements in Romania*, Appendix B, pp. 35-39.
9. *Ibid.*, Appendix C., pp. 40-41.
10. Nicolae Ceausescu, *Expunere la Plenara C.C. al P. C. R., 20 noiembrie 1972* (Bucharest, Editura politica, 1972), p. 9; also, Ceausescu, *Romania On The Way*, VII, 818.
11. Notes, November 17, 1972, Folder JDE Notes-Meeting with President August 7-December 13, 1972, Ehrlichman Notes, Nixon Presidential Materials Project.
12. Memorandum, Richard K. Cook to the President, November 21, 1972, Folder Ex TA March 1-14, 1973, Box 6, (TA) Trade, Subject Files, WHCF, Nixon Presidential Materials Project.
13. Report, August 13, 1974, p. 22, Folder TA 6 Trade Centers, Box 30, Subject Files, WHCF, GRF Library.
14. U. S. Congress, House, Committee on Banking and Currency, Hearings Before the Subcommittee on International Trade, *International Economic Policy*, 93rd Cong., 2d Sess., 1974, p. 326, hereafter, Hearings Before the Subcommittee on International Trade, *International Economic Policy*, 1974; Report, Status of U.S. Economic Matters with Poland, Romania, and Yugoslavia, 2pp., Folder Rom 6/24/75, Box 315, Seidman Collection, GRF Library.
15. *DOS Bulletin*, January 29, 1973, pp. 119-123.
16. NYT, December 23, 1972, p. 4.
17. Staar (ed.), *Yearbook on International Communist Affairs, 1973* , pp. 65-66.
18. Jones, *Soviet Influence in Eastern Europe*, pp, 85ff; Ross, "The Warsaw Pact," 1984, p. 273.
19. Pregelj, "Most-Favored-Nation Policy Toward Communist Countries," 1987, p. 5.

20. "Shumlin Interview," Attachment, Memorandum, Larry Brady to Peter M. Flanigan, January 24, 1973, Folder Ex TA; January 12-31, 1973, Box 5, TA Trade, Subject Files, WHCF, Nixon Presidential Materials Project.

21. Stern, *Water's Edge*, p. 56.

22. Memorandum, Deane R. Hinton to Peter Flanigan, January 3, 1973, 2pp., Folder Ex TA; January 3-11, 1973, Box 5, TA Trade, Subject Files, WHCF, Nixon Presidential Materials Project; Memorandum for the Files from Peter Flanigan, January 4, 1973, 2pp., Folder CF FG 6-11 1/Flanigan, Peter; 71-74, Box 15, Confidential Files, Subject Files, WHSF: WHCF, Nixon Presidential Materials Project.

23. Report, Comprehensive Trade Legislation: Issues and Options (The Office of the Special Representative for Trade Negotiations), January 8, 1973, pp. 35-38, Folder Trade Legislation 1973, Box 17, Marina Whitman, Staff Members and Officers Files, WHCF, Nixon Presidential Materials Project.

24. When Peter Flanigan put together all the materials relevant to the Trade Reform Bill of 1973 the result was sixty-eight pages under the rubric, "Trade Legislation," and dated January 11 (See, Folder Ex, TA; January 3-11, Box 5, TA Trade, Subject Files, WHCF, Nixon Presidential Materials Project).

25. U.S., *Congressional Record*, 93d Cong., 1st Sess., 1973, CIXX, 1581-1582.

26. Author interview of Corneliu Bogdan, April 11, 1987.

27. Memorandum, Larry Brady to Peter M. Flanigan, January 24, 1973, Folder Ex TA; January 12-31, 1973, Box 5, TA Trade, Subject Files, WHCF, Nixon Presidential Materials Project.

28. Stern *Water's Edge*, p. 57; U. S. Congress, House, H.R. 3910, A Bill to prohibit most-favored treatment, 93th Cong., 1st Sess., 1973.

29. For a detailed discussion see, Stern, *Water's Edge*, pp. 59ff; Memorandum, Herbert Stein to Peter Flanigan, George Schultz, February 7, 1973, 9pp., Folder Ex TA; February 1973, Box 6, (TA) Trade, Subject Files, WHCF, Nixon Presidential Materials Project.

30. U. S. Congress, *A Strategy for International Trade Negotiations. Report by Senator Abraham Ribicoff to the Committee on Finance, United States Senate*, 93rd Cong., 1st Sess., 1973, p. 5.

31. Peter Peterson resigned in November 1972.

32. Destler, *Making Foreign Economic Policy*, pp. 151-152.

33. Garthoff, *Detente and Confrontation*, p. 325.

34. Memorandum, Peter Flanigan to Helmut Sonnenfeldt, March 19, 1973, Folder Ex FG 6-6; 3/1/73-4/30/73, Box 3, FG 6-6 NSC, Subject Files, WHCF, Nixon Presidential Materials Project.

35. Memorandum, Peter Flanigan to George Schultz, March 22, 1973, Folder Ex CO 158; 3/1/73-3/31/73, Box 73, CO, Subject Files, WHCF, Nixon Presidential Materials Project.

36. Memorandum, Richard K. Cook for the President, February 26, 1973, Folder (CF) TA Trade 71-74, Box 61, Confidential Files, Subject Files, WHSF:WHCF, Nixon Presidential Materials Project.

37. *Idem.*, Background and Talking Points, Recommended Telephone Call,

the President to Wilbur Mills, March 15, 1973, 2pp.

38. *Idem.*, Memorandum, Peter Flanigan to the President, March 16, 1973, 3pp.

39. *Idem.*, Memorandum, H. R. Haldeman to Peter Flanigan, March 17, 1973.

40. Memorandum, Peter Flanigan to Secretary of State *et al.*, March 19, 1973, Folder Ex FG 11; 3/1/73-3/31/73, Box 6, FG 11 (State), Subject Files, WHCF, Nixon Presidential Materials Project; Memorandum, William R. Pearce to Peter Flanigan, March 15, 1973, 8pp., Folder Ex TA; March 6-23, 1973, Box 6 (TA) Trade, Subject Files, WHCF, Nixon Presidential Materials Project.

41. *Historic Documents, 1973* (Washington, D.C.: Congressional Quarterly Inc., 1973), p. 381.

42. Kissinger, *Years of Upheaval*, pp. 252-253.

43. Stern, *Water's Edge*, pp. 60-61.

44. Memorandum, Peter Flanigan to Henry Kissinger, April 2, 1973, Folder Ex TA; March 23-31, 1973, Box 6, (TA) Trade, Subject Files, WHCFF, Nixon Presidential Materials Project; *Idem.*, Memorandum, Peter Flanigan to the President, March 28, 1973, 4pp.

45. Memorandum for the Files, April 6, 1973, Folder Ex CO 158; 4/1/73-4/30/73, Box 73, CO, Subject files, WHCF, Nixon Presidential Materials Project.

46. Author interview of Corneliu Bogdan, April 11, 1987.

47. Aurel Ghibutiu, "Recent Developments in Trade Relations between Romania and the United States," *East West Trade: Theory and Evidence*, eds. Josef Brada and V. S. Somanath (Bloomington, Indiana: International Development Institute, 1978), Table 5.

48. NYT, February 25, 1973, p. 1.

49. U.S., *Congressional Record*, 93d Cong., 1st Sess., 1973, CIXX, 6136-6138.

50. Memorandum, Helmut Sonnenfeldt to Henry Kissinger, March 5, 1973, Folder Ex CO 125 Romania; 1/1/73, Box 64, CO, Subject File, WHCF, Nixon Presidential Materials Project.

51. Department of Commerce Study on Bilateral Long-Term Trade Agreements with Socialist Countries, Attachment, Memorandum, Secretary of Commerce to George P. Schultz, August 16, 1973, pp, 1-2, Folder Ex TA5 Trade Agreements; 6-9 1973, Box 66, TA Trade, Subject Files, WHCF, Nixon Presidential Materials Project.

52. U. S. Congress, House, Committee on Ways and Means, Hearings Before the Subcommittee on Trade, *Waiver of Freedom of Emigration Requirement to the Socialist Republic of Romania and the Hungarian People's Republic.* 96th Cong., 1st Sess., 1979, pp. 334-335.

53. Eugen Dijmarescu and Emil Paica, "RomControl Data: A Case Study," *East-West Trade*, eds. Brada and Somanath, 1978, pp. 116ff.

54. John K. Ryans, Jr., Anant R. Negandhi and James C. Baker (eds.), *China, The U.S.S.R. and Eastern Europe: A U. S. Trade Perspective* (Kent, OH: The Kent State University Press, 1974), pp. 137ff; U. S. Congress, House,

Hearings Before the Committee on Ways and Means, *Trade Reform*, 93rd Cong., 1st Sess., 1973, pp. 3525-3528. Hereafter, House Committee on Ways and Means, *Hearings on Trade Reform*, 1973. Romania borrowed nearly $13 million in Eximbank credits to finance the plant's construction (House, Subcommittee on International Trade, *International Economy Policy*, 1974, p. 383).

55. Press Release, April 10, 1973, 13pp., Folder Trade legislation, 1973, Box 17, Marina Whitman, Staff Members and Officers Files, WHCF, Nixon Presidential Materials Project; U. S. Congress, *Trade Reform Act of 1973. Message from the President of the United States, Transmitting a Draft of Proposed Legislation To Promote the Development of an Open, Nondiscriminatory and Fair World Economic System, To Stimulate the Economic Growth of the United States, and To Provide the President with Additional Negotiating Authority Therefore, and For Other Purposes*, 93d Cong., 1st Sess., 1973.

56. Kissinger, *Years of Upheaval*, p. 987.

57. *Ibid.*, p. 1234, n10.

58. *Facts on File*, 1973, p. 364.

59. Kissinger, *Years of Upheavel*, pp. 253-254.

60. Author interview with Harry Barnes, July 19, 1987.

61. Notes, April 20, 1973, Folder JDE Pres Notes; Jan 4-May 2 1973, Box 14, Ehrlichman Notes, Nixon Presidential Materials Project.

62. Stern, *Water's Edge*, p. 71; Memorandum, Richard K. Cook for the President, April 19, 1973, Folder Ex CO 158; 5/1/73-5/31/73, Box 73, CO, Subject Files, WHCF, Nixon Presidential Materials Project.

63. *Ibid.*

64. U. S. Congress, House, Committee on Ways and Means, *Prepared Statements of Administration Witnesses, Submitted to the Committee on Ways and Means at Public Hearings, Beginning on May 9, 1973; And other Materials Relating to The Administration Proposal Entitled the "Trade Reform Act of 1973,"* 93d Cong., 1st Sess., 1973.

65. House Committee on Ways and Means, *Hearings on Trade Reform*, 1973, pp. 5273ff.

66. Destler, *Making Foreign Economic Policy*, p. 153.

67. Agenda/Briefing, Meeting with Chairman Wilbur Mills (D-ARK), July 25, 1973, 4pp. Folder (CF) TA Trade; 71-74, Box 61, Confidential Files, Subject Files, WHSF, Nixon Presidential Materials Project.

68. Richard F. Staar (ed.), *Yearbook on International Communist Affairs, 1974* (Stanford, CA: Hoover Institution Press, 1974), pp. 62-67; William Zimmerman, "Soviet Relations with Yugoslavia and Romania," *Soviet Policy in Eastern Europe*, ed. Sarah Meiklejohn Terry (New Haven, CT: Yale University Press, 1984), p. 138; Ronald H. Linden, "Romanian Foreign Policy in the 1980s," *Romania in the 1980s*, ed. Daniel Nelson (Boulder, CO: Westview Press, Inc., 1981), pp. 222-223.

69. Memorandum, David N. Parker to Al Haig, October 12, 1973, Folder CF CO-125 Romania; 1971-74, Box 8, Confidential Files 69-74, Subject Files,

WHSF:WHCF, Nixon Presidential Materials Project.

70. Memorandum, Helmut Sonnenfeldt to Henry Kissinger, March 5, 1973, Folder Ex CO 125 Romania; 1/1/73, Box 64, CO, Subject File, WHCF, Nixon Presidential Materials Project.

71. President Nixon also invited Henry Kissinger, Mel Laird, Ambassador William Pearce, and William Timmons of the CIEP, to attend.

72. Agenda/Briefing, Meeting with Rep. Al Ullman (D-ORE) and Herman Schneebeli (R-PA), September 12, 1973, 3pp., Folder (CF) TA Trade; 71-74, Box 61, Confidential Files, Subject Files, WHSF:WHCF, Nixon Presidential Materials Project.

73. Agenda/Briefing, Meeting with Republican Leaders, September 26, 1973, 11pp., Folder (CF) FG31-1, Legislative Leadership; 1971-74, Box 21, Confidential Files, Subject Files, WHSF:WHCF, Nixon Presidential Materials Project.

74. *Ibid.*, p. 6.

75. [National Policy Panel of the United Nations Association of the USA] *United States Foreign Policy and Human Rights: Principles, Priorities, Practice* (New York: United Nations Association of the United States of America, Inc., 1979), p. 21.

76. *Ibid.*, p. 22.

77. Kissinger, *Years of Upheaval,* p. 990.

78. Garthoff, *Detente and Confrontation*, p. 356.

79. Destler, *Making Foreign Economic Policy*, pp. 155ff; Garthoff, *Detente and Confrontation*, p. 357.

80. Destler, *Making Foreign Economic Policy*, pp. 165-166; Memorandum, Al Haig to the President, November 6, 1973, Folder (CF) TA Trade; 71-74, Box 61, Confidential Files, Subject Files, WHSF:WHCF, Nixon Presidential Materials Project; *Idem.*, Letter, Richard Nixon to Carl Albert, November 15, 1973.

81. Memorandum, David N. Parker to Al Haig, October 12, 1973, Folder CF CO-125 Romania; 1971-74, Box 8, Confidential Files 69-74, Subject Files, WHSF:WHCF, Nixon Presidential Materials Project.

82. *The End of a Presidency*, p. 231.

83. Draft memorandum on the Romanian proposal for Conclusion of Long Term Economic and Industrial Cooperation Agreement. Willis C. Armstrong to East-West Trade Policy Working Group, November 13, 1973, 7pp., Folder Ex CO 125 Romania; 1/1/73. Box 64, CO, Subject Files, WHCF, Nixon Presidential Materials Project; Ceausescu, *Romania On The Way*, IX. 621.

84. *Ibid.*, pp. 579-580.

85. *Ibid.*, p. 552.

86. Lists of gifts received by Nixon during his Presidency. Available at Nixon Presidential Materials Project.

87. Ceausescu, *Romania On The Way*, IX, 644.

88. U.S., *Congressional Record*, 93d Cong., 1st Sess., 1973, CIXX, 39383.

89. Author interview of Corneliu Bogdan, April 11, 1987.

90. [U. S. Department of Commerce] *East-West Trade: American-Romanian Economic Accords, 1973-1974,* i-vii, 31pp., Folder Rom 6/24/75, Box 315, Seidman Collection, GRF Library.
91. *Ibid.,* pp. 6-8.
92. Guest List, December 4 1973, Folder Ex FG 11; 12/1/73-12/31/73, Box 8, FG 11 (State), Subject Files, WHCF, Nixon Presidential Materials Project.
93. *Public Papers of the Presidents of the United States, Richard Nixon,1973* (Washington, D.C.: U. S. Government Printing Office, 1975), pp. 992-994.
94. *Ibid.,* pp. 997ff.
95. [U. S. Department of Commerce] *East-West Trade: American-Romanian Economic Accords, 1973-1974,* i-vii, 31pp., Folder Rom 6/24/75, Box 315, Seidman Collection, GRF Library.
95. *Ibid.,* p. 9.
96. Ceausescu, *Romania On The Way,* IX, 651.
97. *Ibid.,* pp. 663-665.
98. *Ibid.,* p. 658; NYT, December 8, 1973, p. 51.
99. This reception came near to being a disaster for the Romanians. At their meeting on December 4, President Nixon accepted Ceausescu's invitation to visit the Romanian Embassy on the following evening. This would give the Romanian chief of state the chance to perform, as a host, a standard manoeuvre of diplomatic gamesmanship. However, the planned reception was somehow cancelled; perhaps some one on the Embassy staff misunderstood or misplaced a signal. But whatever the reason, the Department of State pitched-in to help the Romanians make up for lost time in making the preparations. The White House observed that, "Protocol is scrambling to assist the Romanians in putting together a reception. The attendees will *probably* be the Chiefs of the Diplomatic Mission . . . The reception will *probably* begin at 6 p.m. with Diplomatic Chiefs arriving first, and the other special guests arriving at 6:30 p.m." Stephen Bull advised the White House that if "my probablies are correct," the President should arrive at 6:30 p.m. (Memorandum, Stephen Bull to David Parker, December 4, 1973, 2pp., Folder CF CO-125 Romania; 1971-74, Box 8, Confidential Files 69-74, Subject Files, WHSF:WHCF, Nixon Presidential Materials Project.
100. *Public Papers of the Presidents, Richard Nixon, 1973,* pp. 994-996.
101. *Ibid.,* p. 1004.
102. Draft Memorandum to the President, Attachment, Memorandum, Peter Flanigan to Henry Kissinger, November 30, 1973, 7pp., Folder Ex TA Trade; November 73, Box 7, TA (Trade), Subject Files, WHCF, Nixon Presidential Materials Project; Memorandum [for the President] From Henry Kissinger, Meeting with Secretaries Kissinger and Schultz, December 3, 1973, 3pp., Folder (CF) TA Trade; 71-74, Box 61, Confidential Files, Subject files, WHSF:WHCF, Nixon Presidential Materials Project.
103. *Ibid.,* p. 2.
104. Draft Memorandum to the President, November 30, 1973, pp. 1-5.

105. Letters to Congressional Leaders, December 3, 1973, Folder (CF) TA Trade, 1971-1974, Box 61, Confidential Files, WHCF, Nixon Presidential Materials Project.

106. Memorandum, George Schultz to Secretary of State *et al.*, January 10, 1974, Folder Ex FG 11; 1/1/74-1/31/74, Box 8, Subject Files (State), WHCF, Nixon Presidential Materials Project.

107. Destler, *Making Foreign Economic Policy*, pp. 171ff; Kissinger, *Years of Upheaval*, pp. 991ff.

108. Memorandum, Helen B. Junz to Mr. Truman, April 1, 1974, 2pp., Folder Trade Reform Act of 1973, Box B99, Burns Papers, GRF Library.

109. Destler, *Making Foreign Economic Policy*, p. 169.

110. Memorandum, W. D. Eberle to Henry Kissinger, March 4, 1974, 3pp., Folder Ex TA (Trade); March 74, Box 8, TA Trade, Subject Files, WHCF, Nixon Presidential Materials Project.

111. *Idem.*, Letter, Henry Jackson to William D. Eberle, March 1, 1974, 2pp.

112. Kissinger, *Years of Upheaval*, p. 992. Kissinger admits that Jackson's pressure undoubtedly contributed to the large number of approvals.

113. *Ibid.*, p. 992,

114. *Ibid.*, p. 993.

115. U. S. Congress, Senate, Hearings Before the Committee on Finance, *The Trade Reform Act of 1973*, 93rd Cong., 2d Ses., 1974, pp. 453-459.

116. *Ibid.*, p. 452.

117. Stern, *Water's Edge*, pp. 141-142.

118. Kissinger, *Years of Upheaval*, p. 994.

119. *Facts on File*, 1974, p. 191.

120. *DOS Bulletin*, April 29, 1974, pp. 465-466; Hearings Before the Subcommittee on International Trade, *International Economic Policy*, 1974, p. 299.

121. *Ibid.*, pp. 357-358.

122. Richard F. Staar (ed.), *Yearbook on International Communist Affairs, 1975* (Stanford, CA: Hoover Institution Press, 1975), pp. 68-69.

123. Brown, *Eastern Europe and Communist Rule*, p. 269.

124. Author interview of Corneliu Bogdan, April 11, 1987.

125. Vladimir Tismaneanu, "The Tragicomedy of Romanian Communism," *Eastern European Politics and Societies*, Vol. 3, No. 2 (Spring 1989), p. 370; also, Fischer, *Nicolae Ceausescu*, pp. 160-161.

126. Socor, "The Limits of National Independence in the Soviet Bloc," 1976, p. 725.

127. Ceausescu, *Romania On The Way*, IX, 280.

128. *Ibid.*, X, 48.

129. [U. S. Department of Commerce] *East-West Trade: American-Romanian Economic Accords, 1973-1974*, pp.12ff, Folder Rom 6/24/75, Box 315, Seidman Collection, GRF Library.

130. Report, May 17, 1976, pp. 20-21, 33-34, Folder TA 6 Trade Centers, Box 30, Subject Files, WHCF, GRF Library.

131. U. S. Congress, A Compendium of Papers Submitted to the Joint Eco-

nomic Committee, *East European Economies, Post-Helsinki*, 95th Cong., 1st Sess., 1977, pp. 1242ff, hereafter, Joint Economic Committee of the Congress, *East European Economies*, 1977.

132. Ibid., p. 1343; U. S. Department of Commerce] *East-West Trade: American-Romanian Economic Accords, 1973-1974*, pp.26ff, Folder Rom 6/24/75, Box 315, Seidman Collection, GRF Library.

133. Senate Committee on Finance, *Trade Reform Act of 1973*, 1974, pp. 1786ff.

134. Memorandum, W. D. Eberle to Henry Kissinger, April 17, 1974, 2pp, attachment, Folder Ex TA (Trade); April 74, Box 8, TA Trade, Subject Files, WHCF, Nixon Presidential Materials Project.

135. Kissinger, *Years of Upheaval*, pp. 994-995.

136. *Ibid.*, p. 995.

137. *Ibid.*, p. 996.

138. *Ibid.*

139. Stern, *Water's Edge*, p. 209.

140. *Ibid.*, pp. 996-997.

141. Nixon, *Memoirs*, p. 1031.

142. *Ibid.*, p. 1034.

143. Memorandum for the Record from Jack Marsh, June 19, 1974, Folder Office of the Assistant for Defense and International Affairs, John March, Jan-Aug 74, Box 65, Ford Vice Pres Files, GRF Library.

144. Letter, Claude S. Brinegar to the President, September 12, 1974, 2pp., Folder CO125 Rom; 8/9/74-12/31/74, Box 43, CO125, WHCF, GRF Library.

145. U. S. Congress, House Committee on Foreign Affairs, Hearings Before the Subcommittee on Europe, *Detente*, 93rd Cong., 2d Sess., 1974, p. 508.

146. See the interview given by Mr. Ceausescu to reporters from *U.S. News & World Report*, June 19, 1974. The interview was reprinted in Ceausescu, *Romania On The Way*, X, pp. 336ff.

147. Newhouse, *War and Peace in the Nuclear Age*, p. 246.

148. Destler, *Making Foreign Economic Policy*, p, 173.

149. *Ibid.*

150. Gerald R. Ford, *A Time to Heal: The Autobiography of Gerald R. Ford* (New York: Harper & Row, 1979), p. 139.

151. Newhouse, *War and Peace in the Nuclear Age*, p. 247.

152. Garthoff, *Detente and Confrontation*, pp. 453ff.

153. Destler, *Making Foreign Economic Policy*, p. 173.

154. Newhouse, *War and Peace in the Nuclear Age*, pp. 246-247.

155. *Congress and the Nation: A Review of Government and Politics. Volume IV, 1973-1976* (Washington, D.C.: Congressional Quarterly Inc., 1977), p. 133. Also, Garthoff, *Detente and Confrontation*, pp. 458ff.

156. Senate Subcommittee on International Finance, *The Export-Import Bank and Export Controls in U.S. International Economic Policy*, 1974, pp. 22-23.

157. Garthoff, *Detente and Confrontation*, p. 454; Spero, *The Politics of*

International Economic Relations, p. 373; Beverly Crawford, "Western Control of East-West Trade Finance: The Role of U.S. Power and the International Regime," *Controlling East-West Trade and Technology Transfer*, ed. Gary K. Bertsch, 1988, pp. 298-299; Harry Gellman, "The Rise and Fall of Detente: Causes and Consequences," *U.S.-Soviet Relations: The Next Phase*, ed. Arnold L. Horelick (Ithaca, NY: Cornell University Press, 1986), p. 65. For an interesting retrospective by Ambassador Stevenson see, Adlai E. Stevenson and Alton Frye, "Trading with the Communists," *Foreign Affairs*, Vol. 68, No. 2 (Spring 1989), pp. 53-71.

158. [Senate] Committee on Foreign Relations, and [House] Committee on International Relations, *Legislation on Foreign Relations Through 1976: Legislation, Treaties, and Related Documents*, [95th Cong., 1st Sess.], February 1977, II, 306, hereafter, Joint Committee Print, *Legislation on Foreign Relations Through 1976*, 1977; U. S. Congress, House, Committee on Banking, Currency and Housing, Hearings Before the Subcommittee on International Trade, Investment and Monetary Policy, *Oversight Hearings on the Export-Import Bank*, 94th Cong., 2d Sess., 1976, pp. 5-6.

159. Schedule Proposal from Henry Kissinger, August 24, 1974, 2pp., Folder CA125 Rom; 8/9/74-12/31/74, Box 43, CO125 WHCF, GRF Library.

160. *Ibid.*; Weekly Compilation of Presidential Documents, Aug-Sept 74, p. 1080, GRF Library.

161. *DOS Bulletin*, November 25, 1974, pp. 730-732.

162. U.S. *Congressional Record*, 93d Cong., 2d Sess., 1974, CXX, D781.

163. U.S. Congress, Senate, Hearing Before the Committee on Finance, *Emigration Amendment to The Trade Reform Act of 1974*, 93rd Cong., 2d Sess., 1974, p. 53.

164. *Ibid.*, p. 54.

165. Pregelj, "Most-Favored-Nation Policy Toward Communist Countries," 1987, p. 7.

166. The United States adopted GSP in 1968, four years after its introduction at the United Nations Conference on Trade and Development in 1964 (see, U. S. Congress, House, Committee on Ways and Means, *Overview and Compilation of U. S. Trade Statutes*, 100th Cong., 1st Sess., 1987, pp. 10ff).

167. U.S., *Congressional Record*, 93d Cong., 2d Sess., 1974, CXX, 39525.

168. U.S., *Congressional Record*, 93d Cong., 2d Sess., 1974, CXX, 39822.

169. Garthoff, *Detente and Confrontation*, p. 459.

CHAPTER XIII

AN AMERICAN-ROMANIAN TRADE AGREEMENT, AND MFN

Negotiating the Trade Agreement

Ford's approval of the Trade Act of 1974 and Moscow's rejection of the 1972 Trade Agreement with the United States gave new life to American-Romanian relations. Bucharest and Washington were free to resume MFN talks without having them subordinated to Soviet-American trade discussions.

1974 had closed on a positive note between America and Romania. On December 13, the two countries signed a five year extension of their Agreement on Cultural and Scientific Exchanges and Cooperation.[1] A month later, on the same day that Kissinger announced the Soviet decision to reject the 1972 Soviet-American trade agreement, George Macovescu, Romania's Foreign Minister, invited Ambassador Barnes to his office. Macovescu wanted to know if the United States was ready to negotiate an MFN agreement which would include a satisfactory approach to the emigration question.[2] Barnes indicated Washington's willingness, and two-track talks began the following day, one with the Romanian Ministry of Foreign Trade, and the other with Macovescu's office to resolve the emigration issue.[3]

While the negotiations continued for the next two months, the end was never in doubt. On January 28, the East-West Trade Policy Committee approved a scenario for signing the trade agreement extending MFN treatment to Romanian products.[4] The Committee also agreed that the Eximbank should await Congressional approval of the trade agreement before making any new credit commitments to Romania. Further, the Committee anticipated that negotiations would soon commence for an LTA with Bucharest.[5]

This January prognosis continued in spite of some Romanian trade practices which raised concern in Washington. During the past years, the United States had sold Portugal corn. During the winter of 1974-75, Washington put corn sales on "hold" to Lisbon until the Agriculture Department could assess America's Spring corn crop. The Portuguese looked for other suppliers, and Bucharest responded selling them 175 thousand metric tons of corn purchased earlier from the United States. Romania's action was not done for economic reasons, since there was little profit to be made. Rather, Ceausescu approved the sale in order to increase Romania's political influence in Western Europe. The State Department was angry and notified Barnes that Bucharest was not to purchase corn from the United States without government approval, until the Portuguese issue was solved.[6]

However, this issue did not affect the bilateral trade negotiations. The main trade issue, which took weeks to resolve, concerned America's need for a Romanian assurance prohibiting product dumping on the American economy. Due to her non-market economy, Romania had cheap labor and could manufacture products inexpensively. Both labor and management in America wanted guarantees that Romania would not export such a large number of specific products as to threaten or actually disrupt a particular product market.[7]

The other track of negotiations concerned emigration. This was a sensitive issue. Ceausescu repeatedly stated that there was no linkage between MFN and emigration. However, as Barnes pointed out, this "was for home consumption." America wanted assurances that "people could leave in some reasonable fashion."[8] However, Bucharest could not simply surrender control over an internal issue as significant as emigration. Equally important, Romania refused to put anything in writing which linked emigration to trade. As a result, negotiations slowed while Barnes, and the Romanian negotiator, Nicolae Nicolescu, searched for an emigration formula acceptable to both sides. By March 18, the trade negotiations were nearly complete, but the emigration issue needed more time. Consequently, the State Department decided to complete the trade agreement, but withhold it from Congress until the entire Romanian "package" was complete. This package included emigration assurances, resumption of Eximbank credits, and the Trade Agreement with provisions for reciprocal MFN treatment.[9]

Meanwhile, the Ford Administration continued to implement various aspects of the Trade Act of 1974. Title V authorized the President to join with 18 other developed countries in implementing GSP. This permitted the United States to provide duty-free treatment, within specified limits, to a broad range of manufactured and semi-manufactured products, for a period of up to 10 years. On March 24, the President designated a number of countries as "beneficiary developing countries" making them eligible for GSP treatment. He also identified about 25 countries, one of which was Romania, as "under consideration" for designation as a "beneficiary developing country."[10] Bogdan saw the President on the same day of the announcement and conveyed Ceausescu's gratitude with this initial determination. A Romanian choral group accompanied the Ambassador, and gave Ford a message from Ceausescu.[11] The note emphasized the importance of the Joint Declaration of Principles he had signed with Nixon in December, 1973, and renewed his invitation for the President to visit Bucharest.[12] As an aside, the fact that the choral group had a message for Ford, rather than Bogdan was typical of Ceausescu. Whenever he wanted to deal directly with the American President, he would send a message through anyone who had access to the Oval Office.

In Bucharest, negotiations had completed the trade part of the treaty, and on April 2, Ambassador Barnes and Ion Patan, the Romanian Minister of Foreign Trade and International Economic Cooperation, signed a three year trade agreement. The terms provided for reciprocal MFN and envisioned that two-way trade during the next three years would triple the value of two-way trade between 1972 and 1974. There were safeguards to prevent market disruption, and protections for industrial rights, processes and copyrights. Finally, the agreement enabled firms and corporations to establish offices and do business in each other's country, and to set up government commercial offices on a reciprocal basis.[13]

With trade negotiations completed, Bucharest and Washington addressed the more difficult issues involved in emigration. Section 402 of the Trade Act of 1974 contained three parts. Sections (a) and (b) prohibited the United States from extending MFN treatment, granting government credits or negotiating a commercial agreement with any nonmarket economy country, such as Romania, if the country (1) denied its citizens the right or opportunity to emigrate; (2) imposed more than a nominal tax on emigration; or (3) imposed more than a nominal charge on any citizen who wanted to emigrate.

However, Section 402 (c) of the Trade Act, which was the Jackson compromise, permitted the President to waive the prohibitions in Sections (a) and (b) for 18 months for any Communist country, if he reported to Congress that (1) he had determined that the "waiver for that country would substantially promote the objectives of freedom of emigration"; and (2) he had received "assurances that the emigration practices of that country would henceforth lead substantially to the achievement of the objectives of freedom of emigration." The 18 month period commenced January 3 when Ford signed the Trade Act into law, and expired on July 3, 1976. Thereafter, extensions could be continued by Presidential order at one year intervals, unless either house passed a resolution of disapproval.[14]

Negotiators worked to find a formula which would permit the President to waive the emigration prohibitions in Section 402. The problem was the form of the "assurance" that Romania could give without appearing to permit the United States to influence its internal policies on emigration. Both Barnes and Bogdan worked from their respective Embassies to resolve the problem. By mid-April, Washington and Bucharest settled on a formula. Romania would give no written assurance concerning her emigration practices. However, Ceausescu would give oral assurance to the President that Romania would live up to the provisions of the Joint Statement of Principles signed in Washington on December 5, 1973. This Nixon-Ceausescu agreement stated that both countries would "contribute to the solution of humanitarian problems on the basis of mutual confidence and good will." Ford accepted this formula and in so doing circumvented the intent of Section 402 (c). Since Romania refused to put any assurances into writing, the President became the sole source of assurance that a Presidential waiver of the emigration prohibitions in Section 402 (a) and (b) would lead to freer emigration practices in Romania.[15]

In his foreign policy address to Congress on April 10, the President indicated his interest in improving commercial relations with the Communist world.[16] Two weeks later, on April 24, he submitted a Romanian "package" to the legislature. The package included a proclamation to extend MFN treatment to Romanian products, the trade agreement signed on April 2, and an Executive Order waiving subsections (a) and (b) of Section 402 of the Trade Act. The waiver referred to the Declaration of December 5, 1973, and Ford indicated that he had "been assured that if and when such problems arise they will be solved, on a reciprocal basis, in the spirit of that Declaration. Accordingly, I am convinced that the emigration practices of Romania will lead substantially to the achievement of the objectives of Section 402 of the Act."[17] This initial waiver was extremely important since it could not be debated by Congress. However, either House could disapprove subsequent requests for an annual extension of the emigration waiver.

Congress and the Trade Agreement

On April 24, concurrent resolutions appeared in the House and Senate. Both called for the approval of the American-Romanian trade agreement including its provision to extend MFN treatment to Romanian products.[18] The House Ways and Means Subcommittee on Trade began hearings on the trade treaty on May 7. The opening remarks of the Chairperson, Edith Green of Oregon, firmly established Congress's disapproval of the waiver formula accepted by the President. Green noted that "despite the clarity of language, intent and legislative history of the waiver, the language of the President's report is not clear since it does not refer directly to assurances from Romania on its emigration practices. We hope that this question will be clarified during this hearing."[19] The parade of witnesses that testified quickly fell into two groups. The first, composed principally of corporate representatives, were nearly unanimous in their support of the trade agreement and Romanian MFN. Their reasons were obvious. Most businesses saw Eastern Europe as a new market for sales as well as a source of cheap labor and inexpensive production.[20] Among those testifying were representatives of the East-West Trade Council, the World Trade Club of New York, and Hugh Donaghue of Control Data Corporation, the only American corporation to establish a joint venture arrangement with Romania. Support also came from B'nai B'rith International and from Barbu Niculescu of the League of Free Romanians. [21]

The second group opposed the trade agreement and MFN. They included representatives from the AFL-CIO, leaders of the stone, glass and clay industries which feared competition from cheaper Romanian products, and members of ethic organizations. This latter group included Reverend Florian Galdau of the American-Romanian Committee for Assistance to Refugees who used the hearings as a forum to facilitate Jewish emigration from Romania. Galdau would appear at nearly every Romanian hearing for the next 12 years. Representatives from Hungarian organizations also appeared at this hearing, notably Z. Michael Szaz of the American Hungarian Foundation. He would be nearly as persistent as Galdau in his opposition to granting Romania MFN, because of Bucharest's treacherous treatment of its Hungarian minorities.[22]

While the House hearings indicated this division of opinion, without question the majority of testimony supported the trade agreement and MFN. While Administration spokesmen came under fire from the Subcommittee for the language of the Presidential waiver, the general sentiment of committee members was to support the agreement. However, Congress did not want to lose an opportunity to criticize the Administration, nor to reduce its new found influence in foreign policy. The new STR Ambassador, Frederick Dent, and Arthur Hartman of the State Department were especially harassed by committee member William Archer of Texas. He asked Hartman "why is it that you cannot tell this Congress today with a certainty that they [Romania] are not in violation of the very document that they signed?" Hartman was trapped. He could not go into details about the formula without indicating that Romania indeed had not given any written assurances to alter its emigration policy. Consequently, his answers to Archer appeared weak and emphasized the "political delicacy" of the situation.[23] This approach, however, had value. Congress's failure to recognize the "political delicacy" of the Soviet-American trade and emigration arrangements had forced Moscow to abort the agreement. The Subcommittee on Trade did not want the Romanian treaty to come to a similar end.

Congress's critical attacks on Ford's waiver alarmed Bogdan. He asked for a meeting with Vice President Nelson Rockefeller on May 14.[24] The Ambassador wanted the Administration's view on the progress of the Romanian treaty. Two-way trade with America had topped $400 million in 1974, and Bogdan wanted MFN in order to increase Romania's trade with the United States.[25] Bucharest's 1976-1980 economic plan called for significant increases in exports. She had successfully begun to develop Third World markets, especially since 1973. These made her less dependent on CMEA, and gave greater global credibility to the Ceausescu regime.[26] However, Bucharest needed Western technology and heavy industrial equipment in order to implement her economic goals. American MFN was important for this purpose, and Bogdan wanted Rockefeller to know that Romania would do everything it could to facilitate Congressional passage of the trade agreement.

During their meeting, Rockefeller tried to reassure Bogdan that in spite of the criticism, Congress would approve the trade package. The

Vice President also confirmed that he would speak to the delegates at the first Washington meeting of the United States-Romanian Economic Council scheduled to begin on May 29. Council membership included some leading American businessmen such as Mark Shepard of Texas Instruments, Ralph Weller of Otis Elevator and Gabriel Hauge of the Manufacturers Hanover Trust.[27]

On the 29th Rockefeller addressed the Council at the Metropolitan Club in Washington. He congratulated them on the work and told the members that he was "hopeful" that the trade agreement would be approved by Congress by mid-Summer.[28] Later in the evening, Secretary of Commerce Rogers Morton addressed the Council and reiterated the Vice President's remarks. On May 30, the Council concluded its meeting and elected Milton Rosenthal, President of Engelhard Minerals and Chemicals Corporation, to succeed Gabriel Hauge as President of the American delegation.

On June 2, the United States and Romania signed a cotton textile agreement,[29] and four days later the Senate Finance Committee began hearings on the trade treaty. The hearings were scheduled for two days, June 6 and July 8. On the first day, Russell Long's committee heard a number of concerns. The AFL-CIO maintained its opposition to Romanian MFN because of the number of jobs it would cost American labor.[30] Rabbi Miller, Chairman of the Conference of Presidents of Major American Jewish Organizations, expressed concern about the limited number of Jews permitted to emigrate to Israel. Miller wanted Congress to withhold its decision on the Romanian trade agreement pending improved Jewish emigration.[31] Michael Szaz repeated his remarks made at the House hearings opposing MFN because of Romania's discriminatory practices towards its Hungarian minority.[32] While other witnesses supported the Romanian package, there was a real concern at the Romanian Embassy whether or not the Finance Committee would recommend approving Romanian MFN. The main concern of the Committee was on the issue of Jewish emigration.

Ceausescu visits Ford

The Senate action reaffirmed Bogdan's fears. He had already notified Ceausescu that the hearings focused far more on emigration than anticipated.[33] The Ambassador wanted Ceausescu to personally intervene and speak with the American President. On June 4, Ford agreed to a meeting. Ceausescu was visiting South America and would stop-over in Washington on June 11 for a two hour visit en route home to Romania.[34]

Ceausescu shared Bogdans's concerns. He wanted more trade with America to counteract growing Soviet pressure to cooperate more with CMEA programs. The oil embargo of 1973 had dramatically increased the world oil prices. This caused Moscow severe economic hardship because she had agreed to sell oil to CMEA countries from 1971 to 1975 at the average world price for the preceding five year period.(1966-1970) In 1974, the Soviets pressed to have this so-called "Bucharest formula" revised to meet the spiraling oil prices. In 1975, Moscow renegotiated intra-CMEA oil prices. The new price was two-thirds of the world oil price. While this arrangement appeared generous from the Soviet viewpoint, it placed an enormous economic burden on the CMEA countries. Although Romania was one of the first East European countries to begin an oil conservation program, the effect of the higher petroleum prices meant that Ceausescu had to increase his foreign exports.[35] He also needed to reduce his imports to alleviate Romania's $500 million trade deficit. Further, he had industrialized Romania with Western credits and by 1975, they accounted for one-third of Romania's total debt.[36] MFN would open America's consumers to Romanian products, and as Bogdan said "you can sell almost anything in the United States, of any value, from junk to quality."[37]

The meeting received little press coverage. However, during their talks, Ford indicated that to assure passage of the trade agreement, Romania had to increase the number of Jews it permitted to emigrate. While disavowing all linkage between MFN and emigration, Ceausescu assured the President that Jewish emigration would increase.[38] Within weeks Bucharest dramatically increased the number of Jews it permitted to emigrate to Israel. In May, 46 Jews had emigrated, in June, 199, in July, 403.[39]

During the one month delay between Finance Committee hearings, Romanian-American business relations continued to develop. Negotiations, which began earlier in the year between Bucharest and the Department of Agriculture for a multiyear agricultural accord, continued. Phil Campbell, the Undersecretary of Agriculture visited Bucharest at the end of May to help complete the negotiations.[40] Meanwhile, the Island Creek Coal Company, a subsidiary of Occidental Petroleum, completed its negotiations with Romania and signed a framework agreement on July 1. While the terms needed Washington's approval, the arrangement called for Island Creek and Romania to enter a joint venture to open a new Virginia coal mine. Romania would invest $50 million for a one-third interest in the mine and receive one-third of the mine's coking coal.[41]

On July 8, Long's committee resumed hearings on the Romanian Trade Agreement. Administration officials began the testimony led by STR Ambassador Frederick Dent. Jesse Helms of North Carolina led the rebuttal. He had a personal quarrel with the President. Ford's waiver not only waived the provisions of Section 402 of the Trade Act, but it also waived Section 409, which he had sponsored and which he had never intended to have waived. Section 409 promoted free emigration of very close relatives of persons residing in the United States from nonmarket countries seeking trade.[42] During the December, 1974 debates on the Trade Act, the Senate approved a "technical amendment" to Section 409 which placed it under the same waiver language as Section 402. Helms was furious with his colleagues. "Senatorial courtesy lapsed even to the extent that I was not informed of the proposed action." The ultra-conservative Senator saw the entire issue of emigration and Section 409 as a moral issue. By issuing his waiver, Ford "flunked" the "very first test of the moral authority with which Congress has invested the emigration standards of the Trade Act."[43] Helms wanted nothing to do with Romania. "There is nothing that the Romanians are selling that we cannot do without. . . . The plain fact is that Romania is desperate to get this agreement, and we ought to hold Romania's feet to the fire to get concessions on human rights."[44]

While Helms' statement was directed as much against his Senatorial colleagues as the Administration, his identification of emigration practices and human rights would prove to be a most troublesome development for Romania in subsequent years. By accepting the Jackson-Vanik emigration language as a criterion for MFN, Romania unknowingly opened her internal politics to Congressional scrutiny. Over the next decade, emigration would be of secondary importance to MFN renewal. The new criterion, which did not exist in the Trade Act of 1974, would emphasize Romania's human rights practices.

While there was other criticism of the Administration, especially concerning the language of the President's waiver, there was considerable testimony at the July 8 hearings in support of MFN. Several witnesses noted Romania's increased Jewish emigration, and viewed it as evidence of Ceausescu's assurances.[45] Business leaders again testified, and the Finance Committee received three times the number of communications concerning the trade agreement as had their House counterpart. While some of these letters were written to free relatives from Romania, many were from major corporations which endorsed the President's waiver. Further, the Committee received a large number of letters in support of MFN from Romanian ethnic organizations such as the Romanian Baptist Association of the United States and Canada, the National Confederation of American Ethnic Groups, Union and League, and from Valerian Trifa, Bishop of the Romanian Orthodox Episcopate of America.[46]

Both the House Ways and Means Committee and the Senate Finance Committee supported the President's package. The House and Senate scheduled final debate for the last week of July, prior to their August recess. The Administration anticipated approval and planned for the trade agreement to come into force during the President's visit to Bucharest on August 2-3.[47]

On July 22, thirty-eight House members sent Ford a petition asking him to talk with Ceausescu about the plight of the Hungarian minority in Romania. In addition, they were concerned about religious minorities, especially evangelistic Protestant denominations. They understood that their people were harassed, and had many of their human rights curtailed, particularly in the areas of housing, jobs, education, and religious instruction.[48] Among the signatories were Philip Crane and Larry McDonald, both of whom would continue to speak out against human rights violations in Romania.

The floor debates went smoothly. In the Senate, Jackson and Ribicoff both supported the Romanian treaty. Further, Rabbi Miller, Chairman of the Conference of Presidents of Major American Jewish Organizations, sent a letter to the Senate indicating his group's support of Romanian MFN in light of the increased Jewish emigration. On July 25, the Senate voted 88-2 to approve the Romanian treaty.[49]

Meanwhile, the House received a report from its Committee on International Relations describing a recent visit made by several of its members to Romania. The report was very positive and contrasted Bucharest's ease of emigration practices with those of Moscow. The report particularly noted that Romania had not interfered with Jewish religious freedom, and that Bucharest had maintained relations with Israel throughout the Yom Kippur War.[50] On July 28, the House approved the treaty by a vote of 355-41.[51]

Ford Visits Bucharest

While Congress voted on the trade treaty, President Ford left for Europe on July 26 to sign the Helsinki Agreement, or Final Act.[52] This agreement stemmed from a 1966 Soviet suggestion for an all European conference on political detente and economic cooperation. Gradually this offer came to include the United States, principally to allay Western fears of Soviet encroachment following the Czechoslovakian invasion. Initial talks for a Conference on Security and Cooperation in Europe began at the foreign ministers level in Helsinki in July, 1973, and grew to include 35 nations– all of Europe, except Albania, plus the United States and Canada.

The Final Act contained three sections, or baskets, of jointly accepted objectives. Basket I set forth ten principles largely dealing with military security in Europe. However, tucked in among these was Principle VII which dealt exclusively with human rights. All of the signatory powers agreed to conform to the purposes and principles of the Charter of the United Nations and the Universal Declaration of Human Rights. Principle VII confirmed the "right of the individual to know and act upon his rights and duties."[53]

Basket II concerned cooperation in the fields of economics, science, technology and the environment. This section also encouraged measures to facilitate East-West trade. Basket III focused on human rights which included measures to reunite families and to promote a freer exchange of peoples, information, culture and education. Any disputes which arose under this section would be settled by the states concerned under "mutually acceptable conditions." The document concluded with a provision for a follow-up conference to meet in two years to review compliance and develop new measures to facilitate European security and cooperation.[54]

On August 1, after visiting West Germany and Poland, President Ford visited the Finnish capital and along with the representatives from 34 other nations, signed the Helsinki Agreement. Ceausescu signed for Romania and in a subsequent speech alluded to the importance of "humanitarian problems" which would require greater attention in the future. While accepting the humanitarian principles in the Final Act, he noted that more time should be paid to humanitarian questions linked "to the struggle against drugs, drug-addiction, [and] criminality." Ceausescu wanted to counter the prevailing view that Basket III was imposed on the Communist world by the West. He wanted Basket III to focus on problems more common to the Capitalist world.[55]

Ceausescu supported the Helsinki Agreement because it provided definite gains for Romania. Under the confidence-building measures outlined in Basket I, notification was required of military maneuvers involving over 25,000 men taking place within 250 kilometers of a national frontier. This limited the "intervention-through-maneuver" evidenced in the Soviet invasion of Czechoslovakia. Bucharest also chose to view the Final Act as a whole document, rather than as three sections. By so doing, the prohibitions in Basket I against interference in a country's domestic affairs excluded Western support of dissidents or reforms within Romania.[56] Finally, by signing the document, Romania participated in an international arena which included the world's two greatest powers.

Following the signing Ceausescu hurried back to Bucharest to await the arrival of President Ford. The President was only spending a night in Romania and had no time to see the countryside. Ceausescu did not mind, since the Romanian farmers were working feverishly to recover from the July floods, the worst since 1970. The raging water had killed 60 people, damaged 270 factories, destroyed homes and inundated 800,000 hectares of agricultural land.[57] As a result, food shortages would appear in the cities by mid-August, and the problem of food supply and distribution would become a major concern of both government and party for the rest of the year.[58]

Ford arrived at Otopeni airport on August 2. Ceausescu greeted him and the two drove in a motorcade through throngs on cheering spectators to Scinteia Square where the Mayor of Bucharest, Gheorghe Cioara, gave Ford the keys to the city.[59] That evening, Ceausescu hosted Ford at a state dinner and in his toast noted that it had been six years to the day that he had welcomed the first President of the United States to ever visit Romania.[60] The following day, the two leaders met at the Peles Castle in Sinaia and signed a joint communique which brought the Romanian-American Trade Agreement into force.[61] The joint acceptance of the treaty meant that Romanian products were eligible for MFN treatment, and that Bucharest was again eligible to receive Eximbank credits, suspended since December, 1974. While the trade agreement did not exclude Romania from export controls, it did increase her ability to export glass and glassware, clothing, wooden furniture, sheet steel, and leather footwear to the United States.[62]

To some, especially the defector Ion Pacepa and David Funderburk, America's Ambassador to Romania from 1981-1985, the agreement meant that Ceausescu could implement project "Horizon," an operation designed to secure Western technology without limiting his Stalinist-type control over Romania.[63] According to Pacepa, who was the former head of the Romanian secret police, Ceausescu told him before his defection in 1978 that "Horizon" was successful. Before it, he had "barely a dozen intelligence officers over in America. Now I have five times that many, the Ambassador included, and in a couple of years it'll be ten times as many. And what has America gotten out of it all? Shit, nothing but shit."[64]

Initial Fruits of the Treaty

With the trade treaty signed, negotiations on an agricultural agreement moved rapidly along. In early September, Angelo Miculescu, the Romanian Deputy Prime Minister and Minister for Agriculture, arrived in Washington. On the eleventh, he and Secretary of Agriculture Earl Butz signed two protocols to increase agricultural trade and cooperation. The former assured Romania that she could purchase needed agricultural commodities from the United States, provided they were available, and envisioned long term purchasing arrangements.[65] The Protocol on Cooperation in Agriculture called for a greater exchange of information on crop development and disease. To facilitate the exchange, both sides agreed to establish a working committee which would meet annually.[66] However, within weeks of the signing, the Agriculture Department indicated that due to lack of funds, its participation in a working committee would be minimal. Romania, too, had difficulties in allocating staff for a working committee, and Bucharest cancelled the first meeting scheduled for February, 1976.[67] The group would finally meet in Bucharest in 1977.[68]

The agricultural protocols proved to be the first of a number of arrangements between Bucharest and Washington which flowed from the Romanian-American Trade Agreement. On September 21, the National Science Foundation agreed to support joint research projects and seminars with the Romanian National Council for Science and Technology.[69] On October 8, Dr. H. Guyford Stever, the Director of the NSF and the President's Science Advisor, visited Bucharest for three days. He met with Ceausescu and the two talked about Romania's interest in developing nuclear energy plants and in space research. In 1974, the United States gave Bucharest a gift of about $16,000 worth of enriched uranium for use in its Triga research reactor. Ceausescu hoped that the American scientific community would continue to help Romania develop breeder reactors, light water reactors and laser technology.[70]

During October and for the next several months, American and Romanian officials crossed the Atlantic in a broad range of exchanges including education, health and transportation. The United States Department of Transportation set up its first "task-sharing cooperative" with an East European country which involved parallel research on psychological and medical factors used in the selection of railroad employees.[71]

Ion Patan, the Deputy Prime Minister and Romanian Minister of Foreign Trade made the most significant visit during the Fall. On November 3 he arrived in Washington at the head of the Romanian delegation to the Romanian-American Economic Commission. When the Romanians met with their counterparts led by Commerce Secretary Rogers Morton, they showed special interest in discussing increased American investment in Romania, joint ventures, and financial and banking cooperation. Morton's delegates countered with the difficulties several American firms had in dealing with Bucharest. Taxes and fees were high, office equipment was scarce and adequate housing was limited. In addition, Romania's centralized economic system prohibited American businesses from dealing with end-users.[72] In turn, the Romanians expressed frustration over export license delays and refusals which hindered joint ventures.[73] After two days of discussions, the delegates agreed to exchange drafts of a Long Term Agreement for Economic, Industrial and Technical Cooperation.[74]

During his stay in Washington, Patan met with President Ford. Ceausescu wanted Romania included in the United States system of tariff preferences for developing countries, the GSP. The Administration had given Bucharest such assurance in early 1975, and Ford had repeated this assurance to Ceausescu during his August visit. Nonetheless, Patan raised the issue again. And again, Ford repeated the pledge, providing Bucharest guaranteed that American interests would be fairly compensated in cases where Romania nationalized property. Patan quickly gave Ford the requisite guarantee,[75] and one week later, on November 10, the President designated Romania as a GSP beneficiary. The White House letter to Congress justified the President's decision on the basis that Romania belonged to the GATT and the IMF, and had maintained an independent foreign policy.[76] On January 1, 1976, the United States implemented a GSP program scheduled to extend through 1985. On that same day, Romania began her GSP eligibility.[77]

This meant that within dollar and volume limits, Bucharest could export items, from a list of 2,724 commodities, duty free to the United States.[78]

By January, 1976, with MFN and GSP Romania was ready to increase her trade with the United States. She had completed or signed 55 agreements with American firms and had 47 others in negotiation.[79] Further, of those 55 agreements, 71% were with Fortune 500 firms. Trade with America's corporate giants appealed to Romania for these were the companies which had the technology Bucharest so desperately sought. Further, because they were large companies, they could absorb the initial costs of negotiations which were exceedingly high compared to dealing with market economies.[80] The cost of negotiations became such that in 1978, the Department of Commerce issued a report on "Trading and Investing in Romania," which emphasized the excessive time involved in dealing with Romania's Foreign Trade Organizations. Since only written contracts were valid in Romania, everything had to be put in writing resulting in "extensive, often exhaustive, discussions of contract details."[81]

The new contracts meant an increase in Romanian imports. To offset this trade, Bucharest worked vigorously to expand her exports, especially in the areas of iron plating and textiles. In 1975, Romania shipped $133 million worth of goods to America. In 1976, she would sell $198 million and in 1977, $233 million. More important from Romania's viewpoint, her improved trade status would reduce America's bilateral trade advantage from $146 million in 1974 to $26 million in 1977.[82]

Romania's status as a "developing" country enabled Ceausescu to secure financial benefits from the industrialized Northern countries, without surrendering her affiliation with the Southern states. In 1963, seventy-seven nations from Latin America, Asia and Africa cosponsored a Joint Declaration of the Developing Countries in the United Nations General Assembly. This manifesto asked UNCTAD, the United Nations Conference on Trade and Development, to expand markets for less developed countries' manufactures, without requiring reciprocal concessions on their part.[83] As a result of their Declaration, the cosponsors became known as the Group of Seventy-Seven, and the name remained although the total group membership soon grew to more than 100 nations. Ceausescu wanted to join the Group. Throughout the 1970s he had made expanded relations with the developing nations a major priority in Romanian foreign policy. Less-developed nations could provide Romania with cheap raw materials, and markets for manufactures that would be unacceptable to the West because of their inferior quality.

Further, by linking herself politically to Third World countries, Romania would bolster her image of pursuing an autonomous foreign policy and be in a position to play a larger role in world affairs. Due to Ceausescu's efforts, the Group of Seventy-Seven accepted Romania as a member at its Manila Conference in January, 1976.[84] Bucharest's continued support of causes of the less developed countries won her even greater recognition among Third World nations. In August, 1976, the Conference of the Non-Aligned States granted Romania "guest status" in the organization. Considering that Romania was a member of the Warsaw Pact, this recognition was a coup for Ceausescu.[85]

Meanwhile Romania and the United States continued to exchange visits of high level government officials, and working level commercial delegations. Following Secretary Butz's visit to Bucharest in November, 1975,[86] the Romanians sent delegates from the Machine Building[87] and Light Industry ministries.[88] On April 29, Ioan Ursu, Chairman of the Romanian National Council for Science and Technology, arrived in Washington to meet with senior officials at the State Department to lobby for greater technological exchange between the two countries, especially in the area of nuclear energy.[89] In the midst of these visits, some serious negotiations took place to further implement the MFN provisions of the trade agreements. On June 4, the United States and Romania signed a three year renewable Maritime Agreement according each other's vessels MFN treatment within the ports and waters of both countries.[90]

The First Waiver Extension

In spite of this rash of negotiations and talks, the real rhythm of Romanian-American relations was set by the language of the Jackson-Vanik amendment. The Trade Act established a time schedule for the President to renew his emigration waiver without which Romania would be ineligible for MFN. The legislation stipulated that within 18 months of the Act becoming law, which was January 3, 1975, the President could waiver requirements of Section 402. He simply had to inform Congress that he had made a determination, on the basis of assurances from Romania, that Bucharest's emigration practices would lead substantially to freer emigration. The initial eighteen month period expired July 3, 1976, and thereafter extensions would be made annually. The legislation called for the President to submit a waiver request thirty days prior to expiration. This meant that the President had to annually submit his request to Congress by June 3.

During the first year of the waiver, Congress had until October 15 to act on the President's request. If Congress took no negative action, the waiver automatically extended until July 3 of the following year. Thereafter, the President would submit his request 30 days in advance of expiration, and Congress had until September 1 to rescind the waiver by a majority vote of either House. If Congress did not disapprove the waiver, it automatically extended until the following July.[91]

As a result of these provisions, Romanian emigration, and, later, human rights practices, came under intense Congressional and White House scrutiny annually between the months of February and August. On February 19, 1976, the White House received a letter from Ronald Mottl, a Congressman from Ohio, registering concern over Bucharest's poor treatment of German and Hungarian workers in Romania. He further indicated that the issue of family reunification was extremely slow and bogged down by the Romanian government. Mottl wanted the President to raise these issues directly with Ceausescu.[92] This first letter was quickly followed by several others until March 25, when Congressman Philip Crane of Illinois sent a petition to the President signed by 60 of his colleagues. They reminded Ford that MFN renewal was contingent on Romanian emigration policies. According to Crane, Ceausescu not only had not fulfilled his earlier promises, but he had threatened to further restrict the rights of Hungarians and Germans to join their families abroad. The petitioners hoped that the President could resolve this problem before Congress had to vote on Romanian MFN renewal.[93]

Opposition to Romanian MFN came also from representatives of the clear sheet glass industry. Libbey-Owens-Ford and Pittsburgh Plate Glass accused Romania of selling clear sheet glass at less than fair value in the United States. They filed a complaint in March with the Treasury Department under the Antidumping Act of 1921. The United States Customs Service investigated the complaint. The Service later determined that while Romania had sold glass at less-than-fair value, there would be no restrictions imposed because the sale had caused no injury to the American glass industry.[94] The speed with which this complaint was filed was an early indication that Romanian MFN renewal would be constantly opposed by special business interests in America.

A further source of concern for Bucharest was an article which appeared in the March 22, 1976, *Washington Post* entitled "A Soviet-East European 'Organic Union'." Helmut Sonnenfeldt told a Chiefs of Mission meeting in London in December, 1975, that he envisioned an "organic union" developing between Eastern Europe and the Soviet Union. Newspapers quickly jumped on the story. Sonnenfeldt was close to Kissinger, and the "Sonnenfeldt Doctrine" became a national headline. If the Counselor's remarks were true, they meant that the United States accepted Soviet domination in Eastern Europe.[95] East European ethnic groups across America called for an explanation. Were Sonnenfeldt's remarks an indication of a major change in American foreign policy? Tito and Ceausescu queried the White House seeking reassurance.[96] As the uproar continued, the House Subcommittee on International Security and Scientific Affairs agreed to hold hearings on the "Sonnenfeldt Doctrine."

On April 12, Sonnenfeldt testified before the Subcommittee. He deplored the "misunderstandings" that had arisen because of the newspaper reports alleging that he advocated the consolidation of Soviet control in Eastern Europe. "Nothing could be further from the truth," he said, "I emphatically do not advocate Soviet domination or subjugation of the countries of Eastern Europe." He totally supported the Administration's policy toward Eastern Europe which recognized the "independence, sovereignty and autonomy" of all countries.[97] When asked about the meaning of the word "organic," Sonnenfeldt explained that it was a phrase frequently used among academic groups to "contrast with a relationship based on force and repression." He wanted relations between Moscow and Eastern Europe to be based on a natural, or "organic," state-to-state relationship, rather than the "inorganic" relationship of oppression and military power which presently existed.[98] During the testimony, Representative Paul Findley of Illinois asked Sonnenfeldt what he would tell Ceausescu if the Romanian President called him concerning his alleged December statements. The State Department official reiterated his support of the promises President Ford made in Bucharest, which recognized Romania's "national sovereignty" and called for continued "normal and productive relations" between the two countries.[99]

The hearings served a purpose. They gave Sonnenfeldt an opportunity to explain his remarks and in so doing reassured Tito and Ceausescu that the United States did not intend to curb her relations with Eastern Europe. However, the hearings did not convince everyone that there was not at least some truth in the "Sonnenfeldt Doctrine." In an interview with Bogdan in 1987, the former Ambassador believed that Sonnenfeldt meant "organic" within the traditional definition. He meant "to send a signal that the United States was ready to accept concrete terms of a Soviet sphere of influence in Eastern Europe" in return for Moscow ending her efforts to secure power in Western Europe. According to Bogdan, Sonnenfeldt's remarks were in response to Communist efforts to "move into Portugal." "The Portuguese situation is the key to Sonnenfeldt."[100] While critics can challenge the substance of Bogdan's views, the fact remains that the phrase "Sonnenfeldt Doctrine" was used to indicate an American strategy to divide Europe into two spheres of influence.

A week after the Sonnenfeldt hearings, the East-West Foreign Trade Board sent the President a reminder that if he wanted to continue Romanian MFN, he had to submit a waiver to Congress before June 3. If the waiver expired, Romania would lose MFN and the availability of government credits. Further, the authority for the Romanian Trade Agreement would lapse. The Board had considered the waiver renewal at its March 22 meeting, and recommended that the President ask Congress for an extension.[101]

In early May the State Department prepared material for the President's emigration waiver, in accordance with the provisions of the Trade Act of 1974.[102] Aware of growing Congressional concern about minority discrimination in Romania, the Department sent a note to several Congressmen to assuage their fears. It reminded them that the Romanian government imposed restrictions on civil liberties, such as travel, freedom of assembly, freedom of speech, and religious practices, which were considered excessive by Western standards. However, the restrictions applied to all Romanian citizens, regardless of their ethnic or religious background. Further, due to the history of Hungarian-Romanian antagonism, any restrictions imposed would be especially resented by the Hungarians and immediately viewed as discriminatory.[103]

On June 2, Ford asked Congress to extend his authority to waive the freedom of emigration requirements of Section 402 for another year. Ford's letter reminded Congress of Romania's independent foreign policy, and the fact that she was the only CMEA member of the IMF, World Bank and the GATT. Further, the Trade Agreement had markedly increased the flow of emigration from Bucharest to both Israel and the United States. In the ten month period between July 1, 1975 and April 30, 1976, nearly twice as many people had left Romania than in any preceding twelve month period during the past 20 years. As a result, the President urged Congress to extend the emigration waiver for 12 months.[104]

1976 was a Presidential election year. The White House and Congress focused their attention on the Republican and Democratic party conventions. Consequently, Congressional hearings on the emigration waiver did not begin until September. In the interim, however, American-Romanian relations continued to flourish. At the same time that the President sent his request to Capitol Hill, the first American Exposition and Congress for the biomedical, hospital and public health fields, held outside the United States, opened in Bucharest.[105] On June 12, representatives of the Department of Commerce and the Licensing Executives Society began a week long visit to Romania. Their purpose was to provide both Washington and the American business community with a better understanding of the procedures and regulations regarding the trade of technology intensive products in Romania.[106]

A few days after this group departed, Treasury Secretary Simon arrived in Bucharest at the invitation of the Finance Minister, Florea Dumitrescu. During his two day visit, he talked with Prime Minister Manescu and Deputy Prime Minister Patan as well as with other government officials.[107] The purpose of Simon's visit was to tell the Romanians what was required under the Jackson-Vanik amendment. He stressed that Congress was concerned about human rights issues in Romania, and that he could not guarantee that Congress would approve the emigration waiver.[108] Romania had to increase the number of exit visas to both Israel and the United States in order to win Congressional support of the waiver.

Simon and Patan also discussed the problems involved in joint ventures. To date, American business had only entered one joint venture, and that was done by Control Data Corporation. Other Western nations too were reluctant to deal with Romania. Six Western firms had established joint ventures in Romania, but the average negotiating period was two years. This was far too long for most American firms. Further, Romania appeared unwilling to accommodate the profit motive of American investors, insisting on unrealistic pricing criteria. On a positive note, both men noted the success of the ongoing negotiations for a Long Term Agreement between the two countries.[109]

In between talks with government officials, Simon attended the opening of the Third Session of the United States-Romanian Economic Council on June 23. During the two day meeting, the delegates discussed revisions of the 1976-1980 Romanian Five Year Plan. In contrast to the goals approved at the 11th Party Congress in November, 1974, the revised targets showed significant increases particularly in the area of agriculture. There were also projected increases in the machine building and chemical industries.[110] The Council also discussed ways to increase trade and expand marketing opportunities. Further, the Council members agreed to simplify and expedite the procedures used in pre-arbitral solutions to commercial problems.[111]

Ceausescu responded to Simon's message. He increased the number of Jews emigrating to Israel in July to 237 in contrast to 51 in April. He also increased Romanian emigration to the United States from 77 in May to 111 in June, 96 in July and 104 in August.[112] The Romanian President did not want to lose his trade gains with the United States. The revised Five Year Plan approved by the Central Committee in early July called for approximately a 100% increase in foreign trade.[113] Continued American trade, especially in the areas of agriculture and technology were needed to meet this target. The value of GSP eligible imports from Romania increased 133% between 1975 and 1976. GSP items constituted 10% of America's total imports from Romania in 1976, the largest among them being PVC resins, wooden furniture and machine tools. Bucharest had also found a major market for low-cost men's and boy's suits, and became America's largest supplier.[114] In comparing trade figures for the months of April-June in 1975 and in 1976, Romania increased her exports to the United States from about $18 million in 1975 to $45 million in 1976, while American exports to Bucharest in 1976 only increased by $4 million over the 1975 figure.[115] Further, Romania received a $47 million line of credit from the Commodity Credit Corporation, CCC, to purchase soybeans and soybean meal,[116] and over $5 million in Eximbank loans and guarantees.[117] Consequently, if increased emigration was the price for continued MFN, Ceausescu was willing to cooperate.

On the same day that the Senate Finance Committee began hearings on continuing MFN treatment for Romanian imports, the Democratic presidential candidate, Jimmy Carter, told a B'nai B'rith audience that "if any nation . . . deprives its own people of basic human rights, that fact will shape our own people's attitudes toward that nation's government."[118] Carter's September 8 remarks reflected a small, but growing sentiment in the United States Congress. The Vietnam War and Watergate, coupled with Soviet-Cuban efforts to bring a Communist regime to power in Angola, had moved America toward a more conservative posture; one which would emphasize morality as a consideration in foreign policy. Signs of this change became apparent in the Ford White House. In July, 1975, the President eagerly attended the Apollo-Soyuz Launch at Cape Kennedy. In March, 1976, he eliminated the word "detente" from his campaign literature.[119] The growing power of the movement which linked human rights behavior to American foreign policy would soon become apparent in the Congressional hearings on Romanian MFN.

Meanwhile, the Finance Committee listened to a large number of witnesses. Those opposing continued MFN for Romania represented three groups: labor organizations which feared cheap products, relatives interested in family reunification, and supporters of free emigration and human rights. Mark Richardson, President of the American Footwear Industries Association represented the first group. MFN changed the tariff on Romanian shoes from 20% to 5% and in the process threatened the existence of the footwear industry. The AFL-CIO reinforced Richardson's position and opposed MFN in behalf of all the interests represented by its laborers.[120] The chief spokesman for the second group was Reverend Florian M. Galdau, Chairman of the American-Romanian Committee for Assistance to Refugees. He submitted a list of 109 Romanians who sought exit visas from Romania to join their families in the United States.[121] In addition, the Senate Committee received written testimony from several dozen people documenting Bucharest's refusal to permit family reunification.

The third group included representatives of religious and ethnic organizations who saw emigration restriction as part of a larger issue, human rights violations. Some members of these groups, such as Laszlo Hamos of the Committee for Human Rights in Romania, Michael Szaz, of the American-Hungarian Federation and Jacob Birnbaum of the Center for Russian Jewry and Student Struggle for Soviet Jewry had appeared at the 1975 hearings on Romanian MFN. While Birnbaum used the hearings to increase Jewish emigration, Szaz and Hamos used the hearings to present a litany of injustices that Bucharest perpetrated against the Hungarian minority in Romania.[122] The importance of their testimony was that it expanded the issue of emigration, which was the primary criterion for extending Romanian MFN, to include human rights violations. This theme was supported by Senator James Buckley and Congressman Edward Koch, both of New York.[123]

There were also a number of people who testified before the Finance Committee in favor of renewing Romanian MFN. Administration officials supported the President as did the American Ambassador to Romania, Harry Barnes. In response to emigration questions, he told the Senators that "as far as emigration to the United States is concerned . . . there is a presupposition, I would say, of favorable decisions toward those who want to emigrate." While there were still emigration problems, he stressed the fact that the situation was improving.[124] Rabbi Schindler, who represented the Conference of Presidents of Major American Jewish Organizations, also testified. He supported MFN renewal. The Jewish problem was complicated. There were about 65,000 Jews remaining in Romania, of whom 50% were over the age of 65. These people did not want to leave Romania. Emigration was important to younger Jews. They numbered about 25,000. Therefore, if the current emigration rate continued, within ten years all Jews who wanted to leave Romania could do so.[125] Leaders of several ethnic organizations also supported Romanian MFN. While none of these appeared to testify before the Committee, the Senate received letters from Barbu Niculescu of the American-Romanian Cultural Foundation, Father Mihai Iancu of the Committee for the Defense of Romanian Transylvania and Valeriu Anania of the Romanian Orthodox Missionary Archdiocese in America. The largest contingent supporting Romanian MFN was, as in 1975, representatives of big business. The two key witnesses for corporate America were Mark Sandstrom of the East-West Trade Council and Milton Rosenthal of the United States-Romanian Economic Council. In addition, numerous CEOs wrote letters in support of continued MFN.

Six days later, the House Ways and Means Subcommittee on Trade began one day hearings on extending Romania's MFN. At the outset, House and Subcommittee members received a copy of a report from a Congressional study mission entitled "Developments in U.S. Economic Relations with Romania and Hungary." The Chairman of the House Committee on International Relations, Jonathan Bingham, had visited Romania on May 28-29, and talked with several government leaders including Ceausescu, Macovescu, the Foreign Minister, and Moses Rosen, the Chief Rabbi. Bingham's report stressed the cultural diversity of Romania, but noted that while there were instances of discrimination, the "allegations of 'cultural genocide' leveled by American groups" were "exaggerated."[126] Bingham had talked with Ambassador Barnes who showed him the report the Embassy had made during the Spring concerning the status of Hungarians in Romania. One major Hungarian complaint was cultural starvation. Bucharest limited the number of Hungarian books and magazines that could enter the country. While conceding that this was true, Barnes' report argued that the restrictions were because Bucharest believed that Hungarian publications promoted a pro-Soviet position in foreign policy and encouraged revanchism.[127]

Bingham's report also addressed the issue of emigration. Romania candidly admitted that as a developing country, their policy was to "discourage emigration." Ceausescu could not modernize Romania and at the same time permit a "brain drain" of talented young people to emigrate. Ceausescu viewed the "freedom of emigration" requirements in the Trade Act of 1974 as an intrusion into Romania's internal affairs. However, since Bucharest wanted trade with the United States, it accepted the Jackson-Vanik language and agreed to "act affirmatively on 'humanitarian problems' which might be eased by emigration."[128]

In his talks with Rabbi Rosen, Bingham concluded that there was considerable religious and cultural freedom for the Jewish community in Romania. There were Hebrew classes, a Jewish theater in Bucharest, Kosher restaurants and a bi-weekly Hebrew newspaper. Rosen feared that continued Jewish emigration could destroy the Romanian Jewish community. In 1948 there were 600 rabbis, now there were 3. Lack of Kosher butchers posed an even greater practical problem, and the few that remained spent most of their time travelling from community to community.[129]

In his recommendations, Bingham noted that while the emigration process was beset with hardships and delays, "the Romanian officials, nevertheless, appear to be making a good faith effort to meet their international commitments to act upon and solve humanitarian problems." Further, Congress should review its immigration laws to insure that no unnecessary restrictions were imposed upon Romanians seeking entry into the United States, once Bucharest approved their emigration visas. In conclusion, Bingham recommended that Congress renew Romania's MFN status, partly as a means for her to continue her "bravely independent foreign policy."[130]

The testimony that the House Subcommittee received was similar to that submitted to the Senate Finance Committee. More people testified at the House hearings, while the Senate received more written communications. The House hearings had more Congressmen testify. Of particular importance were statements made by Charles Vanik and Larry McDonald. As co-author of Section 402, Vanik's testimony to extend MFN carried some weight. He argued that MFN continuation would give Romania an "additional opportunity" to indicate its commitment to freer emigration.[131] McDonald, a Representative from Georgia, focused on human rights, an issue he had raised in July, 1975. He wanted the Subcommittee to consider several resolutions he had cosponsored which were designed to warn Bucharest that MFN renewal was contingent upon increased emigration, and upon improved human rights for ethnic and religious minorities.[132]

After the hearings closed, members of both Houses introduced resolutions to disapprove the extension of the President's authority to waiver the freedom-of-emigration requirement. McDonald submitted Resolution 1547 on September 15 and five days later, Jesse Helms of North Carolina introduced an identical resolution, S. 555, in the Senate. While each resolution prompted some discussion, neither was brought to a vote.[133] On October 15, since neither house had taken any action on the President's request to waive Section 402 of the Trade Act, the waiver and MFN treatment were automatically extended through July 3, 1977.

While Bucharest appreciated the extension, the entire process emphasized the fragile nature of Romanian-American relations. The future was defined in one year units. The Trade Act of 1974 required the President annually to request Congress to approve, or not disapprove, a waiver of the freedom-of-emigration language in Section 402 of the Trade Act. The mandate that this be an annual event meant that the MFN provisions of the three year Romanian-American Trade Agreement could only be depended upon for one year. For without the annual waiver, the President could not continue to extend MFN treatment to Romania.

The uncertainty that this situation produced forced Ceausescu to be more practical in his relations with Moscow. In June, he put an end to an ongoing debate between Romanian and Soviet historians as to the history of Bessarabia and the ethnic background of its inhabitants. He announced that "certain problems inherited from the past . . . should not affect the cooperation and solidarity" between the parties and peoples of Romania and the Soviet Union.[134]

In August, the Romanian President led a delegation of high-ranking government officials to the Crimea. Ceausescu and Brezhnev met and their staffs discussed increased trade between the two countries during the 1977-1980 period. While 14 protocols emanated from these talks, the major result was an improved atmosphere between the two countries.[135] This cordiality continued into November when Brezhnev visited Bucharest, for the first time in a decade. At the state dinner given the Soviet leader on November 22, Ceausescu indicated that while there were still "some differences of opinions on non-essential questions," Romania gave "pride of place to the development of the relations of friendship, alliance and collaboration with the Soviet

Union."[136] While there were no agreements reached during the visit, Brezhnev did invite Ceausescu to Moscow and if nothing else, the visit maintained cordial bilateral relations.[137]

The Last Months of the Ford Presidency

Brezhnev's visit coincided with the arrival of an American delegation led by Commerce Secretary Elliot Richardson. He came to sign a Long-Term Agreement on Economic, Industrial and Technical Cooperation with Romania. First talked about four years earlier, the ten year agreement took fourteen months to negotiate. On November 21, Richardson and Ion Patan signed the accord which supplemented the United States-Romanian Trade Agreement. The Romanians divided international activity into two distinct categories: trade and cooperation. Trade was straight import-export transactions. Cooperation lacked clear definition but included several characteristics such as product marketing, research and development, financing arrangements and technology transfers.[138]

The LTA was a lengthy document which defined Romania as a "developing" country, but suggested that she might become "developed" over the ten years of the agreement. The accord offered protection to American investors against expropriation or contract impairment, and provided measures to improve business facilities and information exchanges.[139] While Romania had signed LTAs with other Western nations, the American agreement alone contained an annex which set out general principles for the organization and operation of equity joint ventures in both countries.[140]

In addition to signing the LTA, Richardson also signed a Fisheries Agreement which regulated Romania's fishing rights within American fishery conservation zones.[141] Immediately thereafter, the Commerce Secretary led the American delegation to join their Romanian counterparts for the third annual meeting of the Joint Romanian-American Economic Commission. The two-day session began on November 22 and focused primarily on steps both sides could take to implement the proposals made in the LTA. Other topics included Romania's credit needs and Washington's anti-dumping regulations.

The LTA, Fisheries accord, and a December Airworthiness Agreement, insuring that Romanian made gliders exported to the United States met American aviation standards, ended the Ford Administration's initiatives to improve United States-Romanian relations.[142] The American people had chosen to restore a Democrat to the White

House after eight years of Republican rule. Jimmy Carter would take office as President of the United States in January, 1977.

Notes

1. *DOS Bulletin*, February 17, 1975, pp. 232-233.
2. Harry G. Barnes, Jr., "Impressions of Romania," *The United States and Romania*, ed. Paul D. Quinlan, p. 126; Author interview of Harry Barnes, July 19, 1987.
3. *Ibid*.
4. Summary record of East-West Trade Policy Committee Meeting of January 28, 1975, p.3, Folder East-West Foreign Trade Board, Box 55, William Seidman Papers, GRF Library. Nixon organized the East-West Trade Policy Committee on June 25, 1974, the day after the resignation of Peter Flanigan as Executive Director of the CIEP. Ambassador Eberle, the STR, replaced Flanigan at the CIEP (Letter, Peter Flanigan to the President, June 24, 1974, Folder CF FG 6-11 1/Flanigan, Peter, Box 15, Confidential files, Subject files, WHSF:WHCF, Nixon Presidential Materials Project); *Idem.*, Richard Nixon to Peter Flanigan, June 24, 1974, 2 pp; Joint Committee Print, *Legislation on Foreign Relations Through 1976*, 1977, II, 1140-1144.
5. Memorandum, Raymond J. Albright to Gerald L. Parsky, February 4, 1975, Folder East-West Foreign Trade Board, Box 55, William Seidman Papers, GRF Library.
6. Memorandum Howard L. Worthington to Secretary Simon, February 14, 1975, 2pp., Folder Exports, Box 67, William Seidman Papers, GRF Library.
7. Author interview of Harry Barnes, July 19, 1987.
8. *Ibid*.
9. Memorandum, David M. Evans to J. M. Dunn, March 18, 1975, p. 3., Folder East-West Foreign Trade Board, Box 55, William Seidman Papers, GRF Library.
10. *DOS Bulletin*, April 21, 1975, pp. 506-509.
11. Weekly Compilation of Presidential Documents, Jan-Mar 75, p. 315. GRF Library.
12. Memorandum, Henry Kissinger to the President, April 15, 1975, Folder ME 1/CO 114-127, Box ME 1/CO CO71-158, WHCF, GRF Library.
13. Verzariu and Burgess, *Joint Venture Agreements in Romania*, Appendix D, pp. 42-49; *Scinteia*, April 3, 1975, p. 5; Press Guidance,President Ford to Henry Kissinger, n.d., 3pp., Folder 4/16/75-4/31/75, Box 16, FO 3-2 Subject Files, WHCF, GRF Library.
14. U. S. Congress, Senate Committee on Finance, *Background Materials Relating to United States-Romanian Trade and the Extension of the President's Authority to Waive Section 402 of the Trade Act of 1974*, 94th Cong., 2d Sess., 1976, pp. 1-3, hereafter, Senate Committee on Finance, *Background Materials Relating to United States-Romanian Trade, 1976*; Press Materials, 10pp., February 19 - June 9, 1975, Folder Romania, Box 124, Nessen Papers, GRF Library.

15. *Public Papers of the Presidents, Richard M. Nixon, 1973*, p. 998; Author interviews of Corneliu Bogdan, March 19, 1987 and April 3, 1989; Author interview of Harry Barnes, July 19, 1987.

16. Memorandum, Gerald L. Parsky to the Members of the East-West Foreign Trade Board, July 3, 1975, Attachment, Folder East-West Foreign Trade Board, Box 55, William Seidman Papers, GRF Library. This was in striking contrast to the dozens of letters Ford had written to his constituents while still a Congressman from Michigan. Then he strongly opposed "building bridges" with Communist regimes.

17. Press Release of the President's Message to Congress, April 24, 1975, Folder TA5; 4/1/75-4/30/75, Box 29, Subject Files, WHCF, GRF Library.

18. See, H. Con. Res. 252 and S. Con. Res. 35.

19. U. S. Congress, House Committee on Ways and Means, Hearings Before the Subcommittee on Trade, *United States-Romanian Trade Agreement*, 94th Cong., 1st Sess., 1975, p. 3.

20. Paul Marer, "U.S.-Romanian Industrial Cooperation: A Compositite Case Study, *East-West Trade*, eds. Brada and Somanath, 1978, p. 98.

21. House Subcommittee on Trade, *Hearings on United States-Romanian Trade Agreement*, 1975, pp. iii-iv.

22. *Ibid*.

23. *Ibid*., pp. 46-49.

24. Memorandum, Brent Scowcroft, May 14, 1975, Attachment, 3pp., Folder CO125 Rom; 1/1/75-6/30/75, Box 43, WHCF, CO125, GRF Library.

25. House Subcommittee on Trade, *Hearings on United States-Romanian Trade Agreement, 1975*, p. 36.

26. Thomas Barnett, "Romania and the Third World," *Conference of the New England Slavic Association*, Harvard University, April 14, 1989, Charts A and B.

27. *Romanian Bulletin*, The Romanian Library, New York, New York [July 1975], 4pp.

28. Memorandum, George S. Springsteen to Brent Scowcroft, Attachment, May 23, 1975, 6pp., Folder IT100 Romanian-American Economic Commission, Box 13, IT100 WHCF, GRF Library; Idem., Memorandum, Henry A. Kissinger [to the Vice-President] , May 29, 1975, 3pp.

29. *DOS Bulletin*, June 23, 1975. p. 78.

30. U. S. Congress, Hearings Before the Senate Committee on Finance, *Romanian Trade Agreement*, 94th Cong., 1st Sess., 1975, pp. 6-7, hereafter, Senate Committee on Finance, *Romanian Trade Agreement*, 1975.

31. *Ibid*., pp. 24-25.

32. *Ibid*., pp. 56ff.

33. Memorandum, Gerald L. Parsky to Members of the East-West Foreign Trade Board, n.d., Attachment, 3pp., Folder East-West Foreign Trade Board, Box 55, William Seidman Papers, GRF Library.

34. Author interview of Corneliu Bogdan, April 11, 1987.

35. Braun, *Romanian Foreign Policy Since 1965*, pp. 33-34; Hutchings, *Soviet-East European Relations*, p. 193.

36. Joint Economic Committee of the Congress, *East European Economies*, 1977, p. 1357.

37. Author interview of Corneliu Bogdan, April 11, 1987.

38. Memorandum, Mr. Clift to Henry Kissinger, June 5, 1975, Folder CO125; 7/1/75-12/31/75, Box 43, CO125 WHCF, GRF Library.

39. U. S. Congress, Senate Committee on Finance, Hearing Before the Subcommittee on International Trade, *Continuing Most-Favored-Nation Tariff Treatment of Imports from Romania - 1977*, 95th Cong., 1st Sess., 1977, p, 158, hereafter, Senate Subcommittee on International Trade, *MFN Treatment*, 1977.

40. Memorandum, Gerald L. Parsky to the Members of the East-West Foreign Trade Board, September 29, 1975, 6pp., Folder East-West Trade Board, Box 55, William Seidman Papers, GRF Library; Memorandum, NSC to Rustand, June 3, 1975, Folder CA125; 1/1/75-6/31/75, Box 43, WHCF, GRF Library.

41. Background Paper, Romania-Island Creek Joint Venture, n.d., 2pp., Folder Rom 6/24/76, Box 315, William Seidman Papers, GRF Library.

42. Senate Committee on Finance, *Romanian Trade Agreement*, 1975, pp. 125-127.

43. *Ibid.*, p. 125.

44. *Ibid.*

45. *Ibid.*, pp. 114ff.

46. Senate Committee on Finance, *Romanian Trade Agreement*, 1975, pp. iv-v.

47. Memorandum, David M. Evans to J. M. Dunn, July 25, 1975, 6pp., East-West Foreign Trade Board, Box 55, William Seidman Papers, GRF Library.

48. Letter, Congress to the President, July 22, 1975, 5pp., Folder Bucharest Rom, 7/25/75-8/3/75, Box 58, TR 34-3, WHCF, GRF Library.

49. U.S., *Congressional Record*, 93d Cong., 1st Sess., 1975, CXXI, 24936-24948.

50. U. S., Congress, House Committee on International Relations, Report of a Study Mission to the Soviet Union and Four Eastern European Nations, *Soviet Bloc Trade Hopes: Reactions to the Trade Act of 1974*, 94th Cong., 1st Sess., 1975, pp. 18-22.

51. U. S. Congress, Senate Committee on Finance, *United States International Trade Policy and the Trade Act of 1974*, 94th Cong., 2d Sess., 1976, p. 36.

52. Ford, *A Time to Heal*, pp. 298ff.

53. U.S., Congress, Hearing and Markup Before the House Committee on Foreign Affairs and Its Subcommittee on International Organizations, *Human Rights in Eastern Europe and the Soviet Union*, 96th Cong., 2d Sess., 1980, p. 128, hereafter, House Committee on Foreign Affairs, *Human Rights in Eastern Europe and the Soviet Union,* 1980.

54. *Ibid.*, pp. 128ff; Hutchings, *Soviet-East European Relations*, pp. 96-97. For extended presentation of Romanian policy on human rights and security see, Romulus Neagu, *European Security: A Romanian Point of View* (Bucharest: Meridiane Publishing House, 1977), and Vojtech Mastny, *Helsinki, Human*

Rights, and European Security: Analysis and Documentation (Durham, NC: Duke University Press, 1986).

55. Ceausescu, *Romania On the Way*, XI, 963-966.

56. Braun, *Romanian Foreign Policy Since 1965*, pp. 116-117.

57. Richard F. Staar (ed.), *Yearbook on International Affairs, 1976* (Stanford, CA: Hoover Institution Press, 1976), p. 62.

58. *Ibid.*, pp. 62-63.

59. *Romanian Bulletin*, The Romanian Library, New York, New York (September 1975), p. 2.

60. *DOS Bulletin*, September 8, 1975, p. 363.

61. *Romanian Bulletin*, September 1975, p. 2.

62. Briefing Paper, U.S.-Romanian Protocol on Development of Agricultural Trade, nd., 2pp., Tab K, Folder Rom 6/24/76, Box 315, William Seidman Papers, GRF Library.

63. David B. Funderburk, *Pinstripes and Reds: An American Ambassador Caught Between the State Department and the Romanian Communists, 1981-1985* (Washington, D.C.: Selous Foundations Press, 1987), p. 54. Hereafter *Pinstripes and Reds*; Pacepa, *Red Horizons*, p. 23.

64. *Ibid.*

65. Briefing Paper, U.S.-Romanian Protocol on Development of Agricultural Trade, nd., 2pp., Folder Rom 6/24/76, Box 315, William Seidman Papers, GRF Library.

66. *Ibid.*

67. *Ibid*; Background Paper, Cooperation in Scientific Research and Technology (Excluding Nuclear Energy), n.d., 2pp., Folder Rom 6/24/76, Box 315, William Seidman Papers, GRF Library.

68. U.S. Department of Commerce, *Trading and Investing in Romania* ("Overseas Business Reports, "OBR 78-33;Washington, D.C.: U.S. Government Printing Office, September 1978), p. 10, hereafter, Department of Commerce, *Trading and Investing in Romania, 1978*.

69. Background Paper, Cooperation in Scientific Research and Technology (Excluding Nuclear Energy), n.d., 2pp., Folder Rom 6/24/76, Box 315, William Seidman Papers, GRF Library.

70. *Ibid.*

71. *Ibid*; Folder CO125; 7/1/75-12/31/75 Box 43, Executive File, GRF Library.

72. Premeeting briefing, Henry Kissinger to the President, n.d., 3pp., Folder CO125; 7/1/75-12/31/75, Box 43, CO125 WHCF, GRF Library; Background Paper, Cooperation in Scientific Research and Technology (Excluding Nuclear Energy), n.d., 2pp., Folder Rom 6/24/76, Box 315, William Seidman Papers, GRF Library.

73. *Idem.*, Background Paper, American-Romanian Economic Commission, June 16, 1976, 2pp.

74. "American-Romanian Economic Commission Joint Communique,"

Romanian Bulletin, The Romanian Library, New York, New York, (November 1975), p. 3.

75. Premeeting briefing, Henry Kissinger to the President, n.d., 3pp., Folder CO125; 7/1/75-12/31/75, Box 43, CO125, WHCF, GRF Library.

76. U. S. Congress, House Subcommittee on Trade of the Committee on Ways and Means, *Background Material on the Generalized System of Preferences*, 94th Cong., 2d Sess., 1976, p. 72-73, hereafter, Subcommittee on Trade, *Materials on the Generalized System of Preferences*, 1976.

77. U. S. Congress, Senate Committee on Finance, Hearing Before the Subcommittee on International Trade, *Review of the U. S. Generalized System of Preferences*, 96th Cong., 2d Sess., 1980, p. 12.

78. The dollar limit in 1975 for a single product was $26 million and the volume of any product could not exceed fifty percent of the United States market (Background Paper, U.S. Generalized Preferences for Romania, June 8, 1976, Tab 20, Folder Rom; 6.24.76, Box 315, William Seidman Papers, GRF Library.

79. Tsantis, Pepper *et al*, *Romania: The Industrialization of an Agrarian Economy under Socialist Planning*, p. 116.

80. Paul Marer, "U.S.-Romanian Industrial Cooperation," *East-West Trade*, eds. Brada and Somanath, 1978, pp. 92-95.

81. Department of Commerce, *Trading and Investing in Romania*, 1978, pp. 11ff.

82. Department of Commerce, *Trading and Investing in Romania*, 1978, p. 5; Background Paper, U.S.-Romanian Trade Trends, n.d., 9pp., Tab G, Folder Rom; 6/24/76, Box 315, William Seidman Papers, GRF Library; Joint Economic Committee of the Congress, *East European Economies*, 1977, p. 1414.

83. Spero, *The Politics of International Economic Relations*, pp. 63-64.

84. Joint Economic Committee of the Congress, *East European Economies*, 1977, p. 889.

85. Ronald H. Linden, "Romanian Foreign Policy in the 1980s: Domestic-foreign Policy Linkages," *Foreign and Domestic Policy in Eastern Europe in the 1980s*, eds. Michael J. Sodaro and Sharon L. Wolchik (New York: St. Martin's Press, 1983), p. 51.

86. U. S. Congress, House Committee on Ways and Means, Hearing Before the Subcommittee on Trade, *Most-Favored-Nation Treatment with Respect to the Products of the Socialist Republic of Romania*, 95th Cong., 1st Sess., 1977, p. 39, hereafter, House Subcommittee on Trade, *MFN Treatment*, 1977.

87. Background Paper, State of Affairs in American-Romanian Trade and Economic Relations, n.d., 7pp., Tab 12, Folder Rom; 6/24/75, Box 315, William Seidman Papers, GRF Library.

88. U. S. Congress, House Committee on Ways and Means, *Sixth Quarterly Report on Trade Between the United States and Nonmarket Economy Countries, Pursuant to Section 411(c) of the Trade Act of 1974*, 95th Cong., 1st Sess., 1977, p. 10, hereafter, House Committee on Ways and Means, *Sixth Quarterly Report on Trade Between the United States and Nonmarket Economy Countries*, 1977.

89. Background Paper, Cooperation with Romania in the Field of Nuclear Energy, n.d., 6pp., Folder Rom; 6/24/76, Box 315, William Seidman Papers, GRF Library.

90. Background Paper, State of Affairs in American-Romanian Trade and Economic Relations, n.d., 7pp., Tab 12, Folder Rom; 6/24/75, Box 315, William Seidman Papers, GRF Library.

91. U. S. Congress, Senate Committee on Finance, *Background Materials Relating to the United States-Romanian Trade Agreement*, 94th Cong., 1st Sess., 1975, p. 7.

92. Letter, Ronald M. Mottl to The Honorable Gerlad [sic] R. Ford, February 19, 1976, Folder CO125; 1/1/76-3/31/76, Box 43, CO125, WHCF, GRF Library.

93. Memorandum, George Springsteen to Brent Scowcroft, May 8, 1976, Attachments, 15pp., Folder CA125; 4/1/75-5/31/76, Box 44, CO125, WHCF. GRF Library; Letter, Philip M. Crane to the President, March 25, 1976, Attachment, 3pp., Folder CO125; 1/1/76-3/31/76, Box 43, CO125, WHCF, GRF Library.

94. U. S., Congress, House Committee on Ways and Means, Hearing Before the Subcommittee on Trade, *Extension of Most-Favored-Nation Treatment to Romania*, 94th Cong., 2d Sess., pp. 48-49; *Idem.*, *Emigration Waiver to the Socialist Republic of Romania and the Hungarian People's Republic; and Nondiscriminatory Treatment of the Products of Romania*, 95th Cong., 2d Sess., 1978, p. 77. hereafter, House Subcommittee on Trade, *Emigration Waiver to the Socialist Republic of Romania and the Hungarian People's Republic*, 1978; U. S., Congress, House Committee on Ways and Means, *Ninth Quarterly Report to the Congress and the East-West Foreign Trade Board; On Trade Between the United States and the Nonmarket Economy Countries*, 95th Cong., 1st Sess., 1977, p. 23. The Socialist Republic of Romania also agreed to limit its glass exports to the United States to two-thirds of all shipments it made in 1976.

95. U. S., Congress, House Committee on International Relations, Hearings Before the Subcommittee on International Security and Scientific Affairs, *United States National Security Policy vis-a-vis Eastern Europe (The "Sonnenfeldt Doctrine")*, 94th Cong., 2d Sess., 1976, pp.31-40, hereafter, House Subcommittee on International Security, *The Sonnenfeldt Doctrine*, 1976.

96. Background Paper, The "Sonnenfeldt Doctrine" controversy, June 15, 1976, 2pp., Tab 28, Folder Rom; 6/24/76, Box 315, William Seidman Papers, GRF Library.

97. House Subcommittee on International Security, *The Sonnenfeldt Doctrine*, 1976, pp., 1-3.

98. *Ibid.*, pp. 4-5; Background Paper, The "Sonnenfeldt Doctrine" controversy, June 15, 1976, p. 1, Tab 28, Folder Rom; 6/24/76, Box 315, William Seidman Papers, GRF Library.

99. House Subcommittee on International Security, *The Sonnenfeldt Doctrine*, 1976, p. 25.

100. Author interview of Corneliu Bogdan, April 11, 1987.

101. Memorandum, William E. Simon to the President, April 19, 1975, Folder CO125; 4/1/75-5/31/76, Box 44, CO125, WHCF, GRF Library.

102. Executive Order, Administration of the Trade Agreements Program [March 27, 1975], 10pp., Folder, TA5 Trade; 3/19/75-3/31/75, Box 29, Subject Files, WHCF, GRF Library.

103. Memorandum, George Springsteen to Brent Scowcroft, May 8, 1976, Attachments, p.3, Folder CA125; 4/1/75-5/31/76, Box 44, CO125, WHCF, GRF Library.

104. Senate Committee on Finance, *Background Materials Relating to United States-Romanian Trade*, 1976, pp. 7-8. In a 1987 interview with Ion Pacepa, the Romanian said that Israel paid about $2,500 in cash for each Jew emigrating to Israel(NYT October 14, 1987, p. 5).

105. Letter, Richard D. Parsons to Steven K. Herlitz, August 10, 1975, Attachments, 5pp. Folder TA6 Trade Centers, Box 30, Subject Files, WHCF, GRF Library.

106. Letter, William E. Simon to the President, October 21, 1976, Attachment, 49pp., p. 8, Folder East West Foreign Trade Board [Sixth] Quarterly Report, Box 56, William Seidman Papers, GRF Library, hereafter, Simon to Ford, Sixth Quarterly Report, October 1976.

107. House Committee on Ways and Means, *Sixth Quarterly Report on Trade Between the United States and Nonmarket Economy Countries*, 1977, pp.4-5.

108. Background Paper, Talking Points for Press Conference in Romania, n.d., 2pp., Tab 4, Folder Rom; 6/24/75, Box 315, William Seidman Papers, GRF Library.

109. Briefing Paper, Romanian Joint Venture Implementation, June 16, 1976, 4pp., Tab 27, Folder Rom; 6/2/4/76, Box 315, William Seidman Papers, GRF Library.

110. Richard F. Staar (ed.), *Yearbook on International Communist Affairs, 1977* (Stamford, CA: Hoover Institution Press, 1977), p. 66.

111. Simon to Ford, October 21, 1976, p. 6, Sixth Quarterly Report.

112. Senate Subcommittee on International Trade, *MFN Treatment*, 1977, pp. 157-158.

113. Ceausescu, *Romania On the Way*, XIII, 205ff; "Romania Under Sixth Five-Year Plan," *Romanian Bulletin*, The Romanian Library, New York, New York, September. 1976, p. 2.

114. This was possible because the suits were not subject to quantitative import restraints (Senate Subcommittee on International Trade, *MFN Treatment*, 1977, p. 159).

115. Simon to Ford, Sixth Quarterly Report, October 1976. p. 32.

116. *Ibid.*, p. 22.

117. The major portion of this was a $4.5 million guarantee for the purchase of communications cable (*Ibid.*, p. 25).

118. David McLellan, *Cyrus Vance*(New York: Rowman Pubs., 1985), p. 71.

119. Newhouse, *War and Peace in the Nuclear Age*, p. 262.

120. U. S. Congress, Senate Committee on Finance, Hearing Before the In-

ternational Trade, *Continuing Most-Favored-Nation Tariff Treatment of Imports from Romania*, 94th Cong., 2d Sess., 1976, pp. 34, 139ff. Hereafter, Senate Subcommittee on International Trade, *MFN Treatment*, 1976.

121. *Ibid.*, pp. 226-233.

122. See, Senate Subcommittee on International Trade, *MFN Treatment*, 1976.

123. Senate Subcommittee on International Trade, *MFN Treatment*, 1976, pp. 6, 135-136.

124. *Ibid.*, pp. 39-40.

125. *Ibid.*, pp. 40-41.

126. U. S. Congress, House Committee on Ways and Means, Hearing Before the Subcommittee on Trade, *Extension of Most-Favored -Nation Treatment to Romania*, 94th Cong., 2d Sess., 1976, pp. 95-100, hereafter, House Subcommittee on Trade, *MFN Treatment*, 1976.

127. Background Paper, Information About Romania's Magyars, n.d., 8pp., Tab 14, Folder Rom; 6/24/76, Box 315, William Seidman Papers, GRF Library.

128. House Subcommittee on Trade, *MFN Treatment*, 1976, pp. 99-100.

129. *Ibid.*, pp. 102-103.

130. *Ibid.*, pp. 109-110

131. *Ibid.*, p. 117.

132. *Ibid.*, pp. 166-167.

133. See, U.S., *Congressional Record*, 94th Cong, 2d Sess., 1976, Vol CXXII, Parts 24, 26, and 27.

134. Shafir, *Romania: Politics, Economics and Society*, p. 3; Staar (ed.), *Yearbook on International Communist Affairs, 1977* , p. 67.

135. Robert R. King, "Romania and the Soviet Union," *Eastern Europe's Uncertain Future: A Selection of Radio Free Europe Research Reports*, eds. Robert R. King and James F. Brown (New York: Praeger, 197), pp. 55-61.

136. Ceausescu, *Romania On the Way,* XIII, 547-551.

137. Staar (ed.), *Yearbook on International Communist Affairs, 1977* , p. 68,

138. Joint Economic Committee of the Congress, *East European Economies*, 1977, pp. 1244-1245; Verzariu and Burgess, *Joint Venture Agreements in Romania*, p. 13.

139. Ibid.; Leonte Tismaneanu and Rolica Zaharia, *Present and Prospect in Romania's Social and Economic Development*, trans. Andrei Bantas (Bucharest, Meridiane Publishing House, 1977), pp. 145-147.

140. Verzariu and Burgess, *Joint Venture Agreements in Romania*, pp. 1251ff; for a complete text see, Verzariu and Burgess, *Joint Venture Agreements in Romania*, Appendix F, pp. 63-68.

141. U. S. Congress, House Committee on Ways and Means, Hearing Before the Subcommittee on Trade, *Most-Favored-Nation Treatment with Respect to the Products of the Socialist Republic of Romania*, 95th Cong., 1st Sess., 1977, p. 40.

142. *Ibid.*, p. 40.

CHAPTER XIV

HUMAN RIGHTS AND ROMANIAN-AMERICAN RELATIONS, 1977-1979

Congress, Carter and Human Rights

Human rights moved to a position of prominence under the Carter Administration, and ultimately this would affect Romanian-American relations. The increased concern about human rights was in part due to Jimmy Carter's public support of the issue as well as to Congressional efforts to link the availability of foreign assistance programs with a country's human rights practices. Congress also saw this linkage as a means to increase its role in designing foreign policy, normally the preserve of the Executive Branch of government.

Sustained Congressional interest in human rights first began in 1973. The moral issues involved in Vietnam and Watergate, coupled with the Administration's role in the Chilean coup, offended several members of Congress. Particularly ired was Donald Fraser, a Democratic Congressman from Minnesota, and member of the House Foreign Affairs Committee.[1] As Chairman of the Subcommittee on International Organizations and Movements, later renamed the Subcommittee on Human Rights and International Organizations, he made human rights and American foreign policy a major focus of the Subcommittee's attention. After holding 15 hearings in 1973, the Subcommittee managed to get Congressional support to include Section 32 in the Foreign Assistance Act of 1973 which expressed a "sense of Congress" that the President should deny any economic or military aid to any government which imprisoned its citizens for political purposes.[2]

Fraser's Subcommittee issued a report in 1974 entitled "Human Rights in the World Community: A Call for U.S. Leadership." The report boldly urged the United States to become involved in human rights in other countries. The rationale was that countries had the responsibility to guarantee their citizens human rights. But when the "government is itself the perpetrator of the violations, the victim has no recourse but to seek redress from outside his national boundaries."[3] Fraser's Subcommittee held more than 150 hearings over the next five years with testimony from more than 500 witnesses. The emphasis was on countries which were involved in "gross violations" of human rights, including torture, imprisonment, and murder. However, the fact of the hearings and the amount of testimony, much of it from government witnesses, educated many people on the need for America to take a more active role to improve all human rights practices world wide.[4]

In July, 1974, Fraser urged the State Department to appoint someone to insure that human rights were made a factor in determining America's foreign policy. On August 14, Robert Ingersoll, the Deputy Secretary of State, indicated that this would be done.[5] However, Fraser saw little change. Although Nixon had resigned, Henry Kissinger was still Secretary of State and he showed no interest in human rights. National security, not human rights, was the driving force behind foreign policy. If a particular country were viewed as strategic for American security, its human rights practices were not significant.[6] As a result, Fraser introduced an amendment to the Foreign Assistance Act of 1974. Section 502B directed the President to end military aid to governments engaged in a pattern of "gross violations of internationally recognized human rights," unless "extraordinary circumstances" warranted such assistance. Congress approved the non-binding amendment in December, 1974.[7] A year later, Congressman Tom Harkin of Iowa, extended the language of 502B to link economic aid, as well as military aid, to human rights. His amendment became Section 116 of the Foreign Assistance Act of 1961.[8]

Fraser's hearings, along with Section 502B and Section 116, which quickly became known as the "Harkin Amendment," placed greater pressure on the State Department. In 1975, the Department had American Embassies in specific countries prepare reports on the host country's human rights practices. However, Kissinger refused to make them public, declaring that all states violated human rights, and there was no reason for the United States to single out particular countries.[9]

Congress tried a different tact. In 1976 it established the United States (Helsinki) Commission of Security and Cooperation in Europe, CSCE. This twelve member bipartisan commission monitored East-West human rights. The legislature also required the President to submit a semiannual report to Congress on each of the Eastern Bloc country's implementation of the Helsinki Agreement. Further Congressional amendments to the Foreign Assistance Act of 1961 established a Coordinator of Human Rights and Humanitarian Affairs in the Department of State, thereby fulfilling Ingersoll's promise to Fraser made two years earlier.[10]

Carter's arrival in the White House certainly appeared to be a victory for human rights supporters. When he announced his presidential candidacy in December, 1974, he said "that this country [should] set a standard within the community of nations of courage, compassion, integrity, and dedication to basic human rights and freedoms."[11] Throughout his campaign, he repeated his interest in human rights. On January 20, 1977, the new President used his Inaugural Address to tell the American people that his government was committed to human rights. He also had broadcast a global message stating that while the United States "alone cannot guarantee the basic rights of every human being to be free of poverty and hunger and disease and political repression . . . the United States can and will take the lead in such effort."[12]

Carter's new Secretary of State, Cyrus Vance, shared the President's commitment to improving human rights.[13] He had indicated his views in a memo to Carter in October, 1976. Following the inauguration, he told a press conference that rather than being "strident or polemical," he preferred to use "quiet diplomacy" to improve an individual nation's human rights practices.[14] While critics would argue that Carter was inconsistent in his human rights policy, and was "too quiet" in his diplomacy,[15] the new President did make some significant changes. He upgraded the Office of Human Affairs to the Bureau of Human Rights and Humanitarian Affairs headed by an Assistant Secretary of State. Further, he appointed Patricia Derian to lead the Bureau. She was the founder of the Mississippi Civil Liberties Union and organizer of the biracial Loyalist Mississippi Democratic Party, that unsuccessfully challenged the all-white delegation to the 1968 Democratic Party Convention.[16] Finally, Carter appointed Deputy Secretary of State Warren Christopher to lead a committee to actively coordinate foreign aid programs with a country's human rights practices. Within a short time, the "Christopher Committee" forced many Adminstration officials to become more aware of the relationship between human rights violations and America's foreign policy.[17]

The enthusiasm of the new Administration for human rights encouraged Congressional supporters. They quickly tied "Harkin Amendments" to numerous foreign aid programs so that by the end of 1978, the "gross violations" criterion applied to the Food for Peace Act as well as to OPIC and Eximbank credits.[18] Further, Congress made Section 502B binding, forcing the President to certify in writing to Congress that extraordinary circumstances existed which warranted that Congress grant military aid to a country guilty of gross human rights violations.[19]

While the thrust of Congressional and Executive action was aimed to punish "gross violators" of human rights, the discussion and hearings raised nearly everyone's level of consciousness about human rights. Therefore, if any country applied to the United States for special treatment, such as MFN or an annual emigration waiver, its human rights practices quickly came under scrutiny. This was the new climate under which Romanian-American relations would have to function.

Romania and Human Rights

Among the issues which faced the Carter Adminstration when it first took office was the need for a policy toward Eastern Europe. The Jackson-Vanik Amendment limited White House initiatives and curtailed flexibility. The only issue which legally mattered was a nation's emigration practices. On January 10, a Carter Presidential Transition Team report recommended that the Administration formulate a new economic policy toward Eastern Europe and the Soviet Union.[20] The policy should expand bilateral trade, and encourage greater East European participation in the world economic system, including North-South talks and multilateral trade negotiations.[21] Finally, the policy should emphasize differentiation, giving preference to countries which were "relatively more liberal internally and/or more independent of the Soviet Union."[22] This would mean, in the final analysis, that as long as Romania pursued a foreign policy somewhat independent of Moscow, her human rights practices could be open to limited criticism.

Carter's election did little to interrupt the normal flow of Romanian-American relations. Before the inauguration, the congressional Commission on Security and Cooperation in Europe (CSCE) held hearings in Washington to review compliance on Basket II, the economic basket, of the Helsinki Final Act. Romania was mentioned by various witnesses during the January 13-14 testimony. However, since the Commission was primarily interested in economic issues, the question of Romanian human rights never came into focus. In his testimony, Milton Rosenthal, Chairman of the United States-Romanian Economic Council, put the issue of Basket II and Romania in simple perspective. "An American businessman has one basic mission. It is to produce and sell the largest quantity of goods and services on the basis of honorable profit to the company for which he is working."[23] This goal made no mention of human rights practices.

The only slowdown to "business as usual" between Bucharest and Washington was new faces. Carter replaced Elliott Richardson with Juanita Kreps as Secretary of Commerce, while Bucharest had sent Nicolae Nicolae to replace Bogdan in June, 1976.[24] In February, 1977, Nicolae officially met Kreps and the two talked about means for increased trade. Nicolae also indicated that Romania supported Carter's concerns about human rights. [25]

However, events in Bucharest belied Nicolae's statement. A small group of dissidents, led by the writer Paul Goma wrote an "open letter" to the Belgrade Conference, which would convene in June to review compliance with the Helsinki Final Act. The February 18 letter criticized Romania's human rights practices. In spite of the Romanian Constitution, a copy of which he appended to the letter, the Ceausescu regime showed no respect for "civil liberties, the right to work, to education, to association, the right to free speech, press assembly, meetings and demonstrations, the freedom of conscience, the inviolability of person, home, the secrecy of correspondence and telephone conversations." Equally disregarded was the right to free movement of peoples, ideas and information.[26] Although there were only eight signers of this letter, the public nature of it embarrassed Ceausescu. He accused Goma of being a traitor, and encouraged him and his dissident followers to leave Romania.[27]

International response to Goma's letter was checked by the violent earthquake which erupted in Romania on March 4. The Bucharest region was most affected. The earthquake killed 1,570, injured 9,300, and left nearly 35,000 families homeless. The total damage exceeded $1 billion and the destruction of petroleum, chemical and petrochemical industries in Ploesti dealt a severe blow to the Romanian economy.[28] American Congressmen quickly responded. Led by Senators Edward Kennedy, of Massachusetts, and Jacob Javits, of New York, the Senate passed a resolution on March 14 expressing the sympathy of the American people and resolved that the United States should do all that was possible "to assist the people of Romania in their hour of need."[29]

On March 24, Senator Edward Kennedy of Massachusetts and Jacob Javits of New York introduced a bill authorizing $20 million in humanitarian assistance for Romania. Similar legislation appeared in the House. While debate was limited, both bills contained specific language noting that the relief funds in no way "endorsed any measure undertaken by the Government of Romania which would suppress human rights." On April 18, Jimmy Carter signed the legislation into law.[30]

The reason for the human rights language was that a number of Congressmen, led by Edward Koch of New York, became alarmed about stories that continued to emanate from Romania indicating the government's callous approach to human rights. Koch had kept Goma's outcry before his colleagues.[31] Soon information spread that Bucharest had arrested and imprisoned Goma and several other dissidents.[32] During the Spring, several Baptist and Pentecostal clergymen and believers spoke out against discrimination in employment and education. In their letter to the United States CSCE, Josif Ton, Pavel Niculescu and Avril Popescu asked the Commission to inform the upcoming Belgrade Conference of Bucharest's violation of their right of freedom of association.[33] There was also an incident involving Vlad Georgescu, a well known Romanian historian who had taught in several American universities. The government arrested Georgescu and threatened him with charges of treason for defaming Ceausescu and the Romanian government. He was particularly friendly with Harry Barnes, the American Ambassador to Romania. In anticipation that he might be in trouble with the authorities, Georgescu gave Barnes a copy of some essays he had written a couple of days earlier. Following the arrest, Romanian police cordoned off the American Embassy and allowed only employees to enter. Bucharest notified Barnes that if he gave them Georgescu's papers, they would release the historian. Barnes refused and Georgescu remained in jail for six weeks.[34] Following his release from prison, Georgescu fled Romania and went to work for Radio Free Europe at the Romanian desk in Munich.[35]

While few in number, these stories fueled the anti-Communist elements in Congress, and proved disturbing to human rights advocates. More significant, however, was a drop in Romanian emigration, which undermined the arguments of those who supported continued MFN. The statistics for the first three months of 1977 indicated a sharp decrease in the number of people permitted to emigrate to the United States and Israel. 291 people came to the United States from January-March, 1976, compared to 140 during the same period in 1977. Similarly, in 1976, 659 people left Romania for Israel between January and March, while only 221 had done so in 1977.[36]

In May, the Senate Judiciary Committee sent a staff team to visit Romania, and make a first-hand report on the earthquake disaster. The team, led by Dale deHaan, Counsel to the Committee, and Jerry Tinker, staff consultant, arrived in Bucharest on May 1 and departed May 4. The two travelled extensively throughout the affected area. They talked with Ambassador Barnes and discussed the earthquake and other elements of American-Romanian relations with President Ceausescu and the Minister of Foreign Affairs, George Macovescu.[37] Without question, they told Ceausescu of Congress' growing concern about Romania's human rights practices. They particularly stressed the present importance of the issue since Congress would soon consider the President's request to extend the emigration waiver for another year.

In his remarks to deHaan and Tinker, Ceausescu told them quite candidly that Romania did not have an emigration policy, but it recognized that emigration on a case-by-case basis was sometimes necessary for humanitarian reasons. The Romanian position clearly rested on Bucharest's fear of a "brain drain." Romania was a developing country and needed to retain the people it had trained and educated. The major exceptions to case-by-case emigration involved some government-to-government contacts involving ethnic Germans seeking to go to West Germany and Jews desiring to go to Israel.[38]

However, Ceausescu understood deHaan and Tinker's warning. Within a week of their departure, Ceausescu issued an amnesty providing full pardons for individuals serving less than five year imprisonments, and partial ones for those interned from five to ten years. The amnesty affected about 28,000 persons, including political prisoners and dissidents, such as Paul Goma and Vlad Georgescu.[39]

Aware of Koch's recent attacks on Romania's human rights record, Ceausescu made the most of a visit by the American business tycoon, Armand Hammer. The Chairman of Occidental Petroleum Corporation was in Bucharest to complete an agreement which permitted Romania to invest in the Island Creek Coal Company, a Virginia subsidiary of Occidental Petroleum. Ceausescu gave Hammer two letters, one for Congressman Koch, the other for Koch's friend, Rabbi Arthur Schneier, both signed by Romania's Chief Rabbi, Moses Rosen. Both May 27 letters were similar. They thanked Koch for his interest in Romania but urged him to be aware that he was "deliberately disinformed about the real situation."[40] Rosen was convinced that as a "good Jew" and an "honest man," Koch would "not continue an action which is against the truth and against the vital interest of our community."[41]

Congress and the President's Emigration Waiver, 1977

Meanwhile, the State Department and the Treasury gathered data and recommended that the President request Congress to extend the emigration waiver of Section 402 of the Trade Act of 1974. On June 2, Carter submitted his waiver recommendation. In his request to Congress, the President noted the increased trade between the United States and Romania, and emphasized Bucharest's relative independence from Moscow. Further, the waiver extension would provide Washington with continued access to government officials in Romania which could facilitate family reunification and improved emigration practices. Carter did indicate that his Administration would monitor Romanian emigration, and if Bucharest's performance did not comply with the intent of the waiver, "I would want to reconsider my recommendation." Further, the President promised that he would bring to the attention of the Romanian government "any actions or emigration trends" which did not conform to the assurances they had made "in the past to treat emigration in a humanitarian manner."[42] These latter statements were the first time a President had showed a willingness to reconsider the emigration waiver in the event of Romanian noncompliance.

The Presidential waiver request meant that either house of Congress had until September to disapprove the recommendation, otherwise, the waiver would continue for another 12 months and with it, Romanian MFN. Ceausescu totally understood this legislative timetable and over the years, there developed an annual Summer ritual between Washington and Bucharest. The highpoint of the ritual normally being a significant increase in the numbers of people permitted to emigrate from Romania to the United States and Israel. For years, the May through October figures would be higher than those of other months.

In addition to increased emigration, Ceausescu aimed to reassure the United States and the world of its human rights concerns. On June 17, two days after the Helsinki review conference opened in Belgrade, Romania and Hungary issued a joint communique. They recognized the existence of a minority question in each country, and agreed to resolve the issue using norms adopted by the United Nations.[43]

Increased emigration and Hungarian accords did not convince everyone in Congress that Ceausescu intended to improve his human rights practices. On June 22, Representative McDonald introduced a resolution in the House, H. 653, to disapprove the Presidential request for a waiver extension. The House referred the resolution to its Ways and Means Subcommittee on Trade, which according to Section 152 (c)(1) had 30 days to report the resolution following its introduction. If the committee took no action within that time period, it was discharged from its obligation to consider the resolution and any other resolution introduced on the same issue. Therefore the Subcommittee had until July 22 to take action on McDonald's resolution.[44]

On June 27 the Senate Finance Committee's Subcommittee on International Trade began hearings on continuing Romanian MFN. Administration officials began the testimony led by Alan Reich, the Deputy Assistant Secretary of Commerce for East-West Trade. In supporting the President's request, Reich summarized American-Romanian commercial relations since 1975. He noted that eleven United States businesses had set up commercial offices in Bucharest, while three firms had signed major contracts with Romania. Wean United and Lipe-Rollway had each signed agreements to sell $23 million worth of equipment to Bucharest, while Armand Hammer's Island Creek Coal Company's contract called for the sale of nearly $2 billion worth of high grade metallurgical coal. This also included an advance payment by Romania of $53 million to assist in the development of the coal mine.[45]

Reich did not mention that much of Romania's purchases depended on Eximbank credits. As of June 8, 1977, Bucharest owed the Eximbank $84.3 million, of which $75.4 were in direct loans.[46] Further, few people noticed that Romania's indebtedness to the United States was but a small portion of Bucharest's financial obligations. Although Ceausescu exhorted Romania's Foreign Trade Organizations to increase exports, he continued to borrow heavily to fulfill Romania's economic plans which called for rapid industrialization.[47] By October, 1977, he owed the IMF $363 million, the World Bank, $697 million and the Eurocurrency market, more than $125 million.[48]

Matthew Niemetz, Conselor for the State Department presented the Subcommittee on International Trade with the Administration's position on Romania's emigration practices. He noted the June communique issued by Ceausescu and General Secretary Kadar of Hungary, and assured the Subcommittee that Romania accepted a commitment to help carry out the reunification of divided families as provided in the Helsinki Final Act. He concluded by noting the recent improvement in emigration to the United States. More Romanians had come to the United States during the period January-May in 1977 than had during the same months in 1976. Emigration to Israel, however, showed a significant decline in 1977, and Niemetz attributed this to a decrease in the number of Jews who wished to depart.[49]

While the number of witnesses testifying at the hearings was about the same as in 1976, the number of communications and letters was substantially less. Adminstration supporters included the regular representatives from corporate America, most of whom had commercial relations with Bucharest, as well as represcntatives from the Romanian community such as Barbu Niculescu, of the American-Romanian Cultural Foundation, who had testified in 1976, and a newcomer representing the academic community, Dr. Radu Florescu, President of the Society for Romanian Studies.[50]

Representatives of the Jewish community wanted Congress to adopt the President's suggestion of monitoring Romania's emigration practices before approving the waiver request. Dr. William Korey of B'nai B'rith International informed the Subcommittee of Romania's emigration application process. The procedure was arbitrary, burdensome, lengthy and costly, equivalent to a month's salary for all the fees needed for emigration. Korey wanted Congress to use the waiver extension as leverage to improve Bucharest's emigration practices.[51] Jacob Birnbaum, the National Director of the Center for Russian and East European Jewry and Student Struggle for Soviet Jewry, reiterated Korey's remarks. Rather than take a position on the waiver extension, both men urged Congress to implement a monitoring procedure to facilitate Jewish emigration[52]

Few witnesses came before the subcommittee in opposition to the President's request. The prime exception being Laszlo Hamos of the Committee for Human Rights in Romania. His lengthy testimony emphasized Bucharest's continued efforts to suppress the civil liberties, human rights and cultural development of Hungarians in Romania. In addition, the Subcommittee did receive a number of letters opposing the emigration waiver including correspondence from the AFL-CIO, the American-Hungarian Federation and the National Association of Americans of Romanian Descent in the United States.[53]

In between the Senate and House hearings, which began in mid-July, the Administration had a couple of opportunities to bolster support for the emigration waiver. On July 7, the President spoke to business leaders and trade officials attending the Fourth Session of the United States-Romanian Economic Council. He reviewed the current status of the waiver legislation and encouraged the Council to continue its efforts to facilitate and expand the two-way trade.[54]

The second opportunity involved Senator Jackson. On June 24, the Senator wrote the President concerning Romania's erratic emigration process. Bucharest quickly processed emigration applications during Congressional hearings, but showed little interest in assisting emigrants during the remainder of the year. Therefore, Jackson wanted the President to indicate whether he thought "that a consistent Romanian policy of freer emigration, without artificial difficulties or unnatural delays" was essential to justify continuing the waiver. Jackson implied that he wanted a written response.[55]

Jackson had shown that he could be a formidable opponent to an Administration, especially in issues concerning Eastern Europe and the Soviet Union. Jackson had also unsuccessfully campaigned against Carter for the Democratic party's presidential nomination. The President had already indicated that he wanted to develop a new policy toward the Communist world which had greater flexibility than that afforded by the Jackson-Vanik Amendment. Senator Robert Dole of Kansas had just introduced a bill, S. 1415, to modify the Jackson-Vanik Amendment to extend CCC credits to nonmarket economies. Jackson opposed the bill and feared that Carter would support the legislation. Jackson expressed his concern to Vance on July 14, but the Secretary of State indicated that the Administration neither opposed nor supported the Dole bill.[56]

Jackson was little consoled by Vance's reply and that, coupled with Carter's failure to respond to his June 24 letter, forced the Senator to become more belligerent toward the Administration. Due to Jackson's persistence, Carter met with his National Security Advisor, Zbigniew Brzezinski, and later with his Secretary of State, Cyrus Vance. The result was Jackson received two letters. The first, from Brzezinski dated July 20, told the Senator what he wanted to hear. William Hyland, of Brzezinski's staff had talked with Richard Perle of Jackson's staff and learned that the Senator wanted Romania to show a "tendency" to handle each case as quickly as possible, realizing that there would be some exceptions.[57] Hyland also talked with Ambassador Barnes, who agreed that this was a realistic approach.[58] Brzezinski's letter assured Jackson that Romanian officials agreed that the "tendency" of their policy would be to eliminate "artificial difficulties or unnatural delays," but reserved their right to determine each case individually. Of the 240 cases Jackson had brought to the attention of Romanian authorities, they had acted on 210. "The implication being that they would act expeditiously, if not agreeing to the abstract principle."[59]

Jackson received a second letter on July 26, this one from the President. Carter acknowledged that he had "always had doubts that the Jackson-Vanik Amendment served the purpose of increasing Jewish out-migration from the Soviet Union. However, I stated last fall that this law would be enforced. As Secretary Vance has said, we do not support S. 1415," Dole's bill which would restrict the intention of the Jackson-Vanik Amendment.[60]

While the Administration mollified Jackson, the House Subcommittee on Trade began its hearings on the President's waiver request. In preparation for the hearings, Subcommittee members received an Administration memo on June 29, noting Romania's emigration performance. The memo concluded that in spite of a developing cyclical pattern, there was an overall moderate upward trend in the number of emigration visas granted since January, 1975.[61] Additional briefing material included a synopsis of Romania's emigration procedures prepared by the American Embassy in Bucharest. At the outset, an applicant was aware that the Bucharest officially discouraged emigration. Therefore, the applicant was viewed as either a deserter, an ingrate, or possibly a traitor. As for reunification, Bucharest believed that family members living outside Romania should return home. With these standards as starting points, the government's emigration process was, as could be anticipated, burdensome and lengthy.

The procedure involved a two part application. First the applicant had to file a preliminary form containing vital statistics, including a notice from the place of work that the applicant's services were no longer needed, and that the applicant had no further contractual obligations and did not work on state secrets. Waiting time could take three weeks, two months, or longer. If this first application was denied, the appeal process was essentially a dead end, unless the Embassy intervened. If the application was approved, the applicant completed a four page document indicating work experience, education, financial status, and emigration destination. The applicant sent this form to the local passport office which forwarded it to the Passport Commission in Bucharest. Normal bureaucratic delays, coupled with the government's official position, resulted in applicants frequently waiting from six months to a year to receive a decision. During that time, the government would try to discourage the applicant from leaving the country. If approval were granted, the applicant had to obtain clearance stamps and sever relations with the state. This took between two and six months. Once the stamps were obtained, the applicant would receive a passport and exit ticket. The American Embassy knew of no instance of any emigrant who, having received approval to emigrate, was refused a passport and exit ticket.[62]

The July 18 hearing was lengthy with nearly twice the number of witnesses testifying than appeared before the Senate Subcommittee. The Administration sent five representatives, including Ambassador Barnes, to support the President. Of the more than 20 witnesses who followed, the vast majority supported the waiver. Business representatives from Control Data Corporation, Island Creek Coal Company, Moody International, and Promethean Corporation joined with Congressmen John Breaux of Louisiana, Edward Derwinski and Paul Findley of Illinois, and Christopher Dodd of Connecticut in support of MFN renewal. While Jacob Birnbaum of the Center for Russian and East European Jewry would use the hearings to encourage emigration, and remain neutral on the issue of the Presidential request, Rabbi Israel Miller, representing the Conference of President of Major American Jewish Organizations, urged approval of the request for one more year as a means to increase Romanian emigration. However, he added a caveat. If Jewish emigration did not improve during the next year, his organization would not support another Presidential waiver.[63]

The opposition included familiar faces. Laszlo Hamos of the Committee for Human Rights in Romania and Reverend Florian Galdau of the American-Romanian Committee for Assistance to Refugees both described in great detail Romania's record of emigration harassment and minority discrimination. They were joined by Representative Larry McDonald, the author of House Resolution 653 who called for the disapproval of the President's request. The opposition testimony focused on human rights abuses, while those in support focused on increased trade and argued that without the waiver, Romania would lose MFN. In turn, Washington would lose its principal means of leverage to force Bucharest to increase emigration and to improve her human rights practices.

After the hearings ended, the Subcommittee on Trade voted on McDonald's resolution to deny the emigration waiver. By voice vote, the Subcommittee unanimously reported House Resolution 653 unfavorably to the Committee on Ways and Means. Three days later, the Ways and Means Committee reported the resolution unfavorably to the House.[64]

While this recommendation essentially killed McDonald's resolution, several Congressmen, led by Representative Koch, tried to have the bill brought to the House floor for a vote during the first week of August. Ironically, at the same time, there were developments in Romania which could have added a bit of fuel to the opposition fires, had they been known. On August 1, miners in the Jiu Valley coal mining towns of Petrosani, Vulcan and Lupeni went on strike against the government demanding better work conditions and improved quality in food and consumer goods. As the number of miners demonstrating and striking increased to the tens of thousands, Ceausescu cut short his Black Sea vacation and flew to the Jiu Valley. He met with the striking miners on August 3, made a number of promises for which the workers agreed to return to the mines. While unrest would continue for several weeks and force the government to send troops to the area in September to maintain order, the crisis passed. The entire incident went generally unnoticed by both Congress and the American public until reports in the Fall described the uprising.[65]

Meanwhile in Congress, the opposition efforts came to a sudden end. Koch's August 2 efforts to have the House vote on McDonald's resolution failed. For on the following day, Representative Vanik moved to table the resolution and the House agreed.[66] On September 1, since neither house had voted a resolution of disapproval, Congress implicitly approved the emigration waiver and Romania retained her MFN treatment for another year. Congressional inaction was due to a number of factors. First, the earthquake had produced a humanitarian response to Romania, one of condolence rather than punishment. Second, Carter's identification with human rights gave greater credibility to his assurances to Congress that the waiver would lead to freer emigration practices. Third, the President's pledge to monitor Romania's behavior and a willingness to reconsider his position if Bucharest failed to keep its assurances won support for his waiver renewal. Fourth, trade was continuing to expand. Fifth, Romania's foreign policy appeared to challenge Soviet efforts to control Eastern Europe's behavior, and Congress wanted to reward Bucharest for its autonomy. And sixth, the need for an annual renewal of the emigration waiver, and therefore continued MFN, appeared to many to give Washington leverage to negotiate improved emigration and human rights practices in Romania.

Continued MFN was important to Ceausescu because it strengthened his relations with the West, which was a needed building bloc in his efforts to balance Bucharest's relations with Moscow. Soviet-Romanian relations had improved since Brezhnev's 1976 visit to Bucharest. The earthquake had given the Soviets an opportunity to assist Romania, and Moscow had responded. In late March, Ceausescu noted that relations between the two countries had "greatly developed."[67]

However, closer ties to Moscow did not mean that Ceausescu would abandon Romania's independent foreign policy. During the last half of 1977, he maintained relations with Israel, the Arab world, and China, and competed with the Soviets for Third World trade and influence. Romania also supported the Eurocommunist movement, much to Moscow's chagrin. Ceausescu praised the autonomous position taken by Santiago Carrillo, the leader of Spain's Communist party, and author of *Eurocommunism and the State*, and invited the Spaniard to stay at his vacation villa, which Carrillo did in a much publicized visit. This incident, coupled with Ceausescu's normal maverick behavior, threatened to end the recent improvement in Soviet-Romanian relations. To prevent such a rupture, Ceausescu paid homage to Moscow, and visited the Kremlin on the occasion of the 60th anniversary of the Bolshevik Revolution.[68]

EPG, Aggrey and Human Rights

Meanwhile in Washington, the Carter Administration tried to get a handle on foreign economic policy, a problem which had beset every President. When he arrived in Washington, he inherited the CIEP. But his transition team had already decided to establish a new economic coordinating group, the Economic Policy Group, EPG. This organization began shortly after the inauguration under the leadership of Michael Blumenthal, the new Treasury Secretary. The reasons for the EPG was that first, the CIEP was a Republican creation, and second, there was a sense that the CIEP had outlived its usefulness. Its statutory authority, granted in 1972, would expire on September 30, 1977, and the new Administration was willing to let the CIEP die of its own accord. In the interim, the President appointed Gus Weiss as the CIEPs Acting Executive Director.[69]

On September 15 the House Subcommittee on International Economic Policy and Trade began hearings on the process involved in coordinating America's international economic policy. In his testimony before the Subcommittee, Blumenthal urged Congress to not renew the

CIEP. The new EPG resembled the troika of the Kennedy-Johnson period which involved the Treasury, Office of Management and Budget and the Council of Economic Advisors. This small group could far more easily coordinate America's foreign economic policy than the large and unwieldy CIEP. Congress agreed, and on September 30 Gus Weiss resigned as Acting Director of the CIEP.[70] As an aside, Carter did not throw out all Republican institutions. He continued the East-West Foreign Trade Council established by Ford, and appointed Blumenthal to chair the group.[71]

In continuing to set its own mark on government, the Carter Administration reviewed foreign service postings and decided to appoint a new Ambassador to Romania. On September 27, Carter nominated O. Rudolph Aggrey as Ambassador to replace Harry Barnes.[72] Aggrey's appointment made a statement, one which, if a defector's story is to be believed, did not please Ceausescu. According to Pacepa, the fact that Aggrey was black infuriated Ceausescu.[73] The Romanian President ignored the fact that he was a career diplomat, who had already served as envoy to Senegal and Gambia.[74] One reason Carter undoubtedly chose Aggrey was to remind Ceausescu that the White House believed in human rights and human equality. Congress approved Aggrey's appointment unanimously.

From October to March, American-Romanian relations continued in a normal fashion. On October 10, the two countries exchanged notes to facilitate visa issuance.[75] In early November, the Romanian delegation of the Joint Romanian-American Economic Commission arrived in Washington led by Ion Patan, the Deputy Prime Minister and Minister of Foreign Trade. After a meeting with Vice President Walter Mondale on November 1,[76] Patan joined Commerce Secretary Juanita Kreps and her delegates on November 2 to open the Fourth Session of the Council. During the two day meeting, government officials from both countries reaffirmed the goal of a $1 billion two-way trade by 1980. A review of the first couple of years of MFN indicated that America's leading exports to Romania were bituminous coal and agricultural products including soybeans, cattle hides, unmilled wheat and yellow corn. In return, 32% of Romania's exports consisted of fuel oil and gasoline. Administration officials on both sides were eager to explore new markets. While current two-way trade was nearly $500 million, with the United States having a $30 million net advantage, both Ceausescu and Carter needed more export trade.[77]

Romania needed increased exports to implement her Five Year Plan, as well as to offset losses incurred by the disastrous earthquake.[78] Further, expanded trade was essential because Ceausescu intended to tell the National Party Congress in December that Romania would be a developed country by 1985.[79] Carter, too, needed more exports to reduce the largest trade deficit in American history. By the end of 1977, the United States would have a $27 billion deficit, in contrast to a $6 billion debt in 1976.[80] While this shortfall was primarily the result of practices of the preceding Administrations, the American public would not view the figures in that light. Before the meeting adjourned, Patan singled out several areas for new American investment including petrochemicals, fertilizers, combustion engineering, and electronics.[81]

Meanwhile, the Administration and Congress maintained an interest in human rights. In late October, the House Subcommittee on International Organizations, chaired by Donald Fraser, held hearings to review the Administration's policy on human rights and American foreign policy. At no time during the testimony did Romania come under scrutiny for its human rights practices. The thrust of the hearings was to examine America's policy toward countries guilty of "gross violations."[82] Six weeks later, the President proclaimed December 10 Human Rights Day and called for Americans to observe Human Rights Week beginning December 10, 1977. The date marked the anniversary of the United Nations adoption of the Universal Declaration of Human Rights in 1948.[83]

Ceausescu undoubtedly thought that he had resolved some of his human rights problems when he encouraged Paul Goma to leave Romania in November for a year long exile.[84] However, the issue of Hungarian persecution reappeared. Hungarians in Budapest accused Romania of carrying out an apartheid-like policy toward Hungarians in Transylvania.[85] Hungarians in Bucharest joined in the protest led by Karoly Kiraly, an ethnic Hungarian who had been a member of the Romanian Communist Party hierarchy until his resignation in the mid-1970s. In January, 1978, he wrote a memo to the Party in which he claimed the Party discriminated against Hungarians and other minorities. A copy of the memo arrived in the West and appeared in the *Manchester Guardian*, the *London Times* and the *Washington Post*. Kiraly accused the government of fraudulent behavior. It preached noble principles, but pursued discriminatory practices which limited educational, cultural and employment opportunities of non-Romanians.[86] While Kiraly would be reassigned to manage a canning factory in Tirgu Mures, the issue of Romanian human rights did not go away. The Baptist ministers, Ton and Niculescu, who had accused Bucharest of discrimination in 1977, continued their criticism. In February, the Ceausescu regime pressured the Baptist church and both men were banned from preaching.[87]

To counter growing reports in the West about Romanian discrimination, Ceausescu invited Amnesty International to visit the country in February, 1978. The government cooperated with the human rights monitoring organization, and the subsequent report did not indicate any particularly abnormal discriminatory practices.[88] In March, Ceausescu told a Joint Plenum of the Councils of Working People of Magyar and German Nationality that "a number of shortcomings still exist in our activity, that mistakes are still made," but he assured the delegates that the Party would "eliminate" these errors.[89] He also alluded to Kiraly and other dissidents describing them as people who had to "cover up their helplessness . . . by . . . speaking ill in every way" of those who were able and willing to sacrifice to continue the struggle toward Communism.[90]

Meanwhile, human rights continued to be a major topic of discussion in Washington. The Carter Administration had struggled for over a year to develop a human rights policy, as distinct from human rights statements. Finally, on February 17, 1978, Carter signed Presidential Directive 30 which defined America's policy. The elements were not new, but for the first time they were combined into a single policy. The United States set priorities in its human rights objectives, foremost being no support to governments guilty of gross violations of human rights, unless there were "exceptional circumstances." Washington would work on a global scale to reduce government violations of civil, political, economic and social rights of people. Finally, America would reward countries that improved its human rights practices through more generous aid programs.[91]

The problem with the policy was consistency. Vance had indicated the problem the day after the inauguration. He wrote Carter a note supporting the President's commitment to human rights, but asking how he intended to respond to the question that would continually be asked: Why did America criticize some governments, and not others, on what appeared to be similar human rights violations. The President admitted that in dealing with about 150 nations, "it was not possible to let any one factor be the sole or dominant one" in making a decision.[92] Nonetheless, the President believed that in spite of the inconsistency, "American idealism was a practical and realistic approach to foreign affairs, and moral principles were the best foundation for the exertion of American power and influence."[93]

In practice, Carter viewed human rights violations differently when they occurred in a country governed by a rightist dictatorship or in a state under Communist control. He believed that American condemnation of human rights violations in conservative regimes could be more effective "than in Communist countries, where repression was so complete that it could not easily be observed or rooted out."[94] And therein laid the basis for Carter's annual renewal of Romania's emigration waiver. He saw the waiver and MFN as one of the few means America had to affect human rights change in Romania. Whether the mechanism worked was not the issue. The fact that the waiver and MFN kept alive a means for change was the purpose of annual renewal.

Ceausescu Visits Carter

Meanwhile, the Administration prepared for a White House visit by President Ceausescu. Carter's invitation to Ceausescu stemmed from President Ford's visit to Romania in 1975. While the arrangements for the visit had been underway for several months,[95] the April date would prove particularly valuable to Ceausescu. Carter had bypassed Romania on his first East European tour in December, 1977, when he visited Poland. Then Carter had hosted Yugoslavia's President Tito, and had signed a bilateral agreement with Hungary on March 17 extending MFN treatment to Budapest. On April 7, the President sent a waiver of the freedom-of-emigration restriction along with the Hungarian treaty to Congress for approval.

Five days later, Ceausescu arrived in Washington. The Romanian President believed in personal diplomacy. He wanted to make sure that Carter's recent overtures to other East European countries did not mean that Romania had fallen into disfavor. He wanted to assure Carter that he too cared about human rights, and that the two men could work together to expand bilateral relations. Finally, he wanted to meet with business leaders, especially those in the fields of energy technology and petrochemicals, to discuss new commercial ventures. He also wanted to move quickly in this area before a most-favored-nation Hungary became a competitor with Romania for American investment and business.

At 10:30 a.m. on April 12 Carter officially welcomed President and

Mrs. Ceausescu in the Oval Office of the White House.[96] The opening remarks of both Presidents mentioned human rights, and this would be one of the recurrent themes throughout Ceausescu's six day visit. Later Carter praised Ceausescu for his mediation efforts in the Middle East.[97] In the afternoon, Barbara Walters, an ABC Television Commentator interviewed the Romanian President. In response to a question concerning human rights, Ceausescu praised his country's efforts and reiterated his view that he saw human rights in a broad context which included disarmament, the right to work, and the right to an education.[98]

On the evening of the twelfth, Carter and Ceausescu exchanged toasts at a state dinner in the Romanian President's honor. Carter indicated that both men had the ability to resolve human rights problems, "perhaps in different means and at different rates of advance . . ." In his toast, Ceausescu agreed that human rights were important and that "we fully respect these rights and consider them sacred – if I may say so – and everything has to be done for them to be asserted."[99]

The second day of his visit was no less busy. At breakfast at the Blair House, he met with about a dozen Senators interested in furthering American-Romanian relations, including a special session with Henry Jackson. Crossing Pennsylvania Avenue, he had an hour long private meeting with Carter from which came a Joint Declaration. The two reaffirmed their commitment to the Joint Statement signed in December, 1973. They also agreed to promote and facilitate trade, including a long term MFN agreement, which would take into consideration Romania's special status as a developing country. Finally, they promised to cooperate in the settlement of humanitarian issues, including family reunification.[100]

A few hours later Ceausescu attended lunch at the National Press Club. The journalists asked him questions on human rights and ethnic minority issues. At the outset Ceausescu made it clear that "as regards human rights . . . one must set out from the observance of independence and non-interference in the internal affairs of other countries." He threw the press a rhetorical question. "Who else could take care of the multiple human rights problems existing in the United States than the U.S. Government?" As for the issue of ethnic minorities, he identified the accusers as "malevolent people that have fled their country . . . and [who] hope to damage the friendly relations between Romania and Hungary."[101] Before leaving Washington, Ceausescu met with members of the House Committee on Foreign Relations. During a question and answer session, he mentioned "I do no know why some of the Hungarians in the U.S.A. are concerned with problems which are of no concern to the Romanian citizens of Hungarian nationality in Romania." There was "no discrimination" in Romania.[102]

For the next three days, Ceausescu flew across the United States to meet with leaders of industry and business. He visited the Sequoyah Atomic Power Plant and the headquarters of Combustion Engineering in Chattanooga, Tennessee. He made two stops in Texas, one in Dallas to visit Texas Instruments and Dresser Industries and another in Houston to see the NASA Space Center and to visit the Cameron Iron Works. On April 15 he arrived in New Orleans, Louisiana. He spoke with members of the International Trade Center and noted that New Orleans was a major port of export to Bucharest. He also visited offshore drilling rigs in the Gulf of Mexico. He finished his tour with a two day visit to New York City, where he was greeted by demonstrators protesting his treatment of ethnic Hungarians.[103] On his last day, Ceausescu talked with a host of industrial giants including David Rockefeller of the Chase Manhattan Bank, Gabriel Hauge, of Manufacturers Hanover Trust, and Milton Rosenthal, Chairman of the United States-Romanian Economic Council.[104]

Upon his return to Romania, Ceausescu took action to show Carter that his promises were not set on sand. On April 18 he granted 47 Romanians passports and exit visas to leave the country.[105] Considering that this number was nearly equal to a Winter month's emigration, the gesture carried weight. Ceausescu may also have granted the visas to deflect a new source of criticism in Romania. On April 2, nine Baptists, including the banned preacher, Pavel Niculescu, organized the Committee for Defense of Religious Liberty and Conscience, or ALRC. The Committee's purpose was to inform the West about religious persecution in Romania. The group also called for "free religion in a free state."[106] While Ceausescu's passport approvals did not address the religious issue, they did provide evidence that Romania was not insensitive to human rights, and would respond to individual needs.

The 1978 Presidential Waiver Request

On June 2 President Carter sent Congress his request for an emigration waiver for Romania and began the annual Summer ritual of emigration waiver hearings. In his recommendation to Congress, the President noted the overall increase of emigration from Romania, especially to West Germany. However, the President did not tell Congress that this increase was due to an arrangement between Bonn and Bucharest. Romania promised to allow approximately 11,000 ethnic Germans to emigrate annually to West Germany in return for credits and payments of up to 8,000 DM per person.[107] Carter noted his concern about the decline in Jewish emigration figures, but added that a number of high-level talks had "led to the favorable resolution of many emigration and humanitarian problems."[108] Carter also notified the legislature that he had determined that the Romanian-American Trade Agreement should be renewed for an additional three years because the United States had maintained a satisfactory balance of trade with Romania, and both countries had reciprocally reduced trade barriers.[109]

Congress showed little opposition toward renewing the emigration waiver and the three year trade agreement. Ceausescu's April visit, coupled with Carter's 1977 pledge to monitor Romania's emigration practices, silenced most critics. In fact, no member of Congress introduced any resolutions of disapproval before or during the hearings. Legislative opposition was also curtailed by the strength of the Administration's presentation made at the outset of the hearings. From the opening testimony before the House Ways and Means Subcommittee on Trade, Administration officials addressed the issue of emigration, and especially Jewish emigration to Israel. On June 15, William Luers, Deputy Assistant Secretary of State for European Affairs reviewed the State Department's role in increasing Jewish emigration to Israel. In effect, the Department played no direct role. Washington did not give Romania lists of Jews who wished to emigrate to Israel. The Department, however, did provide such lists to the Israeli Embassy in Bucharest, thereby making the issue one between Israel and Romania. President Ceausescu and Premier Begin had discussed the matter of Jewish emigration and they were trying to work out a solution. One of the problems was that Israeli authorities did not want all of the Romanian Jews who wanted to emigrate to Israel. This was the reason the United States did not become directly involved. Furthermore, Washington did not want to support only those Jews who wanted to emigrate to Israel. What about those that wanted to emigrate to Canada, or France, or elsewhere?[110]

In response to queries concerning numbers, Luer's noted that the official American Embassy emigration figures were less than the actual number of emigrants. There were two reasons for this. First, many Romanians who actually wished to emigrate to another country applied for permission to emigrate to the United States, since they believed that this increased their chances of approval. Once the Romanian government approved their emigration license, they were free to emigrate to any country which would accept them. Second, a number of Romanians applied for entry into the United States from third countries as refugees, and were not included in Washington's emigration figures. Unless a person received a visa at the American Embassy in Bucharest, the emigrant would not be recorded in the Embassy statistics.[111]

The Administration had its regular supporters from business and ethnic organizations including Barbu Niculescu of the American-Romanian Cultural Foundation and George Crisan of the Romanian Baptist Association of the United States and Canada. Crisan said he had travelled through Romania and had spoken to Hungarian-speaking Baptist leaders. He asked them if they were any discrimination against them. They replied, "Brother George, there is none."[112] While Rabbi Israel Miller, representing the Conference of Presidents of Major American Jewish Organizations, did not appear before the House Subcommittee, he did send a letter indicating the organization's continued support of the President's waiver. Last year he had threatened to withhold support if emigration did not improve.[113]

Opposition figures also testified before the Subcommittee led by Laszlo Hamos, who submitted a massive report documenting the heinous atrocities perpetrated by the Romanian government against Hungarians. Hamos received a new source of support. For the first time, the Coordinating Committee of Hungarian Organizations in North America and the Committee of Transylvania sent a representative. Istvan Gereben presented a statement from Louis Lote, the head of the organizations, which reaffirmed Hamos's allegations.[114] Gereben and Lote would frequently join Hamos to annually oppose the President's waiver request.

Jacob Birnbaum, the National Director of the Center for Russian and East European Jewry, took a much stronger stand in 1978 than in previous years. He wanted Congress to suspend approval of the waiver. Jewish emigration to Israel had drastically declined during the past 5 years. In 1973-74, 4,000 Jews emigrated to Israel. In 1977-78, approximately 1,000 would emigrate. He urged Congress to suspend the waiver and MFN, until Romania increased the number of Jews permitted to emigrate to Israel.[115] While supportive of Birnbaum's position, Reverend Florian Galdau, of the American-Romanian Committee for Assistance to Refugees, would not go so far as to actually suspend the waiver. He wanted Congress not to renew the waiver, unless Bucharest agreed to increase the number of people free to emigrate for family reunification.[116]

The House hearings also acted as a forum for anyone who had a complaint about Romania. Most notable in the 1978 testimony was the case of John Tudor, who alleged that the Romanian government had nationalized his inheritance. On June 9, 1944, Constatin Orghidan wrote her last will and testament awarding all she owned to Ion Ungureanu, who changed his name to John Tudor when he emigrated to the United States. The will clearly left Tudor a large collection of old coins. The State Department had intervened for Tudor for several years. Carter had mentioned the case to Ceausescu during his April visit. On May 30, the Romanian government again officially notified Tudor that the decision made by the Romanian courts in 1946, awarding the coins to the Romanian Academy, remained in effect. Tudor wanted the Subcommittee to support his claim against Bucharest for unlawfully seizing his rightful property.[117]

Several weeks later, on July 12, the Senate Finance Committee's Subcommittee on International Trade began its one day hearings on the President's emigration waiver. Administration witnesses and those testifying in support of continuing and expanding relations with Romania were essentially the same people who had appeared before the House Subcommittee. Opposition figures too were similar with a couple of new faces. Dimitrie Apostoliu, President of the American-Romanian National Committee for Human Rights, and Reverend Alexander Havadtoy, of the Hungarian American Committee of the State of Connecticut, both criticized Bucharest's human rights practices, with Havadtoy especially emphasizing Romania's record of religious persecution.[118]

Since the hearings did not produce any resolutions to disapprove the emigration waiver, the Legislature implicitly extended the waiver and Romanian MFN until July, 1979. Congressional inaction also renewed the American-Romanian trade agreement for another three years.

Pacepa and Goma

The end of the hearings normally meant that Romanian-American relations would again be put on the back burner, until the following Spring. This cycle was generally repeated during the Fall and Winter of 1978-79 with only a few aberrations. Within a couple of weeks of the Senate hearings, Ion Pacepa, the head of DIE, the Romanian intelligence agency, defected to the West. He was in West Germany on official business when he disappeared from his hotel and was flown to the United States by the CIA. Because of his close relationship with Ceausescu, and his access to all forms of correspondence, including sensitive military and political material, his defection was a serious source of irritation between Bucharest and Washington. Moscow was also concerned, because of Pacepa's knowledge of Warsaw Pact information. The Administration said nothing about the defection, and the only information carried in the American press came from the West German daily, *Die Welt*. In September, State Department Counsellor Matthew Nimitz flew to Bucharest to "sooth" Ceausescu, but the Romanian President's displeasure was not easily mollified.[119] The main casualty appeared to be Nicolae Nicolae. Ceausescu recalled Nicolae and appointed Nicolae Ionescu as Romania's new Ambassador to the United States.[120] Pacepa's defection gradually disappeared as a source of friction between the two countries until 1987, when the defector published *Red Horizons, The Chronicles of a Communist Spy Chief*. This book would become a *cause celebre* and a major source of embarrassment between Washington and Bucharest.

A second source of irritation for Ceausescu occurred in early October, when Paul Goma shared his experiences in Romania with members of the Commission on Security and Cooperation in Europe. He told Representative Dante Fascell of Florida, Chairman of the Commission, that "human rights in Romania are not being violated – they do not exist. The right of the government is the only one that exists – the right to do what it pleases." Goma also described how Bucharest used psychiatric imprisonment to silence dissidents. His testimony moved several Congressmen, especially Robert Dole, to speak out against Romania's human rights practice and to read into the Congressional Record a litany of abuse supplied by the Romanian Dignity Association and the Committee for Human Rights in Romania, led by Laszlo Hamos.[121]

Bucharest-Moscow-Washington

While Pacepa and Goma had given American-Romanian relations a slight setback, Ceausescu's relations with Moscow deteriorated rapidly during the last half of 1978. Much to Moscow's chagrin, Ceausescu tried to have the Belgrade Conference curb Warsaw Pact maneuvers, along with those of NATO, but without success. The Romanian leader then continued to seek support outside of CMEA, especially in West Germany and Great Britain. Further, unlike Moscow, Romania supported the Camp David accords on the Middle East. Ceausescu also continued to support Eurocommunism and in May visited Beijing, China. In return, Hua Guofeng reciprocated and for the first time in history, a Chinese leader came West. He stayed in Bucharest for six days. During that time he tried, with limited success, to use Romania as another forum from which Beijing could challenge Moscow for leadership of the world Communist movement.

In October, Soviet-Romanian talks in Bucharest solved little. Moscow was still displeased at Ceausescu's foreign policy which appeared to deliberately deviate from that of the Soviet Union. The fact of the matter was that Ceausescu did consciously pursue foreign policy interests alien to Moscow. By so doing Romania gained greater flexibility in the international arena and was sure to win support in the United States, and other Western countries, for her maverick behavior.

At the November 22-23 Warsaw Pact Political Consultative Meeting held in Moscow, Romania continued to antagonize the Soviets. Ceausescu refused to join her allies in condemning the Camp David accords, refused to endorse a proposal for all the Warsaw Pact members to increase their defense expenditures, and denounced Moscow's efforts to increase military integration through some sort of supranational command structure.[122] After the meeting, Ceausescu returned to Bucharest and spoke to representatives of the military justifying his opposition to increased military expenditures at the expense of the "people's material and spiritual welfare."[123]

As tensions mounted between Bucharest and Moscow, the Carter Administration finally defined its East European policy. Testifying before the House Subcommittee on Europe and the Middle East in September, William Luers of the State Department, announced that America intended to "recognize and support the individuality of each country and seek to work out our relations directly, and bilaterally."[124] The Brezhnev-Ceausescu feud, which continued to heat up throughout the Fall, as evidenced by public statements from both capitals, gave Carter the opportunity to implement his new East European policy. He decided to support Romania.

On December 8, Michael Blumenthal arrived in Bucharest. The stop was not in his original itinerary. The Treasury Secretary had just completed four days of trade talks in Moscow and two in Bonn, West Germany, when he received Carter's instructions to visit Romania before returning to Washington.[125] Blumenthal carried a message from the

President which he announced at the Otopeni Airport. His visit was "to reaffirm to the Romanian people and to President Ceausescu the importance we attach to Romanian independence and to U.S.-Romanian friendship."[126] Blumenthal met with the Foreign Minister Stefan Andrei and on the following day spent ninety minutes in private talks with Ceausescu. He left for Washington at noon on December 9.[127]

The Blumenthal mission was one of the most direct interventions in Warsaw Pact politics ever made by an American President. Apparently Carter's advisors feared possible Soviet military action against Romania, especially since Brezhnev had alluded to Ceausescu's "demagogic" behavior.[128] Few of Carter's staff thought that Ceausescu might have used the Warsaw Pact disagreement as a means to suppress growing Romanian opposition to his method of leadership. In January, 1978, Ceausescu had celebrated his 60th birthday and the media portrayed the President as a messiah and demi-God. In March he had made sweeping changes in party and state leadership, which, if nothing else, intensified his personal control of Romania.[129] As opposition to his "cult of personality" mounted, what better way for Ceausescu to bolster his authority, than to taunt Moscow and let the Soviets become the target of Romanian displeasure.[130] Further, the growing tension between Moscow and Beijing gave Ceausescu the opportunity to annoy Moscow with impunity. Tempers would finally cool in January, 1979, following a brief visit by Andrei to the Kremlin. At the meeting, both sides agreed not to widen the gulf any further between them.[131]

American-Romanian relations in 1978 ended as they began, with treaties. In January, both countries had exchanged notes regulating cotton textile trade, and in December they extended their cultural, scientific and technical exchange programs for another two years, through 1980. Bilateral trade had continued to increase in 1978 reaching a two-way total of $664 million, making Romania America's second largest East European trading partner next to Poland.[132] However, for the first time in history, Washington had a trade deficit with Romania. Ceausescu's efforts to increase exports and decrease imports had succeeded, and Bucharest enjoyed a $27 million trade advantage with the United States.[133]

Notes

1. Jeffrey D. Merritt, "Unilateral Human Rights Intercession: American Practice under Nixon, Ford, and Carter, *The Diplomacy of Human Rights*, ed. David D. Newsom (New York: University Press of America, 1986), p. 44.

2. David P. Forsythe, *Human Rights and U.S. Foreign Policy: Congress Reconsidered* (Gainesville: University Presses of Florida, 1988), p. 8.

3. John Salzberg, "A View from the Hill: U.S. Legislation and Human Rights," *The Diplomacy of Human Rights*, ed. David D. Newsom, (New York: University Press of America, 1986), p. 15.

4. *Ibid.*, p. 16.

5. *Ibid.*, p. 17.

6. Merritt, *The Diplomacy of Human Rights*, ed. David D. Newsom, 1986, pp. 44-45.

7. *Ibid.*, p. 45.

8. U. S. Congress, House Committee on Foreign Affairs, Hearings Before the Subcommittee on International Organizations, *Human Rights and U. S. Foreign Policy*, 96th Cong., 1st Sess., 1979, p. 1. For more on human rights legislation see, Forsythe, *Human Rights and U.S. Foreign Policy*, p. 60, and U.S. Congress, House Committee on Foreign Affairs, Hearing Before the Subcommittee on Human Rights and International Organizations, *Status of U.S. Human Rights Policy, 1987*, 100th Cong., 1st Sess., 1987.

9. Salzberg, *The Diplomacy of Human Rights*, ed. David D. Newsom, 1986, p. 18.

10. Lynne A. Davidson, "The Tools of Human Rights Diplomacy with Eastern Europe," *The Diplomacy of Human Rights*, ed. David D. Newsom (New York: University Press of America, 1986), p. 26.

11. Jimmy Carter, *Keeping Faith: Memoirs of a President* (New York: Bantam Books, 1982), p. 143.

12. *Facts on File*, 1977, pp. 25-26.

13. See, Carter, *Keeping Faith*, p. 50.

14. Cyrus Vance, *Hard Choices: Critical Years in America's Foreign Policy* (New York: Simon and Schuster, 1983), pp. 46, 441.

15. See Carter, *Keeping Faith*, p. 145,

16. McLellan, *Cyrus Vance*.p. 73-74.

17. Forsythe, *Human Rights and U.S. Foreign Policy*, p. 57.

18. U. S. Congress, House Committee on Foreign Affairs, Hearings Before the Subcommittee on International Organizations, *Human Right and U.S. Foreign Policy*, 96th Cong., 1st Sess., 1979, p. 84.

19. Forsythe, *Human Rights and U.S. Foreign Policy*, p. 52.

20. Briefing Paper, Normalization of US Economic Relations with the Communist Countries, n.d., 2pp., [A Summary of Developing International Economic Issues; 1/10/77] Folder Economics (Gen), Box 194, Domestic Policy Staff, Eizenstat, JC Library.

21. U. S. Congress, Joint Economic Committee, *East European Economies: Slow Growth in the 1950s*, Vol. I: *Economic Performance and Policy*, 99th Cong., 1st Sess., p. 545; U. S. Congress, House Committee on Foreign Affairs, Report Prepared for the Subcommittee on Europe and the Middle East by the Foreign Affairs and National Defense Division, CRS, *U. S. Relations with the Countries of Central and Eastern Europe*, 96th Cong., 1st Sess., 1979, pp. 6-7. Hereafter,

House Committee on Foreign Affairs, *U.S. Relations with the Countries of Central and Eastern Europe*, 1979.

22. Zbigniew Brzezinski, *Power and Principle: Memoirs of the National Security Adviser, 1977-1981* (New York: Farrar, Straus, and Giroux, 1983), p. 297.

23. U.S. Congress, Hearings Before the Commission on Security and Cooperation in Europe, *Basket II - Helsinki Final Act; East-West Economic Cooperation*, 95 Cong., 1st Sess., 1977, p. 48.

24. According to Pacepa, Nicolae was a member of the Departamentul de Informatii Externe (DIE), the Romanian counterpart of America's Central Intelligence Agency (CIA) (Pacepa, *Red Horizons*, p. 252).

25. Memorandum, Jack Watson to the President, February 24, 1977, Folder CO130; 1/20/77-12/31/77, Box CO-51, WHCF, JC Library.

26. Mastny, *Helsinki, Human Rights, and European Security*, p. 195.

27. The Washington Post, February 19, 1977, p. 21.

28. Andreas C. Tsantis, Roy Pepper et al., *Romania: The Industrialization of an Agrarian Economy Under Socialist Planning* (Washington, D.C.: The World Bank, 1979), pp. 390-391; U. S. Congress, House Committee on Ways and Means, *Tenth Quarterly Report to the Congress and the East-West Foreign Trade Board, On Trade Between the United States and the Nonmarket Economy Countries*, 95th Cong., 1st Sess., 1977, p. 13; Ceausescu, *Romania On the Way*, XIV, 136-137. A melodramatic account of the earthquake and its aftermath can be found in a series of brief vignettes with the collective title, "Valiant and Courageous, In Full Unity, Romanian People Got Through the Trial Successfully," *Agerpres*, n.d., pp. 1ff.

29. Staff Report, Humanitarian Assistance to Earthquake Victims in Romania (Prepared for the Use of the Committee on the Judiciary, United States Senate), May 28, 1977, p. 4, hereafter, *Staff Report, Humanitarian Assistance*, 1977.

30. *Ibid.*, pp. 4, 57; The Washington Post, April 20, 1977, p. 6.

31. U.S. *Congressional Record*, 95th Cong., 1st Sess., 1977, CXXIII, 8735-8736.

32. Walter D. Connor, "Dissent in Eastern Europe: A New coalition?" *Problems of Communism*, Vol. XXIX (January-February 1980), p. 10.

33. Judy Dempsey, "Religion in the Soviet Union and Eastern Europe," *The Soviet Union and Eastern Europe*, ed. Schopflin, p. 601.

34. Barnes, "Impression of Romania," *The United States and Romania*, ed. Paul D. Quinlan, pp, 127-128.

35. Vlad Georgescu, "Romania in the 1980s: The Legacy of Dynastic Socialism," *Eastern European Politics and Societies*, Vol. 2, No. 1, (Winter 1988), p. 88.

36. Staff Report, Humanitarian Assistance, 1977, pp. 44-47.

37. *Ibid.*, p. 5.

38. *Ibid.*, pp. 42-44.

39. Letter, Frank Moore to Jerome A. Ambro, June 23, 1977, 2pp., Folder CO130; 1/20/77-12/31/77, Box CO 51, WHCF, JC Library; Letter, Zbigniew Brzezinski to Stu Eizenstat *et al*, May 16, 1977, 2pp. Folder Foreign Affairs-

Human Rights, Box 208, Eizenstat Domestic Policy Staff, JC Library.
40. Letter, Moses Rosen to Ed Koch, May 27, 1977, 2pp., Folder CO130; 1/20/77-12/31/77, Box CO 51, WHCF, JC Library.
41. *Idem*, Letter, Moses Rosen to Arthur Schneier, May 27, 1977.
42. *Public Papers of the Presidents of the United States,Jimmy Carter,1977* (Washington, D.C.: U. S. Government Printing Office, 1978), I, 1055-1057.
43. U. S. Congress, House Committee on International Relations, Hearings Before the Subcommittee and the Middle East, *U. S. Policy Toward Eastern Europe*, 95th Cong., 2d Sess., 1978, p. 162. Coincidentally, on the same day, Washington and Bucharest completed months of negotiations and signed a four year agreement on trade in wool and man-made fiber textiles, This extended an interim agreement signed on January 17, 1977. Vladimir M. Pregelj, "U.S. Commercial Relations with Communist Countries: Chronology of Significant Actions Since World War II, and Their Present Status," Economic Division, Congressional Research Service, March 30, 1984, p. 9.
44. House Subcommittee on Trade, *MFN Treatment*, 1977, p. 4.
45. Senate Subcommittee on International Trade, *MFN Treatment*, 1977, pp. 5-9; Background Paper, Eximbank Financing of Major Romanian Projects, n.d., 2pp.,Tab 24, Folder Rom; 6/24/76, Box 315, William Seidman Papers, GRF. The Treasury Department refused to approve the joint venture agreement signed between Romania and the Island Creek Coal Company. The problem was whether or not the Internal Revenue Service would permit the joint venture to operate as a "cost company." The IRS refused to recognize the joint venture as a cost company because it would give unfair tax advantages to Occidental Petroleum, which was the parent company of the Island Creek Coal Company. The IRS ruling forced Occidental to restructure its arrangement with Romania into a long term purchase agreement, rather than as a joint venture(Background Paper, Romania-Island Creek Joint Venture, June 6, 1976, 2pp., Tab N, Folder Rom; 6/24/76, Box 315 William Seidman Papers, GRF). In July, Bucharest purchased a third interest in the coal company enabling Romania to buy 35% of the mine's production, purchasing about one-half of that at cost (The Washington Post, July 12, 1977, p. A12).
46. U. S. Congress, Senate Committee on Finance, Hearing Before the Sub-committee on International Trade, *Continuing the President's Authority to Waive the Trade Act Freedom of Emigration Provisions*, 95th Cong., 1st Sess., 1977, p. 22.
47. A. Detesan and D. Porojan, *Export: Probleme si Solutii* (Bucharest: Revista economica, 1977); Tismaneanu and Zaharia, *Present and Prospect in Romania's Development*, p. 135. B
48. Tsantis, Pepper *et al.*, *Romania*, p. 130.
49. Senate, Subcommittee on International Trade, *MFN Treatment*, 1978, pp. 16-21.
50. *Ibid.*, p. 134.
51. *Ibid.*, pp. 23-27.

52. *Ibid.*, pp. 42-43.
53. *Ibid.*, pp. 111, 117, 142.
54. Letter, President Carter to Romanian-U.S. Economic Council, July 7, 1977, Folder CO130; 1/20/77-12/31/77, Box Co-51, CO, WHCF, JC Library.
55. Letter, Henry M. Jackson to the President, June 24, 1977, Folder Fo 3-2/CO 130; 1/20/77-1/20/81, Box FO-32, Foreign Affairs, WHCF, JC Library.
56. Memorandum, Zbigniew Brzezinski to the President, July 22, 1977, 2pp., Folder Foreign Affairs-Human Rights, Box 208, Eizenstat, Domestic Policy Staff, JC Library.
57. Letter, Zbigniew Brzezinski to Henry Jackson, July 20, 1977, Folder FO 3-1/CO130; 1/20/77-1/20/81, Box FO-32, Foreign Affairs, WHCF, JC Library.
58. *Idem.*, Memorandum, William G. Hyland to Zbigniew Brzezinski, July 18, 1977. Barnes asked to see Brzezinski, but the National Security Advisor refused (Note, July 14 [1977], Folder FG 6-12; 6/6/77-9/30/77, Box FG-89, Fed Govt Orgs, WHCF, JC Library.
59. Letter, Zbigniew Brzezinski to Henry Jackson, July 20, 1977, Folder FO 3-1/CO130; 1/20/77-1/20/81, Box FO-32, Foreign Affairs, WHCF, JC Library.
60. Ms. Letter, Jimmy Carter to Scoop Jackson, July 26, 1977, Folder Foreign Affairs-Human Rights, Box 208, Eizenstat, Domestic Policy Staff, JC Library.
61. House Subcommittee on Trade, *MFN Treatment*, 1977, p. 5.
62. *Ibid.*, pp. 19-21.
63. *Ibid.*, p. 58.
64. House, Subcommittee on Trade, *Emigration Waiver to the Socialist Republic of Romania and the Hungarian People's Republic; and Non Discriminatory Treatment of the Products of Romania*, 95th Cong., 2nd Sess., 1978, pp. 2-3.
65. NYT, November 27, 1977, pp. 1,3. For a different perspective on the story of the Jiu Valley see, "The Jiu Valley – Valley of Joy," *Agerpres*, April 18, 1953.
66. U. S. *Congressional Record*, 95th Cong., 1st Sess., 1977, CXXIII, 26214-26220, 26528-26532.
67. Richard F. Staar (ed.), *Yearbook on International Communist Affairs, 1978* (Stanford, CA: Hoover Institution Press, 1978), p. 61.
68. *Ibid.*, pp. 61-62.
69. Order, April 5, 1977, Folder FG 6-10/A CIEP, Box FG 83, FG WHCF, JC Library.
70. *Idem.*, Letter to Gus Weiss from Jimmy Carter, September 24, 1977.
71. Order, March 24, 1977, Folder FG 118/A, Box FG 181, FG WHCF, JC Library.
72. *Public Papers of the Presidents, Jimmy Carter, 1977*, II, 1673-1674.
73. Pacepa, *Red Horizons*, p. 11.
74. The Washington Post, September 28, 1977, p. 7.
75. *DOS Bulletin*, December 1977, p. 874.

76. Memorandum for the File, Christine Dodson to Denis Clift, November 1, 1977, Folder CO 130; 1/20/77-12/31/77, Box CO-51, CO WHCF, JC Library.

77. House Subcommittee on Trade, *Emigration Waiver to the Socialist Republic of Romania and the Hungarian People's Republic*, 1978, Table 3.

78. Ceausescu, *Romania On the Way*, XV, 244-245.

79. *Ibid.*, p. 252.

80. U.S. Congress, Senate Committee on Commerce, Science, and Transportation, Hearing, *National Export Program*, 95th Cong., 2d Sess., 1978, p. 84.

81. *Commerce America*, November 21, 1977, p. 28; *Commerce America*, January 30, 1978, p. 27.

82. See, U. S. Congress, House committee on International Relations, Hearing Before the Subcommittee on International Organizations, *Human Rights and United States Foreign Policy: A Review of the Administration's Record*, 95th Cong., 1st Sess., 1977,

83. *Public Papers of the Presidents, Jimmy Carter, 1977*, II, 2086-2087,

84. Connor, "Dissent in Eastern Europe: A New Coalition?," *Problems of Communism*, 1980, p. 11.

85. The ethnic composition of Transylvania had been a concern of American diplomats since 1944., A memo in September of that year concluded that because of its tripartite ethnic composition – Romanian, Hungarian, and Saxon – the region ought to be made independent (Memorandum on Transylvania, September 12, 1944, 4pp., Folder Romanian Surrender, Box 3, Harry Howard Papers, HST Library).

86. "The Hungarian View: An Interview with Karoly Kiraly," *East European Reporter*, Vol. 2, No. 3 (1987), p. 48; Richard F. Staar (ed.), *Yearbook on International Communist Affairs, 1979* (Stanford, CA: Hoover Institution Press, 1979), p. 65; Pacepa, *Red Horizons*, p. 147.

87. "The Hungarian View: An Interview with Karoly Kiraly," *East European Reporter*, 1987, p. 48; Schopflin, *The Soviet Union and Eastern Europe*, p. 601.

88. U. S. Congress, Report Submitted to the House Committee on Foreign Affairs and the Senate Committee on Foreign Relations by the Department of State, *Country Reports on Human Rights Practices for 1979*, 96th Cong., 2d Sess., 1980, p. 656.

89. Ceausescu, *Romania On the Way*, Vol. XV, p. 501.

90. *Ibid.*, p. 514.

91. Brzezinski, *Power and Principle*, p. 126.

92. Carter, *Keeping Faith*, p. 145.

93. *Ibid.*, p. 143.

94. *Ibid*.

95. Memorandum, Robert King to Zbigniew Brzezinski, February 7, 1978, Folder CO 130; 1/20/77-12/31/77, Box CO-31, CO WHCF, JC Library.

96. Lieutenant General Pacepa, who accompanied Ceausescu on this visit, remembers that when the American military band played the Romanian

national anthem, it played "Fatherland Romania," which was the anthem of pre-communist Romania, rather than the new anthem Ceausescu himself had introduced to the Socialist Republic. The general confesses he was "dumbfounded" by the gaffe. But his political instincts were still alert enough to notice that "Ceausescu's fingers were furiously agitated" (Pacepa, *Red Horizons*, p. 264).

97. Author interview of O. Rudolph Aggrey, October 26, 1989, Washington, D.C.

98. *President Nicolae Ceausescu's State Visit to the U.S.A.: April 12-17, 1978* (Bucharest: Meridiane Publishing House, 1978), pp. 87ff.

99. *Ibid.*, pp. 100-103.

100. *Ibid.*, pp. 112-116.

101. *Ibid.*, pp. 121-122; Ceausescu, *Romania On the Way*, XVI, 57ff.

102. *Nicolae Ceausescu's State Visit to the U.S.A*, pp. 133-134.

103. Pacepa, *Red Horizons*, pp. 280-281; Letter, George Roman to the Honorable Jimmy Carter, April 8, 1978, 2pp., Folder CO 130; 1/20/77-1/20/81, Box CO-52, CO WHCF, JC Library; *Idem.*, Letter, Jim Purks to George Roman, April 20, 1978.

104. *Nicolae Ceausescu's State Visit to the U.S.A*, pp. 182-188.

105. CSM, April 18, 1978, p. 10.

106. U. S. Congress, House Committee on Ways and Means, Hearing Before the Subcommittee on Trade, *Trade Waiver Authority Extension*, 97 Cong., 1st Sess., 1981, p. 251; Schopflin, *The Soviet Union and Eastern Europe*, p. 60. Due to government pressure, the Baptist Union would exclude all nine cofounders from the Baptist church in 1979.

107. Vlad Georgescu, "Romania in the 1980s: The Legacy of Dynastic Socialism," *Eastern European Politics and Society*, Vol. 2, No. 1 (1988), p. 90 n57.

108. *Public Papers of the Presidents of the United States, Jimmy Carter, 1978* (Washington, D.C.: U.S. Government Printing Office, 1979), I, 1031-1033.

109. *Ibid.*, pp. 1032-1033.

110. House Subcommittee on Trade, *Emigration Waiver to the Socialist Republic of Romania and the Hungarian People's Republic*, 1978, pp. 106-107.

111. *Ibid.*, pp. 68-71.

112. *Ibid.*, pp. 142-143.

113. *Ibid.*, p. 347.

114. *Ibid.*, p. 145.

115. *Ibid.*, pp. 185ff.

116. *Ibid.*, p. 167. Galdau's persistence brought results. On June 20, 1978, Adalbert Rosinger received permission to emigrate to Israel as a direct result of Galdau's lobbying. Rosinger had been convicted in 1960 of "economic crimes," and his sentence involved a large fine. It was on June 8 that Ceausescu removed the fine and permitted him to leave Romania (see, Memorandum, Peter Tarnoff to Zbigniew Brzezinski, June 30, 1978, Folder CO 130; 5/1/78-12/31/78, Box CO-52, CO WHCF, JC Library).

117. House Subcommittee on Trade, *Emigration Waiver to the Socialist*

Republic of Romania and the Hungarian People's Republic, 1978, pp. 87-89, 116-118, 304-308.

118. *Ibid.*, pp. 140ff.

119. *The Washington Post*, August 9, 1978, p. A17; CSM, September 12, 1978, p. 7.

120. *Public Papers of the Presidents of the United States, Jimmy Carter, 1978*, II, 2059.

121. *The Washington Post*, October 13, 1978, p. 16.

122. Hutchings, *Soviet-East European Relations*, p. 107.

123. Ceausescu, *Romania On the Way*, XVII, 226.

124. Statement By William H. Luers, Deputy Assistant Secretary of State for European Affairs, Before the Subcommittee on Europe and the Middle East of the House International Relations Committee, September 7, 1978, 36pp., Folder FG 33-11; 10/1/77-12/31/78, Box FG-151, Fed Govt Orgs, WHCF, JC Library. For elaboration on the point see, Scott McElwain, "The United States and Central Europe: Differentiation or Detente?," *East European Quarterly*, Vol. XXI, No. 4 (Winter 1987), pp. 457-461.

125. NYT, December 7, 1978, p. 14.

126. NYT, December 9, 1978, p. 1.

127. *The Washington Post*, December 10, 1978, p. A25.

128. NYT, December 7, 1978, p. 14.

129. The Washington Post, December 10, 1978, p. A25.

130. Walter M. Bacon, Jr., "Romania: Neo-Stalinism in Search of Legitimacy," *Current History* (April, 1981), p. 170.

131. Richard F., Staar (ed.), *Yearbook on International Communist Affairs, 1980* (Stanford, CA: Hoover Institution Press, 1980), p. 66.

132. U.S. Department of Commerce, *World Trade Outlook for Eastern Europe, Union of Soviet Socialist Republics and People's Republic of China*, Overseas Business Report 79-24 (Washington, D.C.: U.S. Government Printing Office, September, 1979), p. 7; *Twenty-Third Annual Report of the President of the United States on the Trade Agreements Program: 1978*, p. 64.

133. U.S. Congress, House Committee on Ways and Means, *Seventeenth Quarterly Report to the Congress and the East-West Foreign Trade Board, on Trade Between the United States and the Nonmarket Economy Countries*, 96th Cong., 1st Sess., 1979, p. 38.

CHAPTER XV

"HOSTAGES, ALWAYS
THE HOSTAGES"

Romanian-American Relations: January-June, 1979

During the last two years of the Carter Administration, the relative importance of American-Romanian relations declined. Washington's attention in 1979 focused on recognition of Red China, Khomeini's Islamic revolution, the SALT II agreement, the fall of the American Embassy in Tehran, the 444 day hostage crisis, and the Soviet invasion of Afghanistan.

The Administration's support of Romania carried over into Congress at the beginning of the new year. In January, Senator George McGovern gave the Committee on Foreign Relations a report on his Summer visit to Romania.[1] The ten page summary gave an historical overview of Romania, emphasizing her nationalism and desire for economic and political independence. McGovern credited Romania with "pioneering detente" with Nixon's 1969 visit, and noted Ceausescu's continued willingness to take foreign policy initiatives quite independent of Moscow, most notably in the Middle East. While the report noted that emigration procedures were lengthy and burdensome, the fact was that "there has been a dramatic improvement" in the number of people permitted to leave Romania during the past several years. McGovern met Ceausescu, whom he described as "among the world's leading proponents of arms control," and without question was impressed by the Romanian President. In sum, the report gave evidence that America's East European policy, designed as it was to encourage political independence among the Warsaw Pact countries, had made measurable gains in Romania. Washington should continue to expand her relations with Bucharest.[2]

A couple of weeks later, on February 5, Senator Adlai Stevenson of Illinois and Representative Les AuCoin of Oregon introduced virtually identical bills which contained a general amendment to the freedom-of-emigration provision. While designed primarily to help the President develop the new Beijing-Washington axis, the legislation would also have applied to Romania. The proposal gave the President, rather than Congress, the power to waive the emigration provisions of Section 402 of the Trade Act, and he could do so for up to five years. If passed, Romania could have received a multiyear MFN agreement. However, Carter decided that he did not need new legislation to promote Chinese-American relations, and without Administration support, neither bill moved out of committee.[3]

Meanwhile developments in Romania appeared to question the favorable impression made by McGovern's report. In February, a small group of dissidents organized the Free Trade Union of Romanian Workers (SLOMR). Led by Dr. Ionel Cana and Gheorghe Brasoveanu, the group pledged to "fight for the respect of the rights of Romanian citizens" especially in the field of labor. SLOMR complained about unemployment, forced retirement, and poor wages. In March, the government arrested SLOMR leaders. The remaining dissidents notified friends in the West of the government's crackdown on their organization. Human rights advocates in France and later America rallied to SLOMR's defense, but without success. However, the attention that the incident generated would provide fuel to those who argued that Romania had little respect for human rights.[4]

From March through May, American-Romanian relations continued to expand. On March 14, the two countries signed a protocol to increase exchanges of agricultural information especially in the use of grains for animal feed.[5] On April 4, Juanita Kreps arrived in Bucharest at the head of the American delegation to the Fifth Session of the Joint Romanian-American Economic Commission. She was met at the airport by Cornel Burtica, the new Minister of Foreign Trade and head of the Romanian delegation.

The two day conference opened on April 5 and among the topics discussed was Romania's request that Washington liberalize her export controls and expedite the license application process. In addition, Bucharest wanted to expand its financial relations with America and for this reason, the Romanian Bank of Foreign Trade decided to establish a branch office in the United States. Both sides indicated satisfaction with the recently signed cooperation contracts between several American firms and Bucharest to manufacture products in Romania. The initial success of these cooperative ventures, which included the manufacture of electronic watches, multiplex capacitors, and memory magnetic tapes, encouraged delegates from both countries to explore additional cooperative projects.

Both sides pointed with the pride to the ongoing efforts of the Joint Working Group on Agricultural Cooperation and Trade, and the American delegates asked that Romania make available detailed trade statistics to attract more American businesses to Bucharest.[6] At the close of the session, Kreps and Burtica signed an economic protocol summarizing the main points of discussion.[7] This document signing was important to Ceausescu, not necessarily because of the contents of the agreement, but as an end in itself. The Romanian President could show this as evidence of an active and autonomous foreign policy. Frequently, the daily newspaper, *Scinteia*, would mention the latest protocol or accord the government signed.

In May, while the Commerce and State Departments prepared data for the President's annual emigration renewal request for Romania, Senator Claiborne Pell presented a report to the Foreign Relations Committee on a recent visit that he and five other Senators had made to Bucharest. As part of a tour to Eastern Europe and the Middle East, the Senate delegation visited Romania on November 20-21. The report noted both Ceausescu's authoritarianism and Romania's independent foreign policy. Bucharest maintained an active and independent role in CSCE, and used it as a major forum through which she could influence European affairs and protect her interests and territorial integrity from Moscow.[8]

Pell's delegation noted Romania's "largely disappointing" implementation of the Helsinki Final Act's humanitarian provisions, but called attention to her improved emigration record to the United States over the past three years. The delegation spent more than two hours talking with Ceausescu. As a counter to Ceausescu's request for multiyear MFN, the Senators pointed out that bilateral relations would continue as long as Romania responded to the emigration issue. As for the issue of discrimination towards Hungarians in Romania, the delegation talked with the Vice President of the Grand National Assembly, Mr. Fejes. He was an ethnic Hungarian and said that "ethnic Hungarians in

Romania do not view it as a major issue." Further, Ceausescu and the Hungarian Communist Party leader Janos Kadar frequently met and monitored minority rights in each other's country.[9]

While the Senate Foreign Relations Committee reviewed the Pell report, which overall supported continued relations with Romania, the House Subcommittee on International Organizations began hearings on May 2 on Human Rights and American Foreign Policy. The principal Administration spokesman was Warren Christopher, the Deputy Secretary of State. He declared that "human rights are a central facet" of American foreign policy.[10] In reviewing the Carter Administration's record on human rights, he especially emphasized the annual report to Congress begun in 1977, which reviewed human rights practices in countries receiving American development or security assistance. The 1979 report covered 650 pages and 115 countries.

Christopher described the Administration's approach to human rights as a "dramatic" change from the past. Human rights issues, such as the fate of political prisoners, were now discussed "face-to-face" between diplomats forcing governments to confront the issue, rather than letting it be "conveniently ignored" as was the case in previous administrations.[11] While the major focus of his testimony concerned countries which received foreign assistance or security support, he did note the situation in Eastern Europe and the Soviet Union. Human rights remained a "serious source of concern, but even there, we have seen some positive signs."[12] Not once in his testimony did he mention Romania, even though in May, State Department records indicated that there were 328 unresolved family reunification cases with Bucharest.[13] Although these cases involved over 700 people, this problem was not the focus of human rights in 1979. Human rights advocates focused their efforts on "gross violations," not on family reunification problems and emigration practices.

While various Congressional committees and subcommittees heard reports on human rights, the Administration continued to expand its relations with Romania. On May 9, the President met with Beatitude Justin, the Patriarch of the Romanian Orthodox Church. The Bishop had asked for the meeting primarily to tell the President that there was religious freedom in Romania. He was touring the United States in connection with the 50th anniversary of the founding of the Romanian Orthodox Church in America. He also wanted to counter the influence of Valerian Trifa, the Bishop and leader of the Romanian Orthodox Episcopate of America. After years of investigation, the United States

Justice Department had decided to bring Trifa to trial to strip him of his American citizenship for alleged crimes against Jews in Romania during World War II.[14]

Carter agreed to the meeting because of the close relationship the Orthodox Church had with the Romanian government. The closeness, however, forced some American citizens of Romanian heritage to follow Trifa. Consequently, Justin was critically received by some members of the Romanian Orthodox faith as well as by Baptists who identified the Bishop with Ceausescu's repressive religious policies. Carter wanted to capitalize on these allegations of persecution. During the meeting, he urged the Patriarch to "be a voice for religious freedom in Romania." Carter added that because of America's "deep commitment to human rights, we strongly believe that religious freedom is a right which must be protected and cherished."[15]

America's Trade Deficit

On June 1, Carter sent his annual recommendation to waive the freedom-of-emigration requirements in Section 402 of the Trade Act of 1974. In his letter to Congress, the President based his decision on the successful resolution of "many emigration and other humanitarian problems" as a result of high-level bilateral talks.[16] While there would be some opposition to the President's request, Congress was ready to extend the emigration waiver and Romanian MFN for another year. The primary reason for this attitude was the status of the American economy. In the last year of the Ford Administration, America had a trade deficit of nearly $9 billion. In 1977, the deficit leaped to $29 billion and in 1978 to $31 billion. The Consumer Price Index indicated a 6.5% annual rate of inflation in 1977, a 7.7% for 1978, and experts predicted a double digit inflation rate for 1979, which proved correct at 11.3%.[17]

American business blamed the Administration's export control policy for much of the country's economic woes. The 1969 Export Administration Act had limited the President's discretionary power over dual-use items, those which could be used for either peaceful or military purposes. In most instances, the Act prohibited their export to Communist countries. The business community opposed this arrangement. Manufacturers and exporters complained most strongly about losing sales when comparable goods were readily available in foreign markets. Economic controls also created a "worldwide image of the United States as an unreliable supplier" and had forced foreign buyers to look elsewhere.

Finally, exporters reported considerable delay in the export licensing process which had forced buyers to cancel orders and purchase their goods from foreign vendors.[18]

As a result of these dissatisfactions, Congress aimed to revise the 1969 Export Administration Act to limit the President's foreign policy export control authority. Hearings began in February and continued through the end of April, in the process making more Congressmen aware of America's trade deficit and economic problems. The House Subcommittee on International Economic Policy and Trade, which held the hearings, wanted to establish criteria to regulate the President's foreign policy use of export controls. These criteria included the product's availability from other sources, the effect of exports and the overall effectiveness of the restriction.[19] The Administration opposed the concept of criteria, and the most Carter would concede was that the President would "give weight" to the foreign availability of a product prior to making an export control decision.[20]

During the lawmaking process, the President won some concessions from Congress. The 1979 Export Administration Act superseded the 1969 Act and its amendments and called for the President to take into consideration a number of factors before using export controls as a means to implement foreign policy. The legislation noted that these factors, which included foreign availability of a product, need not dictate the President's decision. The 1979 Act also contained provisions to expedite the export licensing process, and retained the 1974 amendment which gave the Defense Department "veto" power over exports controlled for national security purposes. The new act, signed into law in September, extended the President's export control authority through September, 1983.[21]

Trade expansion was also the subject of the ongoing Tokyo Round of the GATT talks which, after six and one-half years, finally concluded in April, 1979. The Multilateral Trade Negotiations, MTN, produced lower tariffs on manufactured products, and, for the first time, established codes to regulate nontariff barriers.[22] Romania participated in these discussions and as an indicator that she too favored greater trade, announced in May the inauguration of a regular shipping service using container vessels between Constanta and several ports along the eastern seaboard of the United States.[23]

The net result of the Export Administration Act hearings and the conclusion of the Tokyo Round of GATT talks was a heightened awareness among Congressmen that increased export trade was of vital importance to the American economy. This was the prevailing climate when the President asked Congress for an emigration waiver for Romania. The Administration quickly pointed out that Washington had reversed its trade imbalance with Romania during the first four months of 1979. America had exported $164 million worth of goods to Romania and imported only $90 million.[24]

Congress and the 1979 Waiver

On June 14, Richard Schulze of Pennsylvania, Larry McDonald of Georgia and Robert Dornan of California introduced a resolution in the House, H. Res. 317, disapproving the waiver extension for Romania.[25] They argued that Romania had consistently violated human rights, institutionalized emigration obstacles, persecuted Hungarians and operated forced labor camps to construct the Black Sea-Danube River Canal. The resolution went to the House Ways and Means for consideration.[26]

Eight days later the House Ways and Means Subcommittee on Trade began two days of hearings on the President's request which recommended an emigration waiver for both Romania and Hungary. On June 22, Administration witnesses appeared before the Subcommittee. Charles Vanik chaired the meeting and in his introductory remarks supported the waiver for Romania. Emigration figures showed that the former cyclic pattern had ended. Monthly numbers no longer showed an increase during the months immediately preceding and during the waiver hearings. Bucharest's emigration to America indicated a consistent pattern.[27] Vanik noted that emigration to Israel had again declined, but justified this on the basis that the remaining Jews in Romania, approximately 35,000 were mostly elderly people who did not want to leave their homeland. Further, Romanian authorities had assured Washington that "all Jewish applicants in 1979 have been resolved."[28]

Administration witnesses confirmed the Chairman's remarks. Those from the State and Commerce Department stressed the increase in bilateral trade and America's growing trade advantage with Romania. Most of the other supporters of the emigration waiver were familiar faces to the more senior members of the Subcommittee. The American Romanian Cultural Foundation sent a representative while George Crisan testified in behalf of the Romanian Baptist Fellowship and Nicolas Bucur for the American Romanian National Institute. Congressmen Millicent Fenwick of New Jersey, Edward Derwinski and Paul

Findley continued to support the waiver. The only real change evident among supporters was in the ranks of big business. In past hearings, there was a veritable parade of witnesses supporting the President's request. In 1979, business supported the waiver by mail, rather than by personal appearance.

The opposition too included a number of familiar faces led by Laszlo Hamos. The most interesting testimony of the day came from Dimitrie Apostoliu of the American Romanian National Committee for Human Rights. He told Chairman Vanik that while he wanted to testify before the Subcommittee, he was frightened to do so. He and seventeen others in the room were on a hunger strike for family reunification in Romania. However, there were also fifteen Romanian secret police agents in the room. These people frightened him and he was afraid that they would bring harm to family members of the hunger strikers who were still in Romania. Vanik said he had no police available to protect him. But, the Chairman was willing to let him testify confidentially in writing. Apostoliu refused because he had learned from "American founders" that you should speak out clearly on human rights. However, since the Romanian continued to show concern about his safety, Vanik refused to let him testify on the basis that he had no means to protect the welfare of Apostoliu, his fellow hunger strikers, and their families in Romania.[29] By day's end, there was still a number of people who wanted to testify on the Romanian and Hungarian emigration waivers. Vanik announced that the hearings would continue on July 9. The delay was due to emigration negotiations in Bucharest and to the traditional July 4 celebrations.

The negotiations stemmed from the continued decline in Jewish emigration from Romania to Israel. In 1974, 3,700 Romanians emigrated to Israel, in 1977, 1,500 emigrated, in 1978, 1,200 emigrated and during the first five months of 1979, only 254 Romanians had left for Israel.[30] This dramatic decline greatly concerned the American-Jewish community. In an effort to resolve the problem, representatives from the Conference of Presidents of Major American Jewish Organizations went to Bucharest in June to talk directly to the Romanian authorities. Aided by Ambassador Ionescu and Corneliu Bogdan, Romania's former Ambassador to the United States, the American delegation negotiated an arrangement with Chief Rabbi Rosen and the Romanian government. Bucharest agreed to permit any Romanian Jew to emigrate to Israel, and assured the Conference of Presidents that Jewish applications would be expeditiously processed.

As Bogdan described the solution, "anyone who wanted to go to Israel could go."[31]

On July 6, the Conference of Presidents sent an aide-memoire to Congress indicating the settlement. Three days later, Vanik resumed the House Subcommittee on Trade's hearings on the emigration wavier. Without question, the success of the Bucharest negotiations undermined much of the opposition's support. Nonetheless, Congressman Richard Schulze, who was the author of House Resolution 317 to disapprove the President's waiver request for Romania, maintained his position and focused on Bucharest's continued persecution of Hungarians. Schulze called attention to Amnesty International's recent condemnation of Romania for its human rights violations.[32] Schulze received support from a new organization, the International Human Rights Law Group, which was a non-profit legal organization funded by the Ford Foundation and the Rockefeller Brothers Fund. Amy Young-Anawaty testified for the Group and reiterated Schulze's concern for the oppressed Hungarians in Romania.[33] Other opposition spokesmen emphasized Bucharest's record of religious persecution especially against various Christian sects and dissident Orthodox movements.[34]

Three days after the hearings ended, the House Ways and Means Committee voted on Schulze's resolution of disapproval. The arrangement on Jewish emigration to Israel coupled with the bulk of supporting testimony and Congress's predisposition toward trade expansion, enabled the Committee to defeat the resolution 26-10. On the following day, the Committee forwarded the resolution to the floor of the House.[35]

Before the Senate held hearings on the President's emigration waiver, the United States-Romanian Economic Council began its Sixth Session in Washington, D.C. on July 16. The business delegations from both countries agreed to increase trade particularly in the areas of machine building equipment and in the petro-chemical industries. At the close of the two day sessions, the two heads of delegations, Milton Rosenthal of the United States and Vasile Voloseniuc of Romania, signed a joint communique affirming their support of continued MFN treatment for Romania.[36]

On July 19, Abraham Ribicoff, the Chairman of the Senate Finance Subcommittee on International Trade, began hearings on the President's waiver request. The opposition sent more witnesses to publicly testify against the President's request than had appeared during the

House hearings. Dimitrie Apostoliu told the Subcommittee about the cooperation of Romanian officials in a world wide Soviet spy network, which included agents in Washington, D.C. and in New York City.[37] A number of witnesses told of religious persecution in Romania. Reverend Alexander Havadtoy of the Calvin United Church of Christ spoke of Romania's refusal to rebuild damaged Reformed churches. Not only did the government fail to provide funding, but it also prohibited the use of Western monies to rebuild the churches.[38] Senator Dole questioned Bucharest's harassment of the so-called neo-Protestants which included the Adventists, Pentecostalists and Reform Baptists. Members of these congregations had lost their jobs, had their salaries withheld for months at a time, and had experienced great delay in getting permits for prayer services. Brutus Coste of the Truth About Romania Committee sent written evidence to support Dole's testimony.[39]

The issue of Jewish emigration indicated a split within the ranks of the American-Jewish community. Jacob Birnbaum of the Center for Russian and East European Jewry was unwilling to take at face value the recent assurances made by the Romanian government to permit free Jewish emigration to Israel. Birnbaum saw no reason to assume that Romania would change its past practice concerning Jewish emigration. For that reason, he urged Congress not to renew the waiver unless Romania gave written assurances to comply with the Jackson-Vanik Amendment.[40] In contrast, Jack Spitzer sent a letter from the Conference of Presidents of Major American Jewish Organizations. This was the organization that had sent representatives to Bucharest in June and negotiated the right for Jews to freely emigrate to Israel. Spitzer's letter gave "an unqualified endorsement to another extension" of Romanian MFN.[41]

The Administration received support from Senators Henry Jackson and Jacob Javits. Both agreed that serious questions existed concerning Romania's human rights practices. However, they were pleased with Bucharest's recent assurances concerning Jewish emigration, and wanted to give Romania the chance to implement these pledges.[42] Other supporters who testified included Arthur Downey, the Director of East-West Trade for the United States Chamber of Commerce as well as Milton Rosenthal, of the United States-Romanian Economic Council. Similar to the House hearings, representatives from American industries used letters rather than personal appearance to indicate their support for the President's waiver request.[43]

The Senate hearings ended after one day of testimony. On July 25, the House voted down Schulze's resolution of disapproval by a vote of 271-126.[44] Since there was no resolution of disapproval in the Senate and neither house took any further action on Romanian emigration, the waiver authority automatically extended through July 2, 1980.

However, on August 3, 76 members of the House signed a letter and sent it to President Carter with a copy to President Ceausescu. The Congressmen urged the President to insure that Romania kept its promises made to the Conference of Presidents of Major American Jewish Organizations. This was the primary reason that the House had supported the President's waiver. The letter indicated that if Bucharest did not implement its assurances, MFN renewal would be jeopardized. Further the letter indicated that Congress was also concerned about Romania's human rights practices.[45]

This was the first time Congress had indicated in writing that they viewed emigration as part of the larger issue of human rights. This theme was repeated and made more specific by the Senate Finance Committee on August 23. Russell Long, Chairman of the Finance Committee sent President Carter a statement which the Committee had adopted. While urging the Administration to be more aggressive in its monitoring of Romanian emigration, the statement's last paragraph made a leap from the Jackson-Vanik emigration requirement to human rights concerns. The Committee noted that

> within the human rights framework, though not always directly related to emigration, the Committee has continued to receive allegations of cultural repression and violations of individual human rights against ethnic minorities. . . . The Committee is deeply concerned about these charges and wishes to indicate its intent to carefully monitor this situation, reviewing the record in detail next year.[46]

The Administration's response to both letters was bland.[47] Carter refused to link emigration to human rights. He knew that Romania could never abide by Congressional standards. Therefore, he wanted to keep the issues distinct in order to maintain MFN as a mechanism to influence change in Bucharest. However, not all Congressmen shared this view, and beginning in 1979, a number of legislators decided to make human rights practices, including emigration, the primary criterion for waivering Section 402 of the Trade Act of 1974.

The "Trifa Affair"

While Congress considered Romanian MFN, the Administration become involved in a sordid affair which could have proved most embarrassing to the United States had Romania chosen to make it so. On July 30, 1979, the Justice Department initiated denaturalization proceedings against Valerian Trifa, Bishop of the Romanian Orthodox Church in America. The "Trifa Affair", as it was popularly called, was a series of events stemming from 1941 through 1984, culminating in Trifa's deportation from the United States to Portugal, where he died in 1987.

Trifa arrived in the United States in 1950 and became Bishop of the Romanian Orthodox Church of America in 1952, after bitter factional fighting. During the struggle, evidence emerged concerning Trifa's past association with the Iron Guard, a Fascist organization in Romania. As a student leader in the Iron Guard, he allegedly led an antisemitic uprising in Bucharest on January 21-24, 1941. He was tried *in absentia* by a Romanian court in 1941, and condemned to life imprisonment. According to State Department documents, Trifa denied taking part in the uprising, and no evidence emerged that proved his involvement. By 1955, the controversy about his past had subsided sufficiently for him to deliver the opening prayer at a session of the United States Senate in May of that year.[48]

In 1957, Trifa became a naturalized citizen, but his past did not go away. When Dr. Charles H. Kremer, a Romanian-born dentist, learned that Trifa was a citizen, he notified the American Immigration and Naturalization Service of Trifa's alleged past. As President of the Romanian-Jewish Federation of America, Kremer continued to pressure Washington to investigate Trifa. He testified before the 1975 Senate hearings on the Romanian-American Trade Agreement, telling the Finance Committee members all about Trifa's past. The Administration finally agreed to act, and in June the Justice Department began an investigation of Trifa.[49]

The investigation gathered speed after Radio Free Europe, RFE, broadcast a 45 minute interview with Trifa on May 1, 1979. The broadcast offended a number of people, including two employees of RFE, Edgar Rafael and Jacob Popper, who recalled his activities in the Iron Guard. Their complaints to the station managers fell on deaf ears. Several of these people informed Elizabeth Holtzman, Chairwoman of the House Judiciary Subcommittee on Immigration, Refugees and International Law, about the interview, and the indifference displayed by the RFE Administration toward the complaints.[50]

Using her committee position, Holtzman pressed the Justice Department to hasten its investigation. On July 30, 1979, with evidence supplied by the Romanian government, the Department began proceedings to strip Trifa of his naturalized citizenship. To make sure that the proceedings would move briskly along, Holtzman notified the President of Trifa's background.[51] She anticipated that his concern for human rights would facilitate the judicial proceedings. On October 28, 1980, the Justice Department began deportation proceedings against Trifa.[52]

The proceedings continued well into 1982. Finally, Trifa admitted that he had lied about his past, and agreed to leave the United States rather than continue the deportation hearings. On October 7, the Justice Department announced its intent to deport Trifa.[53] After two years of searching for a country which would accept Trifa, the former Iron Guardist left the United States in August, 1984, for Portugal. He lived in Estorial, Portugal, until he died on January 28, 1987.[54] His nemesis, Dr. Kremer, died five months later, still frustrated that Trifa never faced a war crimes trial in Israel.[55] While the Trifa Affair gained considerable press, it never affected American-Romanian relations.

Reaction to Khomeini

Meanwhile, developments between Washington and Bucharest continued to run smoothly throughout the late Summer and Fall of 1979. In September, the two countries exchanged notes further regulating America's imports of Romanian wool and manmade fiber textiles.[56] These exchanges occurred periodically in response to American textile manufacturer's complaints concerning Romania's cheap imports. In the following month, *Agerpres* announced that both countries intended to increase their two-way trade to over $1 billion.[57] On the same day, the White House announced that Secretary of State Vance would visit Romania and Yugoslavia later in the year. The notice indicated that Vance's visit to Bucharest was at the request of Foreign Minister Andrei.[58]

However, the Vance trip was quickly cancelled. On November 4, 1979, Iranian students seized the American Embassy in Tehran. They captured fifty Americans and announced they would hold them hostage until the United States returned the ousted Shah, Mohammed Risa Pahlevi, to Iran to stand trial for crimes against the Iranian people. The Shah was in New York under medical care. Vance's East European tour quickly fell to the wayside, as the White House focused nearly all its attention on securing the release of the hostages.

Events in Iran also affected Bucharest. During the 1970s, Romania had purchased much of her oil from Iran under very favorable terms, including barter; Romania swapped industrial equipment for oil. By 1978, Iran supplied about 65% of Romania's oil imports.[59] However, in late 1978, as part of a successful effort to depose the Shah, oil workers cut off all oil exports from Iran. By the Spring of 1979, the loss of Iranian oil was offset by increased production from other oil-producing states especially Saudi Arabia. However, the Iranian action did bring about an oil shortage for about 6 months, and enabled OPEC to increase oil prices by more than 10% in 1979.[60] Romania was especially affected by the Shah's fall, and was forced for the first time to import oil from the Soviet Union.

Ceausescu's efforts to rapidly industrialize Romania during the 1970s had placed heavy demands on energy resources. Energy shortages appeared as early as 1976, but Ceausescu continued to raise the targets for industrial production. Essential for Romania's continued growth were petrochemical exports which accounted for about one-fourth of Romania's hard currency earnings.[61] The events in Tehran forced Ceausescu to rely far more on internal oil and coal production than ever before. He urged Romanians to reduce their energy needs. On July 26, 1979, Bucharest announced that effective August 1 individual tourists motoring in Romania would have to purchase gasoline with hard currency. Due to strong protests by the East European governments, Ceausescu agreed to postpone implementing the decree until August 10, by which time most East Europeans had completed their Summer vacation.[62]

By the fall of 1979, Ceausescu knew that many of the projected targets of the 1976-1980 Five Year Plan would not be met. The decrease in domestic resources, especially oil and gas, and the world energy crisis combined to lower Romania's industrial growth rate, which had been one of the highest in the world. In 1978, industrial production grew at 9% rather than at the 10.6% target. In 1979, industry grew at only 8% in contrast to the planned 11.5%.[63]

Within this economic climate, Ceausescu convened the Twelfth Party Congress on November 19. During the five day meeting, Ceausescu introduced the new Five Year Plan for 1981-1985, which called for an annual growth rate of 7.5%. Although this was higher than any other CMEA country, it was substantially less than envisioned by the 1976-1980 plan. Ceausescu also called for increased foreign trade. He wanted the total volume to increase by 50-57% between 1981 and 1985. However, exports had to exceed imports, and therefore Romanian production would focus on goods which would yield a high currency return.[64] Implicitly this meant that Romania's consumer needs would continue to be neglected in favor of the export market. The Congress adopted two other plans for the period 1981-1990. One focused on scientific research and technological development and emphasized greater use of electronics and robotics for industrial use. The other called for more investment in geological exploration, and coal and oil production in order to make Romania energy self sufficient by 1990.[65]

Throughout the Congress delegates lavished praise on Ceausescu confirming his pre-eminent position in Romanian political life. However, before the meeting ended, an 84 year old delegate and one of the founders of the Romanian Communist Party, Constantin Pirvculescu addressed the Congress. According to observers, he attacked Ceausescu accusing him of putting his personal interests before those of the country. He attacked the Congress for refusing to address Romania's problems, and he announced that he would not vote for Ceausescu's re-election as Secretary General of the Party.[66] This outburst was certainly not expected, and Ceausescu's supporters quickly hooted down Pirvulescu, stripped him of his delegate's credentials and ousted him from the meeting. Thereupon the Congress unanimously reelected Ceausescu to a five year term as Secretary General of the party.

The Soviets Invade Afghanistan

1979 ended with a bang. On December 27, the Soviet Union invaded Afghanistan. Carter responded swiftly. Within a week he placed a grain embargo on the Soviet Union, and threatened to boycott the Moscow Olympic games if Moscow did not remove its troops from Afghanistan.[67] On January 23, 1980, the President presented Congress with the "Carter Doctrine," a guarantee that any attempt by any outside force to secure control of the Persian Gulf would be regarded as an assault against America's vital interests. Similar to the regional framework of the Truman Doctrine, Carter pledged to use all means, including military force, to insure the independence and integrity of the Persian Gulf area.[68]

The Soviet invasion was also felt in Romania. Ceausescu feared that if Moscow were willing to incur world criticism by invading Afghanistan, how much easier would it be for the Soviets to crush an independent

Communist Balkan state. While he thoroughly opposed the invasion, he did not want to draw a great deal of attention to his views. Consequently, Romania registered its disapproval by silence. Bucharest alone refused to attend the Warsaw Pact foreign ministers meetings in Moscow, where all the other Pact members signed communiques supporting the new government in Afghanistan and implicitly endorsing the Soviet invasion.[69] When the United Nations General Assembly voted to condemn the Soviet invasion on January 14, the Romanian delegate abstained. However, during the floor debate the Romanian delegate, Teodor Marinescu, noted that the situation posed a "serious danger to peace and the continuation of the policy of detente," and called for the withdrawal of all foreign troops from Afghanistan.[70]

Moscow wanted more than silence from Bucharest. On January 31, Soviet Foreign Minister Andrei Gromyko visited Romania and talked with Ceausescu. On February 2, the two men issued a communique that blamed the Afghan situation on the "accumulation of unsolved international issues" and implied that the real problem was the "interference of the imperialist forces in the internal affairs of other states."[71] The communique was sufficiently vague to accommodate the foreign policy goals of both countries. However, Gromyko's visit did result in a more positive attitude by Ceausescu. In April, the Romanian President sent Babrak Karmal a congratulatory message on his reelection as President of Afghanistan.[72]

Meanwhile, American-Romanian relations continued without interruption and featured a number of exchange visits. On January 11, Charles Vanik arrived in Bucharest at the head of a Congressional trade review mission to East Europe. The delegation spent two days in Romania and met with Cornel Burtica, the Minister of Foreign Trade and President Ceausescu. Both sides indicated their pleasure with the current status of trade and spoke optimistically of a $1 billion two-way trade in 1980.[73] Several hours later Ceausescu received Jack Spitzer, Chairman of B'nai B'rith and the Conference of Presidents of Major American Jewish Organizations. Included in the meeting was Dr. Moses Rosen, Romania's Chief Rabbi, and the discussion focused on implementing the assurances given the previous July concerning Jewish emigration to Israel.[74]

In recognition of Romania's stand in the Afghanistan situation, the State Department sent Under Secretary of State David Newson to Bucharest on January 28. Newson brought Ceausescu a message from President Carter. Following their meeting, *Agerpres* reported that both men had agreed on the importance of non-interfering in the internal affairs of others.[75] Washington continued to send representatives to Bucharest in February. On the eleventh, an American delegation led by Stephen Palmer, the Deputy Assistant Secretary of State for Human Rights arrived in Bucharest to attend the first Romanian-American Round Table on Human Rights. Mr. Gheorghiu, President of the Academy of Social and Political Science, led the Romanian team and the two groups discussed civil and human rights issues. The *Agerpres* release noted that the discussions proceeded in an "atmosphere of mutual understanding and regard, occasioning a sincere exchange of opinions."[76] In Communist jargon this meant that there was some disagreement, but not enough to be described as a "frank" exchange of views. However, the fact that there was a meeting indicated that Romania recognized the importance of human rights to the Carter Administration, and Ceausescu did not want to be in disfavor with both Washington and Moscow at the same time.

Throughout the next several months there was only one unpleasant incident that developed between the two countries, and it did not affect the overall ambience that developed between American and Romania. In late February, a Washington-based Romanian diplomat, Nicolae Horodinca, asked for political asylum for himself, his wife and their three year old daughter. However, when his wife, Cristina, learned of his intent to defect, she wanted to return to Romania with their child. What happened next is open to speculation. According to the State department, Cristina and her daughter went to National Airport to return to Romania. She fainted while waiting for the airplane, and, after recovering and talking with medical personnel, changed her mind and decided to stay with her husband. *Agerpres* described the incident as "a typical case of kidnapping" and the subsequent statements of the State Department were "a cock and bull story" to cover up the truth.[77] The Romanian press reported that the Romanian Foreign Ministry had requested the return of Cristina and her daughter to Bucharest. By June, 1981, both had returned to Romania.[78] Since then Washington has released no further information on the incident, nor has *Agerpres*.

On April, 22 the Sixth Session of the Joint Romanian-American Economic Commission convened in Washington for a two day meeting. The Romanian Embassy announced that Bucharest had signed export and import contracts worth approximately $150 million with more than 40 American firms in the past few months. Further, Bucharest agreed to open two new trade promotion offices in Atlanta and in Houston bringing the total to five including Chicago, Los Angeles and New York. The United States delegation was especially satisfied with the two-way trade since America showed a surplus of $171 million in 1979, and the early figures in 1980 indicated an even greater surplus.[79] Following the meeting, members of the Romanian delegation visited Houston and Los Angeles, and signed several commercial agreements in energy related areas.[80]

From Vance to Brzezinski

Within a week of the Commission's meeting, there was a major change in the Carter Administration. Secretary of State Cyrus Vance resigned. From the outset of his Presidency, Carter had hoped to establish a foreign policy process which avoided the extreme centralization that occurred during the Nixon Administration. He wanted the Secretary of State to be his principal advisor on foreign affairs with the National Security Adviser playing a less assertive role. He also envisioned the Secretary of State to educate the American public about foreign policy.[81] Carter chose Vance because he was intelligent, honorable, had sound judgement, and was not easily flustered. Carter appointed Zbigniew Brzezinski his National Security Advisor because he was bright, outgoing and outspoken, who was willing to "serve as a lightning rod – to take the blame for unpopular decisions made by others."[82]

Carter believed that the different strengths of the two men matched their roles and permitted a natural competition between the two organizations which produced better advice. However, Brzezinski was aggressive and ambitious, and his natural affinity for the spotlight gradually reduced Vance's influence on the President. The incident which precipitated Vance's resignation was Carter's decision to follow Brzezinski's advice and send a military mission to rescue the American hostages in Iran. The President agreed to the rescue effort while Vance and his wife were on vacation. When the Secretary of State returned, and learned of the decision, he submitted his resignation effective after the mission.[83] On April 24, the President had to abort the rescue mission after learning that two of the original eight rescue helicopters never reached Iran, and only five of the remaining six could lift off.[84] On April 27, Carter appointed Senator Edmund Muskie Secretary of State, instead of the Acting Secretary of State, Warren Christopher, whom Vance had recommended.[85]

On May 16, Brzezinski received a delegation from the Romanian

Grand National Assembly. The legislators arrived at the invitation of the American Congress to reciprocate Vanik's visit in January. The delegation led by Nicolae Giosan, talked with a number of Congressmen as well as Secretary of Agriculture Robert Bergland and Milton Rosenthal of the United States-Romanian Economic Council.[86] The timing of the visit was propitious for two weeks later, Jimmy Carter sent the annual emigration waiver recommendation to Congress. This time the request included Romania, Hungary and the People's Republic of China. Carter justified his May 28 recommendation for Romania on the basis of Bucharest's improved emigration record. He also cited the success of high-level bilateral consultations which he believed would continue to insure favorable resolution of emigration and humanitarian problems.[87]

Romania's Debt Problems

On the following day, Ceausescu addressed the party's Central Committee and criticized them for the number of "shortcomings and drawbacks" that confronted Romania's economy.[88] The economic restructuring announced in 1978, which called for a new economic mechanism, had not taken hold. The new system encouraged enterprises to assume greater responsibility for production and to become profit making. The profits would be shared by workers and management. However, people were more interested in the profits, than in the production efficiency needed to produce them.[89] Ceausescu did note that some of the problems in Romania's economy were influenced by international developments especially rising interest rates and the "soaring price of oil." However, he played down these issues in favor of blaming the central authorities for mismanagement and poor organization.[90]

Ceausescu's concern was legitimate. Romania's economy was in a crisis situation most evident by her increasing external debt. In the early 1970s, Bucharest borrowed from Western commercial and governmental financial markets to underwrite her rapid industrialization. At the outset, most of her borrowing was from government sources. However, by 1980, 69% of her gross hard currency debt was owed to commercial lenders. The shift from official to commercial borrowing indicated a growing debt management problem in Romania, since commercial credits had shorter maturities and higher interest rates than government loans. In fact, by the end of 1980, nearly 43% of Romania's commercial debt had a maturity of less than one year.[91]

A principal reason for Romania's indebtedness was not so much her earlier borrowings, but her growing trade deficit. In the 1960s and 1970s, Romania had frequently borrowed abroad to compensate for raw material and other industrial shortfalls. While this policy of import substitution brought impressive successes, especially between 1973 and 1977, the policy now exacerbated Romania's problems. Romania had become dependent on energy and other raw material imports to export manufactured and agricultural goods to the West. These imports steadily increased in price while, simultaneously, Romania's hard currency exports declined in volume and value, in part due to poor quality. As a result, Romania's trade declined, and she was forced to borrow to finance the deficit. By 1979, Romania's hard currency debt was $6.7 billion.[92]

In 1980, Romania's trade deficit exceeded $3 billion. Typical was her two-way trade with the United States which showed a deficit of $171 million in 1979, and $410 million in 1980. To finance the debt, Bucharest again turned to Western commercial and governmental financial markets and by year's end her external debt was $10.3 billion.[93]

In June, 1980, Ceausescu again had to borrow, but this time he turned to governmental rather than commercial sources. To allay creditor's concerns about Romania's finances, he permitted the IMF to publish information on the government's financial operations. As a result, the IMF signed a $1.4 billion Stand-by Arrangement with Romania. These monies would be available in 1981 to support Bucharest's promise of "economic reform and stabilization efforts." Ceausescu also approached the World Bank and received four loans totalling $325 million for several long term projects including transportation, irrigation and fruit and livestock production.[94]

To offset his growing trade imbalance with the West, Ceausescu turned toward CMEA to increase trade. At the June 17-18 meeting of the CMEA Council in Prague, the Romanian delegate, Premier Ilie Verdet, called for a "speedy" implementation of CMEA's 1981-1985 Coordinated Plan. Verdet criticized the delays which caused domestic planning bottlenecks. He ended his speech calling for a "deepening of cooperation" among CMEA countries, particularly in the areas of fuel, energy sources and raw materials.[95] This surprising *volte face* by Bucharest indicated the growing crisis in Romania's economy. The situation had become sufficiently critical for Romania to purchase nearly 25% of her oil imports from Moscow.[96] Consequently, Ceausescu's criticisms and exhortations at the Central Committee meeting in May were certainly appropriate. Moreover, they also indicated that

Bucharest would reconsider its targets for the 1981-1985 Five Year Plan, and not release its "final" version for another year.

Congress and the 1980 Waiver

Meanwhile in Washington, the President's waiver request prompted Congress to hold its annual hearings. On June 10, the House Subcommittee on Trade listened to testimony from about thirty witnesses, most of whom spoke in support of extending the President's emigration waiver authority to Romania. The thrust of the testimony focused less on emigration, and more on increased trade, religious persecution and human rights violations.

Romania's emigration figures indicated that this was not an issue in 1980. 2,886 Romanians came to the United States and nearly 13,000 went to West Germany.[97] The Jewish emigration issue, too, played a much smaller role in the hearings, in part because of the arrangements made in the Summer of 1979, between the Romanian government and the Conference of Presidents of Major American Jewish Organizations. 1,061 Romanian Jews emigrated to Israel in 1980.[98] While this number was below emigration levels which existed prior to MFN, few people, save Jacob Birnbaum, complained. Briefing materials to Subcommittee members also reduced the focus on Jewish emigration. The materials included a description of Israeli immigration procedures which noted that "Israeli Embassy policy toward Jewish emigration from Romania must be regarded as passive. The Embassy intervenes in individual cases only infrequently, and it claims not to have any means of knowing who is granted Romanian exit documents for Israel, much less who applied." Further, Israel did want all those who Bucharest permitted to leave. Immigration into Israel depended on the applicant's eligibility under the Israeli law of return.[99]

Unlike 1979, representatives of business and industry appeared in person to testify before the Subcommittee. Christopher Stowell of WJS/Moody International Corporation and Harvey Weisenfeld of UOP Incorporated joined Administration officials in support of the President's waiver request. The testimony of these people along with letters from Atalanta Corporation, Control Data Corporation, Lipe-Rollway, and the East-West Trade Council all noted America's substantial trade surplus with Romania.

Those in opposition to the President's request continued to develop their 1979 strategy of viewing emigration as part of the larger issue of human rights. Since Romania had improved its emigration record, opposition forces decried Romania's persecution of religious minorities and human rights practices. Congressman Larry McDonald told of the Underground Church in Romania, a refuge for believers. He told of people sent to "slave labor camps," not because of their "alleged" crimes, but because they wanted to worship God.[100] John Larwood, of the American Conservative Union, and Reverend Galdau, of the American Romanian Committee for Assistance to Refugees, corroborated McDonald's testimony and called for religious freedom in Romania.[101]

Romania's persecution of its Hungarian minority was well documented by veteran witnesses led by Laszlo Hamos and Istvan Gereben along with newcomers, Tamas and Christina de Kun of the American-Transylvania Federation of Washington. Other human rights witnesses which called attention to Romania's abusive practices included Amy Young-Anawaty of the International Human Rights Law Group and Dimitrie Apostoliu of the American-Romanian National Committee for Human Rights. Most of these witnesses were able to develop their testimony in greater detail than normal due to the questioning of Subcommittee member, Richard Schulze, one of the authors of the 1979 House Resolution 317 disapproving the President's waiver.

Three days after the hearing, Jimmy Carter and Nicolae Ceausescu exchanged messages celebrating 100 years of diplomatic relations between the two nations. Both notes mentioned the intensity of relations during the past 15 years, looked forward to another century of further cooperation, and ignored mentioning human rights.[102]

On July 21, the Senate held its hearings. The Subcommittee on International Trade listened to testimony from Counselor Rozanne Ridgway of the State Department along with a considerable number of witnesses from the business community. Mark Sandstrom of Atalanta Corporation joined Preston Brown of the International Commodities Export Company, Simon Chilewich of Chilewich Corporation, Stephen Gans of VITCO and Arthur Ronan of Rockwell International to publicly attest to the merits of continuing the waiver and Romanian MFN. Both government officials and business leaders noted Romania's improved emigration record and the successful trade relationship which existed between the two countries.

The opposition focused, as it had at the House hearing, on religious persecution and human rights violations. The hearing Chairman, Abraham Ribicoff, allotted only 10 minutes for the combined testimony of Jacob Birnbaum, Reverend Galdau, and Mr. Cyrus Gilbert Abbe, all of whom opposed the President's request. Laszlo Hamos submitted a 50 page statement on Romanian discrimination against Hungarians,[103] and Amnesty International submitted a country report on Romania which raised serious questions about Bucharest's laws which specifically prescribed imprisonment and other penalties for the non-violent exercise of certain human rights.[104]

The Subcommittee received a record high number of letters from individual Romanians seeking help to reunite family members. The cause of the unusual volume was twofold. First, living conditions in Romania continued to worsen. Ceausescu's continued emphasis on export production reduced the availability of consumer products. As a result, many more Romanians wanted to leave their homeland, and this was evident in the increase in defection and escape stories which appeared in the American press during the Summer of 1980.[105] Second, according to the testimony of Birnbaum and Ribicoff, Romania had recently agreed to permit numerous people to emigrate including people convicted of economic crimes and Jewish survivors of the holocaust.[106] American-Romanians who sought family reunification saw these developments as an opportunity which should be quickly seized, and they immediately wrote to the Subcommittee for help.

Following the hearing, neither house took any action on the President's waiver recommendation, until August 27 when Richard Schulze introduced House Resolution 775 to disapprove the waiver extension. The Resolution never left the House Ways and Means Committee, and the President's authority automatically extended through July 2, 1981.[107]

"Business as Usual"

During the last months of 1980, the Carter Administration worked to secure the release of the American hostages in Iran, and to win reelection in November. American-Romanian relations moved into their normal Fall pattern of "business as usual." On September 15 delegates to the Seventh Session of the United States-Romanian Economic Council met in Neptun, Romania. During the next two days, discussion concentrated on market access and contract implementation in the the chemical, service, electronics, energy, agriculture and food-processing industries. Both sides expressed satisfaction that the 1976 goal of a $1 billion two-way trade in 1980 would be realized.[108] At the end of the session, President Ceausescu had a private meeting with Robert Smith and J.J. Hillsley of Control Data, the only American company which had a joint venture arrangement with Romania.[109]

The upbeat nature of the talks at the Economic Council hid Bucharest's fear of the economic and political ramifications of recent events in Poland. In July, the Polish government raised meat prices. Polish workers protested, demanding pay increases to meet the rising cost of living. Labor unrest intensified and on August 14, the workers seized control of the Lenin Shipyards in Gdansk. The strikes continued and expanded outside the Baltic region involving hundreds of thousands of workers. On September 6, Stanislaw Kania replaced Edward Gierek as Poland's Communist Party Secretary. The workers formed their own independent labor union, Solidarity, under the leadership of Lech Walesa.

The speed of events took Ceausescu by surprise. Although he espoused non-interference in internal affairs of another country, he wanted to make sure that the Polish example did not take hold in Romania. Throughout the last weeks of August and into early September, the Romanian President went on a whirlwind speaking tour talking to workers across the country. He congratulated them on their hard work, and their commitment to building a multilaterally developed socialist society in Romania.[110] On September 9 he announced a change in the 1980 state budget. He cut 16% of the defense budget and diverted the funds to improve the people's standard of living.[111]

The American delegation to the Economic Council had scarcely left Romania before Bucharest received another economic shock. On September 22, Iraq attacked Iran's oil fields and refineries. Tehran retaliated and within days, both countries halted all oil exports. The war immediately cancelled two agreements signed between Romania and Iran. In April, 1980, Tehran agreed to supply Bucharest with 100,000 barrels of oil a day at the world price of $35 per barrel. In July, the two countries signed a separate accord which provided for Romania to barter agricultural products and farm equipment for additional oil.[112] Although Romania remained neutral, the war effectively reduced the world's oil supply by about 3.5 billion barrels a day. Oil prices soared, and OPEC did not agree until December on a price of $41 per barrel.[113] Romania's oil needs would force her further into debt.

Meanwhile in Washington, the House Committee on Foreign Affairs had begun hearings on Human Rights in Eastern Europe and the Soviet Union in preparation for the upcoming Helsinki Review meeting in Madrid. The Committee met on September 16 and 24 and examined each of the East European countries' five year implementation of the

Final Act. The report on Romania noted her policy of internal repression, but noted that Bucharest would respond to human rights issues raised by Western countries.[114] While the hearings did not impact American-Romanian relations, they did precipitate a response from Ceausescu. On October 29, in an interview with the Norwegian Daily, *Aftenposten*, the Romanian President criticized America's emphasis on freedom-of-emigration. "Nobody can have a better future in another place but at home! That is why we have not encouraged the tendency of some people of being enticed by delusive promises. We consider that such a stand actually expresses the humanitarian character of our policy–of defending the right of the individual to be truly free, to build a happy life where he was born."[115]

On November 4, Americans elected Ronald Wilson Reagan as their 40th President. Jimmy Carter received only 41% of the popular vote. The fact that on the previous day Washington and Bucharest had signed a new four year agreement on trade in wool and man made fiber textiles did not produce many election day votes.[116] Neither did the fact that during 1980, Romania had become the largest East European market for American exports with a combined two-way trade in excess of $1 billion.[117] For in truth, Romanian-American relations played no role in the Presidential election. In assessing the election results as he left the White House for the last time, Carter told his Chief of Staff Hamilton Jordan, "1980 was pure hell–the Kennedy challenge, Afghanistan, having to put the SALT Treaty on the shelf, the recession, Ronald Reagan, and the hostages . . . always the hostages! It was one crisis after another."[118]

Notes

1. *Romanian Bulletin*, The Romanian Library, New York, New York, September, 1978, p. 2; U.S. Congress, Senate Committee on Foreign Relations, *Perspectives on Detente–Austria, Romania, and Czechoslovakia*. A Report by Senator George McGovern, 96th Cong., 1st Sess., 1979.
2. *Ibid*.
3. Pregelj, "Most-Favored-Nation Policy Toward Communist Countries," 1987, pp.. 13-14; U.S. Congress, Senate Committee on Banking, Housing, and Urban Affairs, A Report Submitted by the Subcommittee on International Finance, *U.S. Export Policy*, 90th Cong., 1st Sess., 1979, p. 33.
4. Staar (ed.), *Yearbook on International Communist Affairs, 1980*, pp, 63-64; House Committee on Foreign Affairs, *U.S. Relations with the Countries of Central and Eastern Europe*, 1979, p. 77; Janusz Bugajski and Maxine Pollack, *East European Fault Lines: Dissent, Opposition, and Social Activism* (Boulder CO:

Westview Press, 1989), p. 196; [Amnesty International] *Romania: Human Rights Violations in the Eighties* (London: Amnesty International Publications, 1987), p. 7.

5. FBIS, EEU, March 14, 1979, p. H14.

6. Agreed Minute of the Fifth Session of the Joint American-Romanian Economic Commission (Bucharest, April 6, 1979), pp. 1-10; "U.S.-Romanian Joint Commission Session Spotlights Improvement in Trade Relations," *Business America* (May 7, 1979), pp. 10-11.

7. FBIS, EEU, April 6, 1979, p. H4.

8. U.S. Congress, Senate Committee on Foreign Relations, *Visit to Eastern Europe and the Middle East by the Senate Delegation to the Twenty-Fourth Meeting of the North Atlantic Assembly*, A Report by Senator Claiborne Pell, 96th Cong., 1st Sess., 1979, p. 8.

9. *Ibid.*, p. 12.

10. Zbigniew Brzezinski, *In Quest of National Security*, ed. Marin Strmecki (Boulder, CO: Westview Press, 1988), p. 105.

11. U.S. Congress, House Committee on Foreign Affairs, Hearings Before the Subcommittee on International Organizations, *Human Rights and U.S. Foreign Policy*, 96th Cong., 1st Sess., 1979, p. 16.

12. *Ibid.*, p. 27.

13. House Committee on Foreign Affairs, *U.S. Relations with the Countries of Central and Eastern Europe*, 1979, p. 76.

14. Briefing Paper, Courtesy Visit and Photo with the Patriarch of the Romanian Orthodox Church, May 8, 1979, 2pp., Folder CO 130; 5/1/78-12/31/78, Box CO-52, CO WHCF, JC Library.

15. *Ibid.*, p. 2.

16. *Public Papers of the Presidents of the United States, Jimmy Carter, 1979* (Washington, D.C.: U. S. Government Printing Office, 1980), I, 979.

17. U.S. Bureau of the Census, *Statistical Abstract of the United States 1984* (Washington, D.C.: U.S. Government Printing Office. 1983), pp. 494, 831.

18. [Department of Commerce] *Report of the President on Export Promotion Functions and Potential Export Disincentives*, September 1980, pp. 7-12.

19. U.S. Congress, House Committee on Foreign Affairs, Hearings and Markup Before the Subcommittee on International Economic Policy and Trade, *Extension and Revision of the Export Administration Act of 1969*, 96th Cong., 1st Sess., 1979; Memorandum, Cyrus Vance to the President, March 26, 1979, p. 4, Folder Export Policy, Box 205, Eizenstat, Domestic Policy Staff, JC Library.

20. *Ibid.*, p. 5; *Idem.*, Memorandum, Rick Hutcheson to Cyrus Vance, W. Michael Blumenthal and Juanita Kreps, April 4, 1979.

21. Bela Csikos-Nagy and David G. Young (eds.), *East-West Economic Relations in the Changing Global Environment. Proceedings of a Conference held by the International Economic Association in Budapest, Hungary, and Vienna, Austria* (New York: St Martin's Press, 1986), p. 183; William J. Long, "The Execu-

tive, Congress, and Interest Groups in U.S. Export Control Policy: The national Organization of Power," *Controlling East-West Trade and Technology Transfer*, ed. Gary K.Bertsch, pp. 48-51; Romain Yakemtchouk, "Le systeme americain de controle d'exportations de produits et de technologies sensibles: L'E.A.A. de 1979," [Brussels] *Studia Diplomatica*, Vol XXXVII, No. 4 (1984), 451-460; U.S. Congress, House Committee on Ways and Means, *Overview and Compilation of U.S. Trade Statutes*, 100th Cong., 1st Sess., 1987, p. 102; Long, *U.S. Export Control Policy*, pp. 71-73.

22. Spero, *The Politics of International Economic Relations*, p. 115.

23. *Scinteia*, May 11, 1979, p. 6.

24. U.S. Congress, House Committee on Ways and Means, Hearings Before the Subcommittee on Trade, *Waiver of Freedom of Emigration Requirement to the Socialist Republic of Romania and the Hungarian People's Republic*, 96th Cong., 1st Sess., 1979, p. 47. Hereafter, House Subcommittee on trade, *Waiver of Freedom of Emigration Requirement*, 1979.

25. *Ibid.*, p. 10.

26. U. S. Congress, Senate Committee on Finance, Hearing Before the Subcommittee on International Trade, *Continuing the President's Authority to Waive the Trade Act Freedom of Emigration Provisions*, 96th Cong., 1st Sess., 1979, p. 53. Hereafter, Senate Subcommittee on International Trade, *Continuing the President's Authority to Waive the Trade Act Freedom of Emigration Provisions*, 1979.

27. U.S. Congress, House Committee on Ways and Means, Hearing Before the Subcommittee on Trade, *Trade Waiver Authority Extension*, 96th Cong., 2d Sess., 1980, pp. 46-47. Hereafter, House Subcommittee on Trade, *Trade Waiver Authority Extension*, 1980.

28. House Subcommittee on Trade, *Waiver of Freedom of Emigration Requirement*, 1979, pp. 1-2.

29. *Ibid.*, pp. 140-141.

30. *Ibid.*, p. 381.

31. U.S. Congress, Senate Committee on Finance, Hearing Before the Subcommittee on International Trade, *Extension of the President's Authority to Waive Section 402 (Freedom of Emigration Requirements) of the Trade Act of 1974*, 96th Congs., 2d Sess., 1980, pp. 119, 208, hereafter, Senate Subcommittee on International Trade, *Extension of the President's Authority to Waive Freedom of Emigration Requirements*; Author interview of Corneliu Bogdan, January 11, 1989.

32. House Subcommittee on trade, *Waiver of Freedom of Emigration Requirement,* 1979, pp. 266-269.

33. *Ibid.*, pp. 339-340.

34. *Ibid.*, pp. 208ff.

35. U.S. Congress, House Report 96-336, *Disapproval of Extension of Presidential Authority to Waive Freedom of Emigration Requirements Under Section 402 of the Trade Act of 1974 with Respect to Romania*, 96th Cong., 1st Sess.,

1979, 10pp.; Forsythe, *Human Rights and U.S. Foreign Policy*, p. 39.
36. FBIS, EEU, July 19, 1979, pp. H1-2.
37. Senate Subcommittee on International Trade, *Continuing the President's Authority to Waive the Trade Act Freedom of Emigration Provisions*, 1979, pp. 230ff.
38. *Ibid.*, pp. 219ff.
39. *Ibid.*, pp. 34, 412ff.
40. *Ibid.*, pp. 39-40.
41. *Ibid.*, p. 40.
42. Letter, Robert F. Drinan *et al.* to President Carter, May 25, 1978, 3pp., Folder CO 130; 1/1/78-12/31/78, Box CO-52, CO WHCF, JC Library; *Idem.*, Letter, Zbigniew Brzezinski, June 7, 1978.
43. See, *Ibid.*, pp. iii-iv for a list of witnesses.
44. U.S. *Congressional Record*, 96th Cong., 1st Sess, 1979, CXXV, 20660; Forsythe, *Human Rights and U.S. Foreign Policy*, p. 39.
45. Letter, Ted Weiss *et al.* to the President, August 3, 1979, 6pp., Folder CO130; 1/1/70-12/31/79, Box CO-52, CO WHCF, JC Library.
46. Letter, Russell B. Long to the President, August 23, 1979, Attachment, p. 2, Folder CO130; 1/1/79-12/31/79, Box CO-52, CO WHCF, JC Library.
47. Letter, Nelson C. Ledsky to Ted Weiss, August 31, 1979, 2pp., Folder CO130; 1/1/79-12/31/79, Box CO-52, CO WHCF, JC Library.
48. Memorandum, Richard A. Christensen to Michael B. Smith, January 20, 1972, 2pp., Folder Ex CO 125 Romania; 1/1/71, Box 63, CO Subject Files, WHCF, Nixon Presidential Materials Project.
49. U.S. Congress, Senate Committee on Finance, Hearings, *Romanian Trade Agreement*, 94th Cong., 1st Sess., 1975, pp. 94-96.
50. Letter, Elizabeth Holtzman to Dante B. Fascell, December 20,, 1979, 2pp., Folder FG 6-12; 5/1/77-1/20/81, Box FG-91, Fed Gvt Orgs, WHCF, JC Library. The broadcast schedule of Radio Free Europe was greatly expanded during the Carter administration, because Carter was convinced that both the Voice of America and Radio Free Europe were important means of penetrating the Iron Curtain (Declaration, Jimmy Carter to the Congress of the United States, March 22, 1977, 2pp., Folder IT; 1/20/77-1/20/81, Box IT-2, WHCF, JC Library).
51. Memorandum, Zbigniew Brzezinski to Stu Eizenstat, February 12, 1980, Folder FG 6-12; 1/1/80-2/29/80, Box FG-90. Fed Gvt Orgs, WHCF, JC Library.
52. NYT, October 29, 1980, p. A16.
53. NYT, October 8, 1982, p. A1.
54. NYT, January 29, 1987, p. B6.
55. NYT, May 26, 1987, p. D23.
56. *DOS Bulletin*, November 1979, p. 92.
57. FBIS, EEU, October 12, 1979, p. H6.

58. NYT, October 6, 1979, p. 3. Bucharest had wanted either Carter or Mondale to visit. Neither, however, showed any interest in making the trip. Vance's visit was a sop to the Romanian regime (See, Matt Nimetz to Cyrus Vance, June 5, 1979, Folder CO130; 1/1/79-12/31/79, Box CO-52, CO WHCF, JC Library). Also, Ceausescu had earlier invited former President Nixon to make a private visit to Romania, but that too was refused (CSM, September 22, 1978, p. 2).

59. CSM, August 16, 1979, p. 7.

60. Spero, *The Politics of International Economic Relations*, pp. 312-313.

61. Richard F. Staar (ed.), *Yearbook on International Communist Affairs, 1981* (Stanford, CA: Hoover Institution Press, 1981), p. 288.

62. Staar (ed.), *Yearbook on International Communist Affairs, 1980*, pp. 66-67.

63. *Ibid.*, p. 63; Staar (ed.), *Yearbook on International Communist Affairs, 1981*, p. 288.

64. Ceausescu, *Romania On the Way*, XIX, 197-198. See also, *Directivele Congresului al XII-LEA al Partidului Comunist roman cu privire la Dezvoltarea Economico-Solciala a Romaniei in Cincinalul 1981-1985, si Orientarile de Perspectiva Pina in 1990* (Bucuresti: Editura Politica, 1979), pp. 49-51.

65. Helgard Weinert and John Slater, *East-West Technology Transfer, The Trade and Economic Aspects* (London: Organization for Economic co-operation and Development, 1986), pp. 82-87.

66. Fischer, *Nicolae Ceausescu*, p. 240; Hutchings, *Soviet-East European Relations*, p. 130; Trond Gilberg, "Romania's Growing Difficulties," *Current History* (November 1984), p. 377.

67. When Moscow refused to remove its troops, Carter imposed a unilateral ban on all strategic high technology exports. This action effectively prohibited the export of many dual use products (*Congressional Quarterly*, February 25, 1989, p. 402).

68. Brzezinski, *Power and Principle*, pp. 444-445; *Public Papers of the Presidents of the United States, Jimmy Carter, 1980-1981* (Washington, D.C.: U. S. Government Printing Office, 1981), III, 2337.

69. Hutchings, *Soviet-East European Relations*, p. 110.

70. *Ibid.*

71. *Ibid.*, pp. 110-111.

72. Staar (ed.) *Yearbook on International Communist Affairs, 1981*, p. 291.

73. *Agerpres*, January 12, 1980, p. 1; CSM, January 24, 1980, p. 11.

74. *Ibid.*

75. FBIS, EEU, January 29, 1980, p. H2.

76. FBIS, EEU, February 14, 1980, p. H1.

77. FBIS, EEU, March 11, 1980, pp. H1-2.

78. CSM, June 4, 1981, p. 2.

79. *Business America*, July 28, 1980, p. 22; U.S. Department of Commerce,

East-West Trade Update: A Commercial Fact Sheet for U. S. Business. Overseas Business Report 80-25 (Washington, D.C.: U.S. Government Printing Office, August, 1980), pp. 10-11.

80. House Subcommittee on Trade, *Trade Waiver Authority Extension*, 1980, p. 55.

81. Crabb and Mulcahy, *Presidents and Foreign Policy Making*, p. 275; Carter, *Keeping Faith*, p. 54.

82. *Ibid.*, pp. 52-54.

83. McLellan, *Cyrus Vance*, pp. 159-161.

84. Hamilton Jordan, *Crisis: The Last Year of the Carter Presidency* (New York: G. P. Putnam's Sons, 1982), pp. 272-273.

85. Vance, *Hard Choices*, p. 412.

86. FBIS, EEU, May 19, 1980, pp. H2-3.

87. *Public Papers of the Presidents of the United States, Jimmy Carter,1980-1981*, II, 980-982.

88. Ceausescu, *Romania On the Way*, XX, 70.

89. *Ibid.*, pp. 94-95.

90. *Ibid.*, pp. 70ff.

91. U. S. Congress, Joint Economic Committee, *East-West Trade: The Prospects to 1985*, 97th Cong., 2d Sess., 1982, p. 242.

92. *Ibid.*, p. 264.

93. Bureau of the Census, *Statistical Abstract of the United States,1989* (Washington, D.C.: U.S. Government Printing Office, 1989), Table 1372.

94. Assetto, *The Soviet Bloc in the IMF and the IBRD*, pp. 153-156.

95. Hutchings, *Soviet-East European Relations*, p. 180.

96. Ronald H. Linden, *Communist States and International Change; Romania and Yugoslavia in Comparative Perspective* (Boston: Allen & Unwin, 1987), p. 7.

97. U.S. Congress, House Report No. 97-743, *Disapproval of Extension of Presidential Authority to Waive Freedom of Emigration Requirements Under Section 402 of the Trade Act of 1974 with Respect to Romania*, 97th Cong., 2d Sess., 1982, p. 4.

98. *Ibid.*

99. U.S. Congress, House Committee on Ways and Means, Hearing Before the Subcommittee on Trade, *Trade Waiver Authority Extension*, 96th Cong., 2d Sess., 1980, p. 14.

100. *Ibid.*, p. 106.

101. *Ibid.*, pp. 123, 146.

102. *DOS Bulletin*, August 1980, p. 61.

103. Senate Subcommittee on International Trade, *Extension of the President's Authority to Waive Freedom of Emigration Requirements*, 1980, pp. 281ff.

104. *Ibid.*, pp. 159ff.

105. See, NYT, June 28, 1980, p. 3; NYT, July 5, 1980, p. 4; NYT, August 14, 1980, p. 15.

106. Senate Subcommittee on International Trade, *Extension of the Presi-*

dent's Authority to Waive Freedom of Emigration Requirements, 1980, pp. 5-6; 105ff.

107. Pregelj, "Most-Favored-Nation Policy Toward Communist Countries," 1987, p. 18.

108. RFE, Romania Situation Report/14, October 10, 1980, pp. 7-8.

109. FBIS, EEU, September 18, 1980, p. H2.

110. Ceausescu, *Romania On the Way*, XX, 330ff.

111. Staar (ed.), *Yearbook on International Communist Affairs*, 1981, p. 290.

112. RFE, Romania Situation Report/10, July 22, 1980, pp. 7-8.

113. Spero, *The Politics of International Economic Relations*, p. 313.

114. House Committee on Foreign Affairs, *Human Rights in Eastern Europe and the Soviet Union*, 1980, pp. 17-21.

115. Nicolae Ceausescu, *Human Rights in the Contemporary World* (Bucharest: Editura Politica, 1985), p. 47.

116. Pregelj, *U.S. Commercial Relations with Communist Countries*, 1984, p. 13.

117. *Twenty-Fifth Annual Report of the President of the United States on the Trade Agreements Program, 1980-1981*, p. 119.

118. Jordan, *Crisis*, p. 7.

CHAPTER XVI

REAGAN, HUMAN RIGHTS AND THE CHADHA CASE

From Carter to Reagan

Moments after Ronald Reagan's inauguration on January 20, 1981, Tehran freed the American hostages. The timing was deliberate, designed to complete the humiliation of Jimmy Carter. Few people credited the hostage release to Carter's persistent efforts to negotiate their freedom. Rather, most Americans believed that Reagan's election, resulting from a conservative groundswell in America, frightened Tehran into releasing the prisoners.

Reagan's election pleased Bucharest. Romanian's believed that Republicans liked Romania. Both Nixon and Ford had visited their country, Carter had not. Reagan's rhetoric appealed to Ceausescu. He believed that Reagan's tough stance toward the Soviet Union would improve Romania's relations with Washington, as a reward for Bucharest's continued dissent from Moscow. Ceausescu reacted to Reagan's words, and ignored his actions including his decision in April to end Carter's grain embargo against the Soviet Union.[1]

American-Romanian relations developed slowly under the new Administration, primarily due to the President's near assassination on March 30, 1981. As Reagan walked out of a Washington, D.C. hotel, John Hinckley fired six shots at the President, one hitting him in the chest. While the President underwent surgery, Alexander Haig, the Secretary of State, told the press corps that he was "in charge here." Haig's statement was undoubtedly meant to reassure the American public that the government was operating efficiently. However, many members of the Administration believed that Haig meant exactly what he said, which was a deliberate affront to the Vice President, who, by the 25th amendment, took "charge" of the government. Haig's reputation never recovered from this statement, and fifteen months later he resigned.[2] In contrast, Reagan recovered quickly and left the hospital on April 11. However, he did not resume the full regimen of the Presidency for several months, and in the interim, Vice President George Bush represented the President.

On May 14, Commerce Secretary Malcolm Baldrige led an American delegation to the Seventh Session of the Joint Romanian-American Economic Commission meeting in Bucharest. While there, Baldrige visited President Ceausescu and gave him a message from President Reagan which conveyed good wishes, and looked forward to increased bilateral relations.[3] During the two day meeting of the Commission, the delegates explored new ways of expanding trade especially in the chemical and metallurgical fields. Romania signed contracts with several American companies during the meeting including General Electric, 3-M, Schaffer Grinding Company, Pitman-Dreitzer, and the Vitco Company.[4] The Bucharest delegation also sought cooperation with American firms to produce United States brand-name cigarettes and to grow tobacco.[5] The American delegation showed special interest in assisting Romania develop her new aviation industry, especially in the construction of civilian aircraft, one of the areas targeted for growth in Bucharest's 1981-1985 Five Year Plan.[6] As usual, the session ended with both sides signing the ritual protocol which outlined areas of agreement and indicated new fields of economic opportunity.[7]

As the session ended in Bucharest, Stefan Andrei met with Secretary of State Haig in Washington. In addition to discussing international issues of common interest, Andrei wanted to insure that the new Administration would continue to support Romanian MFN, and recommend renewal of the three year trade agreement due to expire in 1981. Andrei also wanted Reagan's support to secure more loans from the United States.[8] After their discussion, Haig arranged for Andrei to meet the President. On May 16, the Romanian Foreign Minister gave Reagan an invitation from Ceausescu to visit Bucharest.[9] Further, he lobbied the President to make a determination to approve a $120 million loan from the Eximbank. Romania needed the money to purchase steam turbine generators from General Electric to construct nuclear power stations in Romania. By law, the President had to approve any Eximbank loans in excess of $50 million by certifying that the loan was in America's "national interest." Four days after Andrei's visit, Reagan made determination No. 81-7 which approved the loan.[10]

As a result of an invitation from the Romanian Grand National Assembly, a delegation from the House Armed Services Committee visited Bucharest on May 29-30 as part of a tour of Eastern Europe. Led by Melvin Price from Illiniois, the ten member bipartisan delegation met with Ilie Ceausescu, Vice Chairman of Defense, Foreign Minister Andrei and on May 30, with President Ceausescu. Throughout the discussions on both days, the Romanians reminded the Americans of Bucharest's independent foreign policy, and the successful bilateral trade relations existing between the two countries.[11] Bucharest had obviously timed the visit to lobby the Congressmen, including Richard Schulze of Pennsylvania, an outspoken critic of Romania's human rights practices, to support Reagan's expected recommendations to continue Romanian MFN and to extend the bilateral trade agreement for another three years.

Reagan and Human Rights

On June 2, President Reagan sent Congress his recommendation to extend the Romanian emigration waiver for another twelve months. In defending his request, he noted Bucharest's increased rate of emigration which brought more than 2,800 people to the United States. This was twice the 1979 figure. The waiver would also enable Washington to dialogue with Bucharest on family unification issues as well as other humanitarian problems.[12] The President also notified Congress that he had determined to renew the Romanian-American Trade Agreement for three more years since there was a satisfactory balance of concessions in trade and services between the two countries.[13]

While the President's rationale for extending the waiver was consistent with his predecessor, many members of Congress were concerned that Reagan was not sufficiently sensitive to the issue of human rights. Several weeks earlier, the President had nominated Ernest Lefever to replace Pat Derian as the new head of the Bureau of Human Rights and Humanitarian Affairs. Lefever's nomination acted as a lightning rod to human rights advocates. During the Carter years, Lefever was a leading critic of the Administration's human rights policies arguing that it alienated friendly authoritarian regimes. Lefever had publicly advocated abolishing human rights legislation, or at best, to make human rights an anti-Communist policy. He had written that to do otherwise was to "trivialize" human rights.[14]

Members of the Senate Foreign Relations Committee used Lefever's confirmation hearings as a means to chastize the Reagan Administration for its apparent indifference to human rights issues. One of the President's first appointments was Jeane Kirkpatrick as Ambassador to the United Nations. She was one of the most outspoken critics of Carter's human rights policy.[15] On March 31, Secretary of State Haig had outlined the Administration's view on human rights. The main threat to human rights was the expansion of Communism. This might mean that at times Washington would support friendly authoritarian regimes, with repressive human rights practices, in order to thwart Soviet aggression.[16] This position became an adjunct to the much heralded "Reagan Doctrine" which promised American support to popular insurgencies against Communist domination.[17] Reagan described the Soviet Union as an "evil empire," which inspired conspiracy and promoted political terrorism through "wars of liberation." The President intended to use all of his executive authority, including export controls, to stem the Soviet tide.[18]

On June 5, members of the Senate Foreign Relations Committee who opposed Reagan's human rights policy, the "Reagan Doctrine," or who were annoyed by Lefever's arrogance during the hearings, voted 13-4 to recommend that the Senate reject the President's nominee.[19] Hours after the Committee's action, Lefever asked the President to remove his name from nomination. Reagan would leave the Bureau of Human Rights and Humanitarian Affairs without a leader until October when he nominated Elliott Abrams to the post. On November 20, the Senate confirmed the nomination without controversy, even though Abrams was the son-in-law of Norman Podhoretz, the hawkish editor of *Commentary* magazine.[20]

Romania's Increasing Indebtedness

In between Lefever's rejection and the House hearings on the President's emigration waiver request, Romania received a $1.5 billion loan from the IMF. The package included immediate funds and standby credit spread over three years. The need to borrow stemmed from a variety of factors, internal and external, all of which worked to weaken Romania's economy. The prime indicator of Romania's economic woes was her increasing hard currency debt to the Western industrialized states. In 1975, Romania owed about $2.5 billion to the West, in 1980, she owed $8.8 billion, and by the middle of 1981, her debt was approximately $10 billion.[21] The major cause of Romania's indebtedness was her increasing dependence on imported oil to offset declining domestic production. Ceausescu's five year plans required substantial energy sources to implement the goal of rapid heavy industrialization. Romania's domestic oil production peaked in 1976 at 14.7 million metric tons, and declined to 11.5 million in 1980. Oil imports in 1976 represented 3.3% of consumption, whereas by 1981, they equalled 40%. The fall of the Shah of Iran and the subsequent Iran-Iraq War threatened to shut off Romania's traditional oil supply. In fact, the war did reduce oil availability, and forced Bucharest to fill its petroleum needs through spot market prices. This, in turn, increased the cost of oil refining to the point at which it was no longer lucrative, thereby eliminating one of Bucharest's major export products.[22]

Agriculture was another problem. Traditionally viewed as less important than industrial development, Romania's food production had declined in recent years. This was in part due to a slow recovery from the 1977 earthquake, as well as from poor weather in 1980 and 1981. To exacerbate the problem, Bucharest viewed food principally for its export value, as a means to offset her increasing foreign trade deficit. As a result, food shortages appeared throughout Romania, especially in the urban areas. Newspaper reports noted sporadic unrest in Romania due to the general unavailability of fresh produce in the marketplace.[23]

Romania's economic policies also contributed to her declining economy. On the one hand, Bucharest eagerly sought commerical relations with the West. Early on she joined the IMF, World Bank and the GATT. Ceausescu had made increased exports to the West a major theme of his economic messages during the past decade. At the same time, however, Ceasescu encouraged a xenophobic climate in Romania which discouraged contact between Romanians and foreigners. As a result, few Romanians knew about world prices, Western trade markets or banking practices. Consequently, some of Romania's borrowing was made without realistic thoughts of repayment, particularly when interest rates skyrocketed on short term commerical debt.[24] In an effort to stem her foreign trade deficit, Bucharest announced Foreign Trade Law No. 12 in December, 1980. This legislation required any organization desiring to import goods, to show export earnings that would offset import costs.[25] In addition, the government urged its Foreign Trade Organizations to use barter to pay for Western imports.[26]

Other factors which contributed to Romania's economic plight included the West's belief in the Moscow "umbrella theory." This view held that in the final analysis, the Soviet Union would guarantee Western loans to CMEA countries. While the Soviets did, on occassion, provide hard currency to some of its satellites, Romania was not a favorite son.[27] In fact, a popular Romanian joke in 1981 asked what telephone number in Moscow should Bucharest call for fraternal assistance. The answer was: 56-68-80, recalling Soviet help in Hungary, Czechoslovakia and Poland.[28]

Changing Western commercial attitudes toward the Communist world also affected Romania's economy. Commencing in 1980, Western nations restricted trade with Moscow in response to the Soviet invasion of Afghanistan. And then, on March 26, 1981, one of the West's favorite CMEA countries defaulted on its loans. Poland had a hard currency debt of $26 billion with a projected $11 billion trade deficit for 1981. The Polish government announced that it could not pay its external debts, and requested its creditors to reschedule debt payments.[29] The Polish default surprised the West, and forced many creditors to question whether Romania was another Poland. As a result, few banks were willing to extend credit to Bucharest without guarantees. Consequently, Romania negotiated a $1.5 billion loan package with the IMF on June 15. As part of the arrangement, Bucharest agreed to avoid any debts in arrear service, to reduce its trade deficit, and to undertake a long term program of management and financial reform. These terms were similar to those proposed in Romania's 1978 "new economic mechanism," most of which had not been implemented.[30]

Congress and the 1981 Waiver

One week later, the House Subcommittee on Trade held a one day hearing on the President's emigration waiver extension request. This proved to be the last House hearing until 1986 at which a large number of businessmen appeared to testify in support of the President's recommendation. In the following years, representatives from religious and human rights interests would dominate the oral testimony heard by the Subcommittee. A significant reason for this development was Romania's new economic policies which increased exports and reversed its deficit trade balance with America.

1980 had produced the highest trade balance for the United States in its two-way trade with Bucharest since World War II. The recent IMF loans certainly gave no indication that this trade balance would significantly change. As a result, business leaders from Action Tungsram, the Chilewich Corporation, WJS Moody International, and the UOP and Vitco Corporations were most willing to support continued MFN treatment for Romanian products. These men echoed the reports presented by representatives from the Commerce and Treasury Departments, as well as from the Office of the United States Trade Representative. According to Treasury representative Robert Cornell, Romania was "a good customer." She bought American manufactures and government surplus agricultural produce. Further, Bucharest was a "reliable supplier" of petroleum related products.[31] Government officals pointed to Romania's increased emigration to both the United States and West Germany, and emphasized Bucharest's continued independence in foreign policy. While Jewish emigration to Israel had declined during the past two years, Administration officials believed that this was due in large measure to the declining Jewish population in Romania. John Scanlan of the State Department noted that "many of the remaining Romanian Jews are elderly; others may have jobs or family ties; some may not wish to emigrate."[32] Although criticized by Administration opponents, Scanlan's remarks had the support of O. Rudolph Aggrey, America's Ambassador to Romania during the Carter Administration. According to Aggrey some of the Jews did not want to leave Romania. They preferred to "fight in their own way, rather than switch sides" and come to the United States.[33]

Opposition witnesses challenged the Administration's position on emigration. They also continued to maintain the link between emigration and the larger issue of human rights. Encouraged by Subcommittee member, Richard Schulze, author of the 1980 resolution to deny Romania MFN, several people gave detailed testimony concerning the extent of religious persecution in Romania, including continued impediments to Jewish emigration. Jacob Birnbaum used the hearings to once again point out the failure of Romania to permit Jewish emigration to Israel. Due to his organization's "intensive Washington campaign," Bucharest issued 105 passports in May to Jews emigrating to Israel, in contrast to 28 in April. Birnbaum believed that the annual potential for Jewish emigration to Israel was not less than 3-4,000. He wanted the Administration to use MFN renewal as a lever to force Bucharest to fulfill this potential Jewish emigration quota.[34] Birnbaum's proposal received support from a frequent witness, Attorney Cyrus Gilbert Abbe, and from first time respondent, Congressman John LeBoutillier of New York.[35]

Reverend Pavel Nicolescu, of the Romanian Baptist Church, made his first appearance before the Subcommittee. He had left Romania in 1979 under duress and explained Bucharest's emigration practices and policy of religious discrimination. He provided the Congressmen with a list of people who Romania would not allow to emigrate for the purpose of family reunification. He was the new Director of ALRC, the Committee for the Defense of Religious Freedom and Conscience. This organization began in Romania in April, 1978, was forced to dissolve, and he had reorganized it in America in May, 1981. Most of his testimony dealt with specific individuals whose right to worship or to emigrate were denied.[36] Reverend Galdau supported Nicolescu's testimony noting especially the case of Father Gheorghe Calciu-Dumitreasa. Bucharest arrested him on March 10, 1979, and sentenced him to ten years of hard labor for saying in one of his sermons, "the Communist ideology is depressing. Anyone who believes in Christ should reject it."[37] Calciu's arrest was surprising since he was a member of the Orthodox Church which normally supported Ceausescu and the government. However, Calciu was a maverick, whose criticism of Romania's religious and human rights practices reached an international audience. He had appealed to Pope John Paul II for help, and had described the oppressive conditions in Romania to intellectuals in Western Europe. Prior to his arrest, Calciu had provided spiritual leadership to a group of Romanian workers and intellectuals who tried to establish a Free Labor Union of Working People in Romania, known as SLOMR.[38] As a result, Calciu was a *cause celebre* and his release was frequently called for by human rights activitists and leaders of religious groups in America during the annual waiver hearings in Congress. While the opposition was quite specific in its descriptions of human rights abuse, the overwhelming testimony supported the President's request. As a result, no member of the House introduced a motion to disapprove the waiver extension.

The Senate Finance Subcommittee on International Trade opened its one day of hearings on July 27. Of the 15 subcommittee members, only the Chairman, John Danforth, attended along with Robert Dole, the Chairman of the Committee on Finance. In his opening remarks, Dole noted that he was cochairman of the Helsinki Commission and as such intended to support the President's request. However, he was distressed by reports that people wanting to emigrate from Romania were under constant harassment. He told those waiting to testify that "we have a new day in this committee, a new leadership in this committee." Dole pledged to monitor the emigration process in Romania before the next extension.[39]

In addition to this warning, the major difference between the two hearings was that fewer businessmen appeared before the Senate Subcommittee. As a result, the oral testimony emphasized Romania's human rights practices toward religious and ethnic minorities. Laszlo Hamos steadfastly presented evidence indicating Bucharest's continued efforts to destroy the remnants of Hungarian culture. Dimitrie Apostoliu decried Romania's human rights practices as did Michael Szaz. Nina Shea of the International League for Human Rights remained neutral on the issue of renewing Romanian MFN, but believed the hearings were a useful vehicle to identify, and hopefully, to eliminate human rights violations in Romania.

After the hearing, Romanian-American relations continued on a "business as usual" course. In August, several members of the House Agriculture Committee visited Bucharest, met with Romanian agriculture officials and visited President Ceausescu.[40] A week later, on August 20, Ceausescu received a delegation from the Union and League of Romanian-American Societies in the United States and Canada. The group, led by John Copacea, came to Bucharest at the invitation of the Romania Association. At the close of their visit, *Agerpress* reported that Copacea attributed the rapid socio-economic progress in the "fatherland" to Ceausescu's leadership and activity.[41] 1981 would be the last year in which neither house introduced a resolution disapproving the President's emigration waiver request. In September, Congressional inaction automatically extended Romanian MFN for one year and the Romanian-American Trade Agreement for three years.

Debt Rescheduling

Meanwhile, Ceausescu's efforts to end Romania's trade deficit were successful. In 1982, Bucharest showed a trade surplus of $1.5 billion as imports from the West declined by 45%.[42] However, the Romanian people paid for the trade surplus. Ceausescu's economic program required Romanians to raise food for export, not for domestic consumption. In October, 1981, the government established criminal penalties from six months to five years imprisonment for "hoarding" food. A week later, Ceausescu introduced grain rationing programs.[43] However, austerity programs need time to produce results. Consequently, on November 3, Bucharest asked her Western creditors permission to postpone payments for up to six months.[44] A couple of weeks later, the IMF officially recognized Romania in arrears on her debt payment, and suspended further payments on the Standby Agreement signed in June.[45] Although Ceausescu refused to admit that there were any fundamental problems in Romania's economy, he removed two senior party officials from the Central Committee in late November. He blamed Virgil Trofin and Vasili Ogirlaci for Romania's coal shortages, accusing them of falsifying production figures and tolerating inefficiency.[46]

By the end of 1981, Romania's foreign debt had increased to $11.4 billion. She was unable to meet interest payments, and Western banks refused to make more funds available. The IMF pressed Romania to discuss her financial situation with her creditors. Reluctantly Ceausescu agreed, and in early January representatives from nine Western banks arrived in Bucharest.[47] On January 29, the banks agreed to reschedule $4 billion worth of Romanian payments due within the next 18 months.[48]

The reschduling process was lengthy and would take until December, 1982, to complete. The needs of four groups of creditors had to be addressed, among them were commercial banks, 15 governments of the industrialized countries, informally known as the Paris Club, central banks primarily representing OPEC interests, and commercial suppliers.[49] The process was lengthy, but far easier because of the Polish experience. The banks moved quickly, but the process still took nearly a year, primarily because Romanian decisions could only be made at the highest level. Consequently, negotiations frequently stalled in the absence of direction from Bucharest.[50]

Meanwhile in Washington, the "golden years" of Romanian-American relations, a Bogdan description, were about to come to an end. On August 28, 1981, President Reagan nominated David B. Funderburk as America's new Ambassador to Romania replacing O. Rudolph Aggrey.[51] Although he had studied in Romania and was familar with the language, Funderburk's appointment was made principally due to the work of Senator Jesse Helms of North Carolina.[52] Prior to his nomination, Funderburk had written, *If the Blind Lead the Blind*, a book highly critical of Communism.[53] While his writing and conservatism raised liberal eyebrows, the Senate confirmed his appointment early in October. His supporters, Helms among them, expected that Funderburk would bring a new dimension to the American Embassy in Bucharest, and in fact he proved to be a significant force in altering American-Romanian relations. Later he wrote *Pinstripes and Reds,* his first person account of what he discovered in Bucharest. There was a conspiracy in Romania between the "pinstripes" of the State Department and the "Reds" in Bucharest. This alliance always opposed his interests, which were in keeping with the traditional values of America.

Funderburk's nomination along with the questions raised at the Congressional hearings on Romania concerning emigration, religious persecution, and human rights practices, forced Andrei to meet with Secretary of State Haig on September 29, and with several members of Congress two days later. He reassured Haig and the legislators, including Richard Schulze, of Ceausescu's commitment to human rights. He reminded them that while Romania did not encourage emigration, the 1980 emigration figures indicated that Bucharest certainly did not prevent people from leaving their homeland.[54]

While Romania spent the next several months trying to meet her foreign debt payments, Washington focused on events in Poland. Warsaw's efforts to stabilize her economy through austerity produced substantial unrest throughout the country. The Solidarity Union challenged the new government of Wojciech Jaruzelski, and demanded free elections and drastic economic reforms. Jaruzelski responded on December 13, 1981, imposing martial law throughout the country. The military crushed wildcat strikes and arrested union leaders. Reagan blamed Moscow for the decision to establish marital law in Poland. On December 29, the President imposed sanctions against the Soviet Union. Among other things, the sanctions required American firms to obtain government licenses for sales of oil and natural gas equipment to Moscow. To add teeth to the measure, Reagan ordered the Commerce Department to stop processing all applications for such licenses.[55] Reagan's sanctions and the subsequent animosity between Moscow and Washington carried over to the Helsinki review conference in Madrid. On February 12, 1982, Western delegates including Alexander Haig used the meeting to renew their attacks on Poland's martial law decree. By implication, and sometimes by direct statement, Western delegates accused the Soviet Union of forcing Warsaw to implement the decree.[56]

Without hours of the meeting, Haig arrived in Bucharest at the urgent request of President Ceausescu. While Haig would later say that the visit was in response to a long-standing invitation, his arrival appeared to be a hurried affair.[57] The Romanian leader feared that further animosity between the superpowers could force Moscow to insist on orthodox behavior by all of the East European satellites, including

Bucharest. Ceausescu wanted to warn Haig of this possibility and urge moderation in Washington's dealings with Moscow and Warsaw over the issues of maritial law and economic sanctions.[58] In addition, the Romanian President wanted to sound out Haig on the possibility of additional aid from the United States to help Romania through its economic crisis. Ceausescu requested $1 billion. However, Haig gave the President little encouragement. Congress and the budget mitigated against such largess.[59] Before Haig left, Ceausescu indicated that he would be interested in visiting the President during the summer. He could tie such a visit into the United Nations Second Special Session on Disarmament. Haig promised to deliver the message to Washington, but Reagan never extended an invitation.[60]

A week after the Secretary of State returned to Washington, the President gave proof of Haig's rejoinder to Ceausesu's request for aid. On February 20, Reagan denied Bucharest a CCC loan for $65 million over the objections of the State and Agriculture Departments.[61] However, Haig's visit did have some tangible results for Bucharest. On February 25, the State Department announced that the federal government would reimburse two private banks, the European American Bank of New York City and the Chicago International Bank, $5.8 million because Romania failed to meet its scheduled payments. More important, neither the banks nor Washington moved to declare Romania in default, since this would seriously have affected Bucharest's credit position.[62] On the following day, the two countries completed a separate set of negotiations and exchanged notes extending their program for scientific and technological cooperation begun in 1979.[63]

As part of her debt rescheduling, Romania had to continue to revise her annual economic plans in order to increase exports. On March 31 Ceausescu told members of the party Central Committee that "we must . . . find new ways of cutting back imports and insuring a positive commerical balance." Each sector of the economy "must bring a profit; each leu spent must produce a profit."[64] Shortly thereafter Bucharest passed a series of draconian measures to reduce energy consumption not tied to export needs. The government shut off street lights, reduced electric bulb wattage for home use to a bare minimum, and severely curtailed public transportation.

Ceausescu's committment to rapidly developing a trade surplus was clearly shown in May. On the twenty-first he removed Cornel Burtica from his post as Minister of Foreign Trade and International Economic Cooperation. Burtica was a senior member of the party and a long time associate of Ceausescu.[65] Burtica's fall from grace was complete when Ceausescu purged him from the party and publicly explained his actions at the meeting of the Enlarged Plenum of the Central Committee on June 1-2, 1982. He told the delegates that

> I should not like anyone to have the impression that the steps we have recently taken at the Ministry of Foreign Trade . . . are just routine measures or that they have been taken only because action was not taken in the spirit of economic efficiency. Wrong, comrades! In the foreign trade activity state money was embezzled and stolen; it was stolen, but it was also badly managed.[66]

At this June Central Committee meeting, Ceausescu informed the delegates that Romania had ended the developmental phase of the "dictatorship of the proleteriat," and had entered a new phase in its march toward Communism, the "state of worker democracy."[67] While this change was primarily intended to continue the dominant position of the Communist Party in Romania, it also gave an additional reason for party members to work harder, to be more productive, and to increase the country's national wealth. Simply put, a state of worker democracy should not have a trade deficit.

Ceausescu's efforts to reduce imports and expand exports were sufficient to permit the IMF to reschedule a major portion of Romania's hard currency debt. In June, the IMF released monies for Bucharest suspended since the previous November. On July 28, the Paris Club, agreed to reschedule 80% of Romania's arrears from 1981 and 1982, totaling about $400 million. This reschedule, which was limited to medium and long term debt, gave Bucharest a three year grace period followed by seven semi-annual payments. Negotiations with commercial banks continued until November.[68]

Meanwhile relations between Bucharest and Washington had continued without strain. In February, 1982, the House Committee on Foreign Affairs began year long hearings on "Religious Persecution as a Violation of Human Rights." Romania was never an object of special interest during the 10 days of testimony.[69] However, the fact that the hearings extended throughout the year, made more Congressmen aware that religious persecution did exist, and was an abuse of a person's human rights. This new awareness, rather than any evidence which surfaced during the hearings, would affect Congressional perceptions toward Bucharest during the annual hearings to extend Romanian MFN.

In April, Ceausescu appointed Micea Malita to replace Nicolae

Ionescu as Ambassador to the United States. Malita had a graduate degree from New York University, and had served for several years as Romania's Ambassador and Permanent Representative to the United Nations in Geneva. Ceausescu anticipated that Malita's knowledge of America, and reputation as a scholar would enable him to influence Congress to renew Romania's MFN status.[70]

Reagan's 1982 Waiver

On June 2, 1982, President Reagan asked Congress to extend his waiver authority because continuation of the emigration waiver would substantially promote the objectives of Section 402 of the Trade Act of 1974. However, the President indicated that he was "concerned about Romania's emigration record this year and suggested it be reexamined." Reagan's concern was not with emigration to America, for about 2,400 people had emigrated to the United States in 1981. Rather, he was "gravely" concerned about the decline in Romanian Jewish emigration to Israel. In his message to Congress, the President stated that the 1979 agreement between Bucharest and American Jewish leaders was not working. There was a considerable backlog of unresolved long-standing emigration cases involving at least 652 people. Further, Romania had not improved its emigration procedures. They were cumbersome and "plagued with obstacles for those who merely wish to obtain emigration application forms." All of these factors clearly demonstrated that Romania's emigration policy "clearly contravenes the intent and purpose of the Jackson-Vanik Amendment." In closing, Reagan told Congress that while he was willing to extend Romanian MFN this year, he intended to inform Bucharest that "unless a noticeable improvement in its emigration procedures takes place, and the rate of Jewish emigration to Israel increases signficiantly, Romania's MFN renewal for 1983 will be in serious jeopardy."[71]

Reagan's statement had to be seriously considered by Bucharest. This was the President who had no qualms about using trade as a foreign policy weapon regardless of the provisions and implications of the 1979 Export Administration Act. Reagan had removed Carter's embargo on grain sales to Moscow in April, 1981, but had quickly restored trade sanctions against the Soviet Union six months later. On June 22, 1982, Reagan extended the December, 1981, prohibitions on exporting oil refining and natural gas equipment to the Soviets to all foreign subsidiaries of American firms. The President wanted to stop, or at least slow down, Moscow's efforts to build a natural gas pipeline into Western Europe. He did not want the Soviets to increase their influence in the West through energy availability.[72] If Reagan was willing to upset American corporations and allied governments, he certainly would have little difficulty in terminating Romanian MFN.

On the same day that the President sent his waiver request to Congress, a group of 31 Senators sent Reagan a letter indicating that as of then, they were "unpersuaded" that another extension of MFN would improve Romania's emigration practices.[73] The new Romanian Ambassador launched an intensive lobbying effort of his own on Capitol Hill, even before he officially presented his credentials to the White House on June 25.[74] Malita sought out Congressmen who wanted specific emigration cases resolved and urged Bucharest to comply.

Meanwhile, Nicolae Constantin, Romania's new Foreign Trade Minister, arrived in Washington to attend the Eighth Session of the Joint Romanian-American Economic Commission scheduled to open on June 28. During the two day meeting, Commerce Secretary Baldrige and Constantin discussed a wide range of topics, especially the extension of Romanian MFN. Bucharest also wanted to add to the list of products she could export under GSP. At the close of the session, both delegations agreed to support the work of the United States-Romania Economic Council, and to continue to work to improve trade relations between the two countries.[75]

While in Washington, Constantin and the Romanian delegation met with several government officials including Under Secretary of State Lawrence Eagleburger, the United States Trade Representative William Brock and William Draper III, the President of the Eximbank. Before returning to Bucharest, Constantin visited American businessmen and bankers in Houston, Chicago and New York.[76] As Constantin worked to promote Romania's future relations with Washington, Ceausescu revived the past. In reponse to a personal invitation from the Romanian President, Richard Nixon arrived in Bucharest on June 28. Ceausescu wined and dined the former President recalling their joint efforts which culminated in Romania receiving MFN in 1975.[77]

Meanwhile, Malita worked vigorously to accomodate the specific emigration requests made by Congressmen. Dante Fascell would later testify to the success of Malita's work. As Chairman of the U.S. Commission on Security and Cooperation in Europe, Fascell had names of families seeking reunification. He submitted this list quarterly to Bucharest for resolution. From October, 1981 until April, 1982, Romania resolved all but 15 cases. During Malita's first two months in Washington, Bucharest approved 61 cases for emigration.[78]

Part of this increase was due to the rhythmic nature of Romanian-American relations. The monthly emigration figures from May to October were traditionally higher than those in the other months. While Congress normally attributed this increase to the timing of its annual debate over continued Romanian MFN, this year, a number of legislators singled out Malita for his personal intervention to resolve family reunification cases.[79] Malita's high visibility coupled with Bucharest's expeditious response to his requests, gave a degree of credence to his assurances of emigration cooperation unequaled since Bogdan.[80] Due to Malita's work, more Romanians emigrated to the United States in 1982 than in 1981. However, of greater importance was the increase in the number of Romanian Jews who emigrated to Israel. Prior to Malita's arrival, 350 Jews emigrated to Israel during the months of January through May, 1982. In June, 131 emigrated and this was the lowest number for any month during the rest of the year with October registering the highest with 255.[81]

On July 12, the House Subcommittee on Trade began two days of hearings on the President's emigration waiver request. The parade of witnesses included old and new faces, most of whom opposed the President's recommendation. The hearings saw a signficiant increase in the number of people willing to give oral testimony, however the increase was not due to more corporate representation. The business community was reluctant to defend tariff reductions and GSP support for a country which contributed to America's trade deficit.

Ceausescu's efforts to reduce imports and increase exports produced a significant turn around in the trade balance between Washington and Bucharest by the end of 1981. During that year, the United States exported $504 million worth of products but imported $612 million for a trade deficit of $108 million.[82] In 1980, America had a trade surplus with Romania of about $400 million. In essence, Romania had affected a half billion dollar change in the two-way trade in one year. Further, the early reports for 1982 indicated a major reduction in the total value of two-way trade with a still greater surplus for Romania.[83]

The government had forewarned the business community that East-West trade would decline. The East European economies had to reduce their hard currency debt, and they faced inadequate energy supplies and declining agricultural production. Increased competition from Japan and Western Europe further reduced markets for American exports.[84]

As a means to reduce her hard currency debt, Romania increased her two-way trade with Moscow by more than 25% between 1980 and 1981.[85] Ceausescu had showed considerable restraint in his dealings with the Soviet Union and CMEA since early 1981. In February, 1981, he told the Soviet Party Congress of "the ascending course of relations of warm friendship and solidarity" between the two parties.[86] Nearly eighteen months later, he reminded members of the Romanian Communist Party's Central Committee of the role played by the Soviet army in Romania's emancipation from Fascism. The "historic act of 23 August 1944 . . . [was] . . . provided by the victories of the Soviet . . . armies."[87] Ceausescu's austerity programs coupled with her increased trade within the Communist Bloc meant that America's bilateral trade surplus with Romania was a thing of the past. Since Romania preferred selling to buying, American businessmen were less willing to take the time to appear before Congress to support MFN. Rather, they would send their testimony in writing to the appropriate committee.

However, the same could not be said for critics of Romania's human rights practices. In July the House Subcommittee members heard testimony from numerous organizations including the Christian Legal Defense and Education Fund, East Watch International, East/West News Service, the American-Romanian Committee for Assistance to Refugees, and the Christian Rescue Effort for the Emancipation of Dissidents. Ernest Gordon represented this latter organization and described the harassment, and sometimes imprisonment, of neo-Protestants, and religious dissenters. Many who testified gave specific examples of police brutality and government discrimination toward Christian evangelists. Dimitrie Apostoliu of the American Romanian National Committee for Human Rights appeared, and, as usual, added his unique touch to the hearings. In closing his testimony he screamed: "Down terrorism! Down Communism! Up Jesus! Up Ronald Reagan! Long live (sic) to freedom! God bless America!"[88]

Spokesmen representing Hungarians in Romania also appeared and opposed the President's recommendation. Joining Laszlo Hamos were Tamas A. de Kun of the American Transylvanian Association, Louis Lote of the Committee of Transylvania, Istvan Gereben of the Coordinating Committee of Hungarian Organizations in North America and Michael Szaz of the National Confederation of America Ethnic Groups, Inc. Each of these men had appeared before the Subcommittee in previous years. Each presented evidence that Bucharest pursued a conscious policy of discrimination with the purpose of destroying the remnants of Hungarian culture in Romania.

While much of the testimony opposed the Administration's position, the Subcommittee did hear from several representatives of ethnic and religious groups who supported Reagan. Among them were Thad Lempicki of the American-Romanian Cultural Foundation, Reverend Danila Pascu of the Romanian Radio Hour, and Reverend A.S. Lucaciu of the Romanian-American Baptist Fellowship. The representatives of the two major Jewish organizations continued to split their opinion. Jacob Birnbaum of the Center for Russian and East European Jewry viewed the hearings as a vehicle to facilitate Jewish emigration from Romania. As a result, he remained neutral on the issue of continuing Romanian MFN, for once discontinued, the hearings would end.[89] In contrast, Jack Spitzer of B'nai B'rith International and the Conference of Presidents of Major Jewish Organizations supported the President's recommendation. While agreeing that Romania's emigration process was cumbersome, he noted that "I suppose bureaucracy in the United States, too, can be construed to be onerous. I am sure the congressional committee is concerned about that too."[90]

One of the final pieces of testimony the Subcommitee received was a statement from Dante Fascell. The Congressman, who was Chairman of the United States Commission overseeing implementation of the Helsinki Accords, was annoyed at Romania's manipulation of emigration. Bucharest always increased exit visas during the months Congress held MFN hearings. While critical of this approach, Fascell supported the President's recommendation. If nothing else, annual MFN hearings increased Romanian emigration.[91]

However, not all Congressmen shared Fascell's view. On the final day of hearings, July 13, Robert Dornan of California along with Richard Schulze of Pennsylvania introduced House Resolution 521 to disapprove the President's waiver extension and to terminate Romanian MFN. Three days later, Jesse Helms of North Carolina and Steven Symms of Idaho introduced a similar resolution in the Senate, S. Res. 428. In introducing his resolution, Dornan told House members that he did not think that Romania had promoted the objectives of Section 402 of the Trade Act of 1974. He and his colleagues had received numerous accounts of harassment of Baptists, Pentacostals and other Christians. Hungarians were the target of forced assimilation while Jewish emigration was restricted.[92] Helms repeated these arguments in the Senate and both men agreed that they and their cosponsors could no longer support the President's recommendation.[93]

In the interim between the end of the House hearings on July 13 and the beginning of the Senate hearings on August 10, Malita and Bucharest worked diligently to increase Romanian emigration, especially the number of Jews permitted to leave for Israel. Bucharest had only granted 54 exit visas to Israel in the months of May and June combined. In July, she issued 131, and in August, 155.[94] In addition, Bucharest resolved several outstanding cases of interest to particular members of Congress. Eleven political prisoners, found guilty of smuggling Bibles into Romania, received amnesties.[95] Bucharest also agreed to begin a series of discussions with the Conference of Presidents of Major American Jewish Organizations, and later in the Fall with Administration officials on improved emigration procedures.[96]

On the day before the Senate hearings began, the *New York Times* carried an article by Moses Rosen, Romania's Chief Rabbi. To date, the Romanian government had permitted 93% of the post-World War II Jewish population to emigrate. The remaining Jews had a full and active program of worship and social service. In May, Edgar Bronfman, President of the World Jewish Congress visited the Central Synagogue in Bucharest and told the worshippers that "it is no small accomplishment that in a socialist society, Jewish life in every aspect can so flourish." Rosen argued that the testimony presented before the House Subcommittee was incorrect, and urged those who sought to "make Jews the scapegoat" to prevent renewed MFN, to stop their activity. "The lives, institutions and free emigration of Romanian Jews" should not be drawn into issues overwhich they have no control, responsibility or interest.[97]

As usual the Senate Subcommittee on International Trade's hearing had fewer people testifying before it than before the House hearings. No representative of business appeared for the Senate hearing, with the exception of Milton Rosenthal, chairman of Engelhard Corporation, who annually represented the United States-Romanian Economic Council at the MFN hearings. As a result, the vast majority of witnesses represented ethnic and religious groups and they repeated their testimony given at the House hearings. There were only two new voices, a letter from the 1776 Conservative Club which opposed Romanian MFN,[98] and a statement by Reverend Donald Kyer, Director of Frontline Fellowship, a Christian missionary organization, which supported the President's recommendation.[99]

However, the recent activity of Malita and Bucharest had an impact on the Senate. The Chairman of the Subcommittee on International

Trade, Senator Danforth of Missouri, introduced the first witness, Senator Henry Jackson, as "without any doubt the leader in Congress on the whole question of human rights in Eastern Europe and in emigration policy." Jackson totally supported the President. He believed that Section 402 of the Trade Act had done precisely what he and Charles Vanik intended. "Tens of thousands of people, Christians, Jews and others, have been able to emigrate because of the amendment . . . .Its provisions constitute indispensable leverage in the on-going bargaining for freer emigration." Jackson informed the Subcommittee members that he had just received a letter from Ambassador Malita dated August 2, which committed Bucharest to "make further progress in the field of procedures of emigration, including the question of reducing the time period required for processing the applications." Jackson accepted Malita's assurances, and believed that MFN renewal was the "wise course to follow."[100]

Jackson's testimony won over all but the most die-hard conservatives. The Senate Finance Committee, which was charged with considering the Helms-Symms resolution disapproving the President's recommendation, took no action effectively killing the measure for 1982. However, two days later, on August 13, the Finance Committee supported a new resolution, S. Res. 445, introduced by Robert Dole. While not binding on the President, the "Sense of the Senate" resolution called for the Administration to enter into talks with Bucharest for the purpose of securing "credible assurances" that Romania would expedite her emigration procedures. Further, the resolution urged the Adminstration to address the issue of Romania's repression of religious groups and ethnic minorities. The Senate did recognized that "these issues raise more general human rights concerns that are not the subject of the President's determination under the Jackson-Vanik Amendment to renew MFN for any country." However, if Romania refused to deal with this issue, the Administration should pursue it in other international fora concerned with human rights issues.[101] Following its August recess, the Senate passed Dole's "Sense of the Senate" resolution on September 24.

Meanwhile on August 12, the House Ways and Means Committee adversely reported out the Dornan-Schulze disapproval resolution. The Committee based its action on Romania's willingness to enter serious negotations with the United States to reach an "understanding" on the emigration issue. On August 18 the House of Representatives agreed to postpone indefinitely the Dornan-Shulze resolution.[102] This action automatically extended Romanian MFN through July 2, 1983.

Human Rights and the Education Tax

A few weeks after the hearings, Jack Spitzer followed-up on Bucharest's July invitation and visited Romania during the first week in September. As spokesman for the Conference of Presidents of Major American Jewish Organizations, Spitzer spent five days visiting government and religious leaders in Romania. All assured him that applications to Israel and the United States would be processed and ruled upon within six months. Spitzer spoke to Ceausescu about non-Jewish issues as well, especially the alleged persecution of neo-Protestant groups. Bucharest had arrested 11 fundamentalist Evangelicals for distributing Bibles in Romania. Although Ceausescu had amnestied them during the Summer, Spitzer was concerned about their arrest in the first place. The Romanian President indicated that they were arrested for "economic crimes." Since they sold Bibles for their own profit, they undermined the efforts of legitimate religious organizations which depended on the sale of Bibles for their livelihood.[103]

A few days later, Ambassador Max Kampelmann, the head of the American delegation to the Helsinki review conference in Madrid, arrived in Bucharest. He met with Foreign Minister Andrei and explained that there was growing concern in Congress over Romania's human rights practices. Family reunification and other emigration issues were serious issues to several legislators, and he suggested that Romania resolve specific cases including that of Father Calciu.[104]

On October 5, the Assistant Secretary of State for Human Rights, Elliott Abrams arrived in Bucharest to implement the "Sense of the Senate" resolution passed in late September. He met with Romanian State Secretary Aurel Duma and the Deputy Foreign Minister, Maria Groza, daughter of Petru Groza, the postwar "Ploughman's Front" Prime Minister.[105] Abrams had heard a rumor that Romania intended to impose an education tax on emigrants.[106] When he raised this issue with the Romanian officials, he was given oral assurance that this was not the case. Rather, Bucharest promised to respond to emigrant applications within six to nine months, and to cease harassment of would-be emigrants.[107]

Abrams later met with religious leaders, including Justin Moisescu, Patriarch of the Romanian Orthodox Church, and informed them of particular Congressional concerns, including Bible distribution, and religious freedom.[108] He also raised the issue of minority rights with Romanian officials, noting especially the treatment of ethnic Hungarians. However, Bucharest denied that there were any religious or ethnic problems in Romania.[109]

Upon his return from Bucharest, Abrams granted an interview to Radio Free Europe in which he described his talks as "constructive." However, he described the Romanian regime as "an extremely oppressive Communist dictatorship" with a "deplorable, terrible" human rights record.[110] RFE broadcast the interview on October 18, which did little to improve American-Romanian relations. Nonetheless, on the following day, Ceausescu met with the American representatives to the Ninth Session of the United States-Romanian Economic Council. He commended the delegates for their achievement in promoting improved economic relations between the two countries.[111] He especially noted Romania's foreign debt problem, and indicated that it would be liquidated "in a few years – and I believe we shall do it sooner than others would think." Since Romania did not intend to apply for any further loans, Ceausescu clearly indicated that the only type of trade he was interested in pursuing was one which was either balanced or which produced a trade surplus for Bucharest.[112]

three days later, Bucharest surprised Washington. On October 22 the Romanian State Council announced the enactment of an "Education Repayment Decree" effective November 1. The new legislation, numbered Decree 402, perhaps to counter Section 402, the Jackson-Vanik Amendment, required persons wishing to emigrate from Romania to reimburse the state for the costs of secondary and higher education.[113] To complicate matters, Article 2 of the decree required that repayment be made in hard currency.[114] Since Bucharest prohibited its citizens from owning hard currency, payment would have to be made from sources outside Romania. The amount of payment varied but, depending on the level of education, could approach $20,000.[115]

Washington's responded with predictable outrage. Administration officials and Congressmen both viewed the Decree as further evidence of Romania's inhumane practices. The assurances given Abrams were lies. However, few analysts could explain the rationale behind Ceausescu's actions. Without question, he was deliberately enticing the United States Congress to terminate Romanian MFN. One popular explanation was that Ceausescu had concluded that MFN would not be renewed, and he wanted to "preempt" any such action by exerting his own authority to implement policies which were "internal" in nature. Ceausescu may also have wanted to slow down the "brain drain" from Romania. The tax only affected those who had received more than a compulsory education. Decree 402 made it clear that anyone who sought higher education implicitly made a commitment to remain in the country, and to use that education for the improvement of Romania.[116]

Ambassador Bogdan, however, gave a significantly different interpretation. Agreeing that Ceausescu may have thought that Congressional renewal of Romanian MFN was questionable, Bogdan suggested that Ceausescu imposed the education tax in order to withdraw it. He knew that Washington would criticize the decree and exert pressure on Bucharest. Congress would threaten to terminate MFN were the decree enforced. As a result, Ceausescu could suspend the decree, and in the process let the United States believe that through MFN renewal it could affect Romania's internal policies. This thinking would encourage Congress to do precisely what Ceausescu wanted, namely, to support the President's waiver, and renew Romanian MFN.[117]

Meanwhile, debt rescheduling negotiations continued between Bucharest and her commercial banks creditors. The banks finally accepted the formula adopted by the Paris Club in June, 1982, and on December 7, the banks agreed to restructure the $1.7 billion debt. Romania would repay 80% of her 1981 arrears and 1982 principal over six and a half years, with three years' grace. The remaining 20% would be paid by March, 1983.[118]

Ten days later, on December 16, Ceausescu told the National Party Conference delegates that Romania would have a trade surplus of about $1.8 billion for 1982.[119] He commended his audience for their hard work but exhorted them to work even harder. He wanted Romania to supply 90% of its domestic energy needs. To do this, party cadre and government officials would have to intensify labor productivity and economic efficiency. Foreign exports had to increase. By 1985, he wanted Romania's foreign debt halved, and completely eliminated by 1988.[120]

Ceausescu aimed to capitalize on Romania's economic success. In January, 1983, Bucharest notified its creditors, both the Paris Club and commercial lenders, that it would withhold repayment of $1.4 billion in debt principal due in 1983. Ceausescu was willing to pay all interest installments during the year, but wanted to reschedule principal payments. The foreign lenders agreed. Romania's trade surplus, commitment to internal austerity to promote foreign exports, and foreswearing of further hard currency loans were signs that Romania was serious about her debt repayments.

The 1982 rescheduling process made the 1983 negotiations easier. In May, Bucharest and the Paris Club agreed to reschedule $148 million through 1989. Five weeks later, on June 23, Romania made a similar arrangment for $601 million with her commercial lenders. The terms of both negotiations were only slightly less generous than those of 1982, requiring Romania to immediately repay 30% of her obligation rather than the 20% negotiated the previous year.[121]

While Bucharest rescheduled its debt, reaction to Ceausescu's education tax continued in Washington. Within days of Ceausescu's November 1, 1982, announcement, State Department representatives met with Romania's Deputy Foreign Trade Minister, Paula Prioteasa. The officials told her that the education tax put Romania's MFN in "serious jeopardy." America required non-market economy countries to have a free emigration policy, or an assurance that waiving such a requirement would promote such a policy.[122]

Although criticism of Ceausescu's decree continued to grow in Washington, most aspects of American-Romanian relations continued without interruption. On November 30, the two countries exchanged notes extending their programs of cooperation and exchange in areas of culture, science and technology for another two years.[123] Two weeks later, President Reagan made his annual proclamation recognizing December 10 as Human Rights Day. In his remarks, he noted the depressing situation in Poland where a military regime aimed to "crush Solidarity," but he made no mention of Romania's efforts to stifle emigration.[124] A couple of months later, the Administration would extend and amend its 1980 agreement with Romania on trade in wool and manmade fiber textiles.[125]

While Administration officials decided to use a quiet approach to resolve the tax issue, several Congressmen used the decree as a podium issue to publicly denounce Romania's human rights practices. On December 15, Marjorie Holt of Maryland told her House colleagues of the recent arrest of several Hungarian intellectuals in Transylvania. Among them was the well known ethnic Hungarian poet, Geza Szocs. Their crime involved publishing a samzidat, or underground paper, called *Ellenpontok* (Counterpoint) which criticized Bucharest's human rights practices.[126] Further, the authorities believed that Szocs and his associates were responsible for smuggling a memorandum to Vienna for transmittal to the Madrid Conference on Security and Cooperation in Europe. The message described Romania's continued discrimination against the Magyars in Transylvania. Holt saw the education tax as simply one more step in Bucharest's policy of discrimination, and urged her colleagues to make the renewal of Romanian MFN contingent on Bucharest improving its human rights record.[127]

On December 21, Representative Robert Dornan of California added his support to Holt's recommendation. He believed that Bucharest consciously supported a policy designed to destroy Magyar culture in Romania.[128] While both Congressmen pointed to specific instances of apparent discrimination, neither noted that Bucharest's actions may have been prompted by recent events in Moscow. On November 10, Leonid Brezhnev died. Two days later, the Central Committee of the Communist Party of the Soviet Union elected Yuri Andropov as his successor. Prior to his election, Andropov served in the Central Committee's Department for Liaison with Ruling Communist States. He was known for his opposition to East European autonomy.[129] Further, Bucharest viewed him as so pro-Hungarian, that following his election, party officials held special meetings to discuss means of preventing any Budapest sponsored aggression in Transylvania.[130]

On January 10, the White House sent Lawrence Eagleburger, the Undersecretary of State for Political Affairs, as a special envoy to request Ceausescu to cancel the education tax. No emigrant had been forced to pay the tax to date, because those leaving had received their exit visas prior to November 1. However, Reagan wanted Ceausescu to know that his recommendation to waive the emigration language in the Jackson-Vanik Amendment was contingent upon Romania not enforcing the tax decree. In his meeting with Ceausescu and Foreign Minister Andrei, Eagleburger "laid the cards on the table." Reagan would not recommend continued Romanian MFN if the tax decree were enforced. This did not mean that Ceausescu had to rescind the decree; non-enforcement was sufficient to maintain the present status of American-Romanian trade relations.[131]

Nine days later, a House of Representatives delegation led by Tom Lantos of California arrived in Bucharest by invitation of the Romanian Grand National Assembly. This was part of a reciprocal exchange visit program inaugurated several years earlier. Lantos and his colleagues met with Ceausescu and reiterated Eagleburger's warning: neither the

Administration nor Congress were sympathetic to renewing Romanian MFN in view of the emigration decree.[132]

Both Eagleburger and Lantos failed to stop Romania from implementing the education tax. The first instance of enforcement occurred two days after Ceausescu spoke with the Congressional delegation. On January 21, Bucharest required Margareta Paslaru Sencovici to pay $7,400 for education expenses prior to emigration.[133] In another case, two engineers wishing to come to the United States were told they had to pay at least $20,000 apiece before they could leave.[134] By mid-February, the American Embassy knew of at least 24 cases in which persons approved for emigration had to repay the state for education costs before they could receive passports. These cases involved people going to Holland, Italy, West Germany and Canada.[135]

Since quiet diplomacy had failed, the Administration made its concerns public. On March 4, President Reagan declared that Romania's education decree conflicted with the "letter and spirit of Section 402 of the Trade Act of 1974." Therefore, he intended to terminate Romanian MFN and other benefits effective June 30, 1983, "if the education repayment decree remains in force on that date."[136] The announcement was well timed. It gave American importers three months in which to protect their interests, and it gave Ceausescu time to reconsider his position.

Reagan's promise to terminate MFN carried considerable weight. This was not an idle threat. The President had already discontinued MFN treatment to Polish products on November 1, 1982, three days after the Polish government disbanded Solidarity.[137] If he was willing to end a twenty-two year relationship with Warsaw, the President would most certainly have few qualms about severing an eight year relationship with Bucharest, a relationship which now contributed to America's trade deficit.

Bucharest quickly responded to the President's announcement. *Agerpres* called Reagan's threat unjustifiable. "It is a form of American pressure and interference in the domestic affairs of Romania, and it cannot be accepted."[138] However, the rhetoric did not indicate that Romania wanted to sever relations with Washington. On March 30, Milton Rosenthal met with Ceausescu. The chairman of the United States delegation of the United States-Romanian Economic Council saw the Romanian President as a tourist. However, he brought with him a message from the White House. Reagan did not want to terminate MFN, but would do so unless Ceausescu suspended enforcement of the education tax.[139]

In spite of statements to the contrary, Ceausescu began to reconsider his position. He did not want to lose American MFN, and the immediacy of this reality was constantly reinforced by David Funderburk, America's Ambassador to Romania, as well as by events in the United States. American newspaper coverage of Romania ridiculed the Bucharest regime. The New York Times carried an article on the government's most recent decree requiring official permission for anyone to own or purchase a typewriter. Further, people with typewriters had to submit a sample of the print to the police as a means to identify the publishers of samzidat literature.[140] Congressman Mark Siljander of Michigan recounted the typewriter decree to his colleagues in the House on May 11. He described the typewriter as a "vital tool for the human rights and religious rights movements in Romania," and the government's decree was yet another reason to deny Romania MFN.[141]

As pressure mounted, Ceausescu decided to concede. On May 17, he sent Stefan Andrei to Washington. The Foreign Minister told Vice President George Bush that while Romania would not rescind its decree, it would not impose an educational tax on prospective emigrants.[142] In turn, Washington indicated that the President would recommend that Congress approve the emigration waiver.

Whether or not Bogdan was correct in his analysis that the education tax was designed to improve relations with the West, the measure worked. By suspending the decree, Ceausescu received a stronger endorsement of MFN renewal from the Administration than he initially believed possible. In addition, since the education tax affected all emigrants, not just those going to America and Israel, Bucharest was able to use the tax to make money. Since its agreement with West Germany in 1978, Bonn had paid about DM 5,000 for each ethnic German who left Romania and settled in West Germany. In order to suspend the new educational tax, Hans-Dietrich Genscher visited Bucharest on May 31 to negotiate a new financial arrangment. While not publicized, the West German Foreign Minister apparently agreed to a figure of DM 7,000 as compensation to Bucharest for each German emigrant.[143] Whatever the motive, Ceausescu's education tax produced some very tangible short term gains. However, in the long run, the tax was a painful reminder, especially to human rights advocates, that Romania viewed these rights in terms of trade and hard currency.

Congress and the 1983 Waiver

On June 3, 1983, President Reagan sent his recommendation to waive Section 402 of the Trade Act of 1974. He was willing to continue MFN with Romania because Bucharest had permitted nearly 20,000 people to emigrate in 1982. Further, President Ceausescu had assured him that Romania would "not require reimbursement to the State of education costs as a precondition to emigration," and would not create other economic or procedural barriers to emigration. As a result, the President believed that the waiver continuation would "substantially promote" the objectives of the Jackson-Vanik Amendment.[144]

In spite of the assurances, resolutions to disapprove the President's request soon appeared in both houses of Congress. On June 29, Jesse Helms introduced Senate Resolution 171 disapproving the waiver extension. On the following day, Philip Crane introduced a similar resolution in the House, H. Res. 256. In explaining his reasons for opposing the President's recommendation, Crane said that he frankly did not believe Ceausescu's promises. He cited the Administration's semi-annual report to the Commission on Implementing the Helsinki Final Act. The document covered the period December, 1982 through May, 1983, and in it the White House stated that "there had been no overall improvement in the Romanian divided family record during the six month reporting period." The report also cited Bucharest for its "extensive harassment in Romania of religious, political and cultural dissidents."[145] Crane concluded that if this was the Administration's view of Romania, why should anyone accept Ceausescu's assurances at face value.

The House Subcommittee on Trade held a one day hearing on July 14 on the question of renewing the President's waiver extension request for Romania, Hungary and the People's Republic of China. The roster of witnesses was similar to 1982. Few businessmen took the time to appear before the House Subcommittee, while numerous representatives from human rights and religious organizations presented oral testimony. In all, fewer people testified at the hearings and the majority of those who did opposed granting the waiver extension. In contrast, much of the correspondence the Subcommittee received represented corporate interests supporting the President's recommendation.

Administration witnesses began the testimony and introduced a new argument to support the President's waiver request. For the first time, the Commerce Department stressed the impact that non-renewal of Romanian MFN would have on the United States. Franklin Vargo, the Deputy Assistant Secretary of Commerce for Europe, explained that

without MFN the competitiveness of 90% of Romania's exports to the
United States would be adversely affected. As a result, Romania would
sell her products to Japan, Taiwan, South Korea and Western Europe.[146] However, since Romania's new economic policies called for a
least a balanced bilateral trade, Bucharest would reduce American imports to compensate for her lost trade. As a result, the United States
would lose about $200 million worth of exports which meant 6,000 fewer
American jobs. Vargo noted that America was Romania's third largest
supplier and her third largest customer. About 200-250 American companies did business based largely or wholly upon merchandising Romanian products in the United States. Termination of Romanian MFN
would adversely affect these companies.[147] In concluding his statement,
Vargo noted that if America refused to renew Romanian MFN,
Bucharest would be forced to reorient part of her trade back to Moscow
and CMEA, thereby defeating one of the primary reasons America first
began trading with individual East European countries.[148]

Administration officials also justified MFN renewal by pointing to
the increased number of people leaving Romania. Others further argued that without MFN, Washington would have little leverage to affect
Romania's internal policy. To wit, the President's threat to curtail MFN
forced Bucharest to suspend her education tax.[149] Additional support
for the President's waiver came through letters from businessmen and
the oral testimony of veteran witnesses from such organizations as the
Romanian-American Baptist Fellowship and the American-Romanian
Cultural Foundation.

Taking a somewhat neutral position in the testimony was Dante Fascell, Chairman of the U.S. Commission on Security and Cooperation in
Europe. However, his testimony was important because it supported the
concept that there was linkage between the Jackson-Vanik Amendment
emigration requirements and the larger issue of humanitarian rights. In
some ways, Fascell was a bridge between the two issues. Since Romania
had signed the Helsinki Final Act, Bucharest obliged itself to "abide by
international human rights standards" if they wanted to engage in cooperative efforts and trade with other countries. Fascell saw the hearings
as a means to decide if the "continued facilitation of bilateral trade with
. . . [Romania] . . . serves humanitarian objectives" embodied in the letter and spirit of the Helsinki Accords.[150]

No one took issue with Fascell's linkage of MFN and humanitarian
concerns, although Dole's "Sense of the Senate" resolution ten months
earlier noted that the Jackson-Vanik language made only emigration a

criterion for continued MFN. The Chairman of the United States CSCE Committee supported the President's waiver request because MFN had affected Romania's decision to suspend its education tax. On the other hand, Fascell questioned the sincerity of Romania's commitment to human rights. Bucharest's "continuing violation and inadequate protection of civil and political, religious and minority rights set forth in the Helsinki Final Act provide a bleak backdrop to the emigration issue." Improved emigration figures alone did not give a true picture of the issue. "Behind virtually every one of these departures were months and often years of harassment and procedural and economic obstacles." In conclusion, while Fascell would not oppose MFN renewal, he hoped that Romania would facilitate the release of some longstanding emigration cases which had special support in Washington, such as that of Father Calciu, as good-faith evidence of their assurances.[151]

Those opposing the President's recommendation appeared in large number before the Subcommittee. They focused their testimony on Bucharest's constant discrimination against Jews, Pentecostals, Baptists and Hungarians. Jacob Birnbaum appeared to present the plight of Romanian Jews, while Istvan Gereben and Michael Szaz described Bucharest's efforts to destroy Hungarian culture and tradition. Laszlo Hamos read Geza Szoc's letter to the Madrid Conference, and provided extensive information on Romania's abominable record on human rights.[152] The Subcommittee received numerous letters from organizations such as the Association of the Former Romanian Political Prisoners, the American-Transylvanian Association, and the National Association of Americans of Romanian Descent in the United States, all of which opposed MFN renewal.

When the Subcommittee ended its hearing on July 14, 1983, no member suspected that this would be the last House hearing on Romanian MFN until 1986. On June 23, the Supreme Court had made a decision in the case of the *United States Immigration and Naturalization Service v. Chadha* which declared that legislative vetoes of Executive decisions were unconstitutional. This clearly raised the issue of the constitutionality of a House resolution disapproving a Presidential emigration waiver.

The case involved Jagdish Rai Chadha, an East Indian born in Kenya, who was came to the United States on a non-immigration student visa in 1966. The visa expired on June 30, 1972, and he was eligible for deportation. Chadha asked the Immigration and Naturalization Service, INS, to suspend his deportation for fear of racial persecution were he to return to Kenya. The INS heard his case, and the judge agreed on June 25, 1974, to suspend deportation on the basis that he had resided continuously in the United States for over seven years, was of good moral character and would suffer "extreme hardship" if deported. On the same day the judge informed Congress of his decision in accordance with the 1952 INS Act which permitted Congressional review of deportation suspensions. The INS Act permitted either house to veto a suspension. On December 16, 1975, the House vetoed Chadha's deportation suspension.

Chadha appealed the veto on the grounds it was unconstitutional. Various appellate boards refused to hear the appeal since they were not able to rule on constitutional issues. With support from Public Citizen, a non-profit organization, Chadha managed to have the Supreme Court hear the case in February, 1982. On June 23, 1983, by a vote of 7 to 2, the Supreme Court ruled the veto unconstitutional. The Court reasoned that according to Article 1 of the Constitution, the legislative process required approval by a majority of both Houses of Congress and "presentment to the President" for his action. The House action was clearly unconstitutional.[153]

The Supreme Court reaffirmed its decision two weeks later in two more cases. In *Process Gas Consumers Group v. Consumers Energy Council of America* and in *United States Senate v. Federal Trade Commission* the Court confirmed that virtually all existing legislative veto provisions were invalid.[154] Since these rulings affected over 200 pieces of legislation, the House Committee on Foreign Relations held three days of hearings on the implications of the Chadha case commencing July 19.

The Foreign Relations Committee solicited comments from private constitutional lawyers, Library of Congress specialists in American law, the Attorney General's Office, and the State Department. The bulk of the testimony concluded that a one-House veto of a Presidential recommendation was definitely illegal, a two-House veto was probably illegal since Article 1 required bicameralism and presentment to the President for action. Simply put, Congress could not make law without permitting the President a means to respond.[155]

Meanwhile, as the Foreign Relations Committee held its hearings, the House Subcommittee on Trade considered Representative Crane's June 30 resolution disapproving the President's waiver extension recommendation. The Subcommittee reported the resolution unfavorably to the House Ways and Means Committee. On July 26, the Ways and

Means Committee concurred with their vote and recommended that the House disapprove Crane's resolution.[156]

On July 29, the Senate Subcommittee on International Trade held a hearing on the President's waiver request. The impact of the Chadha case overshadowed the one day of testimony. Only twelve people showed up to testify in addition to Administration witnesses. Joining Hamos and Szaz in opposing the waiver was Lucian Orasel who represented a conservative coalition called the American-Romanian Relations Committee and Ms. Ildiko Trien, who wanted to make MFN renewal contingent on Romania ending its discrimination toward Hungarians.[157] Jack Spitzer, Senator Henry Jackson and Milton Rosenthal of the United States-Romanian Economic Council all supported the President. Nina Shea of the International League for Human Rights wanted increased emigration, while Jeri Laber of Helsinki Watch wanted Congress to review Romanian MFN every six months. His logic was that if an annual review improved Romania's human rights practices for about six months of the year, then a semi-annual review would force Bucharest to be even more mindful of humanitarian issues.[158]

The main focus of the testimony, however, concerned the impact of the Chadha case. State Department personnel reassured the Senate that the Administration intended to continue the process called for under the Jackson-Vanik language. The President would continue to make an annual determination and consult with Congress on continued MFN. Michael Matheson, legal advisor to the State Department, explained that the Chadha case did not end Congress's role in renewing MFN. Chadha prohibited Congress from unilaterally vetoing an Executive recommendation without the President having an opportunity to respond. The Crane resolution in the House was unconstitutional. However, were both houses to pass a joint resolution of disapproval and send it to the President, he would be free to approve it or veto it. In the event of the latter, both houses could override the veto the same way they could any Presidential veto.[159] Additional testimony from Attorney Peter Ehrenhaft confirmed Matheson's interpretation of the Chadha decision.[160]

In light of this legal advice, the Senate Subcommittee on International Trade chose to take no action on Jesse Helms's June 29 resolution of disapproval. On August 1, the House decided to postpone action on Representative Crane's motion indefinitely.[161] Consequently, since both houses refused to take any action, Romania retained her MFN status for another year. The Chadha case crippled Congressional efforts to use MFN renewal as a lever to force Bucharest to improve its human rights and emigration practices.

Notes

1. Nestor Ratesh, "The American Connection," *Romania, 40 Years (1944-1984)*, ed. Vlad Georgescu ("The Washington Papers, No. 115"; New York: Praeger, 1985), pp. 65-66; Newhouse, *War and Peace in the Nuclear Age*, p. 339.
2. Alexander Haig, *Caveat: Realism, Reagan and Foreign Policy* (New York: Macmillan Pub., Co., 1984, p. 160.
3. "Trend in Romania is Toward Slower Growth on Higher Base," *Business America*, June 15, 1981, pp. 15-16.
4. U.S. Congress, House Committee on Ways and Means, Hearing Before the Subcommittee on Trade, Trade Waiver Authority Extension, 97th Cong., 1st Sess., 1981, p. 66. Hereafter, House Subcommittee on Trade, *Trade Waiver Authority Extension*, 1981.
5. *Business in America,* June 15, 1981, p. 16.
6. David C. Bowie, "Romania Open to Western Help in Carrying Out Ambitious Plans to Expand Its Aircraft Industry," *Business America*, April 20, 1981, pp. 11-13; The United States and Romania had exchanged notes in January, 1981, extending their agreement relating to civil air transport (*DOS Bulletin*, April 1981, p. 49).
7. FBIS, EEU, May 18, 1981, p. H3.
8. *Ibid.*, pp. H1-2
9. NYT, May 16, 1981, p. 1.
10. RFE, Situation Report, Romania/11, June 12, 1981, p. 2. ; *Twenty Sixth Annual Report of the President of the United States on the Trade Agreements Program, 1981-1982*, p. 95.
11. FBIS, EEU, June 2, 1981, pp. H1-2.
12. *Public Papers of the Presidents of the United States, Ronald Reagan, 1981* (Washington, D.C.: U. S. Government Printing Office, 1981), p. 479.
13. *Ibid.*, p. 480.
14. Forsythe, *Human Rights and U.S. Foreign Policy: Congress Reconsidered*, p. 121.
15. Friedbert Pfluger, "Human Rights Unbound: Carter's Human Rights Policy Reassesed," *Presidential Studies Quarterly*, Vol. XIX, No. 4 (Fall 1989), p. 711.
16. *Ibid.*
17. Robert W. Tucker, "Reagan's Foreign Policy," *Foreign Affairs*, Vol. 68, No. 1 (1989), p. 13.
18. Crabb and Mulcahy, *Presidents and Foreign Policy Making*, pp. 280-281; Long, *U.S. Export Control Policy*, p. 80.
19. *Congress and the Nation*, Vol. VI (1981-1984), p. 141.
20. Forsythe, *Human Rights and U.S. Foreign Policy: Congress Reconsidered*, p. 122.

21. U. S. Congress, Joint Economic Committee, *East-West Trade: The Prospects to 1985*, 97th Cong., 2d Sess., 1982, p. 264; Assetto, *The Soviet Bloc in the IMF and the IBRD*, p. 153.

22. Richard F. Staar (ed.), *Yearbook on International Communist Affairs, 1982* (Stanford, CA: Hoover Institution Press, 1982), p. 461; U. S. Congress, Joint Economic Committee, Selected Papers, *East European Economies: Slow Growth in the 1980s*. Vol. 2, *Foreign Trade and International Finance*, 99th Cong., 2d Sess., 1986, p. 33, hereafter, Joint Economic Committee, *Foreign Trade and International Finance*, 1986; and, U. S. Congress, Joint Economic Committee, Selected Papers, *East European Economies: Slow Growth in the 1980s*. Vol. 3, *Country Studies on Eastern Europe and Yugoslavia*, 99th Cong., 2d Sess., 1986, pp. 492ff. Hereafter, Joint Economic Committee, *Country Studies on Eastern Europe and Yugoslavia*, 1986.

23. NYT, March 9, 1981, p. A4; NYT, April 26, 1981, p. L15.

24. Joint Economic Committee, *Country Studies on Eastern Europe and Yugoslavia*, 1986, p. 513.

25. *Ibid.*, p. 501.

26. CSM, January 13, 1981, p. 10..

27. Joint Economic Committee, *Foreign Trade and International Finance*, 1986, p. 154.

28. Thomas W. Simons, Jr., "Approaching Relations with Eastern Europe in the Late 1980s," Occasional Paper No. 12, (East European Program, The Wilson Center, Washington, D.C., n.d.), p. 10.

29. Joint Economic Committee, *Foreign Trade and International Finance*, 1986, pp. 245ff. On the resolution of the Polish debt issue see, Fischer, *Nicolae Ceausescu*, pp.250-251; Csikos-Nagy and Young, *East-West Economic Relations in the Changing Global Environment*, pp. 104-105; Assetto, *The Soviet Bloc in the IMF and the IBRD*, pp. 153ff.

30. Joint Economic Committee, *Country Studies on Eastern Europe and Yugoslavia*, 1986, p. 503.

31. House Subcommittee on Trade, *Trade Waiver Authority Extension*, 1981, p. 54.

32. *Ibid.*, p. 45.

33. Author interview of O. Rudolph Aggrey, October 26, 1989.

34. House Subcommittee on Trade, *Trade Waiver Authority Extension*, 1981, pp. 102-103.

35. *Ibid.*, pp. 107, 380.

36. *Ibid.*, pp. 254-257.

37. *Ibid.*, p. 372.

38. Bugajski and Pollack, *East European Fault Lines*, pp. 167-168.

39. U.S. Congress, Senate Finance Committee, Hearing Before the Subcommittee on International Trade, *Most Favored Nation Status for Romania, Hungary and China*, 97th Cong., 1st Sess., 1081, p. 35.

40. FBIS, EEU, August 17, 1981, p. H1.

41. FBIS, EEU, August 21, 1981, pp. H1-2.

42. Assetto, *The Soviet Bloc in the IMF and the IBRD*, p. 156.
43. Staar(ed.), *Yearbook on International Communist Affairs, 1982*, pp. 461-462.
44. NYT, November 4, 1981, p. D4.
45. Joint Economic Committee, *Country Studies on Eastern Europe and Yugoslavia*, 1986, p. 504.
46. NYT, December 5, 1981, p. 7.
47. NYT, January 14, 1982, p. D2.
48. NYT, January 30, 1982, p. 31.
49. Joint Economic Committee, *Foreign Trade and International Finance*, 1986, p. 200.
50. *Ibid.*, p. 206.
51. *Public Papers of the Presidents of the United States, Ronald Reagan, 1981*, p. 740.
52. David B. Funderburk, *Pinstripes and Reds: An American Ambassador Caught Between the State Department and the Romanian Communists, 1981-1985* (Washington, D. C.: Selous Foundation Press, 1987), p. vii.
53. *Ibid.*, pp. 3-4.
54. RFE, Romania Situation Report/21, October 16, 1981, pp. 4-5; FBIS, EEU, October 2, 1981, p. H1.
55. *Congress and the Nation*, Vol. VI., p. 145.
56. *The Washington Post*, February 13, 1982, p. A20.
57. *DOS Bulletin*, April 1982, p. 47.
58. NYT, February 13, 1982, p. 3; NYT, February 14, 1982, p. 14; FBIS, EEU, February 16, 1982, p. H1; *DOS Bulletin*, April 1982, p. 48.
59. Alexander M. Haig, Jr., *Caveat: Realism, Reagan, and Foreign Policy* (New York: Macmillan Publishing Company, 1984), p. 258.
60. Robert Weiner, "The U.S. Policy of Differentiation Toward Romania," *The United States and Romania*, ed. Paul D. Quinlan, p. 137.
61. *Boston Sunday Globe*, February 21, 1982, p. 2.
62. NYT, February 26, 1982, p. D15.
63. *DOS Bulletin*, May 1982, p. 79.
64. FBIS, EEU, April 7, 1982, p. H2.
65. Robert Wesson (ed.), *Yearbook on International Communist Affairs, 1983* (Stanford, CA: Hoover Institution Press, 1083), pp. 326-327.
66. Ceausescu, *Romania On the Way*, XXIV, 118.
67. *Ibid.*, p. 54.
68. Joint Economic Committee, *Country Studies on Eastern Europe and Yugoslavia*, 1986, p. 505; Joint Economic Committee, *Foreign Trade and International Finance*, 1986, p. 163.
69. U. S. Congress, House, Hearings and Markup Before the Committee on Foreign Affairs and Its Subcommittee on Human Rights and International Organizations, *Religious Persecution as a Violation of Human Rights*, 97th Cong., 2d Sess., 1983.
70. RFE, Romania Situation Report/8, May 4, 1982, pp. 7-8.

71. *Public Papers of the Presidents of the United States, Ronald Reagan, 1982* (Washington, D.C.: U. S. Government Printing Office, 1982), I, 720-721.

72. U.S. Congress, House Committee on Foreign Affairs, Hearing Before the Subcommittees on Europe and the Middle East, *East-West Economic Issues, Sanctions Policy, and the Formulation of International Economic Policy,* 98th Cong., 2d Sess., 1984, p. 13, hereafter, House Subcommittees on Europe and the Middle East, *East-West Economic Issues,* 1984.

73. RFE, Romania Situation Report/11, June 15, 1982, p. 16.

74. FBIS, EEU, June 29, 1982, p. H1.

75. "Romanian Foreign Trade Minister Visits United States, Reviews Trade Relations with Secretary Baldrige," *Business America,* July 12, 1982, p. 16; U.S. Congress, Senate Committee on Finance, Hearing Before the Subcommittee on International Trade, *Review of the President's Decision to Renew Most-Favored-Nation Status for Romania, Hungary, and China,* 97th Cong., 2d Sess., 1982, p. 52, hereafter, Senate Subcommittee on International Trade, *Review of the President's Decision to Renew Most-Favored-Nation Status,* 1982.

76. *Business America,* July 12, 1982, p. 16; *Scinteia,* July 1, 1982, p. 6.

77. Ceausescu, *Romania On the Way,* XXIV, 189-190.

78. U.S. Congress, House Committee on Ways and Means, Hearings Before the Subcommittee on Trade, *Extension of MFN Status to Romania, Hungary, and the People's Republic of China,* 97th Cong., 2d Sess., 1982, p. 390, hereafter, House Subcommittee on Trade, *Extension of MFN Status,* 1982.

79. U. S., *Congressional Record,* 97th Cong., 2d Sess., 1982, CXXVIII, E3160.

80. Mastny, *Helsinki, Human Rights, and European Security,* pp. 139-140.

81. U.S. Congress, House Committee on Ways and Means, Hearing Before the Subcommittee on Trade, *Presidential Recommendation to Continue Waivers Applicable to Romania, Hungary, and the People's Republic of China, and to Extend the Trade Act Waiver Authority,* 98th Cong., 1st Sess., 1983, p. 17, hereafter, House Subcommittee on Trade, *Presidential Recommendation to Continue Waivers,* 1983.

82. U.S. Department of Commerce, *U.S. Foreign Trade Highlights, 1988* (Washington, D.C.: U.S. Government Printing Office, 1988), pp. 86, 91.

83. *Ibid.*

84. U. S. Congress, Joint Economic Committee, *East-West Commercial Policy: A Congressional Dialogue with the Reagan Administration,* 97th Cong., 2d Sess., 1982, p. 52.

85. U. S. Congress, Joint Economic Committee, Selected Papers, *East European Economies: Slow Growth in the 1980s.* Vol. I, *Economic Performance and Policy,* 99th Cong., 21st Sess., 1985, pp. 32-33, hereafter, Joint Economic Committee, *Economic Performance and Policy,* 1985.

86. Ceausescu, *Romania On the Way,* XXI, 522.

87. *Ibid.,* Vol. XXIV, p. 24.

88. *Ibid.,* p. 202.

89. *Ibid.,* pp. 117ff.

90. *Ibid.*, p. 113.
91. *Ibid.*, pp. 389ff.
92. *Ibid.*, pp. 257ff.
93. U.S., *Congressional Records*, 97th Cong., 2d Sess., 1982, CXXVIII, S8526.
94. House Subcommittee on Trade, *Presidential Recommendation to Continue Waivers*, 1983, p. 17.
95. This was reported in the Helsinki Watch report of July 29, 1983. See, U.S. Congress, Senate Committee on Finance, Hearing Before the Subcommittee on International Trade, *Continuation of the President's Authority to Waive the Trade Act Freedom of Emigration Provisions*, 98th Cong., 1st Sess., 1983, p. 143, hereafter, Senate Subcommittee on International Trade, *Continuation of the President's Authority*, 1983.
96. *Ibid.*; Lynne A. Davidson, "Romania, CSCE and the Most-Favored-Nation Process, 1982-1984," *The Diplomacy of Human Rights*, ed. David D. Newsom, 1986, p. 191.
97. NYT, August 9, 1982, p. 15.
98. Senate Subcommittee on International Trade, *Review of the President's Decision to Renew Most-Favored-Nation Status*, 1982, p. 180.
99. *Ibid.*, p. 123.
100. *Ibid.*, pp. 34-36.
101. U.S. Congress, Senate Report 97-522, *U.S. Goals for Upcoming Consultations with the Socialist Republic of Romania*, 97th Cong., 2d Sess., 1982, 3pp.
102. U.S., Congressional Record, 97th Cong., 2d Sess., 1982, CXXVIII, H6538-H6359.
103. RFE, Romania Situation Report/18, October 26, 1982, pp. 8-9.
104. Funderburk, *Pinstripes and Reds*, p. 160; RFE, Romania Situation Report/18, October 26, 1982, p. 9.
105. *Ibid.*, p. 10.
106. Senate Subcommittee on International Trade, *Continuation of the President's Authority*, 1983, p. 144.
107. *Ibid*; Lynne A. Davidson, *The Diplomacy of Human Rights*, ed. David D. Newsom, 1986, p. 192.
108. FBIS, EEU, October 8, 1982, p. H2; RFE, Romania Situation Report/18, October 26, 1982, p. 11.
109. *Ibid.*
110. Ratesh, "The American Connection", *Romania, 40 Years (1944-1984)*, ed. Vlad Georgescu, p. 68.
111. FBIS, EEU, October 20, 1982, pp. H1-2.
112. Ceausescu, *Romania On the Way*, XXIV, 497ff.
113. Senate Subcommittee on International Trade, *Continuation of the President's Authority*, 1983, p. 38; U.S. Congress, Senate Committee on Foreign Relations, Staff Report, *Human Rights Issues in United States Relations with Romania and Czechoslovakia*, 98th Cong., 1st Sess., 1983, p. 3, hereafter, Senate Committee on Foreign Relations, *Human Rights Issues in United States Rela-*

tions with Romania and Czechoslovakia, 1983.

114. *Scinteia,* November 6, 1982, p. 5.

115. RFE, Romania Situation Report/21, December 8, 1982, p, 7.

116. Senate Committee on Foreign Relations, *Human Rights Issues in United States Relations with Romania and Czechoslovakia,* 1983, pp. 6-7.

117. Oral interview with Corneliu Bogdan by the authors, January 11, 1989. The speculation in Washington was that Bogdan's retirement from government service at the end of 1982 was due to his opposition to the education tax (NYT, December 28, 1982, p. A6).

118. NYT, December 8, 1982, p. D9; Joint Economic Committee, *Foreign Trade and International Finance,* 1986, p. 250.

119. Ceausescu, *Romania On the Way,* XXV, 18.

120. *Ibid.,* p. 35. For a summary of Romania's "1983 Plan" see, RFE, RAD Background Report/54 (Romania), March 15, 1983, 12pp.

121. Joint Economic Committee, *Foreign Trade and International Finance,* 1986, p. 165; Joint Economic Committee, *Country Studies on Eastern Europe and Yugoslavia,* 1986, p. 506; NYT, January 4, 1983, p. D6.

122. RFE, Romania Situation Report/3, February 19, 1983, p. 16.

123. *DOS Bulletin,* February 1983, p. 86.

124. *Public Papers of the Presidents of the United States, Ronald Reagan, 1982,* II, 1591.

125. *DOS Bulletin,* May 1983, p. 92.

126. FBIS, EEU, November 26, 1982, p. H3; FBIS, EEU, March 29, 1983, p. BB2.

127. U.S., *Congressional Record,* 97th Cong., 2d Sess., 1982, CXXVIII, H9921.

128. *Ibid.,* p. E5391.

129. Wesson (ed.), *Yearbook on International Communist Affairs, 1983,* p. 335.

130. J. F. Brown, "Conservatism and Nationalism in the Balkans: Albania, Bulgaria, and Romania" *Central And Eastern Europe: The Opening Curtain?,* ed. William E. Griffith (Boulder, CO: Westview Press, 1989), p. 285.

131. Funderburk, *Pinstripes and Reds,* p. 134.

132. FBIS, EEU, January 20, 1983, p. H1.

133. Funderburk, *Pinstripes and Reds,* p. 135.

134. Senate Committee on Foreign Relations, *Human Rights Issues in United States Relations with Romania and Czechoslovakia,* 1983, p. 8.

135. *Ibid.*

136. *Public Papers of the Presidents of the United States, Ronald Reagan, 1983* (Washington, D.C.: U. S. Government Printing Office, 1983), I, 329.

137. For more on the question of Polish sanctions see, Bruce W. Jentleson, "The Western Alliance and East-West Energy Trade," *Controlling East-West Trade and Technology Transfer,* ed. Gary K. Bertsch, 1988, pp. 332ff. Also, House Subcommittees on Europe and the Middle East, *East-West Economic Issues,* 1984, pp. 15ff.

138. FBIS, EEU, March 5, 1983, p. H1; RFE, Romania Situation Report/5, March 17, 1983, pp. 5-6.
139. FBIS, EEU, April 1, 1983, p. H1; Funderburk, *Pinstripes and Reds*, p. 134.
140. NYT, April 24, 1983, p. D20.
141. U.S., Congressional Record, 98th Cong., 1st Sess., 1983, CXXIX, E2179-2180.
142. FBIS, EEU, May 20, 1983, p. H1; NYT, May 19, 1983, p. A3.
143. RFE, Situation Report, Romania/10, June 7, 1983, p. 2.
144. *Public Papers of the Presidents of the United States, Ronald Reagan, 1983*, I, 817-818.
145. U.S., *Congressional Record*, 98th Cong., 1st Sess., 1983, CLXIX, E3315.
146. House Subcommittee on Trade, *Presidential Recommendation to Continue Waivers*, 1983, p. 64.
147. *Ibid.*, pp. 23-24.
148. *Ibid.*, p. 65.
149. *Ibid.*, pp. 17, 60ff.
150. *Ibid.*, p. 300.
151. *Ibid.*, p. 301.
152. *Ibid.*, pp. 172-173.
153. Barbara Hinkson Craig, *The Legislative Veto: Congressional Control of Regulation* (Boulder, CO: Westview Press, 1983), pp. 139ff; and, Barbara Hinkson Craig, *Chadha: The Story of an Epic Constitutional Struggle* (New York: Oxford University Press, 1988). On the same topic see, Administrative Conference of the United States, "Legislative Veto of Agency Rules after INS v. Chadha; Twenty-seventh Plenary Session Discussion, December 15, 1983" (Washington, D.C.: U.S. Government Printing Office, 1984); Paul Lansing and Eric C. Rose, "The Granting and Suspension of Most-Favored-Nation Status for Nonmarket Economy States: Policy and Consequences," *Harvard International Law Journal*, Vol. 25, No. 2 (Spring 1984), pp. 329-351; Joint Economic Committee, *Economic Performance and Policy*, 1985, p. 576.
154. Administrative Conference of the United States, "Legislative Veto of Agency Rules after INS v. Chadha; Twenty-seventh Plenary Session Discussion, December 15, 1983" (Washington, D.C.: U.S. Government Printing Office, 1984), p. i.
155. U.S. Congress, Hearings Before the House Committee on Foreign Affairs, *The U.S. Supreme Court Decision Concerning the Legislative Veto*, 98th Cong, 1st Sess., 1983, p. 243.
156. U.S. Congress, House Report No. 98-315, *Disapproval of Extension of Waiver Authority Under the Trade Act of 1974 to the Socialist Republic of Romania*, 98th Cong., 1st Sess., 1983, pp. 1-2.
157. Senate Subcommittee on International Trade, *Continuation of the President's Authority*, 1983, pp. 249, 265.
158. *Ibid.*, pp. 131ff.
159. *Ibid.*, pp. 45ff.

160. *Ibid*., pp. 59ff.

161. U.S. *Congressional Record,* 98th Cong., 1st Sess., 1983, CXIX, H6034-6037.

CHAPTER XVII

THE CHANGING JACKSON-VANIK CRITERIA: EMIGRATION BECOMES HUMAN RIGHTS

Romania's Road to Economic Recovery

American-Romanian relations declined sharply during the next two years. In September, 1983, Vice President Bush promised continued American support for Bucharest. In December, 1985, Secretary of State George Schultz threatened to end MFN if Romania did not significantly improve her human rights practices. A major reason for the decline was the continued development of Ceausescu's cult of personality, a cult which permitted little deviation. Ceausescu had dissidents arrested and imprisoned for any number of "crimes" from selling Bibles to questioning his authority. Romania's decision to eliminate its hard currency debt chopped American exports to Bucharest by nearly two-thirds, thereby curtailing business support for Romanian MFN. This support was needed to counterbalance those who opposed Romanian MFN on the grounds of her poor human rights record. Finally, the election of Mikhail Gorbachev as General Secretary of the Communist Party of the Soviet Union, replacing Konstantin Chernenko who died on March 10, 1985, too made an impact on Romanian-American relations. Gorbachev's support for detente, denuclearization, and world peace ended the "Romanian deviation." His willingness to embrace Ceausescu's foreign policy goals signaled an end to the image that Bucharest pursued a "maverick' foreign policy, an image which the White House had historically rewarded with MFN. Without a "maverick" foreign policy, the totalitarianism of Ceausescu stood naked, and few wanted to publicly support an oppressive regime.

Although Reagan's decision to deploy 572 intermediate range missiles in Europe in December, 1983, provided fuel for Ceausescu's calls for denuclearization, his words fell on many deaf ears. After the Soviets shot down the commercial Korean Airliner, Flight 007, killing 269 passengers, Moscow-Washington relations hit a new low. Ceausescu's message had no Western audience. Reagan appeared to be correct: the Soviets were an "evil empire," and Ceausescu's call for the great powers to turn their swords into plowshares appeared foolish.[1]

In mid-September, 1983, Vice President Bush visited Romania and Hungary. During his September 18-19 stopover in Bucharest, he met with Ceausescu and other high ranking government officials. The talks concerned America's decision to deploy intermediate range missiles in Western Europe, and the need for the two countries to work together to implement the Helsinki Accords.[2] At the state dinner given Bush on the night of September 18, the Vice President used his dinner toast to emphasize the importance of human rights to the future of American-Romanian relations. "Now the time has come not only for words but for deeds. We must work together to ensure that the ideals of Helsinki and Madrid are given concrete expression, particularly in human rights, including human contact and emigration."[3]

The major critic of the visit was the American Ambassador to Romania, David Funderburk. The Administration refused to listen to his advice. In an August, 1983, meeting in the White House, Funderburk had recommended to both Reagan and Bush that America had to pursue a hard line with Ceausescu. The Romanian President cared "little for human rights or religious freedom."[4] When Bush came to Bucharest he talked briefly with Funderburk, but did not invite the Ambassador to his meeting with Ceausescu. Funderburk saw this as one more example of Washington's naivete resulting from the State Department's collusion with the Communists in Bucharest. The Ambassador believed that Bush "caved in" to Romanian and State Department pressure to "exclude" him from the meeting. Ceausescu did not approve of Funderburk's outspoken position on human rights.[5]

Before returning to Washington, Bush completed his East Europe tour with a visit to Vienna. Here he made the Adminstration's first public statement of its East European policy. Bush told the Austrian Foreign Policy Association on September 21, that America's policy was one of "differentiation—that is, we look to what degree countries pursue autonomous foreign policies, independent of Moscow's direction, and to what degree they foster domestic liberalization—politically, economically, and in their respect for human rights." He went on to specify that the United States would "engage in closer political, economic and cultural relations" with Romania, rather than with Czechoslovakia and Bulgaria who continued to "flagrantly violate the most fundamental human rights."[6]

Two weeks after Bush's visit, the American delegation to the Ninth Session of the Joint Romanian-American Economic Commission arrived in Bucharest. Originally scheduled for the previous Spring, the United States postponed the meeting because it was unclear whether or not Romania would retain its MFN status. However, with this resolved, Secretary of Commerce Malcolm Baldrige brought the American delegation to the October 5 meeting.

During the two day session, both sides looked for new ways to increase their two-way trade to $2 billion. Talks also indicated that Romania intended to use the newly available Eximbank $120 million credit line to purchase two large steam turbine generators from the General Electric Company. When the meeting closed on October 7, both delegations signed a protocol outlining specific measures for increasing trade and cooperation in the areas of power engineering, electronics, machine building, chemistry and agriculture.[7]

Although Romania wanted to expand trade, she did not necessarily want to increase imports. Ceausescu's economic plans called for even more belt-tightening on the part of the Romanian consumer. In September, Bucharest announced a new system of worker remuneration. The plan linked wages to production quotas. If production exceeded the quota, workers would be bonused in proportion to the excess. If production was under, for whatever reason, worker's salaries would be similarly affected. This really meant that the factory worker would underwrite the government's historic inability to have needed materials available and on time at production sites.[8]

In November, the government made a patriotic appeal to reduce nonproductive energy consumption by an additional 50%. Citizens should limit themselves to one low-wattage light bulb per room, limit their use of electrical appliances, and curtail night time activities.[9] Bucharest also reintroduced compulsory food deliveries to the state, abolished in 1956,[10] and called for an accelerated program of horse breeding so that by 1986, the country could use horse drawn vehicles for transportation.[11] In December, the *New York Times* carried an article describing conditions in Bucharest.

> Restaurants, hotel lobbies and government offices are cold and dark . . . At dusk, which arrives in midafternoon . . . the city goes dim, with no neon lights or glimmers from shop windows. The most important currency in the local economy is Kent cigarettes. . . . It is particularly important to have Kents, for example, if one is to go to a hospital; otherwise services like changing the bed will be unlikely.[12]

The government tolerated the Kent cigarette based black market, since it did not interfere with Romania's efforts to reduce its hard currency debt. Without question Bucharest had curtailed Romania's dependence on foreign products. Imports from Western countries fell by two-thirds between 1980 and 1983, while Romanian exports only declined by about 30%. The rapidly increasing trade surplus caused concern in the Common Market. Romania was the first CMEA country to sign an agreement with the EEC, and did so in 1980. However, Ceausescu's austerity program had destroyed the anticipated volume and direction of the two-way trade. The EEC's deficit with Romania increased from $59 million in 1980 to $710 million in 1982, and was well on the way to surpassing that sum in 1983.[13] A further indication of Romania's success was its decision in February, 1984, to cancel its last tranche of standby credit from the IMF. Bucharest's growing trade surplus enabled her to be less dependent on foreign creditors, and their irksome rules and regulations.[14]

The main beneficiary of Romania's new trade policy was CMEA. In 1980, only 38% of Romania's total trade was with CMEA countries. In 1983, the trade reached 53%. Since Bucharest refused to increase her hard currency debt through Western purchases, Ceausescu looked to purchase technology, raw materials and petroleum from CMEA with soft currencies and barter. While still not tolerating any Soviet efforts to make CMEA a supranational organization, Bucharest was willing, and at times eager, to participate in new ventures with its East European neighbors. Relieved by the death of Andropov in February, 1984, and seeing no threat in his replacement, Konstantin Chernenko, Ceausescu agreed in March to participate in a CMEA summit, the first in 13 years. However, the June 12-14 meeting did not produce any significant outcomes, save Moscow's insistence that CMEA countries pay her current world oil prices for petroleum purchases.[15] Soviet efforts for greater economic integration continued to fail. Romania's desire to increase her participation in CMEA was solely due to her present economic situation, and not to any change in political or economic philosophy.[16]

Meanwhile, American-Romanian relations continued without much excitement. On December 8, 1983, Florida Congressman Sam Gibbons of the House Ways and Means Committee led a Congressional delegation to Bucharest. Following the two day visit, Gibbons submitted a lengthy report to members of the Ways and Means Committee on March 29, 1984. He described the meeting with Ceausescu as "very positive and optimistic with respect to future bilateral relations." On the issue of religious freedom, Ceausescu explained Romania's policy noting that there was "full liberty" for the 14 religious cults recognized by the government. In response to Gibbon's concerns about some of the evangelical sects, such as the Baptists, the President noted that all religious cults had to be registered. "Several Baptist sects were recognized by the government, and another one was not needed." Ceausescu insisted that the system of established cults worked well and that "other governments should not interfere in this internal matter."[17]

Romania's economy was the other major topic of discussion. The Romanian President conceded that aside from the world recession, Bucharest had contributed to its own indebtedness. The government had permitted too many enterprises to borrow money from foreign creditors. Subsequent meetings with Andrei and the Minister of Foreign Trade, Vasile Pungan, did not alleviate Congressional concerns about the future of Romanian-American commercial relations. Gibbon's report concluded that business opportunities for American companies were on the decline, partly due to the "considerable presence and involvement of France, the Federal Republic of Germany and Japan." The delegation did not think that the $2 billion figure for two-way trade mentioned at the United States-Romanian Economic Council meeting the previous October was realistic. The report recommended that America should continue her bilateral relations with Romania, but surmised that further efforts to liberalize trade would depend on Romania's human rights practices.[18]

Human rights was also the focus of a second Romanian-American Round Table meeting held in Washington from February 27-29, 1984. Elliott Abrams, the Assistant Secretary of State for Human Rights, and Maria Groza, Romania's Deputy Foreign Minister, co-chaired the session which focused on the provisions of the Helsinki Final Act.[19] While nothing specific came out of the meeting, Romania's human rights practices continued to be a concern to American government officials.

In early May, 190 members of the House formed a Congressional Human Rights Caucus. On May 14, the group sent Ceausescu a letter indicating its "distress" over Romania's continued human rights violations of the Helsinki provisions. The letter noted a number of anti-Semitic articles which appeared in Romanian literary and popular press, especially the poems written by Corneliu Vadim Tudor in the July 29, 1983 issue of *Septamana*. The Caucus also noted its concern about the "direct and calculated persecution of fundamentalist Christians," and Bucharest's efforts to destroy the remnants of Hungarian culture in Romania. The letter closed hoping that Ceausescu would find solutions to these problems "during this period" when the President would make his determination concerning MFN renewal.[20]

Congress and the 1984 Waiver

On May 31, President Reagan sent two communiques to Congress. The first, a memorandum, indicating his decision to renew the Romanian-American Trade Agreement signed in 1975 for an additional three years.[21] The second was a message indicating his decision to extend Romania's emigration waiver for another year. In justifying his decision, he emphasized Romania's continued willingness to let people emigrate especially to the United States and West Germany. Since emigration to Israel had declined somewhat in 1983, the President assured Congress that he intended to "monitor closely" Romania's procedures for emigration to Israel. He particularly noted Romania's assurances and performance that it would not impose an education tax on prospective emigrants. As a result, he believed that a waiver extension would continue to substantially promote the goals of the Jackson-Vanik Amendment.[22]

The Chadha case clearly affected Congress. No one introduced a resolution of disapproval, and the House refused to hold hearings on the President's waiver extension. However, on June 20, Philip Crane introduced a resolution in the House, H.R. 5901, which called for the repeal of the waiver provisions of the Jackson-Vanik Amendment. This would leave in force only the original, more restrictive, freedom-of-emigration requirement. If approved, Crane's resolution would extend MFN treatment to a Communist country only if the President reported semi-annually to Congress that the country was not in violation of the freedom-of-emigration requirement.[23] The House took no action on Crane's resolution in 1984.

However, the House did hold hearings on "Protecting and Promoting Religious Rights in Eastern Europe and the Soviet Union" which gave human rights advocates an opportunity to speak out against religious discrimination. While most of the speakers at the June 12 hearing directed their wrath at the Soviet Union, Reverend John Butosi, Bishop of the Calvin Synod Conference of the United Church of Christ in Bridgeport, Connecticut, pointed to Romania's discrimination against Hungarians in Transylvania. Most of the Hungarians were either Catholic or Protestant, and as such Hungarian believers had a four-fold problem in Romania: "the burden of being Hungarians in a Romanian state, non-Communist in a Communist state, Protestant or Roman Catholic in an Orthodox environment, and Evangelical Christians in a state-controlled church."[24]

While Butosi's remarks added little new information, his testimony was another indication of the dogged persistence of those human rights advocates who wanted Washington to make human rights and religious freedom criteria for American foreign policy and foreign aid decisions. Bucharest was well aware of this development and knew that the Chadha case had bought them time. In 1984, the United States hosted the Summer Olympics. When the Soviet Union decided to boycott the event in retaliation for Carter's boycott of the 1980 Moscow olympics, Romania became the only Warsaw Pact country to participate in the Los Angeles games. This fact did not go unnoticed in the American press. Newspapers recalled America's love affair with former Romanian olympic gymnasts Olga Korbut in 1972 and Nadai Comaneci in 1976. While Mary Lou Retton's gold medal in the women's gymnastics made her America's sweetheart, many observers were also thrilled by the performance of Ecaterina Szabo, who led the Romanian gymnastic team to to a gold medal in Los Angeles.

On August 8 the Senate Subcommittee on International Trade held hearings on the President's emigration waiver determination. Witnesses were fewer than at past hearings, undoubtedly due to the Chadha decision which rendered one-house resolutions useless. In fact, only one business person appeared to testify, Joseph Torsani of Prudential Lines, and only seven corporations sent letters supporting Romanian MFN. As a result, nearly all of the testimony opposed the President's waiver and focused on three issues: Bucharest's record of religious persecution, ethnic discrimination and emigration harassment.[25]

Many veteran witnesses presented testimony including Laszlo Hamos, Istvan Gereben, and Lucian Orasel, all opposing the President's recommendation. Of particular note was the testimony of Holly Burkhalter, representing Helsinki Watch. She testified that after numerous requests, Romania had finally agreed to let a Helsinki Watch delegation visit the country provided the visit was made after the American Congress completed its 1983 MFN review. The organization agreed, and made little reference to Romania's human rights record in its 1983 publication. However, once the Congressional process ended, Bucharest reneged and cancelled the visit.[26] Nonetheless, Burkhalter did not use her testimony to avenge the cancellation.

While decrying the abuse of would-be emigrants from Romania, the human rights advocate described a growing problem for emigrants to the United States. American immigration regulations made it impossible for Romanian emigrants to enter the United States. America's emigrant quota for Romania was far smaller than the number of prospective immigrants. To alleviate the problem, Washington had established a special Third Country Processing program for Romanians in the mid-1970s. Under this program, Romanians with exit visas, who were ineligible to enter the United States as immigrants, could travel to Rome for processing as "refugees" and as such come to America.

However, the 1980 Refugee Act set quotas on the number of Romanian "refugees" eligible for entry to the United States. In 1982, the quota was 2,300 and in 1983, the Act projected a maximum of 1,300. However, the backlog of cases coupled with America's continued insistence that Bucharest "let her people go," rendered the Third Country Processing program ineffective. In September, 1982, Washington severed the Rome connection. At present, according to Burkhalter, the United States worked solely on a quota system which could not accommodate the thousands of Romanian applicants for immigrant visas.[27]

One of the last pieces of testimony was a letter from Dante Fascell, Chairman of the United States Helsinki Commission on Security and Cooperation in Europe. While the Deputy Assistant Secretary of State, Mark Palmer, had reminded the hearing that its function was to review Romania's emigration performance,[28] Fascell saw the MFN review in a much broader framework. The letter of the Jackson-Vanik Amendment stipulated emigration, but Fascell believed "that the spirit of the legislation embraces wider human rights topics, such as the freedoms of conscience, expression and association, religious liberty and minority rights."[29]

While he described Romania's emigration record as mixed, and its human rights record as poor, Fascell did not oppose the President's recommendation. Bucharest did respond to particular humanitarian cases, and its monthly rate of emigration no longer reflected the cyclic pattern typical of the late 1970s. He concluded that while each year the decision to renew Romanian MFN became more difficult, the recommendation to extend "rested on the calculation that humanitarian aims would better be served by granting MFN than by its denial."[30]

Certainly Ceausescu understood this assumption for on August 20, he commuted Father Calciu's 10 year sentence, and released him from prison. Ceausescu hoped to profit from Szabo's gymnastic performance, and America's conclusion that Romania's participation in the Summer Olympics was proof positive of her continued independence in foreign policy. Calciu's release had been the object of widespread international pressure, especially from a number of human rights supporters in Congress. Ceausescu's decision was surely designed to capitalize on the groundswell of positive feelings for Romania generated by the Olympics, and as a sign that Romania deserved MFN renewal. Apparently Congress agreed and since neither House introduced any action of disapproval, Romania retained her MFN status through July, 1985.

However, Congressional silence did not necessarily mean Congressional approval. The Chadha ruling had limited Congressional review, and forced both houses to use legislation as the means to indicate their human rights concerns. The ten year statutory authority for GSP, or General System of Preferences, was due to expire on January 3, 1985. This program provided unilateral, non-reciprocal duty-free tariff treatment to about 3,000 articles from 140 developing countries, including Romania.[31]

The Administration asked Congress to extend the authority for an additional ten years. The Senate considered the legislation in May and the House in September. During the debates, Congress amended the renewal legislation to include human rights concerns. In order for goods to receive GSP treatment, a country had to provide "internationally recognized worker rights." These included the right of association, the right to organize and bargain collectively, a prohibition on the use of any form of forced or compulsory labor, minimum wage for children and acceptable working conditions including wages, hours of work, safety and health regulations.[32] The President signed the GSP renewal into law on October 30, 1984. As events developed, Romania's unwillingness to provide the required "worker rights" would terminate her GSP relationship with the United States in March, 1987.

In December, the Administration reminded Romania of Washington's concern for human rights on several occasions. At the Tenth Session of the Joint Romanian-American Economic Commission meeting in Washington, Malcolm Baldrige told his Romanian counterpart, Vasile Pungan, about the recent legislation and Congress's growing interest in human rights as a criterion for American foreign policy.[33] On December 10, President Reagan made his annual proclamation concerning Human Rights Day,[34] and a few hours later, American and Romanian delegates met for the Eleventh Session of the United States-Romanian Economic Council in Bucharest. Although composed primarily of business representatives, the American delegation urged Ceausescu to show greater concern for Washington's human right's interests. However, the Romanian President ignored the issue in his opening remarks to the Council, and urged the representatives to find new avenues for increased trade. He hoped that in the near future, two-way trade would exceed $2 billion.[35]

Ceausescu refused to link trade and human rights. In fact, he did not think there was any human rights problem in Romania, and said as much at the Thirteenth Party Congress. In his opening address to the delegates on November 19, he told them that some foreign observers wondered what kind of democracy existed in Romania. Romanian democracy "is an expression of unity of interests, because antagonistic classes were liquidated in the Socialist Republic of Romania. The Romanian nation is made up of friendly social classes and categories sharing the same interests: to build a new society free of oppressors, a society of social equality and justice."[36] He urged his colleagues to "make every effort to strengthen friendship and brotherhood among all the country's citizens regardless of nationality."[37]

Romania's Economy

The Thirteenth Party Congress approved the Eighth Five Year Plan, 1986-1990, with long range guidelines through the year 2000. While the program called for increased dependence on domestic energy and raw materials, the success of the Five Year Plan depended on a 60% increase in labor productivity over that of the preceding Five Year Plan.[38] In reviewing Romania's economic growth during the past several years, debt reduction and the opening of the Danube-Black Sea Canal, promised for over a decade, led the list of economic achievements. In conclusion the Congress agreed that by the year 2000, Romania would be a multilaterally developed industrial-agrarian country, whose productivity would place it among the most advanced countries in the world.[39]

Implementation of the new Five Year Plan required Romania to increase her CMEA trade and to improve relations with Moscow. In 1983, 53% of Romania's trade was with socialist states. Two years later that share had increased to 57%.[40] As Bucharest turned more toward CMEA, Ceausescu became more critical of the organization's shortcomings. At the June, 1985, CMEA meeting in Warsaw, Romanian Prime Minister Constantin Dascalescu called for an increase in intra-CMEA trade based on a more efficient utilization of each country's industrial capacity. At times Romania's factories were idle, and this was due to poor management on the part of CMEA. Dascalescu wanted CMEA to help member states with their individual domestic economic problems. Romania was willing to do its part. She had already signed bilateral trade and cooperation agreements through the year 2000 with Poland, Bulgaria and East Germany, and negotiations for similar accords were underway with Czechoslovakia and Hungary. Romania also favored new multilateral investment projects, provided the benefits accrued equally to each of the participants. To date, most projects involved Moscow and were located in Soviet territory. This arrangement frequently left CMEA investors unable to anticipate their investment benefits. Before the meeting ended, the Romanians asked their colleagues to work on a plan to more efficiently utilize each country's industrial capacity.[41]

Needing cheaper fuel and more raw materials from Moscow, Romania was the first East European country to call for the renewal of the Warsaw Pact. Ceausescu made this statement in November, 1984, and gave Romania's approval to the twenty year extension in May, 1985. In the interim, Bucharest negotiated a five year trade agreement with Moscow, which indicated that the growing shift in Romania's trade from West to East would continue. In 1982, 17% of Bucharest's trade was with Moscow, in 1984, the figure rose to 22% and to 26% in 1985. All in all, a rather spectacular increase. Romanian exports to the Soviet Union consisted mainly of steel and industrial machinery, aircraft and weapons, rolling stock, oil equipment, food, and some consumer goods.

In turn, Moscow increased its deliveries of raw materials, especially iron ore, natural gas and oil.[42]

The Cult of Personality and Human Rights

In addition to the economy, the other major development in Romania during the first part of 1985 focused on the ever-increasing adulation proffered to the Romanian President. Ceausescu's cult of personality appeared to have no bounds. By 1985, he was the only pre-1965 leader in power, and 42 of the 47 members of the Party's Executive Committee were elected since 1965.[43] His penchant for rotating cadres, which included replacing Stefan Andrei as Foreign Minister with Ilie Vaduva, prevented any one party member from becoming a threat to the President. The only exceptions to this practice were family members, especially his wife Elena and their youngest son, Nicu. However, their ability to grow in power was simply an extension of the President's cult of personality. Elena was the object of her own campaign of public adoration while Nicu, whose reputation as a playboy, and an unpleasant one at that, became an alternate member of the Party's Political Executive Committee.[44]

Throughout 1985 Romanians were reminded of Ceausescu's overwhelming importance to the nation's socialist development. Newspapers and media produced seemingly endless praise of Nicolae Ceausescu on the occasion of his birthday, January 26; the twentieth anniversary of his election as General Secretary, March 26; and, the twentieth anniversary of the historic Ninth Party Congress on July 24.[45] At the Plenary meeting of the Party's Central Committee on March 27, Ceausescu thanked the delegates for their vote of confidence expressed by unanimously nominating him for reelection as President of Romania. In what he undoubtedly considered to be a humble statement, he told his listeners that

> as far as I am concerned, as a son of my people, as a loyal soldier of the Party for over fifty years, I have done my best to serve the cause of social and national liberation, the cause of progress, democracy and socialism in Romania, and, since the Party put me in the high office of General Secretary, I have not had a moment's rest, day and night, I may say, my thoughts have been of how better to serve the cause of the people, of the Party, of what action to take so that the wonderful ideals of the socialist and communist society may come true on Romania's soil.[46]

To those in the audience who listened and believed, they knew they were fortunate to have a leader who worked day and night to implement his goals for his people. The growth of Ceausescu's cult of personality meant that fewer people had individual identities. Ceausescu's *persona* overshadowed other people's achievements. Individuality, of person or group, was realized only in conjunction with Ceausescu. Those without this relationship lacked identity, and correspondingly could claim no equality in human rights. As the pyramidial effect of the cult grew, more Romanians were denied their basic freedoms. These people rapidly became the subject of considerable discussion in Congress and in the American press.

The issue which gained the most attention in the United States in 1985 was Romania's unwillingness to accord freedom to religious groups not recognized by the government's Department of Cults. The early seeds of religious discord which appeared in the early 1980s continued to sprout. American based Christian movements encouraged these developments, and supported some of the neo-Protestant sects. In addition, Bucharest's decision to bulldoze churches to build concrete palaces for the party and the ruling family infuriated religious believers. They interpreted the bulldozing as further evidence of Bucharest's policy of religious persecution. The government's actions made religion an issue even among non-believers. Bucharest's decision to bulldoze churches, such as the historic Vacaresti monastery built in 1724 and the Mihai Voda monastery dating from 1591, produced a public outcry among intellectuals throughout the Western world.[47]

Evidence of a religious revival in Romania mounted. More Bibles appeared in circulation, more people attended recognized churches, and more underground religious movements appeared. Many believers who were disenchanted with the Orthodox Church joined recognized fundamentalist Christian Churches, such as Baptist, Adventist, Pentecostal and the Brethren. Some joined non-recognized denominations such as the Jehovah's Witnesses, Christian Scientists and the Mormons. While still others joined the two officially banned churches, the Uniate, or Eastern-rite Catholic Church, and the Army of the Lord, consisting mainly of dissident Orthodox believers.[48]

Organizations such as Helsinki Watch and Amnesty International published reports on Bucharest's harassment of religious cults. The reports also noted the governments alleged discrimination against ethnic

Hungarians.[49] Other news media, such as the *East European Reporter*, gave its Western readers information about a new "underground resistance movement," Romanian Democratic Action, formed by workers interested in reviving the goals of SLOMR, dissolved in 1979. The new organization called for free trade unions and improved human rights.[50]

While the Chadha case continued to project a dark shadow over the value of Congressional review of Romanian MFN, the case did not prevent Congressmen from showing their displeasure with Bucharest's callous approach to human rights and matters of conscience. Early in 1985, Philip Crane reintroduced a bill to repeal the President's waiver authority under the freedom-of-emigration provisions. America would only grant MFN to those non-market economy countries that fully complied with the Jackson-Vanik language. On March 21, Representative Dornan introduced the "Slave Labor Act of 1985" which prohibited MFN treatment to any imports from a Communist regime. Dornan defined "Communist" as any nation which the Department of Defense determined deprived its citizens of basic human rights, or exported terrorism beyond its national borders.[51]

Meanwhile, Ceausescu decided to replace his Ambassador. He recalled Micea Malita, who had been particularly effective in protecting Romanian MFN, and replaced him with Nicolae Gavrilescu.[52] Ceausescu made this decision in large measure because he knew that David Funderburk intended to resign his Ambassadorial post in Bucharest. Funderburk was totally frustrated with America's foreign policy toward Romania which he described as "largely misconceived and ineffective."[53]

On May 8, Funderburk paid his farewell visit to Ceausescu, and returned to Washington.[54] He wasted little time in telling the American public of his disenchantment with the State Department. In an interview with the *Washington Post*, he told reporters that Romania's record on human rights made "a mockery of declared U.S. policy goals." For example, when Ceausescu suspended his education tax and permitted hundreds of Romanians to emigrate, most of those given exit visas were not qualified for admission to the United States. "We were outfoxed by Ceausescu."[55] In concluding his interview, he blamed former Undersecretary of State Lawrence Eagleburger and his proteges for hiding the truth from the Reagan Administration. His Embassy reports had told the Department about increased Soviet-Romanian contacts, technology transfers to Moscow through American sales to Bucharest, and Romania's growing weapons industry, which made her the fifth largest weapons exporter in the world in 1982. However, these reports were ignored by "people in Washington" who defended Ceausescu "because their jobs, promotion, careers depend on proving they were right about Romania."[56]

One day after Funderburk's outburst, the House Subcommittee on Human Rights and International Organizations held hearings on "Human Rights in Romania." Only five people appeared at the hearings, four of whom represented human rights advocacy organizations. Jeri Laber of Helsinki Watch, Robert Sharlet of Amnesty International, Nina Shea of the International League for Human Rights and Laszlo Hamos of the Committee for Human Rights in Romania all condemned Bucharest's human rights practices. Significantly, this was the first time that Helsinki Watch had called for an end to Romanian MFN. All of those opposed to the President's recommendation distinguished between Romania's emigration record, and her discriminatory behavior toward religious and ethnic minorities.[57]

Even the lone Administration representative, conceded that "individual and collective liberties" were "severely limited" in Romania. Gary Matthews, the Deputy Assistant Secretary of State for Human Rights and Humanitarian Affairs, agreed that religious rights in Romania were "significantly uneven," and that the Department was concerned about "the degree of cultural freedom enjoyed by Romania's ethnic minorities." However, in justifying the Administration's continued support of Romanian MFN, Matthews pointed to Bucharest's independence in foreign policy and her improved emigration record. Further, due to the annual MFN review, Washington had been able to exercise considerable influence in Bucharest through top level discussions. These had resulted in the resolution of several important family reunification cases, and had brought Father Calciu's release from prison.[58]

The hearings acted more as a catalyst than a catharsis for Congress. On May 23, Representative Mark Siljander of Michigan introduced a bill which would expand the Jackson-Vanik language to prohibit MFN treatment to any country which discriminated against its citizens on the basis of religious, cultural or ethnic orientation.[59]

Congress and the 1985 Waiver

Ten days later, President Reagan sent a message to Congress indicating that he had determined that while emigration problems still existed, Romania's performance had continued to improve and warranted MFN renewal.[60] On the same day, June 3, the Administration signed a new agreement with Bucharest regulating trade in steel products.

On July 10, Senator Robert Dole told his colleagues of his recent visit to Romania during the last week in May. In a meeting with Ceausescu, the Romanian President indicated he wanted to expand trade with the United States, especially in the area of technology. Dole suggested that relations would improve were Romania able to resolve a number of special interest emigration cases, particularly that of Father Calciu. Ceausescu had released Calciu from prison the previous August, however, the priest was unable to travel about and was essentially under house arrest. Dole also mentioned the case of Dorin Tudoran, a prominent writer, who was on a hunger strike protesting the government's unwillingness to let him and his family emigrate.

Ceausescu had countered Dole's requests, with one of his own. He would like to see the United States expedite its emigration processing procedures. Bucharest had granted exit visas to thousands of Romanians to go to America, but due to Washington's slowness, these people were unable to leave Romania. In concluding his presentation to the Senate, Dole recognized that there were limitations on the type of relationship America could have with a totalitarian regime. However, "because of such differences in principles and policies, it is important that we keep doors of communication open" as a means to affect changes important to the United States.[61]

The overall positive tone of Dole's report seemed to fly in the face of newspaper accounts of Romania's most recent efforts to denigrate religious believers. In June, the *New York Times* and *Wall Street Journal* carried reports that Bucharest recycled Bibles into toilet paper. Rolls of paper contained fragments of biblical verses. The Romanian government had permitted the World Reformed Alliance to ship 20,000 Bibles to the Reformed Church in Transylvania. The Alliance shipped the Bibles during the late 1970s and early 1980s. However, no one knows the number of Bibles which actually reached church congregations. The undistributed Bibles arrived at the paper and pulp combines at Braila and Bistrita, where they were recycled into toilet paper and first appeared in state retail stores in February, 1985.[62]

These reports along with stories of more bulldozed churches and arrested clergymen encouraged House members Tony Hall of Ohio, Chris Smith of New Jersey and Frank Wolf of Virginia to make a fact-finding mission to Romania in early July. Sponsored by the Christian Response International, a Swiss-based human rights organization, the Congressmen toured Bucharest and several outlying areas. They were taken back by the numerous accounts they heard about the beatings and torture given to prisoners of conscience. Following their return to Washington, they wrote a note to Ceausescu on July 16 asking him to end the government's policy of religious repression.[63] As evidence mounted that Bucharest pursued a systematic policy of repression, Congressman Philip Crane introduced a resolution in the House on July 23 disapproving the President's waiver request. While Crane and his colleagues knew that the resolution, if approved, was probably unconstitutional, they wanted to make known their objections to Ceausescu's policies.[64]

On the same day that Crane introduced his resolution in the House, the Senate held hearings on the President's emigration waiver recommendation. A review of the evidence indicated that corporate America was no longer willing to testify in support of Romanian MFN. No business representative appeared at the hearings aside from Milton Rosenthal, who, as Chairman of the American section of the United States-Romanian Economic Council, made a *pro forma* appearance. While one can argue that business executives did not want to waste their time testifying at a hearing that had little impact on the President's decision, the fact that only one corporation sent a letter supporting the President indicated a major turnabout by the business community.

This flight of corporate America away from supporting Romanian trade was especially surprising in 1985. Business lobbyists had worked for two years to amend the Export Administration Act to reduce controls to facilitate West-West and East-West trade. The 1979 Export Administration Act had expired on September 30, 1983. Congress only extended the act temporarily through March, 1984, thereafter the President continued to administer export controls through Executive Order 12470 until Congress finally passed the Export Administration Amendments Act of 1985. One of the principal reasons for the two year debate was over the issue of technology exports to the Soviet Bloc. Business representatives frequently cited a National Academy of Sciences study which estimated that the government's restrictive export controls cost the country $9.3 billion in short term gains, and more than $17 billion in long term gains in 1985 alone.[65] The bill which the President signed into law on July 12, 1985, reduced controls on many "low technology" items, such as personal computers, and limited the Commerce Department's authority to deny export licenses for products readily available from foreign sources.[66]

Considering the amount of money and time that corporate America spent on lobbying Congressmen to liberalize Washington's trade regu-

538 TWEAKING THE NOSE OF THE RUSSIANS

lations, an appearance at an Romanian MFN hearing would have posed little problem. However, Bucharest had lost much of its attractiveness. While two-way trade had remained at about $1 billion, its composition had dramatically changed since 1980. In that year, America showed a $400 million trade surplus on a two-way trade total of a billion dollars. In 1984, while the volume remained the same, Romania had a surplus of $644 million and in 1985, Bucharest would increase its surplus to $674 million. In the process, American exports declined from $722 million in 1980, to $249 million in 1984, and to $208 million in 1985.[67]

As fewer American corporations did business with Romania, some of those that did had complaints. Business with Romania was not based simply on commercial and economic considerations. Rather, Bucharest considered other factors in each transaction such as debt repayment, bilateral trade balances, and the political implications of the arrangement. Another complaint was that Bucharest officials frequently cancelled appointments, sometimes with only a few hours notice.[68] While many of these problems were common to dealing with non-market economies and Third World countries, they were still irksome, and especially so when the Romanian government urged its people and industries to become independent of foreign imports.

Without business representatives at the Senate hearing, there were few spokesman supporting continued Romanian MFN. Even the Administration refused to send its normal delegation of three or four witnesses. Edward Derwinksi, Counselor of the State Department, was the sole Administration representative. He began by reminding the members of the Subcommittee on Trade that the Jackson-Vanik amendment only linked trade to emigration. Congress's annual review of MFN renewal had looked at issues beyond the amendment's language. MFN renewal did "not constitute U.S. endorsement of internal development or satisfaction with the internal situation" in a country. To the contrary, continued MFN created opportunities for Washington to work to improve a country's emigration and human rights performance.[69]

Derwinski told the Senators of a recent success made possible by America's willingness to accord Romania MFN. He had visited Bucharest in June, and began negotiations for a new emigration arrangement with Romania. Frequently, Bucharest gave emigration visas to citizens who proved to be ineligible for admission to the United States. These would-be emigrants became "trapped" between the regulations of the two countries. According to the new agreement, Romania would only issue exit visas to individuals certified as eligible by the

American Embassy for admission into the United States. He expected to complete the negotiations within a couple of weeks.[70]

Derwinski also told the Subcommittee that due to the leverage afforded by MFN renewal, Washington could resolve special interest emigration cases. He was especially pleased to inform them that Bucharest had agreed to permit both Father Calciu and Dorin Todoran to leave Romania. While both of these cases had considerable public support, Derwinski indicated that of the 23 special cases given Bucharest in June, 11 were already resolved and he expected the remainder would be soon approved.[71]

The Counselor's position had a few supporters at the hearing. One of these was O. Rudolph Aggrey, America's former Ambassador to Romania during the Carter Administration. Aggrey saw MFN as important to America as a vehicle to encourage change in Romania.[72] However, another former Ambassador testified to the contrary. The recently resigned David Funderburk told the Senators that America should withdraw MFN from Romania. Withdrawal would not push Romania closer to Moscow, and it would not result in greater persecution of religious believers, since the government's policy was already repressive. As for viewing MFN as a reward to Bucharest for her independent foreign policy, Funderburk argued that Romania had little autonomy. Rather, "Romanian disinformation has kept the reality of Romanian foreign policy collaboration with the Soviets and internal repression from the world."[73]

For a change, all of the spokesmen for the Jewish community agreed. Jacob Birnbaum, Jack Spitzer and Albert Friedman, National Editor of "Der Yid", the largest Yiddish language newspaper in the world, all supported continuing MFN for Romania. Abandoning his normal neutral position, Birnbaum noted that in recent years he had learned that the number of persons emigrating to Israel was much larger than reported. About 50% of the Romanian Jews who arrived in Israel had not registered with Jewish communal offices in Bucharest before leaving, and consequently there was no record of their destination.[74]

However, more witnesses agreed with Funderburk than with the Administration. Reverend Havadtoy of the Calvin Reformed Church described the Bible recycling process, and saw that as a sufficient reason to deny Romania MFN.[75] Others, such as Jeffrey Collins of the Christian Response International wanted to suspend Romanian MFN until she improved her human rights record.[76] Still others, led by Hamos and Szaz, called for an end to Romanian MFN on the basis of her discriminatory practices against ethnic Hungarians. The bulk of the written testimony received by the Subcommittee also called for an end to Romanian MFN.

After the hearings closed, several Senators indicated their complete frustration with Romania's continued refusal to improve its record on human rights, and at their own inability to affect change as a result of the Chadha ruling. Consequently nineteen members of the Senate sent a letter to Ceausescu notifying him of their concern about Romania's repression of religious believers, emigration applicants and ethnic minorities. The Senators hoped that Ceausescu would address these issues since they raised the question of whether continued MFN was "really mutually beneficial."[77]

During the next few weeks, Derwinski finished negotiations on the new emigration procedure with Bucharest, and Calciu and Todoran arrived in the West.[78] On August 30, President Reagan nominated Roger Kirk, a career Foreign Service Officer, to replace Funderburk as America's Ambassador to Romania.[79] Kirk's confirmation hearings brought no surprises, and he presented his credentials to President Ceausescu on November 29, 1985.

By the end of August, since Congress took no action to disapprove the President's waiver, including no House debate on Crane's resolution of disapproval, Romania retained her MFN status for another year. However, this extension did not put an end to Congressional concern about Bucharest's human rights practices.

From Emigration to Human Rights

The 1985 hearings proved to be a watershed in the Congressional review of Romanian MFN. Derwinski's efforts to separate the Jackson-Vanik emigration requirements from Romania's human rights practices as the sole criterion for renewed MFN fell on deaf ears. Emigration was no longer an issue. Representatives of the Jewish community had few complaints about Bucharest's emigration practice, while the new emigration arrangement agreed to in August could resolve the backlog of emigrants waiting to come to America. The arguments of those opposed to extending Romanian MFN in the 1985 hearings rested almost exclusively on Bucharest's internal policies toward religious dissidents and ethnic minorities. Congress wanted to change the rules. Ceausescu had accepted emigration, but, according to the former Romanian Ambassador Corneliu Bogdan, he "did not make any commitments on Bibles or churches."[80]

The Twelfth Session of the United States-Romanian Economic Council meeting in Bucharest from September 10-12 proved to be the highpoint of Washington-Bucharest relations for the remainder of 1985.[81] The delegates agreed to find new ways to expand bilateral trade, and representatives from several American firms signed agreements with several Foreign Trade Organizations.[82] Milton Rosenthal used his arrival visit with President Ceausescu to remind him of Congress's growing concern about Romania's human rights practices.

Five weeks later, Representatives Smith, Wolf and Hall introduced legislation to temporarily suspend Romanian MFN. The three men had visited Romania during the summer, written a letter to Ceausescu about their observations, but had received no reply. The hearings had not shown any change of policy on the part of Bucharest. Consequently, the Congressmen decided to introduce HR 3599 which, if enacted, would place Romania on "probation" for six months. During this time, the Administration could assess whether the level of progress on the issues of religious freedom and human rights justified restoring Romania's MFN status.[83]

On November 1, Paul Trible of Virginia and William Armstrong of Colorado introduced a parallel bill in the Senate, S. 1817. In explaining the legislation, the Senators focused on Bucharest's record of religious persecution citing, among other issues, the Bible-into-toilet paper matter.[84] Two weeks later, Trible attended hearings on "Religious Persecution Behind the Iron Curtain" as a member of the Senate Subcommittee on European Affairs. While the thrust of the hearings was to determine religious conditions in the Soviet Union, some witnesses included statements about Romania.[85]

The chief Administration witness was Richard Schifter, the new Assistant Secretary of State for the Bureau of Human Rights and Humanitarian Affairs. Schifter replaced Elliott Abrams who became Assistant Secretary for Inter-American Affairs following Reagan's reelection. Schifter began his testimony with an overview of religious conditions in each of the Soviet Bloc countries. He described Romania as having "the most mixed and complex religious situation" in Eastern Europe. In spite of persistent persecution by the state, religious groups were growing at a tremendous rate.[86]

Trible pressed Schifter to expand his testimony on Romania, and explain why the Administration consistently renewed Bucharest's MFN in spite of her human rights record. Schifter defended the State Department's position using the argument that Romania's independent foreign policy warranted continued American MFN. Romania had taken a number of steps which furthered American foreign policy interests. Bucharest limited its participation in the Warsaw Pact, opposed Moscow's invasion of Czechoslovakia and Afghanistan, and absented itself in the United Nations rather than join other Bloc countries in anti-American resolutions. Using the 39th General Assembly as an example, Schifter compared Romania and America's voting pattern, and noted that Bucharest was the only East European country which did not vote against the United States on 10 key issues.[87]

Trible quickly countered. Using the 38th General Assembly, he compared the two countries voting record on all plenary votes. Noting that Israel voted with the United States 93.3% of the time, West Germany, 82%, Romania 16.3%, and the Soviet Union, 13.8%. There was little difference between Moscow and Bucharest's support of Washington's positions in the United Nations.[88] Further, this voting record indicated that Romania showed little independence from Moscow and consequently, the Administration ought not reward Bucharest for something she did not do. In closing, Trible urged his colleagues and the Administration to review America's East European policy and examine its goals and means in light of present developments in the Soviet Bloc.[89]

Trible was not alone in calling for a policy review. The House Foreign Relations Committee had held hearings in early October to examine America's policy toward Eastern Europe. Following testimony by members of the Administration and representatives of the academic community, a Congressional Research Service report concluded that the Reagan Administration had only provided a "few broad policy statements" concerning Eastern Europe. In reviewing testimony made by Administration witnesses at numerous Congressional hearings, the report noted that continuity appeared to be the main focus of the Administration. And this continuity meant continuing the previous Administration's policy of differentiation. Each country would be seen as distinct, and not as part of an Eastern Bloc.[90]

As though to reinforce this view, the State Department announced on November 14, that Secretary of State George Shultz would make his first visit to Eastern Europe. The press release stated that his purpose in visiting Romania, Hungary and Yugoslavia was to seek better bilateral relations with members of the Warsaw Pact, "rather than treating them merely as part of the Soviet Bloc."[91] However, Shultz's visit to Romania had an unannounced purpose as well.

Growing Congressional anger at Bucharest's record of religious repression had finally made an impact on the President. Although he had annually proclaimed December 10 as Human Rights Day, 1985 was the first time that he included Romania in his introductory remarks. He noted that in Eastern Europe the hopes and aspirations of millions of people for religious freedoms and civic rights remained alive in spite of years of persecution. "In Romania, religious persecution includes the destruction of Bibles."[92] Reagan knew that the Administration's efforts to renew Romanian MFN would meet ever growing Congressional opposition unless Bucharest curbed its repressive practices.

As the number of Congressmen grew who were embarrassed by the Administration's continued support for Romania, the President realized that soon there would be enough votes to pass legislation terminating MFN. This process would by-pass the Chadha restrictions, and force the President to either accept the legislation or veto it. If he chose the latter, he would risk having Congress either override the veto, or take out its frustrations with the White House by jeopardizing other Administration sponsored legislation. The simplest solution was for Bucharest to improve its human rights record. Shultz's visit was designed primarily to convey this message personally to the Romanian President.

While Schultz prepared for his East European visit, Ceausescu prepared his countrymen for another winter of hardship and austerity. In a speech at a Plenary Meeting of the Party's Central Committee on November 13, he told the delegates that Romania needed to increase the amount of meat available for export. Each county had a quota it had to deliver to the state. Whatever meat was available beyond the quota would remain in the county. He suggested that the extra meat could come from using the heads of the animals, these would stay in the county.[93] Two weeks later, Romanians complained that all the local butcher shops had for meat were "pig's heads."[94] Other austerity measures included mandates that temperatures in private homes and public institutions not exceed 54 degrees, all restaurants and places of entertainment close by 10 p.m., and household bulbs not exceed 40 watts.[95]

On December 15, George Schultz arrived in Bucharest. He carried with him two messages, one from Reagan to Ceausescu and the other from Representative Robert Michel of Illinois to Foreign Minister Vaduva. Michel had met Vaduva earlier when the Foreign Minister was a member of the Romanian parliament. When Shultz learned of this relationship, he asked Michel to write a letter describing the intensity of Congress's growing concern about Romania's human rights record. Michel was also affiliated with the Nazarene Christians, a group persecuted by Bucharest.[96]

In his talks with Ceausescu, Shultz warned the Romanian leader that MFN renewal was contingent on Romania taking some significant steps to improve her human rights practices. Schultz explained that there was a definite link between American-Romanian relations and views on Capitol Hill. Although not admitting that there were any human rights problems in Romania, Ceausescu agreed to establish a new mechanism to resolve "the broad range of rights issues." Regular discussions would take place in Washington between Romanian Embassy officials and Edward Derwinski, the State Department Counselor, and in Bucharest between Roger Kirk, the American Ambassador, and Foreign Minister Ilie Vaduva.[97]

At the close of the meeting, Schultz described his talks with Ceausescu as "candid and frank."[98] He agreed with Ceausescu's earlier remarks to the press, that bilateral relations "could be better." The purpose of his meeting with Ceausescu was "to discuss some of the reasons why it isn't better and to see if some things can be done about it."[99] If nothing else, Schultz had clearly told Ceausescu that if Romania wanted American MFN, Bucharest would have to change its repressive policies.

Notes

1. For elaboration on these issues see Harrington and Racheotes, *Masters of War, Makers of Peace*, pp. 299ff.
2. FBIS, EEU, September 19, 1983, p. H1.
3. *DOS Bulletin*, November 1983, p. 17.
4. Funderburk, *Pinstripes and Reds*, p. 117.
5. *Ibid.*, pp. 163-165.
6. Raymond L. Garthoff, "Eastern Europe in the Context of U.S.-Soviet Relations," *Soviet Policy in Eastern Europe*, ed. Sarah Meikeljohn Terry, 1984, pp. 338-339; Nestor Ratesh, "The American Connection," *Romania, 40 Years (1944-1984)*, ed, Vlad Georgescu, pp. 70-75; Joint Economic Committee, *Economic Performance and Policy*, 1985, pp. 557ff; William H. Luers, *Foreign Affairs*, 1987, pp. 979ff.
7. RFE, Situation Report, Romania/18, October 27, 1983, pp. 8-9; FBIS, EEU, October 12, 1983, p. H1.
8. Richard F. Staar (ed.), *Yearbook on International Communist Affairs, 1984* (Stanford, CA: Hoover Institution Press, 1984), p. 364.

9. *Ibid.*

10. Vlad Georgescu, *Eastern European Politics and Societies*, 1988, p. 74; Everett M Jacobs, "Agriculture," *The Soviet Union and Eastern Europe*, ed. George Schopflin, 1986, p. 441.

11. Gabor Hunya, "New Developments in Romanian Agriculture," *Eastern European Politics and Societies*, Vol. 1, No. 2 (1987), p. 268.

12. NYT, December 24, 1985, p. 2.

13. RFE, Situation Report, Romania/20, December 31, 1983, pp. 15-16.

14. Serban Orescu, "Multilaterally Developed Romania: An Overview," *Romania, 40 Years (1944-1984)*, (ed.), Vlad Georgescu, p. 26.

15. Christopher Coker, *The Soviet Union, Eastern Europe, and the New International Economic Order* ("The Washington Papers, No. 111;" New York: Praeger, 1984), pp. 21-26.

16. Richard F. Staar (ed.), *Yearbook on International Communist Affairs, 1985* (Stanford, CA: Hoover Institution Press, 1985), p. 326.

17. U.S. Congress, House Committee on Ways and Means, Subcommittee on Trade, *Report on Trade Mission to Central And Eastern Europe*, 98th Cong., 2d Sess., 1984, pp. 62-63.

18. *Ibid.*, pp. 64-71.

19. FBIS, EEU, March 5, 1984, p. H1.

20. U.S. Congress, Senate Committee on Finance, Hearing Before the Subcommittee on International Trade, *Continuing Presidential Authority to Waive Freedom of Emigration Provisions*. 98th Cong., 2d Sess., 1984, pp. 471-472, hereafter, Senate Subcommittee on International Trade, *Continuing Presidential Authority to Waive Freedom of Emigration Provisions*, 1984. Tudor was very explicit and denunciatory. The Jews, he said, are "thieves and corrupters, people with no conscience and no sense of loyalty, who have no patriotic links whatsoever to their country and only think of how to exploit it" (*Ibid.*), p. 51.

21. *Public Papers of the Presidents of the United States, Ronald Reagan, 1984* (Washington, D.C.: U. S. Government Printing Office, 1984), I, 779.

22. *Ibid.*, pp. 769-770.

23. Pregelj, "Most-Favored -Nation Policy toward Communist Countries," 1987, p. 19.

24. U.S. Congress, Hearing Before the Senate Committee on Foreign Relations, *Protecting and Promoting Religious Rights in Eastern Europe and the Soviet Union*, 98th Cong., 2d Sess., 1984, p. 38.

25. See, Senate Subcommittee on International Trade, *Continuing Presidential Authority to Waive Freedom of Emigration Provisions*, 1984.

26. *Ibid.*, p. 27.

27. *Ibid.*, pp. 40-41.

28. *Ibid.*, p. 5.

29. *Ibid.*, p. 335.

30. *Ibid.*, p. 339.

31. U.S,. Congress, House Report No. 98-1090, *Generalized System of Preferences Renewal Act of 1984*, 98th Cong., 2d Sess., 1984, p. 1.

32. U.S., Congress, House Committee on Ways and Means, *Trade Legislation Enacted Into Public Law, 1981 Through 1988*, 101st Cong., 1st Sess., 1989, p. 130.

33. FBIS, EEU, December 6, 1984, p. H1.

34. *Public Papers of the Presidents of the United States, Ronald Reagan, 1984*, II, 1883.

35. Ceausescu, *Romania On the Way*, XXVIII, 149-151; FBIS, EEU, December 13, 1984, p. H4.

36. Ceausescu, *Romania On the Way*, XXVIII, 118, 119.

37. *Romania: Congresul al XIII-LEA al P.C.R.: Documents and Events* (Bucharest, 1984), p. 75.

38. Ceausescu, *Romania On the Way*, XXVIII, 54-55.

39. *Ibid.*, pp. 58-59.

40. Georgescu, *Eastern European Politics and Societies*, Vol. 2 No. 1, p. 77; *International Affairs: A Monthly Journal of Political Analysis*, Moscow, Progress Publishers, 1985, No. 3, p. 147.

41. RFE, Situation Report, Romania/13, September 11, 1985, p. 3-6.

42. Georgescu, *Eastern European Politics and Societies*, Vol. 2 No. 1, p. 77; Linden, *Communist States and International Change*, p. 169.

43. Fischer, *Nicolae Ceausescu*, p. 211.

44. *Ibid.*, p. 171; Shafir, *Romania*, pp. 99-100. On the rise to power of the Ceausescu family see *Yearbook on International Communist Affairs, 1985*, ed. Richard F. Staar (Stanford, CA: Hoover Institution Press, 1985), p. 327-328.

45. *Ibid.*, p. 327.

46. Ceausescu, *Romania On the Way*, XXVIII, 377.

47. *DOS Bulletin*, August 1985, p. 59.

48. RFE, Background Report, Religious Trends in Eastern Europe, October 10, 1986, pp. 49-50; Senate Subcommittee on International Trade, *Continuing Presidential Authority to Waive Freedom of Emigration Provisions*, 1984, p. 53.

49. *Amnesty International Report, 1986* (London: Amnesty International Publications, 1986), pp. 299-300.

50. Vladimir Tismaneanu, "New Underground Union," *East European Review* (Autumn 1988), p. 57

51. Pregelj, "Most-Favored-Nation Policy toward Communist Countries," 1987, p. 19.

52. *Scinteia*, April 4, 1985, p. 5.

53. U.S. *Congressional Record*, 99th Cong., 1st Sess., 1985, CXXXI, S6140.

54. FBIS, EEU, May 9, 1985, p. H4.

55. U.S. *Congressional Record*, 99th Cong., 1st Sess., 1985, CXXXI, S6140.

56. *Ibid.*, p. S6141

57. See, U.S. Congress, House Committee on Foreign Affairs, Hearing Before the Subcommittees on Europe and the Middle East and on Human Rights and International Organizations, *Human Rights in Romania*, 99th Cong., 1st Ses., 1985.

58. *DOS Bulletin*, August 1985, p. 59.

59. U.S. Congress Senate Committee on Finance, Hearing Before the Subcommittee on International Trade, *MFN, Status for Hungary, Romania, China, and Afghanistan*, 99 Cong., 1st Sess., 1985, pp. 172-173, hereafter, Senate Subcommittee on International Trade, *MFN Status for Romania*, 1985.

60. *Public Papers of the Presidents of the United States, Ronald Reagan, 1985* (Washington, D.C.: U. S. Government Printing Office, 1985), I, 708-709.

61. U.S. *Congressional Record*, 99th Cong., 1st Sess., 1985, CXXXI, S9222.

62. RFE, Background Report/95 (Romania), August 30, 1985, pp. 1-2.

63. U.S. Congress, House Committee on Ways and Means, Hearing Before the Subcommittee on Trade, *Most-Favored-Nation Trading Status for the Socialist Republic of Romania, the Hungarian People's Republic, and the People's Republic of China*, 99th Cong., 2d Sess., 1986, p. 11, hereafter, House Subcommittee on Trade, *MFN Status*, 1986.

64. Pregelj, "Most-Favored-Nation Policy Toward Communist Countries," 1987, p. 20.

65. Martin J. Hillenbrand, "East-West Economic Relations, Export Controls, and Strains in the Alliance," *Controlling East-West Trade and Technology Transfer*, ed. Gary K. Bertsch (1988), p. 385.

66. Long, U.S. Export Control Policy, pp. 93-94. For more on this bill see, [Export Administration Subcommittee of the President's Export Council] "Coping with the Dynamics of World Trade," Volume II, Appendix, pp. 240-255 (December 1984); Joint Economic Committee, *Economic Performance and Policy*, 1985, pp. 570ff; U.S. Congress, House Committee on Ways and Means, *Overview and Compilation of U.S. Trade Statutes*, 100th Cong., 1st Sess., 1987, pp. 102ff.

67. [U.S. Department of Commerce] Statistical Abstract of the United States 1989 (Washington, D.C.: U.S. Government Printing Office, 1989), Table No. 1372.

68. Moore and Nove, "Perspectives of American Importers," *East-West Trade*, eds. Brada and Somanath, 1978, pp. 33-35.

69. Senate Subcommittee on International Trade, *MFN Status for Romania*, 1985, p. 53.

70. *Ibid.*, p. 54.

71. *Ibid.*

72. *Ibid.*, pp. 66-67.

73. *Ibid.*, pp. 94-95.

74. *Ibid.*, pp. 146, 365, 69.

75. *Ibid.*, pp. 99ff.

76. *Ibid.*, pp. 96ff.

77. U.S. Congress, Senate Committee on Finance, Hearing Before the Subcommittee on International Trade, *MFN Status for Romania*, 99th Cong., 2d Sess., pp. 200-202.

78. U.S. Congress, Senate Committee on Foreign Relations, Hearing Before the Subcommittee on European Affairs, *Romania: Most Favored Nation Status*, 99th Cong., 2d Sess., 1986, pp. 26-27.

79. *Public Papers of the Presidents of the United States, Ronald Reagan, 1985*, II, 1025.

80. Author interview of Corneliu Bogdan, January 11, 1989.

81. Ceausescu, *Romania On the Way*, XXIX, 45.

82. FBIS, EEU, September 10, 1985, pp. H1-2

83. House Subcommittee on Trade, *MFN Status*, 1986, p. 11; Senate Subcommittee on International Trade, *MFN Status for Romania*, 1986, pp. 207-209.

84. U.S. *Congressional Record*, 99th Cong., 1st Ses., 1985, CXXXI, S14684-14688.

85. U.S. Congress, Senate Committee on Foreign Relations, Hearing Before the Subcommittee on European Affairs, *Religious Persecution Behind the Iron Curtain*, 99th Cong., 1st Sess., 1985, p. 1.

86. *Ibid.*, pp. 15-16.

87. *Ibid.*, pp. 31-32.

88. For a different view see, Robert Weiner, *Romanian Foreign Policy and the United Nations* (New York: Praeger, 1984).

89. Senate Subcommittee on European Affairs, *Religious Persecution Behind the Iron Curtain*, 1985, p. 33.

90. U.S. Congress, House Committee on Foreign Affairs, Hearings Before the Subcommittee on Europe and the Middle East, *U.S. Policy Toward Eastern Europe, 1985*, 99th Cong., 1st Sess., 1985, pp. 241ff.

91. CSM, November 14, 1985, p. 2.

92. *DOS Bulletin*, February 1986, p. 87.

93. Ceausescu, *Romania On the Way*, XXIX, 157.

94. FBIS, EEU, November 27, 1985, p. H9.

95. CSM, November 12, 1985, p. 1.

96. NYT, December 16, 1985, p.1; *The Washington Post*, December 16, 1985, p. 12.

97. NYT, December 16, 1985, p.1; *The Washington Post*, December 16, 1985, p. 12.

98. FBIS, EEU, December 16, 1985, p. H3.

99. *The Washington Post*, December 16, 1985, p. 12.

CHAPTER XVIII

MFN LOST

Special Senate Hearings on Romania's Human Rights

America's image of Romania would continue to decline through 1988. Gorbachev's dynamic foreign policy stole Ceausescu's thunder. Since many of Moscow's initiatives embodied earlier Romanian positions, Bucharest lost its American image as an Eastern Bloc nation pursuing a foreign policy independent of Moscow. Once this image vanished, all that remained for Americans to see was a Romania which repressed religious freedom and denied its people basic human rights. Administration efforts to continue extending MFN, not only lost supporters in Congress, but forced many legislators to take foreign policy matters into their own hands.

While Schultz's December, 1985, visit had produced more avenues for human rights discussions, his trip did not bring about any significant changes in Romania's internal policies. The newspapers described the aftermath of the Schultz visit as "business as usual." The Romanian Minister of Religious Cults, Ioan Cumpanas, told reporters, "our policy toward religion will not change. We will listen to your specific requests, but policy is policy."[1] In early February, the *Washington Post* carried a report on religion in Romania. To meet the requirements of the Jackson-Vanik emigration language, Romania had, over the years, given Jews preferential emigration status. As Bucharest increased its religious repression, many Christians announced their conversion to Judaism to facilitate their emigration from Romania. The number of these "converts" had grown sufficiently for Rabbi Rosen either to reject conversion applicants, or to withhold their certificates of conversion for several years to insure the religious sincerity of the applicant.[2]

These types of stories, coupled with the questionable success of the Shultz's mission, encouraged human rights advocates in the Senate to call for a review of American-Romanian relations. On February 26, 1986, the Foreign Relations Subcommittee on European Affairs held hearings to assess the effectiveness of the Administration's policy of "differentiation" toward Bucharest. Among the Subcommittee members were two outspoken critics of Romania's domestic policies, Senators Trible and Helms.[3] In prior years, each had introduced legislation opposing Romanian MFN.

As a member of the Subcommittee, Trible wasted little time informing his colleagues and the Administration witnesses as to his concerns . He did not want to continue to conduct "business as usual" with Bucharest. Romania was a repressive regime with an "abysmal human rights record." The country maintained the "highest proportion of security personnel to population . . . engaged in active procurement of Western technology for the Soviet Union," and trained and supported the PLO and other terrorist groups. "I have to ask: is this the kind of government we ought to be dealing with . . . ? I think not." Trible indicated that he was not alone in his views, and unless the Administration could prove that Romania were altering her ways, he and his colleagues would "insist" that Romania lose her MFN treatment.[4]

Administration witnesses from the Office of U.S. Trade Representative, and the Departments of State and Commerce presented testimony throughout the morning and early afternoon. Among the arguments used to justify the President's annual recommendation to extend Romanian MFN were: (1) according to present legislation, emigration performance was the sole criterion for MFN renewal; (2) Romania pursued an independent foreign policy; and (3) MFN provided Washington leverage to affect change in Romania.[5] While no Senator would debate the leverage argument, the *Christian Science Monitor* carried a story the day after the hearings which suggested that one of the main supporters of this leverage argument was Bucharest. As one Romanian official told a reporter, "if you don't like things now, just take away MFN status. Whatever you have now, you won't have then."[6]

The Administration officials conceded that Romania's recent history of internal repression was "deplorable."[7] However, the Assistant Secretary of State, Mark Palmer, did not find Bucharest's behavior out of character for a Communist country. He compared Romania's religious practices with Albania where neither church nor clergyman could legally exist.[8] Trible countered. He was "intrigued" by the way Palmer compared Romania "with the worst of nations and suggests, for some reason, that Romania represents something good." Trible also challenged the State Department's contention that Romania followed an independent foreign policy. In the 39th General Assembly of the United Nations, Romania voted with the United States only 10.1% of the time, less than that of Hungary, East Germany, Bulgaria and the Soviet Union.[9]

Chairman Larry Pressler of South Dakota described one of the reasons businessmen no longer looked to Romania for new trade. Bucharest took between 6 to 8 months to approve a Western firm's application to open a business office, charged high rents, restricted personnel hires, and forced companies to pay high costs for telecommunications equipment. Joseph Dennin of the Commerce Department agreed, but noted that these problems were frequently addressed during the meetings of the Joint Romanian-American Economic Commission.[10]

During the afternoon, most of the witnesses provided evidence critical of the Administration's policy. Representatives Smith, Wolf and Hall, who had earlier introduced House resolutions disapproving the President's waiver request, reiterated their opposition. The only surprise came from Jeri Laber of Helsinki Watch. 1985 was the first time in three years that the organization had opposed MFN renewal. However, this year members of the organization found themselves in a "quandary." On the one hand, Romania was the most "egregious offender" of human rights in Eastern Europe. On the other hand, MFN was America's principle means of leverage to modify Bucharest's behavior. As a result, the organization proposed suspending Romanian MFN for six months. During this time Washington could assess Romania's commitment to internationally recognized human rights, and the results of the assessment would determine MFN resumption.[11]

While this solution appeared practical, the Commerce Department representative quickly pointed out that a temporary suspension of MFN would have the same effect as a permanent suspension. Once MFN was suspended, trade would not "bounce back quickly after a reinstatement of MFN." Since trade took a long time to develop to become mutually advantageous, any interruption produced loss of confidence and loss of profit. Further, American importers would be the initial losers in a temporary suspension. They were bound by purchase orders at contracted prices, and they would have to pay the additional duties imposed on the

Romanian imports.[12] Finally, any temporary suspension of MFN at this point in time would interrupt a major sale of power turbines for Romania's nuclear energy program, a sale which would generate about 1,000 new jobs and keep 6,000 other workers employed.[13] In sum, temporary suspension was not economically viable from the American standpoint. Ironically, two years later to the day, Romania would terminate her privileged trade status with America, rather than accept the temporary suspension of MFN.

Bucharest and Moscow

Concern about Romania's human rights practices extended far beyond Washington. As Ceausescu's cult of personality continued to grow, its corresponding requirement to intensify repression of difference and individuality began to embarrass other Eastern Bloc countries. Most disturbed was Budapest, which believed that Ceaùsescu deliberately intended to eliminate Magyar culture in Romania. Budapest television permitted journalists and newscasters to publicly criticize Romania's repressive practices.[14] These telecasts had little precedent among Eastern Bloc nations, which had traditionally agreed not to criticize the internal politics of a fellow CMEA country.

At the same time that Bucharest told the United Nations Human Rights Committee in January, 1986, that there was no deprivation of freedom in Romania, new efforts to organize dissidents into political action groups appeared.[15] The short-lived Romanian Association for the Defense of Human Rights began in 1986 with chapters in Bucharest, Sibiu and Reghin. Their charter included a thorough critique of Romania's human rights record. Other dissidents viewed themselves as heirs to the platforms of the longtime outlawed Liberal Party and National Peasants Party. In November, 1985, a small group of dissidents formed Romanian Democratic Action. Its goals were similar to those of the old Liberal Party, and called for parliamentary democracy and a mixed economy. In 1986, several people formed the National Peasant Youth Group which wanted guaranteed civil liberties.[16] While these groups had neither political influence nor large membership, as underground organizations they provided the West with still more evidence of Romanian repression.

Demands for greater political and social freedom also came from Moscow. While the American Congress considered the future of American-Romanian relations, Ceausescu attended the 27th Congress of the CPSU. The February 24-28 meeting was the first Party Congress under Gorbachev's control. He seized the moment, and made the 27th Congress an historic meeting. The watch words were *perestroika*, or restructuring, and *glasnost*, or openness. According to Gorbachev, perestroika was a policy "of accelerating the country's social and economic progress and renewing all spheres of life." [17] Glasnost meant the "democratization of the atmosphere;" a need for "more light!" The Party should know everything, "truth" was the main goal.[18]

The 27th Congress adopted the 12th Five Year Plan, 1986-1990, and set up economic guidelines through the year 2000. Gorbachev saw increased consumer goods as Moscow's primary goal, followed by overall economic growth and continued appropriations for defense.[19] The new party leader wanted to improve the life of the Soviet citizen, this meant restructuring economic priorities. The Soviet Union lacked competent managers, and those with the most talent served in the military-industrial complex. To provide increased consumer goods, Gorbachev had to curb military development to transfer competent management staffs to operate consumer oriented industries.

However, no domestic improvement was possible without a favorable international environment. Gorbachev recognized the multipolar and interdependent nature of contemporary international relations.[20] He was willing to make "peaceful coexistence" not a a tactical "breathing spell," but the long term goal of Soviet foreign policy. Confrontational foreign policies were incompatible with improved consumer living. Consequently, Gorbachev called for nuclear arms reductions, and peaceful means of conflict resolution. While these changes would all take time, too much for some critics, the 27th Congress of the CPSU certainly made the Soviet citizen the object of Moscow's attention. The Congress also indicated that those citizens would have far greater freedom, socially, politically and economically, than they had ever known under any previous Communist leader.

The day before the Congress closed, Ceausescu addressed the delegates. Needless to say, he had little intent to implement *perestroika* and *glasnost* in Romania. However, rather than be fractious, Ceausescu emphasized the "diversity of paths to socialism." While commending Gorbachev's call for disarmament, he believed that any agreement between East and West depended on proposals made by both sides. This statement implicitly criticized Gorbachev since Moscow had recently rejected Reagan's latest proposal without providing an alternative.[21]

Before leaving Moscow, Ceausescu and Gorbachev met privately on

February 28. The Romanian and Soviet media gave identical press releases which described the talks as "friendly and frank," indicating that there were differences of opinion. One issue which rankled Gorbachev was Ceausescu's illusion to the fact that Moscow appeared slow to take the initiative in disarmament.[22] The two men also talked about economic issues without resolution. Prominent in their talks was Romania's reluctance to sign a long term bilateral accord with Moscow for technological and economic cooperation through the year 2000. In November, each of the CMEA nations, except Romania, had signed agreements with Moscow legalizing and promoting enterprise-to-enterprise foreign contracts within the Bloc.[23] Gorbachev hoped that Romania would sign a similar agreement in the future.

While Ceausescu refused to make any commitments in February, he knew that he would soon have to reach an agreement with Moscow. His near fanatical commitment to eliminate Romania's hard currency debt meant that exports held "prime place" in the economy. In February, he told members of the Central Committee that "everyone should understand that export tasks are not optional;" they were "compulsory."[24] In return, the cost of imports had to be reduced. Bucharest needed cheap sources of energy and raw material, and that criterion forced Romania to increase her dependence on the Soviet Union. During the last week in May, Ceausescu returned to Moscow and signed a bilateral accord agreeing to the provisions of the CMEA Complex Program for economic and technological cooperation through the year 2000. As a result, Romania increased her food exports to Moscow in return for increased deliveries of energy and raw materials.[25] By 1987, Soviet sources reported that the two countries had established five joint ventures, four in Moscow, one in Romania.[26]

Congress, Human Rights and the 1986 Waiver

Meanwhile, the issues raised at the Senate hearings in Washington in February, continued to irritate a number of Congressmen. To some, Romania appeared daily to become more repressive. On March 27, Larry Pressler, who had chaired the February hearings, and Richard Lugar of Indiana introduced a " Sense of the Senate" resolution. S. Res. 372 urged the State Department to encourage Romania to improve its record on human rights and religious freedom before the Senate began its 1986 MFN deliberations.[27]

Although two weeks later, Ceausescu told the Swiss daily, *Tribune de*

Geneve, that "in Romania there is no human rights problem," members of the House disagreed.[28] On May 1, Gus Yatron of Pennsylvania urged his colleagues to adopt a resolution similar to that introduced by Pressler and Lugar in the Senate. As Chairman of the Subcommittee on Human Rights and International Organizations, he wanted Romania to release its political prisoners, ensure the free distribution of Bibles, improve its treatment of ethnic minorities, and continue to work on resolving outstanding emigration cases.[29]

On May 20, Philip Crane asked House members to support his request that the President not renew Romanian MFN. He had visited Bucharest the previous July. He recounted conversations he had with Catholic priests and Pentecostal and Baptist clergymen. All described the government's inhuman treatment of prisoners of conscience. From the Romanian people's viewpoint, America's continued renewal of MFN meant that Washington did not care about Bucharest's repressive policies.[30] On the following day, Paul Trible echoed Crane's sentiments and urged the Senate to pass legislation suspending Romanian MFN for 6 months.[31]

While these exhortations did not produce any legislation, they were certainly early warning signals that MFN renewal would face strong opposition. Legislation had already been introduced the previous November by Representatives Smith, Wolf and Hall in the House and by Senators Trible and Armstrong in the Senate suspending Romanian MFN for six months. Ambassador Gavrilescu's reports attested to the growing Congressional unrest. On June 2, Ceausescu responded. He announced a new amnesty which granted full pardons for people serving up to five years imprisonment, and reduced sentences for those serving between five and ten years. The major beneficiaries were prisoners of conscience, many of whom were freed, while others had their sentences shortened by about two to three years.[32]

The amnesty was well timed. Accounts of Ceausescu's decision, along with a State Department announcement that Bucharest intended to permit 1,000 more people to emigrate than scheduled, appeared in the American press on June 3.[33] Coincidentally, this was the same day that President Reagan notified Congress of his decision to extend the emigration waiver authority for Romania, and renew her MFN. In his message, Reagan noted Romania's improved emigration record, but shared the concerns of Congress regarding Bucharest's restrictions on religious liberties. His decision to extend was made with "difficulty." He urged Ceausescu's regime to permit "substantial importation" and "legal distribution" of Protestant Bibles, and to ease government restrictions against Nazarenes and "unofficial" Baptists. Further, he wanted Bucharest to ease measures that discouraged construction and repair of churches, and which had forced the demolition of a number of these religious facilities for building code violations. The State Department would "vigorously" pursue these issues and give him progress reports every six months.[34]

Reagan knew that his message had two audiences. This first part was designed to reduce Congressional opposition to his decision. However, the remaining portion indicated that the White House was far less bothered by Romania's religious practices than was the legislature. He noted that Bucharest's efforts "to discourage religion should not be allowed to overshadow the widespread practice of religion in Romania especially among the Protestant denominations." Protestantism was growing faster in Romania than in any other country in Eastern Europe. At present, Romania had over 1,000 functioning Baptist churches, more than 4,000 churches of other denominations and some 8,100 Orthodox churches.[35] Implicitly, the President suggested that these were not insignificant numbers in a country the size of Oregon.

On June 10, 1986, the House Subcommittee on Trade held hearings on the President's decision for the first time since 1983. While most of the witnesses represented human rights organizations, several businessmen appeared at the hearings and nearly a dozen sent letters supporting the President's position.

Congressmen Hall, Wolf and Smith presented the initial testimony, and called for Congress to adopt their resolution, H.R. 3955, to suspend Romanian MFN for six months. Wolf described Romania's human rights record as a "knee jerk" reaction to Congressional pressure. When the Senate Foreign Relations Subcommittee on Trade held hearings the previous July, Romania released Father Calciu. When The Senate Foreign Relations Committee held hearings in March, Bucharest released more dissidents. And now, when "this distinguished committee" considered adding language to a trade bill which would suspend Romanian MFN, Ceausescu permitted another 1,000 Romanians to emigrate.

Wolf noted that President Reagan told Congress that he made his decision to renew MFN because it contributed to "important exchanges on human rights and emigration." Wolf argued that "if the situation in Romania demonstrates a success in this regard, then the status of foreign policy and U.S. influence abroad is in serious trouble."[36] As a member of the Subcommittee, and as a person totally in agreement with

Wolf's position, Phil Crane asked the Congressmen questions so that
they could expand their testimony, and elaborate on Bucharest's
appalling human rights record. Smith explained that Romania's Department of Cults recognized 14 religious denominations, and, when
interviewed, leaders of these groups urged Congress to renew Romania's MFN. The recognized religions survived by staying "within very
carefully defined parameters," which included not criticizing the government. Ceausescu employed a policy of "selective terror" against those
who did criticize.[37] By arbitrarily arresting some dissidents rather than
others, the government undermined any opposition efforts to mount a
large protest.

The last witnesses before the noon recess was Counselor Derwinski
of the State Department, who was accompanied by Thomas Lynch, the
Desk Officer for Romania, and several other State Department
officials. Derwinski decided to provide Subcommittee members with a
copy of his prepared statement, and use his remaining time to challenge
the "pattern" of the morning's testimony. He reminded his audience that
the Jackson-Vanik Amendment related to emigration. "It is not
intended to provide for religious freedom in Romania or anywhere
else." Romania also maintained some foreign policy "postures" which
America considered useful and independent of Moscow. He called them
"postures" because some Congressmen thought that Romania adopted
foreign policy positions solely for tactical reasons. Some of these
postures included facts, the fact that Warsaw Pact countries did not
practice maneuvers in Romania, the fact that Romania did not
participate in the invasion of Czechoslovakia, and the fact that presently
two United States naval vessels would enter the Black Sea and visit the
Romanian port of Costanza. Romania had also just resolved a family
unification case at the request of Phil Crane. While some would argue
that "the Romanian authorities do this just to maintain Jackson-Vanik
benefits," he believed that the opposite was true. Jackson-Vanik gave
the United States leverage to facilitate family reunification cases, and to
maintain emigration.[38]

During the afternoon, the Subcommittee heard testimony covering a
wide range of positions. Those supporting the President's decision included representatives from a number of export-import companies, who
had obvious reasons for wanting Romania to retain her MFN. Shortly
after the hearings, several of those who testified joined a new business
lobby, ABIT, American Businesses for International Trade. This group
aimed to insure that their trade interests were represented at appropri-

ate Congressional hearings, which would include those involving Romania in 1987.[39]

Other Administration supporters included Warren Eisenberg and Alfred Moses who replaced Jack Spitzer as the representative of the B'nai B'rith and the Conference of Presidents of Major American Jewish Organizations. They saw a six month suspension of MFN as useless, it would not bring the Romanians "into line." Romania did not need MFN, she could live without it. The present system of Congressional review was effective and should be maintained.[40] John Crossley, who represented the Christian Rescue Effort for Emancipation of Dissidents, Eastwatch International and Reference Point: Reality, not only concurred but challenged the testimony of Congressmen Wolf, Smith and Hall. Crossley had visited Romania over 30 times in the past ten years. He had monitored Romanian human rights throughout this period. Americans failed to realize that Romania was an "Orthodox country." There were 18 million orthodox believers in Romania. This gave the Orthodox Church a position of power similar to that of the Catholic Church in Poland. Listening to some Congressional testimony, one would assume that "Romania is a Baptist country, and that pastors being hung by their wrists is a matter of daily occurrence. It is really just not that way."[41]

Congressman Steny Hoyer from Maryland spoke at the hearings as Co-chairman of the United States Helsinki CSCE Commission. He recognized that Romania's continued poor record on human rights made a decision to renew MFN more and more difficult both for the Administration and for Congress. However, he opposed the present options under Congressional consideration. A six month suspension was tantamount to revocation. Further, were Romania willing to accept the suspension, would or could Bucharest affect the changes Congress wanted within six months? Furthermore, would the "explicit introduction of preconditions beyond emigration, such as respect for religious and minority rights, make leverage more or less feasible?" Finally, if Congress passed legislation to broaden the Jackson-Vanik criteria, would this adversely affect Washington's future relations with Moscow and other Eastern Bloc countries? While the present system had its flaws, he believed it was better than the proposed alternatives.[42]

Former Ambassador David Funderburk led the opposition to the President's decision. "What does it take to wake up the U.S. Government to the reality of Romania's tyrannical regime and its threat to U.S. national security interests?" Funderburk attacked the State Department for naivete in dealing with Bucharest. He described Romania's "endless disregard for basic human rights," and urged Congress to revoke Romanian MFN.[43] The Heritage Foundation representative, Juliana Geran Pilon, agreed with Funderburk as did Laszlo Hamos. While Pilon suggested that Ceausescu's independent foreign policy positions received prior approval from Moscow,[44] Hamos vilified the regime's treatment of ethnic Hungarians as "tales of horror" and called for Congress to no longer indulge the "brutal dictator," Nicolae Ceausescu.[45] While representatives from Helsinki Watch and Christian Response International shared the views of Hamos and Pilon, they preferred to suspend, rather than revoke, Romania's MFN to affect desired changes.[46]

Two days after the hearings closed, Representative Crane introduced a resolution to the House, H.R. 475, to disapprove the extension of the President's waiver authority with respect to Romania. However, since the Senate introduced no parallel resolution, Crane moved to discharge the House Ways and Means Committee from considering H.R. 475. However, he used his July 29 discharge motion to urge his colleagues to draft legislation making human rights the criteria for awarding MFN to a Communist country.[47] Curiously, no one questioned why he did not make human rights practices the criterion for all countries seeking MFN treatment from the United States. After considerable discussion of Romania's human rights record, which included supporters of MFN renewal, the House decided to table Crane's discharge motion by a vote of 216-190.[48] The vote indicated that there was insufficient support for any motion of disapproval in the House, and effectively ended discussion on H.R. 3599, calling for a six month suspension of Romania's MFN.

On August 1, the Senate Subcommittee on International Trade held a one day hearing on Romanian MFN, including S. 1817, the Trible-Armstrong resolution to suspend Romanian MFN for six months. The Administration sent Assistant Secretary of State, Rozanne Ridgway, to present the President's position. Simply put, Romania had fulfilled the emigration requirement of the Jackson-Vanik Amendment. Further, the arrangements worked out with Bucharest the previous summer worked. Romania no longer granted exit visas to the United States without prior approval of the candidate's eligibility from the American Embassy. This prevented people from being "trapped" between the two country's regulations. Ridgway noted that the President had made his decision only with great difficulty, in spite of Romania's emigration record. "What is it that today makes our task here more challenging than its has ever been?" she asked. "It is, I believe, as the President's June 3 report to Congress made clear, the associated questions of religious rights issues and the treatment of the Romanian people across a broad range of human rights principles."[49]

Ridgway aimed to steal the thunder from Administration opponents. She conceded that dealing with Bucharest forced the United States to make "tough choices" involving moral issues. She agreed that the Ceausescu regime destroyed churches on the pretext of building code violations, she agreed that the regime systematically interfered with individual freedoms, and she agreed that Romania had implemented draconian economic measures to offset economic mismanagement.[50] While all of these issues were significant, none had to do with the Jackson-Vanik emigration requirement. Under questioning, she told Senator John Danforth of Missouri that "one has to walk right straight down the line. Jackson-Vanik is emigration." Congress established a criterion, and two countries accepted the standard, Romania and Hungary. If Congress wanted to change the standard, then it could. However, "if we are prepared to say, now, it wasn't emigration, it was something else; it was a broader view, and we now wish to go by that standard and Romania cannot meet it, then you also have to be prepared – for the people standing in line for emigration – to say to each of them, sorry, it is all over."[51]

Franklin Vargo, of the Commerce Department, was the other Administration witness. He attacked the concept of MFN suspension. From the vantage point of business, there was no difference between termination and suspension. "Temporary suspension would not merely be a strong warning." Once severed, albeit for six months, market relationships could not easily be restored. More than 130 firms did business with Romania. Suspension would force American importers to find new suppliers, while Romania would find new sources for needed imports. American exporters could not simply move back into Romania after six months and ask their West German and Japanese competitors to give them back their suspended markets.[52]

Further, suspended MFN would not prove critical to Romania's economy. She would lose about $300 million in exports to the United States, which represented only 5% of Romania's annual exports to the West. MFN suspension would also impact the American labor force. The Romanian export market was about the same size as Austria, and larger than Greece or Finland. The Commerce Department estimated that MFN interruption would cost America about 5,000 jobs, without any guarantee that the MFN suspension would improve Romania's human rights record.[53]

One of the few voices supporting the Administration's position was Senator Pressler, co-author of the March, 1986, "Sense of the Senate" which urged Romania to improve her human rights practices. Pressler had just returned from a meeting with Ceausescu in Bucharest.[54] The Senator had reached the conclusion that the Jackson-Vanik language only applied to emigration. To broaden it to include human rights concerns was "not only fraught with danger, but also virtually useless in dealing with the Soviet Bloc." Those legislators who wanted to terminate or suspend Romanian MFN were in effect unilaterally "changing the rules." There was no reason to assume that MFN suspension would bring about any human rights improvements in Romania. "Life in Romania is no tea party; conditions are harsh, the economy is in shambles, and the government offers few guarantees for human freedoms." However, 160,000 Romanians now resided in the West as a result of the leverage afforded by annual MFN renewal. "Legal emigration on such scale is not an option anywhere else in the Soviet Bloc. Make no mistake – if Romania's MFN status is suspended or revoked, Romania will retaliate by restricting or eliminating emigration."[55]

Equally impassioned pleas supporting MFN suspension came from those opposing the Administration's position. Although Senator Trible and Congressman Wolf were unavailable for testimony, since there were attending the funeral of former Governor Dalton of Virginia, Congressmen Dodd, Smith and Hall led the opposition.[56] They had support from representatives of Christian Response International, the Heritage Foundation, and the International Human Rights Law Group, and all called for a six month suspension. They based their argument on the moral ground that continued MFN implied American approval of Romania's systematic violation of internationally recognized human rights, especially the right to religious freedom. Representative Hall reminded the Senators that the House had just narrowly defeated Crane's resolution disapproving the President's waiver authority. Hall believed that had Crane's bill called for temporary suspension of MFN, it would have passed. He hoped the Senate would pass the Trible-Armstrong resolution.[57]

In spite of Hall's plea, the Senate took no action on Romanian MFN. However, their absence of action did not minimize the growing opposition against another MFN renewal. Even Bucharest took heed of Hall's warning. 190 members of the House had voted against Romania in

1986, compared to 126 in 1979 who supported Schulze's resolution of disapproval, compared to the 41 in 1975 who opposed the initial trade agreement. If the House could swing 10 votes, it could pass legislation affecting Romanian MFN.

In an effort to counter Romania's negative image in America, Ceausescu agreed in September to print 5,000 Cornilescu Bibles for the Romanian National Baptist Union. This was the Bible preferred by the Protestants, and the printing would be the first authorized since the 1920s.[58] However, the action would prove to be too little, too late. Congressional concern about human rights had grown steadily over the past ten years. While Romania had its monitors, other Congressmen served as watch-dogs for other nations' human rights practices. In September, Congress passed legislation imposing economic sanctions against South Africa for her disregard of human rights and pursuit of apartheid policies. Reagan vetoed the bill on September 26. Six days later both Houses of Congress overrode the veto, giving Reagan one of his most important foreign policy defeats.[59] The override indicated that human rights had sufficient Congressional support to make it a matter of importance for the Administration.

On the same day that the Senate overrode Reagan's veto, Paul Trible capitalized on the mood of his colleagues and asked them to support a "Sense of the Senate" resolution condemning Romania for persecuting its citizens for religious or political reasons, and for repressing Hungarian and other ethnic minorities. Quickly thirteen Senators joined Trible as co-sponsors and the Senate approved the non-binding resolution.[60]

Congressional interest in human rights, especially the South African issue, encouraged the American press to publicize human interest stories, especially those involving human rights abuse. Reports about life in Bucharest soon appeared. The *New York Times* carried a lengthy article by David Binder entitled "The Cult of Ceausescu,"[61] while *The New York Review of Books* described Romania as "unique." She was the only country in which a person could be sentenced to five years for purchasing too much food, the only country in which a person could work 46 hours a week and need 4 hours a day to shop for groceries, and was led by the only East European leader who preferred to compose lyrics for his country's new national anthem rather than entrust the task to a poet.[62]

The press gave numerous accounts of Romania's repression of her German and Magyar populations. The fact that Romania had the largest percentage of ethnic minorities, totalling 12%, of any country in

Eastern Europe, went unnoticed by most reporters.[63] Most stories described the plight of the ethnic Hungarians, whose very culture Bucharest aimed to destroy. These stories were partly fueled by Budapest. After several years of trying quiet diplomacy to improve conditions for Hungarians in Romania, Budapest made its complaints public. In creating the most open conflict among East European countries known in the Soviet Bloc, Hungarian television programs criticized Ceausescu's "cult of personality."[64] Reports that both countries had compiled accounts of each other's atrocities, in the form of histories of Transylvania, appeared in the *New York Times* in December, 1986.[65]

During the same month, the *East European Reporter* published an interview with Karoly Kiraly, who had remained in Romania following his 1978 criticism of the government. In answering questions concerning Bucharest's suppression of Hungarian culture, Kiraly made several interesting observations. Until about 1984, Ceausescu spoke of "nationalities living together." This concept recognized national minorities. Now the regime spoke of "Romanians of different languages," which denied ethnicity. Kiraly believed that Bucharest intended to "Romanise" Romania. The number of students attending ethnic schools had declined dramatically, especially the number of Transylvanian youth attending Hungarian schools. As for MFN, he had formerly supported the annual renewal. He had believed that "what is good for the country is also good for the people." This was no longer the case. "The state is incapable of strengthening the country's economy, or relieving the poverty of its people even if it can trade favorably." Consequently MFN suspension would send an "important" message to Bucharest concerning her human rights practices.[66] Kiraly's interview, although more interesting than others, proved to be but one among many stories which continued to appear well into the Spring.

Reagan and Human Rights

The press accounts affected the White House. In November, Reagan sent John Whitehead to tour Eastern Europe, including a stop in Bucharest. While there is no record of his conversation with Ceausescu, Whitehead subsequently wrote that the foreign policy goals of the Reagan White House clearly included the "observance of fundamental human rights."[67] Whitehead was Shultz's second-in-command, and in his talks with the Romanian President, he certainly advised him of Romania's declining image in America, and possibly informed him of a forthcoming announcement from the White House.

The President did not mention Romania in his 1986 Human Rights Day remarks, as he had the previous year.[68] However, he did notify Congress on January 2, 1987, of his decision to remove Romania from the list of beneficiary developing countries entitled to GSP. The 1984 amendments to the Trade Act of 1974 made "worker rights" a criterion for continued participation in GSP. Reagan decided that Romania had taken no steps to afford her workers internationally recognized worker rights, and so notified Congress that Romanian products would cease to have GSP tariff treatment effective March 1, 1987.[69]

Reagan's decision affected about 5% of Romania's exports to the United States. Of this approximately $40 million worth of goods, most items would only bear the slightly higher MFN rates and not lose competitiveness in the marketplace.[70] As for the reasons behind the President's decision, he either was genuine in his concern for human rights, or wanted to throw Congress a bone, to keep them quiet. Either reason, however, produced the same effect. Those Congressmen who opposed Romanian MFN saw the President's decision as a sign that the White House was willing to punish Romania for her human rights behavior. Furthermore, a White House announcement on February 23 to restore MFN status to Poland, suspended since 1982, gave further credence to the view that the Administration would use trade privilege to reward or punish a country for its human rights behavior. The Warsaw government had given amnesty to political prisoners in September, 1986, and three months later included three former Solidarity members in a government advisory council.[71] To Congressmen concerned about human rights, Reagan's action appeared to reward Poland for her political liberalization.

Congress and Romania's Human Rights

Eager to capitalize on what appeared to be new White House thinking, Representatives Smith, Hall and Wolf introduced a resolution to the House on February 25, 1987. H.R. 1250 called for a six month suspension of Romanian MFN. During this period the Administration would monitor Romania's human rights practices, especially in the area of religious freedom. If Romania showed "substantial progress" in halting its practice of persecution and repression, the President could restore Romania's MFN subject to Congressional approval. If there was no progress, MFN would be suspended for another six months.[72] In introducing the legislation, Smith told his colleagues that he hoped the bill would send a "clear message to the Romanians that respect for human rights is the cornerstone of United States-Romanian relations."[73]

The resolution was well timed. The State Department had just released its *Country Reports on Human Rights Practices for 1986*. The report noted that political dissent was not tolerated in Romania. Criticism of the regime and its policies were "suppressed by the ubiquitous Department of State Security." In the area of human rights, major discrepancies existed between "generally accepted standards" and Romanian practice. While the report noted that religious practice was active and widespread in Romania, the government frequently restricted non-approved religious denominations, especially evangelical sects. Members of these groups came under government surveillance, often lost their jobs and social benefits, and were subject to police intimidation, beatings, and arrest.[74]

The fact that this was an Administration oriented report encouraged more Congressmen to support the Smith-Hall-Wolf resolution. By early March, 234 members of the House had co-signed a letter to Secretary of State Shultz regarding the human, cultural and self-determination rights of ethnic Hungarians in Romania.[75] On March 25, the House Foreign Affairs Committee unanimously supported a "Sense of Congress" resolution condemning Romania's repressive policies toward ethnic Hungarians. [76]

Meanwhile, Ceausescu tried to counter the growing tide in Congress. He invited a group of 60 American businessmen, most of whom were members of the United States-Romanian Economic Council, to visit Romania. He met the group on March 24, and urged them to lobby Congress to end the annual renewal of MFN. This was the "single problem" which interfered with long term business agreements. Romania needed multiyear MFN.[77] While the businessmen listened, they knew there was another problem as well. Ceausescu's decision to pay off Romania's foreign debt by severely restricting imports had given Bucharest a $503 million trade surplus with the United States in 1986. Corporate America saw Bucharest's continued commitment to this trade pattern as a problem, and to some, a more important problem than MFN renewal.

On Capitol Hill, Congressmen continued to register their disapproval of Romania's domestic policies. On March 30, Tony Hall reminded his House colleagues to support H.R. 1250 suspending Romanian MFN.[78] A week later, Representative Ernest Konnyu of California, who was an

Hungarian immigrant, introduced a bill, H.R. 1953, suspending Romanian MFN for one year or longer, until Romania provided all people religious freedom and ended her repression of ethnic Hungarians.[79]

The Eleventh Session of the Joint Romanian-American Economic Commission began its two day meeting in Bucharest on April 21. The American delegation was normally chaired by the Secretary of Commerce. However, as an indication of its displeasure with Romania, Washington sent the Deputy Secretary of Trade, Clarence Brown to lead the American contingent. Ilie Vaduva, Romania's Minister of Foreign Trade, continued to chair the Romanian delegation. While not intending to do so, the *Agerpres* release indicated that little was accomplished. While both sides paid lip-service to a goal of a $2 billion two-way trade, the newspaper account indicated no new areas for trade or investment.[80] Before leaving, Brown talked with Ceausescu. The Deputy Secretary emphasized the need for Romania to improve her human rights record. Ceausescu countered with a request for multiyear MFN.[81] There is little evidence to suggest that either side heard what the other said.

The day after the meeting, Senator Trible introduced a bill to suspend Romanian MFN for six months. S. 1093 required the President to report to Congress every 60 days on the human rights situation in Romania, including such issues as freedom of emigration, religious, political and ethnic rights, and access to Bibles and restoration of places of worship.[82] Over in the House, Representatives Konnyu and Lantos of California along with John Porter of Illinois introduced legislation on April 27 to suspend Romanian MFN until Bucharest recognized and protected fundamental human rights.[83]

Supporters of suspending Romanian MFN were unsure of the Administration's position. They anticipated that in the final analysis, the White House would defer to State Department pressure, and recommend MFN renewal. The State Department did not want to terminate Romania's MFN. If nothing else, the annual renewal process gave the Department diplomatic leverage to affect change in Romania. However small the changes, they justified continued MFN from the Department's viewpoint.

The Chadha case had made change by Congressional resolution unconstitutional. Legislation approved by both houses and signed by the President was the only way Romania could lose her MFN. Separate legislation affecting Romania could be initiated, but, even if both houses concurred, the President could easily veto the bill. In this event, few

Congressmen would incur the wrath of the President by overriding him on a relatively insignificant issue. Consequently, proponents of MFN suspension looked to amend a major piece of legislation, a bill significant enough to enable Congress to override a veto if necessary. Such a bill already was in Congress. Romania's trade surplus with the United States was merely the tip of an iceberg. In 1986, America had a trade deficit of $156 billion, which continued to grow to $171 billion by the end of 1987. The House had passed trade legislation in 1986, but without any Senate action, H.R. 4800 died. However, the continued deficit and notion by some legislators that the American economy was growing less competitive, encouraged members of both houses to initiate trade legislation. On January 6, 1987, Representative Gephardt of Missouri, along with 180 cosponsors, introduced H.R. 3, the Trade and International Economic Policy Reform Act. Similar to H.R. 4800, the bill was all encompassing including provisions for trade remedy reforms, new negotiating authorities, export enhancement, and agricultural exports. On February 2, 1987, Senator Bentsen of Texas, with 56 cosponsors, introduced S. 490, the Omnibus Trade Act of 1987, which contained many of the same provisions of the House bill.

The importance and significance of the trade bill soon marked it as a target for amendment by many special interest groups. On April 28, Representative Wolf urged his colleagues to support an amendment to H.R. 3 suspending Romanian MFN for six months.[84] His amendment embodied the provisions of the Trible bill introduced earlier in the week in the Senate.

On April 30, the House debated Wolf's amendment. Dan Rostenkowski of Illinois led the opposition. While agreeing with Wolf that conditions in Romania needed improvement, MFN suspension was not the answer. In fact, such a move would remove a major means of American leverage in Romania.[85] After additional debate, the House voted and accepted the amendment by a vote of 232 to 183.[86] Shortly thereafter, the House passed H.R. 3 with the Wolf amendment as Section 1501 of the trade bill. The vote gave Wolf and his followers half a loaf. The Senate still had to adopt a similar amendment.

Bucharest, Budapest and Moscow

The House vote was not Ceausescu's only source of irritation. Hungarian-Romanian relations, too, had taken a turn for the worse. The Hungarian delegate to the Third CSCE Review in Vienna had raised the issue of the poor treatment given Hungarians in neighboring states. However, these initial statements, made in December, 1986, had not mentioned Romania by name. The Romanian delegate to Vienna tried to prevent further discussion of the Hungarian minority question on the basis that it interfered with Romania's internal affairs.[87]

This soon produced a "tit for tat" approach between Hungary and Romania. Ceausescu convened a meeting of the Councils of Working People of Magyar and German Nationality in February, 1987. The delegates all agreed that there was no nationality problem in Romania.[88] Ceausescu accused Budapest of falsifying Transylvania's history, and of promoting themes prominent during the Nazi era.[89] A few days later, the Hungarian delegate to Vienna announced that Budapest would cosponsor a human rights proposal initiated by Canada and Yugoslavia. This was the first time a Bloc country had cosponsored a Western human rights resolution.[90] As the debate between Budapest and Bucharest became more heated, each country used media to publicize its position. The Western press quickly joined in promoting the discord. Human rights issues generated large readerships and the status of ethnic Hungarians in Transylvania quickly gained international attention, including the interest of a number of American Congressmen.

While Hungarian-Romanian relations deteriorated, Ceausescu received more bad news. Gorbachev wanted to visit Bucharest. Soviet Foreign Minister Eduard Shevardnadze had raised the issue the previous October,[91] and by May, Romania was the only Warsaw Pact country Gorbachev had not visited. Ceausescu reluctantly acquiesced. There were no two Warsaw Pact leaders as ideologically apart than Ceausescu and Gorbachev. Ceausescu had already announced that *glasnost* and *perestroika* were not needed in Romania. Further, Gorbachev's foreign policy initiatives had usurped Ceausescu's role in international relations. When Gorbachev embraced arms reductions, Ceausescu's "peace initiatives" fell by the wayside. Since Gorbachev wanted to improve relations with China, Ceausescu's efforts to mediate between the two powers were no longer needed.[92] Gorbachev's leadership had significantly reduced Romania's international role, and the effect of this decline was clear in Washington. Without her image of pursuing a "maverick" foreign policy, Romania had no shield behind which she could hide her human rights record.

Why then did Ceausescu agree to Gorbachev's visit? He had little choice. His decision to eliminate Romania's foreign debt, forced him to seek non-hard currency imports. Moscow had the energy sources and raw materials to make Romania's factories work. Romanian-Soviet trade grew 47% from 1985 to the end of 1986. Soviet technicians, experts and purchasing agents had reappeared in Romania after nearly 20 years. Soviet and Romanian specialists worked together to link Romania to CMEA's Mir unified power grid, to construct a gas pipeline through Romania to supply Soviet energy to Bulgaria, Greece and Turkey, and to build a nuclear power plant near Piatra Neamt. Moscow also agreed to help Ceausescu implement his latest Five Year Plan by delivering Soviet equipment to modernize Romania's metallurgical, machine-building and chemical industries.[93]

Gorbachev began his three day visit to Bucharest on May 25, 1987. Romanian radio and television broadcast live his arrival and the welcoming ceremony at Otoponi Airport. The Romanian people were confused by Gorbachev. His visit was the first made by a Soviet leader since 1976, and his eagerness to talk to people in the crowds made many people uneasy. Ceausescu had often engaged in "Russian bashing" as a means to promote his brand of national Communism. Further, Bucharest frowned on Romanians talking to foreigners. Consequently, the people were afraid to respond to Gorbachev.[94] However, Gorbachev was not afraid to speak out. He made this clear at the State Dinner given him the day of his arrival. He told his audience that Romanian-Soviet relations needed a "qualitative change." Expanded relations depended on improved product quality, and this could be best achieved by greater CMEA integration.[95]

On the following day, Gorbachev spoke to an audience of several thousand hand-picked officials at a Friendship Rally in Palace Square, Bucharest. Aware that his address was to be broadcast live over Romanian radio and television, he decided to take advantage of this opportunity to spread his message of reform to the Romanian people. He told them that he understood that Romania had "a number of difficult problems" which affected "daily life." Moscow too had problems, but had found a solution. The guiding theme of Soviet life was *perestroika*, the "restructuring of all aspects of the life of society–unprecedented in scale, revolutionary in nature." Further, in January, 1987, the CPSU Central Committee embraced "democratization," an openness which was "an indispensable condition for the development of democracy." Were these twin pillars a panacea to Soviet problems? "Of course not. After all, openness and criticism affect the interests of real people. . . .

Socialism is dear to all of us, we all want it to look as attractive as possible. But if some shortcomings are hushed up, they will then inevitably grow."[96]

Although *glasnost* and *perestroika* were the main points of the address, they were not the only issues which provoked Ceausescu. Gorbachev wanted Romania to participate more fully in CMEA. He also discussed a couple of points which had special implication for Romania. Social and economic restructuring required competent personnel, not people promoted because of nepotism. As for nationality problems, Gorbachev reminded his audience that Lenin attached great importance "to everything that had to do with national relations, and the great sensitivity and tact that he demanded in dealing with these problems. I think that Lenin's behests on this score are still topical today."[97]

During his final day in Romania, Gorbachev visited residential districts, markets – which overflowed with food for the occasion, schools and urban areas.[98] Before departing, the two leaders signed a joint communique. The language indicated that Ceausescu had agreed to be more cooperative within CMEA. The press release stated that both men agreed to assume "responsibility" not only for the welfare of their own countrymen, but to the "common cause of socialism."[99] Further, Romania agreed to establish mixed enterprises with Moscow to produce goods for Third World export; an arrangement reminiscent of the Sov-Roms after World War II. Ironically, the communique indicated far greater agreement in foreign affairs, than Romania liked to profess, and far less agreement internally than would be expected between two socialist countries.

A few days after Gorbachev left, Ceausescu sent a delegation to Budapest to discuss the nationalities issue. Apparently Gorbachev refused to mediate the squabble, but encouraged bilateral talks to end the dispute. However, press statements following the talks indicated that the two sides were far apart. Since Ceausescu refused to admit that there was a nationalities problem, Budapest's requests to improve conditions for ethnic Hungarians in Romania fell by the wayside.[100] Without resolution, each country chose to go its own way. Budapest decided to keep public Romania's mistreatment of ethnic Hungarians through the press and international fora; a decision which would provide more ammunition for Congressmen in Washington. If Bucharest's human rights practices were criticized by a fellow Warsaw Pact country, those practices were certainly below the standards required for MFN renewal.

Trade Bills and Romanian MFN

Meanwhile in Washington, advocates of suspending Romanian MFN were celebrating their recent success in Congress. The House vote on April 30 to approve the trade bill included a six month suspension of Romanian MFN. These advocates were further heartened by testimony given a week later before the United States CSCE. The May 5 hearings focused on the status of Hungarian minorities in Romania and Czechoslovakia. Thomas Simons, a Deputy Assistant Secretary of State, presented the Administration's position. The White House had no intention of becoming involved in the Hungarian-Romanian debate concerning the treatment of ethnic minorities, nor in the dispute concerning historical rights to Transylvania. The President had nothing to gain by taking sides in the debate. Consequently, Simons limited his statement to Romanian MFN. Renewal was primarily based on Romania's emigration policy in terms of the Jackson-Vanik criteria. And within this construct, MFN renewal had made real progress measured by the thousands of Romanian emigrants now living in the West.[101]

However, most of the others who either testified or submitted written statements felt no such constraints. They viewed the hearings as an opportunity to provide as much evidence as possible about Romania's mistreatment of its ethnic Hungarians. Testimony included a presentation by Laszlo Hamos, in behalf of Geza Szocs, a report from Helsinki Watch and lengthy statements from Michael Szaz of the American-Hungarian Federation and Istvan Gereben of the Coordinating Committee of Hungarian Organizations.[102]

In an effort to counter the changing mood in Congress, Romanian Ambassador Gavrilescu launched a vigorous campaign. He sought support from the academic community. Meeting with professors, he described Romania's problem as an image problem created by a few religious groups in the United States.[103] The Romanian Embassy invited representatives from a number of religious denominations to attend a choral presentation by forty Jewish boys and girls from Iasi singing Yiddish songs.[104] On May 8, a delegation from the Romanian Grand National Assembly arrived in Washington. They met with Speaker of the House, Jim Wright, talked with Senate and House committee chairpeople, and visited John Whitehead, the Deputy Secretary of State. Throughout their stay, the delegation members lobbied everyone they could to support Romanian MFN.[105]

However, Representatives Hall and Wolf retaliated in Congress. In a last minute effort to discourage the President from requesting his annual waiver, both men elaborated on the reasons why the House had adopted their amendment to suspend Romanian MFN. They aimed their May 27 and May 28 remarks directly at the White House. Wolf asked his audience whom the Administration would support: a repressive Romanian regime, or the Romanian people?[106]

The Last Waiver

On June 2, 1987, President Reagan sent his decision to Congress. Romania would keep its MFN. In an attached statement, the President again indicated that the decision was "exceptionally difficult" to make. He had carefully weighed the strong criticisms made of Romania's human rights record. He shared the concerns of Congress and others about Romania's violations of basic human rights. However, MFN helped people. MFN had made possible the reunification of thousands of family members. MFN was a means to affect change in Romania, and he was not about to risk these benefits.[107]

In spite of the fact that the House had already indicated its position on Romanian MFN, the Subcommittee on Human Rights and International Organizations held hearings on "Human Rights in Romania and Its Implications for U.S. Policy and Most Favored Nation Status." Representatives Smith, Hall and Wolf began the testimony. The three were extremely disappointed by the President's decision. MFN no longer helped a "substantial number of people" as Reagan suggested.[108] In completing his testimony, Frank Wolf remarked that "the citizens of Romania are looking to Premier Gorbachev as the great liberator, the champion of human rights, because they see the continuation of MFN by the United States as support of President Ceausescu."[109]

The only other witnesses called before the Subcommittee were Richard Schifter, Assistant Secretary of State for Human Rights and Humanitarian Affairs, and Thomas Simons, Deputy Assistant Secretary of State. Schifter presented the rationale for the President's decision. Conceding that there still were problems within the emigration process, the Administration believed that the "situation in Romania is better today that it would have been without MFN." The President was well aware of Congress's concerns and took special note of the House's vote to suspend MFN. In making his decision, he made a judgement call and decided that he could not "in good conscience end MFN at this time."[110]

Much due to the fact that the Chairman of the Subcommittee, Gus Yatron, wholeheartedly supported Representatives Smith, Hall and Wolf, he permitted the three Congressmen to sit with the Subcommittee and participate in questioning the witnesses. They vented their anger over the President's decision on Schifter. They questioned him on everything from Romania's affiliation with the PLO to Bucharest's efforts to sell Dacia automobiles in America.[111]

The questioning grew intense. Hall told Schifter, "I get the impression when you read your statement and the way you have answered questions that you have not read your own human rights reports of not only a couple of years ago, but this year, because it seems to me—." Schifter interrupted. "Congressman, that is simply not so. I certainly do read the reports, and I have read the report on Romania." The questioning continued. Hall accused Schifter of being "cynical" and "not particularly an advocate of human rights, especially when it comes to Romania." Schifter finally exploded. He said, "Congressman, let me just tell you something. Just last week, I was in the concentration camp in Poland, in which my mother and father were gassed to death. I know more about human rights, sir, than you do."[112]

Schifter's outburst ended the nastiness. The questioning continued but soon both sides realized that there was no room for compromise. Schifter had described the President's decision as a "judgement call." This meant that there were arguments supporting two positions. The President had heard both sides, and he had made a decision. In choosing to renew MFN, he had consciously chosen not to suspend MFN.

Two days later, during a Senate discussion of the Omnibus Trade and Competitiveness Act of 1987, William Armstrong, of Colorado, and Christopher Dodd, of Connecticut, along with several other Senators, proposed amending the bill to suspend Romanian MFN for six months. The cosponsors knew that if the Senate approved the amendment, which was identical in language to that approved by the House on April 30, a final trade bill passed by both houses would include MFN suspension. In view of the Chadha decision, this was the only way Congress could override the President's MFN renewal decision.

Since Senate approval was crucial, Armstrong made a lengthy impassioned plea to his colleagues. The purpose of the suspension was to make it "unmistakably clear to the Government of Romania that we are dead serious about human rights." The suspension was not termination. MFN would be automatically restored after six months without the President or Congress taking any action. Thereafter, MFN would be renewed every six months depending on a Presidential determination that Romania had made "substantial progress in halting the persecution . . . of its citizens on religious and political grounds, and the repression. . . . of Hungarians and other ethnic minorities within Romania." Congress could override the President's decision by passing a joint resolution of disapproval.[113]

Armstrong reminded the Senate of America's responsibilities as the "leader of the free world." The purpose of the amendment was to show that America was "serious about linkage" between MFN status and human rights and emigration.[114] He cited a recent article written by Mihai Botez, a Romanian dissident whom Bucharest refused to let emigrate. Botez noted that through MFN, "the West has proved to be associated with the most incompetent, backward, and injurious to the people alternative of Communism."[115] Armstrong did not intend to let this association continue.

Senators Lloyd Bentsen of Texas, Bob Packwood of Oregon and John Danforth of Missouri led the opposition. They rested their arguments on two points: numerous leaders of the Jewish community opposed the suspension, and the annual MFN renewal process was an effective lever to promote emigration and to affect Romanian policy.

As the debate continued, evidence mounted in favor of suspension. Senators spoke of bulldozed churches and Bibles-into-toilet paper, referred to reports by Helsinki Watch and Amnesty International, described the beatings and tortures imposed on Magyar and German minorities, and cited the statements of Ambassador Funderburk and the defector, Ion Pacepa. In a last minute effort to stave off defeat, Senator Bentsen moved to table the suspension amendment. When the Senate defeated the motion to table, the handwriting was on the wall. Within minutes, Armstrong called for a vote on the amendment. By rollcall, the Senate supported the suspension 57 to 36.[116] The second half of the Congressional loaf was complete. Now all that was left was for Congress to pass the trade bill and have the President sign the legislation into law.

With hindsight, the Senate vote on June 26, 1987, sent an unmistakably clear signal to Romania that Congress had changed the rules for MFN. The vote was also the first time Congress had acted honestly in over a decade. Prior to 1987, resolutions disapproving Romanian MFN ignored the Jackson-Vanik criterion of emigration, and created new criteria: human rights, religious freedom, and minority equality. In the past, the legislature had lacked the votes, and perhaps the courage, to legally change the rules accepted by Bucharest in 1976. The House and

Senate amendment served as a public notice of the new criteria needed for Romania to retain her MFN status. MFN was linked to human rights performance as well as to emigration figures.

Ceausescu reacted predictably. He described the Senate vote as a "hostile act."[117] However, he also tried to maintain a "business as usual" attitude toward the United States. He met with Jack Spitzer, the honorary chairman of B'nai B'rith, on June 29, and discussed the recent Senate action. Spitzer hoped that Congress's actions would not affect Jewish emigration from Romania.[118] On the following day, Bucharest and Washington exchanged notes extending and amending their 1984 textile agreements.[119] The Romanian Deputy Prime Minister, Dimitrie Ancuta, and several other high ranking officials attended an Independence Day reception at the American Embassy, and Ceausescu sent Reagan a telegram recognizing the occasion.[120]

Meanwhile, the White House pressured the Senate to reconsider its vote to suspend Romania's MFN. Since the Senate had not completed debate on the trade bill, John Danforth, who had opposed the June 26 vote, introduced an amendment on July 15 which would give the President discretionary authority to suspend Romanian MFN. The President could decided not to suspend, if he reported to Congress that such application "would make it more difficult to improve human rights practices in Romania or to enhance opportunities for emigration of persons from Romania."[121]

Danforth's amendment seemed to ignore the just published Amnesty International Report on "Romania: Human Rights Violations in the Eighties."[122] But this publication did not pass unnoticed by Senator Armstrong, cosponsor of the original amendment. He had the entire document printed in the Congressional Record. Armstrong described Danforth's proposal as a "killer amendment." It reversed the position the Senate took on June 26. Worse, "this is a feel good killer amendment. This is an amendment by which Senators may reverse their position and yet affords them an opportunity to feel good about what they are doing." The amendment placed responsibility for MFN suspension on the White House, and not on Congress. This was the essence of a "feel good" amendment.[123]

The debate lasted over two hours, and opponents and proponents replayed the same arguments heard during the June debate. Armstrong feared that if the amendment came to the floor for a vote, too many Senators might reverse their position. Consequently, he moved to table Danforth's motion. The Senate agreed by a vote of 53 to 44, with 13

Senators switching votes.[124] The crisis had passed. Six days later, the Senate approved the trade bill with Armstrong's amendment, 71 to 27.[125]

On July 30, the House Subcommittee on Europe and the Middle East held hearings on the President's June 2 determination to renew Romanian MFN. In many ways this hearing was a grand *deja vu*. The House had considered Romanian MFN and human rights practices on April 30 during the trade debates, and held hearings on Bucharest's human rights record on June 24.

Rozanne Ridgway, the Assistant Secretary of State for European and Canadian Affairs, was the sole witness. She presented the Administration's opposition to the Congressional amendments. Six month suspension would cost Washington the limited access and influence it had on Romanian policy. Further, MFN restoration would be far more difficult than suggested by its proponents. The new amendment broadened the Jackson-Vanik mechanism. It required "substantial progress" in a variety of human rights areas. What was "substantial"? If the Administration worked for six months to resolve four family reunification cases, was this "substantial"? Successive administrations had opposed broadening the Jackson-Vanik criteria, and the Reagan Administration did so as well.[126]

Committee member Tom Lantos began the questioning, and made a couple of statements that clearly indicated the difference between human rights in 1987, and human rights in 1975. Emigration numbers "is a total misreading of Jackson-Vanik. . . . It is my humble opinion that it is a perversion of Jackson-Vanik if the Department uses emigration figures as an index of how human rights are observed in a country." "Human rights are indivisible . . . You will be talking about emigration figures, and we will be talking about human rights in general. That is our concern."[127]

Although not a member of the Subcommittee, Frank Wolf took advantage of his friendship with Tom Lantos to join in the questioning. While not attacking Ridgway with the same venom he used on Schifter, Wolf took advantage of the situation to continue to criticize the Administration. He complained to Ridgway that if the Administration was so opposed to the MFN suspension legislation, why did they not talk to supporters of the amendments. Wolf portrayed the Administration as aloof. Sponsors of the bills had asked to see the President, but he refused to see them. "Never once did you, did Under Secretary Whitehead, did Secretary Shultz, did anyone in the White House call to say listen, we have sincere problems with this and let's go over this language. . . . On other issues when the Administration is interested in having my vote . . . they are not reluctant to call." But no one called anyone in either the Senate or the House.[128]

Ridgway concluded her testimony reminding the Congressmen that MFN also had an economic aspect. MFN suspension was tantamount to revocation. Contracts were not written for six months. She was not there to defend American business, however, it was an issue that Congress should keep in mind.[129] However, House and Senate supporters of MFN suspension had only one thought in mind, to pass the trade bill with its Romanian amendment. As a result, neither the House nor the Senate passed any resolution disapproving the President's waiver, and Romanian MFN automatically extended through July, 1988.

The Omnibus Trade Bill

Supporters of the suspension amendments turned their attention to a House-Senate conference committee which began deliberations in September. The conference was huge, involving 199 members divided into 17 subgroups responsible for ironing out differences in the 1,000 page bill. Work was slow and came to a halt following the October 19, 1987, stock market crash. When the Democratic leadership met early in 1988, it placed the Omnibus Trade Bill at the top of its agenda. [130]

In the meantime, American delegations continued to visit Bucharest. On September 1, Ceausescu received representatives of the United States Commission on Security and Cooperation in Europe. Led by Congressman Steny Hoyer from Maryland, the group was on a tour of Europe and accepted an invitation by the Grand National Assembly.[131] In mid-October, Romania hosted a pictorial exhibit, "Contemporary American Architecture." Louis Luan, the Assistant Secretary of State for Commerce, accompanied the exhibit and talked with Stefan Andrei, former Foreign Minister and now Romania's Deputy Prime Minister. Luan assured Andrei that in spite of Congressional action, the Administration wanted Romania to retain MFN.[132]

On October 19, Ceausescu welcomed the Fourteenth Session of the United States-Romanian Economic Council. Norman Heller, President of PepsiCo Wines and Spirits International, led the American delegation. Much of the discussion during the three day meeting focused on designing new markets and broadening business opportunities in both countries in the event Romania lost her MFN.[133]

Meanwhile, Congressmen Wolf kept the House abreast of the latest news of religious persecution in Romania. On September 17, he told colleagues that two more churches were bulldozed to the ground to make way for a boulevard, the Victory of Socialism Boulevard.[134] On the twenty-first, he reported that the dissident writer, Duimiru Mircescu, was sent to a psychiatric hospital, to silence him during Gorbachev's May visit to Bucharest.[135]

While Wolf reminded his colleagues of the need to suspend Romanian MFN, State Department officials argued the opposite. Deputy Secretary of State John Whitehead told reporters on October 16, that MFN suspension "might make it harder" for America to influence change in Romania. Two weeks later, Assistant Secretary of State Ridgway and Helmut Sonnenfeldt, gave the same message in their testimony to the U.S. Commission on Security and Cooperation in Europe.[136]

The October stock market crash which forced the House-Senate conference committee to postpone its work on the trade bill also postponed Romanian MFN suspension. As a result, Congressman Wolf, along with Senators Armstrong and Helms, all influential advocates of suspension, met with President Reagan on November 12. They urged the President to issue an Executive Order suspending Romania's MFN. Reagan agreed to consider the request.[137] However, when he presented his semiannual Helsinki Agreement Implementation Report on December 5, he made no comment about Romanian MFN.[138]

Meanwhile in Bucharest, events developed which would give Wolf and his colleagues even more ammunition. On November 15, workers in the Steagul Rozu truck and vehicle plant in Brasov marched out of their factory toward the center of town, where they were joined by a number of spontaneous sympathizers. The object of their anger was Ceausescu and the party as evidenced by their sacking party headquarters and smashing Ceausescu photographs and pictures.[139]

Ostensibly, the demonstration followed a government notice that due to a decline in the plant's production, several workers would be reassigned to other parts of the country. The remainder would have their pay cut, since the latest decrees tied productivity to salary.[140] However, there were other factors which prompted this first major demonstration in ten years. Principal among them was Ceausescu's program of economic austerity. Foreign goods had nearly vanished from the shelves. Ceausescu continued to blame everyone but himself and his family for Romania's continued poor economic performance. On October 5, he told the delegates at the Central Committee Party Plenum that there were no shortages of raw materials, machinery or spare parts. The problem was "miscalculation, misconduct, and mismanagement" by officials at all levels, but especially in the energy sector.[141] A week labor he extended blame to include his CMEA partners. He told them at the 43rd Session in Moscow, that they should provide more fuels and raw materials for Romania's industries, and provide more markets for her manufactures. To go further, since Romania was still a "developing" country, she should be given special preference from her industrially developed allies.[142]

Ceausescu's austerity especially affected Brasov. Situated higher in the hills, the city had winter temperatures normally below freezing. Further, the government's insistence on growing food for export left little produce for the Romanian people, and the availability of that was frequently delayed by the government's poor distribution system. Consequently, consumers sought food in the "second economy" or black market. Here the currency was Kent cigarettes and foodstuffs not seen in years were available for purchase. With the smaller paychecks, the workers at the Steagul Rozu plant could scarcely buy Kent cigarettes.[143] They were angry. They did not want to go through another winter of freezing cold and limited supplies of rationed food. While the demonstration was short-lived, the fact that the workers took to the streets, in a country whose secret police force was omnipresent, indicated that there was a limit to the degree of deprivation people were willing to tolerate.

Ceausescu quickly responded. Ignoring statements by Silviu Brucan that the overwhelming majority of Romanian Communists would disapprove of any repressive measures against the demonstrators, Ceausescu went about arresting several alleged leaders of the march.[144] However, he also announced a few days later at the National Party Congress an increase of 10% in basic wages between the summer of 1988 and 1990. He also promised greater supplies of meat and consumer goods.[145]

Representative Smith did not let the Brasov demonstration pass unnoticed in Congress. On December 15, he gave his colleagues a vivid description of the incident, albeit exaggerated. "Thousands of Romanian men and women . . . risked their jobs and faced arrest to protest publicly the repressive policies of the Ceausescu regime. . . . We owe it to them to pick up their banner in the West and plead for their rights and basic needs."[146] On the eighteenth, Frank Wolf again reminded House members of Romania's plight,[147] and three weeks later Smith and Wolf visited Romania. The Congressmen wanted to see Ceausescu, and urge him to permit international organizations, such as Amnesty International or Helsinki Watch to make an independent survey of Romania's human rights practices.[148]

Ceausescu refused to see the Congressmen. He had no desire to meet with two of the principals responsible for Romania's collapsing relations with Washington. Further, Ceausescu had reached the conclusion that continued MFN was not worth the trouble caused by America's efforts to interfere in Romania's domestic affairs. He conveyed this message at a meeting the Congressmen had with Ioan Totu, Romania's Foreign Minister. Bucharest had no interest in having outside organizations monitor her internal policies.[149]

Ceausescu Rejects MFN

On January 26, 1988, Ceausescu celebrated his 70th birthday. The party propaganda apparatus eulogized the "saintly modesty" of the General Secretary. On the following day, Ceausescu granted his seventeenth amnesty releasing all prisoners serving sentences of ten years or less. Sentences in excess of ten years were halved, and life sentences commuted to 20 years imprisonment.[150]

As the House-Senate conference committee prepared to resume its work on the trade bill, Representative Hall and his colleagues went to work to keep Congressional attention focused on suspending Romanian MFN. On February 1, Hall told House members that Charter 77, a Czechoslovakian based organization, decried the plight of Romania's people who were forced to live in a country where there was "neither heat nor light."[151] During the next three days, Congressmen Konnyu and Lantos along with Senator Armstrong all made speeches describing the inhumane conditions of life under Ceausescu. None mentioned the recent amnesty.[152]

As pressure mounted, the Administration made one last attempt to force change in Romania. On February 5, Reagan sent Whitehead to Bucharest. The Deputy Secretary of State carried a special Presidential message for Ceausescu. However, neither the message nor Whitehead's talks with the Romanian President produced any results. Whitehead told the press that "I must say in all candor that I was disappointed at not being able to convey successfully to President Ceausescu the deep feelings that my country has about human rights, and the importance of individual freedoms. . . . He seemed to resent my mention of these subjects."[153]

During his two day visit, Whitehead hosted a reception at the American Embassy. He later reported that "a number of guests were discouraged by police from meeting with me and gained access to the residence only after considerable difficulty. . . . Others were prevented from coming at all."[154] Three weeks later, Whitehead told a Human Rights Forum in New York that during his visit he "experienced first-hand evidence of Romania's human rights problems. Militia men followed my every movement by car or by foot." He saw no efforts to reform Romania's "bleak" economic situation. "The leadership, fixed on a Draconian campaign to reduce foreign debt, is either unaware of or unmoved by the growing economic chaos which has caused severe deprivation to Romanian citizens . . . "[155]

Ceausescu's treatment of Whitehead was a clear signal that continued MFN was not worth the effort America demanded. In looking at MFN from a Romanian viewpoint, former Ambassador Aggrey concluded that MFN meant "Jews, Hungarians and Christians."[156] As early as September, 1985, Romanian officials told the New York Times that there was a "limit to what we can accept . . . for MFN status."[157] Ceausescu knew that the trade bill would ultimately be passed, and with it new terms for MFN, terms which required major reforms in Romania's human rights practices. He was unwilling to make those changes. "So," according to Bogdan, "he decided to cut his losses and come out of it a hero."[158] Shortly after Whitehead left, Ceausescu notified Washington that Romania no longer wanted American MFN.[159]

Meanwhile, the House Subcommittee on Human Rights and International Organizations held hearings on "Recent Developments in U.S. Human Rights Policy." The State Department's recent publication of its Country Report on Human Rights Practices in 1987 precipitated the February 10 and 17 hearings. Testifying before the Subcommittee, Christopher Smith pointed to the Department's report on Romania. "The poor human rights picture in Romania in 1987 showed no improvement." As further evidence, Smith cited the recently published Red Horizons by Ion Pacepa describing it as a work which clearly showed the Ceausescu regime for what it truly was, a fraud.[160]

While Ceausescu told the State Department that he no longer wanted MFN, his notice also indicated that he wanted Washington to make the announcement public, not Bucharest. Since Ceausescu indicated that he did not intend for MFN termination to restrict other bilateral agreements or to sever friendly relations, Washington agreed to work out a timetable for the announcement.[161] In the meantime, members of the House-Senate conference committee on the trade bill learned of Ceausescu's decision, and quietly removed the Romanian suspension amendments from the legislation.[162]

On February 26, 1988, the State Department announced that Romania had "decided to renounce renewal of most-favored-nation subject to the terms of the Jackson-Vanik agreement." As a result, the Administration would not exercise its waiver authority, and Romanian MFN would expire on July 3, 1988. In addition, effective July 3, Romania would be ineligible for any United States government export credits through programs such as the Commodity Credit Corporation or the Eximbank.[163]

On the following day, *Agerpres* carried an article noting that Romania had informed Washington that it no longer accepted MFN renewal under the Jackson-Vanik terms. Bucharest attributed MFN problems to "certain hostile circles . . . [which] . . . used the annual renewal of . . . [MFN] . . . as a means to slander and interfere in Romania's domestic affairs." The press noted that when Bucharest conveyed its decision, the government asked for bilateral consultations to "clarify problems linked" to MFN. However, Washington had ignored this request and made the announcement prior to any bilateral talks. The article concluded on a positive note that Romania wanted to continue bilateral relations with the United States, and looked forward to eliminating obstacles impeding greater cooperation.[164] Three days later, the two countries exchanged notes extending their textile agreements through January, 1989.[165]

Without question, Ceausescu's MFN decision decreased international pressure on his domestic policies. However, within a week he found a new way to gain international criticism. In early March he convened the All Country Conference of People's Councils' Chairmen to launch his plan of "village systemization," a massive scheme to eliminate half of Romania's 13,000 villages by the year 2000. The people affected would be moved to agro-industrial centers where peasants would live in a community of residential dwellings.[166] Within days, West Germany and Hungary protested the plan. Many of the villages scheduled for destruction were home to ethnic Germans and Hungarians. Ceausescu's plan seemed to be one more step in his effort to destroy the remaining elements of German and Magyar culture. Budapest was most sensitive to the "systemization" plan in light of her continued poor relations with Bucharest. Ethnic Hungarians fled by the thousands across the border to Hungary requesting permanent residence. As tensions mounted,

Hungary permitted a huge, unofficial anti-Romanian demonstration in Budapest on June 27, 1988.[167] Bucharest responded. It described the demonstration as "chauvinistic" and "antisocialist," and closed the Hungarian Consulate in Cluj-Napoca, Transylvania, and ordered its staff to leave Romania within 48 hours.[168]

In an effort to resolve the situation, Ceausescu offered to meet with Karoly Grosz, the new party leader in Hungary. They met on August 28 in the Romanian border town of Arad. However, the talks stalled on the "systemization" issue. Budapest wanted Ceausescu to halt the program. He refused, but would permit Hungary to send a delegation to monitor the program's implementation.[169] By year's end, Hungarian-Romanian relations remained tense.

Meanwhile, Ceausescu tried to maintain relations with American businesses. A few weeks after the State Department's February announcement, the Romanian leader sent a message to the United States-Romanian Economic Council urging them to work to restore MFN. He also told his Foreign Trade Organizations to maintain the same volume of trade after MFN ended.[170] In May, he invited a group of 65 American businessmen to Bucharest. They arrived on May 3, led by Robert Robertson, vice president of ABIT, the American Businessmen for International Trade. Ceausescu spoke to the group on May 4 and urged them to work with Romanian officials to find new avenues for greater economic cooperation.[171] He especially encouraged them to reach agreements which would be unaffected by MFN termination.[172] Two weeks later, Ceausescu repeated the message in *Lumea*, adding that Romania would continue to negotiate "in good faith" with American industries and supply quality products to American markets.[173]

Ceausescu's call for greater trade had an eager audience. Businessmen on both sides of the Atlantic had worked vigorously to promote sales before the July, 1988, MFN termination date. During the first six months of 1988, American exports to Romania equalled $122 million, in contrast to $193 for the whole of 1987. Similarly, Romanian exports to the United States totalled $475 million for the first half of 1988, compared to $782 for 1987.[174] However, both sides knew that without MFN, government credits and guarantees, little new business would develop. Moreover, changes in Eastern Europe made new markets available, especially in Hungary which had MFN, credits and guarantees. Companies accustomed to dealing in East-West trade, as well as those venturing into the field for the first time, saw Budapest and other East European cities far more attractive than Bucharest.

On June 3, Reagan sent his annual waiver message to Congress. This year, for the first time since 1975, the waiver did not apply to Romania. The President told Congress that he was permitting the waiver to expire.[175] At the end of the month, the President issued a proclamation noting that effective July 3, Romanian imports, including those still in warehouses, would no longer receive MFN treatment.[176] American-Romanian relations had entered a new phase, one which would give Washington little leverage with which to influence Romanian policy.

Notes

1. CSM, February 27, 1986, p. 11.

2. *The Washington Post*, February 18, 1986, p. C14.

3. U.S., Congress, Senate Committee on Foreign Relations, Hearing Before the Subcommittee on European Affairs, *Romania: Most Favored Nation Status*, 99th Cong., 2d Sess., 1986, p. 1. Hereafter, Senate Subcommittee on European Affairs, *Romania: MFN Status*, 1986.

4. *Ibid.*, pp. 2-3.

5. *Ibid.*, pp. 5-45.

6. CSM, February 27, 1986, p. 11.

7. Senate Subcommittee on European Affairs, *Romania: MFN Status*, 1986, p. 100.

8. *Ibid.*, p. 11.

9. *Ibid.*, pp. 11-12.

10. *Ibid.*, p. 36.

11. *Ibid.*, p. 54-55.

12. *Ibid.*, p. 112.

13. *Ibid.*, p. 31.

14. Richard F. Staar (ed.), *Yearbook on International Communist Affairs, 1987* (Stanford, CA: Hoover Institution Press, 1987), p. 336.

15. [Amnesty International] *Romania: Human Rights Violations in the Eighties* , 1987, p. 11.

16. Bugajski and Pollack, *East European Fault Lines*, pp. 137-139.

17. Mikhail Gorbachev, *Perestroika: New Thinking for Our Country and the World* (New York: Harper & Row, Publishers, 1987), p. 10.

18. *Ibid.*, p. 75.

19. Abraham Becker *et al.*, *The 27th Congress of the Communist Party of the Soviet Union: A Report from the Airlie House Conference*, Rand/UCLA Center for the Study of Soviet International Behavior (December 1986), p. 26.

20. Joseph S. Nye, Jr., *et al.*, *How Should America Respond to Gorbachev's Challenge? A Report of the Task force on Soviet New Thinking* (New York: Institute of East-West Security Studies, 1987), pp. 17.

21. RFE, Situation Report, Romania/4, March 25, 1986, pp. 4-5.

22. *Ibid.*, p. 5.

23. Valerie Bunce, "Decline of a Regional Hegemony: The Gorbachev

Regime and Reform in Eastern Europe," *Eastern European Politics and Societies*, Vol. 3, No. 2 (Spring 1989), p. 253.

24. Ceausescu, *Romania On the Way* , XXIX, 306.

25. Staar (ed.), *Yearbook on International Communist Affairs, 1987*, p. 337; RFE, Situation Report, Romania/4, March 25, 1986, p. 7.

26. Vlad Georgescu, *Eastern European Politics and Societies*, Vol.. 2, No. 1, 78, n27.

27. U.S. *Congressional Record*, 99th Cong., 2d Sess., 1986, CXXXIII, S3730-S3731.

28. Ceausescu, *Romania On the Way*, XXIX, 429.

29. U.S. *Congressional Record*, 99th Cong., 2d Sess., 1986, CXXXII, E1491-E1492.

30. *Ibid.*, pp. H3014-H3017.

31. *Ibid.*, p. S6283.

32. [Amnesty International] *Romania: Human Rights Violations in the Eighties*, 1987, p. 9.

33. NYT, June 3, 1986, p. 1.

34. *Public Papers of the Presidents of the United States, Ronald Reagan, 1986*, (Washington, D.C.: U.S. Government Printing Office, 1986), I, 713.

35. *Ibid.*, p. 16.

36. House Subcommittee on Trade, *MFN Status*, 1986, pp. 18-19.

37. *Ibid.*, p. 31.

38. *Ibid.*, pp. 47-48.

39. U.S. Congress, Hearing Before the Commission on Security and Cooperation in Europe. Part II. National Minorities in Eastern Europe: The Hungarian Minorities in Romania and Czechoslovakia, *Implementation of the Helsinki Accords*, 100th Cong., 1st Sess., 1987, p. 19, hereafter, Congressional Commission on Security and Cooperation in Europe, *The Hungarian Minorities in Romania and Czechoslovakia*, 1987.

40. House Subcommittee on Trade, *MFN Status*, 1986, pp. 118-119.

41. *Ibid.*, p. 229.

42. *Ibid.*, pp. 127-130.

43. *Ibid.*, pp. 139-142.

44. *Ibid.*, pp. 149-150.

45. *Ibid.*, p. 192.

46. *Ibid.*, pp. 106-110, 204.

47. U.S. *Congressional Record*, 99th Cong., 2d Sess., 1986, CXXXII, H4963-H4973.

48. Ibid., p. H4973.

49. U.S. Congress, Senate Committee on Finance, Hearing Subcommittee on International Trade, *MFN Status for Romania*, 99th Cong., 2d Sess., 1986, pp. 41-42. Hereafter, Senate Subcommittee on International Trade, *MFN Status for Romania*, 1986.

50. *Ibid.*, p. 43.

51. *Ibid.*, p. 61.

52. *Ibid.*, pp. 51, 135.
53. *Ibid.*, p. 52.
54. RFE, Situation Report, Romania/11, October 2, 1986, p. 33.
55. Subcommittee on International Trade, *MFN Status for Romania*, 1986, p. 71.
56. *Ibid.*, p. 13.
57. *Ibid.*, p. 33.
58. U.S. Congress, Report Submitted to the Committee on Foreign Relations, Senate, and Committee on Foreign Affairs, House, by the Department of State, *Country Reports on Human Rights Practices for 1986*, 100th Cong., 1st Sess., 1987, p. 1018; *The Washington Post*, September 16, 1986, p. 22.
59. Long, U.S. *Export Control Policy*, p. 98.
60. U.S. *Congressional Record*, 99th Cong., 2d Sess., 1986, CXXXII, S14698-S14700.
61. NYT, November 30, 1986, VI, 32ff.
62. "In the Land of Decree 408," *The Economist*, November 15, 1986, p. 50; "Birth and Death in Romania," *The New York Review of Books*, October 22, 1986, pp. 10-18.
63. *The Washington Post,* October 25, 1986, p. A20.
64. *Ibid.*
65. NYT, December 27, 1986, p. 5.
66. "The Hungarian View: An Interview with Karoly Kiraly,"*East European Reporter*, Vol. 2, No. 3, pp. 436-48.
67. John C. Whitehead, "The Department of State: Requirements for an Effective Foreign Policy in the 1990s," Presidential Studies Quarterly, Vol. XIX, No.1 (Winter 1989), p. 14; NYT, November 5, 1986, p. 8.
68. *Public Papers of the Presidents of the United States, Ronald Reagan, 1986*, II, 1616-1618.
69. U.S., Congress, Communication from the President of the United States, *Removal of Romania and Nicaragua and Suspension of Paraguay from the List of General System of Preference Eligible Countries*, 100th Cong., 1st Sess., 1987, p. 1.
70. Susanne S. Lotarski, "Eastern Europe's Economic Plans May be Dimmed by Harsh Winter," *Business America*, March 30, 1987, p. 16.
71. Karen Dawisha, *Eastern Europe, Gorbachev and Reform: The Great Challenge* (New York: Cambridge University Press, 1988), pp. 246-248.
72. U.S. Congress, H.R. 1250, 100th Cong., 1st Sess., 1987.
73. U.S. *Congressional Record*, 100 Cong., 1st Sess, 1987, CXXXIII, H796, H7999, H836.
74. U.S. Congress, Report Submitted to the Committee on Foreign Relations, Senate, and Committee on Foreign Affairs, House, by the Department of State, *Country Reports on Human Rights Practices for 1986*, 100th Cong., 1st Sess., 1987, pp. 1012, 1018.
75. U.S. *Congressional Record*, 100 Cong., 1st Sess, 1987, CXXXIII E936.
76. *Ibid.*, pp. E1479-E1480.

77. Nicolae Ceausescu, *An Independent Foreign Policy for Peace and Cooperation*, ed. J. Van Kloberg, III (n.p.: The Political Science Library, n.d.), pp. 140-141; "Romania's Big Squeeze," *Eastern Europe Newsletter*, Vol. 1, No. 2 (June 17, 1987), p. 6.

78. U.S. *Congressional Record*, 100th Cong., 1st Sess., 1987, CXXXIII, E1175.

79. *Ibid.*, pp. E1407-E1408.

80. FBIS, EEU, April 27, 1987, p. H1.

81. FBIS, EEU, April 24, 1987, p. H1; RFE, Situation Report, Romania, June 19, 1987, p. 10.

82. U.S. *Congressional Record*, 100th Cong., 1st Sess., 1987, CXXXIII, S5489-S5490.

83. U.S. Congress, H.R. 2175, 100th Cong., 1st Sess., 1987.

84. U.S. *Congressional Record*, 100th Cong., 1st Sess., 1987, CXXXIII, H2546.

85. *Ibid.*, pp. H2862-H2866.

86. *Ibid.*, pp. H2867-H2868.

87. Richard F. Staar (ed.), *Yearbook on International Communist Affairs, 1988* (Stanford, CA: Hoover Institution Press, 1988), p. 309.

88. *The R.C.P. National Policy; A Just, Highly Scientific, Realistic and Humanitarian Policy. Joint Meeting of Magyar-German-Nationality Working People's Councils, February, 1987*, p. 73.

89. NYT, April 4, 1987, p. 5; NYT, May 21, 1987, p. 14.

90. Staar (ed.), *Yearbook on International Communist Affairs, 1988*, p. 310.

91. RFE, Situation Report, Romania, May 29, 1987, p. 3.

92. Otto Pick, "Problems of Adjustment: The Gorbachev Effect in Eastern Europe,"*SAIS Review*, Vol. 8, No. 1, 1988, pp. 70-72.

93. RFE, Situation Report, Romania, May 29, 1987, pp. 19-22.

94. *Ibid.*, p. 7.

95. *Ibid.*, pp. 8-9.

96. "Making the Working People's Life Richer and Fuller – Rumanian-Soviet Friendship Rally," *The Current Digest of the Soviet Press*, Vol. 39, No. 21 [June 24, 1987].

97. *Ibid.*

98. NYT, May 31, 1987, p. 5.

99. RFE, Situation Report, Romania, May 29, 1987, p. 16.

100. Staar (ed.), *Yearbook on International Communist Affairs, 1988*, p. 310.

101. Congressional Commission on Security and Cooperation in Europe, *The Hungarian Minorities in Romania and Czechoslovakia*, 1987, pp. 5-6.

102. *Ibid.*

103. Author interview of Ambassador Gavrilescu, May 21, 1987.

104. NYT, May 10, 1987, p. L5.

105. FBIS, EEU, May 11, 1987, p. H1.

106. U.S. Congressional Record, 100th Cong., 1st Sess., 1987, CXXXIII, pp. H3983, E2082.

TWEAKING THE NOSE OF THE RUSSIANS

107. *DOS Bulletin*, August 1987, p. 57.
108. U.S. Congress, House Committee on Foreign Affairs, Hearing Before the Subcommittee on Human Rights and International Organizations. *Human Rights in Romania and Its Implications for U.S. Policy and Most Favored Nation Status*, 100th Cong., 2d Sess., 1987 p. 18. Hereafter, House Subcommittee on Human Rights, *Human Rights in Romania*, 1987.
109. *Ibid.*, p. 21.
110. *Ibid.*, pp. 31-44.
111. *Ibid.*, pp. 65, 63.
112. *Ibid.*, pp. 59-60.
113. U.S. *Congressional Record*, 100 Cong., 1st Sess., 1987, CXXXIII, S8788-S8789.
114. *Ibid.*, p. S8789.
115. *Ibid.*, p. S8791.
116. *Ibid.*, pp. S8810-S8811.
117. FBIS, EEU, June 29, 1987, p. R1.
118. FBIS, EEU, July 2, 1987, p. R1.
119. *DOS Bulletin*, October 1987, p. 69.
120. FBIS, EEU, July 6, 1987, pp. R3-4; FBIS, EEU, July 6, 1987, p. R1.
121. U.S. *Congressional Record*, 100th Cong., 1st Sess., 1987, CXXXIII, S9963.
122. [Amnesty International] *Romania: Human Rights Violations in the Eighties* , 1987.
123. U.S. *Congressional Record*, 100th Cong., 1st Sess., 1987, CXXXIII, S9982.
124. *Ibid.*, p. S9994.
125. WSJ, July 22, 1987, pp. 3, 10.
126. U.S. Congress, House Committee on Foreign Affairs, Hearing Before the Subcommittee on Europe and the Middle East, *United States-Romania Relations and Most-Favored-Nation [MFN] Status for Romania*, 100th Cong., 1st Sess., 1987, pp. 23-25. Hereafter, House Subcommittee on Europe and the Middle East, *MFN Status for Romania*, 1987.
127. *Ibid.*, p. 26.
128. *Ibid.*, p. 41.
129. *Ibid.*, p. 49.
130. *Congressional Quarterly Almanac* (Volume XLIV), 100th Congress, 2nd Session, 1988 (Washington, D.C.: Congressional Quarterly Inc., 1989), p. 216.
131. FBIS, EEU, September 2, 1987, p. 29.
132. FBIS, EEU, October 19, 1987, p. 57.
133. FBIS, EEU, October 22, 1987, p. 16; FBIS, EEU, October 20, 1987, p. 41.
134. U.S. *Congressional Records*, 100th Cong., 1st Sess., 1987, CXXXIII, H7598.
135. *Ibid.*, p. H7636.
136. RFE, Situation Report, Romania/2, January 28, 1988, p. 22.

137. *The Washington Post*, November 13, 1987, p. A10.
138. RFE, Situation Report, Romania/2, January 28, 1988, p, 23.
139. *Eastern Europe Newsletter*, Vol. 1, No. 13, November 25, 1987, p. 2.
140. *Ibid.*
141. RFE, Situation Report, Romania/12, November 6, 1987, pp. 4-5.
142. *Ibid.*, pp. 13-14.
143. NYT, November 22, 1987, p. 9; "Bang went Brasov," *The Economist*, November 21, 1987, pp. 52-53; "Down With the Dictator," *Newsweek*, December 28, 1987, pp. 27-28.
144. Vladimir Tismaneanu, "Ceausescu at Seventy," *East European Reporter*, Vol. 3, No. 2 (March 1988), p. 60.
145. *Ibid.*, pp. 61-62; Staar (ed.), *Yearbook on International Communist Affairs, 1988*, p. 308.
146. U.S. *Congressional Record*, 100th Cong., 1st Sess., 1987, CXXXIII, E4828.
147. *Ibid.*, p. H11684.
148. RFE, Situation Report, Romania/2, January 28, 1988, p. 23.
149. *Ibid.*
150. See "Romania," [Amnesty International] *Human Rights in Eastern Europe and the Soviet Union; Excerpts from The 1989 Amnesty International Report* (New York: Amnesty International, 1989).
151. U.S. *Congressional Record*, 100th Cong., 2d Sess., 1988, CXXXIV, E96.
152. *Ibid.*, pp. H58, S469-S470. E169.
153. NYT, February 7, 1988, p. 6.
154. *Ibid.*
155. *DOS Bulletin*, May 1988, p. 55.
156. Author interview with O. Rudolph Aggrey, October 26, 1989, Washington, D.C.
157. NYT, September 29, 1985, p. 21.
158. Author interview with Corneliu Bogdan, January 11, 1989.
159. Mihai Botez *et al.*, "Round Table: A Turning Point in United States-Romanian Relations," *Journal of the American Romanian Academy of Arts and Sciences*, No. 12 (1989), p. 37; *DOS Bulletin*, May 1988, p. 43.
160. U.S. Congress, House Committee on Foreign Affairs, Hearings Before the Subcommittee on Human Rights and International Organizations, *Recent Developments in U.S. Human Rights Policy*, 100th Cong, 2d Sess., 1988, pp. 35-36.
161. Author interview with Corneliu Bogdan, January 11, 1989.
162. NYT, February 27, 1988, p. 3; *DOS Bulletin*, May 1988, p. 43; U.S. Congress [Conference Committee] *Summary of the Conference Agreement on H.R. 3, The Omnibus Trade and Competitiveness Act of 1988* [100th Cong., 2nd Sess.], 1988.
163. *DOS Bulletin*, May, 1988, p. 43.
164. FBIS, EEU, February 29, 1988, p. 47.
165. *DOS Bulletin*, September 1989, p. 93.

166. Richard F. Staar (ed.), *Yearbook on International Communist Affairs, 1989* (Stanford, CA: Hoover Institution Press), p. 354.

167. CSM, June 27, 1988, p. 7.

168. Staar (ed.), *Yearbook on International Communist Affairs, 1989*, p. 356.

169. Ibid.

170. Author interview of Corneliu Bogdan, January 11, 1989.

171. FBIS, EEU, May 5, 1988, p. 61.

172. FBIS, EEU, May 6, 1988, p. 55.

173. FBIS, EEU, May 18, 1988, p. 44.

174. [Department of Commerce], *U.S. Merchandise Trade Position in Midyear 1988* (Washington, D.C.: U.S. Government Printing Office, 1988), pp. 14, 19.

175. June 3, 1988, *Weekly Compilation of Presidential Documents*, Vol. 24, No. 23, p. 748.

176. June 28, 1988, *Ibid.*, No. 26, pp. 877-878.

CHAPTER XIX

POSTSCRIPT: BUCHAREST, DECEMBER 25, 1989

The First Year Without MFN

The authors planned to end this book with MFN termination, and during the following year and a half, nothing developed which warranted additional comment. However, on December 25, 1989, newspapers and radio broadcasts blared the same news and the television confirmed it: Nicolae and Elena Ceausescu were dead. Ousted, arrested, tried and executed, the "Genius of the Carpathians" and his wife were shot following a quick military trial.[1]

A Romania without Ceausescu gave rise to all sorts of possibilities, including the resumption of MFN relations between Washington and Bucharest. This consideration warranted an extension of the book through February, 1990, by which time both Congress and the Administration had taken steps signaling that a new era in American-Romanian relations could begin.

The period following MFN termination neither curtailed American-Romanian relations, nor Congressional criticism of Romania's human rights practices. Ceausescu and the White House wanted to maintain relations. The Romanian-American Trade Agreement was still in force, and the Department of State and the Bucharest Foreign Ministry continued to extend bilateral commercial accords through 1990. Of particular note were those agreements concerning cotton textiles, manmade fibers, and civilian aviation transportation.[2]

Congress, on the other hand, continued its condemnation of

Romania's human rights record. In August, 1988, Senator Frank Lautenberg and twenty-six cosponsors introduced a "Sense of the Senate" resolution. This asked for the President to inform Ceausescu that neither MFN nor other favorable trading privileges would be restored until Romania reformed its human rights practices and stopped destroying Hungarian villages in the name of "systemization." The Senate unanimously approved the non-binding resolution on August 10.[3] A month later the House and Senate introduced legislation which ended Romania's eligibility for OPIC programs, because of her "deteriorating" human and workers rights record.[4] In October, Representative Konnyu reminded his colleagues of the devastation Ceausescu wreaked on Hungarians in Transylvania. 8,000 villages were scheduled for destruction. As living conditions deteriorated, over 12,000 Romanians had fled to Hungary in search of refuge. Konnyu wanted Congress to abrogate the Trade Agreement, freeze all Romanian assets in the United States and consider recalling America's Ambassador from Bucharest.[5]

Corporate America did not share Konnyu's wrath. In spite of Romania's deteriorating human rights image, American businesses still wanted to trade with Bucharest. On November 10, the 15th Session of the United States-Romanian Economic Council opened in New York City. Delegates from both countries explored new ways to expand trade.[6] American business hoped that its Romanian trade would not follow the Polish-American example. In the years following Poland's loss of MFN, her two-way trade with America fell by 50%, from about $1.1 billion in 1980 to about $500 million annually between 1983 and 1986.[7] However, ads and goodwill could not offset the growing global awareness of Romania's callous approach to human rights. By early 1989, *The Economist* wrote that "if Communism has an evil emperor, he is Nicolae Ceausescu."[8] This image, coupled with Bucharest's success in reducing its dependence on foreign imports produced a significant decline in Romanian-American trade; a decline which at the outset appeared to parallel the Polish-American model. In 1988, two-way trade totalled about $940 million.[9] For the first six months of 1989, total trade equalled $204 million with Romania enjoying a trade advantage of over $80 million.[10]

Meanwhile, Romania's human rights practices continued to attract Congressional attention. In January, 1989, soon after Romania had signed the CSCE Vienna Concluding Documents, Bucharest announced that she would only implement those human rights provisions she considered valid.[11] On February 28, Representative Hoyer of Maryland informed his colleagues of this development.[12] The United Nations also turned its attention toward Romania. Much due to Hungarian efforts, the United Nations Human Rights Commission finally responded to numerous complaints. On March 10 it passed a resolution condemning Romania's human rights practices. Hungary joined the United States, West European and South American states in supporting this resolution, which passed 21-7.[13] The United Nations further appointed Joseph Voyname to investigate Romania's human rights abuses including those against religious and national minorities.[14]

On March 14, Hoyer again addressed his House colleagues. As Co-chairman of the United States CSCE, he felt obliged to keep the legislature abreast of Romania's human rights practices. He told them of the recent UN action, noting that as could be anticipated, Bucharest refused to permit any UN representative the right to investigate Romania's internal practices. Hoyer also mentioned the recent treatment accorded several dissidents accused of publishing an "independent manifesto."[15] This open letter criticized Ceausescu's policies. The six signers, all well known Communists, were Gheorghe Apostal, Alexandru Birladeanu, Constantin Parvulescu, Silviu Brucan, Cornelius Manescu and Grigore Raceanu. In addition to harassing the signers, Ceausescu arrested and accused Raceanu's adopted son, Mircea, of treason.[16]

Romanian Human Rights

While the White House deplored Bucharest's actions, Administration officials did not want to impose any sanctions. The feeling was that the letter, itself, would cause sufficient damage to Ceausescu's government.[17] The White House, however, did show its disapproval by making no comment following Ceausescu's announcement that Romania had paid off all of her foreign debt, as of April 1, 1989.[18] The EEC was equally noncommittal, and later decided to officially suspend all negotiations on an economic accord pending an improvement in Bucharest's human rights record.[19] Romania's new solvency also attracted little attention among American businessmen. Ceausescu's continued austerity program kept foreign imports to a minimum. By the end of September, 1989, the Commerce Department reported the total value of Romanian-American two-way trade was $356 million, with only $102 million in American exports.[20]

Not all Congressmen shared the Administration's reluctance to impose sanctions against Bucharest. Continuing stories of Romanians fleeing across borders to Hungary and Yugoslavia appeared in the national press. By May, 1989, Hungary had given refuge to thousands of Romanian citizens.[21] In response to this growing outcry against Ceausescu's repressive regime, Congressmen Smith, Hall and Wolf, introduced House Resolution 2765 on June 27. The measure, had it passed, would have prohibited America from importing any wine, cheese, meat or other agricultural product from Romania.[22]

As waves of liberal change crashed through Eastern Europe, Bucharest built barriers along the Hungarian-Romanian border to prevent thousands more from fleeing persecution and misery.[23] At an East-West human rights Congress in Paris, the Hungarian delegate, Andre Erdos, equated Romania with South Africa, and described the border barriers as the new "Berlin Wall."[24] On July 19, Senator Pell of Rhode Island proposed an amendment to the Foreign Relations Authorization Act of 1990. The "Sense of the Senate" amendment, which was later adopted, supported the House boycott of food exports from Romania, urged the Secretary of State to consider sanctions, and recommended termination of Romanian air service with the United States.[25] In support of the amendment, Senator Pressler described Bucharest's support of Libyan terrorists, recounted Romania's history of selling Jews to Israel for hard currency and described the effect of systemization on Hungarian culture.[26]

In August, the United Nations received a report on Romanian human rights smuggled out of Bucharest. In 1985, a subcommittee of the UN Human Rights Commission assigned Dumitru Mazilu to make a report on youth and human rights in Romania. Ceausescu agreed to the request apparently to enhance the career of his son, Nicu, who was Minister of Youth at the time. Professor Mazilu's completed report severely criticized the Ceausescu regime. In one sentence Mazilu wrote "In Romania, one single leader, one single name, is cultivated continuously, insistently, exasperatingly–that of the Dictator." Bucharest refused to let the report leave the country, and prohibited Mazilu from leaving as well. In July, 1989, Mazilu's report arrived in the West and was forwarded to the UN.[27] Publication of Mazilu's report brought quick response from Bucharest. Romania attempted to censure the UN Human Rights Center in Paris which had published the document.[28]

Romania's abusive practices continued to receive global censure. The Administration refused to send a delegation to the Joint Romanian-American Economic Commission, while the Council of Europe's Parliamentary Assembly asked its member states to impose sanctions on

Romania.[29] In October, Representative Hall told House members about the pastor of an Hungarian Reformed church in the Transylvanian city of Timisoara. Pastor Laszlo Tokes was an outspoken critic of Ceausescu's human rights practices, particularly those which discriminated against Hungarians. Several of Tokes' parishioners were bold in their defense of their pastor's views, especially Erno Ujvarossy, an engineer who had helped restore the church. Wolf told the House of Ujvarossy's murder, implying that it was the work of the dreaded Securitate, the para-military police force fanatically loyal to Ceausescu.[30]

Two weeks later, Ceausescu provided his critics with more ammunition. He instructed the Romanian delegation to the CSCE review in Sofia to block a thirty-five nation environmental agreement. He opposed the human rights provision in the document permitting citizens to express their views on ecological issues.[31] On November 14, Congressman Wolf told the House that "we need to be watching Romania." While events such as the collapse of the Berlin Wall and popular uprisings in Czechoslovakia and Bulgaria had captured the world's attention, America must not forget the inhuman conditions which still existed in Romania.[32] On the following day, Dennis DeConcini of Arizona gave his Senate colleagues the same message.[33]

As world condemnation of Ceausescu's regime mounted, delegates gathered in Bucharest for the Fourteenth Party Congress. The Palace Hall was draped with banners proclaiming "Ceausescu, Romania, Freedom." Inside, the 71 year old Ceausescu assured his audience that he had no intention of stepping down from the post he had held for twenty-four years. He condemned the changes which were occurring in the Warsaw Pact countries, and reassured the party apparatchiks that he would continue to pursue Romania's national socialist path. At the close of the meeting, on November 24, the delegates unanimously reelected Ceausescu as party leader for another five years.[34]

Several days later, United Press International announced that Olympic gymnast Nadia Comaneci had defected and crossed into Hungary.[35] On Friday, December 1, she flew to the United States and spent the weekend in New York City. However, what could have been a star-spangled welcome in the United States quickly ended. She had chosen to leave Romania with her lover, Constantine Panait, a married man, whose wife, Maria, appeared quite surprised by her husband's television appearance with Comaneci. Within a few days, Nadia's defection disappeared from the press, and with it her opportunity to capitalize on a celebrated escape.

Tokes and Timisoara

On December 17, the man who two months earlier Representative Tony Hall had brought to the attention of his House colleagues, became internationally known. When Ceausescu's Securitate forces came to evict Pastor Laszlo Tokes from his Hungarian Reformed Church, Hungarians and Romanians surrounded the church in Timisoara to prevent his eviction. The Securitate opened fire, killing an undetermined number of people. The demonstrators chanted "Down With Ceausescu" and demanded food. On December 18, as the riots continued in Timisoara, Bucharest closed Romania's frontiers. However, this did not keep news of the uprising from spreading to the West. Budapest television and radio continued to monitor events in Timisoara, emphasizing the violence and the Securitate's willingness to shoot unarmed people including children.[36]

The television reports produced reactions as they had following the video accounts of the events in Tiananmen Square in Beijing, six months earlier. On December 19, the White House condemned the "brutal use of force" against the demonstrators.[37] Undoubtedly Congress would have responded with even harsher measures, but the legislature was not in session during the revolution.

On December 20, Ceausescu labelled the demonstrators "hooligans" and called for a pro-government rally in Bucharest for the following day.[38] Demonstrators poured into the center of town on December 21, chanting pro-democracy slogans. Ceausescu called out the military. Shots rang out and tanks appeared on the main streets of downtown Bucharest. The demonstrators remained, and their courage was broadcast through Yugoslavian, Czechoslovakian, French and Soviet news agencies. On the twenty-first, the State Department again called on Bucharest to cease its "brutal" repression of the Romanian people.[39] The Romanian Embassy refused to answer telephone calls from the State Department. Finally, the Department sent a courier to the Embassy and summoned Ambassador Stoichici to meet with Deputy Secretary of State Lawrence Eagleburger. At the meeting, the White House formally protested Romania's brutality.[40] Following the meeting, the State Department indicated that it was seriously considering reducing the few remaining ties the United States had with Romania.[41]

Ceausescu's declaration of a nation-wide state of emergency did nothing to curb the demonstrators. Units of the Romanian army refused to obey orders, joined the demonstrators and turned their weapons against the Securitate. As chaos swept Bucharest, the State Department ordered the evacuation of all non-essential personnel from the United States Embassy.[42] The Department also issued a travel advisory, warning Americans to leave Romania, asking others to postpone their plans to enter the country.[43]

The Bush Administration and the National Salvation Front

When Ceausescu appeared on the balcony of the Presidential Palace, the protestors burned his picture, booed, and screamed "Down With the Dictatorship."[44] Unable to silence the demonstrators, Ceausescu and his wife ran to the roof of the Palace, jumped into a waiting helicopter, and fled Bucharest. Within hours, a provisional government formed called the National Salvation Front. Its interim leader was Corneliu Manescu, a former Foreign Minister. The new government seized control of the radio station, and, according to the British Broadcasting Corporation, announced "Romania is now free. Ceausescu is Down."[45]

Fighting continued for the next several days between the Army, which supported the National Salvation Front, and the Securitate which supported Ceausescu. Fighting was especially severe around the state television station in Bucharest which became the headquarters of the provisional government. The National Salvation Front used the television to keep Romania and the world informed of the revolution. By nightfall on the twenty-second, Free Romanian Television, as the station was now called, announced the capture of Nicolae and Elena Ceausescu. While mystery still surrounds the details of their capture, the two were put into an armored car and would be kept there for three days. News of the arrest encouraged the revolutionaries. People cut out the socialist symbols from the Romanian flag, and by the end of the month the government would adopt the tricolor flag and proclaim "Romania" as the country's official name.

In the meantime, the Bush Administration welcomed the revolution's success, and offered to send $500,000 in emergency medical aid to the victims of the revolution. However, Washington noted that it would postpone shipment of the supplies until the fighting subsided.[46] Also in Washington, the Romanian Embassy denounced Ceausescu and declared its loyalty to the new revolutionary government. However, this switch of sides did little to calm the demonstrators outside the Embassy. One woman responded to the new loyalty announcement by screaming in Romanian through a bull-horn, "Come out and we'll hang you by your tongues."[47]

As the fighting continued, neither side claimed victory. The continuing broadcasts from the television station was the only proof that the National Salvation Front was still in power. Front members appeared disorganized and frightened. On December 24, Secretary of State James Baker announced that the United States would follow France's lead, and support the Soviets if they chose to intervene in Romania.[48] However, within 24 hours, the crisis had passed. On Christmas Day, the new head of the National Salvation Front, Ion Iliescu, announced the execution of Nicolae and Elena Ceausescu following a brief military trial. The two were found guilty of genocide, destroying public property, undermining the state's economy and power structure and of trying to steal state funds deposited in foreign banks.[49]

On December 26, Romanian television showed the dead bodies of Nicolae and Elena to the world. While the White House criticized the National Salvation Front for not giving the Ceausescus a public trial, Washington did recognize the Front as the legitimate government of Romania.[50] The State Department instructed America's Ambassador, Alan Green, who had replaced Roger Kirk a couple of months earlier, to work with the new regime.[51]

While historians will later analyze the reasons for Ceausescu's fall, suffice to say that among the causes, five quickly come to mind. First, Romania's human rights record had isolated the country from the West, and proved an embarrassment to her Warsaw Pact neighbors, especially the Soviet Union. Second, although Ceausescu proudly announced that Romania had paid off her foreign debts, he had no intention of changing the country's economic plans which continued to call for increased food exports. Third, the weather forecast predicted a harsh Winter, and without economic relief, more food and increased fuel and electricity, thousands of people would probably die from starvation and the cold. Fourth, Ceausescu's abusive practices came under fire even by fellow Communists and former leaders of the Party as seen in the March, 1989, letter. Finally, Ceausescu was a hated man, and this hatred united all the dissident groups in Romania for a common purpose. The people had tolerated harassment, arrest, imprisonment, starvation and cold, but they would not tolerate murder. When the Securitate fired on fellow Romanians in Timisoara, killing women and children, there appeared to the people no alternative but to oust the hated dictator. Ceausescu's death was necessary for most of the people because it guaranteed that he could never again kill the men, women and children of Romania.

Ceausescu's death did not end the fighting, but it did slow it down.

The Securitate forces had lost the political reason for their militancy; Ceausescu could not return to power. Some members of the Securitate chose to continue fighting, because they feared that if they surrendered they would be killed by the revolutionaries. Others, abandoned their weapons and moved into the crowds hoping to gain anonymity. As the fighting subsided, the United States prepared to send its promised supplies to Romania.[52] A couple of days later, Secretary of State Baker clarified his December 24 announcement that the United States would support Soviet intervention in Romania. On December 30, Baker explained that his statements were made within a "hypothetical" context.[53]

By December 31, Romania's provisional government had announced that there would be multiparty elections in April to establish a new government for Romania. In addition to the National Salvation Front, which was politically left, there were several new parties in Romania. Largest among them was the conservative National Christian Peasants Party and the Liberal Party, both of which were new versions of their outlawed predecessors.[54] As the membership in these parties and others grew, they demanded inclusion in the provisional government. While the National Salvation Front initially balked, it eventually agreed to form a National Unity Council with multiparty representation. By early February, the Front announced that there would be free elections on May 20, to form Romania's new government.[55]

In spite of making contradictory statements, one day outlawing the Communist party and the death penalty, and on a later day reinstating them both, the provisional government gradually became more stable. In the process, there were leadership changes, and none more disheartening than the death of Corneliu Bogdan on January 1, 1990.[56] The former Romanian Ambassador to the United States had fallen into disfavor with Ceausescu in 1982, and never regained political prominence until after the dictator's death. The provisional government quickly made him Deputy Foreign Minister, and principal government liaison with the Western press agencies. Other notable leadership changes included Silviu Brucan, a former Minister to the United States, and Dimitru Mazilu, the former United Nations human rights investigator. Both men resigned angry over policies pursued by the National Salvation Front. There will undoubtedly be more leadership changes as the country comes to grip with the fact that Ceausescu's death ended the main source of unity among Romania's dissidents.

Throughout the Romanian revolution, Congress was out of session. However, on January 24, one day after the Second Session of the 101st

Congress convened, legislators responded to the developments in Bucharest. Representative Stanford Parris of Virginia introduced a concurrent "Sense of Congress" resolution calling for the President to "immediately reextend MFN trading status" to Romania.[57] Recalling the economic help France gave to the fledgling American government in 1778, he urged his colleagues to cosponsor this resolution and bring it quickly to the House floor for approval.[58]

While Parris spoke, Bucharest recalled two diplomats from the United States, Ion Stoichici, her Ambassador to America, and Petre Tansie, her Ambassador to the United Nations.[59] On the following day, Virgil Constaninescu arrived in Washington to represent Romania's new government.[60]

In Congress on January 25, Congressmen Wolf and Hall responded to Parris' resolution. Wolf had just returned from Romania. He was "hopeful" that there would be significant changes, especially in the area of human rights. However, he was also "skeptical," because many of the leaders of the provisional government were old faces. He did not mean to discredit them, but he wanted Congress to wait until Romania held free elections before the legislature took any steps to restore MFN. In the interim, America could send information on the "tools of democracy," and provide her with humanitarian assistance. Hall completely agreed with Wolf, and the two urged Congress to withhold MFN until after Romania held "open, free, fair and verifiable elections."[61]

Wolf's message was apparently heard on the other end of Pennsylvania Avenue. On February 11, Secretary of State Baker arrived in Bucharest. He promised Romania $80 million in food aid composed of 500,000 tons of grain and 7,500 tons of butter. He was unsure whether the aid would be made as an outright grant, or as a loan with favorable repayment terms, or as a combination of both. Echoing the sentiments of Wolf and Hall, Baker told Iliescu that all other form of assistance depended on Bucharest holding free elections and improving its human rights practices.[62]

Clearly the future of Romanian-American relations rests with Bucharest. If the scheduled free elections are held, and the new government promotes religious and nationality toleration, Bucharest and Washington may well enter a new "golden" age of diplomatic and commercial relations.

Notes

1. *L'Express*, April 14, 1989, p. 56.

2. *DOS Bulletin*, October, 1989, p. 88; *DOS Bulletin*, November, 1989, p. 92.

3. U.S. Congress, Senate, *Legislative Activities Report of the Committee on Foreign Relations, January 6, 1987-October 21, 1988,* 100th Cong., 2d Sess., 1988, p. 86.

4. U.S. Congress, House Report 100-922, *Amending the Foreign Assistance Act of 1961 With Respect to the Activities of the Overseas Private Investment Corporation, and to Make Supplemental Authorizations of Appropriations for the Board of International Broadcasting,* p. 7, 100th Cong., 2d Sess., 1988, hereafter, House, *Amending the Foreign Assistance Act of 1961,* 1988. U.S. Congress, Senate Report 100-500, *Miscellaneous International Affairs, Authorizations Acts of 1988,* p. 7, 100th Cong., 2d Sess., 1988. Hereafter, Senate, *Miscellaneous International Affairs Authorizations Act of 1988.*

5. U.S. *Congressional Record,* 100 Cong., 1st Sess., 1988, Vol. CXXXIV, E3319.

6. FBIS, EEU, November 16, 1988, p. 50.

7. U.S. Department of Commerce, *U.S. Foreign Trade Highlights* (Washington, D.C.: U.S. Government Printing Office, 1988), pp. 86, 91.

8. *The Economist*, April 22, 1989, p. 16.

9. "Trade Statistics," *BLOC: The Soviet Union and Eastern Europe Business Journal*, Vol. 1, No. 1 (1989), p. 42.

10. Author Telecon, Romanian Desk Officer, U.S. Department of Commerce, December 13, 1989.

11. "Chronology 1989," *Foreign Affairs*, Vol 69, No. 1, p. 230; U.S., *Congressional Record*, 101st Cong., 1st Sess., 1989, Vol. CXXXV, E554.

12. *Ibid.*

13. *Ibid.*, p. E780, E1859. The Soviet Union, Bulgaria, the Ukraine and East Germany refused to participate in the vote.

14. U.S., *Congressional Record*, 101st Cong., 1st Sess., 1989, Vol. CXXXV, E1859.

15. *Ibid.*, p. E 780.

16. RFE, Soviet/East European Report, April 1, 1989, p. 1.

17. CSM, March 30, 1989, p. 7.

18. Nicolae Ceausescu, *Speech Delivered at the Plenum of the Central Committee of the Romanian Communist Party, June 27-28, 1989* (Bucharest: Filaret Presses, 1989), p. 6.

19. RFE, Soviet/East European Report, December 10, 1989, p. 4.

20. Author Telecon, Romanian Desk Officer, U.S. Department of Commerce, February 13, 1990.

21. CSM, May 8, 1989, p. 19; RFE, Soviet/East European Report, July 20, 1989, p. 4.

22. U.S., *Congressional Record*, 101st Cong., 1st Sess., 1989, Vol. CXXXV, H3257.

23. CSM, July 10, 1989, p. 6.

24. *Ibid.*

25. U.S., *Congressional Record*, 101st Cong., 1st Sess., 1989, Vol. CXXXV, S8215.

26. *Ibid*, p. S8216.

27. NYT, August 30, 1989, p. A13; Robert Weiner, "Romanian-American Relations During the Glasnost Period," Conference of the AAASS, Chicago, November 2, 1989, pp. 8-9. Bob is at the University of Massachusetts, Boston.

28. NYT, August 20, 1989, p. A13.

29. RFE, Weekly Record of Events in Eastern Europe, September 21-28, 1989, p. 20.

30. U.S., *Congressional Record*, 101st Cong., 1st Sess., 1989, Vol. CXXXV, E3453.

31. Dialog Computer Data Base, No. 0503854, UPI report from Bulgaria by Patricia Koza, November 2, 1989.

32. U.S., *Congressional Record*, 101st Cong., 1st Sess., 1989, Vol. CXXXV, H8523.

33. *Ibid*., p. S15748.

34. The Boston Globe, November 25, 1989, p. 4.

35. Dialog Computer Data Base, No. 0508243, UPI report from Hungary by Erika Laszlo, November 30, 1989.

36. CNN News, December 19, 1989.

37. Dialog Computer Data Base, No. 0511352, UPI report from Washington, December 19, 1989.

38. *The Economist*, January 6, 1990, p. 44.

39. Dialog Computer Data Base, No. 0511837, UPI report from Washington, December 21, 1989.

40. WSJ, December 22, 1989, p. A4.

41. Dialog Computer Data Base, No. 0511838, UPI report from Washington by Jim Anderson, December 21, 1989.

42. Dialog Computer Data Base, No. 0512054, UPI report from Belgrade by Nesho Djuric, December 22, 1989.

43. Dialog Computer Data Base, No. 0512060, UPI report from Budapest by Erika Laszlo, December 22, 1989.

44. *Ibid*.

45. *Ibid*.

46. Dialog Computer Data Base, No. 0512177, UPI report from Washington by Frank Csongos, December 23, 1989.

47. NYT International, December 24, 1989, p. 15.

48. Dialog Computer Data Base, No. 0512286, UPI report from Washington by Frank Csongos, December 24, 1989. In addition to political and economic reasons, Soviet interest in intervening may have stemmed from Gorbachev's desire to help an old friend, Ion Iliescu, the head of the National Salvation Front.

49. *The Boston Globe*, December 26, 1989, p. 3.

50. *Los Angeles Times*, December 26, 1989, p. A13.

51. Green was an Oregon businessman and a supporter of Bush's presidential campaign.

52. *Los Angeles Times*, December 28, 1989, p. A19.
53. *Los Angeles Times*, December 30, 1989, p. A17.
54. *Eastern Europe Newsletter*, Vol. 4, No. 1, January 8, 1990, p. 2; RFE, Soviet/East European Report, January 10, 1990, p. 2.
55. *The Boston Globe*, February 1, 1990, p. 16.
56. *Newsweek*, January 15, 1990, p. 65.
57. U.S., *Congressional Record*, 101st Cong., 2d Sess., 1990, Vol. CXXXVI, H70-H72.
58. *Ibid.*, p. H72.
59. NYT, January 24, 1990, p A8.
60. NYT, January, 25, 1990, p. A9.
61. U.S., *Congressional Record*, 101st Cong., 2d Sess., 1990, Vol. CXXXVI, H95-H98.
62. *The Boston Globe,* February 12, 1990, p. 10; CNN News, February 11, 1990.

CHAPTER XX

CONCLUSIONS

A case can be made that over most of the past fifty years, two hyphens are needed to understand American-Romanian relations; one between Bucharest and Washington, and one between Washington and – lots of countries. During World War II, United States-Romanian relations lived in the shadow of America's relations with Greece and Poland. Later Washington's affiliation with Bucharest, had to parallel Moscow's affiliation with Tokyo and Rome. After the Tehran Conference in 1943, the road to Bucharest was always designed with Moscow in mind. By the time World War II ended, Washington had forfeited any position of power in Romania to the Soviets. The reasons were legion, but the reality was clear: Romania was not geographically significant to the Pentagon within the framework of Germany, Italy and Japan. Tehran clearly gave the Soviets a freehand to remake the Balkans in their own image. When America finally developed a policy for Eastern Europe, Romania had identity only within a Russian context; Bucharest was the "most Sovietized" of the satellite states.

From 1950 through 1975 overtures to Bucharest were made with an eye to affecting Moscow. Washington aimed first to de-Stalinize and later to de-satellitize Romania. The country slowly became viewed as a "Latin island in a Slavic sea;" an island which Kennedy wanted to reach through "penetration" and Johnson by "building bridges." But the motives were always the same: to weaken Soviet control, not, necessarily, to strengthen Romania. The Johnson-Nixon policy of "differentiation" was old wine in new bottles; America's first "differentiation" was in 1948, when Truman rewarded Yugoslavia for her deviation from Moscow. The Johnson-Nixon "carrot and stick" program aimed to do the same for Bucharest, and under a Ceausescu, the policy could work. While Yugoslavia was not Romania, Tito and Ceausescu both promoted national Communism. Ceausescu's distinctive path to socialism came from being distinct from Moscow. Washington labelled this policy "maverick," and rewarded Romania for pursuing it because this kind of independence could possibly reduce Soviet control in the Balkans.

President Nixon's historic visit to Romania in 1969 had little to do with Romania. True he had a "soft spot" for the country because of the reception he received in 1967, but the principle reason for the visit was to "tweak the nose of the Russians." Nixon's commitment to multipolarity meant that America would seek new power connections, and none was more important to the White House than China. If Bucharest was a conduit to Beijing, then a Romanian visit was important. Ceausescu's "tous azimuts" foreign policy complemented Nixon's multipolarity, for both Presidents wanted to find alternatives to bipolar relations with Moscow. Further, Ceausescu needed Western technology and greater independence from CMEA, while Washington wanted to encourage the "de-coupling" of Eastern Europe from Soviet hegemony.

If Romanian MFN was "only a phone call away" in 1972, the reason Nixon never dialed Mills was because Romania was not worth a legislative IOU. Romania's importance, even with Nixon, remained within the post World War II context of Soviet-American relations. From the outset of Nixon's first Administration, Moscow closely monitored Ceausescu's and Bogdan's efforts to secure MFN. In some ways, the Kremlin let Bucharest test the waters. When they were found favorable, Brezhnev moved into the picture, and in 1972 Moscow signed a trade agreement with Washington, which promised the coveted MFN. Moscow's arrival abruptly ended Romania's endeavors, and Bucharest had to wait until the Soviet negotiations collapsed.

Since the Jackson-Vanik language was aimed at Moscow, all non-market economy countries had to deal with Washington within a context orchestrated for Soviet-American relations. During the early years of MFN, the Administration cited Romania's independence in foreign policy as justification for annual renewal. During the first half of the 1980s, advocates of continuing Romanian MFN, in spite of her human rights record, emphasized Bucharest's denunciation of the Soviet invasion of Czechoslovakia, criticism of Moscow's Afghanistan policy, obstructionism within the Warsaw Pact, and her participation in the Los Angeles Summer Olympics, defying Moscow's boycott. Even at the end, Romania's loss of MFN, was affected by Moscow. Gorbachev's foreign policy was more "maverick" than Ceausescu's. By adopting many of Romania's longtime foreign policy demands, especially those which had distinguished her from Moscow, Gorbachev stripped Bucharest of her "maverickness." What remained was an ugly reality of human abuse and deprivation, that even Moscow found distasteful.

As Gorbachev moved beyond detente, toward a 21st Century Europe, Washington's continued tolerance of Romania's behavior became a hindrance to future Soviet-American relations. While the issue of human rights provided a legitimate reason for Congress to want to terminate MFN, the reason had been there since 1948. While human rights advocates have taken credit for Ceausescu's decision to end MFN, Congress would not have forced his hand had not Gorbachev supported human rights and freedoms, long the rhetoric of Washington. How could America continue to reward a country, whose human rights practices were criticized by Moscow.

The human rights issue is significant in Romanian-American relations. Within a couple of years following World War II, Washington raised the issue of human rights in Bulgaria, Hungary and Romania. However, the principle reason was to point attention to the immorality of Communism. This rationale continued until late into the 1950s. Once the claims issue was solved, America's interest in Romanian human rights vanished, and would not reappear until the Jackson-Vanik Amendment.

The importance of this Amendment was not in its emigration language. Rather, the Amendment gave Congress a foothold in foreign policy, normally the domain of the Administration. The Jackson-Vanik proposal did what Bricker had tried to do in the 1950s. However, the aura of an Eisenhower was sufficient to undermine Bricker; Ford had no such aura, nor could he have had in light of Watergate. The Jackson-Vanik Amendment gave Congress an opportunity to influence foreign policy, an influence coveted by many legislators. However, unlike the Administration, Congress did not always have access to national security information. Congress was unaware of Romania's mediation during the Vietnam War. Later, the White House was initially prohibited from informing Congress about Moscow's willingness to permit 55,000 Jews to annually emigrate. Nonetheless, Congress wanted to influence foreign policy, and could do so under the rubric of emigration.

To curb Congressional efforts to enlarge its foreign policy power, the White House, until 1981, kept Romanian MFN renewal hearings focused almost exclusively on the literal interpretation of the Jackson-

Vanik Amendment. Jewish emigration was the only factor for consideration. True, some Congressmen raised questions about the treatment of neo-Protestants and Hungarians, but they were few in number. The Jewish issue was the prime focus, and Bucharest finally agreed to resolve the problem. For all intents and purposes, the July 1979 arrangement with Romania settled the issue of Jewish emigration. Congress did not mind that the upsurge in emigration to West Germany and Israel was because Bonn and Jerusalem paid for each emigrant in hard currency. Congress also showed little concern with the fact that because of America's quotas, many Romanians, Jews and non-Jews, could not enter the United States. Further, not once in more than a dozen years, did any person testify before Congress about the number of Americans who returned to Romania. Interviews with Ambassadors Barnes and Aggrey indicated that, while the number was not large, there were people who chose to live in Romania rather than in the United States.[1]

As human rights became more popular in Congress, few legislators knew that America's commitment to human rights was not as strong as Congressional rhetoric would suggest. For a variety of reasons, some of which involved encroachments on America's internal policies, Washington had not ratified several major international treaties on human rights. Included among these were the UN Covenant on Civil and Political Rights, the UN Covenant on Social, Economic and Cultural Rights, and the Organization of American States Convention on Human Rights.[2]

While some few Congressmen complained about the mistreatment accorded religious and ethnic minorities in Romania, the issue of Romanian human rights did not come to the fore until there was a change in the pattern of American-Romanian two-way trade. Through 1980, America enjoyed a very favorable trade balance. However, commencing in 1981, the reverse quickly became true. And with this development, human rights became a criterion for MFN renewal. Romanian MFN renewal went through three phases: the first focused on Jewish emigration, the second emphasized Hungarian persecution and Jewish emigration, and the third dealt with Bucharest's policies toward Hungarians and non-recognized religious denominations.

The third phase began in the early 1980s. Ceausescu's economic austerity programs and commitment to repay Romania's foreign debt crippled America's exports to Bucharest. As business declined, so too did the number of corporate witnesses who took time to testify before

MFN renewal hearings. This development occurred at about the same time that the Jewish emigration issue was resolved, and Carter's departure from the White House, having successfully kept emigration distinct from human rights during his Administration. The result of all this was that now the vast majority of witnesses who trooped before Congressional hearings on Romanian MFN testified about Bucharest's heinous human rights record.

To be sure, Ceausescu also did his part to help focus Congressional attention. Ever since his visit to North Korea, Ceausescu had worked on developing an omnipotent position for himself in Romania. His cult of personality became apparent in 1974, and continued to grow in an unhindered fashion. Reminiscent of the Fascist theoretician, Giovanni Gentile, who said you only have existence within the state, Ceausescu held a similar view: life was through identification with Ceausescu. His cult forced all who did not accept him into becoming dissenters, and he did not tolerate dissent. A direct correlation began to develop between the intensity of the cult, and the size of the dissident population. Samzidat literature appeared in cities across Romania, in spite of the typewriter decree. Romania's policy of non-emigration did not affect those who chose to flee the country; their application process was only hindered by border guards and barriers, neither of which worked very well. Those who fled told stories of deprivation. Ceausescu's obsession to repay Romania's foreign loans meant that food was raised for export, not for domestic consumption. Animal heads were the primary source of meat for the average consumer, unless they had Kent cigarettes and access to the "second economy."

As these reports multiplied, they found a larger audience in Congress. The changing climate in both Washington and Bucharest should have altered American-Romanian relations in 1983. House advocates in favor of suspending or terminating MFN were sufficient in number to have effectively challenged the annual Presidential waiver request. However, the Chadha findings postponed all Congressional action. In 1983, there was insufficient support in the Senate to pass bicameral legislation affecting Romania's MFN.

For the next several years, Ceausescu continued to show a genuine disregard of his people's human rights. His economic policies had worked. By the mid-1980s, Romania had an annual trade surplus of about $1.5 billion. Much of this money was earmarked to repay foreign loans, some was diverted into developing a Ceausescu legacy, and none was allocated to improve the Romanian standard of living. Probably the symbol which best reflected Ceausescu's indifference to the needs of his people, was the construction of his new palace. Nearly three football fields in length, one field wide, and thirteen stories tall, the mammoth structure devoured billions of lei, which could easily have been used to increase food, fuel and electricity to thousands of Romanian people.

During the interlude between 1983 and 1986, the American Senate began to reconsider its position toward suspending Romanian MFN. Traditionally the Senate was less inclined to take quick action than the House. Senators were less responsive to their constituencies than were House members. Senators only needed voter support every six years, and represented a state-wide constituency. They liked to think that they saw issues from a national perspective. They believed that their House colleagues, who were elected every two years from small districts, were far more responsive to their voters and more parochial in their thinking.[3] As a result, groundswell movements took longer to affect the Senate.

However, Ceausescu's continued demagoguery forced even the most benign Senators to face up to Romania's human rights practices. The result was that Congress changed the rules. In 1974, the Jackson-Vanik criterion was emigration. In 1987, Jackson-Vanik meant human rights, religious freedom and minority equality. While Ceausescu was not the major reason for this change, his behavior certainly contributed to this new definition. What is also certain, is that if he had continued in power, the distinction between Romania being guilty of human rights violations, or being a "gross violator" of human rights, was only a short time away. Congress's decision in 1987 to forge forward and suspend Romanian MFN for human rights reasons was long overdue. While Romania might not have violated Section 402 of the Trade Reform Act of 1974, Bucharest had certainly violated the conscience of most legislators in America, and representatives in other international fora. When Hungary joined the Western nations to censure Romania's human rights practices, Congress needed no further evidence to end MFN treatment.

The emphasis on MFN suggests that trade was the primary object of Romanian-American relations. While this certainly was the view of corporate America, it rarely was the view of the government. In fact, the last time the Administration had viewed trade with Eastern Europe from an essentially economic viewpoint was during the closing years of World War II. During that period, Washington envisioned a post-war world open to American exports. Without question, the United States was the dominant economic power in the world. By 1950, she would produce 52% of the world's gross national product. America intended to use this power to insure the victory of democracy, and the spread of capitalism throughout the world.

However, the spread of Communism into Eastern Europe and China prompted the United States to view the world in bipolar terms. At that point, trade became a weapon. America's obsession with destroying Communism often muddied the waters as to whom the enemy was. "Linkage" played a very important part in America's foreign economic policy between 1948 and 1958. During these years, America linked foreign aid to the trade practices of her allies. Washington threatened sanctions against countries who received Marshall Plan funds, if they shipped or transshipped goods to the Communist world which the United States considered prohibited for export. Washington's export controls affected West-West trade as well as East-West trade.

However, America's export control policy was not developed without considerable disagreement among Cabinet members. Until 1958, the Commerce Department viewed trade restriction as the norm for East-West trade. The Department believed that trade only benefitted the Communist world. They saw dual-use in nearly all goods, and had lists of hundreds of commodity categories prohibited for export. The Department of Defense was even more stringent, and, to this day, maintains a veto over the export of many items considered potentially threatening to America's national security.

In contrast, the State Department, except when America was at war, saw trade as a weapon to increase America's influence in the world. The Department consistently supported fewer restrictions than did the Commerce and Defense Departments. The Department also opposed linkage language, which in the 1950s took the form of *quid pro quos*. While they would normally concede that some linkage had value, the Department drew a line at embargoes. It totally opposed embargoes or embargo-type programs. In addition to the illegality of an embargo, a concept which honestly bothered few members of the Administration, the Department's objections rested on three issues. First, the Communist Bloc was too self sufficient, and had enough illegal trade sources to defeat an embargo. Second, and more important, the greater the trade restrictions, the less leverage America had to influence the behavior of particular Communist countries. Third, restrictive trade prohibited Western Europe from importing much needed raw materials from Eastern Europe. Unlike the Commerce Department, the State Department accepted the traditional "breadbasket-workshop" relationship between East and West Europe.

While the Korean War would diminish the differences between the departments, the death of Stalin, pressure from COCOM allies, and Moscow's New Course restored the division of opinion between State and Commerce for the next several years. The effectiveness of the Soviet peace offensive along with America's new sense of security built upon her growing nuclear arsenal, encouraged American businessmen to look to Eastern Europe for new markets. Khrushchev's 1958 trade overtures gave further encouragement to this movement, and by the early 1960s, Washington had negotiated a trade agreement with Poland, and in 1964 with Romania. However, the Vietnam War curbed further development of this new trade pattern. Congress did not want the United States to sell products to Eastern Europe for transshipment to North Vietnam. By the end of the decade, peace negotiations had begun, and Nixon and Kissinger decided to resume America's "differentiation" policy toward Eastern Europe. Again, the purpose was the same; trade was a means to affect change, not an end in itself.

Neither the Administration nor Congress ever questioned the view that trade with Eastern Europe was essentially political in nature. And certainly Romania was no exception. American trade with Bucharest had too many impediments to be economically successful. Non-market economies have non-convertible currencies and limited product convertibility. Romania frequently required credit or financial guarantees, and wanted to make repayment through barter or countertrade. To complicate matters, Ceausescu's cult of personality produced a Romanian xenophobia. Foreigners were not welcomed into the country, and Bucharest became more unaware of Western financial and trading practices. Further, Romanian-American trade negotiations were so lengthy, that only major corporations could afford to underwrite the talks. By the early 1980s, even some of these companies began to close shop, due to Ceausescu's increasing call of greater Romanian self sufficiency. Bucharest's trade philosophy was quite simple, and quite mercantilistic: Romania should always increase exports, and reduce imports.

As the two-way trade balance disproportionately favored Bucharest, American trade lost its primary role in Romania. Ceausescu's commitment to austerity made her less dependent on American exports, one of which was American influence. Romania's debt crisis and subsequent economic policies, ended Congress's ability to use trade to affect Bucharest's human rights policies. Having shifted much of Romania's trade to CMEA and the Third World, Ceausescu no longer had to accommodate Congressional demands and Administrative pressure to conform to America's human rights standards. No MFN did not mean no trade; it simply meant no more American influence in Romanian affairs.

In reviewing the years of MFN hearings, and the subsequent termination, a question quickly comes to mind: What happened to the Romanian lobby? At the outset, there were three elements of support for Romanian MFN: big business, Congressional indifference to human rights issues and the Administration. However, the first two of these disappeared during the 1980s. Romania's commitment to debt reduction cut American exports by two-thirds, and with it corporate support for continued MFN. The Carter Presidency made human rights a campaign issue. Americans welcomed a moral agenda as a means to overcome their guilt and embarrassment caused by Watergate and the Vietnam War. Human rights organizations appeared over night, both regionally and nationally. Congressional candidates paid at least lip-service to human rights issues to insure support at the ballot box. A "Moral Majority" took credit for Reagan's election, and supported their President when he identified the Communist world as an "evil empire." Fueled by reports from emigres, and stories in samzidat literature smuggled to the West, human rights organizations called on Moscow and other East European states to "let their people go," and to give freedom to those that remained. Congressmen slowly jumped on the bandwagon and joined in monitoring human rights practices in leftist regimes. Conservative America defended policies in rightest governments, and tended to punish leftist ones for the same practices.

The third supporter of Romanian MFN was the Administration. Using the literal interpretation of the Jackson-Vanik Amendment, every President was able to determine that Romania had fulfilled the legal criteria for MFN renewal. Congress and the Administration had chosen improved emigration as the criterion for all non-market economy nations seeking American MFN. At the time Washington made the decision, emigration seemed a logical choice because Soviet Bloc countries generally refused to permit their citizens to emigrate. Furthermore, the emigration criterion had the approval of Moscow. The Soviets unofficially agreed to accept increased emigration, especially Jewish emigration, as a means to insure Congressional approval of the recently signed Soviet-American Trade agreement. Although the agreement collapsed when the linkage became public, emigration remained the criterion.

For the next decade, the Administration assiduously demanded all non-market economies to accept the emigration language as the criterion for American MFN. Budapest and Beijing joined Bucharest in unofficially accepting the linkage. However, the human rights movement in the decade following the Romanian-American Trade Agreement expanded to include a host of concerns. Emigration was still an issue, but of less significance than in 1975. To many Congressmen, the Administration suffered from "tunnel vision." There was more to human rights than emigration. While the White House conceded this point in the early 1980s, it did nothing to remedy the situation. After years of frustration, Congress seized the initiative. It accepted the 1974-75 logic of linking human rights performance to MFN, but defined human rights in the language of 1987. Emigration remained a concern, but only one of many. An Administration laden with anti-Communist rhetoric would be hard pressed not to finally accept a Congressional demand for an across-the-board improvement in Romania's human rights as a precondition for continued American MFN.

As Romanian MFN supporters dwindled, its opponents increased. Throughout most of the Twentieth Century, Hungary and Romania have maintained fractious relations brought on by a number of problems, not the least of which are competing national claims to Transylvania. Hungarian and Romanian immigrants brought their hostilities with them as baggage when they settled in America. While exact figures are hard to come by, there are about 80,000 Romanian-Americans in contrast to nearly 450,000 Hungarian-Americans.[4] In addition to the difference in number, there is also a difference in attitude between these two ethnic groups. According to Ambassador Aggrey, Romanian-Americans are more conscious of being American, while Hungarian-Americans remind a listener of their ethnic roots.[5]

The lobbying efforts of each of these groups certainly supports Aggrey's views. Hungarian-Americans appeared religiously at Romanian MFN hearings from their inception. They based their opposition to MFN renewal on Romania's systematic discrimination against ethnic Hungarians. In contrast, representatives of Romanian-American groups appeared to lack organization. While nearly all Romanian-Americans opposed the Ceausescu regime, few could agree on a common program. Some Romanians supported the return of the monarchy, while others wanted a democracy. To make matters worse, many Romanians wanted to sever relations with Bucharest to punish the Communists for forcing them to leave their homeland, and become separated from their families. Perhaps the one unifying factor among Romanians, was an intense dislike of Nicolae Ceausescu. This shared feeling brought some Romanians together in a variety of small organizations which cried out against Bucharest's human rights record. Among the more prominent organizations were the Faith and Liberty Institute begun in Washington, D.C. by Father Calciu, the London-based World Union of Free Romanians, and the League for Human Rights in Paris which frequently worked with Amnesty International.

A final factor which contributed to the demise of Romanian support was Mikhail Gorbachev. The new Soviet leader embraced many of Ceausescu's peace initiatives, and in so doing ended Romania's "maverick" identify. The argument that American MFN rewarded Bucharest for her independence from Moscow was no longer valid. Stripped of this protection, Ceausescu's regime laid bare for inspection, and its record of human rights violations forced even Romania's supporters to think twice about extending MFN, a privilege normally thought of as a reward for good behavior.

The Christmas execution of Nicolae and Elena Ceausescu raises the question of American-Romanian relations in the post-Ceausescu era. As of March, 1990, developments are far too muddled to make much more than an educated guess. One thing is certain. Ceausescu's death destroyed the one unifying factor among all dissidents and critics. Now those who found fault with Ceausescu have the choice of not repeating his mistakes, of not becoming the people's enemy. If the new government can bring Romanian human rights practices into the mainstream of Western acceptability, and open her economy for investment, development and trade, American-Romanian relations might well resume, and prosper. Further, in view of the on-going changes in Eastern Europe and the Soviet Union, America might be able to finally establish a relationship with Romania which is not based on "tweaking the nose of the Russians."

Notes

1. Author interview of Ambassadors Harry Barnes, July 19, 1987, and O. Rudolph Aggrey, October 26, 1989.

2. Forsythe, *Human Rights and U.S. Foreign Policy: Congress Reconsidered*, pp. 2-3.

3. For an interesting elaboration on this point, see Ross K. Baker, *House and Senate*(New York: W.W. Norton, 1989).

4. Memo for Kuropas, pp. 1-6, East-West Trade, Box D74, Special Files, Press Secretary, GRF Library.

5. Author interview of O. Rudolph Aggrey, October 26, 1989.

BIBLIOGRAPHY

Archival Materials

From the National Archives

Department of State(DOS) Decimal Files, 1945-1949
Joint Chiefs of Staff Files, 1946-1956
Office of Strategic Services (OSS) Research and Analysis Reports (R&A), 1950-1956
National Security Council (NSC) Policy Papers, Record Group 273 5W1
Record Groups: 59, 84(Foreign Service Posts, DOS, Bucharest, 1946-1955), LM 102-103, 469(Special Representative, Paris, Trade and Finance Division), 1949-1951
Papers of Harry Howard

From the Harry S. Truman Presidential Library

Naval Aide Files
President's Secretary Files(NSC Meetings)
President's Subject Files
Papers of Thomas C. Blaisdell
Oral Interview Transcripts of:
    John C. Campbell
    Mark F. Ethridge
    Edwin McCammon Martin
    H. Freeman Matthews
    G. Frederick Reinhardt

From the Dwight D. Eisenhower Presidential Library

Ann Whitman Files
CFEP (Council of Foreign Economic Policy), Records, Policy Papers, Confidential Files, Office of the Chairmen
Clarence R. Randall Journal

National Security Council(NSC), Policy Papers, Record Group 273 5W1
White House Central Files(WHCF), Confidential Files, Office Files
White House Office Files (WHOF), Special Assistant NSC
Papers of:
  Phillip Arreda
  Joseph Rand
  Charles W. Thayer
Oral Interview Transcript of Robert Thayer

From the John F. Kennedy Presidential Library

National Security Files(NSF), Departments and Agencies Country Files
Pre-Presidential Papers, Transition Files
White House Central Files(WHCF)
Papers of Orville Freeman
Oral Interview Transcript of William Crawford

From the Lyndon B. Johnson Presidential Library

Administrative History, Department of Commerce
Administrative History, Department of State
Interagency Task Force
National Security Council(NSC) Country File
National Security Files(NSF), Aides Files: McGeorge Bundy
National Security Files(NSF), Committee Files: Miller Committee
National Security Files (NSF) Name Files: Francis Bator Memos
Outside Task Forces
White House Central Files(WHCF), Country Files

From the Nixon Presidential Materials Project

Martin Anderson Files
Marina Whitman Files
White House Central Files(WHCF): Confidential Files: Country, National Security Council(NSC), State Department, Subject Files: Country, Tariffs(TA)
White House Special Files(WHSF), Staff Memos and Office Files(SMOF) of John Ehrlichman, H. R. Haldeman
Papers of:
  John Ehrlichman
  Peter Flanigan
  H. R. Haldeman

From the Gerald R. Ford Presidential Library

Vice Presidential Files
Executive Files: Country
White House Central Files(WHCF), Subject Files: Trade, Country Files

Papers of:
Arthur Burns
Ron Nessen
William Seidman

From the Jimmy Carter Presidential Library
White House Central Files(WHCF), Country Files: Romania, Federal Government Organizations, Foreign Affairs
Papers of Stu Eizenstat

Other Unpublished Materials

John Campbell, "The American Outlook on the Balkans, 1944-1946," presented at the AAASS Annual Conference, Honolulu, Hawaii, November, 1988.
Robert Weiner, "Romanian-American Relations During the Glasnost Period," presented at the AAASS Annual Conference, Chicago, Illinois, November, 1989.

Author Interviews With

Ambassadors O. Rudolph Aggrey, Harry Barnes, Corneliu Bogdan, William Crawford and Nicolae Gavrilescu
John Ehrlichman
H.R. Haldeman
Herbert Stein

Books

Academia Republicii Populare Romine, Institutul de Cercetari Economice. *Dezvoltarea Economica a Rominiei, 1944-1964*. Bucuresti: Editura Academiei Republicii Populare Romine, 1964.
Academia de stiinte sociale si politice a Republicii Socialiste Romania, Institutul de cercetari economice. *Eficienta si crestere economica; Comunicari prezentate la sesiunea stiinficica organizata in cinstea semicentenarului Partidului Comunist Roman, aprille, 1971*. Bucuresti: Editura Academie Republicii Socialiste Romania, 1972.
Acheson, Dean. *Present at the Creation; My Years in the State Department*. New York: W. W. Norton & Company, Inc., 1969.
Adler-Karlsson, Gunnar. *Western Economic Warfare, 1947-1967: A Case Study in Foreign Economic Policy*. Foreward by Gunnar Myrdal. "Stockholm Economic Studies, New Series, IX," Stockholm: Almqvist & Wiksell, 1968.
Albu, Alexandru D. *Cooperapea Economica Internationala a Republicii Socialiste Romania*. Craiova: Editura Scrisul Romanesc, 1979.

Allen, Richard V. (ed.). *Yearbook on International Communist Affairs 1968*. Stanford, CA: Hoover Institution Press, 1969.

Ambrose, Stephen E., *Nixon: The Education of a Politician, 1913-1962*. New York: Simon and Schuster, 1987.

[Amnesty International] *Amnesty International Report 1986*. London: Amnesty International Publications, n.d.

_____. *Amnesty International Report 1987*. London: Amnesty International Publications, n.d.

_____. *Romania: Human Rights Violations in the Eighties*. London: Amnesty International Publications, 1987.

Assetto, Valerie J. *The Soviet Bloc in the IMF and the IBRD*. Boulder, CO: Westview Press, 1988.

Baker, Ross K. *House and Senate*. New York: W.W. Norton, 1989.

Baldwin, Robert E. *Nontariff Distortions of International Trade*. Washington, D.C.: The Brookings Institution, 1970.

Basic Principles of Romania's Foreign Policy. (Joint Meeting of the CC of the RCP, the State Council, and the Romanian Government, August 21, 1968; Special Session of the Grand National Assembly of the Socialist Republic of Romania, August 22, 1968). Bucharest: Meridiane Publishing House, 1968.

Bertsch, Gary K. (ed.). *Controlling East-West Trade and Technology Transfer: Power, Politics, and Policies*. Durham, NC: Duke University Press, 1988.

Bethlen, Steven, and Volgyes, Ivan (eds.). *Europe and the Superpowers: Political, Economic, and Military Policies in the 1980s*. Boulder, CO: Westview Press, 1985.

Bohlen, Charles E. *Witness to History, 1929-1969*. New York: W. W. Norton & Company, Inc., 1973.

Borisov, O.B., and Koloskov, B. T. *Sino-Soviet Relations, 1945-1973: A Brief History*. Moscow: Progress Publishers, 1975.

Brada, Josef C., and Somanath, V. S. *East-West Trade: Theory and Evidence*. "Studies in East European and Soviet Planning, Development, and Trade, No. 27," Bloomington, IN: International Development Institute, 1978.

Braun, Aurel. *Romanian Foreign Policy Since 1965: The Political and Military Limits of Autonomy*. New York: Praeger Publishers, 1978

Brown, J. F. *The New Eastern Europe: The Khrushchev Era and After*. New York: Frederick A. Praeger, Publishers, 1966.

_____. *Eastern Europe and Communist Rule*. Durham, NC: Duke University Press, 1988.

Brug, Phillip D., and Holbik, Karel. *American-East European Trade: Controversy, Progress, Prospects*. Washington, D.C.: National Press, Inc., 1969.

Brzezinski, Zbigniew. *Power and Principle: Memoirs of the National Security Adviser, 1977-1981*. New York: Farrar, Straus, and Giroux, 1983.

_____. *In Quest of National Security*. Edited and annotated by Martin Strmecki. Boulder, CO: Westview Press, 1988.

Bucur, Nicholas A., Jr. *Ceausescu of Romania, Champion of Peace*. Cleveland, OH: Quills and Scrolls, 1981.

Bugajski, Janusz, and Pollack, Maxine. *East European Fault Lines: Dissent,*

Opposition, and Social Activism. Boulder, CO: Westview Press, 1989.

Byrnes, James F. *All In One Lifetime*. New York: Harper & Brothers, Publishers, 1959.

_____. *Speaking Frankly*. New York: Harper & Brothers, Publishers, 1947.

Campbell, John C. *American Policy Toward Communist Eastern Europe: The Choices Ahead*. Minneapolis: The University of Minnesota Press, 1965.

_____. *The United States in World Affairs, 1945-1947*. New York: Harper & Brothers, Publishers, 1947.

Candea, Virgil. *An Outline of Romanian History*. Bucharest: Meridiane Publishing House, 1977.

Carter, Jimmy. *Keeping Faith: Memoirs of a President*. New York: Bantam, 1982.

Ceausescu, Ilie, Constantiniu, Florin, and Ionescu, Mihail E. *A Turning Point in World War II: 23 August 1944 in Romania*. "East European Monographs, Boulder," New York: Columbia University Press, 1985.

Ceausescu, Ilie (ed.). *War, Revolution, and Society in Romania: The Road to Independence*. "Social Science Monographs, Boulder," New York: Columbia University Press, 1983.

Ceausescu, Nicolae. *Comertul exterior si cooperarea economica internationala*. Bucuresti: Editura Politica, 1980.

_____. *Cuvintare la Incheierea Lucrarilor Consfatuirii cu Activul de Partid si de Stat din Domeniul Comertului Exterior si Cooperarii Economice Internationale, 14 Februarie 1975*. Bucuresti: Editura Politica, 1975.

_____. *An Independent Foreign Policy for Peace and Cooperation*. Edited by J. Van Kloberg, III. [Washington, D.C.] The Political Science Library [n.d.].

_____. *The Five Year Plan: A New Stage of Progress and Prosperity in the Life of the Romanian People in the Flourishing of Socialist Romania*. Bucharest: Agerpres, 1966.

_____. *The R.C.P. National Policy: A Just, Highly Scientific, Realistic and Humanitarian Policy*. Bucharest: Agerpres, February 1977.

_____. *Report of the Central Committee on the Activity of the Romanian Communist Party in the Period between the Eleventh Congress and the Twelfth Congress, and the Party's Future Tasks, November 9, 1979*. Bucharest: Meridiane Publishing House, 1979.

_____. *Report on Romania's Short-Term and Long-Term Economic and Social Development; On the Improvement of the Planned Management of Society and the Development of Socialist Democracy, the Growth of the Leading Role of the Party in Building Socialism and Communism; On the International Activity of the Party and State. Presented at the National Conference of the R.C.P., July 19, 1972*. Bucharest: Meridiane Publishing House, 1972.

_____. *Romania On the Way of Completing Socialist Construction*. Volumes: I-III. Bucharest: Meridiane Publishing House, 1969.

_____. *Romania On the Way of Building Up the Multilaterally Developed Socialist Society*. Volumes IV-XXXII. Bucharest: Meridiane Publishing House, 1970-1989.

_____. *Der Rumanische Standpunkt: Thesen zur Nationalen und International Politik*. Freiburg im Bresgau: Verlag Rombach & Co., 1973.

_____. *Session of the Grand National Assembly of the Socialist Republic of Romania, July 24-26, 1967*. Bucharest: Agerpres, 1967.

Chalet, Jean Anne. *La Roumanie, Alliee rebelle*. Tournai: Casterman, 1972.

[Chamber de commerce de la Republique Socialiste de la Roumanie] *Le Developpement economique de la Roumanie dans le quiquennat, 1976-1980*. Bucharest: 1975.

Chamber of Commerce of the Socialist Republic of Romania. *Expansion of Romanian Economy Over 1971-1980*. Bucharest: Chamber of Commerce of the Socialist Republic of Romania, 1969.

_____. *Romania's Economic Development Over 1966-1970*. Bucharest: Chamber of Commerce of the Socialist Republic of Romania, 1966.

Churchill, Winston S. *The Second World War*, Vol. IV: *The Hinge of Fate*. Boston: Houghton Mifflin Co., 1950.

_____. *The Second World War*, Vol. VI: *Triumph and Tragedy*. Boston: Houghton Mifflin Co., 1953.

Cioranesco, George *et al*. (eds.). *Aspects de relations sovieto-romaines: Retrospectives et orientations*. Paris: Minard, 1967.

_____. *Aspects de relations sovieto-romaines, 1967-1971. Securite europeenne*. Paris: Minard, 1971.

Cline, Ray S., Miller, James Arnold, and Kanet, Roger E. (eds.). *Western Europe in Soviet Global Strategy*. Boulder, CO: Westview Press, 1987.

Coker, Christopher. *The Soviet Union, Eastern Europe, and the New International Economic Order*. Foreword by Stanislaw S. Wasowski. "The Washington Papers, No. 111," New York: Praeger, 1984.

Cordier, Andrew W., and Foote, Wilder (eds.). *Public Papers of the Secretaries-General of the United Nations*. Vol. 1: *Trygve Lie, 1946-1953*. New York: Columbia University Press, 1969.

_____. Vol. II: *Dag Hammarskjold, 1953-1956*. New York: Columbia University Press, 1972.

Crabb, Cecil V., and Mulcahy, Kevin V. *Presidents and Foreign Policy Making: From FDR to Reagan*. Baton Rouge: Louisiana State University Press, 1986.

Craig, Barbara Hinkson. *Chadha: The Story of an Epic Constitutional Struggle*. New York: Oxford University Press. 1988.

_____. *The Legislative Veto: Congressional Control of Regulation*. Boulder, CO: Westview Press, 1983.

Csikos-Nagy, Bela, and Young, David G. (eds.). *East-West Economic Relations in the Changing Global Environment. Proceedings of a Conference Held by the International Economic Association in Budapest, Hungary, and Vienna, Austria*. New York: St. Martin's Press, 1986.

Daniels, Robert V. (ed.). *A Documentary History of Communism*. rev. ed. Vol. II: *Communism and the World*. Hanover, NH: University Press of New England, 1984.

Davids, Jules. *The United States in World Affairs*. New York: Harper & Row, Publishers, 1965.

Davis, Lynn Etheridge. *The Cold War Begins: Soviet-American Conflict over Eastern Europe*. Princeton, NJ: Princeton University Press, 1974.

Dawisha, Karen. *Eastern Europe, Gorbachev and Reform: The Great Challenge*. New York: Cambridge University Press, 1988.

Dennett, Raymond, and Johnson, Joseph E. (eds.). *Negotiating With the Russians*. n.p., World Peace Foundation, 1951.

DeSantis, Hugh. *The Diplomacy of Silence: The American Foreign Service, the Soviet Union, and the Cold War, 1933-1947*. Chicago: The University of Chicago Press, 1979.

Destler, I.M. *Making Foreign Economic Policy*. Washington, D.C.: The Brookings Institution, 1980.

Detesan Al, and Porajan, D. *Export probleme si solutii*. Bucuresti: Editara de revista economica, 1977.

Deutscher, Isaac. *Russia, China, and the West: A Contemporary Chronicle, 1953-1966*. Edited by Fred Halliday. Baltimore: Penguin Books, 1970.

Donovan, Robert J. *Tumultuous Years: The Presidency of Harry S. Truman, 1949-1953*. New York: W. W. Norton & Company, 1967.

Drachkovitch, Milorad M. (ed.). *Yearbook on International Communist Affairs 1966*. Stanford, CA: The Hoover Institution on War, Revolution and Peace, 1967.

Eisenhower, Dwight D. *Waging Peace, 1956-1961: The White House Years*. Garden City, NY: Doubleday & Company, Inc., 1965.

Ellison, Herbert J. (ed.). *The Sino-Soviet Conflict: A Global Perspective*. Seattle: University of Washington Press, 1982.

_____. (ed.). *Soviet Policy toward Western Europe: Implications for the Atlantic Alliance*. Seattle: University of Washington Press, 1983.

Feis, Herbert. *Churchill, Roosevelt, Stalin: The War They Waged and The Peace They Sought*. Princeton, NJ: Princeton University Press, 1957.

Fejto, Francois. *A History of the People's Democracies: Eastern Europe Since Stalin*. Translated by Daniel Weissbort. New York: Praeger Publishers, 1971.

Ferrell, Robert H. (ed.). *Off The Record: The Private Papers of Harry S. Truman*. New York: Harper & Row, Publishers, 1980.

Fischer, Louis. *The Road to Yalta: Soviet Foreign Relations, 1941-1945*. New York: Harper & Row, Publishers, 1972.

Fischer, Mary Ellen. *Nicolae Ceausescu: A Study in Political Leadership*. Boulder, CO: Lynne Rienner Publishers, 1989.

Fischer-Galati, Stephen (ed.). *Eastern Europe in the Sixties*. New York: Frederick A. Praeger, Publishers, 1963.

_____. *Man, State, and Society in East European History*. New York: Praeger Publishers, 1970.

_____. *The New Rumania: From People's Democracy to Socialist Republic*. Cambridge, MA: The M.I.T. Press, 1967.

_____. *Twentieth-Century Rumania*. New York: Columbia University Press, 1970.

Floyd, David. *Rumania: Russia's Dissident Ally*. New York: Frederick A. Praeger, Publishers, 1965.

[Ford, Gerald R.] *A Time to Heal: The Autobiography of Gerald R. Ford*. New York: Harper & Row, Publishers, 1979.

Forsythe, David P. *Human Rights and U.S. Foreign Policy: Congress Reconsidered*. Gainesville: University Presses of Florida, 1988.

Funderburk, David B. *Pinstripes and Reds: An American Ambassador Caught Between the State Department and the Romanian Communists, 1981-1985*. Foreward by Congressman Philip M. Crane. Washington, D.C.: Selous Foundations Press, 1987.

Funigiello, Philip J. *American-Soviet Trade in the Cold War*. Chapel Hill: The University of North Carolina Press, 1988.

Gaddis, John Lewis. *The Long Peace: Inquiries Into the History of the Cold War*. New York: Oxford University Press, 1987.

_____. *Strategies of Containment: A Critical Appraisal of Postwar American National Security Policy*. New York: Oxford University Press, 1982.

_____. *The United States and the Origins of the Cold War, 1941-1947*. New York: Columbia University Press, 1972.

Garthoff, Raymond L. *Detente and Confrontation: American-Soviet Relations from Nixon to Reagan*. Washington, D.C.: The Brookings Institution, 1985.

Georgescu, Vlad (ed.). *Romania, 40 Years (1944-1984)*. Foreward by Eugen Weber. "The Washington Papers, No. 115," New York: Praeger, 1985.

Gheorghiu-Dej, Gheorghe. *Artikel und Reden, Dezember, 1955-Juli 1959*. Bukarest: Politischer Verlag, 1959.

_____. *Concerning the Foreign Policy of the Government of the Rumanian People's Republic*. Bucharest: Publishing House of the Rumanian Institute for Culture, 1955.

_____. *Situatia internationala si politica externa a republicii populare romine*. Bucuresti: Editura politica, 1960.

Gilberg, Trond. *Modernization in Romania Since World War II*. New York: Praeger, 1975.

Gorbachev, Mikhail. *Perestroika: New Thinking for Our Country and the World*. New York: Harper & Row, Publishers, 1987.

Gordon, Lincoln *et al. Eroding Empire: Western Relations with Eastern Europe*. Washington, D.C.: The Brookings Institution, 1987.

Gormly, James L. *The Collapse of the Grand Alliance, 1945-1948*. Baton Rouge: Louisiana State University Press, 1987.

Graebner, Norman A. (ed.). *The National Security: Its Theory and Practice, 1945-1960*. New York: Oxford University Press, 1986.

Graham, Lawrence S. *Romania: A Developing Socialist State*. Boulder, CO: Westview Press, 1982.

Granick, David. *Enterprise Guidance in Eastern Europe: A Comparison of Four Socialist Economies*. Princeton, NJ: Princeton University Press, 1975.

Griffith, William E. (ed.). *Central and Eastern Europe: The Opening Curtain?* Boulder, CO: Westview Press, 1989.

Grub, Phillip D., and Holbik, Karel. *American-East European Trade: Controversy, Progress, Prospects*. Washington, D.C.: The National Press, Inc., 1969.

Hacker, Jens. *Der Ostblock: Enstehung, Entwicklung und Struktur, 1939-1980*.

Baden-Baden: Nomos Verlagsgesellschaft, 1983.

Haig, Alexander M. Jr. *Caveat: Realism, Reagan, and Foreign Policy.* New York: Macmillan Publishing Company, 1984.

Hale, Julian. *Ceausescu's Romania: A Political Documentary.* London: George G. Harrap & Co., Ltd., 1971.

Hardy, Chandra S. *Rescheduling Developing-Country Debts, 1956-1981: Lessons and Recommendations.* Washington, D.C. Overseas Development Council, 1982.

Harriman, W. Averell, and Abel, Elie. *Special Envoy to Churchill and Stalin, 1941-1946.* New York: Random House, 1975.

Harrington, Joseph, and Racheotes, Nicholas. *Masters of War, Makers of Peace.* Littleton, MA: Copley Publishing Group, 1987.

Harvey, Mose L. *East-West Trade and United States Policy.* Foreword by Robert D. Murphy. New York: National Association of Manufacturers, 1986.

Herring, George C. (ed.). *The Secret Diplomacy of the Vietnam War: The Negotiating Volumes of the Pentagon Papers.* Austin: University of Texas Press, 1983.

Hersh, Seymour M. *The Price of Power: Kissinger in the Nixon White House.* New York: Summit Books, 1983.

Hess, Stephen. *Organizing the Presidency.* Washington, D.C.: The Brookings Institution, 1988.

Hinton, Harold C. *Communist China in World Politics.* Boston: Houghton Mifflin Company, 1966.

Holzman, Franklyn D. *The Economics of Soviet Bloc Trade and Finance.* Boulder, CO: Westview Press, 1987.

Horelick, Arnold L. (ed.). *U.S.-Soviet Relations: The Next Phase.* Ithaca, NY: Cornell University Press, 1986.

[Cordell Hull] *The Memoirs of Cordell Hull.* 2 volumes. New York: The Macmillan Company, 1948.

Hutchings, Robert L. *Soviet-East European Relations: Consolidation and Conflict.* Madison: University of Wisconsin Press, 1987.

Ionescu, Ghita. *The Break-up of the Soviet Empire in Eastern Europe.* New York: Penguin Books, 1965.

_____. *Communism in Romania, 1944-1962.* New York: Oxford University Press, 1964.

_____. *The Politics of the European Communist States.* New York: Frederick A. Praeger, Publishers, 1967.

_____. *The Reluctant Ally: A Study of Communist Neo-Colonialism.* London: Ampersand Ltd., 1965.

Jackson, Marvin R., and Woodson, James D. Jr. *New Horizons in East-West Economic and Business Relations.* "East European Monographs, Boulder," New York: Columbia University Press, 1984.

Johnson, Lyndon B. *The Vantage Point: Perspectives of the Presidency, 1963-1969.* New York: Holt, Rinehart and Winston, 1971.

Jones, Christopher D. *Soviet Influence in Eastern Europe: Political Autonomy and the Warsaw Pact.* New York: Praeger, 1981.

Jordan, Hamilton. *Crisis: The Last Year of the Carter Presidency*. New York: G. P. Putnam's Sons, 1982.

Jowitt, Kenneth. *Revolutionary Breakthroughs and National Development: The Case of Romania, 1944-1965*. Berkeley: University of California Press, 1971.

Kalb, Marvin, and Abel, Elie. *Roots of Involvement: The U.S. in Asia, 1784-1971*. New York: W. W. Norton & Company, Inc., 1971.

Karnow, Stanley. *Vietnam, A History*. New York: The Viking Press, 1983.

Keefe, Eugene K. *et al. Romania: A Country Study*. Washington, D.C.: U.S. Government Printing Office, 1979.

Kennan, George. *Memoirs, 1925-1950*. Boston: Little, Brown & Co., 1967.

Kertesz, Stephen D. (ed.). *East Central Europe and the World: Developments in the Post-Stalin Era*. South Bend, IN: University of Notre Dame Press, 1962.

_____ (ed.). *The Fate of East Central Europe: Hopes and Failures of American Foreign Policy*. South Bend, IN: University of Notre Dame Press, 1956.

_____. *The Last European Peace Conference: Paris 1946 – Conflict of Values*. New York: University Press of America, Inc., 1986.

King, Robert R., and Brown, James F. *Eastern Europe's Uncertain Future: A Selection of Radio Free Europe Research Reports*. New York: Praeger, 1977.

Kinnell, Susan K. (ed.). *Communism in the World Since 1945*. Foreword by Herbert J. Ellison. Santa Barbara, CA: ABC-CLIO, 1987.

Kiraly, Bela K., Lotze, Barbara, and Dreisziger, Nandor F. (eds.). *The First War Between Socialist States: The Hungarian Revolution of 1956 and Its Impact*. Volume XI of *War and Society in East Central Europe*. "Social Science Monographs, Brooklyn College Press," New York: Columbia University Press, 1984.

Kissinger, Henry. *White House Years*. Boston: Little, Brown and Company, 1979.

_____. *Years of Upheaval*. Boston: Little, Brown and Company, 1982.

Kolko, Gabriel. *The Politics of War: The World and United States Foreign Policy, 1943-1945*. New York: Vintage Books, 1968.

Kovrig, Bennett. *The Myth of Liberation: East-Central Europe in U.S. Diplomacy and Politics Since 1941*. Baltimore: The Johns Hopki᠎s University Press, 1973.

Khrushchev, Nikita. *Khrushchev Remembers*. Translated by Strobe Talbott with an Introduction by Edward Crankshaw. Boston: Little, Brown & Co., 1970.

_____ *Khrushchev Remembers: The Last Testament*. Edited by Strobe Talbott. Boston: Little, Brown & Company, 1974.

Laird, Robbin F., and Hoffmann, Erik P. (eds.). *Soviet Foreign Policy in a Changing World*. New York: Aldine Publishing Company, 1986.

Leiss, Amelia C., with Dennett, Raymond (ed.). *European Peace Treaties After World War II: Negotiations and Texts of Treaties with Italy, Bulgaria, Hungary, Rumania, and Finland*. Millwood, NY: Kraus Reprint Co., 1976.

Lendavi, Paul. *Eagles in Cobwebs*. New York: Anchor Books, 1969.

Linden, Ronald Haly. *Bear and Foxes: The International Relations of the East*

European States, 1965-1969. "East European Monographs, Boulder," New York: Columbia University Press, 1979.

_____. *Communist States and International Change: Romania and Yugoslavia in Comparative Perspective.* Boston: Allen & Unwin., 1987.

Loewenheim, Francis L., Langley, Harold D., and Jonas, Manfred (eds.). *Roosevelt and Churchill: Their Secret Wartime Correspondence.* London: Barrie & Jenkins, 1979.

London, Kurt (ed.). *Eastern Europe in Transition.* Baltimore: The Johns Hopkins Press, 1966.

Long, William J. *U.S. Export Control Policy: Executive Autonomy vs. Congressional Reform.* New York: Columbia University Press, 1989.

Lundestad, Geir. *The American Non-Policy Towards Eastern Europe, 1943-1947.* New York: Humanities Press, 1975.

Macartney, C. A., and Palmer, A. W. *Independent Eastern Europe: A History.* London: Macmillan, 1966.

[Machinery and Allied Products Insitutite] *U.S. Technology and Export Controls.* [n.p.] Machinery and Allied Products Institute, 1978.

Marer, Paul, and Montias, John Michael (eds.). *East European Integration and East-West Trade.* Bloomington: Indiana University Press, 1980.

Marer, Paul (ed.). *US Financing of East-West Trade: The Political Economy of Government Credits and the National Interest.* Bloomington: Indiana University Press, 1975.

Mastny, Vojtech. *Helsinki, Human Rights, and European Security: Analysis and Documentation.* Durham, NC: Duke University Press, 1986.

Matley, Ian M. *Romania: A Profile.* New York: Praeger Publishers, 1970.

McMillan, Carl H. (ed.). *Changing Perspectives in East-West Commerce.* Lexington, MA: Lexington Books, 1979.

McLellan, David S. *Cyrus Vance.* New York: Rowman Publishers, 1985.

McNeal, Robert H. (ed.). *International Relations Among Communists.* Englewood Cliffs, NJ: Prentice-Hall, Inc., 1967.

McNeill, William Hardy. *America, Britain, & Russia: Their Co-Operation and Conflict, 1941-1946.* New York: Johnson Reprint Corporation, 1970.

Medvedev, Roy. *China and the Superpowers.* Oxford: Basil Blackwell,1986.

Millis, Walter, with Duffield, E. S. (ed.). *The Forrestal Diaries.* New York: The Viking Press, 1951.

Montias, John Michael. *Economic Development in Communist Rumania.* Cambridge, MA: M.I.T. Press, 1967.

Morris, Roger. *Richard Milhous Nixon: The Rise of an American Politician.* New York: Henry Holt and Company, 1990.

Mosely, Philip. E. (ed.). *The Soviet Union, 1922-1962: A Foreign Affairs Reader.* Foreword by Hamilton Fish Armstrong. New York: Frederick A. Praeger, Publishers, 1963.

Nelson, Daniel N. (ed.). *Romania in the 1980s.* Boulder, CO: Westview Press, 1981.

Newhouse, John. *War and Peace in the Nuclear Age.* New York: Alfred A. Knopf, 1989.

Newsom, David. D. *The Diplomacy of Human Rights*. New York: University Press of America, 1986.

Nixon, Richard. *Leaders*. New York: Warner Books, 1982.

_____. *The Memoirs of Richard Nixon*. New York: Grosset and Dunlap, 1978.

Notter, Harley. *Postwar Foreign Policy Preparation, 1939-1945*. Washington, D.C.: U.S. Department of State, 1949.

Nove, Alec. *East-West Trade: Problems, Prospects, Issues*. "The Washington Papers, Volume 6." London: Sage Publications, 1978.

Otetea, Andrei (ed.). *The History of the Romanian People*. New York: Twayne Publishers, Inc., 1970.

Oudes, Bruce (ed.). *From: The President. Richard Nixon's Secret Files*. New York: Harper & Row, Publishers, 1989.

Pacepa, Ion Mihai. *Red Horizons: Chronicles of a Communist Spy Chief*. Washington, D.C.: Regnery Gateway, 1987.

Partidului Comunist Roman. *Directivele congresului al xii-lea al Partidului Comunist Roman, cu privire la dezvoltarea economico-sociala a Romaniei in cincinalul 1981-1985, si orientarile de perspectiva pina in 1990*. Bucuresti: Editura politica, 1979.

_____. *Documente ale Partidului Comunist Roman; Culegere sintetica. Politica externa a Romaniei socialiste*. Bucuresti: Editura politica, 1972.

_____. *Documente ale Partidului Comunist Roman; Culegere sintetica. societatea socialista multilateral dezvoltata*. Bucuresti, Editura politica, 1972.

_____. *Hotarirea Comitetului Central al Partidului comunist roman, cu privire la indeplinirea planului cincinal 1971-1975*. Bucuresti: Editura politica, 1976.

Paterson, Thomas G. *Meeting the Communist Threat: Truman to Reagan*. New York: Oxford University Press, 1988.

The Pentagon Papers: The Defense Department History of the United States Decisionmaking on Vietnam. The Senator Gravel Edition. 4 vols. Boston: Beacon Press, 1971-1975.

Pestieau, Caroline, and Henry, Jacques. *Non-Tariff Trade Barriers as a Problem in International Development: A Study in Two Parts*. n. p., The Canadian Economic Policy Committee, 1972.

Pethybridge, Roger (ed.). *The Development of the Communist Bloc*. Boston: D C. Heath and Company, 1965.

Porter, Ivor. *Operation Autonomous: With S.O.E. in Wartime Romania*. London: Chatto and Windus, 1989.

President Nicolae Ceausescu's State Visit to the U.S.A., April 12-17, 1978. Bucharest: Meridiane Publishing House, 1978.

Public Papers of the Presidents of the United States: Jimmy Carter (1977-1981). 9 vols. Washington, D.C.: U.S. Government Printing Office, 1977-1982.

Public Papers of the Presidents of the United States: Dwight D. Eisenhower (1953-1961). 8 vols. Washington, D.C.: U.S. Government Printing Office, 1960-1961.

Public Papers of the Presidents of the United States: Gerald R. Ford (1974-1976). 6 vols. Washington, D.C.: U.S. Government Printing Office, 1975-1979.

Public Papers of the Presidents of the United States: Lyndon B. Johnson (1963-1969). 10 vols. Washington, D.C.: U.S. Government Printing Office, 1965-1970.

Public Papers of the Presidents of the United States: John F. Kennedy (1961-1963). 3 vols. Washington, D.C.: U.S. Government Printing Office,1961-1964.

Public Papers of the Presidents of the United States: Richard M. Nixon (1969-1974). 6 vols. Washington, D.C.: U.S. Government Printing Office, 1970-1975.

Public Papers of the Presidents of the United States: Ronald Reagan, (1981-1987). 12 vols. Washington, D.C.: U.S. Government Printing Office, 1982-1989.

Public Papers of the Presidents of the United States: Harry S. Truman (1945-1953). 7 vols. Washington, D.C.: U.S. Government Printing Office, 1961-1966.

Quinlan, Paul D. *Clash Over Romania: British and American Policies toward Romania: 1938-1947.* A.R.A. Volume 2. Los Angeles: American Romanian Academy of Arts and Sciences, 1977.

_____ (ed.). *The United States and Romania: American-Romanian Relations in the Twentieth-Century.* A.R.A. Volume 6. Los Angeles: American Romanian Academy of Arts and Sciences, 1988.

Rafael, Edgar R. *"Entwicklungsland" Rumanien; Zur Geschichte der "Umderfinierung" eines sozialistischen Staates.* Munchen: R. Oldenbourg Verlag, 1977.

Republica Socialista Romania. *Comertul Exterior al Republicii Socialiste Romania, 1974. Culgere de date statistice.* Bucharest: 1974

Romania Yearbook, 1977. 3rd ed. Bucharest: Editura stiintifica si enciclopedica, 1977.

Romania, Documents and Events. Congresul al xiii-lea al P.C.R. Bucharest: Agerpres, 1984.

_____. *Communique, On the Fulfillment of the 1986 Single National Plan of the Economic and Social Development of the Socialist Republic of Romania.* Bucharest: Agerpres, 1987.

_____. *Meeting of the Executive Political Committee of the CC of the RCP.* Bucharest: Agerpres, 1987.

Romanian Communist Party. *Directives of the Tenth Congress of the Romanian Communist Party Concerning the 1971-1975 Five-Year Plan, and the Guidelines for the Development of the National Economy in the 1976-1980 Period.* Bucharest: Agerpres, 1969.

_____. *Directives of the Central Committee of the Romanian Communist Party, On the Perfecting of Management and Planning of the National Economy Approved at the Plenary Meeting, October 5-6, 1967.* Bucharest: Agerpres, 1967.

Rubinstein, Alvin Z. *Soviet Foreign Policy Since World War II, Imperial and Global.* 2nd ed. Boston: Little, Brown, and Company, 1985.

Ryans, John K., Negandhi, Anant R., and Baker, James C. *China, the U.S.S.R. and Eastern Europe: A U.S. Trade Perspective.* Kent, OH: The Kent State University Press, 1974.

Schoenbaum, Thomas J. *Waging Peace and War: Dean Rusk in the Truman, Kennedy, and Johnson Years.* New York: Simon and Schuster, 1988.

Schopflin, George (ed.). *The Soviet Union and Eastern Europe.* New York: Facts on File Publications, 1986.

Seton-Watson, Hugh. *Eastern Europe Between the Wars, 1918-1941.* New York: Harper & Row, Publishers, 1967.

_____. *The East European Revolution.* 3rd ed. New York: Frederick A. Praeger, Publishers, 1956.

Shafir, Michael. *Romania: Politics, Economics and Society. Political Stagnation and Simulated Change.* Boulder, CO: Lynne Rienner Publishers, Inc., 1985.

Sherwood, Robert E. *Roosevelt and Hopkins: An Intimate History.* Harper & Brothers, Publishers, 1948.

Simon, Jeffrey. *Cohesion and Dissension in Eastern Europe: Six Crises.* New York: Praeger, 1983.

Singleton, F. B. *Background to Eastern Europe.* London: Pergamon Press, 1965.

Smyser, W. R. *Refugees, Extended Exile.* Foreword by Leo Cherne. "The Washington Papers, No. 129," New York: Praeger, 1987.

Sodaro, Michael J., and Wolchik, Sharon L. (eds.). *Foreign and Domestic Policy in Eastern Europe in the 1980s: Trends and Prospects.* New York: St. Martin's Press, 1983.

Spero, Joan Edleman. *The Politics of International Economic Relations.* 3rd ed. New York: St. Martin's Press, 1985.

Spigler, Iancu. *Economic Reform in Rumanian Industry.* London: Oxford University Press, 1973.

Staar, Richard F. *et al.,* (eds.). *Yearbook on International Communist Affairs, 1969.* Stanford, CA: Hoover Institution Press, 1970.

_____. *Yearbook on International Communist Affairs, 1970.* Stanford, CA: Hoover Institution Press, 1971.

_____. *Yearbook on International Communist Affairs, 1971.* Stanford, CA: Hoover Institution Press, 1971.

_____. *Yearbook on International Communist Affairs, 1972.* Stanford, CA: Hoover Institution Press, 1972.

_____. *Yearbook on International Communist Affairs, 1973.* Stanford, CA: Hoover Institution Press, 1973.

_____. *Yearbook on International Communist Affairs, 1974.* Stanford, CA: Hoover Institution Press, 1974.

_____. *Yearbook on International Communist Affairs, 1975.* Stanford, CA: Hoover Institution Press, 1975.

_____. *Yearbook on International Communist Affairs, 1976.* Stanford, CA: Hoover Institution Press, 1976.

_____. *Yearbook on International Communist Affairs, 1977.* Stanford, CA: Hoover Institution Press, 1977.

_____. *Yearbook on International Communist Affairs, 1978*. Stanford, CA: Hoover Institution Press, 1978.

_____. *Yearbook on International Communist Affairs, 1979*. Stanford, CA: Hoover Institution Press, 1979.

_____. *Yearbook on International Communist Affairs, 1980*. Stanford, CA: Hoover Institution Press, 1980.

_____. *Yearbook on International Communist Affairs, 1981*. Stanford, CA: Hoover Institution Press, 1981.

_____. *Yearbook on International Communist Affairs, 1982: Parties and Revolutionary Movements*. Stanford, CA: Hoover Institution Press, 1982.

Staar, Richard F. (ed.). *Yearbook on International Communist Affairs, 1984: Parties and Revolutionary Movements*. Stanford, CA: Hoover Institution Press, 1984.

_____. *Yearbook on International Communist Affairs, 1985: Parties and Revolutionary Movements*. Stanford, CA: Hoover Institution Press, 1985.

_____. *Yearbook on International Communist Affairs, 1986: Parties and Revolutionary Movements*. Stanford, CA: Hoover Institution Press, 1986.

Stanciu, Ion, and Cernovodeanu, Paul. *Distant Lands: The Genesis and Evolution of Romanian-American Relations*. "East European Monographs, Boulder," New York: Columbia University Press, 1985.

Stebbins, Richard P. *The United States in World Affairs*. New York: Harper & Row, Publishers, 1965.

Stern, Paula. *Water's Edge: Domestic Politics and the Making of American Foreign Policy*. Westport, CT: Greenwood Press, 1979.

Stevenson, Richard W. *The Rise and Fall of Detente: Relaxations of Tension in US-Soviet Relations, 1953-1984*. Urbana: University of Illinois Press, 1985.

Sugar, Peter F. (ed.). *Native Fascism in the Successor States, 1948-1945*. Santa Barbara, CA: ABC-CLIO, 1971.

Sulzberger, C. L. *An Age of Mediocrity: Memoirs and Diaries, 1963-1972*. New York: Macmillan Publishing Co., Inc., 1973.

_____. *A Long Row of Candles: Memoirs and Diaries, 1934-1954*. New York: The Macmillan Company, 1969.

Summerscale, Peter. *The East European Predicament: Changing Patterns in Poland, Czechoslovakia and Romania*. London: Gower, 1982.

Szulc, Tad. *The Illusion of Peace: Foreign Policy in the Nixon Years*. New York: The Viking Press, 1978.

Talbott, Strobe. *The Master of the Game: Paul Nitze and the Nuclear Peace*. New York: Alfred A. Knopf, 1988.

Terry, Sarah Meiklejohn (ed.). *Soviet Policy in Eastern Europe*. New Haven, CT: Yale University Press, 1984.

Tismaneanu, Leonte, and Zaharia, Rolica. *Present and Prospect in Romania's Social and Economic Development, 1977*. Bucharest: Meridiane Publishing House, 1977.

Tananbaum, Duane. *The Bricker Amendment Controversy: A Test of Eisenhower's Political Leadership*. Ithaca, NY: Cornell University Press, 1988.

Tsantis, Andreas C., and Pepper, Roy. Romania: *The Industrialization of the Agrarian Economy under Socialist Planning*. Washington, D.C.: The World Bank, 1979.

Ulam, Adam. *Stalin, The Man and His Era*. New York: The Viking Press, 1973.

Vance, Cyrus. *Hard Choices: Critical Years in America's Foreign Policy*. New York: Simon and Schuster, 1983.

Vasilescu, Corneliu. *Romania in International Life*. Bucharest: Meridiane Publishing House, 1969.

Weiner, Robert. *Romanian Foreign Policy and the United Nations*. New York: Praeger, 1984.

Wesson, Robert (ed.). *Yearbook on International Communist Affairs, 1983: Parties and Revolutionary Movements*. Stanford, CA: Hoover Institution Press, 1983.

Wheeler-Bennett, John, and Nicholls, Anthony. *The Semblance of Peace: The Political Settlement After the Second World War*. New York: St. Martin's Press, 1972.

Wienert, Helgard, and Slater, John. *East-West Technology Transfer; The Trade and Economic Aspects*. London: Organisation for Economic Cooperation and Development, 1986.

Wolff, Robert Lee. *The Balkans in Our Time*. New York: W. W. Norton & Company, Inc., 1967.

Zagoria, Donald S. *The Sino-Soviet Conflict, 1956-1961*. Princeton, NJ: Princeton University Press, 1962.

Zamfir, Alexandru, and Rapcea, Constantin. *Strategia competitivitatii in comertul international*. Bucuresti: Editura politica, 1976.

Articles and Periodicals

Becker, Abraham, et al. "The 27th Congress of the Communist Party of the Soviet Union: A Report from the Airlie House Conference," Rand/UCLA Center for the Study of Soviet International Behavior, December, 1986.

Bacon, Walter M., Jr. "Romania: Neo-Stalinism in Search of Legitimacy," *Current History* (April, 1981), 168-172.

Campbell, John C. "Diplomacy on the Danube," *Foreign Affairs*, Vol. 27, No. 2 (January 1949), 315-327.

Clabaugh, Samuel F., and Allen, Richard V. "East-West Trade, Its Strategic Implications. Analysis and Inventory of Congressional Documents, 1959-1963." Washington, D.C., The Center for Strategic Studies, 1964.

Clabaugh, Samuel F., and Feulner, Edwin J., Jr. "Trading With the Communists." Washington, D.C., The Center for Strategic Studies, 1968.

Clarke, Duncan L. "Why State Can't Lead," *Foreign Policy*, No. 66 (Spring 1987), 128-134.

Fischer, Mary Ellen. "Political Leadership in Rumania under the Communists," *International Journal of Rumanian Studies*, Vol. 5, No. 1 (1987), 7-32.

Galdi, Theodor W., and Shuey, Robert D. "U.S. Economic Sanctions Imposed Against Specific Foreign Countries, 1979 to the Present" (Report No. 87-949

F), Washington, D.C., Library of Congress, Congressional Research Service, December 1, 1987.

Georgescu, Vlad. "Romania in the 1980s: The Legacy of Dynastic Socialism," *Eastern European Politics and Societies*, Vol. 2, No. 1 (Winter 1988), 70-93.

Lansing, Paul, and Rose, Eric C. "The Granting and Suspension of Most-Favored-Nation Status for Nonmarket Economy States: Policy and Consequences," *Harvard International Law Journal*, Vol. 25, No. 2 (Spring 1984), 329-351.

Holliday, George. "Issue Brief: Trade (Updated October 9. 1987)," Washington, D.C.: Library of Congress, Congressional Research Service, n.d.

"The Hungarian View: An Interview with Karoly Kiraly," *East European Reporter*, Vol. 2 No. 3 (1987), 46-48.

Hunya, Gabor. New Developments in Romanian Agriculture," *Eastern European Politics and Societies*, Vol. 1, No. 2 (Spring 1987), 255-276.

Jackson, Marvin R. "Economic Development in the Balkans Since 1945 Compared to Southern and East-Central Europe," *Eastern European Politics and Societies*, Vol. 1, No. 3 (Fall 1987), 393-455.

Lawson, Colin. "The Soviet Union and Eastern Europe in Southern Africa: Is There a Conflict of Interest," *International Affairs*, Vol. 59, No. 1 (Winter 1982/1983), 32-40.

Luers, William H. "The U.S. and Eastern Europe," *Foreign Affairs*, Vol. 65, No. 5 (1987), 976-994.

Lugar, Richard G. "A Republican Looks at Foreign Policy," *Foreign Affairs*, Vol. 66, No. 2 (1987), 249-262.

McElwain, Scott. "The United States and Central Europe: Differentiation or Detente?," *East European Quarterly*, Vol. XXI, No. 4 (Winter 1987), 451-468.

Mondale, Walter F., Senator. "East-West Trade: A Congressional Perspective," *New York University Center for International Studies Policy Papers*, Vol. 3, No. 3 (January, 1970).

Mushkat, Marion. "Kann ein Kleiner Staat sich selbst verteidigen? Die rumanische Version." Berichte des Bundesinstituts fur ostwissenschaftliche und internationale Studien [Bonn, Bundesrepublik Deutschland] Juni, 1979.

[National Policy Panel, United Nations Association of the USA] *United States Foreign Policy and Human Rights: Principles, Priorities, Practice*. n.p., United Nations Association of the USA, December, 1979.

Netea, Vasile. "Actions et ecrits contre le Diktat de Vienne," *Revue roumaine d'histoire*, Vol. XIII, Nos. 5-6 (1974), 765-788.

Pick, Otto. "Problems of Adjustment: The Gorbachev Effect in Eastern Europe," *SAIS Review*, Vol. 8, No. 1 (Winter-Spring 1988), 57-74.

Piquet, Howard S. "The Unconditional Most-Favored-Nation Policy of the United States," Washington, D.C., Library of Congress, Legislative Reference Service, February 12, 1947.

Pregelj, Vladimir N. Most-Favored-Nation Treatment of Foreign Trading Partners by the United States: A Summary" (Report No. 86-17 E), Washington, D.C.: Library of Congress, Congressional Research Service, January 28, 1986.

_____. "U.S. Commercial Relations with Communist Countries: Chronology of Significant Actions Since World War II, and their Present Status" (Report No. 84-67 E), Washington, D.C., Library of Congress, Congressional Research Service, March 30, 1984.

Radio Free Europe, *Research*, 1980-1989.

Radio Free Europe, *Situation Reports*, 1980-1989.

"Romania: Opposition Tangle," *Eastern Europe Newsletter*, February 10, 1988.

Skurski, Rogers. "Trade and Integraton in East Europe," *Current History* (November, 1982), 357-361.

Socor, Vladimir. "The Limits of National Independence in the Soviet Bloc," *Orbis* (Fall 1976), 702-704.

Spiegelman, James M., (ed). "International Symposium on Export-Import Interrelationships." Special Publication No. 11. Washington, D. C.: National Center for Export-Import Studies, January 1986.

Stevenson, Adlai E., and Frye, Alton. "Trading With the Communists," *Foreign Affairs*, Vol. 68, No. 2 (1989), 53-71.

Svec, Milan. "The Prague Spring: 20 Years Later," *Foreign Affairs*, Vol. 66, No. 5 (1988), 981-1001.

Tismaneanu, Vladimir. "Ceausescu's Socialism," *Problems of Communism*, Vol. XXXIV, No. 1 (January-February, 1985), 50-66.

_____. "Ceausescu at Seventy," *East European Reporter*, Vol. 3, No. 2 (March 1988), 60.

_____. "The Tragicomedy of Romanian Communism," *Eastern European Politics and Societies*, Vol. 3, No. 2 (Spring 1989), 329-347.

Trachtenberg, Marc. "A 'Wasting Asset': American Strategy and the Shifting Nuclear Balance, 1949-1954," *International Security*, Vol. 13, No. 3 (Winter 1988/89), 5-49.

Tucker, Robert W. "Reagan's Foreign Policy," *Foreign Affairs*, Vol. 68, No. 1 (1989), 1-27.

Tudor, Gheorghe. "Cincinalul 1986-1990 – etapa calitativ superioara pe drumul fauririi societatii socialiste multilateral dezvoltate," *Anale de istorie*, Anul XXXII, No. 5 (1986), 3-17.

Whitehead, John C. "The Department of State: Requirements for an Effective Foreign Policy in the 1990s." *Presidential Studies Quarterly*, Vol. XIX, No. 1 (Winter 1989), 11-24.

Congressional Committees

House of Representatives

House. Committee on Banking and Currency and the Subcommittee on International Trade. *Continuation of authority for Regulation of Exports and Amending the Export Control Act of 1949*. Hearings, 89th Cong., 1st Sess., May 5, 13, 20, and 21, 1965.

House. Committee on Banking and Currency, Subcommittee on International

Trade. *To Extend and Amend the Export Control Act of 1949.* Hearings 91st Cong., 1st Sess., May 22, 23; June 4, 11; and July 24, 1969.

_____. *Extension of the Export Administration Act of 1969.* Hearing, 92nd Cong., 2d Sess., May 30, 1972.

_____. *International Economic Policy. Hearings,* 93rd Cong., 2d Sess., April 22, 23, 24, 25, 26, 29, 30; May 1 and 2, 1974.

House. Committee on Banking, Currency and Housing, Subcommittee on International Trade, Investment and Monetary Policy. *Briefing on East-West Trade.* Hearing, 94th Cong., 1st Sess., March 19, 1975.

_____. *Oversight Hearings on the Export-Import Bank.* Staff Report and Recommendations. 94th Cong., 2d Sess., May 10 and 11, 1976.

House. Committee on Energy and Commerce, Subcommittee on Oversight and Investigations. *Services for Exporters from the U. S. Government.* Committee Imprint, 98th Cong., 2d Sess., November, 1984.

House. Committee on Foreign Affairs, *Special Studies Series on Foreign Affairs Issues,* Vol. I: *Soviet Diplomacy and Negotiating Behavior: Emerging New Contest for U.S. Diplomacy.* House Document No. 96-238, 96th Cong., 1st Sess. [December,1979].

_____. *Selected Executive Session Hearings of the Committee, 1951-56,* Vol. XIV: *U.S. Foreign Policy and the East-West Confrontation,* 1980.

_____. *The U.S. Supreme Court Decision Concerning the Legislative Veto.* Hearings, 98th Cong., 1st Sess., July 19, 20, and 21, 1983.

House. Committee on Foreign Affairs, Subcommittee on Europe. *Report of the Special Study Mission to Europe, On Policy Toward the Satellite Nations.* House Report No. 531, 85th Cong., 1st Sess., June 4, 1957.

_____. *Recent Developments in the Soviet Bloc.* Hearings, 88th Cong., 2d Sess., February 18, 19, 25; March 4 and 10, 1964.

_____. *Conditions in the Baltic States and in Other countries of Eastern Europe.* Hearings, 89th Cong., 1st Sess., May 17 and 18, 1965.

_____. *Recent Developments in East-West Relations.* Hearing, 89th Cong., 2d Sess., October 18, 1966.

_____. *East-West Trade.* Hearings, 90th Cong., 2d Sess., January 30; February 20, 21, 27, 28; March 7 and 27, 1968.

_____. *Detente.* Hearings, 93rd Cong., 2d Sess., May 8, 15, 22; June 10, 12, 26; July 17, 25, and 31, 1974.

House. Committee on Foreign Affairs, Subcommittee on Europe and the Middle East. *U. S. Relations with the Countries of Central and Eastern Europe.* Report, 96th Cong., 1st Sess., December 1979.

_____. *East-West Relations in the Aftermath of Soviet Invasion of Afghanistan.* Hearings, 96th Cong., 2d Sess., January 24 and 30, 1980.

_____. *U.S. Policy Toward Eastern Europe, 1985.* Hearings, 99th Cong., 1st Sess., October 2 and 7, 1985.

_____. *United States-Romanian Relations and Most-Favored-Nation [MFN] Status for Romania.* Hearing, 100th Cong., 1st Sess., July 30, 1987.

House. Committee on Foreign Affairs, Subcommittees on Europe and the Middle East, and on Human Rights, and on International Organizations. *Human*

Rights in Romania. Hearing, 99th Cong., 1st Sess., May 14, 1985.

House. Committee on Foreign Affairs, Subcommittees on Europe and the Middle East, and on International Economic Policy and Trade. *East-West Economic Issues, Sanctions Policy, and the Formulation of International Economic Policy.* Hearing, 98th Cong., 2d Sess., March 29, 1984.

_____. *United States Trade Relations with Eastern Europe and Yugoslavia.* Hearing, 100th Cong., 1st Sess., October, 28, 1987.

House. Committee on Foreign Affairs, Subcommittee on Foreign Economic Policy. *East-West Trade.* Hearing, 83rd Cong., 2d Sess., February 16, 1954.

_____. *The Involvement of U.S. Private Enterprise in Developing Countries.* Hearings, 90th Cong., 1st Sess., July 18; August 1, 8, 9, 27; September 12, 13, 19; and October 25, 31, 1967.

_____. *Overseas Private Investment Corporation.* Hearings, 91st Cong., 1st Sess., August 5, 6, 12, September 16, and 18, 1969.

_____. *Overseas Private Investment Corporation.* Hearings, 93rd Cong., 1st Sess., May 22, 29, 31, June 5, 7, 12, 13, 19, and 20, 1973.

_____. *Overseas Private Investment Corporation.* Hearing, 93rd Cong, 2d Sess., March 20, 1974.

House. Committee on Foreign Affairs, Subcommittee on Human Rights and International Organizations. *Religious Persecution as a Violation of Human Rights.* Hearings and Markup, 97th Cong., 2d Sess., February 10; March 2; May 25; July 27 and 29; August 5 and 10; September 23; December 1 and 14, 1982.

_____. *Status of U.S. Human Rights Policy, 1987.* Hearing, 100th Cong., 1st Sess., February 19, 1987.

_____. *Human Rights in Romania and Its Implications for U. S. Policy and Most Favored Nation Status.* Hearing, 100th Cong., 2d Sess., June 24, 1987.

_____. *Recent Developments in U.S. Human Rights Policy.* Hearings, 100th Cong., 2d Sess., February 10 and 17, 1988.

House. Committee on Foreign Affairs, Subcommittee on International Economic Policy and Trade. *Commercial Lending to the Soviet Bloc.* Hearing, 100th Cong., 1st Sess., November 17, 1987.

_____. *Extension and Revision of the Export Administration Act of 1969.* Hearings and Markup, 96th Cong., 1st Sess., February 15, 22; March 7, 8, 14, 15, 21, 22, 26, 27, 28; April 3, 4, 24, 25, and 26, 1979.

_____. *Review of Activities of the Overseas Private Investment Corporation.* Hearings, 96th Cong. [1st and 2d Sess.], July 17, 1979, and February 7, 1980.

House. Committee on Foreign Affairs, Subcommittee on International Operations. *Allegations Concerning the Romanian Service of Radio Free Europe.* Hearing, 96th Cong., 2d Sess., February 21, 1980.

House. Committee on Foreign Affairs, Subcommittee on International Organizations. *Human Rights and U.S. Foreign Policy.* Hearings, 96th Cong., 1st Sess., May 2, 10; June 21; July 12; and August 2, 1979.

_____. *Human Rights in Eastern Europe and the Soviet Union.* Hearing and Markup, 96th Cong., 2d Sess., September 16 and 24, 1980.

House. Committee on International Relations. *Soviet Bloc Trade Hopes:*

Reactions to The Trade Act of 1974; Report of a Study Mission to the Soviet Union and Four Eastern European nations. Committee Print, 94th Cong., 1st Sess., June 28, 1974.

_____. *Selected Executive Session Hearings of the Committee, 1943-50*, Vol. II: *Problems of World War II and Its Aftermath*, 1976.

House. Committee on International Relations, Subcommittee on Europe and the Middle East. *U.S. Policy Toward Eastern Europe.* Hearings, 95th Cong., 2d Sess., September 7 and 12, 1978.

House. Committee on International Relations, Subcommittee on International Economic Policy and Trade. *Human Rights and United States Foreign Policy: A Review of the Administration's Record.* Hearing, 95th Cong., 1st Sess., October 25, 1987.

House. Committee on International Relations, Subcommittee on International Economic Policy and Trade. *Coordination of United States International Economic Policy.* Hearing, 95th cong., 1st Sess., September 15, 1977.

House. Committee on International Relations, Subcommittee on International Security and Scientific Affairs. *United States National Security Policy vis-a-vis Eastern Europe (The "Sonnenfeldt Doctrine').* Hearings, 94th Cong., 2d Sess., April 12, 1976.

House. Committee on International Relations, Subcommittee on International Trade and Commerce. *Status of Claims Settlements with Nonmarket Countries: East German Claims Bill (H.R. 14642).* Hearings, 94th Cong., 2d Sess., August 25 and 26, 1976.

House. Committee on Ways and Means. *Trade Expansion Act of 1962.* Hearings, 87th Cong., 2d Sess., March 12, 13, 14, 15, 16, 19, 20, 21, 22, 23, 26, 27, 30; April 2,3, 4, 5, 6, 9, 10 and 11, 1962.

_____. *Foreign Trade and Tariff Proposals.* Hearings, 90th Cong., 2d Sess., June 4, 5, 10, 11, 12, 13, 14, 17, 18, 19, 21, 24, 25, 26, 27, 28; July 1 and 2, 1968.

_____. *Prepared Statements of Administration Witnesses, Submitted to the Committee on Ways and Means at Public Hearings Beginning on May 9, 1973; And Other Material Relating to the Administration Proposal Entitled The "Trade Reform Act of 1973," (H.R. 6767),* May 14, 1973.

_____. *Trade Reform.* Hearings, 93rd Cong., 1st Sess., May 9, 10, 11, 14, 15, 16, 17, 18, 21, 22, 23, 24, 29, 30, 31; June 1, 6, 7, 8, 11, 12, 13, 14, and 15, 1973.

_____. *Third Quarterly Report to the Congress and the East-West Foreign Trade Board, On Developments in Trade Between the United States and the Nonmarket Economies,* 94th Cong,, 1st Sess., September 30, 1975.

_____. *Fifth Quarterly Report on Trade Between the United States and Nonmarket Economy Countries, Pursuant to Section 411(c) of the Trade Act of 1974,* 94th Cong., 2d Sess., August 9. 1976.

_____. *Sixth Quarterly Report on Trade Between the United States and Nonmarket Economy Countries, Pursuant to Section 411 (c) of the Trade Act of 1974,* 95th Cong., 1st Sess., October 21, 1976.

_____. *Eighth Quarterly Report to the Congress and the East-West Foreign*

Trade Board, On Trade Between the United States and the Nonmarket Economy Countries, 95th Cong., 1st Sess., December 30, 1976.

_____. *Ninth Quarterly Report to the Congress and the East-West Foreign Trade Board, On Trade Between the United States and the Nonmarket Economy Countries*, 95th Cong., 1st Sess., March 31, 1977.

_____. *Tenth Quarterly Report to the Congress and the East-West Foreign Trade Board, On Trade Between the United States and the Nonmarket Economy Countries*, 95th Cong., 1st Sess., June 30, 1977.

_____. *Thirteenth Quarterly Report to the Congress and the East-West Foreign Trade Board, On Trade Between the United States and the Nonmarket Economy Countries*, 95th Cong., 2d Sess., March 31, 1978.

_____. *Fourteenth Quarterly Report to the Congress and the East-West Foreign Trade Board, On Trade Between the United States and the Nonmarket Economy Countries*, 95th Cong., 2d Sess., June 30, 1978.

_____. *Seventeenth Quarterly Report to the Congress and the East-West Foreign Trade Board, On Trade Between the United States and the Nonmarket Economy Countries*, 96th Cong., 1st Sess., April 2, 1979.

_____. *Disapproval of Extension of Presidential Authority to Waive Freedom of Emigration Requirements Under Section 402 of the Trade Act of 1974 with Respect to Romania*. Report No. 96-336, 96th cong., 1st Sess., July 13, 1979.

_____. *Disapproval of Extension of Presidential Authority to Waive Freedom of Emigration Requirements Under Section 402 of the Trade Act of 1974 with Respect to Romania*. Report No. 97-743, 97th Cong., 2d Sess., August 12, 1982.

_____. *Disapproval of Extension of Waiver Authority under the Trade Act of 1974 to the Socialist Republic of Romania*. Report No. 98-315, 98th Cong., 1st Sess., July 26, 1983.

_____. *Generalized System of Preferences Renewal Act of 1984*. Report 98-1090, 98th Cong., 2d Sess., September 27, 1984.

_____. *Comprehensive Trade Policy Reform Act of 1986*. Report No. 99-581, 99th Cong., 2d Sess., May 6, 1986.

_____. *Overview and Compilation of U. S. Trade Statutes*. Committee Print, 100th Cong., 1st Sess., January 6, 1987.

_____. *Trade Legislation Enacted Into Public Law, 1981 Through 1988*. Committee Print, 101st Cong., 1st., January 27, 1989.

House. Committee on Ways and Means, Subcommittee on Foreign Trade Policy. *Foreign Trade Policy*. Hearings, 85th Cong., 1st Sess., December 2, 3, 4, 5, 6, 9, 10, 11, 12, and 13, 1957.

House. Committee on Ways and Means, Subcommittee on Trade. *United States-Romanian Trade Agreement*. Hearings, 94th Cong., 1st Sess., May 7 and 8, 1975.

_____. *Background and Status of the Multilateral Trade Negotiations: Supplement*. 94th Cong., 1st Sess., September 19, 1975.

_____. *Background Material on the Generalized System of Preferences*

(GSP). 94th Cong., 2d Sess., January 19, 1976.

_____. *Extension of Most-Favored-Nation Treatment to Romania*. Hearing, 94th Cong., 2d Sess., September 14, 1976.

_____. *Legislative Proposals on Miscellaneous Tariff and Trade Bills*. Hearings, 95th Cong., 1st Sess., April 26, 27, and 28, 1977.

_____. *Most-Favored-Nation Treatment with Respect to the Products of the Socialist Republic of Romania*. Hearing, 95th Cong., 1st Sess., July 18, 1977.

_____. *Emigration Waiver to the Socialist Republic of Romania and the Hungarian People's Republic; And Nondiscriminatory Treatment of the Products of Romania*. Hearing, 95th Cong., 2d Sess., June 15, 1978.

_____. *Waiver of Freedom of Emigration Requirement to the Socialist Republic of Romania and the Hungarian People's Republic*. Hearings, 96th Cong., 1st Sess., June 22 and July 9, 1979.

_____. *Trade Waiver Authority Extension*. Hearing, 96th Cong., 2d Sess., June 10, 1980.

_____. *Trade Waiver Authority Extension*. Hearing, 97th Cong., 1st Sess., June 22, 1981.

_____. *Extension of MFN Status to Romania, Hungary, and the People's Republic of China*. Hearings, 97th Cong., 2d Sess., July 12 and 13, 1982.

_____. *Presidential Recommendation to Continue Waivers Applicable to Romania, Hungary, and the People's Republic of China, and to Extend the Trade Act Waiver Authority*. Hearing, 98th Cong., 1st Sess., July 14, 1983.

_____. *Report on Trade Mission to Central and Eastern Europe*. Committee Print. 98th Cong., 2d Sess., March 29, 1984.

_____. *Most-Favored-Nation Trading Status for the Socialist Republic of Romania, the Hungarian People's Republic, and the People's Republic of China. Hearing*, 99th Cong., 2d Sess., June 10, 1986.

Senate

Senate. Committee on Banking and Currency, Subcommittee on International Finance. *Extend and Amend The Export Control Act of 1949*. Hearing, 89th Cong., 1st Sess., June 16, 1965.

_____. *East-West Trade*. Hearings, 90th Cong., 2d Sess., June 4, 13, 27; July 17, 24, and 25, 1968.

_____. *Export Expansion and Regulation*. Hearings, 91st Cong., 1st Sess., April 23, 24, 28, 29, and 30; and May 1 and 28, 1969.

Senate. Committee on Banking, Housing, and Urban Affairs. *Use of Export Controls and Export Credits for Foreign Policy Purposes*. Hearings, 95th Cong., 2d Sess., October 10 and 11, 1978.

_____. *U.S. Export Control Policy and Extension of The Export Administration Act*. Hearings, 96th Cong., 1st Sess., March 5 and 6, 1979.

Senate. Committee on Banking, Housing, and Urban Affairs, Subcommittee on International Finance. *The Role of the Export-Import Bank and Export Controls in U.S. International Economic Policy*. Hearings, 93rd Cong., 2d Sess.,

April 2, 5, 10,, 23, 25, and 26; May 2, 1974.
_____. *Extension of The Export Administration Act.* Hearings, 94th Cong., 2d Sess., March 22 and 23, 1976.
_____. *Export Policy.* Hearing, 95th Cong., 2d Sess., February 6, 1978.
_____. *U.S. Export Policy.* Report, 90th Cong., 1st Sess., February 1979.
_____. Hearings, 92nd Cong., 2d Sess., March 13 and 14, 1972. *Amending The Export-Import Bank Act and The Trade Act.* Hearings, 96th Cong., 1st Sess., July 12 and 19, 1979.
Senate. Committee on Commerce. *Export Expansion.* Hearings, 89th Cong., 1st Sess., March 17, 18, and 19, 1965.
Senate, Committee on Commerce, Subcommittee on Foreign Commerce and Tourism. *Export Expansion Legislation.* Hearings (Part 1), 93rd Cong., 1st Sess., June 7, 8, and 29, 1973.
_____. *Export Expansion Legislation.* Hearing (Part 2), 93rd Cong., 1st Sess., September 6, 1973.
Senate, Committee on Commerce, Science, and Transportation. *National Export Program.* Hearing, 95th Cong., 2d Sess., September 28, 1978.
Senate. Committee on Finance. *Trade Expansion Act of 1962.* Hearings (Part 1), 87th Cong., 2d Sess., July 23, 24, 25, and 26, 1962.
_____. *Trade Expansion Act of 1962.* Hearings (Part 3), 87th Cong., 2d Sess., August 7, 8, 9, and 10, 1962.
_____. *Foreign Trade Statistics.* Hearings, 89th Cong., 2d Sess., August 31 and September 1, 1966.
_____. *Summary and Analysis of H.R. 10710 - The Trade Reform Act of 1973.* Committee Print, 93rd Cong., 2d Sess., February 26, 1974.
_____. The *Trade Reform Act of 1973.* Hearings, 93rd Cong., 2d Sess., March 4, 5, 6, 7, 21, 22, 25, 26, 27, 28, 29; April 1, 2, 3, 4, 5, 8, 9, and 10, 1974.
_____. *Emigration Amendment to The Trade Reform Act of 1974.* Hearing, 93rd Cong., 2d Sess., December 3, 1974.
_____. *Background Materials Relating to the United States-Romanian Trade Agreement.* Committee Print, 94th Cong., 1st Sess., June 5, 1975.
_____. *Romanian Trade Agreement.* Hearings, 94th Cong., 1st Sess., June 6, and July 8, 1975.
_____. *U. S. International Trade Policy and the Trade Act of 1974.* Committee Print, 94th Cong., 2d Sess., January 29, 1976.
_____. *Background Materials Relating to United States-Romanian Trade and the Extension of the President's Authority to Waive Section 402 of the Trade Act of 1974.* Committee Print, 94th Cong., 2d Sess., August 26, 1976.
_____. *Trade Agreements Act of 1979.* Report No. 96-249, 98th Cong., 1st Sess., July 17, 1979.
_____. U. S. *Goals for Upcoming Consultation with the Socialist Republic of Romania.* Report No. 97-522, 97th Cong., 2d Sess., August 13, 1982.
_____. *Renewal of the Generalized System of Preferences.* Report No. 98-485, 98th Cong., 2d Sess., May 21 1984.
_____. *Comparing Major Trade Bills.* Hearings, 100th Cong., 1st Sess., April 2, 1987.

Senate. Committee on Finance, Subcommittee on International Trade. *Foreign Trade*. Hearings, 92nd Cong., 1st Sess., May 17, 18, 19, 20, and 21, 1971.

_____. *Continuing Most-Favored-Nation Tariff Treatment of Imports from Romania*. Hearing, 94th Cong., 2d Sess., September 8, 1976.

_____. *Continuing Most-Favored-Nation Tariff Treatment of Imports from Romania – 1977*. Hearing, 95th cong., 1st Sess., June 27, 1977.

_____. *Continuing the President's Authority to Waive the Trade Act Freedom of Emigration Provisions*. Hearing, 95th Cong., 2d Sess., July 12, 1978.

_____. *Continuing the President's Authority to Waive The Trade Act Freedom of Emigration Provisions*. Hearing, 96th Cong., 1st Sess., July 19, 1979.

_____. *Extension of the President's Authority to Waive Section 402 (Freedom of Emigration Requirements) of The Trade Act of 1974*. Hearing, 96th Cong., 2d Sess., July 21, 1980.

_____. *Most Favored Nation Status for Romania, Hungary and China*. Hearing, 97th Cong., 1st Sess., July 27, 1981.

_____. *Review of the President's Decision to Renew Most-Favored-Nation Status for Romania, Hungary, and China*. Hearing, 97th Cong., 2d Sess., August 10, 1982.

_____. *Continuation of the President's Authority to Waive the Trade Act Freedom of Emigration Provisions*. Hearing, 98th Cong., 1st Sess., July 29, 1983, July 29, 1983.

_____. *Continuing Presidential Authority to Waive Freedom of Emigration Provisions*. Hearing, 98th Cong., 2d Sess., August 8, 1984.

_____. *MFN Status for Hungary, Romania, China, and Afghanistan*. Hearing, 99th Cong., 1st Sess., July 23, 1985.

_____. *MFN Status for Romania*. Hearing, 99th Cong., 2d Sess., August 1, 1986.

Senate. Committee on Foreign Relations. *A Decade of American Foreign Policy: Basic Documents, 1941-49*. Staff Report, Document No. 123, 81st Cong., 1st Sess., 1950.

_____. *Executive Sessions of the Senate Foreign Relations Committee (Historical Series)*, Vol. III, Part 2, 82nd Cong., 1st Sess., 1951 [Made Public August 1976.]

_____. *East-West Trade*. Hearing, 83rd Cong., 2d Sess., April 9, 1954.

_____. *Status of Nations Under Communist Control*. Hearing, 84th Cong., 1st Sess., June 21, 1955.

_____. *Background Documents on East-West Trade*. Committee Print, 89th Cong., 1st Sess., February 1965.

_____. *East-West Trade*. Hearings, 89th Cong., 1st Sess., February 24, 25, and 26, 1965.

_____. *A Background Study on East-West Trade*. Committee Print (Prepared by the Legislative Reference Service of the Library of Congress), 89th Cong., 1st Sess., April, 1965.

_____. *Shipping Restrictions on Grain Sales to Eastern Europe*. Hearings, 89th Cong., 1st Sess., September 17 and 27, 1965.

_____. *The Communist World in 1967.* Hearing, 90 Cong., 1st Sess., January 30, 1967.

_____. *Funding of Radio Free Europe and Radio Liberty.* Hearings, 92nd Cong., 2d Sess., June 6 and 7, 1972.

_____. *Export Administration Act Amendments.* Hearing, 92nd Cong., 2d Sess., July 19, 1972.

_____. *Detente and a New American Administration.* Report by Senator George S. McGovern, 95th Cong., 1st Sess., February 1978.

_____. *Perspectives on Detente—Austria, Romania, and Czechoslovakia.* Report by Senator George McGovern, 96th Cong., 1st Sess., January 1979.

_____. *Visit to Eastern Europe and the Middle East by the Senate Delegation to the Twenty-Fourth Meeting of the North Atlantic Assembly.* Report by Senator Claiborne Pell, 96th Cong., 1st Sess., May 1979.

_____. *Human Rights Issues in United States Relations with Romania and Czechoslovakia.* Report, S. Rpt. No. 98-38, 98th Cong., 1st Sess., April 1983.

_____. *Human Rights; The Promotion and Protection of Human Rights in Eastern Europe and the Soviet Union.* Hearing, 98th Cong., 1st Sess., [Chicago, Illinois] November 9, 1983.

_____. *Protecting and Promoting Religious Rights in Eastern Europe and the Soviet Union.* Hearing, 98th Cong., 2d Sess., June 12, 1984.

Senate. Committee on Foreign Relations, Subcommittee on European Affairs. *Religious Persecution Behind the Iron Curtain.* Hearing, 99th Cong., 1st Sess., November 14, 1985.

_____. *Romania: Most Favored Nation Status.* Hearing, 99th Cong. 2d Sess., February 26, 1986.

Senate. Committee on Foreign Relations, Special Subcommittee on Security Affairs. *Restrictions on Diplomatic Personnel By and From Iron Curtain Countries.* Committee Print, 83d Cong., 1st Sess., April 23, 1953.

Senate. Committee on Government Operations, Subcommittee on Foreign Aid Expenditures. *Coordination in the Administration of Public Law 480.* 89th Cong., 2d Sess., June 2 and 30, 1966.

Senate. Committee on Government Operations, Permanent Subcommittee on Investigations. *East-West Trade.* Report No. 2621, 84th Cong., 2d Sess., July 18, 1956.

_____. *The Rising Soviet and East European Debt to the West.* Committee Print, 95th Cong., 1st Sess., April, 1977.

_____. *Transfer of Technology and the Dresser Industries Export Licensing Actions.* Hearing, 95th Cong., 2d Sess., October 3, 1978.

Senate. Committee on Interstate and Foreign Commerce. *Export Controls and Policies in East-West Trade.* Report No. 944, 82d Cong., 1st Sess., October 12, 1951.

Joint Committees

Committee on Foreign Relations of the U.S. Senate, and Committee on Foreign Affairs of the U.S. House of Representatives. *Country Reports on*

Human Rights Practices for 1979. Report made by the Department of State, 96th Cong., 2d Sess., February, 4, 1980.

_____. *Country Reports on Human Rights Practices for 1986*. Report, 100th Cong., 1st Sess., February, 1987.

Conference Committee Print. *Summary of the Conference Agreement on H.R. 3; The Omnibus Trade and Competitiveness Act of 1988*. [100th Cong., 2d Sess.] April 19, 1988.

Joint Economic Committee Congress of the United States. *Foreign Economic Policy*. Report, 84th Cong., 2d Sess., January 5, 1956.

_____. *Soviet Economic Prospects for the Seventies*. Compendium of Papers, 93rd Cong.., 1st Sess., June 27, 1973.

_____. *East European Economies, Post Helsinki*. A Compendium of Papers, 95th cong., 1st Sess., August 25, 1977

_____. *Soviet Economy in a Time of Change*. Compendium of Papers, 96th Cong., 1st Sess. October 10, 1979.

_____. *Special Study on Economic Change, Vol. IX: The International Economy: U.S. Role in a World Market*. Studies, 96th Cong,, 2d Sess., December 17, 1980.

_____. *East-West Commercial Policy: A Congressional Dialogue with The Reagan Administration*. Study, 97th Cong., 2d Sess., February 16, 1982.

_____. *East-West Trade: The Prospects to 1985*. Studies, 97th Cong., 2d Sess., August 18, 1982.

_____. *East European Economies: Slow Growth in the 1980's, Vol. I: Economic Performance and Policy*. Selected Papers, 99th Cong., 1st Sess., October 28, 1985.

_____. *East European Economies: Slow Growth in the 1980's, Vol. II: Foreign Trade and International Finance*. Selected Papers, 99th Congress, 2d Sess., March 28, 1986.

_____. *East European Economies: Slow Growth in the 1980's, Vol. III: Country Studies on Eastern Europe and Yugoslavia*. Selected Papers, 99th Cong., 2d Sess., March 28, 1986.

Joint Economic Committee, Congress of the United States, Subcommittee on Foreign Economic Policy. *The Political Stakes in East-West Trade*. A Report on a Factfinding Trip to the U.S.S.R. and Eastern Europe, submitted by Senator Jacob K. Javits, 87th Cong., 2d Sess., February, 1962.

_____. *A Foreign Economic Policy for the 1970's*, Part 6: *East-West Economic Relations*, Hearings, 91st Cong., 1st Sess., December 7, 8, and 9, 1969.

_____. *Economic Developments in Countries of Eastern Europe*. Compendium of Papers, 91st Cong., 2d Sess., April, 1970.

Committee on Foreign Relations [Senate], Committee on International Relations [House]. *Legislation on Foreign Relations Through 1976*. 2 vols. [95th Cong., 1st Sess.] February, 1977.

_____. *Legislation on Foreign Relations Through 1978*. 2 vols. [96th Cong., 1st Sess.] February, March, 1979.

Publications of the U. S. Department of Commerce

U.S. Department of Commerce. *The United States Role in East-West Trade: Problems and Prospects*. An Assessment by Rogers Morton, Secretary, August, 1975.

Bureau of the Census. *Statistical Abstract of the United States 1989*. 109th ed.

Bureau of International Economic Policy and Research. *Trade of the United States with Communist Countries in Eastern Europe and Asia, 1973-75*. International Marketing Information Series, OBR 76-40, October, 1976.

_____. *Trade of the United States with Communist Countries in Eastern Europe and Asia, 1974-76*. International Marketing Information Series, OBR 77-30, June, 1977.

_____. *Trade of the United States with Communist Countries in Eastern Europe and Asia, 1975-77*. International Marketing Information Series, OBR 78-32, September, 1978.

_____. *Trading and Investing in Romania*. International Marketing Information Series, OBR 78-33, September, 1978

_____. *Trade of the United States with Communist Countries in Eastern Europe and Asia, 1976-1978*. International Marketing Information Series, OBR 79-42, December, 1979.

_____. *East-West Trade Update: A Commercial Fact Sheet for U. S. Business*. International Marketing Information Series, OBR 80-25, August, 1980.

_____. *World Trade Outlook for 64 Countries*. International Marketing Information Series, OBR 81-24, September, 1981.

Domestic and International Business Administration, Bureau of East-West Trade. *American-Romanian Economic Accords, 1973-1974*, March, 1975.

_____. *East-West Trade*. Export Administration Report, First Quarter 1974.

_____. *East-West Trade*. Export Administration Report, Second Quarter 1974.

_____. *East-West Trade*. Export Administration Report, Third Quarter 1974.

_____. *East-West Trade*. Export Administration Report, Fourth Quarter 1974.

_____. *East-West Trade*. Export Administration Report, First Quarter 1975.

_____. *East-West Trade*. Export Administration Report. Semiannual, April-September,1975.

_____. *East-West Trade*. Export Administration Report. Semiannual, October 1975- March, 1976.

_____. *East-West Trade*. Export Administration Report. Semiannual, April - September, 1976.

_____. *115th Report on U. S. Export Controls to the President and the Congress*. Export Administration Report. Semiannual, October 1976- March 1977.

_____. Verzariu, Pompiliu, Jr., and Burgess, Jay A. *Joint Venture Agreements in Romania: Background and Implementation*, June, 1977.

_____. *116th Report on U. S. Export Controls to the President and the Congress*. Export Administration Report. Semiannual, April - September, 1977.

_____. *117th Report on U. S. Export Controls to the President and the Congress*. Export Administration Report. Semiannual, October 1977 - March, 1978.

_____. Verzariu, Pompiliu, Bozek, Scott, and Matheson, JeNelle. *East-West Countertrade Practices: An Introductory Guide for Business*, August, 1978.

_____. *118th Report on U. S. Export Controls to the President and the Congress*. Export Administration Report. Semiannual, April 1978 - September 1978.

_____. *119th Report on U. S. Export Controls to the President and the Congress*. Export Administration Report. Semiannual, October 1978 - March 1979.

_____. *120th Report on U. S. Export Controls to the President and the Congress*. Export Administration Report. Semiannual, April 1979 - September 1979

_____. *Selected Trade and Economic Data of the Centrally Planned Economies*, n.d.

International Trade Administration. *1984: U. S. Foreign Trade Highlights*, n.d.

_____. *1985: U.S. Foreign Trade Highlights*, n.d.

_____. *1986: U.S. Foreign Trade Highlights*, n.d.

_____. *1988: U.S. Foreign Trade Highlights*, n.d.

_____. *U.S. Merchandise Trade Position at Midyear 1988*, n.d.

Other Congressional Imprints

Congressional Record, 1968-1990.

Extension of Jackson-Vanik Waiver Authority; Message from the President of the United States. House Document No. 96-137, 96th Cong., 1st Sess., 1979.

_____. House Document No. 96-318, 96th Cong., 2d Sess., 1980.

_____. House Document No. 97-57, 97th cong., 1st Sess., 1981.

Extension of Jackson-Vanik Waiver Authority Granted by Subsection 402 (c) of the Trade Act of 1974; Message from the President of the United States. House Document No. 97-190, 97th Cong., 2d Sess., 1982.

Removal of Romania and Nicaragua and Suspension of Paraguay from the List of General System of Preference Eligible Countries, House Document No. 100-18, 100th Cong., 1st Sess., 1987.

Publications of the U.S. Department of State

American Foreign Relations, Current Documents, 1965. 1968.
American Foreign Relations, Current Documents, 1966. 1969.
American Foreign Relations, Current Documents, 1967. 1969.
The Department of State Bulletin, Vol. XIV, No. 361, June 2, 1946.
The Department of State Bulletin, Vol. LXXII, No. 1860, February 17, 1975.- Vol. LXXXIX, November, 1989.
Foreign Relations of the United States, Diplomatic Papers. The Conferences at Cairo and Tehran, 1943. 1961.
_____. *The Conferences at Malta and Yalta, 1945.* 1955.
_____. *The Conference of Berlin (The Potsdam Conference) 1945.* 2 vols. 1960.
_____. *1945.* Volume II: *General: Political and Economic Matters.* 1967.
_____. *1945.* Volume V: *Europe.* 1967.
_____. *1946.* Volume II: *Council of Foreign Ministers.* 1970.
_____. *1946.* Volume IV: *Paris Peace Conference: Documents.* 1970
_____. *1947* Volume IV: *Eastern Europe; The Soviet Union.* 1972.
_____. *1948* Volume IV: *Eastern Europe: The Soviet Union.* 1974.
_____. *1949* Volume V: *Eastern Europe: The Soviet Union.* 1976.
_____. *1950.* Volume IV: *Central and Eastern Europe: The Soviet Union.* 1980.
_____. *1951.* Volume I: *National Security Affairs; Foreign Economic Policy.* 1979.
_____. *1951.* Volume IV: *Europe: Political and Economic Developments.* 1985.
_____. *1952-1954.* Volume I: *General: Economic and Political Matters.* 1983.
_____. *1952-1954.* Volume II: *National Security Affairs.* 1984.
_____. *1955-1957.* Volume XI: *United Nations and General International Matters.* 1988.

Other Publications of the U.S. Government

Annual Reports of the President of the United States on the Trade Agreements Programs, 1976-1982.
[Battle Act Administrator] *The Strategic Trade Control System, 1948-1956. Mutual Defense Assistance Control Act of 1951; Ninth Report to Congress.*
Comptroller General of the United States. *Clarifying Webb-Pomerene Act, Needed to Help Increase U.S. Exports.* General Accounting Office, August 22, 1973.
_____. *The Government's Role in East-West Trade; Problems and Issues.* General Accounting Office, February 4, 1976.
President's Export Council. *Coping With the Dynamics of World Trade in the 1980's.* December 1984.
United States Tariff Commission. *Considerations Involved in Granting Most-*

Favored-Nation Treatment to the Countries of Eastern Europe. 1971.
_____. *Impact of Granting Most-Favored-Nation Treatment to the Countries of Eastern Europe and the People's Republic of China.* 1974.
Weekly Compilation of Presidential Documents.

Newspapers, Media and Computer Sources
Agerpres
The Boston Globe
Cable Network News
Christian Science Monitor
Current Digest of Soviet Press
Dialog Computer Data Base
East European Reporter
Eastern Europe Newsletter
Foreign Broadcast Information Service, Eastern Europe
Los Angeles Times
Newsweek
New York Review of Books
New York Times
New York Times International
Scinteia
Time
Wall Street Journal
The Washington Post

INDEX